MOON

3124300 648 0486

Lake Forest Library
360 E. Deerpath
Lake Forest, IL 60045
847-234-0636
www.lakeforestlibrary.org

- 2020

OAXAC

CODY COPELAND

D1073789

Contents

Oaxaca

I'll start with a confession: I am madly, absolutely head-over-heels in love with Oaxaca. And I believe in magic. If I'm not careful, the hyper-excited six-year-old inside of me will break through the stiff layer of grown-up I've built around it and let loose a stream of superlatives: *It's a magical place with gigantic flowers and purple trees and clouds for seas and . . .*

I am not alone in using the word "magic" in relation to Oaxaca. It describes the allure of the colors, flavors, festivities, and everything else that's wholly unique to the region. But I believe that when we say it, there is also a tacit understanding that real, unexplainable magic does exist here. How could it not in a place with so many living connections to the ancient past? Certain customs, such as the weekly *día de plaza* (market day), have been practiced continuously here for thousands of years. People in and around the town of Tlacolula have gathered there every Sunday for millennia, and to this day, many agricultural products are still bartered, rather than sold there. The creativity and humor of the Oaxacan people are apparent in everything from their food and their dances to the art they create and the way they dress. A traditional Oaxacan *huipil* (embroidered garment) not only

Clockwise from top left: intricate embroidery from El Istmo; French toast with *tejate* sauce at Oaxaca City's Café Tradición; *papel picado* hanging over the streets of Oaxaca City; demon dancers at La Muerteada; the ancient Árbol del Tule; busy pedestrian street in Oaxaca City's historic center.

dazzles with its colors and designs, it also tells a story about the place where it was embroidered.

I have no problem believing that thousands of years of interaction between this rich collective imagination and the unusual geography here resulted in magic. Oaxaca showed me that the world is not as terrestrial as I'd believed it to be. The otherworldly calcified waterfalls at Hierve El Agua and the megadiverse cloud forests of the Sierra Norte make science fiction seem obsolete. The earth in parts of La Mixteca and the Valles Centrales boasts enough colors to fill a box of crayons. The orchids in the Sierra Mazateca look like fireworks and tentacled creatures, and the Laguna de Manialtepec glows purple at night with the bioluminescent phytoplankton that live there.

No matter how you define it, Oaxaca has a special something that you'll find hard to put into words that don't have metaphysical connotations. It will not cease to surprise you, no matter how much time you spend here. Come and see for yourself. Even if you don't return home believing in magic, you definitely won't go back the same person you once were.

Clockwise from top left: Tuxtepec's crowd-pleasing Flor de Piña dance; a typical Oaxacan street parade called a *calenda;* the baroque facade of the Basílica de Nuestra Señora de la Soledad in Oaxaca City; orchids in Huautla de Jiménez.

11 TOP
EXPERIENCES

1 **Celebrate Day of the Dead:** Oaxaca is the most spectacular and inviting place to experience Día de Muertos festivities (pages 37, 66, and 136).

2 **Explore Oaxaca City:** The energetic capital city teems with bustling markets, art galleries, hip cafés and bars, and excellent restaurants. Don't miss the top-notch museums and colonial architecture (pages 24 and 40).

3 **Journey into the Past:** Travel back in time at pre-Hispanic sites such as the mountaintop capital **Monte Albán** (page 103) and dust-swept **Mitla,** the "Place of the Dead" (pictured, page 119).

4 **Go Mezcal-Tasting:** At *mezcalerías* (mezcal bars) in Oaxaca City and distilleries in the Valles Centrales, you can taste and learn about the culture and production of mezcal, made from the agave plant (pages 62, 115, and 119).

5 **Surf the Pacific Coast:** Oaxaca's beaches boast world-class swells, including the famous "Mexican Pipeline" off Puerto Escondido's Playa Zicatela (pages 241, 263, 268, 275, 291, and 317).

>>>

6 **Trek between the Pueblos Mancomunados:** Nestled in the misty, pine-scented peaks of the Sierra Norte, these remote mountain villages host some of the best ecotourism activities in the state (pages 27 and 143).

7 **Feast on Oaxacan Cuisine:** Venture into bold landscapes of flavor different from anywhere else in the world (page 33).

8 **Get a New Perspective:** Rent a *cabaña* in the quaint mountain town of **San José del Pacífico** to see the sunset above the clouds, from the privacy of your own personal patio (page 229).

9 **Swim atop Frozen Waterfalls:** The strange, towering **Hierve El Agua** might have you double-checking what planet you're on, but the stunning views of the valley below will remind you (page 122).

10 **Learn about Oaxacan Folk Art from the Artists Themselves:** The work of Oaxacan hands is imbued with history, both ancient and recent—and boundless imagination (page 35).

11 **Get Away from It All in Mazunte:** This hippie hideaway of a beach offers fun in the sun during the day and tranquility at night (page 239).

Planning Your Trip

Where to Go

Oaxaca City

The **lively capital city** of Oaxaca de Juárez centers around the shady arcades of the **Zócalo**, or central plaza, from which everything the city has to offer is within walking distance. Just to the southwest are the bustling hives of the **Benito Juárez and 20 de Noviembre markets.** The **cobblestone streets** to the north teem with **art galleries, print shops,** hip **cafés and bars,** Oaxacan and international **restaurants,** and much more of the **green limestone colonial architecture** that give this town its anachronistic character.

Valles Centrales

Sprawling **desert vistas,** ancient **Zapotec ruins,** and quaint **artisan villages** abound

in this region that is often referred to as the Valley of Oaxaca. Spend a day shopping for local **craftwork** in **San Bartolo Coyotepec, Teotitlán del Valle,** or **Arrazola,** stuffing yourself with *barbacoa* along the way. Or admire handiwork dating back millennia at **Monte Albán** and **Mitla.** The otherworldly calcified stone "waterfalls" at **Hierve El Agua** will make you double-check what planet you're on.

Sierra Norte, El Papaloapan, and La Cañada

The dense **cloud forests,** crystal-clear natural **springs,** and **tropical rivers** of the northern regions of Oaxaca offer a hearty buffet of rich experiences for nature lovers. Hike over 100 kilometers (62 mi) of **interconnected mountain**

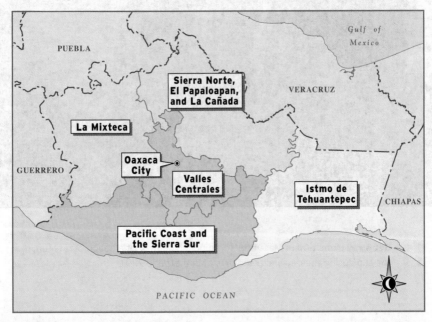

- **FOUR DAYS:** If you've only got four days, spend them based in **Oaxaca City,** enjoying the city the first couple days, and making trips out to towns in the **Valles Centrales.** For something different, spend your last day or two exploring the valleys from a base in **Mitla, Tlacolula,** or whichever town catches your fancy.

- **ONE WEEK:** A full week gives you enough time to do the aforementioned plan, with a few extra days for some adventuring. For those extra three days, you could go camping or stay in a *cabaña* in the **Pueblos Mancomunados** (in the **Sierra Norte**) or **Apoala** (in **La Mixteca**). This latter option will include a stopover in **Nochixtlán,** so take advantage and make sure to grab a meal there. Of course, the **beach** is also an option for those last few days.

cabañas at Balneario Monte Flor in the Sierra Norte

- **TWO WEEKS:** This is the perfect amount of time for experiencing the incredible cultural, gastronomical, and natural gems of **central Oaxaca,** and then heading to the **coast** for a week of beach bumming. You won't find as many ecotourism opportunities in the **Sierra Sur** as you will in the north, but there are great hikes around **San José del Pacífico** and **Pluma Hidalgo.** For that week on the coast, you can bounce from beach to beach, or pick what suits your fancy from **Puerto Escondido, Bahías de Huatulco,** or the hippie beaches around **Puerto Ángel,** and just sit back and relax.

paths of the **Pueblos Mancomunados,** camp out and explore the **caves** at **Nindo-Da-Gé,** and cool off with a dip in the spring-fed **pools** at **Balneario El Zuzul.**

La Mixteca

This lesser-visited region is the **heartland of the Mixtecs,** one of Oaxaca's most prominent indigenous cultures, and home to some of the finest examples of **Dominican architecture** in the state, as well as more **archaeological zones,** such as **Cerro de las Minas.** Visit the bustling weekly market of **Tlaxiaco,** or get away from it

all camping beneath the soaring cliffs of **Apoala.** On top of all this, the **food** is reason enough to make the trip out here.

Pacific Coast and the Sierra Sur

From the southern edge of the Valles Centrales rise the verdant and vertiginous slopes of the **Sierra Madre del Sur.** These mountains are home to **San José del Pacífico,** famous for its magic mushrooms, and **Pluma Hidalgo,** Oaxaca's prize coffee-producing village, as well as the highest peaks in the state. Oaxaca's Pacific coast has **beaches** to suit all tastes, from **surfing**

a refreshing cold coconut on the beach

and nightlife in **Puerto Escondido,** to the **luxury hotels** and vacation homes of **Bahías de Huatulco,** to the quiet **hippie hideaway** of **Mazunte.**

Istmo de Tehuantepec

The inhabitants of these **rich, green lowlands** really know how to party. No matter the time of year, there's a good chance a trip to the Isthmus will coincide with at least one of over a hundred *velas,* local **festivals** to celebrate patron saints and social cohorts. Puerto Escondido may boast the famed "Mexican Pipeline," but the waves off the shores of **Salina Cruz** are also of world-class quality, and the town boasts a number of **surf camps** and board shops.

Know Before You Go

When to Go

Although Oaxaca is located at a tropical latitude, seasonal rains and the mountainous landscape keep the high average temperatures within comfortable ranges. Any time of year is a good time to visit Oaxaca. The **rainy season** runs **May-September.** In Oaxaca City and the Valles Centrales, you can expect dependable afternoon showers that cool everything down nicely, and on the coast the rains will be more frequent and less predictable. Up in the mountains, you might spend an entire day shrouded in eerie clouds. The tropical evergreen forests and rainforests in the north get enough rain year-round to keep their color, but the rest of the state turns a brilliant green during these rainy months.

The green of the deciduous forests on the coast and desert scrub of the Valles Centrales fades when the rains go, but Oaxaca's rich floral biodiversity keeps a rainbow of colors in the land throughout the dry months.

Busy holiday seasons to watch out for are

Day of the Dead, at the end of October and beginning of November. Do not fail to make reservations during this time, as well as at **Christmas,** the two-week Easter holiday called **Semana Santa,** and the month of July, during the **Guelaguetza** season. Christmas and Semana Santa are very busy times on the coast, as people from Mexico City and other parts of the country escape the daily grind on the sunny shores of Oaxaca. If you want the coast basically all to yourself, head there in September, but expect to find fewer services and accommodations, as many close up shop for the low season.

Passports, Tourist Cards, and Visas

Make sure your **passport** has at least six months of validity left on it before you come to Mexico. It's not a guarantee that you won't be allowed in, but it's better not to risk it. You will not need to apply for a tourist visa before traveling.

If you **fly** to Oaxaca, the immigration fee will be included in your plane ticket, and you'll be given a **tourist card** at the airport. Do not lose this, as you'll waste precious time and money replacing it. Make copies of everything once you arrive, and take the copies around when you leave your hotel. Stow the originals in a safe place in your accommodations.

If you **cross at the border,** you will have to stop in the immigration office upon entry and ask for a **tourist visa.** You will be given the card and an **invoice** for the fee, which you will have to pay at a bank in Mexico before you leave. Don't forget to pay for it, and again, don't lose the card!

Vaccinations

Make sure all your basic vaccinations are up-to-date, and get vaccinated for **Hepatitis A** and **B.** If you're planning on doing some bushwhacking in the jungle, seriously consider vaccinations for nasty tropical bugs like **dengue, typhoid,** and **rabies,** just in case. Places like Apoala, in La Mixteca, are home to vampire bats that, although rarely, are known to sometimes bite people. Don't forget bug spray in these areas, either. I've been lucky with mosquito bites in Oaxaca, but you never want to find out what they carry by being their petri dish.

Transportation

The quickest way to get to Oaxaca is by **air,** and with the state's popularity rising, flights are getting very affordable. International airports in **Oaxaca City, Puerto Escondido,** and **Huatulco** connect Oaxaca to the world at large. You can also travel within the state via these airports, but it will be more expensive, and you'll miss all the fun stuff on the ground along the way.

The great thing about Mexico is there is always a bus going your way. The majority of **long-distance buses** in Mexico are comfortable and have bathrooms, but you may be forced to watch a lengthy festival of dubbed Sandra Bullock films and movies about people dying, going to heaven, and coming back to tell the tale. **Oaxaca City, Puerto Escondido,** and **Tehuantepec** are major hubs on the bus routes that go to and from Oaxaca.

Once in Oaxaca, you've got a ton of options for getting around, from **renting a car** to piling into a tiny taxi with five other people and their cargo for next to nothing. For longer distances in Oaxaca, take a 12-15-passenger van called a *suburban.* The companies usually have names like **Transportes Turísticos** or **Autotransportes.** For shorter distances, use the even more local *camionetas* (covered pickups) and *taxis colectivos.* On just about any highway in Oaxaca, you can flag down one of these types of transports, but make sure you're in a safe place for the vehicle to pull over, or they won't stop. Also, don't do it at night, anywhere. Within towns, and to get to towns close to highway intersections, a *mototaxi* will take you around for a coin or two.

Best of Oaxaca City and the Valles Centrales

To get the best overall experience of the cultural and gastronomic wonders of Oaxaca, head to the capital city. With a couple of additional days, it's easy to do day trips to explore the ancient ruins and artisan villages of the Valles Centrales.

Day 1

Start at the **Zócalo**, which gets lively early. It's a great spot to post up and people-watch for a while, as well as to orient yourself, as this is the geographical center of town. From here head southwest and squeeze through the busy aisles of **Mercado Benito Juárez** and **Mercado 20 de Noviembre**, the main gastronomical market that has the best food in town. Eat *mole* here. Stick around here for a while, perusing the **chocolate stores** on Calle Mina to find the flavor you like. Stop by the **Mercado de Artesanías** before heading up to the **Plaza de la Danza** and enjoy artisanal ice cream as you watch the sun set behind the magnificent baroque facade of the **Basílica de Nuestra Señora de la Soledad.**

Day 2

Grab a coffee at **Café Brújula** and take a stroll up the **Andador Macedonio Alcalá,** checking out the **Museo de Arte Contemporáneo; Galería Omar Hernández,** a ceramics gallery; and **IAGO,** the Graphic Arts Institute of Oaxaca. Don't miss the printmaking shops, like **Gabinete Gráfico** and **Espacio Zapata.** If you're really into lithography and other printmaking methods, pick up a **Pasaporte Gráfico**, a map and brochure provided by 12 shops in the Centro. Visit them all and you'll get a discount. Grab your meals at places like **Azucena Zapoteca** and **Tierra del Sol.**

Gabinete Gráfico printmaking shop

the arches and patios of the Zócalo

ceramic skulls in Galería Omar Hernández

Day 3

Spend a few hours in the museum at the **Centro Cultural Santo Domingo,** which boasts a superlative collection of ceramic, turquoise, and gold artifacts discovered at Monte Albán, as well as relics from the colonial period in Oaxaca. Then take a quick tour of the **Jardín Etnobotánico de Oaxaca,** in the old vegetable garden of the Santo Domingo convent. After lunch at **La Olla,** check out some smaller museums, like the **Museo de Filatelia** (Stamp Museum, more interesting than it sounds), and the photography exhibits at the **Centro Fotográfico Manuel Álvarez Bravo.** For dinner and drinks, head to **Expendio Tradición.**

Day 4

For breakfast, head to **Café Tradición,** next to its parent restaurant. It has a French toast served with a sauce made from *tejate* and sprinkled with flower petals that it would be a shame to leave Oaxaca without eating. Spend your last day picking up whatever gifts or souvenirs you still need at artisan cooperatives like **Huizache**

Arte Vivo de Oaxaca, MARO, and **La Casa de las Artesanías.** Or you could do some meandering throughout the Centro, stopping by **Los Arquitos de Xochimilco, Parque El Llano,** and the **Templo de San Matías Jalatlaco.**

Explore the Valles Centrales

Three of Oaxaca's biggest attractions are located in the Valles Centrales and can be visited on **day trips** from Oaxaca City: the ruins of **Monte Albán,** the ancient Zapotec capital; the ruins of **Mitla,** the "Place of the Dead" with its unique stone mosaics; and the calcified waterfalls at **Hierve El Agua.** (Other ruins such as **Yagul** and **Atzompa** are also worth a visit and are much less crowded.)

The **communities** of the Valles Centrales, replete with **imaginative artists** and **delicious food,** are also close enough to make day trips from Oaxaca City.

- Head to **Teotitlán del Valle** and neighboring towns in the Valle de Tlacolula for the brightly colored wool rugs called *tapetes.*
- The psychedelically painted wooden statuettes

the hilltop pyramids at Monte Albán

called *alebrijes* are found in stores all over the state, but the best places to learn about them are **Arrazola** and **San Martín Tilcajete.**

- For ceramics, visit **San Bartolo Coyotepec,** where a potter named Doña Rosa invented the technique for making *barro negro* (black clay pottery) in the 1950s, and **San Antonino Castillo Velasco,** where blind potter José García still works with *barro rojo* (red clay) without the use of his sight.

- **San Antonino Castillo Velasco** is also known for its unique style of *huipil* (embroidered blouse). Another great place to shop for *huipiles* made in this town is the **Friday** market in neighboring **Ocotlán de Morelos.** For **belts** and other embroidered items, head to **Santo Tomás Jalieza.**

- Meat lovers absolutely must make pilgrimages to **Tlacolula** and **Zaachila** for the *barbacoa,* barbecue slow-roasted in an earthen oven for up to eight hours. **Sunday** is a good day to visit Tlacolula, as you can also experience one of the oldest continuously running indigenous markets in the Americas, as well as enjoy the delicious **goat and lamb** *barbacoa.* Zaachila also has goat and lamb daily, but on **Thursday,** during the town's *día de plaza* (market day), you can treat yourself to the local specialty: *barbacoa en rollo* (rolled beef *barbacoa*), which is roasted with avocado tree leaves to give it its distinct flavor.

It's easy to find **tours** to these destinations in Oaxaca City. You can find full-day tours that combine multiple destinations, such as Teotitlán del Valle, Mitla, and Hierve El Agua. It's also very possible to do day trips on your own via **public transport.** Little English is spoken in the Valles Centrales, so if you don't have at least a basic level of Spanish, you're best off going with a tour.

For more day-trip ideas, see page 58.

Trekking the Pueblos Mancomunados

Just 1.5 hours from Oaxaca City by car (and not much longer by bus or *taxi colectivo*), and 1,500 meters (4,921 ft) higher, the **Pueblos Mancomunados** are a world away from the desert below. Translating to "United Villages," this group of seven mountain towns in the Sierra Norte have organized to create and sustain a **paragon of ecotourism** in Mexico. The citizens of these communities, in which the ownership of private property is banned, understand how vital their natural environment is to their livelihood, both in terms of economy and quality of life, and they love sharing it and their culture with others. **Camp out** among the pines, or rent a *cabaña ecoturística* (ecotourism cabin) if you want to get cozy next to the fire when the temperature drops at night. Plan on spending **three days** or so in the Pueblos Mancomunados.

Experience the Landscape

Up here, you'll understand why the Zapotec people call themselves Gente de las Nubes (People of the Clouds). Towns here range 2,000-3,000 meters (6,562-9,843 ft), covering a wide range of vegetation zones, from megadiverse pine-oak forests to the misty, pine-covered peaks at the higher altitudes.

Over 100 km (62 mi) of **mountain roads and footpaths** connect the Pueblos Mancomunados, serving as both hiking trails for visitors and daily commutes for locals. You'll most likely start out in the **gateway town** of **Cuajimoloyas,** the highest of the communities, at 3,000-3,200 meters (9,843-10,500 ft) above sea level. Often shrouded in clouds, it can get chilly, sometimes freezing, so pack appropriately, but when the sun comes out, the slopes heat up nicely and offer breathtaking views of the surrounding landscape. From

a lookout point in the Pueblos Mancomunados

here, you can hike or mountain bike to Benito Juárez, Latuvi, or any of the other towns in the network. You'll also find zip lines, suspension bridges, waterfalls, and more.

Immerse in Local Culture

In between hikes, get to know the People of the Clouds and their way of life better via the many cultural workshops the communities offer.

There are courses in making tortillas, artisanal breads, and jams, as well as in reforestation and sustainable farming efforts.

You can also learn more about the various local plants and herbs used in traditional medicine in the Sierra Norte, or get a Zapotec massage, *limpia* (spiritual cleansing), or *temazcal* (indigenous sweat lodge), and come back down the mountain feeling refreshed.

Wonders of La Mixteca

Home to the Ñuu Savi, or People of the Rain, as the Mixtecs call themselves, the landscapes of La Mixteca are simply mesmerizing. The terrain here ranges from cloudy peaks to lower scrublands with all the colors of the rainbow in the soil and stone. Mixtec legend tells that this land was conquered when a warrior called El Flechador del Sol (The One Who Wounded the Sun with an Arrow) shot the setting sun with his arrow, causing it to bleed red over the hills and winning the land for the Mixtec people. Watch the sun set here, and you might start to question whether or not it's really a myth.

Explore Architectural and Natural Wonders

Traditionally, tourism to this lesser-visited region west of the Valles Centrales has focused on the impressive Dominican architecture in the churches and convents built at the behest of the Spanish during the colonial period. The most impressive are in Yanhuitlán, Coixtlahuaca, Tamazulapan, and Teposcolula, where the *capilla abierta* (open-air chapel) of the Templo y Ex-Convento de San Pedro y San Pablo is the largest of its kind in Latin America. These structures truly are a sight to see, but they aren't the only attractions here. Ecotourism has begun to sprout and develop here, showcasing the best of La Mixteca's gorgeous geography.

Luckily, you can see them on the way to La Mixteca's most beautiful natural wonders, such as La Cascada Esmeralda (Emerald Falls) at the

Parque Natural Yosondúa, south of Tlaxiaco, and Cañón El Boquerón (Bigmouth Canyon), just outside Santo Domingo Tonalá. Observe Yosondúa's waterfalls from its 131-meter (430-ft) suspension bridge, then get lost for hours hiking through the canyon. The walkway pegged into the 400-meter (1,312-ft) cliffs of Cañón El Boquerón offers spectacular views of the canyon walls and river below.

If you can't venture this far into La Mixteca, head to Santiago Apoala, just 1.5 hours north of Nochixtlán. This tiny town perched on a flat shelf is used as a base for exploring the stunning valley of Apoala. Towering cliff walls good for climbing (or simply causing your jaw to drop), waterfalls and caves named after snakes and horse tails, ghostly moss-strewn oak forests, and cave paintings dating back thousands of years will keep you busy and having fun for a few days of camping or in one of the comfortable *cabañas* (cabins).

Savor the Food

I'm not going to lie, the food in La Mixteca is so flavorful and creative that I often curse aloud after taking a bite. Nochixtlán now rivals Oaxaca City for my favorite place to eat in the world. Everything from the street tacos to the *comida corrida* to the rotisserie chicken is absolutely delicious, and a local restaurant there, Cenaduría Chiquirunguis, makes the best *tlayuda* I've had in Oaxaca, so far.

Luckily, the street market in Tlaxiaco operates

the suspension bridge at the Parque Natural Yosondúa

daily, because it will take you more than one day to eat all the yummy stuff there. And don't miss your chance to eat a meal created by one of Mexico's top chefs at **Restaurante El Patio,** inside Hotel del Portal. Chef Ixchel Ornelas Hernández was a contestant on the televised competition *Top Chef Mexico*, and one taste of her *mole negro* with *picadillo* and an olive relish will have you raving on social media about how she should have won.

Mid-October-mid-November, try and make it to **Huajuapan de León,** where the seasonal dish *mole de caderas* is served in the **Restaurante García Peral** at the hotel of the same name. This spicy, soupy *mole* made with goat meat has the always delicious and distinctive *hoja de aguacate* (avocado tree leaf), which makes everything better.

Planning Tips

You'd need **two weeks** to see all the sights in La Mixteca. If you have a **week** or so to explore the region, here's **how best to organize your time:** Base yourself in Nochixtlán (which is a little over an hour from Oaxaca City), do a day in Apoala (and possibly overnight there), and then spend two days exploring the churches on the Dominican Route. Then spend three days in and around Tlaxiaco (including Parque Natural Yosondúa) and/or spend a couple days in and around Huajuapan de León (including a short hike through Cañón El Boquerón).

Sierra Sur and Pacific Coast Adventure

Don't get me wrong, I am all for picking one beach on the coast and moving very little for a week or more, so if that's what you're after, head to one of the coast's three main beach destinations— Puerto Escondido, Puerto Ángel and environs, or Huatulco—and laze away. This itinerary will keep you pretty active, but I've included time for splashing around and sunbathing, as well. The complex ecosystems and rich biodiversity along the coast offer much to see and do, so if you're into exploring, this route will immerse you in the best of what there is to do to get your adrenaline pumping and curiosity piqued.

In the Mountains
DAY 1: SAN JOSÉ DEL PACÍFICO

Leave Oaxaca City by car or *suburban* van by 8am, arriving in **San José del Pacífico** by 11am. Grab a cup of coffee and a bite, throw your stuff in a *cabaña*, and hit the trail. There are lots of great **trails** to wander, just always try to be aware of where you are in relation to the highway, as, even if you get lost, you can always grab a *camioneta* back to town. With or without the psychedelic fungi that San José is known for, a walk through these mountains is sure to inspire awe. For dinner, grab pasta or a steak and some house-distilled mezcal at **La Taberna de los Duendes.**

DAY 2: SAN MATEO RÍO HONDO

After breakfast, **hike** out to **San Mateo Río Hondo,** which takes about 1.5 hours, but take your time to work up an appetite. You'll pass by so many plants, bugs, and birds you've probably never seen before that you'll end up making frequent stops. Eat lunch at **Las Amapolas,** admire the church, and walk back to San José, or get a *camioneta* to take you back to the highway and head south, arriving in **Pluma Hidalgo** for a cup of joe as the sun sets. Stay in town, or have a

night reserved at a **coffee plantation.** You can sleep in a bed at **Finca Don Gabriel,** or out in the fields at **Cerro de la Pluma,** where you'll basically camp out like coffee farmers.

DAY 3: PLUMA HIDALGO

Have your **plantation tour** reserved beforehand. You'll learn a lot about coffee production in Oaxaca, and get to taste a lot, too. You should be able to tour the plantation in the morning and early afternoon, arriving in **Bahías de Huatulco** for a sunset swim.

On the Pacific Coast
DAY 4: BAHÍAS DE HUATULCO

In Huatulco, spend a day exploring the bays and beaches. Head out to **Playa La Entrega,** with a stop for photos from the **Mirador El Faro** (Lighthouse Lookout) on the way, and do some **snorkeling.** Or rent a **bicycle** and pedal through the jungle trails of **Parque Nacional Huatulco** to get to undeveloped beaches like **Playas El Maguey** and **Cacaluta.** Take snacks. In the evening, have dinner on the beach at **Playa Santa Cruz.** Don't forget to take a look at the open-air **Capilla de la Santa Cruz,** which houses one of the four crosses made from a once supposedly indestructible larger one. Enjoy a last dip in the calm waters of the bay and drinks at a *palapa* bar.

DAY 5: LAS CASCADAS MÁGICAS AND FINCA LA GLORIA

Have your transportation out to **Las Cascadas Mágicas** arranged beforehand, ready to leave town by 10am, after coffee and breakfast in **La Crucecita.** Before noon, you'll be jumping off **waterfalls** and swinging on rope swings, splashing around in the thick jungle heat to work up an appetite for lunch. If you didn't get enough coffee up in Pluma, grab a cup at the **coffee farm**

Choose Your Beach

With world-class surfing, primary global sea turtle nesting sites, nudist beaches, and accommodations options from hammocks to camping to rustic *cabañas* to five-star resorts, the Oaxacan coast has a beach for everyone. Here is a list of the best beaches organized by the primary activity (or lack thereof) on them.

SWIMMING

· Playas Manzanillo and Puerto Angelito, Puerto Escondido

· Playa Panteón, Puerto Ángel

· Playa Santa Cruz, Huatulco

SURFING

· Playa Zicatela, Puerto Escondido

· Punta Zicatela, Puerto Escondido

· Barra de la Cruz

SNORKELING

· Playa La Entrega, Huatulco

· Playas Manzanillo and Puerto Angelito, Puerto Escondido

SEA TURTLE OBSERVATION AND RELEASE

· Mazunte

· La Ventanilla, Mazunte

· Playa La Escobilla, east of Puerto Escondido

CROCODILE CONSERVATION

· Lagunas de Chacahua

· La Ventanilla, Mazunte

CAMPING

· Playa San Agustín, Huatulco

· Playa Tangolunda, Huatulco

· Chacahua, Lagunas de Chacahua

the calm turquoise waters of Playas Manzanillo and Puerto Angelito

LETTING IT ALL HANG OUT (NUDISM)

· Zipolite

· Mazunte (topless acceptable)

PARTYING

· Zipolite

· Playa Zicatela, Puerto Escondido

· El Adoquín, Puerto Escondido

SUNSETS

· Punta Cometa, Mazunte

· Playa Marinero, Puerto Escondido

· Punta Zicatela, Puerto Escondido

IN THE LAP OF LUXURY

· Playas Chahué, Tangolunda, and Conejos, Huatulco

· Playa Carrizalillo, Puerto Escondido

Mazunte's Playa Rinconcito

La Gloria and explore the grounds of this lower-altitude plantation. Back in Huatulco by the early evening, relax poolside or on the beach, or get a **massage** or *temazcal* in one of Huatulco's many excellent **spas.**

DAY 6: MAZUNTE

Leave Huatulco on an *urbano* bus by 8am, which should put you in **Mazunte** by 10am. Cool off from the trip on **Playa Rinconcito,** then stop by the **Centro Mexicano de la Tortuga** to learn more about **sea turtle** biology and conservation. In the afternoon, you might take a *camioneta* east down the coast to visit beaches at **San Agustinillo, Zipolite,** and **Puerto Ángel,** but try and make it back to Mazunte an hour before sunset. **Hike** out to the tip of the **Punta Cometa** to watch the sun melt into the Pacific before dinner.

DAY 7: LA VENTANILLA

Start the day off with a tour of the lagoons at **La Ventanilla,** where the **canoe** you take to the conservation center on the island shares the murky mangrove waters with gigantic **crocodiles.** Learn more about the wildlife here on a hike through **jungle trails,** or take a **horseback ride** on the beach. After the tour, kick back on the beach in Mazunte, or visit others you missed, and head to **Puerto Escondido** by late afternoon, arriving by sunset.

DAY 8: PUERTO ESCONDIDO

In Puerto, take some **surf** lessons on the smaller waves off **La Punta Zicatela,** or, if you've already got the skills, grab a board and hit **Playa Zicatela,** one of the world's best surfing beaches. If hanging ten isn't exactly your thing, spend the day checking out the calmer beaches for **swimming.** Start off at **Playa Principal.** From here, you can walk west to **Playas Manzanillo** and **Puerto Angelito.** Get to **Playa Carrizalillo** by sunset, as you won't want to miss the view from the top of the stairs that lead to the beach.

DAY 9: LAGUNAS DE CHACAHUA

Start the day early to take a morning **boat tour** of the **Lagunas de Chacahua.** Once in the town of Chacahua, **surf, swim,** or check out the **crocodile farm** across the inlet. Have your **sunset tour** of the **Laguna de Manialtepec** arranged beforehand, and get back to this lagoon by 4pm or 5pm. Here, do some **bird-watching** on a sunset cruise, and when the sun goes down, splash around in the glowing water with the **bioluminescent plankton** that lives here. You'll be back in Puerto just in time to party on the last night of your trip.

DAY 10: RECREATION AND RELAXATION

Take advantage of your last day on the coast doing whatever you like. Get back on the board and spend all day riding waves, eat too many **shrimp cocktails,** take a **yoga class,** or get a **Zapotec massage** to beat the soreness out of your muscles. In the evening, do some shopping on **El Adoquín** and the **Avenida del Morro,** grabbing some gifts and souvenirs to take home. This isn't *adios,* but rather *¡Hasta la próxima!* (Until next time!).

New Frontiers of Flavor

Oaxaca boasts enough sights, stories, and activities to keep travelers of all types occupied and happy, but for us flavor fiends, it's paradise. To eat here is to venture into landscapes of flavor so different from anywhere else in the world that your tongue might as well be on another planet. What's more, Oaxacan gastronomy is colorful, storied, and spicy enough to satisfy all those other reasons for leaving home.

Start your journey off with a morning cup of **Oaxacan chocolate,** a recipe unique to the state. From here, you can venture forth to other

mole negro, chocolate, and salsa

beverages you won't find anywhere else in the world. For example, the cool, dry nights of the **Valles Centrales** are a key ingredient in the pre-Hispanic drink called *tejate*. The *flor de cacao*, a small flower that isn't actually from the cacao plant, needs these conditions to create the sweet foam that rises to the surface. Also on the itinerary are *espuma*, a different foamy chocolate drink from **Zaachila**, and the *chocolate-atole* of **Teotitlán del Valle**. The Zapotec women of **Juchitán**, in the Istmo de Tehuantepec, make *bupu*, which is similar to the *espuma* of Zaachila (*bupu* means "foam" in Zapotec), but much sweeter.

Most of the **coffee** you try in the state is from **Pluma Hidalgo**, in the Sierra Sur. Pluma coffee is strong and bold, with a heavy acidity. Other regions, such as the Sierra Norte and parts of La Mixteca, produce milder coffees. **Mezcal**, distilled from the maguey (also called agave) plant, is Oaxaca's most famous alcoholic beverage. **Oaxaca City** and the **Valles Centrales** are the best places to taste and learn about mezcal.

From here, we move on to *mole negro,* a plate with ingredients that include chocolate, charred corn tortillas, chiles so rare they're endangered, and a laundry list of seeds, nuts, and spices that cooks elsewhere would break up into numerous dishes. And that's only the first leg on a trip that includes many other distinct and complex *mole* recipes.

The gastronomically intrepid will be delighted to hear that the ancient practice of entomophagy, or eating insects, is alive and well in Oaxaca today. In every market in the state, you'll find vendors of *chapulines,* grasshoppers fried with chiles, garlic, and lime, and experimental chefs in Oaxaca City love jazzing up a plate with the tasty little critters. The worms that live in maguey hearts are eaten here, as well, and often ground up for the *sal de gusano* (worm salt) served with fresh orange slices alongside a glass of mezcal.

The key to the deliciousness of the *tlayuda,* Oaxaca's overgrown version of a quesadilla or tostada, lies in a sneaky little ingredient called *asiento* (vegans beware!), which is the lard left over from frying pork. Hidden under all the

WHERE TO FIND THE BEST FOOD AND DRINK

Here are the best (and in some cases, only) places to sample and learn about these Oaxacan delicacies:

FOOD

- *mole negro* (black *mole*) — available in most parts of state; Restaurante El Patio in Tlaxiaco (La Mixteca) is highly recommended

- *mole de caderas* (goat-meat *mole*) — La Mixteca, primarily in and around Huajuapan de León; also restaurant Tierra del Sol in Oaxaca City; only available seasonally (mid-Oct.-mid-Nov.)

- goat and lamb *barbacoa* (slow-roasted barbecue) — Tlacolula and Zaachila (Valles Centrales)

- *barbacoa en rollo* (rolled beef *barbacoa*) — Zaachila (Valles Centrales); only on Thursday, the town's market day

- *tlayuda* (overgrown quesadilla/tostada) — available statewide; best is found in La Mixteca (try Cenaduría Chiquirunguis in Nochixtlán)

- *garnacha* (deep-fried tostada) — specialty of Tehuantepec, Juchitán, and other towns in the Istmo de Tehuantepec

BEVERAGES

- *tejate* (foam-topped nutty/chocolatey drink) — Oaxaca City and Valles Centrales

- *espuma* (foamy chocolate-based drink) — Zaachila (Valles Centrales)

- *mezcal* — available statewide; best places to taste and learn are Oaxaca City and Valles Centrales

- *coffee* — available statewide; most comes from the coffee plantations of Pluma Hidalgo (Sierra Sur)

beans, cheese, veggies, and meat, the *asiento* is what gives this paragon of tortilla-based food its distinctive flavor.

Go from the gigantic tortilla of the *tlayuda* to the squat little fried ones of *garnachas* of the **Istmo de Tehuantepec.** These tasty snacks are topped with shredded beef, crumbly *queso fresco* cheese, tangy pickled cabbage, and spicy red salsa.

And that cheese . . . the stringy, tangy, oh-so-perfectly melty cheese called **quesillo** was the product of a fortunate accident in **Reyes Etla** over a century ago.

Each recipe in the Oaxacan cookbook is a new adventure through the history and teeming imagination of the people who prepare it, so when a Oaxacan tells you *Buen provecho* (Bon appétit), they're also saying *Buen viaje* (Bon voyage).

Oaxacan Folk Art

The work of Oaxacan hands is imbued with history, both ancient and recent, as well as boundless imagination. Some crafts, like ceramics, have been produced here for millennia. During the conquest, the indigenous peoples of Oaxaca combined native materials and techniques to the goods and practices introduced by the Spanish. Combine natural dyes sourced directly from the earth with European wool and looms, and add a few centuries of Oaxacan humor and fancy, and you've got the hallucinatory *tapetes* **(wool rugs)** of **Teotitlán del Valle** and other communities.

But at just five short centuries old, rug weaving is barely a teenager in terms of the average lifespan of a Oaxacan folk art. As in other parts of

Mexico, people here have been baking clay since they figured out how to do it over 4,000 years ago. What you'll have a hard time finding elsewhere in Mexico, however, is a town like **Santa María Atzompa,** famous for its **green-glazed, matte-white, and intricate filigree pottery** styles. Recent archaeological investigations on a hilltop just south of the current ceramics market here uncovered a 2,000-year-old kiln, tangible evidence that this art has been produced in the Valles Centrales continually for millennia. And even this one isn't the oldest here, if you, like me, consider gastronomy an art. The *caldo de piedra* **(stone soup)** of San Felipe Usila is believed to predate the discovery of ceramics in the

a potter using traditional methods to form his piece

Americas, as its original recipe doesn't include a bowl, but rather a hollow in a boulder or the sand next to the river now called Río Santo Domingo.

What is truly incredible about these craft traditions is not only how long they have been handed down from generation to generation here in Oaxaca, but also how they are constantly changing to this day. The technique that produces the glossy *barro negro* (**black clay pottery**) of **San Bartolo Coyotepec** was invented by a woman named Doña Rosa in the 1950s. The fantastic *alebrijes* of **Arrazola** and **San Martín Tilcajete** are even younger, and weavers in Teotitlán have recently begun experimenting with their craft by twisting three-dimensional images into their rugs.

All over Oaxaca live expert and creative chefs, basket weavers, embroiderers, jewelry makers, silversmiths, leatherworkers, knife makers, and more, all with unique imaginative styles that add their own voices to the greater communal art form. This wealth of artisanal traditions has filled the *mercados* of the state with gorgeous artifacts that make shopping in Oaxaca unique, personal, and full of fun, exploration, and learning.

WHERE TO FIND FOLK ART

Oaxaca is home to a number of communities that specialize in particular art forms.

- **rugs, tapestries, and other woven items** — Teotitlán del Valle (Valles Centrales)

- *alebrijes* (brightly painted carved wooden figures) — Arrazola and San Martín Tilcajete (Valles Centrales)

- *barro negro* (black clay pottery) — San Bartolo Coyotepec (Valles Centrales)

- *barro rojo* (red clay pottery) — San Antonino Castillo Velasco (Valles Centrales)

- **green-glazed and matte white pottery** — Santa María Atzompa (Valles Centrales)

- *huipiles* (embroidered blouses) — the most popular come from Tehuantepec and Juchitán (Istmo de Tehuantepec); San Antonino Castillo Velasco (Valles Centrales) has a unique style

- **belts and other embroidered items** — Santo Tomás Jalieza (Valles Centrales)

artisanal textiles in Teotitlán del Valle

Best Festivals

If there's one thing Oaxacans love more than their culture, it's celebrating it. Just about any time of year you come, you'll be able to dance and drink and eat to celebrate a patron saint, recipe, indigenous culture, and other things Oaxacans hold dear to their hearts. Here is a list of the state's best festivals, but there are many, many more, so if you see a *calenda* (street parade) coming down the street, don't hesitate to join the party.

Day of the Dead

- **Where:** Oaxaca City, Xoxocotlán, San Agustín Etla, and elsewhere
- **When:** end of October, beginning of November

Oaxaca is renowned for its **Día de Muertos** (Day of the Dead) celebrations. The Day of the Dead is a syncretism of an ancient Mesoamerican holiday with the Catholic days of observance All Souls' Day and All Saints' Day. November 1 and 2 are the official holidays, but celebrations more or less span the months of October and November.

In Oaxaca City, the day passes in a haze of parades, costumes, and dancing in the streets. After nightfall, Oaxaca City is tinged with an eerie orange glow from burning *copal* incense, and a brass band plays an otherworldly dirge at the entrance to the Xoxocotlán Cemetery. Visitors may be invited into the homes of strangers to view altars made to their deceased loved ones. Fireworks are everywhere.

The citizens of San Agustín Etla observe the holiday in their own unique way, with a ghoulish parade called **La Muerteada** on November 1. It's a raucous, alcohol-fueled all-nighter that fills the town's streets with music, fireworks, costumed dancers, and locals and visitors alike.

Guelaguetza

- **Where:** Oaxaca City, Zaachila, and elsewhere

the Dance of the Feather at the Guelaguetza

observing Day of the Dead traditions

decorations at a *vela,* a traditional raucous party in the Istmo de Tehuantepec

- **When:** last two Mondays in July; various dates in other towns

Also called **Lunes del Cerro** (Mondays on the Hill), the **Guelaguetza** is a celebration of the diverse customs and creations of the various cultures tucked away in the eight regions of the state. The official Guelaguetza is held in Oaxaca City on the last two Mondays of July, but communities all over the state have their own Guelaguetza or Los Lunes del Cerro at other times of the year. One of the most popular is in Zaachila, which is also held in July.

Zipolite Nudist Festival

- **Where:** Zipolite
- **When:** first weekend in February

The **Zipolite Nudist Festival** is a three-day, stitch-free celebration of what your momma gave you that includes traditional dances, music, yoga, theater, *calendas,* and more.

Feria Anual de Teposcolula

- **Where:** Teposcolula
- **When:** end of February, beginning of March

At Teposcolula's nearly three-week-long **Feria Anual** (Annual Fair), experience riotous *calendas,* live music, regional foods, and two traditional games: *pelota Mixteca,* a Mixtec ball game played with a heavy rubber glove, and the *juego de batalla,* a game similar to hockey but played with a ball that is on fire.

San Agustinillo Eco Fest

- **Where:** San Agustinillo
- **When:** mid-March

The **San Agustinillo Eco Fest** is a four-day event with conferences on ecology, fishing excursions, photography exhibitions, whale watching, concerts, and more. It's held at the time of year when migrating humpback whales pass by Oaxaca's shores.

Fiestas de Mayo

- **Where:** Istmo de Tehuantepec
- **When:** end of April through May

The people of El Istmo know how to party. They

even have their own word for it: *vela*. The main *vela* season is in May, during the **Fiestas de Mayo,** with the first *velas* beginning at the end of April. A *vela* is typically three nonstop days and nights of drinking, eating, and dancing to the regional musical style known as *el son istmeño.* Even the preparations are turned into celebrations.

Feria Regional de Hongos Silvestres

- **Where:** Cuajimoloyas
- **When:** penultimate weekend in July

The **Feria Regional de Hongos Silvestres** (Regional Wild Mushroom Fair) is a two-day festival of workshops, classes, and hikes focused on identifying, preparing, and consuming edible wild mushrooms. This is not a magic mushroom festival—some species that grow here have medicinal properties, but the majority are for plain old cooking and enjoying.

3 de Octubre Festival

- **Where:** Miahuatlán de Porfirio Díaz
- **When:** October 3

The unique **3 de Octubre Festival** commemorates General Porfirio Díaz leading a battalion to victory against the French here in 1866. The show begins in the afternoon, with a *cabalgata*, a parade of horses. Then at night, a riotous party ensues in the *zócalo*. Kids shoot soapy, sometimes colored water at each other and break confetti eggs over each other's heads. Around the *zócalo*, people set up bamboo cages, and throughout the melee, young folks grab unsuspecting revelers and drag them inside. If you're caught, you'll have to pay a few pesos to make bail—so keep some coins in your pockets.

Feria Gráfica Oaxaca

- **Where:** Oaxaca City
- **When:** October 31 and November 1

If you're in Oaxaca City for Day of the Dead, don't miss the **Feria Gráfica Oaxaca** (Oaxaca Printmaking Fair), held on October 31 and November 1 at Taller Espacio Alternativo (Alternative Space Workshop). The best woodcut, linotype, etching, and other printmaking artists from Oaxaca and elsewhere in Mexico come here to showcase their incredible work.

Mazunte Jazz Festival

- **Where:** Mazunte
- **When:** mid-November

The biggest festival on this stretch of coastline is the **International Jazz Festival of Mazunte.** Not strictly a jazz event, this three-evening festival usually includes genres such as rock, reggae, afrobeat, *trova*, and more.

Noche de Rábanos

- **Where:** Oaxaca City
- **When:** December 23

During the colonial period, farmers would carve religious images into giant radishes to catch the eyes of shoppers in the Christmas market on December 23. The **Noche de Rábanos** (Night of the Radishes) was formalized into an official competition in 1897, and farmers have been carving like crazy to one-up each other ever since. Farmers from the surrounding valleys proudly display their large arrangements of vegetal nativity scenes and aspects of Oaxacan life and culture in the Zócalo in the late afternoon; judging begins around 9pm.

Oaxaca City

For a year and a half, I lived in a small town at the edge of the desert two hours south of Oaxaca de Juárez. A quick van ride after work on Friday would get me here just in time to check into Hotel Chocolate for the weekend and spend the rest of the night darting in and out of bars and *mezcalerías* (mezcal bars), breakfast on my mind. I've come three times for Día de Muertos, followed enough boisterous *calendas* (street parades) down the Andador Macedonio Alcalá to need an extra hand to count them on, and eaten so many chiles rellenos at my favorite stall in the 20 de Noviembre market that the folks there don't even hand me a menu anymore. Still, this energetic city has something new in store for me every time I visit.

Getting to know this small but endlessly surprising city doesn't

Highlights

Look for ★ to find recommended sights, activities, dining, and lodging.

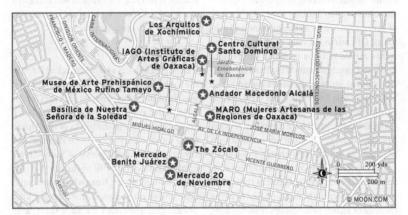

★ **The Zócalo:** Like a heart, the vibrant main square pumps life through the city, with cultural activities and live music to keep you on your toes—literally. Join the dance (page 48).

★ **Mercado Benito Juárez:** The city's main market is abuzz with both locals and visitors socializing and shopping for everything from textiles to fried grasshoppers (page 49).

★ **Basílica de Nuestra Señora de la Soledad:** This 17th-century baroque cathedral is one of the best places in town to catch the sunset—plus you can enjoy artisanal ice cream in the adjoining Jardín Sócrates (page 50).

★ **Museo de Arte Prehispánico de México Rufino Tamayo:** This breathtaking collection of pre-Hispanic carved stone and ceramic artwork was the personal trove of painter Rufino Tamayo (page 50).

★ **Andador Macedonio Alcalá:** This cobblestoned pedestrian walkway lined with cafés, bars, and art galleries leads like a main artery to another of Oaxaca's vital organs, the Templo de Santo Domingo (page 52).

★ **Centro Cultural Santo Domingo:** Housed in the masterpiece 16th-century church complex of the same name, this museum exhibits Oaxaca's most important archaeological discoveries (page 54).

★ **Los Arquitos de Xochimilco:** Residents have used the arches of the 18th-century San Felipe Aqueduct to frame the front doors of their homes, creating fantastic photo ops (page 56).

★ **IAGO (Instituto de Artes Gráficas de Oaxaca):** Founded by the renowned artist Francisco Toledo, IAGO has a small exhibition space, an extensive arts library, and a store selling hauntingly beautiful artwork (page 72).

★ **MARO (Mujeres Artesanas de las Regiones de Oaxaca):** This women's artisan co-op sells handiwork from all regions of the state at some of the best prices in town (page 72).

★ **Mercado 20 de Noviembre:** Oaxaca's main gastronomic market is home to the tastiest food in town, as well as the unique dining experience of the **Hall of Grilled Meats** (page 81).

happen overnight, or in a day, or even years. A first trip here is like stubbing your toe on a hypnotizingly beautiful rock that, upon closer inspection, is merely the capstone of a great pyramid that doesn't cease to astonish as you remove the layers.

This time it was the green in the limestone. Founded two years after the infamous arrival of Hernán Cortés, the entire Centro Histórico was built of *cantera verde*, a quarry stone distinct in Mexico for its light tinge of green somewhere between mint and seafoam. Of course I'd seen the columns and saints carved into the facade of the Templo de Santo Domingo many times before, and already posed for pictures under the arches of Los Arquitos de Xochimilco, but the way I was rubbernecking at buildings I'd seen dozens of times before, you'd have thought it was my first day in town. The color goes so well with the light of a sunset that it's hard to look away.

Maybe it's all the color everywhere else. Subtle tones aren't really Oaxaca's thing, and turning a corner in the capital is like twisting the tube of a great kaleidoscope. Eye-catching colors dominate the scene everywhere you go, in the elaborate embroidery of the *huipiles* and the psychedelic skin of the *alebrijes* (painted wooden figures). They're in the bright coats of paint on the houses. In the flowers peeking out of home gardens and hanging in the trees. In the food, the hues as bold as the flavors they represent.

Even Mexicans from other parts of the country (a considerably colorful place itself) will rant and rave about the culture, festivities, and flavors here. Almost everyone, except those from Puebla, will admit that this is the best place to eat *mole,* and there's no denying that Oaxacan cooks are the most creative with it. Everyone knows that this is where people eat *chapulines* (there's no missing the heaps of chile- and lime-flavored fried grasshoppers in the Mercado Benito Juárez), that this is where the best cheese is made, and

that, even though other states produce mezcal, Oaxacan *palenqueros* (mezcal producers) are the true experts.

When I consider this and more, I'm baffled by a common trend I see among foreign visitors to Oaxaca. Many travelers are so (understandably) hell-bent on getting to the coast that they think of Oaxaca City as a quick layover, giving it a measly day or two of their itineraries. If you had this in mind, don't take this as a rebuke. I'm only looking out for you. You need to let this place surprise you.

HISTORY

Although Zapotecs and Mixtecs had lived in the Valles Centrales for thousands of years, it was the Aztecs who founded Oaxaca City. In 1486, Aztec emperor Ahuitzotl dispatched a group of warriors to the banks of the Atoyac River in an effort to colonize Zapotec territory. They felled a grove of *guaje* (river tamarind) trees on a hill to the north of the river and built a fort, from which they could keep an eye on Cocijoeza, the Zapotec king of Zaachila, and called the place Huaxyacac (Guaje Point) in Nahuatl. This hill, to the northwest of the Centro (downtown), is now called the Cerro del Fortín, or "Hill of the Small Fort." They began a full-fledged invasion of Zapotec territory in 1495.

The Aztecs' imperialistic plans in the region were thwarted a few decades later by those of Hernán Cortés and his cohort of conquistadors, who arrived in Mexico in 1519. They arrived in Oaxaca the next year and called it Guajaca, also in honor of the trees that grew in abundance in the area. In 1521, after the fall of Tenochtitlán (modern-day Mexico City) Cortés sent Francisco de Orozco to Oaxaca because Aztec emperor Moctezuma had told them that the gold they searched for was here. Among Orozco's company was Friar Juan Díaz, who is remembered as saying the first Catholic mass in Oaxaca. It took place beneath a large tree on the banks of

---

Previous: dancers called Las Chinas Oaxaqueñas; textiles for sale in the Mercado Benito Juárez; the Templo de Santo Domingo.

the Atoyac, where the Templo de San Juan de Dios, in the northwest corner of the Mercado 20 de Noviembre, now stands. Orozco had commands to change the name of the settlement to Segura de la Frontera, but the name didn't stick, and most Spanish settlers kept calling it Guajaca.

After a series of power struggles between different groups of Spanish colonizers sent to Guajaca by Cortés, the town was officially named Villa de Antequera in 1528. In 1532, Spanish king Carlos V officially recognized Antequera as a "very noble and faithful city." This name was changed to Oaxaca (a derivative of Huaxyacac) in 1821, and in 1872, after the death of beloved president of Mexico and native Oaxacan Benito Juárez, it changed again to the current iteration, Oaxaca de Juárez.

The economic boom of tourism began to flourish in Oaxaca in the second half of the 20th century. The archaeological expeditions of Monte Albán, Mitla, and other pre-Hispanic sites, as well as the popularity of folk art like *alebrijes* and *barro negro* (black clay pottery), began to attract curious globetrotters from all over the world (not to mention the hippies drawn to Maria Sabina and her magic mushrooms in Huautla de Jiménez). In the second decade of the 21st century, mezcal joined the ranks of Oaxaca's heavy-hitting tourist attractions, and the industry is currently riding high on this wave, leading to new economic opportunities for Oaxacan mezcal producers and entrepreneurs, who are exporting more than ever and opening up bars, restaurants, and hotels designed to further the knowledge and culture of this artisanal spirit. Oaxaca City was and still is the nucleus of this tourism, a vibrant capital city showcasing the best of what the rest of the state has to offer.

PLANNING YOUR TIME

Three or four unhurried days in Oaxaca City should give you enough time to fully experience the city. If it's your first time here, I imagine you'll be walking around with hearts for eyes, just as I did on my first visit.

Eating in Oaxaca City is an experience you will not find anywhere else in the world. For example, staples of the cuisine here, such as the *chile de agua* (a pepper with good flavor; sometimes spicy) and the cacao-based beverage *tejate,* are pretty much impossible to get outside of the Valles Centrales. If you see a plate made with *chile pasilla mixe* (a pepper with rich, smoky flavor; light, lingering spice), also called *pasilla oaxaqueño,* order it. And don't leave the city without eating at least once in the **Mercado 20 de Noviembre.**

In true Oaxacan fashion, even the colonial **architecture** here is unique. The limestone has a pastel green tinge to it, something like seafoam, or what I like to call zombie-skin green. But you won't find much *cantera verde* elsewhere in the state, where you'll find yellow and pink hues in the church facades, or even in Mexico.

Outstanding examples of colonial architecture in Oaxaca City include the crowd favorite **Templo de Santo Domingo,** at the north end of the **Andador Macedonio Alcalá,** and the **Basílica de Nuestra Señora de la Soledad,** west from the Zócalo down Avenida de la Independencia. You'll see tons of great old architecture on the way, too. Make sure to stop into the **Centro Cultural San Pablo,** housed in the old convent that would have had the grandiose reputation that Santo Domingo now has, had an earthquake not put the kibosh on its original construction.

Immerse yourself in the exciting history and art of Oaxaca in its plethora of world-class **museums.** Two hours or so in the **Centro Cultural Santo Domingo** are obligatory, as you'll see all the riches that archaeologist Alfonso Caso and his team unearthed in Tomb 7 of Monte Albán.

The **Museo de Arte Prehispánico de México Rufino Tamayo** is an art museum with an archaeological bent. Oaxacan native and world-famous painter Rufino Tamayo chose the pieces for their artistic, rather than their archaeological, value, and the collection truly does stand out from regular anthropology museums, showcasing the boundless

Oaxaca City

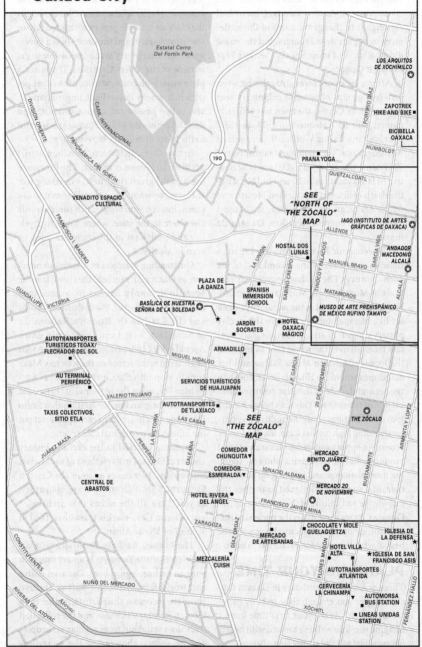

Estatal Cerro
Del Fortín Park

190

LOS ARQUITOS
DE XOCHIMILCO

ZAPOTREK
HIKE AND BIKE

BICIBELLA
OAXACA

HUMBOLDT

PORFIRIO DÍAZ

PRANA YOGA

QUETZALCOATL

CARR. INTERNACIONAL

PANORÁMICA DEL FORTÍN

DIVISIÓN ORIENTE

VENADITO ESPACIO
CULTURAL

SEE
"NORTH OF
THE ZÓCALO"
MAP

IAGO (INSTITUTO DE ARTES
GRÁFICAS DE OAXACA)

ALLENDE

ANDADOR
MACEDONIO
ALCALÁ

FRANCISCO I. MADERO

HOSTAL DOS
LUNAS

MANUEL BRAVO

GARCÍA VIGIL

ALCALÁ

GUADALUPE VICTORIA

LA UNIÓN

PLAZA DE
LA DANZA

SPANISH
IMMERSION
SCHOOL

SABINO CRESPO

TINOCO Y PALACIOS

MATAMOROS

BASÍLICA DE NUESTRA
SEÑORA DE LA SOLEDAD

MUSEO DE ARTE PREHISPÁNICO
DE MÉXICO RUFINO TAMAYO

JARDÍN
SOCRATES

HOTEL
OAXACA
MÁGICO

AUTOTRANSPORTES
TURÍSTICOS TEOAX/
FLECHADOR DEL SOL

ARMADILLO

MIGUEL HIDALGO

J.P. GARCÍA

20 DE NOVIEMBRE

AU TERMINAL
PERIFÉRICO

SERVICIOS TURÍSTICOS
DE HUAJUAPAN

VALERIO TRUJANO

TAXIS COLECTIVOS,
SITIO ETLA

AUTOTRANSPORTES
DE TLAXIACO

LAS CASAS

SEE
"THE ZÓCALO"
MAP

THE ZÓCALO

ARMENTA Y LÓPEZ

PERIFÉRICO

LA VICTORIA

GALEANA

JUÁREZ MAZA

COMEDOR
CHUNQUITA

MERCADO
BENITO JUÁREZ

BUSTAMANTE

CENTRAL DE
ABASTOS

COMEDOR
ESMERALDA

IGNACIO ALDAMA

HOTEL RIVERA
DEL ÁNGEL

MERCADO 20
DE NOVIEMBRE

DÍAZ ORDAZ

FRANCISCO JAVIER MINA

ZARAGOZA

CHOCOLATE Y MOLE
GUELAGUETZA

IGLESIA DE
LA DEFENSA

CONSTITUYENTES

MERCADO
DE ARTESANÍAS

FLORES MAGÓN

HOTEL VILLA
ALTA

IGLESIA DE SAN
FRANCISCO ASÍS

MEZCALERÍA
CUISH

AUTOTRANSPORTES
ATLÁNTIDA

NUÑO DEL MERCADO

CERVECERÍA
LA CHINAMPA

AUTOMORSA
BUS STATION

RIVERAS DEL ATOYAC

Atoyac

XÓCHITL

FERNÁNDEZ FIALLO

LÍNEAS UNIDAS
STATION

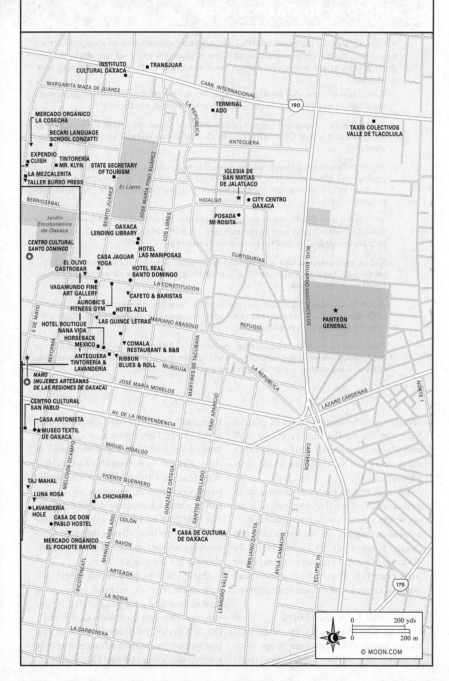

INSTITUTO CULTURAL OAXACA ■ TRANSJUAR

MARGARITA MAZA DE JUÁREZ

CARR. INTERNACIONAL

190

TERMINAL ■ ADO

MERCADO ORGÁNICO LA COSECHA

BECARI LANGUAGE SCHOOL CONZATTI

LA REPÚBLICA

ANTEQUERA

TAXIS COLECTIVOS VALLE DE TLACOLULA

EXPENDIO ▼ CUISH
TINTORERÍA ▼ MR. KLYN

STATE SECRETARY OF TOURISM

LA MEZCALERITA ▼
TALLER BURRO PRESS ■

El Llano

JOSÉ MARÍA PINO SUÁREZ

IGLESIA DE SAN MATÍAS DE JALATLACO

HIDALGO

★ ● CITY CENTRO OAXACA

BENITO JUÁREZ

BERRIOZÁBAL

Jardín Etnobotánico de Oaxaca

CENTRO CULTURAL SANTO DOMINGO ✪

LOS LIBRES

OAXACA LENDING LIBRARY

POSADA ● MI ROSITA

CURTIDURÍAS

EL OLIVO GASTROBAR

HOTEL LAS MARIPOSAS

CASA JAGUAR YOGA

HOTEL REAL SANTO DOMINGO

VAGAMUNDO FINE ART GALLERY

LA CONSTITUCIÓN

CAFETO & BARISTAS ▼

AUROBIC'S FITNESS GYM

HOTEL AZUL ●

5 DE MAYO

LAS QUINCE LETRAS ▼

MARIANO ABASOLO

REFUGIO

PANTEÓN GENERAL ★

HOTEL BOUTIQUE NANA VIDA ■

REFORMA

HORSÉBACK MEXICO ■

COMALA RESTAURANT & B&B ▼

ANTEQUERA TINTORERÍA & LAVANDERÍA ▼

RIBBON BLUES & ROLL ▼

MURGUÍA

MARTÍRES DE TACUBAYA

LA REPÚBLICA

BLVD. EDUARDO VASCONCELOS

LÁZARO CÁRDENAS

MARO ★ (MUJERES ARTESANAS DE LAS REGIONES DE OAXACA) ✪

JOSÉ MARÍA MORELOS

FRAY APARICIO

CARTEROS

NORTE 1

CENTRO CULTURAL SAN PÁBLO ■

AV. DE LA INDEPENDENCIA

CASA ANTONIETA

MUSEO TEXTIL DE OAXACA ● ★

MIGUEL HIDALGO

MELCHOR OCAMPO

VICENTE GUERRERO

GONZÁLEZ ORTEGA

SANTOS DEGOLLADO

TAJ MAHAL ▼

LUNA ROSA ▼

LA CHICHARRA ●

LAVANDERÍA HOLE ■

CASA DE DON PABLO HOSTEL ●

MANUEL DOBLADO

COLÓN

CASA DE CULTURA DE OAXACA ■

ECLIPSE 70

175

MERCADO ORGÁNICO EL POCHOTE RAYÓN

RAYÓN

XICOTÉNCATL

ARTEAGA

LEÁNDRO VALLE

EMILIANO ZAPATA

ÁVILA CAMACHO

LA NORIA

LA CARBONERA

0   200 yds
0   200 m

© MOON.COM

One Day in Oaxaca City

A single day really isn't sufficient to let Oaxaca City sink in (and definitely not enough time to eat everything), but it's sometimes unavoidable. This whirlwind itinerary will take you by the best sights in town, as well as my favorite places to eat, snack, and refuel. We don't have much time, so keep up!

- **8am:** Up and at 'em, y'all! Breakfast will be at **Portal del Marqués,** where owners María and Alfonso serve a delicious house-made jam of homegrown blackberries.

- **9am:** Despite my apparent gusto, it takes me a while to join the land of the conscious, so we'll need to stop in at **Café Brújula,** a block north on the Andador Macedonio Alcalá, for espressos.

- **9:30am:** From here, it's back down to Avenida Independencia, where we'll take a right and stop by the **Catedral de Nuestra Señora de la Asunción** on our way to the **Museo de Arte Prehispánico de México Rufino Tamayo,** a collection of spectacular pre-Hispanic relics.

- **10:30am:** We'll continue west to check out the **Basílica de Nuestra Señora de la Soledad,** three blocks west. In the adjoining **Jardín Sócrates,** we'll grab some *nieves* (artisanal ice cream). Try the *beso oaxaqueño* (Oaxacan kiss).

- **11am:** We'll spend an hour or so wandering the aisles of the **Mercado Benito Juárez,** with a quick stop at the stylish booth **La Flor de Huayapam** to sample some *tejate*, a cacao-based pre-Hispanic drink.

- **Noon:** Lunch at **Mercado 20 de Noviembre.** I'm gonna have a chile relleno and a cup of Oaxacan chocolate because I have a soft spot for cheese and peppers, but you must try the *mole negro* here. Tip the musicians.

- **1pm:** After lunch we'll take a stroll down the **Andador Macedonio Alcalá,** stopping in at the modern ceramics gallery of **Omar Hernández** and at **IAGO,** the Graphic Arts Institute of Oaxaca, founded by iconic Oaxacan visual artist Francisco Toledo.

creativity, rich imagination, and playful humor of the pre-Hispanic people from all over Mexico. The artistic detail preserved in these pieces will have your jaw on the floor for over an hour.

Oaxaca's smaller specialty museums are so well curated that you'll find yourself fully engrossed in a theme you weren't previously interested in. Stop into the **Museo de Filatelia** (Stamp Museum) or the **Museo Textil de Oaxaca** (Textile Museum of Oaxaca) for some beautifully displayed exhibitions, phenomenal artwork, and fun, interesting stories.

High and Low Seasons

High season in Oaxaca City corresponds to the **major festivals** here. From **mid-October to mid-November,** the streets throng with visitors for **Día de Muertos** (Day of the Dead). They fill back up again at the **end of December** for **Christmas** celebrations. The two-week **Semana Santa** (Holy Week) vacation around **Easter** is a popular travel period for Mexican people, and Oaxaca City is a major destination during this time. The month of **July** is also a very busy time here, as people from all over the world come to experience the **Guelaguetza** festival, a celebration of the region's cultures.

Outside of these periods, you should have no problem reserving rooms or just showing up and finding a great place to stay. If your trip coincides with these festivals, especially Día de Muertos, you'll need to book at least two to three months in advance to get the room of your choice (or anything at all).

- **3pm:** I need more coffee. After a quick refueling around the corner at **Coffee Beans,** we'll check out the treasures of Monte Albán in the museum at the **Centro Cultural Santo Domingo.**

- **5pm:** We'll take a 15-minute break in the **Parque Labastida** to rest our trotters and check out the work of local artists who set up shop here. Unless there's music; then we're dancing.

- **5:15pm:** Alright, look alive, folks. Time to go shopping: xylography, or woodcut prints, at **Gabinete Gráfico;** *artesanías* (folk art) at **Huizache Arte Vivo de Oaxaca, La Casa de las Artesanías,** and **MARO,** a cooperative run by over 400 skilled indigenous Oaxacan women; and modern fashions made with traditional textiles at stores like **Shkaála de Micaela** and the boutique of **Liliana del Toro.**

- **7pm:** Time for dinner—and I'll bet you could use a drink after my bossing you around all day. One of the proprietary mezcals of **Expendio Tradición** will be just what you need. We'll share a plate of *botanas* (finger foods), and I recommend absolutely anything else on the menu. I have never not said "Wow" after a first bite here.

- **9pm:** One more sight to see before we hit up the *mezcalerías* (mezcal bars): **Los Arquitos de Xochimilco,** the remains of an 18th-century aqueduct that have been incorporated into surrounding architecture of the neighborhood. Fellow fans of the movie *Nacho Libre* can quote lines with me and snap pics in goofy Jack Black poses under the archway where a scene in the movie was filmed.

- **9:30pm:** We'll try the proprietary brands of mezcal at **Los Amantes** and **El Cortijo** before finishing our *mezcalería* tour at **In Situ,** which boasts the widest variety of distilled agave beverages of any bar of its type in the world.

- **11:30pm:** Back to the Zócalo to finish out the night dancing to the cumbia and salsa rhythms of the marimba band that plays outside **Del Jardín,** at the southwest corner of the square.

And thus ends our fast and furious day in Oaxaca City. I know you'll be back, so we won't say *adiós* but rather *¡Hasta la próxima!* (Until next time!).

ORIENTATION

One of the great things about Oaxaca is how walkable it is. Just about everything you want to see within the city is packed into the **Centro** (downtown district), the nucleus of which is the laurel tree-shaded main square called the **Zócalo.** The block to the north is taken up by the Catedral de Nuestra Señora de la Asunción (Cathedral of Our Lady of the Assumption), whose elaborate baroque facade faces the **Alameda de León,** a smaller, tree-lined plaza named for a famous Oaxacan general and governor. I've always considered this as part of the central plaza as well, so when I refer to the Zócalo, I mean this entire public space.

From here, the streets extend through the Centro in a classic colonial grid pattern,

which would make orientation extremely simple were it not for the sudden changes in street names. Think of the Centro as two halves, north and south, bisected by the **Avenida de la Independencia,** a block north of the Zócalo. All north-south streets change names here, and many east-west streets (but not all) change names at the longitude of the Zócalo, at **Bustamante** to the south, and **Macedonio Alcalá** to the north.

From the Zócalo to the **Templo de Santo Domingo,** six blocks north, stretches the pedestrian street **Andador Macedonio Alcalá,** the main tourist artery of the city, lined with cafés, restaurants, art galleries, and small open-air markets. To keep things simple, you can think of the north half of the

Centro as the touristy side, and the southern half as that of the locals. Businesses north of Independencia cater almost exclusively to tourists, and this section is much more prettified and much less crowded than the south, which—although it offers a lot for visitors— is where Oaxacans are hustling through the streets taking care of business. Because of this division, the southern half is generally much cheaper than the north; if you're on a budget, this is where to look for accommodations.

Sights

★ THE ZÓCALO

The central square of any colonial Mexican city or town is most commonly referred to as the **Zócalo,** but you might hear it called the Plaza de la Constitución, Plaza de Armas, or Plaza Central (Plaza Municipal in smaller towns). Oaxaca's Zócalo is a large plaza with a gazebo at its center and winding walkways through raised gardens, all shaded by gargantuan laurel trees.

The streets of the Zócalo are named *portales* for the broad arcades that face the square; most are full of cafés and restaurants. They are Portal de Clavería to the north, Portal de Flores to the west, Portal de Gobierno to the south, and Portal Benito Juárez to the east. The building on the south side is the **Palacio de Gobierno** (tel. 951/501-8100, 9am-5pm Mon.-Fri.), the entrance of which is often blocked by indigenous protesters occupying the space in response to alleged state violence. These are peaceful demonstrations, and protesters usually sell folk art and other products to fund their causes. For years, the building did not house the state government administrative offices, functioning instead as a museum showcasing the murals of Mexican painter and printmaker Arturo Bustos (1926-2017). Painted in 1980, the three murals represent three stages of Oaxacan history and development: pre-Hispanic Oaxaca, the colonial period, and independence and statehood.

The best point of reference in the city is the **Auditorio Guelaguetza.** It's that giant white, tent-like structure on the **Cerro del Fortín,** which, before the arrival of the Spanish, was called Huaxyacac by the Aztecs who set up a military base at its summit in 1486 in preparation for an invasion nine years later. This marks the farthest northwest point of the Centro, so if you ever get lost, orient yourself in relation to this hill.

In 2018, however, the state government once again took up residence in the limestone building, which dates to 1783. The museum no longer exists, but you can still view the murals in the central stairwell free of charge. If the main entrance is blocked, check the east and west sides of the building.

The church on the north side of the Zócalo is the **Catedral de Nuestra Señora de la Asunción** (Cathedral of Our Lady of the Assumption), an impressive baroque building that, like other churches in Oaxaca, was built stout and heavy because of the earthquakes that are so common in the region. Dating to 1535, it's also simply called the Catedral de Oaxaca. Take 20-30 minutes strolling around inside (free admission), where you'll find high, vaulted ceilings, elaborate stained-glass windows of Saints Paul and Peter, and part of the **Santa Cruz de Huatulco** (Holy Cross of Huatulco). As legend has it, the Spanish explorers who arrived in Huatulco in the 16th century were surprised to find that the people there revered a large wooden cross. They said that it was brought there by a bearded man in a white tunic, and the Spaniards called it a miracle. The story goes that in 1587, English pirate Thomas Cavendish, irked at not finding the riches he'd hoped for, ordered Huatulco to be razed. After the attack, the only thing standing was the cross, but no matter what he tried (hatchets, fire, tying it to his boat),

The Zócalo

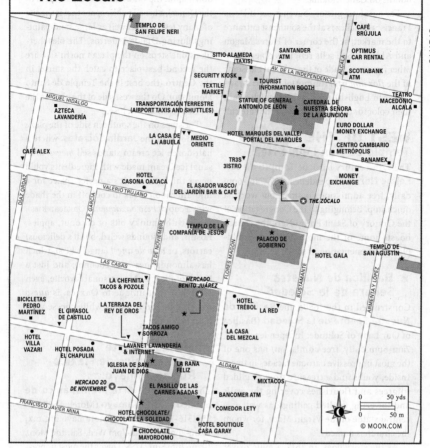

TEMPLO DE SAN FELIPE NERI

CAFÉ BRÚJULA

SITIO ALAMEDA (TAXIS)

SANTANDER ATM

OPTIMUS CAR RENTAL

SECURITY KIOSK

AV. DE LA INDEPENDENCIA

SCOTIABANK ATM

TEXTILE MARKET

TOURIST INFORMATION BOOTH

MIGUEL HIDALGO

AZTECA LAVANDERÍA

TRANSPORTACIÓN TERRESTRE (AIRPORT TAXIS AND SHUTTLES)

STATUE OF GENERAL ANTONIO DE LEÓN

CATEDRAL DE NUESTRA SEÑORA DE LA ASUNCIÓN

TEATRO MACEDONIO ALCALÁ

HOTEL MARQUÉS DEL VALLE/ PORTAL DEL MARQUÉS

EURO DOLLAR MONEY EXCHANGE

CAFÉ ALEX

LA CASA DE LA ABUELA

MEDIO ORIENTE

CENTRO CAMBIARIO METRÓPOLIS

BANAMEX

TR3S 3ISTRO

DÍAZ ORDAZ

HOTEL CASONA OAXACA

VALERIO TRUJANO

EL ASADOR VASCO/ DEL JARDÍN BAR & CAFÉ

MONEY EXCHANGE

THE ZÓCALO

J.P. GARCÍA

TEMPLO DE LA COMPAÑÍA DE JESÚS

PALACIO DE GOBIERNO

TEMPLO DE SAN AGUSTÍN

20 DE NOVIEMBRE

HOTEL GALA

LAS CASAS

FLORES MAGÓN

ARMENTA Y LÓPEZ

BICICLETAS PEDRO MARTÍNEZ

LA CHEFINITA TACOS & POZOLE

MERCADO BENITO JUÁREZ

HOTEL TRÉBOL

LA RED

EL GIRASOL DE CASTILLO

LA TERRAZA DEL REY DE OROS

BUSTAMANTE

LA CASA DEL MEZCAL

HOTEL VILLA VAZARI

HOTEL POSADA EL CHAPULIN

TACOS AMIGO SORROZA

LAVANET LAVANDERÍA & INTERNET

LA RANA FELIZ

ALDAMA

IGLESIA DE SAN JUAN DE DIOS

MIXTACOS

MERCADO 20 DE NOVIEMBRE

EL PASILLO DE LAS CARNES ASADAS

BANCOMER ATM

FRANCISCO JAVIER MINA

COMEDOR LETY

HOTEL CHOCOLATE/ CHOCOLATE LA SOLEDAD

HOTEL BOUTIQUE CASA GARAY

CHOCOLATE MAYORDOMO

0   50 yds
0   50 m

© MOON.COM

---

he couldn't destroy the thing. The cross was later broken down into smaller crosses, and one of them was installed in a side chapel in the southwest corner of the church. The other three are in Mexico City, Puebla, and the Vatican.

AROUND THE ZÓCALO
★ Mercado Benito Juárez

A block south of the southwest corner of the Zócalo, the **Mercado Benito Juárez** (tel. 951/516-2352, 7am-9pm daily) has been the main market for Oaxacans living in the Centro since 1893. It's easy to while away a

few hours strolling the narrow aisles of kaleidoscopic textiles, folk art, leather goods, flowers, ice cream, and much more. Be sure to try the pre-Hispanic cacao-based beverage *tejate* at **La Flor de Huayapam**, in the center of the market.

Although the majority of the booths cater to tourists, many Oaxacans still do their daily shopping here. You'll find fresh meats and fish in the butchers' aisle at the south end, robust coffee from Pluma Hidalgo (Oaxaca's star coffee-growing town) in a tiny stall in the southwest corner, and tortillas and *chapulines* (fried grasshoppers) from the *señoras* you have to squeeze past to get out to the produce booths on Calle Aldama.

For a unique gift or souvenir, see if Doña Francisca Sánchez is at the southeast entrance to the market, at the corner of Flores Magón and Aldama. She sells religious objects and other figurines made of the colorful blossoms of the *flor inmortal* (immortal flower; strawflower in English), the petals of which retain their color for up to 45 years after they are cut.

WEST OF THE ZÓCALO
Templo de San Felipe Neri

The 17th-century baroque **Templo de San Felipe Neri** (Independencia 407, 7am-6pm daily, free admission) is small but worth a quick stop. Belonging to the Congregation of the Oratory of Saint Philip Neri, the church boasts some of the most impressive gold-plated ornamentation in the city.

★ Basílica de Nuestra Señora de la Soledad

Constructed in the 1680s, the **Basílica de Nuestra Señora de la Soledad** (Basilica of Our Lady of Solitude; Independencia 107, 7am-6pm daily, free admission) has one of the most impressive baroque facades in town. Inside, you'll find a treasure trove of gilded filigrees and flourishes covering the walls and towering vaulted ceilings, as well as a central statue of the Virgin Mary, for whom the church is named.

As the story goes, in 1617, a mule driver from Veracruz on his way to Guatemala noticed an extra mule in his train when he got to Oaxaca. When he passed a small chapel dedicated to Saint Sebastian, the mule collapsed. The driver could not get the stubborn thing to stand up and move, so he alerted the authorities of the situation, so as not to arouse suspicion that he was stealing anything. When the police arrived, they removed the mule's load, and the animal died instantly. When they opened the box, they found an image of the Virgin Mary, prompting Bishop Bartolomé Bohórquez to order the basilica to be built in honor of the miraculous event.

The limestone saints in the facade look down upon the **Plaza de la Danza** (Plaza of the Dance), a broad public space that is the site of many festivals, as well as large sand paintings during Día de Muertos. The bleacher-like stone steps on the plaza's north side are the second-best place to catch the sunset in the Centro (the best is the Templo de Santo Domingo). On the west side of the plaza is the Ex Convento de San José.

The steps on the southern side of the plaza lead down to the **Jardín Sócrates,** where a half-dozen ice cream stands sell *nieves*, artisanal ice cream made with ingredients you'd never think to use. It's a perfect place for a mid-afternoon break to cool off in the shade with a cup of *beso oaxaqueño* (Oaxacan kiss), made with chunky bits of coconut, apples, raisins, and (sounds weird, but it's delicious) carrots, or *beso de ángel* (angel's kiss), which has almonds, peanuts, coconut, and just a touch of mezcal. My personal favorite, even though it isn't unique to Oaxaca, is *queso con zarzamora*, or tangy white cheese with blackberries.

★ Museo de Arte Prehispánico de México Rufino Tamayo

The **Museo de Arte Prehispánico de México Rufino Tamayo** (Morelos 503, tel. 951/516-7617, www.rufinotamayo.org.mx, 10am-2pm and 4pm-7pm Wed.-Sat. and Mon., 10am-2pm Sun., US$5) owns the most impressive collection of pre-Hispanic Mexican artifacts I've seen outside of the National Museum of Anthropology in Mexico City. But this is not an anthropology museum. Oaxacan-born painter Rufino Tamayo (1899-1991) curated the collection over two decades, selecting works according to their aesthetic value. In addition to personal interest, his goal was to keep them safe from illegal exportation, as has happened with other priceless Mexican

---

1: the arches and patios of the Zócalo 2: carved skulls at the Museo de Arte Prehispánico de México Rufino Tamayo 3: the Basílica de Nuestra Señora de la Soledad

artifacts. He donated the collection to found the museum and preserve and showcase the exceptional artistic talent of pre-Hispanic peoples from all over Mexico. The 1,059 displayed pieces are arranged into five rooms, each painted one of Tamayo's favorite colors. Works are arranged thematically according to their subject and artistic style.

There are Olmec vases in the shape of crab-walking human figures; Aztec statues of sly, snickering old women; and completely intact life-size Mayan stone carvings. You'll find the grinning face of Tlaloc, the Aztec god of rain, etched into dark, porous volcanic stone, and sections of murals from Teotihuacán and other pieces that still display their original coloring. The collection is in immaculate condition. Such well-preserved detail offers insight into the rich imaginations, deep spiritual lives, and, perhaps most surprisingly, fun senses of humor of the ancient peoples of Mexico.

As far as museums in Oaxaca go, this one is on the pricier end, but it's worth every peso. Printed guides in English, Spanish, and French at the entrance to each room explain the origins and significance of the pieces.

NORTH OF THE ZÓCALO
Centro Cultural San Pablo

Two blocks east of the northeast corner of the Zócalo, the **Centro Cultural San Pablo** (San Pablo Cultural Center; Hidalgo 907, tel. 951/501-8800, www.san-pablo.mx, 10am-8pm Mon.-Sat., 10am-6pm Sun., free admission) has room after room of exhibition space for temporary exhibits that change out regularly but generally showcase the work of contemporary Oaxacan artists and folk art. This whole block (and then some) was once the Convento de San Pablo, the first Dominican convent in Oaxaca, built in the 16th century. It became the Ex Convento de San Pablo after a pair of earthquakes in the early 17th century brought the convent crumbling to the ground; friars moved their operation to the recently finished Santo Domingo Convent.

The brick-paved courtyard spans the block and gives access to both Hidalgo and Independencia. On the Hidalgo side are an exhibition space and a café, and on the north side is the elegant SP Restaurante. Cacti grow up the west wall of the courtyard. Facing east, on your right, you'll see the Retablo de la Virgen del Rosario, a small chapel with a gold-plated altar to the Virgin Mary. The entrance to the left leads to the center's main exhibition space. As in many other small museums in town, curators take full advantage of the beautiful architecture, using it as much as the pieces on loan to create the whole experience of observing art.

The main mission of the friars who lived here was to convert indigenous peoples to Catholicism; for this purpose, they dedicated themselves to learning native Oaxacan languages. This linguistic heritage lives on in the **Biblioteca de Investigación Juan de Córdova** (Juan de Córdova Research Library), which boasts an extensive collection of texts about Zapotec, Mixtec, Mixe, and other indigenous Oaxacan tongues. The library is open to the public, but the books cannot be borrowed.

★ Andador Macedonio Alcalá

The **Andador Macedonio Alcalá** is the main tourist artery of the city, leading north from the Zócalo to the Santo Domingo church via six picturesque, car-free blocks paved with iconic Oaxacan green limestone. Its namesake, violinist and pianist Macedonio Alcalá (1831-1869), composed the waltz "Dios Nunca Muere," now considered to be the de facto anthem of Oaxaca.

This winsome pedestrian walkway is constantly alive with music, art, and festivities. Children sell drawings on the sidewalk, and artists set up easels in **Parque Labastida** to sew the image of the **Iglesia Sangre de Cristo,** the 17th-century baroque masterpiece on the corner with Calle M. Bravo, into the canvas with needle and thread. Four blocks north of the Zócalo, Parque Labastida is a thin, shady public space, usually alive with loquacious students, artists, and dance

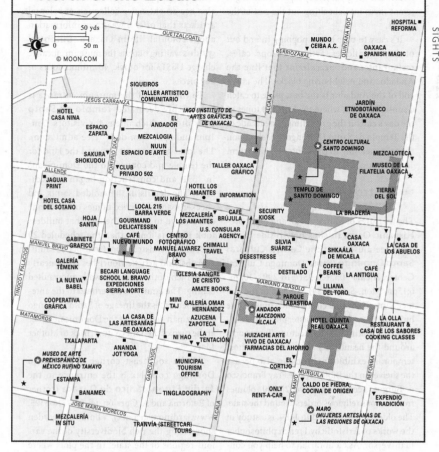

North of the Zócalo

classes. If you're lucky, you'll hear the plaintive wail of Max Cruz's accordion. Max, who is blind, sometimes busks in the street, and it's always pleasant (and more than worth a few pesos as a tip) to stop and listen for 5 or 10 minutes. If you don't catch him on the street, he and violinist Sam McKeone make up Duo Zapocelta, and they play regular gigs at Expendio Tradición and other restaurants, cafés, and cultural venues around town.

Two blocks north of the Zócalo, **MACO (Museo de Arte Contemporáneo de Oaxaca)** (Museum of Contemporary Art of Oaxaca; Alcalá 202, tel. 951/514-2228, www.

museomaco.org, 10:30am-7:45pm Wed.-Mon., US$1) is a gorgeous venue for contemporary art exhibitions. Dating back to the turn of the 18th century, this diligently restored colonial limestone house is called the Casa de Cortés (House of Cortés), although it was never actually owned by the conquistador. The museum's expert curators have two floors of exhibition rooms and two large patios to work with, as well as the Cubo Abierto (Open Cube), a roofless patio reserved for large exhibits. Curators balance the exhibitions between artists from Oaxaca and elsewhere in Mexico and from all over the world. The doors to the Andador are left open during museum hours, allowing passersby a peek that might tempt them into checking out the rest of the rooms.

It's easy to pass hours popping in and out of the art galleries, artisans co-ops, cafés, restaurants, and *mezcalerías* that line the Andador and neighboring blocks. The north end of the Andador is the best place to catch a sunset in town, where the brilliant tones of the day's end on the green limestone facade of the Templo de Santo Domingo will show you the true meaning of the photographer's term "magic hour."

★ Centro Cultural Santo Domingo

The treasures of Monte Albán and other pre-Hispanic Oaxacan sites now reside in the must-see museum at the **Centro Cultural Santo Domingo** (Santo Domingo Cultural Center; Alcalá 505, tel. 951/516-2991, 10am-6:15pm Mon.-Sat., US$4). Housed in the former Santo Domingo church and convent, the building is a shining masterpiece of 16th-century Dominican architecture. Two rooms around the beautifully restored cloister host temporary exhibitions. You can also peruse the shelves in the Biblioteca de Fray Francisco de Burgoa, a collection of over 23,000 volumes from various religious orders around the state. The oldest book, printed in 1484, is a study of the works of Aristotle by French philosopher Juan Versor. Ask a librarian to help you consult a particular book if you're interested. You can view microfilms of books not in a condition to be handled.

The gold is upstairs. A handful of large rooms house a great number of well-preserved ceramic funeral urns, vases, and figurines. The first room to your right after climbing the ornate stairwell is the treasure trove of gold, silver, and turquoise that archaeologists led by Alfonso Caso (1896-1970) discovered in Monte Albán's Tomb 7 in 1931. Filigreed gold earrings decorated with intricately detailed faces and other pieces of jade and silver jewelry glitter in the weak archival light. The star of the show is a human skull covered in a "skin" of turquoise fragments. The museum also has an extensive collection of colonial artifacts that offer a wealth of information about colonial life in Oaxaca. **Bilingual guides** waiting outside the museum entrance charge US$13 for quick, 40-minute tours of key pieces.

To the right of the museum entrance is the lavishly decorated **Templo de Santo Domingo,** which opens for visitors 7am-1pm and 5pm-8pm daily (free admission). The local government donated the land for the temple and convent to the Dominicans in 1551, and construction began immediately. The details in the molded saints and checkerboard-patterned domes of the facade alone serve to justify the fact that builders took 10 years longer than the scheduled 20 to complete construction. Gold-plated saints, cherubs, and artistic flourishes cover nearly every inch of the interior's walls and vaulted ceiling. The family tree overhead in the antechamber traces the lineage of Santo Domingo de Guzmán, founder of the Dominican Order at the turn of the 13th century, back to Mother Mary.

At the southeast corner of the Santo Domingo complex is the entrance to the **Jardín Etnobotánico de Oaxaca** (corner of Reforma and A. Gurrión, tel. 951/516-5325, www.jardinoaxaca.mx), a botanical garden showcasing the rich biodiversity of the various regions of the state. In the plots where Dominican friars once tended to their rows of vegetables, over 800 species of cacti, flowers, and trees endemic to Oaxaca now grow, among artwork by contemporary Oaxacan artists Francisco Toledo (who passed away in 2019) and Luis Zárate. According to Toledo, informational plaques are "visual pollution," so there is no signage, and visitors are not allowed to wander the garden unattended. Scheduled tours in Spanish are at 10am, noon, and 5pm Monday-Saturday and cost US$3.

1: Andador Macedonio Alcalá **2:** Los Arquitos de Xochimilco

English tours are only offered on Tuesday, Thursday, and Saturday at 11am and cost US$5.50. Children 12 and under get in free.

Small Museums

I can't rave enough about the level of talent apparent in the curators of Oaxaca's smaller museums. They have style and an obvious passion for the work they present.

Two blocks east of the northeast corner of the Zócalo, the **Museo Textil de Oaxaca** (Textile Museum of Oaxaca; Hidalgo 917, tel. 951/501-1104, www.museotextildeoaxaca. org, 10am-8pm Mon.-Sat., 10am-6pm Sun., free admission) is a shining example of this curatorial talent. Given the level of skill of Oaxacan textile workers, it's no wonder people from all over the world want to put their work in the hands of curator Alejandro de Ávila Blomberg. The lighting is ingenious: elegantly dim in a darkened room to bring out the rich tones in the pieces and nothing more, and all-white blouses lit from the inside to put the intricate needlework into relief. The museum shows these shirts, shawls, and table runners for what they truly are: fine art.

From Parque Labastida on the Andador, walk one block west on M. Bravo to find the **Centro Fotográfico Manuel Álvarez Bravo** (Manuel Álvarez Bravo Photographic Center; M. Bravo 116, tel. 951/516-9800, diffusion.cfab@gmail.com, 9:30am-8pm Wed.-Mon., free admission). Founded by (surprise) noted Oaxacan artist Francisco Toledo (1940-2019) and named in honor of Mexico's first leading artistic photographer, who passed away in 2002, the museum hosts temporary exhibits by photographers from all over the globe. Also on-site and open to the public is the Fonoteca Eduardo Mata, a music library with over 3,000 recordings of classical, jazz, world, and popular music.

The small but very well-curated **Museo de Filatelia** (Stamp Museum; Reforma 504, tel. 951/514-2375, www.mufi.org.mx, 10am-8pm Mon.-Sat., 10am-6pm Sun., free admission), on the block to the east of the Jardín Etnobotánico, is a lot more fun than philately,

or stamp collecting, sounds. In addition to an extensive collection of postage from all over the world dating back centuries, the museum also has a permanent exhibition of handwritten letters by painter Frida Kahlo, most of which were written to her doctor Leo Eloesser.

★ Los Arquitos de Xochimilco

From Santo Domingo, walk north on Alcalá past the Jardín Carbajal and take a left onto the short pedestrian walkway Calle de Xólotl. At its west end is the Plazuela de la Cruz de Piedra, with its large stone cross statue, and just beyond, **Los Arquitos de Xochimilco,** the remains of the 18th-century San Felipe Aqueduct. This picturesque 300-meter (984-ft) stretch of the waterway, which brought fresh water from the Cerro de San Felipe to the north into the capital until the 1940s, is made of the iconic green *cantera* quarry stone, with its semicircular archways outlined in red brick. The little archways (*arquitos*) now frame the front doors of houses along Calle Rufino Tamayo, named to honor the canonical 20th-century Mexican painter Rufino Tamayo, who was born just a few blocks away.

Painting, however, isn't the only fine art of historical significance associated with Los Arquitos. A scene from the cinematic comedy masterpiece *Nacho Libre* (don't judge me) was filmed under the arch that leads to the quaint cobblestone walkway Marcos Pérez.

Templo de San Matías Jalatlaco

The colorful *barrio* (neighborhood) of Jalatlaco, at the far northeast corner of the Centro, is home to the quirky **Templo de San Matías Jalatlaco** (Hidalgo 211, Barrio de Jalatlaco), three blocks east of Parque El Llano. Built in the late 17th century, the current structure replaced a smaller chapel dedicated to Saint Catherine of Alexandria, and the new church initially remained dedicated to her. However, in the year 1700, it was consecrated to San Matías Apóstol, the apostle chosen to replace Judas Iscariot after that fateful kiss in the garden of Gethsemane. The small church stands out among others in Oaxaca for the geometrical designs, rather than statues of saints, in its facade. Diamonds, rectangles, crosses, and a few floral flourishes adorn the church front, and zigzag designs embellish the tritostyle columns (a baroque architectural feature with decorations only on the pillar's bottom third).

SOUTH OF THE ZÓCALO

The vast majority of the city's tourist attractions are concentrated in the north side of the Centro, but south of the Zócalo, a number of old churches will interest architecture buffs.

At the northwest corner of the Mercado 20 de Noviembre, what's left of the **Templo de San Juan de Dios** (9am-6pm daily, free admission) sits quietly among the daily hustle and bustle of economic activity. The informational plaque is often covered up by the tarps of nopal and tortilla vendors. This is where the first Catholic mass in Oaxaca was said in 1521, when Orozco's expedition stopped to pray in the shade of a river tamarind tree on the banks of the Río Atoyac (the river reached this part of town in the 16th century but was later diverted to avoid the Centro). The temple built to commemorate this event was the first church in Oaxaca, and the whole block once housed the adjoining convent. Earthquakes and fires plagued the complex over the centuries, until it was mostly abandoned in the 19th century. Little by little, the abandoned space was occupied by secular interests. The block officially became the Mercado 20 de Noviembre on January 26, 1890, but the temple remains. Inside, you'll find paintings depicting the first mass in Oaxaca; the baptism of Cocijoeza, king of Zaachila, whose name means "Storm of Obsidian Knives"; and the miraculous Cross of Huatulco.

Other beautiful old churches in this area include the **Templo de la Compañia de Jesús** (on the block just to the southwest of the Zócalo), the **Templo de San Agustín** (at the corner of Guerrero and Armenta y López), and the **Iglesia de San Francisco Asís** (five blocks south of the Zócalo on Bustamante); all were built in the 16th century. The 18th-century **Iglesia de la Defensa** sits quietly tucked away behind laurel trees on the corner of Arteaga and Fiallo.

Recreation and Activities

MOUNTAIN BIKING

Zapotrek Tours (Xolotl 110, tel. 951/502-5957, www.zapotrek.com, 9am-8pm Mon.-Fri., 2pm-6pm Sat.-Sun.) runs full-day cycling tours through owner Eric Ramírez's birthplace, the Valle de Tlacolula. Their La Gente de las Nubes (People of the Clouds) tour (US$120) descends from Cuajimoloyas, in the Sierra Norte, down the mountains into the valley. In addition to having spectacular panoramic views, you'll eat in smoky mountain *comedores* (family-run restaurants) and interact with farmers, business owners, and other residents along the way. Eric and the team practice responsible tourism, which focuses on spreading knowledge of a culture while minimizing negative economic, social, and environmental impact. A Zapotrek tour will show you a side of Oaxaca you wouldn't see otherwise, and includes food, safety gear, and hotel pickup and drop-off.

When ecotourists began coming to Oaxaca in the 1980s in search of bicycles for rent, people pointed them in the direction of the bike shop of Pedro Martínez, one of Mexico's top cyclists at the time. Pedro responded to the demand by opening **Bicicletas Pedro Martínez** (Aldama 418, tel. 951/514-5935, www.bicicletaspedromartinez.com, 9am-8pm Mon.-Sat., 10:30am-4pm Sun.), and he has been taking visitors on exciting cycling adventures ever since. The company will take you down the hill from Monte Albán, visiting craft villages en route to Zaachila in a half day

Day Trips to the Valles Centrales

Oaxaca City is strategically located in the heart of the **Valles Centrales,** a region teeming with spectacular natural wonders, ancient human settlements, and a cornucopia of artisanal traditions, some of which date as far back as when those settlements were actually inhabited. With fascinating places to see less than an hour's drive away, visitors to Oaxaca City have many day-trip options that can be reached easily, whether by a **tour** or via **public transportation.** (Little English is spoken in the Valles Centrales, so if you don't have at least a basic level of Spanish, you're best off going with a tour.)

MONTE ALBÁN, ATZOMPA, AND SANTA MARÍA ATZOMPA

Some expert, eh? Like you needed me to tell you to go to **Monte Albán.** But hear me out. You can enjoy a leisurely jaunt around the ruins of the ancient Zapotec capital and be back in the city in time for lunch. However, I recommend extending your plans to include the **ruins at Atzompa,** a former suburb of the illustrious Zapotec capital on a neighboring hill to the north. Here you'll find living quarters of the lower classes of ancient Zapotec society and the biggest ball court found to date in the greater Monte Albán complex, as well as the reconstructed remains of a 1,300-year-old kiln for baking clay. A visit to Atzompa puts into perspective the size and complexity of one of the first true urban centers in the Americas.

After seeing where Zapotec ancestors once made ceramics, head back down the hill to the town of **Santa María Atzompa** to shop for the **glazed green and matte white pottery** the current residents continue to make.

ZAACHILA, CUILAPAM DE GUERRERO, AND ARRAZOLA

This trip is for the meat lovers, with a bit of history and culture tossed in for good measure. For the best **beef** *barbacoa* (slow-roasted barbecue) you've ever tasted, head to **Zaachila,** in the Valle de Zimatlán, on a **Thursday.** This is when the ancient Zapotec tradition of weekly markets comes to town. Tarps cover the streets for blocks around the Plaza Municipal; under them, vendors sell everything from cheap Chinese FM radios to original Oaxacan folk art, but the real reason to come is to eat. The meat stands in the **Mercado Municipal Alarii** serve the savory local specialty: *barbacoa en rollo.* Most *barbacoa* in the Valles Centrales is goat or lamb, but this recipe is beef wrapped in avocado leaves, which give the meat a flavor so distinctive

(US$78), or all the way to Puerto Escondido, on the coast, in four days (US$420). They also rent bikes (US$13-26 per day; turn in by 8pm) with all the necessary safety gear.

If you plan on exploring on your own, the website **Oaxaca MTB** (www.oaxacamtb.org) is a detailed resource for riding Oaxaca. It has information, including maps, on dozens of routes around Oaxaca City, as well as in the Valles Centrales, La Mixteca, and the Sierra Norte.

HORSEBACK RIDING

Native Canadian Mary Jane Gagnier has explored Oaxaca on horseback since she moved here in 1987. Through her company **Horseback Mexico** (Murguía 403, tel. 951/199-7026, www.horsebackmexico.com), she leads half-day, overnight, and weeklong rides in various locations throughout Oaxaca. Mary regularly competes in endurance races. She and her son Gabriel, a veterinarian and endurance rider himself, are both certified in Basic First Aid by the Red Cross. Their rides are as safe as they are fun.

Prices start at US$100 for half-day rides, US$175 for full-day rides, and US$430 for overnight trips. Mary runs her day rides, as well as a bed-and-breakfast, at her ranch just 20 minutes from Oaxaca City in the Valle de Tlacolula. A night at **Rancho Pitaya** (US$250) includes breakfast, dinner, transfer to and from the house on Murguía in Oaxaca City, and a free welcome margarita. There's that it is difficult to describe. Make sure to stop by the *nieves* stands in the plaza for artisanal ice cream.

After filling up, move on to **Cuilapam de Guerrero** to stand in awe of the extravagant **Dominican architecture** of the 16th-century **Ex Convento de Santiago Apóstol.** This is the site of the execution of Vicente Guerrero, Mexico's second president, who is remembered for abolishing slavery in the country in 1829 during his short term in office.

Finish the day off in **Arrazola,** the "cradle of the *alebrijes,*" the imaginative wood carvings made popular here by Manuel Jiménez in the mid-20th century.

VALLE DE TLACOLULA RUINS TOUR

The **Valle de Tlacolula** is home to Oaxaca's second most famous ruins at Mitla. However, its intricately decorated tombs and plazas aren't the only ancient leftovers to have been discovered here. Three other lesser-known sites offer a wealth of information about the civilization the Spanish encountered and conquered half a millennium ago, and there's a good chance you'll have the sites all to yourself.

Make your first stop at **Dainzú.** Settled around 700 BC, a couple centuries before Monte Albán, it was a major economic and political center in the valley. Like many other settlements, it most likely played a role in the founding of the city on the Sacred Hill.

After a 10-minute drive down the road, you'll find the small site **Lambityeco** right on the highway. The settlement relied heavily on rain, as the inhabitants used river water drained through the area's saline soils to make salt. It's no wonder archaeologists found large masks of the rain god Cocijo here.

Next stop, **Yagul.** The largest and most impressive of these three, it was built on and into a hill just east of Tlacolula. There is a ball court here, as well as a mazelike group of residences and a fortress built into the hill for refuge during attacks. Hike around the hill to take in some truly breathtaking views of the valley and ruins below.

Finally, finish off the ruins tour at **Mitla.** You definitely won't be the only adventurer here, but the "Place of the Dead" is absolutely a must-see for visitors to Oaxaca. If you got up early enough and made good time, you could finish the day off with a dip in the pools at the calcified waterfalls of **Hierve El Agua.**

much more than horseback riding to do here, such as hiking, cooking classes, or exploring the valley on the mountain bikes provided at no extra cost.

YOGA

Yoga is very popular in Oaxaca City, and there are excellent studios in the Centro, as well as retreats outside of the city center. The most centrally located studio is **Ananda Jot Yoga** (Matamoros 200, tel. 951/128-2136, US$5), just a block west of the Andador. Despite the location in the busy Centro, the studio is a quiet, tranquil place that fosters a meditative mindset. Kundalini classes are offered

throughout the week (except Fridays and Sundays), and there is a women-only class on Thursday mornings.

A block south of Parque El Llano, **Casa Jaguar** (Juárez 501, tel. 951/205-4474, US$6) offers classes in other types of yoga, such as hatha, vinyasa, and power yoga. Its beautiful, wood-paneled studio can fit a dozen yogis comfortably. They also have classes for children. For classes in ashtanga, dharma, and yin yoga, as well as meditation and contemporary dance, check the schedule at **Prana Yoga** (Del Carmen 104, tel. 951/198-4413, www.pranayogaoaxaca.com, US$5), in the northwest corner of the Centro.

LEARNING SPANISH

When people ask what brought me to Mexico, the first in a laundry list of reasons is the Spanish language. I had a blast learning Spanish (still do, every day) in this country, with its unique, sarcastic slang, its affinity for double entendres, and its varying and numerous regional vocabularies. Whether you have a week or three months to dedicate to learning, the schools here are dedicated to making sure you come away with tangible results.

I can personally attest to the effectiveness of a **homestay,** where students stay in the homes of friendly locals who, by being hospitable and chatty, provide fun, meaningful learning opportunities throughout the day—and usually meals, as well. I've done two homestays in the past, and both resulted in major advancements in my learning of Spanish. All schools listed here offer this immersive, productive experience in the homes of people around the Centro.

Schools

Lázaro Rojas and his faculty of experienced teachers at **Spanish Immersion School** (Matamoros 502, tel. 951/196-4567, www.spanishschoolinmexico.com, oaxacaimmersion@gmail.com, US$180-280/week) utilize their greatest resource (the amazing city in which they live) to teach practical, usable Spanish effectively and quickly. Lesson plans include shopping trips to the market in which the student does all the talking (teachers help out, if necessary), or fast-paced afternoons catching rides on local buses, teaching Oaxaca as well as the language.

Classrooms really aren't the school's thing, and neither are classes: The school only offers one-on-one lessons. This serves two purposes. First, and most obvious, it allows teachers to focus instruction on the student's individual need. Second, the close teacher/student relationship this engenders (classes can be 2-5 hrs a day) creates trust and comfort in the learning environment.

Spanish Immersion School will also organize excursions, transportation, and accommodation in apartments or a local's home. They'll organize your whole trip for you, if you need it.

Another standout is **Oaxaca Spanish Magic** (Berriozábal 200, tel. 951/516-7316, www.oaxacaspanishmagic.com, oaxacaspanishmagic@yahoo.com, US$120-140/week, US$15/class). To director Flor Bautista, to engender learning in someone is an act of magic, hence the name. Her love for teaching is apparent in how she talks about her job, and how much time she spends there. Both she and students describe the school as a family-style environment, where she hangs out with students, socializing and prompting them to use what they've learned in class. Instruction is hands-on and intensive, fluidly combining grammar with vocabulary. One interesting service they offer is online classes via video call, which gives students the chance to start learning before a trip in order to get acquainted with the basics and to understand and learn more once they arrive.

One of the most experienced schools in town is the **Instituto Cultural Oaxaca** (Juárez 909, tel. 951/515-3404, www.icomexico.com, US$155-195/week). Since 1984, ICO has offered tailor-made instruction at its campus in a gorgeous 19th-century home at the northernmost end of Calle Benito Juárez. Excited students lounge on the green lawns of the courtyard under towering palm trees. The school offers both classroom and one-on-one courses. The weekly rate goes down if you study for multiple weeks.

ICO is a proud sponsor of the Fundación En Via, a microfinance organization that supports women in Oaxaca by helping them finance businesses. Part of En Via's mission is to educate travelers about the benefits of microfinance, so they work with the school to organize tours to villages to get a unique glimpse of Oaxaca and see their system at work.

1: vintage bicycles for rent to get around town
2: learning to make chiles rellenos 3: a typical "classroom" at Spanish Immersion School

Becari Conzatti Language School (Gómez Farías 118, tel. 951/503-8448, www. becariqr.com) now has a second location (M. Bravo 210, tel. 951/514-6076, www.becari.com. mx), providing twice as many learning and volunteer opportunities as before. Becari partners with the Centro de Esperanza Infantil (Children's Hope Center) and four other local organizations to offer discounted Spanish courses in exchange for volunteer hours.

If you just need a bit of practice and help, the **Oaxaca Lending Library** (Pino Suárez 519, tel. 951/518-7077, www.oaxlibrary.org, 10am-2pm and 4pm-7pm Mon.-Fri., 10am-1pm Sat.) hosts a weekly *intercambio* (language exchange) from 10am to noon on Saturdays. The OLL extends its hours to include the afternoon siesta from October until January.

OAXACAN COOKING COURSES

Many hotels and Spanish schools in Oaxaca offer cooking classes as cultural activities or as part of the curriculum. Aside from the satisfaction you'll get from creating something delicious, this is a fun and effective method for practicing your Spanish.

If you have a meal at La Olla, you'll understand why chef Pilar Cabrera is the person you want teaching you to cook Oaxacan cuisine. In addition to crafting the restaurant's toothsome menu, Pilar shares her extensive knowledge of Oaxacan ingredients, recipes, and cooking methods through her school **Casa de los Sabores** (Reforma 402, tel. 951/516-6668, www.casadelossabores. com). Classes (in both English and Spanish; 9:30am-2:30pm Wed. and Fri.) include a shopping trip through the market, cooking class at Pilar's house, mezcal tasting, and, of course, lunch. Group classes cost US$85, and private classes can be arranged with at least two weeks' notice. Those who want to eat without attending the class can join in on the meal for US$30 a person.

Chocolate lovers, take heed! **Oaxaca Profundo Sessions** (no phone, www. oaxsessions.com, oaxacaprofundosessions@ gmail.com) offers their four-hour Food of the Gods Chocolate Sessions (US$31) every weekday morning at 9am. Admittedly, there is more tasting than cooking in these sessions, but it is a fun and delicious way to explore more deeply this divine Oaxacan staple. Their Nectar of the Gods Maguey-Agave Sessions (4pm-6pm Thurs., or by request, US$21) take a similar approach to understanding mezcal and other beverages made from agave. Using venues such as the Centro's local markets as classrooms, the classes are in English and include lots of taste tests.

Entertainment and Festivals

NIGHTLIFE

TOP EXPERIENCE

Mezcalerías (Mezcal Bars)

A unique staple of Oaxaca City nightlife is the *mezcalería*, a bar dedicated to the promotion of knowledge about Oaxaca's signature spirit. The recent economic boom in the mezcal industry has led to new *mezcalerías* sprouting up all over town like wild agave. The idea behind these usually small, intimate bars is to inform visitors about the culture, production, and types of mezcal, not necessarily to get drunk—that is to say, sip it, don't shoot it.

The one not to miss is **In Situ** (Morelos 511, tel. 951/514-1811, www.insitumezcaleria. com, 1pm-11pm Mon.-Sat.), 2.5 blocks west of the Andador. Owners Ulises Torrentera and Sandra Ortíz Brena have worked as hard as museum curators since opening the bar in 2011. Now In Situ boasts the largest selection of mezcals of any bar of its type in the world, all crammed in behind the tiny, six-seat bar. There is more seating in the loft overhead.

On García Vigil, a block west of Santo Domingo, **Mezcalogia** (García Vigil 509, tel. 951/514-0115, 6pm-1am Sat.-Thurs., 6pm-2am Fri.) hosts regular *catas de mezal* (mezcal tastings) and boasts an imaginative menu of cocktails. Signature mixed drinks like the Mercado (*espadín* mezcal, lime, green Chartreuse, and mint), and the soft glow of candlelight on dark-stained wood, attract enough foreign tourists to keep the tables full.

Take a national tasting tour at **Mezcaloteca** (Reforma 506, tel. 951/514-0082, www.mezcaloteca.squarespace.com, 5pm-10pm Mon.-Sat.), where the curators have broadened their search for mezcal to include the entire country. The apothecary-style bar shelves have bottles from Miahuatlán, Matatlán, and Zoquitlán (all in Oaxaca) alongside agave distillates from Durango, Michoacán, Jalisco, and other Mexican states known (though not as well as Oaxaca) for mezcal.

Some *mezcalerías* are owned by proprietary brands and sell only their own mezcals. The best of these is **Los Amantes** (Allende 107, tel. 951/501-0687, www.losamantes.com, 5pm-11pm daily). Try the *reposado* (aged mezcal) if

you find other types of the distillate too harsh; it's triple distilled, lowering the alcohol content and producing a smoother mezcal. Barely bigger than a market booth, the bar becomes a spirited scene with live *ranchera* (a type of traditional Mexican music) beginning at 8pm.

Juan Carlos Mendez opened **El Cortijo** (5 de Mayo 305, tel. 951/514-3939, www.mezcalelcortijo.com, 1pm-11pm Mon.-Sat.) to honor and spread awareness of the work of his grandparents, who hail from Matatlán, the world capital of mezcal. Juan likes to think of himself as a "guide to your mezcal adventure" and uses the compact but cozy space to foment friendship, as well as knowledge of mezcal. The late, world-renowned Oaxacan artist Francisco Toledo designed the stylized bats in the floor tiles, and tin sacred hearts adorn the wall behind the bar.

It's a little out of the way, but **Cuish** (Díaz Ordaz 712, tel. 951/516-8791, www.mezcalescuish.mx, 10am-10pm daily) is worth the trek, especially if you can't find room at the smaller *mezcalerías*. It is five blocks south and three blocks west of the Zócalo, almost to the *periférico* (bypass highway). Cuish also has an *expendio* (store, and much smaller bar) of the same name on the Centro's north side, a block north of Santo Domingo (Alcalá 802,

part of the impressive collection at the mezcal bar In Situ

noon-10pm daily). They boast many types of mezcal. Try the *cuish,* a mezcal made from the *Agave karwinskii* plant. They make it so well, they decided to name the company after it.

If someone in your group isn't enamored of mezcal, **La Mezcalerita** (Alcalá 706, tel. 951/312-1745, noon-1am daily), a block north of Santo Domingo, has an extensive list of craft beers and *pulque,* a fermented beverage made from agave sap. *Pulque* is either served by itself (*natural*) or mixed with fruit juice (*curado*). The bar inside is painted a spirit-lifting turquoise, and there's also lots of room on the terrace to enjoy a mezcal and a snack.

The ghost of Manuel Paz de la Cajiga, who founded **La Casa del Mezcal** (Flores Magón 210, no phone, 11am-2am daily) in 1935, would probably call all these bars a bunch of whippersnappers. Actually, he'd probably just get their patrons drunk. Mezcal isn't for sipping here; it's fuel for the *parranda* (raging party), as anyone who has passed by at 1am and heard the drunken revelers singing along to '80s rock classics will attest.

Bar-Cafés

Cafés by day, bars by night, these cozy little establishments in Oaxaca City tend to have a similar studio-style layout: bar and tables on the ground floor, and a loft-style second floor built above it with seating space on the floor. At **La Nueva Babel** (Porfirio Díaz 224, tel. 951/512-3494, babelmusica@hotmail.com, 9am-2am daily), they passed on the tables for upstairs and opted for floor seating with cushions. The bar is often full of musicians, poets, actors, and dancers, either drinking at the tables or performing on the small ground-floor stage.

Around the corner, **Txalaparta** (Matamoros 208, tel. 951/514-4305, 1pm-3am Mon.-Sat., occasional cover US$1-2) is a bit hard to categorize. The difference in the bar's atmosphere from day to night is, well, night and day. When the sun is out, you can sit around relaxing, puffing away at a hookah; after it sets, you can throw back beers

and cocktails and dance through numerous rooms with vintage furniture and decor.

Armadillo (Mier y Terán 103-B, no phone, 2pm-2am daily), a half block south of the Plaza de la Danza, has a bit more of a dive-bar feel to it. No mixology here, no waterpipes: just cold beer in the fridge and Mexican ska and rock on the radio.

Live Music

The cow skulls and indigenous masks from across the globe hung on the black walls at **Ribbon Blues & Roll** (Pino Suárez 215, no phone, 6pm-2am daily, usually no cover) make it the perfect setting for the growl of a blues singer's voice and the twang of a guitar. Live music is usually Thursday-Saturday, but during the week it's worth stopping by for the draft beer and chicken wings.

Up in the quiet streets on the hillside of the Cerro del Fortín, **Venadito Espacio Cultural** (Panorámica del Fortín 530, tel. 951/393-7613, www.cafebrujula.com, 7:30pm-10pm Mon.-Sat., usually no cover) is an excellent venue to hear local musical talent. The green *cantera* walls and antique instruments decorating the stage set an intimate scene for local singers, rappers, and instrumentalists. Fans of Oaxacan singer Lila Downs should keep an eye out—born in a small town in La Mixteca, she now tours internationally, but when at home, she is known to stop by to enjoy the tunes.

There's little chance you'll miss my favorite place for live tunes in town, the southwest corner of the Zócalo, where **Del Jardín marimba band** gets people's feet moving with classic cumbia, salsa, and Oaxacan songs. They set up every night after the sun goes down, and usually play until midnight or later.

Nightclubs

If the rhythm has still got you after the marimba band in the Zócalo has gone home, head up the Andador to Matamoros and take a left. Halfway down the block, **La Tentación** (Matamoros 101, tel. 951/199-9694,

9:30pm-3am Wed.-Sat., cover charged) has live salsa, cumbia, and merengue Wednesday to Saturday nights.

A block south of Santo Domingo, next to the Iglesia Sangre de Cristo, **Desestresse** (Alcalá 401, tel. 951/514-2453, noon-2am Mon.-Sat., 6pm-2am Sun., cover charged) is known for its drink specials and its very loud techno and house music. Its sublime location gives partiers instant access to the late-night street food along the Andador.

LGBTQ Nightlife

Club Privado 502 (Porfirio Díaz 502, tel. 951/514-8552, 11pm-5am Thurs.-Sat., cover charged)—or El Número, as it's better known, since the art deco numbers of the address are the only signage outside—is Oaxaca City's only gay nightclub. The ambience is open and welcoming to anyone who wants to dance, and dance late. There are other gay bars in Oaxaca City, such as **Luna Rosa** (Colón 300, tel. 951/170-1909, 2:30pm-2:30am Mon.-Sat., 5pm-2am Sun., no cover), with its pink jukebox, and the city's oldest gay bar, **Cervecería La Chinampa** (Bustamante 603, no phone, 5pm-3am daily, no cover), but they don't get as rambunctious as El Número.

FESTIVALS

In his canonical essay collection on Mexican culture titled *The Labyrinth of Solitude,* poet Octavio Paz described his people's party mode with phrases like "*nos desgarramos*" (we tear ourselves open) and "*nos disparamos*" (we fire off like a gun). Oaxacan festivals are a perfect embodiment of this sentiment. As soon as the smoke of one party clears, another fuse is lit, and it's only a matter of time before the next joyous explosion. Everyone's invited. Come dance.

High season in Oaxaca City doesn't correspond to the weather—it follows the festivities. These are grand public affairs where riotous brass bands lead groups of dancing, drinking revelers through the cobblestone streets. Costumes burst with color, and the sparks and smoke of fireworks follow the boisterous processions like thunderstorms sweeping through the desert.

Guelaguetza

Also called **Los Lunes del Cerro** (Mondays on the Hill), the **Guelaguetza** (geh-lah-GEHT-sah) is a celebration of the diverse customs and creations of the various cultures tucked away in the eight regions of the state. The name comes from a Zapotec term meaning "mutual cooperation."

The two official Mondays on the Hill are the last two in July, but the city is ablaze with festivities the entire month. A staple celebration here is the *calenda,* an uproarious procession through the streets with the squeal of clarinets and the low bass bump of tubas at its core. One person leads the band of revelers, spinning a large white globe called a *marmota* on a pole set in a belt holster, and others dance around inside the hollow bodies of *monos,* gigantic figures of men and women with floppy arms and papier mâché heads. *Calendas,* which crowd the streets multiple times during Guelaguetza season, herald the arrival of festivities and invite everyone to join in the fun.

The official event is held in the **Auditorio Guelaguetza,** the large white, tent-like structure on the Cerro del Fortín, northwest of the Centro. There are two shows each Monday, wherein delegations from the various regions of Oaxaca perform their unique dances and then toss food and craft products from home into the cheering crowd. Tickets run US$50-60, but book early, as tickets sell out quickly and are more expensive when people resell them. Check with your hotel or with the **Secretary of Tourism** (Juárez 703, tel. 951/502-1200, www.sectur.oaxaca.gob.mx, 9am-3pm Mon.-Fri.).

Other communities in Oaxaca also hold their own Lunes del Cerro, for which there is no charge. **Zaachila** is known for its **Danza de los Zancudos,** where participants prance around the stage on stilts nearly eight feet tall. Towns like **Teotitlán del Valle** and **Cuilapam de Guerrero** perform the visually stunning **Danza de la Pluma** (Dance of the Feather).

The month of July is packed with other **Fiestas de la Guelaguetza** that celebrate just about anything and everything Oaxaca. The most popular and longest running are the **Festival de los Moles** (Mole Festival), the **Feria Internacional de Mezcal** (International Mezcal Fair), and the **Feria del Tejate y el Tamal** (Tejate and Tamale Fair), but the list goes on and on. Check the website www.viveoaxaca.org for dates and locations.

TOP EXPERIENCE

Day of the Dead

It may sound ironic to call a party "lively" when the guest of honor is the Grim Reaper himself, but Octavio Paz wrote that "our death illuminates our life," and nowhere in Mexico is this more apparent than in Oaxaca, renowned for its **Día de Muertos** (Day of the Dead) celebrations. Imagine the Guelaguetza mayhem in the streets but add ghoulish, ghastly costumes and piles of skulls to the mix. The brass bands in the streets and cemeteries twist their tones into plaintive reminders that yes, he's coming for you too, but not yet. So let's have fun.

Pre-Hispanic Mesoamerican cultures had a very different conception of death than the mortality-obsessed Spaniards who crossed the pond and told the indigenous peoples of Mexico they were doing it all wrong. For Zapotecs, Mayas, Aztecs, and others, death was more like walking through a door to another room, rather than a one-way trip to a hole in the ground. Despite also believing that death led to another form of life, the Christian conquistadors were terrified of such pagan beliefs and, as with many other indigenous images and practices, they syncretized the ancient custom with their own to make it more palatable.

Before the arrival of the Spaniards, Mesoamerican peoples celebrated the holiday in the month they were compelled to call August. In an attempt to convert them, the colonizers moved the fiesta to coincide with the Catholic days of observance All Souls' Day and All Saints' Day on the first two days in November. However, as with other impositions on their beliefs and ways of life, indigenous Mexicans didn't renounce all their former customs. It was common practice to keep the skulls of the dead and display them as reminders of death and rebirth. They stopped using the real skulls of the departed, but indigenous potters picked up the tradition, and decorated ceramic skulls are now the osteal icons of this purely Mexican holiday. **November 1 and 2** are still the **official holidays,** but celebrations more or less span the months of October and November. Some towns, like San Antonino Castillo Velasco, have their cemetery celebration on November 3. Once, on November 22, I was awakened by a parade of dancing skeletons and demons in the street below my hotel in Tlacolula.

Another popular example of syncretism is **La Catrina,** a skeletal representation of a svelte woman who somehow fills out quite nicely the long purple dress she wears, along with a broad-brimmed hat decorated with flowers, feathers, and frills. The image was created by Mexican printmaker José Guadalupe Posada in 1913 and subsequently popularized by muralist Diego Rivera, who depicted her in his mural *Dream of a Sunday Afternoon in the Alameda Central* in Mexico City. She has since become the holiday's modern connection to the Aztec "Lady of Death" Mictecacihuatl, who reigned over Mictlán, the eternal resting place of Aztec souls.

In Oaxaca, this centuries-old cultural concoction begins about a week before the holiday. Oaxacans set up elaborate *ofrendas,* altars to departed ancestors that they decorate with sugar skulls, marigolds, cockscombs, and the favorite foods and drinks of the deceased. The idea is that the dead return to the land of the living for their ethereal family reunion,

1: observing Day of the Dead traditions 2: fantastic figures made of radishes at the Noche de Rábanos competition 3: the Danza de la Pluma (Dance of the Feather) at the Guelaguetza

and it is said that the foods no longer have a taste after the spirits have had their annual snack attack. This is a public family affair, and many people like to show off their *ofrendas* to visitors. Restaurants, bars, art galleries, and other businesses also make altars. The city becomes smoky and tinged with orange from all the burning copal incense. In the evening on November 1, head to the **Panteón General** (Main Cemetery) on Calle del Refugio, just to the west of the Centro, to experience the cemetery decorations and rituals in Oaxaca City.

San Agustín Etla, about 17 km (10.6 mi) north of Oaxaca City, has been celebrating Day of the Dead in its own unique way since 1907, with a ghoulish parade called **La Muerteada**. It's a raucous, alcohol-fueled all-nighter that fills the town's streets with music, fireworks, costumed dancers, and locals and visitors alike.

XOXOCOTLÁN CEMETERY

The cemetery (*panteón* in Mexican Spanish) at **Santa Cruz Xoxocotlán,** about 5 km (3.1 mi) southwest of Oaxaca City, is the quintessence of Day of the Dead celebrations. Families elaborately decorate the tombs as they do *ofrendas* in their homes, and spend all night in the graveyard, eating, drinking, and remembering. A large orchestra provides an eldritch soundtrack to the scene, music that both invites you in and creeps you out. Many tour operators provide transportation to Xoxocotlán for Día de Muertos; to get there super cheap, grab a *colectivo* taxi at the **Sitio La Soledad Xoxocotlán** (US$2) on the Diagonal de Mercaderes, the street on the east side of the Central de Abastos. This is a very popular tourist attraction at this time, and a private taxi trip from the Centro will cost you US$11-20.

Christmas

Even Christmastime is wholly unique here. During the colonial period in Oaxaca, when radishes were introduced to the region by Dominican friars, farmers would carve religious images into giant radishes to catch the eyes of shoppers in the Christmas market on December 23. The practice became so popular that in 1897 the mayor of Oaxaca City formalized the **Noche de Rábanos** (Night of the Radishes) into an official competition, and farmers have been carving like crazy to one-up each other ever since. Farmers from the surrounding valleys proudly display their large arrangements of vegetal nativity scenes and aspects of Oaxacan life and culture in the Zócalo in the late afternoon; judging begins around 9pm.

The magic continues into **Nochebuena** (Christmas Eve) and **El Día de Navidad** (Christmas Day). You've never seen nativity scenes quite like this before. Different from the root-based scenes on December 23, these nativities have the baby Jesus and cohort surrounded by dark-green mosses from the mountains, poinsettias, bromeliads, and other bright tropical and desert flowers, like the *flores inmortales* of San Antonino Castillo Velasco, called "immortal" because they retain their color for up to 45 years after they have been cut. The Zócalo is the best place to see these verdant dioramas.

Christmastime parades are called *posadas,* and they represent the journey Mary and Joseph took and the troubles they had finding accommodations in Bethlehem (no Moon guides back then). Children dressed as biblical characters roam the streets and are welcomed into homes and churches, where they are given food and snacks. Universities often join in the fun with their own *posadas.*

Artisans make special *piñatas* for the *posadas.* However, unlike the traditional papier-mâché figures known the world over, these are made of clay jars. They are usually in the form of seven-pointed stars adorned with tassels, meant to represent the seven deadly sins, and their bright decorations symbolize Satan's fraudulent temptations. But his wiles are no match for Virtue, represented by the stick that eventually breaks the jar open and frees all the goodies inside.

In true Oaxacan celebratory fashion, Christmas Day is only the culmination of a month of festivities. In addition to the Noche de Rábanos, Oaxacans celebrate Mexico's patron saint La Virgen de Guadalupe from the beginning of the month to her official saint day on December 12. Then it's on to celebrating Oaxaca's patron saint, La Virgen de la Soledad, on December 18. Even if you can't be in the city on Christmas Day, you'll find a *calenda* somewhere in town all month long.

ART EVENTS

The best places to find out about art events in Oaxaca are the galleries themselves. They usually have inaugural events for new exhibitions, so these depend on each gallery's schedule. If you're in town for Day of the Dead, don't miss the Feria Gráfica Oaxaca (Oaxaca Printmaking Fair), held on October 31 and November 1 at Taller Espacio Alternativo (Alternative Space Workshop; Porfirio Díaz 41). The best woodcut, linotype, etching, and other printmaking artists from Oaxaca and elsewhere in Mexico come here to showcase their incredible work.

Posters in cafés and on the street advertise many events. The best online resource is Qué Pasa Oaxaca (www.quepasaoaxaca.com), which has a detailed schedule of art events in the city. A big one to look out for is Drama Fest (www.dramafestmx.com), usually held in August and September. Each year this theater festival invites dramaturgs and actors from Mexico and abroad to showcase their talents in Oaxaca City's theaters. For other theatrical performances, check the playbills at the Teatro Macedonio Alcalá (Independencia 900, tel. 951/516-8312, info@teatroalcala.org), which regularly hosts plays and concerts.

Movie buffs will love the volume of film events in Oaxaca City. The mobile cinema club Cinema Cuervo (tel. 951/414-7083) hosts showings all over town. Check their social media accounts or look for their posters around town for information. Billing itself as "simply the best festival experience on the planet," the Oaxaca Film Fest (www.oaxacafilmfest.com) is a weeklong international film festival usually held in mid-October. The ambulatory documentary film festival Ambulante (www.ambulante.org), organized by Diego Luna and Gael García Bernal, stars of the famous Mexican film *Y Tu Mamá También,* travels to cities all over Mexico as well as the United States, El Salvador, and Colombia. It usually comes to Oaxaca in April or May and showcases new documentary films from all over the world. Don't miss a showing if it coincides with your trip.

Shopping

TRADITIONAL MARKETS

Your first shopping stop should be the Mercado Benito Juárez (tel. 951/516-2352, 7am-9pm daily), a block south of the southwest corner of the Zócalo. This is both a tourists' and locals' market, selling everything from souvenir T-shirts to traditional clothing and folk art to tortillas, vegetables, meat, and *chapulines*. It's also one of the best places to try the pre-Hispanic Oaxacan drink *tejate*. The trendy-looking *puesto* (vendor booth) La Flor de Huayapam is run by women from San Andrés Huayapam, the birthplace of the beverage. They have the classic cacao-flavored *tejate,* as well as a drink made with coconuts and one made with *chilacayote* (figleaf gourd) and sweetened with honey.

A number of bakers in the Mercado 20 de Noviembre (20 de Noviembre 512, tel. 951/516-2352, 7am-8pm daily) sell the Oaxacan staple *pan de yema* (egg yolk bread), which is typically served with hot chocolate. Booths on the south side of the market sell *mole* in all its scrumptious variations, and just outside the market you're bound to find the right chocolate to go with your bread in one of the sweet-smelling chocolate factories on Calle Mina. Oaxaca's most famous brand, **Chocolate Mayordomo** (Mina 219, tel. 951/516-1619, www.chocolatemayordomo.com.mx, 7am-9pm daily), is made and sold on the corner of Mina and 20 de Noviembre. I have a soft spot for *chocolate almendrado* (almond-flavored chocolate) from **Chocolate La Soledad** (Mina 212, tel. 951/516-5841, www.chocolatedeoaxaca.com.mx, 7am-9pm daily), as well as its *malteada* (literally "milkshake," but in this context, chocolate milk) mix Choco Pombo. They also make milk and bitter chocolates, as well as other flavors like *vainilla* (vanilla), *canela* (cinnamon), and *moka* (coffee).

From the southwest corner of the Mercado 20 de Noviembre market, walk south a block on 20 de Noviembre and one block west on Zaragoza to get to the **Mercado de Artesanías** (Artisan Market; corner of Zaragoza and J. P. García, no phone, 9:30am-7pm daily). The selection is not as ample as at other places in town, as vendors here focus on the most popular textiles and pottery styles, but prices are generally very good. It's a great place to pick up a rug made in Teotitlán del Valle or *barro negro* ceramics from San Bartolo Coyotepec.

ART GALLERIES AND PRINTMAKING WORKSHOPS

Try turning a corner in Oaxaca City and not finding an art gallery. This is not an extensive list of the galleries but rather a selection of places that really stand out.

You'll see some of the most interesting modern ceramic fine art being made in Oaxaca at **Galería Omar Hernández** (Alcalá 303, tel. 951/516-7302, galeriaoh@gmail.com, 10am-2pm and 3pm-9pm Mon.-Fri.). Omar finds inspiration in some of Oaxaca's most valuable cultural symbols, such as skulls, corncobs, and most notably, his representations of the plastic jugs people use to dole out mezcal during *calendas* and other festivities. Like other impactful Oaxacan artists, he has

found that magical way to use conventionally dark themes and hair-raising motifs to celebrate the lively cultural heritage of his native land.

Another great gallery that deals with similar themes in a different medium is the woodcut printmaking shop **Gabinete Gráfico** (M. Bravo 216, tel. 951/104-9175, gabinetexilografico@gmail.com, http://gabinetegrafico.wordpress.com, 10am-8pm daily). The artists who work and sell here tend to stick to images of people (both with and without flesh), plants, and other symbols representative of Oaxaca, like mezcal and tortillas.

That is not to say there isn't both social power and artistic value to political art. Inspired by the teachers' protests of 2006 that resulted in violent clashes with police, printmaking workshops like **Espacio Zapata** (Porfirio Díaz 509, tel. 951/126-7110, http://espacio-zapata.negocio.site, 11am-8pm Mon.-Sat.) focus their imagery on what they view as injustices committed by the government. The on-site café is a hip place to enjoy a cup of coffee and talk art.

A block west of Santo Domingo, **NUUN Espacio de Arte** (García Vigil 505-A, tel. 951/206-0848, www.nuun.mx, 11am-3pm and 5pm-8pm Mon.-Sat.) takes its name from the Zapotec word for "space." Here you'll find the paintings and sculptures of some of the most well-known, as well as up-and-coming, artists from all over Mexico.

A block to the east of Santo Domingo, **Vagamundo** (La Constitución 210, tel. 951/205-3441, http://vagamundo-fine-art-gallery.negocio.site, 11am-9pm daily) hosts temporary exhibits by well-known artists from all over the world, usually alongside the paintings of famous Oaxacan artists such as Rodolfo Morales and Francisco Toledo.

The photography gallery **Tingladography** (García Vigil 212, tel. 951/268-9769, www.tingladography.com, 11am-2:30pm and 5pm-9pm Mon.-Sat.) bills itself as "El Ladrón de Imágenes" (The Image Thief). *Tinglado* in Spanish means "tangle" or "mess," and that is

Oaxaca City's Thriving Printmaking Scene

The violence that erupted in May and June of 2006, when police opened fire on nonviolent protesters demanding higher pay for teachers, sparked an artistic conflagration that still burns bright. Lithography, xylography, and other types of printmaking existed here before this tragic event, but the art form has definitely gained popularity, and many *talleres de grabado* (printmaking workshops) have sprouted up around town, mostly in the blocks west of the Andador.

In true Oaxacan fashion, a dozen of these workshops have collaborated to support each other and the art form in general. At the workshops listed below, you can pick up a *Pasaporte Gráfico* (Graphic Passport), a free brochure and map to all 12 shops. As you visit shops, ask them to stamp your passport with their unique print, which ends up becoming a cool souvenir on its own. Once you've filled it up, you get a discount at all of them.

Some personal favorites are **Gabinete Gráfico; Espacio Zapata,** which has a café; and **T.A.C.,** which is responsible for a lot of the stickers, stencils, and

Gabinete Gráfico printmaking shop

poster street art you'll see around town. However, each shop has its own unique style and focus, some choosing to concentrate on images of maguey, maize, skulls, and other cultural symbols of Oaxaca, rather than politics. The galleries are listed by their proximity to the Andador.

- **Oaxaca Gráfico,** Macedonio Alcalá 503, tel. 951/516-7236, oaxgrafico@gmail.com, 11am-9pm daily

- **Gabinete Gráfico,** M. Bravo 216, tel. 951/104-9175, gabinetexilografico@gmail.com, 10am-8pm daily

- **Tëmenk,** M. Bravo 301, tel. 951/124-5705, tallertemenk@gmail.com, 10am-9pm daily

- **Cooperativa Gráfica,** Matamoros 305, no phone, cooperativagraficaoaxaca@gmail.com, noon-8pm Mon.-Sat.

- **Espacio Zapata,** Porfirio Díaz 509, tel. 951/126-7110, asarooaxaca@gmail.com, 11am-8pm Mon.-Sat.

- **T.A.C. (Taller Artístico Comunitario),** Porfirio Díaz 510-A, tel. 951/207-9904, urtarte2017@gmail.com, 11am-8pm Mon.-Sat.

- **Siqueiros,** Porfirio Díaz 510, tel. 556/475-1259, espaciosiqueiros@gmail.com, 11am-8pm Mon.-Fri.

- **Hoja Santa,** Porfirio Díaz 400-B, tel. 951/160-3837, tallerhojasanta@gmail.com, 10am-8pm Mon.-Sat.

- **Estampa,** Morelos 511, tel. 951/207-1381, estampa_galeria_oax@hotmail.com, 10am-9pm Mon.-Sat.

- **Jaguar Print,** Tinoco y Palacios 416-A, no phone, tallerjaguarprint@hotmail.com, 10am-9pm Mon.-Sat.

- **La Chicharra,** Xicotencatl 317, tel. 951/165-1911, lachicharra14@hotmail.com, 11am-8pm Mon.-Sat.

- **Burro Press,** Humboldt 100-A, no phone, burropress@gmail.com, 10:30am-3pm and 4pm-8pm Mon.-Sat.

exactly what gallery owner Marcel Rius wants artists to make with the photos he scours markets, closets, and antiques shops to find. For his exhibitions, he invites Mexican and foreign artists to "intervene" in the photos with paint, plastics, and other media, with stunning results. Even if they are messy and tangled, the artists' interventions breathe new life into these images once doomed to be forgotten.

★ IAGO (Instituto de Artes Gráficas de Oaxaca)

Fans of world-renowned Oaxacan visual artist **Francisco Toledo** (www.franciscotoledo. net) must visit **IAGO (Instituto de Artes Gráficas de Oaxaca)** (Graphic Arts Institute of Oaxaca; Alcalá 507, tel. 951/516-6980, 9:30am-8pm Wed.-Mon.), in a gorgeous 18th-century house right across from Santo Domingo. The center has rooms for temporary exhibitions, a printmaking workshop, an extensive art library, a café, and a gift shop full of items emblazoned with his haunting aesthetic.

Toledo, who was born in Juchitán (in the Istmo de Tehuantepec) in 1940, founded the center in 1988. The artist, who died in 2019, is most well-known for his unique mosaics of animals usually not associated with beauty, such as monkeys, alligators, and insects. Among his most popular pieces are his decorative kites, but there are also cool notebooks printed with eerie spiders, shrimps, and pelicans, and framed prints of monkeys, skeletons, and anthropomorphic scorpions made of laser-cut X-ray film. Toledo also made jewelry with this innovative technique. The mastery of his art, his ability to find beauty in what conventionally arouses disgust and fear, is exemplified by these stylish and wearable crocodiles, grasshoppers, crabs, spiders, and scorpions with human legs. He added sparkle to some of the necklaces, bracelets, and earrings with coarsely applied gold film.

ARTISANS COOPERATIVES

Artisans cooperatives are some of the best places to find gifts and souvenirs in Oaxaca. The selections are wide and the prices reasonable, and, best of all, you can be sure that your money is directly supporting the artists in the co-ops.

The artisans at **Huizache Arte Vivo de Oaxaca** (Murguía 101, tel. 951/501-1282, 9am-9pm daily) created this ample and beautiful store on their own, without the help of government grants. There are products from all regions of Oaxaca, and lots of them. Check out the artisanal footwear of Ndavaa, a cooperative enterprise started by women from the town of San Dionisio Ocotepec, in the Valle de Tlacolula.

One block to the west of Huizache (note that Murguía changes to Matamoros at Alcalá), **La Casa de las Artesanías** (Matamoros 105, tel. 951/516-5062, www. casadelasartesanias.mx, 9am-10pm daily) also showcases a large selection of folk art from all eight regions of Oaxaca.

On the block northwest of the Centro Cultural San Pablo, **Andares del Arte Popular** (Journeys in Folk Art; Independencia 1003, tel. 951/688-7593, www. andaresdelarte.business.site, 10am-8pm Mon.-Sat., 11am-6pm Sun.) curates its products like artifacts in a museum. The beautifully arranged displays treat Oaxaca's rich communal art traditions like the fine art they truly are.

★ MARO (Mujeres Artesanas de las Regiones de Oaxaca)

A block south of the Hotel Quinta Real, the all-female artisans co-op **MARO (Mujeres Artesanas de las Regiones de Oaxaca)** (Craftswomen of the Regions of Oaxaca; 5 de Mayo 204, tel. 951/516-6722, http:// maroaxaca.blogspot.com, 9am-8pm daily)

1: Teatro Macedonio Alcalá 2: decorations outside an artisans co-op 3: embroidery from the Istmo de Tehuantepec for sale in Oaxaca City 4: IAGO (Instituto de Artes Gráficas de Oaxaca)

is made up of over 400 women artisans who have organized to provide visitors with what is probably the widest variety of artisanal products in the Centro, all at prices that are fair for both shopper and merchant. When you shop here, you can be sure that your money is going directly to bettering the lives of hardworking residents of Oaxaca. The women I spoke to all said their lives were much more economically stable because of the support of the cooperative.

Furthermore, they have harder-to-find items, such as the wooden masks of the Huave people of the Istmo de Tehuantepec. They are painted black and decorated with fur from goats, cows, or javelinas, as well as pieces of armadillo shell. Conscience note: Some species of armadillos are considered threatened or endangered in this region due to human consumption of the mammals. If you can't purchase a mask without compunction, it's best to move on to the many other beautiful choices.

CLOTHING AND TEXTILES

Aside from the co-ops, the daily open-air markets in the **Alameda de León** and on **Calle Aldama**, on the north side of the Mercado 20 de Noviembre, sell traditional *huipiles* (embroidered blouses) and other garments from all regions of Oaxaca. However, traditional artisans aren't the only folks in Oaxaca selling vivid vestments in the city. A number of designers purchase embroidered fabrics and other artisanal textiles to create fashionable pieces that range in style from casual to formal wear.

Designer Sara Almaraya enlivens denim jackets (mostly for women, but who am I to tell you what to wear?) with the bright primary colors of Oaxaca with floral *huipil* designs and other Mexican iconography. They're for sale at **Shkaála de Micaela** (5 de Mayo 412, tel. 951/516-2285, www.shkaalademicaela.com, 10am-2pm and 4pm-8pm Mon.-Sat.), on the pedestrian street on the south side of Santo Domingo.

With two locations in the Centro, **Moda Textil Rut** (Matamoros 302 and Pino Suárez 311, tel. 951/103-3235, 10am-8pm Mon.-Sat.) incorporates textiles from the eight regions of Oaxaca into modern casual and formal designs for both men and women. They make it a point to work with artisans from all over the state in order to provide clients with a selection that represents the full range of colors, designs, and talent that Oaxaca has to offer the world.

Silvia Suárez (Guirrión 110, tel. 951/516-8633, www.silviasuarez.com, 11am-3pm and 4pm-8pm Mon.-Fri., 11am-8pm Sat., 11am-3pm Sun.) was born in Argentina but has lived in Oaxaca since she was six years old. Since 2001, she has garnered close relationships with needleworkers from all corners of the state in order to find fabrics for her elegantly casual yet fashion-forward attire for women. Without losing the designs' traditional essence, Silvia creates clothing that is as eye-catching as it is wearable in any destination.

Just around the corner from Silvia Suárez, on the block just to the south of Santo Domingo, is the boutique of **Liliana del Toro** (5 de Mayo 400, tel. 951/514-5384, 10am-3pm and 4pm-8pm Mon.-Sat.), who also scouts Oaxaca in search of artisanal textiles and turns them into her own unique style of form-fitting casual and evening-wear pieces for women.

Two blocks west of Santo Domingo, the designers at **Miku Meko** (Allende 207, no phone, mikumeko.oax@gmail.com, 11am-8pm Mon.-Fri.) use fabrics and designs that originate from the Oaxacan coast in their comfortable, earthy garments for men and women. They have a small selection of pieces on sale in the boutique, but the majority of their work is custom-tailored clothing; have them take your measurements if you want something truly unique for your wardrobe.

BOOKSTORES

One of the best English-language bookstores in Mexico is **Amate Books** (Alcalá 307, tel. 951/516-6960, 10:30am-7:30pm Mon.-Sat.,

1pm-7pm Sun.), on the Andador just across from Parque Labastida. Although on the smaller side, Amate fits a lot in on the two rows of shelves and the walls. The selection runs both deep and wide, with a shelf dedicated to books about Oaxaca, as well as lots of classic and modern literature and translations of Mexican authors. As someone who has managed a bookstore in Mexico City, I can't recommend this one highly enough.

In a little nook up by the Jardín Etnobotánico, **La Bradería** (Constitución 110, tel. 951/107-7498, labraderia@gmail.com, noon-8pm Tues.-Sat.) sells books from independent Mexican authors and publishers, as well as notebooks, postcards, prints, and other rarities and *chingonerías*, which translates to something like "cool s**t."

Food

Boy, are you in for a treat. From street tacos to *tlayudas* (think overgrown quesadillas) smeared with *asiento* (lard collected from the pan after cooking pork) to organic health food to the original culinary inventions of the new vanguard of Oaxacan chefs riding high on the wave of the mezcal boom, the extensive range of ingredients, flavors, and prices here offers something for everyone, no matter your tastes or budget.

AROUND THE ZÓCALO

Most of the restaurants around the Zócalo have large menus featuring both traditional Oaxacan cuisine and international meals like club sandwiches and cheeseburgers. You won't find the best of what Oaxacan kitchens have to offer here, but that's not really the point. Eat here for the lively ambience beneath the shade of the towering laurel trees.

Mexican

Located in the Hotel del Marqués, on the north side of the Zócalo, ★ **Portal del Marqués** (Portal de Claveria, tel. 951/514-0688, www.hotelmarquesdelvalle.com.mx, 7am-2am daily, US$6-20) has a broad patio that is a great place for breakfast, with its glass-paneled doors (filled with corn husks and chile peppers) that open up to reveal the bar and grill built of dark-red quarry stones. The morning sun peeks through Calle Miguel Hidalgo to brighten up your alfresco breakfast, and the lively action in the square will get your spirits ready for a busy day. Make sure to ask for the blackberry jam made in-house from blackberries grown in the owners' home garden. It's also a great place for some afternoon *antojitos* (snack foods). Grab an *empanada de mole verde* (green mole empanada with chicken) or some fried tostadas called *garnachas* for a taste of the Istmo de Tehuantepec.

A quick and cheap lunch option is at **Medio Oriente** (Hidalgo 413, no phone, 1pm-10:30pm daily, US$2-3), just to the west of the northwest corner of the Zócalo. This Oaxacan chain specializes in "Arab tacos," a popular fusion of Mexican and Lebanese food that swaps out the traditional corn tortilla for a thick flour one and stuffs it with savory, seasoned pork meat. Spice it up however you like it with salsa, guacamole, and onions and cilantro at the salsa bar.

For some homestyle Oaxacan cooking, try **La Casa de la Abuela** (Hidalgo 616, tel. 951/516-3544, 1pm-9pm daily, US$11-22), which overlooks the northwest corner of the square. Designed to live up to its name, "Grandma's House" cooks fresh tortillas on a traditional *comal* (ceramic hot plate) and serves up Oaxacan favorites in a friendly, homestyle setting. Grandma's specialty, of course, is *mole*. There are five types on the menu, and her personal twist is the *tlayuda* made with *mole negro*. Can't decide? Try the mole sampler, served with shredded chicken and white rice.

The tables on the west side of the Zócalo almost all belong to **Del Jardín** (Portal de Flores, tel. 951/516-2092, 8am-midnight daily, US$6-12) in one of its iterations: **Café, Bar,** and **Cafetería.** The ambience makes up for the passable food (in Oaxaca, if it's not delicious, the place better have something else going for it). It's very lively at night when the marimba band plays classic cumbia, salsa, and Oaxacan songs, and people gather to dance in the southwest corner of the Zócalo.

The best combination of flavor, ambience, and price is the understatedly swanky ★ **Tr3s 3istro** (Portal de Flores 3, tel. 951/501-0407, 9am-11:30pm daily, US$8-15), above Cafetería Del Jardín. The service is impeccable, and the ample menu of traditional *moles* and house specialties does not disappoint. Offered during high seasons, the *degustación de los siete moles* (seven-mole sampler), served with crispy chicken wings, is a great way to try out a number of Oaxaca's *moles* and see which one you like best. Oaxaca City is only a six-hour drive from the coast, so the seafood is always fresh, and oysters are flown in from Baja California daily to stock the oyster bar.

Basque

Just above Café Del Jardín is the award-winning **El Asador Vasco** (The Basque Grill; Portal de Flores 10-A, tel. 951/514-4755, www.asadorvasco.com, 1:30pm-11:30pm daily, US$11-20), with a large menu of the hearty surf and turf of Basque Country. Decorated like a medieval inn where Don Quixote would have regaled diners with outrageous tall tales, El Asador Vasco serves classic Basque fondues and seafood, as well as its namesake, grilled meats like filet mignon and veal au gratin. For its toothsome dishes and spectacular service, the restaurant consistently earns the Achievement of Distinction from DiRoNA (Distinguished Restaurants of North America).

NORTH OF THE ZÓCALO

The north side is where you'll find the fancier restaurants in Oaxaca City, where chefs are more into experimenting with recipes than presenting them traditionally. Catering to tourists, these restaurants sometimes seem to spend more time, effort, and money on their decor and website than they do on the menu—but you'll also find some affordable places where the experiments have produced delicious new twists on Oaxacan flavors.

Mexican

A meal at ★ **Azucena Zapoteca** (Alcalá 303, tel. 951/516-8341, www.restaurante azucenazapoteca.com, 9am-10pm daily, US$8) is a feast for both the eyes and the belly. Its location in a sunny courtyard in the same building as the *alebrijes* gallery Voces de Copal makes it a bright, colorful place for lunch. Having found success at their first location in San Martín Tilcajete (known for its *alebrijes*), Azucena Zapoteca opened this branch in 2018. This isn't one of those restaurants that constantly think up new ways to mix the region's seemingly infinite list of unique ingredients. The kitchen philosophy here is to stick to traditions passed down for generations. There are three original house recipes, but the rest are prepared just like grandma used to, making it a great place to try various Oaxacan mole recipes, like *coloradito, estofado, amarillo,* and *chichilo,* the last of which gets its smoky flavor from tortillas burned to a crisp, ground to a fine powder, and tossed into the pot.

Speaking of pots, esteemed Oaxacan chef Pilar Cabrera runs the kitchen at a restaurant named after them. **La Olla** (Reforma 402, tel. 951/516-6668, www.laolla.com.mx, 8am-10pm Mon.-Sat., US$6) changes out its menu three to four times a year in order to exhibit the wide range of possibilities with all the ingredients available in Oaxaca. Pilar creates the

---

1: Azucena Zapoteca **2:** a typical set lunch called *comida corrida* **3:** food stalls in the Mercado 20 de Noviembre

menu of the day according to a theme schedule—Monday's theme is Good Start, Tuesday is International, and so on, but I recommend showing up for Oaxacan Wednesdays. The rooftop terrace has an excellent view of Santo Domingo, perfect for cocktails at sunset.

The menu measures up to the care they put into the interior design at ★ **Expendio Tradición** (corner of Reforma and Murguía, tel. 951/501-1460, www.expendiotradicion.com, 1pm-1am Mon.-Sat., 1pm-11pm Sun., US$7-12), a masterpiece of modern Oaxacan design. Established by the fifth generation of the Chagoya family of mezcal producers, the restaurant serves four brands of its Mezcales Tradición Chagoya, as well as full-flavored traditional and house recipes. Personal recommendation: fettuccine in cream sauce with shrimp and *queso istmeño* (cheese from El Istmo). Fans of Oaxacan artist Francisco Toledo's work will find his signature geometric style all over the restaurant. The floor and wall tiles, as well as the gate separating the restaurant from the café, are stylized mosaics of an agave plant viewed from above. The restaurant also creates a space for local street artists to perform and earn a little more than they do busking.

The culinary creativity of Expendio Tradición extends to the breakfasts on the menu at the adjoining **Café Tradición** (Reforma 206, tel. 951/514-2191, 8am-8pm daily, US$6-8). The café puts a Oaxacan twist on Mexican and international staples, such as the *chilaquiles* served with Oaxacan *amarillo* mole sauce, and the French toast with a whipped *tejate* cream sauce served with red berries and flower petals.

If you can't make it out to La Mixteca on this trip, get a taste of the region's delicious recipes in the cozy, ranch-style home setting at ★ **Tierra del Sol** (Land of the Sun; Reforma 411, tel. 951/516-8641, www.tierradelsol.mx, 8am-11pm daily, US$8-16). Head chef Olga Cabrera Oropeza, originally from Huajuapan de León, brings the home-style cooking she learned from her grandmothers to Oaxaca City and beyond, having

presented dishes from La Mixteca at international culinary festivals in New York and elsewhere. The *mole de Doña Chonita* is her homage to one of her grandmothers, from whom she gained much of the knowledge she uses in the kitchen.

My first meal at ★ **Las Quince Letras** (The 15 Letters; Abasolo 300, tel. 951/514-3769, 9am-10pm Mon.-Sat., 9am-7pm Sun., $8-12) left tears in my eyes and a surging desire in my chest to call my mom and rant as though I'd fallen in love. And indeed, I had—with the food of owner and head chef Celia Florian. Relax in the shady, cactus-lined courtyard with a refreshing *agua fresca* (fruit drink) and watch the chefs prepare the tortillas for *tetelas* (corn tortilla prepared with beans, grasshoppers, and piquant herbs) and other tasty local delicacies. The menu's absolute musts include the *chiles de agua a la vinagreta*, spicy chiles stuffed with pork and tangy onions prepared with a vinaigrette, and the chef's flavorful interpretation of the famous *empanadas de amarillo* (pork empanadas in *amarillo* sauce) of San Antonino Castillo Velasco. For dessert, try her ingenious *tamal de chocolate* (chocolate tamale).

One of the best breakfasts in town is at ★ **Restaurante Comala** (Pino Suárez 300-A, tel. 951/351-7838, 8:30am-midnight daily, US$3 set breakfast, US$5-10 menu). Owner Carlos Gross, who named his café after the setting of the canonical Mexican novel *Pedro Páramo* by Juan Rulfo, has been serving traditional Oaxacan meals made with fresh, quality ingredients since 1996. The restaurant is sparsely decorated with a few classic Mexican movie posters, but the food makes up for the bare walls. Personal recommendation: the *omelette de flores,* made with *flor de calabaza* (squash flowers) and other petals, served with a piquant red salsa and refried beans. For lunch and dinner, try some shrimp tacos or a hearty *tlayuda.*

On the block to the north of Santo Domingo, you'll recognize **Mundo Ceiba** (Berriozabal 109, tel. 951/192-0419, www.mundoceiba.org, 8am-11pm Mon.-Sat.,

9am-5pm Sun., US$4) by the racks full of bicycles in the back. This *bici café* (bike café) serves up classic Oaxacan breakfasts, tacos, and *tlayudas*, as well as fresh salads and pastas. It's a great place to fuel up before you join them for their *paseos nocturnos en bicicleta* (nighttime bike rides the staff organizes with local cyclists). You'll probably see the group roaming the streets, blaring music and generally having a ball.

Asian

Ramesh Radheshyam, owner of **Mini Taj** (García Vigil 304, tel. 951/501-0000, 11am-10pm daily, US$8-10) has been firing up the tandoor and serving popular Indian dishes since 2010, including curries, naan, samosas, lassis, and more. His curries are made the way they're supposed to be: packed as full of spices and flavors as complex as *mole*.

There are quite a few Chinese food buffets in town, but if you're craving some noodles and dumplings, your only real option is ★ **Ni-Hao Restaurant** (Matamoros 101, tel. 951/507-1606, 9am-9pm daily, US$7). Inside, it is as Mexican as it is Chinese. In the entryway, Chinese dragons snarl next to cigarette-smoking Mexican skulls with flames shooting out of their eyes. Streams of *papel picado* (decorative paper flags) hang over the golden ships and paintings of cranes in the dining room. You should do the same thing with the sauces and mix soy and *salsa macha* to dip your dumplings in (just go easy on the spicy *macha*). The sign outside says Dumpling House, so don't go around looking for Ni-Hao.

Nestled in the cluster of printmakers on Porfirio Díaz, **Sakura Shokudou** (Porfirio Díaz 507, tel. 951/145-6261, 2:30pm-7pm Mon.-Thurs., 2:30pm-8pm Fri.-Sat., US$4-5) serves up ramen, udon, tempura, *yakimeshi* (a fried rice dish), and, of course, sushi—but only for a few hours a day, so it'll have to be lunch or an early dinner.

Tapas

The ample terrace at **El Olivo Gastrobar** (Constitución 207, tel. 951/501-0333, tasca.

elolivo@gmail.com, 2pm-1am Tues.-Sat., 2pm-11pm Sun., US$8-10) has an open, friendly atmosphere for tapas next to the olive and *pochote* trees. The stylish horseshoe-shaped bar downstairs serves draft beer brewed in-house, as well as other local beers. Also on the menu are delicious Spanish-style tortillas, pastas, and gazpacho.

El Olivo's spin-off delicatessen and café **Gourmand** (Porfirio Díaz 410-A, tel. 951/516-4435, deli.gourmand@gmail.com, 9am-1am Mon.-Sat., US$4-6), two blocks west of Santo Domingo, also serves tapas, as well as sandwiches, burgers, Spanish tortillas, gazpacho, sausages, charcuterie, and other Spanish delicacies.

Cafés

Most cafés tend to focus on the coffee and serve only bakery snacks like cookies, cakes, and muffins, but some have full menus with delicious breakfasts, salads, sandwiches, and more.

Oaxaca's most reputable café chain, ★ **Café Brújula** (Alcalá 104 and 407, tel. 951/424-0907, www.cafebrujula.com, 8am-10pm Mon.-Sat., 8am-7pm Sun.), has two locations on the Andador, one close to Santo Domingo and the other closer to the Zócalo. Since 2006, the chain has been devoted to offering guests the highest-quality coffees from all regions of Oaxaca, in settings that add a hip, modern touch to the venerable surroundings of the cafés. Brújula's master roasters extract full-bodied, never bitter flavors from the beans.

A block south of the entrance to the Jardín Etnobotánico, **Café La Antigua** (Reforma 401, tel. 951/516-5761, 8:15am-10pm Mon.-Sat.) serves 100 percent organic, shade-grown coffee cultivated in Santos Reyes Nopal, in the Sierra Madre del Sur. The growers they work with use solar panels and other sustainable equipment and practices. True to its name, the café is decorated with antique grinders, roasters, and other coffee memorabilia, and the patio is sunny and pleasant, with white stucco arches and columns.

Oaxaca City for Vegans

My recommendations may tend to favor the meat eaters (it's the Texan in me; I can't help it), but don't worry, vegans. I haven't forgotten you. Luckily for you, there are a lot of people in Oaxaca who are much more health-conscious than I.

Many restaurants have salads and whatnot, but having witnessed the difficulty of traveling with strict dietary restrictions, I figured I'd make this list of restaurants that stand out for their vegan options.

fresh *chiles de agua* and other veggies outside a market

- **Casa Oaxaca** (Constitución 104-A, tel. 951/516-8531, www.casaoaxacaelrestaurante.com, 1pm-11pm Mon.-Sat., 1pm-9pm Sun., US$16-32), across the street from the Jardín Etnobotánico, may be more well-known for its ribs and rabbit dishes, but Casa Oaxaca hasn't forgotten about vegans. Chef Alejandro Ruiz actually dedicated menu space for vegan plates, such as the blue corn tostada topped with grilled veggies, beet pâté, avocado, and *frijolón*, a large bean endemic to the region.

- The cozy little "green bar" **Local 215 Barra Verde** (Allende 215, tel. 951/390-6890, 8am-6pm Mon.-Sat., US$3), two blocks west of Santo Domingo, is stocked with fresh, locally sourced ingredients. And they do deliveries.

- There are many vegan and vegetarian dishes on the buffet at **Taj Mahal** (Fiallo 314, tel. 951/527-4242, 9am-11pm daily, US$5), which is served from noon to 7pm. The menu also has vegan options, in case you don't make it for the buffet. The restaurant is two blocks east and one block south of the southeast corner of the Zócalo.

- Many stalls serve vegan food in the **Mercado Orgánico La Cosecha** (Alcalá 806, no phone, 8am-5:30pm Wed.-Sun.), two blocks north of Santo Domingo. For something similar on the south side, head to the **Mercado Orgánico El Pochote Rayón** (Rayón 411, no phone, 8am-6pm daily), about four blocks southeast of the Zócalo.

Coffee geeks will want to grab an espresso drink at **Cafeto & Baristas** (Pino Suárez 407-B, tel. 951/187-0022, 8am-9pm Mon.-Sat.), which buys directly from coffee producers in the Sierra Norte and La Mixteca. This little nook two blocks east of Santo Domingo has a variety of brewing methods to satisfy your inner barista's every whim, including Chemex, Moka pot, AeroPress, and more.

The locals' favorite, **Coffee Beans** (5 de Mayo 400-C, tel. 951/162-7171, 8am-1am daily) has a bit more of a bar vibe to it. The dark wood of the furniture and the loft that creates the second floor give the café a cave-like atmosphere that is quite welcoming after

you've been walking around sweating in the bright, hot afternoon sun.

With delicious coffee now available around nearly every corner in Oaxaca, it appears as though the roasters at cozy and bright **Café Nuevo Mundo** (M. Bravo 206, tel. 951/501-2122, www.cafenuevomundo.com, 8am-10pm Mon.-Sat., 8am-9pm Sun., US$4) have achieved what they set out to do in 2002: promote coffee culture and the consumption of local foodstuffs in the city. They source their beans from small growers in Oaxaca and Chiapas. The large menu includes traditional breakfasts, salads, sandwiches, and sweet breads made in the on-site bakery.

SOUTH OF THE ZÓCALO

You'll notice a marked difference between the streets north of the Zócalo and those to the south. Here the streets teem with people, carts, cars, buses, and the cheapest (and in my opinion, best) food in the Centro. There are fantastic restaurants north of the Zócalo, but they are admittedly cooking for tourists. From tiny nooks selling fresh juice and *tortas* (Mexican sandwiches) to affordable terrace bars for buckets of beer and plates of *botanas* (finger foods) to family-run *comedores,* the south is where you'll find delicious everyday Oaxacan food for a fraction of the price. This is not the best area for people with serious personal space issues. It's much more crowded down here, yes, but don't let that deter you. Elbow in and wish those around you, *¡Buen provecho!* (Enjoy your meal!).

★ Mercado 20 de Noviembre

If you leave Oaxaca City without having a meal at the **Mercado 20 de Noviembre** (20 de Noviembre 512, tel. 951/516-2352, 7am-8pm daily, US$2-3), you're doing it wrong. This crowded, hectic, and delicious collection of food stalls is the best introduction to Oaxacan food you can find.

Sandwiched in between the bakers' counters on the north side and the *mole* vendors on the south side, the small diner-style counters serve up fresh hot Oaxacan chocolate with *pan de yema* (egg yolk bread) and other *comida típica* (traditional food) from the region, like *mole negro, enmoladas* (enchiladas made with *mole coloradito*), *enfrijolados* (same, but with a bean sauce), *tlayudas,* chiles rellenos, and more. Just find an empty spot at one of the dozen or so counters, and you're set. Every chef in this market building knows exactly what he or she is doing, and you will not be disappointed. On the market's east side, the butchers of **El Pasillo de las Carnes Asadas** (The Hall of Grilled Meats) grill fresh *tasajo* (thin-cut beef), *cecina* (thin-cut pork), and chorizo (spicy sausage) for hungry carnivores all day long.

Musicians often stroll the aisles, livening up the atmosphere with melodies and rhythm. Support them. They are part of what makes this place a unique eating experience.

Mexican

Locals are so fond of seafood restaurant **La Red** (Las Casas 101, tel. 951/514-6853, noon-8:45pm daily, US$5-8) that waiters sometimes control the regular line out front with a chain pulled across the door. I tend to trust lines for food like this in Mexico, and it is indeed worth the wait. La Red serves seafood specialties from all over Mexico, like *camarones a la diabla* (devilishly spicy shrimp) and *huauchinango a la veracruzana* (red snapper baked in a spicy, Veracruz-style tomato sauce).

Just across the street from the eastside entrance to the Mercado 20 de Noviembre is a narrow *comedor* called **Lety** (20 de Noviembre 105, no phone, 8am-9pm daily, US$3-5). Like the Hall of Grilled Meats on the other side of the street, Lety's alleyway dining area is full of grill smoke, hustling waitstaff, and hungry people. They'll grill you up a mountain of *tasajo, cecina enchilada,* and chorizo, and serve it on a big wicker plate with tortillas and all the fixings.

The Oaxacan taco chain **Mixtacos** (Aldama 105-B, tel. 951/516-8591, www.mixtacos.com, 1pm-1am daily, US$3-4) serves up delicious tacos, *tortas, alambres* (Mexican hash of taco ingredients and cheese), and more at an excellent price. Don't worry: Fast food doesn't mean you have to sacrifice quality. Ingredients are fresh and full of flavor. Standouts include the *gringas* (basically quesadillas) and the *pozole de pollo* (spicy red soup with hominy and chicken). Little *torta* and juice shops (*juguerías*) like **Naganda Juguería** (20 de Noviembre 203, tel. 951/256-6639, 8am-6pm Mon.-Fri., 8am-4pm Sat.) are great places to grab a quick sandwich and glass of fresh juice, then head back out to keep exploring the streets.

If you'd rather rest your feet awhile, head to the shady terrace at **La Terraza del Rey de Oros** (Aldama 304, tel. 951/516-8420, www.reydeoros.com.mx, 8am-11pm daily, US$5-10)

The Hall of Grilled Meats

That frenetic hallway on the east side of the Mercado 20 de Noviembre is **El Pasillo de las Carnes Asadas,** or The Hall of Grilled Meats. Also called El Pasillo del Humo (The Hall of Smoke), for obvious reasons, this is a unique eating experience for carnivores.

If it looks confusing, that's because it is, at first. Smoke rises from meat sizzling on grills while people squeeze by carrying trays of condiments, gripping multiple bottles of Coca-Cola between their fingers, or playing guitar. The thing here is that you order and pay for each part of your meal with a different person. All these people rushing back and forth through the aisle are working, selling tortillas, salsas, grilled onions and *chiles de agua* (good flavor, sometimes spicy), chopped-up onions, cucumbers, tomatoes and cilantro, and beverages.

Order the *carnes* first. Your options are *tasajo* (beef), *cecina enchilada* (seasoned, or "chilied" pork), chorizo, *lomo* (pork loin), and *tripa* (intestines). While they grill it up right there for you, head to the big communal tables at the west end and order whatever else you want for your meal. They'll pile up the meat and grilled chiles on

the smoky Pasillo de las Carnes Asadas

a big basket-like plate and bring it to you. It may seem hectic, but the servers here will make sure you get everything you need. Someone will come by with a tray of veggies and salsas, someone else will take your beverage order, and a different person will bring you tortillas. Someone from the butcher will bring the bill for the meat, and you'll pay everyone else separately for each type of food item at the end of the meal. *¡Buen provecho!*

and kick back with a bucket of cold beer. They have a large selection of *botanas* to accompany the suds, and also open early for breakfast. The terrace offers a nice view of the Templo de San Juan de Dios, the first church built in Oaxaca.

For something healthier, head to the **Mercado Orgánico El Pochote Rayón** (Rayón 411, no phone, 8am-6pm daily), where a cluster of booths serve up salubrious, veggie-heavy meals from Oaxaca and beyond. You'll find fresh seafood, pastas, and stir-fries, and fresh juices, chocolate, and *tejate,* all made with organic ingredients. There is even a stand that sells *cemitas,* large, often messy sandwiches typical of the neighboring state of Puebla, brimming with *quesillo* (Oaxacan cheese) and flavored with *epazote,* a zesty herb that grows in the region.

Comida Corrida

Of Mexico's eating customs, my personal favorite has to be the *comida corrida.* Translating literally to something like "meal on the go," *comida corrida* is a set menu of around five options of premade meals kept hot and ready to be served. It will include an *agua de sabor* (fruit drink), a soup or fruit salad, and *guisado* (literally "stew" or "gravy," but in this case, "main course") options that usually include things like chiles rellenos, enchiladas, *moles,* and *huevos al gusto,* or "eggs how you want 'em." *Comida corrida* is usually served from breakfast to around 4pm or 5pm, sometimes later. It isn't really a dinner option, and it is rarely offered on Sundays.

The blocks south of the Zócalo are home to a number of delicious *comida corrida* options, where you can eat what is basically a fresh, home-cooked meal for US$1.50-3. You'll find consistent quality at **La Rana Feliz** (Aldama 217, no phone, 8am-9:30pm daily, US$2.50), as well as set-menu service in case someone in your party isn't a fan of the daily specials. This is on the north side of the Mercado 20 de Noviembre, just to the left of the entrance.

Small, homey *comedores* usually aren't as done up as more expensive restaurants, and most are just exterior rooms in family homes. On the corner of Aldama and J. P. García is **El Girasol de Castillo** (J. P. García 404, tel. 951/508-9321, 8am-11pm Mon.-Sat., US$1.50), which can accommodate large groups and dietary restrictions if you call ahead. At 4pm, they stop serving *comida corrida* and finish out the day grilling *tlayudas*. One block west, on the corner of Aldama and Díaz Ordaz, **Comedor Esmeralda** (Aldama 510, no phone, 8am-6pm Mon.-Sat., US$1.50) serves *comida corrida* until 6pm. Half a block north, **Comedor Chunquita** (Díaz Ordaz 407-A, no phone, 9am-7pm Mon.-Sat., US$2) stays open until 7pm.

For slightly more of a restaurant-style feel, head to **Café Alex** (Díaz Ordaz 218, tel. 951/514-0715, 7am-9pm daily). The 80 peso (US$4.50) *comida corrida* is about twice as much as in the *comedores,* and service can be spotty, but the atmosphere is pleasant and clean, and the food is very good. They also have a set menu with large portions of traditional Oaxacan food.

Street Food

During the day, you'll find old women with baskets of *empanadas de amarillo,* large quesadilla-like things filled with *mole amarillo* and chicken or pork, on the sidewalks outside the Mercado 20 de Noviembre. They're a delicious treat on the go, but be careful: The filling is usually steaming hot and takes a while to cool down. These empanadas are the famed recipe from the town of San Antonino Castillo Velasco, so if you can't visit, don't miss your chance to try one here.

In the afternoon, taco and *pozole* stands like **Chefinita** (corner of Las Casas and 20 de Noviembre, no phone, 4pm-4am daily, US$2) set up shop along 20 de Noviembre on the blocks by the market. On the *pozole, con todo* means cabbage and guacamole thrown on top of the soup. *Taqueros* (taco makers) like those at **Amigo Sorroza** (corner of Las Casas and 20 de Noviembre, no phone, 5pm-2am daily, US$1.50) mean onion, cilantro, and guacamole when they ask *¿Con todo?* If the stand on this corner is too crowded, head to the Amigo Sorroza taco stand a block south on the corner of 20 de Noviembre and Aldama.

Accommodations

All but a couple of the hotels listed here are family-run businesses with generations of hard work and great stories behind them. Many are masterpieces of architecture and design, and all are staffed by friendly locals and offer a memorable, authentic experience. Perhaps you're considering a peer-to-peer property rental in Oaxaca City. These have their allure and can be tempting, but this type of accommodations simply isn't fair for locals because it drives up rents for those living in an area. Landlords begin to realize that they can make more money renting nightly to tourists than monthly to residents. Furthermore, it can be difficult to tell if a property is owned by an actual resident of the area or a development corporation looking to skirt hotel taxes.

As a general rule, you can expect to find higher hotel rates on the north side of the Centro and more economical ones in the south, but there are a few exceptions. If your trip is planned during a big festival season, such as Día de Muertos, the Guelaguetza, Christmas, or Easter, book at least a few months in advance to get your top pick. Oaxaca City is brimming with visitors during these periods. Rates are generally 10-20 percent higher at these times, as well.

AROUND THE ZÓCALO

The area near the Zócalo has a number of great hotel options for those who want to stay in the heart of the action.

US$50-100

During Guelaguetza season, I was green with envy of the guests at ★ **Marqués del Valle** (Portal de Clavería, tel. 951/514-0688, 951/516-3474, www.hotelmarquesdelvalle.com.mx, US$65 s, US$78 d, US$128 suite), whose balconies were front row seats to the *castillo* (three-story "castle tower" of fireworks) in the Zócalo one night. Cloudy green onyx veined with red adorns the lobby, and the sunroof over the interior common area provides a bright, open environment. The Zócalo is rarely uneventful and can be noisy, but even street-facing rooms do an excellent job of keeping it quiet inside.

On the block just southeast of the Zócalo, **Hotel Gala** (Bustamante 103, tel. 951/514-2251, www.gala.com.mx, US$50 d, US$71 suite) is more luxurious than the facade suggests. The labyrinthine stairways leading to the rooms conjure up the gravity-defying architecture of an M. C. Escher print, and the rooms are decorated with paintings by the hotel's owner, Señora Consuelo Casasnovas. Rooms are cooled with ceiling fans and include TVs and Wi-Fi access.

Casona Oaxaca (Trujano 206, tel. 951/516-4811, www.lacasonaoaxaca.com, US$50 s, US$65 d), a block west of the Zócalo, has over a century of hospitality experience. Established in 1896 under the name Hotel Francia, the hotel has 25 large, high-ceilinged rooms with air-conditioning, TV, and Wi-Fi. On top of the four-star government rating attained after the remodeling and name change in 2013, the hotel's bragging rights include a stay by English poet and novelist D. H. Lawrence, who mentioned Hotel Francia in published letters to friends.

Over US$100

In a house that was part of one of the first construction projects in Oaxaca, the 16th-century Ex Convento de San Pablo, **Casa Antonieta** (Hidalgo 911, tel. 951/688-8517, www.casaantonieta.com, US$162 standard, US$180 junior suite, US$200 suite) has six luxury rooms and suites around a sunny courtyard lined with bare limestone columns and decorated with ferns, vines, and other endemic Oaxacan plants. Like many newer boutique hotels opened in recent years, Antonieta is pet-friendly and offers only a handful of rooms in order to provide superb attention to guests' needs.

NORTH OF THE ZÓCALO

Accommodations north of the Zócalo are generally more expensive than the blocks to the south, but a few budget gems still exist.

Under US$50

One of the best values in the north is the quaint **Hotel Casa Nina** (Carranza 215, tel. 951/153-9772, www.casaninaoaxaca.com, US$25 s, US$36 d, US$42 king suite), three blocks west of Santo Domingo. The rooms, set around a sunny sunken courtyard, are clean and comfortable. Basic rooms include a private bathroom, though it's not en suite; all include a continental breakfast, served until 11:30am. They also rent bikes for US$5 for two hours.

Two blocks to the south of Hotel Casa Nina, **Hostal Dos Lunas** (M. Bravo 404, tel. 951/516-1446, www.hostaldoslunas.com, US$12 dorm, US$39 d, US$47 suite) charges a little more for private rooms but has clean, airy dorm beds for next to nothing. If you have no need for a TV, you'll save US$5 on the double room. Breakfast (included) is served in the shade of the bougainvillea that climbs up and over the courtyard. A cold beer in a hammock on the terrace is a great break from the afternoon sun.

Two blocks east of Santo Domingo, **Hotel Real Santo Domingo** (Pino Suárez 311, tel. 951/503-0767, www.hotelrsd.com, US$40 s,

US$47 d) offers the basics without sacrificing quality. The interior common area may be small, but the murals of Oaxacan landscapes and bright yellow walls give a sense of openness and draw light into the courtyard. The dozen cozy rooms are all doubles with either full or king beds, and all are cooled with ceiling fans.

Eco-conscious visitors will find their utopia at ★ **Las Mariposas** (Pino Suárez 517, tel. 951/515-5854, www.hotellasmariposas. com, US$45 s, US$48 studio), just to the south of the broad, leafy plazas of Parque El Llano. Every detail here was designed to minimize the hotel's impact on the environment and maximize sustainability and the reuse of resources. The gutter system collects the short, fierce summer rains to water the multiple gardens and clean the restrooms. Small hourglasses on suction cups promote sustainable bathing practices, and trash is separated and recycled, and food waste composted. A communal kitchen for guests in standard rooms allows them to prepare meals (studios include a kitchenette), and all rooms include a continental breakfast. The seven studios and 13 rooms are trimmed with dark-stained wood and bright Mexican ceramic tiles, and the ceiling and standing fans are more than sufficient for cooling down in the desert heat. The hotel arranges tours and transportation, and offers useful services like lending sun hats, umbrellas, and shopping bags free of charge.

Perfect for longer stays, ★ **La Casa de los Abuelos** (Reforma 410, tel. 951/516-1982, 951/514-9815, www.casadelosabuelos. net) has one simple but comfy room (US$45/night, US$320/week) and furnished studio apartments with full kitchens (US$60/night, US$400/week), all pleasantly adorned with Oaxacan ceramics and paintings. I'm a sucker for houses painted yellow, and this one is a paragon of my predilection for sunnier colors: buttery-gold walls in harmony with sky-blue moldings and lime-green pillars. Built at the turn of the 18th century, the house was seized from its owner during the Reform Laws of the 1850s. Luis and Ita, current owners, run the property as an homage to what their ancestors passed down to them. Just a block from Santo Domingo, it is right in the heart of the Centro's action.

At the northeast corner of the Centro, just south of the quirky Templo de Jalatlaco, **Posada Mi Rosita** (Aldama 405, Barrio de Jalatlaco, tel. 951/132-6557, US$31 s, US$39 d) is a tranquil, economical option for those who might prefer a bit of distance from the hubbub of the heart of the Centro. The rooms are comfy and pleasant, with light fixtures, curtains, and furniture made with brightly colored artisanal Oaxacan products.

US$50-100

North of Independencia, Calle Díaz Ordaz turns into the shady, tree-lined Manuel Sabino Crespo, where you'll find the unostentatiously elegant **Hotel Oaxaca Mágico** (Crespo 110, tel. 951/501-0228, US$50 s, US$56 d, US$100 t suite). What stands out here is the service. Hotel staff are friendly, knowledgeable, and helpful, even if a service does not bring business to the hotel (for example, they apprised me of the most convenient taxi *colectivo* stops). The flowery terrace boasts a great view of the Cerro del Fortín and the Basílica de Nuestra Señora de la Soledad, a block to the west.

If a free morning meal is important to your stay, look no further than **Comala Bed & Breakfast** (Pino Suárez 300-A, tel. 951/351-7838, https://comala-bed-breakfast.negocio. site, US$55 d), where owner Carlos Gross has been working on the breakfast part of the deal since the late 1990s. In 2018, he added beds to his repertoire, and now has six comfortable double rooms with en suite bathrooms and air-conditioning units (though the rooms could use a bit of decor). In addition to the delectable victuals, the B&B stands out by being pet-friendly, offering massages and yoga, and hosting live jazz on the stylish terrace on the weekends.

The sylvan courtyards and cool covered patios of ★ **Hotel Casa del Sótano** (Tinoco y Palacios 414, tel. 951/516-2494, www.

hoteldelsotano.com.mx, US$60 d, US$66 d king) may surprise you, considering the hotel's name (*sótano* means "basement"), but this brightly painted 17th-century house is no dank, dark cellar. The stairs from the reception lead down into a jungle of elephantine leaves and polychromatic petals, and the 23 rooms flanking it and the second courtyard beyond are airy and full of sun. The on-site restaurant serves coffee, chocolate, mezcal, and Oaxacan meals in the shade of the patios. This is an ideal hotel for those in need of rest and relaxation after the hustle and bustle of exploring Oaxaca.

Named after a saying from the Zapotec people of El Istmo meaning "What a blessing," ★ **Hotel Boutique NaNa Vida** (Murguía 405, tel. 951/501-1285, www.nanavida.com, US$85 d, US$110 junior suite, US$116 junior suite king) truly lives up to the sentiment. Very few hotels in the Centro combine art, culture, service, and location the way NaNa Vida does. With both Santo Domingo and the Zócalo less than 10-minute walks away, it is right in the heart of the action, but the shade beneath the mango, grapefruit, and pomegranate trees offers a quiet respite. Bare green limestone columns and decor from Oaxaca's most famous folk-art villages add to NaNa Vida's Oaxacan aesthetic. On the wall in each of the 14 rooms is a QR code that can be scanned with a cell phone to provide information on the Oaxacan artists whose work decorates the room. Furthermore, the service goes above and beyond expectations. The hotel makes its own artisanal soaps, and guests get to choose from many aromas and ingredients, like chocolate and agave. Kids receive free bracelets from the Istmo, and women receive free *huipiles* with stays of two nights or more.

Over US$100

With a phenomenal view of Santo Domingo, ★ **Los Amantes** (Allende 108, tel. 951/514-

8899, www.hotellosamantes.com, US$230 d suite, US$305 garden suite, US$335 king suite) is a testament to the recent economic boom in the mezcal industry. Owned by the mezcal brand of the same name, the hotel has 10 high-ceilinged suites named after different types of the spirit. Services include complimentary shoe polishing, bike rentals, a pillow menu, and toiletry kits from Italian luxury brand Bulgari. The green limestone distinctive to Oaxaca's Centro frames the hotel's entrance, and Portuguese architect Joao Boto Caeiro is responsible for the minimalist industrial design, providing a sleek modern look to the remodeled colonial structure. The suites were decorated by Oaxacan visual artist Guillermo Olguín, who is also a founder of the mezcalería Los Amantes and a major player in the global promotion of mezcal. Olguín used contemporary Oaxacan paintings and sculptures as well as antique appliances like sewing machines and radios to achieve a perfect fusion of old rustic and new minimalist design in the stylish suites.

Of the hotels in Oaxaca that marry modern design with traditional Oaxacan art, perhaps the best is the visually stunning ★ **Hotel Azul** (Abasolo 313, tel. 951/501-0016, www. hotelazuloaxaca.com, US$185 s, US$215 d, US$325-625 suite). Established in 2010, Hotel Azul boasts design by Oaxaca's most famous artist, the late Francisco Toledo, that blends seamlessly into the original colonial architecture. The Toledo Suite is fully decked out with his trademark style, epitomized by the backlit wall design above the king-size bed, a tessellation of his signature *papalotes* (kites). Along with fellow Oaxacan visual artist Luis Zárate, he designed the mosaics and water fountain that are the centerpiece of the main courtyard. Rubén Leyva and José Villalobos, also prominent local artists, provided the stylized tiles, colorful floor rugs, and other art for the spacious, airy twin and king twin rooms. The service here is as impeccable as one would expect for the price, and each room comes with a gift of a straw sombrero and woven scarf.

The building now home to ★ **Hotel**

1: the sunny courtyard at Hotel Casa del Sótano
2: a courtyard at Hotel Boutique NaNa Vida

Quinta Real (5 de Mayo 300, tel. 951/501-6100, www.quintareal.com, US$336 d, US$445-475 suites) was built in 1576 as a monastery. The nuns were ejected as a result of the Reform Laws of the mid-19th century, and the premises served as a prison, movie theater, and governmental offices until its restoration and conversion into a hotel in 1976. Historical experts worked with the National Institute of Anthropology and History (INAH) to restore fading frescoes and to incorporate the old structure as much as possible into the design, such as the restaurant's Sala de los Cántaros (Pitcher Room), the western wall of which is covered in the clay oil jugs that were found discarded in a corner of the room. Oaxaca City's gorgeous iteration of the luxury hotel brand Quinta Real boasts 81 rooms and 10 suites richly decorated with dark wood furnishings and gracefully artistic lamps and other fittings. Bright blankets and pillows on the beds add a touch of color to the pleasant earth tones of the décor. The hotel's rates definitely reflect the comfort and services, but if you can afford it, stay here. If you can't, at least stop by and ask to look around the ground floor.

Farther northeast is the unapologetically Mexican pink **City Centro** (Aldama 410, Barrio de Jalatlaco, tel. 951/502-2270, www.cityexpress.com, US$170 s, US$175 d). Although the hotel is part of the City Express chain, the design of the rooms and common areas speaks more to its location than its corporate ownership. It may be more subtle than at other hotels, but the Oaxacan touch is there. A gigantic *pochote* (ceiba) tree stands majestic and thorny as the centerpiece of the main courtyard, and the upper terrace boasts a swimming pool as well as a front-row-seat view of the 17th-century Templo de San Matías Jalatlaco. The price includes a traditional Oaxacan breakfast, and the hotel also loans bicycles to guests free of charge.

SOUTH OF THE ZÓCALO

Affordable accommodations abound in the lively blocks south of the Zócalo. It's the perfect area for shoestring budgeteers—you're not gonna get free shoeshines or a pillow menu, but neither do you have to sacrifice cleanliness or safety.

Under US$50

I can personally vouch for the economical hotels ★ **Posada El Chapulín** (Aldama 317, tel. 951/516-1646, US$20 d) and **Emperador** (Díaz Ordaz 408, tel. 951/516-3089, US$15 d no TV, US$17 d). Every time I've stayed in these spartan establishments, I've met friendly, helpful staff, and I've never had a problem with safety or personal property. You can count on the water being hot, as advertised (not always the case in the bargain lodging here), and the ceiling fans are sufficient to keep you cool at night. El Chapulín's bang for your buck makes it a top budget choice, especially when you factor in its proximity to money-saving *comedores,* the food market, and the taco and *pozole* stands on a number of corners on 20 de Noviembre.

Also in this area are the basic but comfortable rooms at **Villa Vazari** (Aldama 409-A, tel. 951/514-6607, US$28 d), with its castle-like bare stone walls and ample light wells that usher the afternoon sunlight in and right up to your doorstep. A big plus is on-site parking rather than the use of a parking lot in another location, as is the case with many hotels in the Centro.

No other hotel in the city embodies the magic of Oaxaca quite like ★ **Hotel Chocolate** (Mina 212, tel. 951/516-3807, www.chocolateymolelasoledad.com/posada, US$17 d twin beds, US$25 t, US$37 d en suite), on the south side of the Mercado 20 de Noviembre. Owned by the chocolate company Chocolate La Soledad, the small cacao-processing plant and store on the ground floor keeps the whole place smelling like the Food of the Gods all day long. To be truthful, what you're paying for here is this aromatic novelty. Guests in the eight two- and three-bed rooms (which feature little more than twin beds, TV, and fans) use shared bathrooms, and the service is about what you'd expect for the rates.

There are two rooms with en suite baths. Even if you're not a guest, stop in to enjoy a *chocomil* (chocolate milk) on the terrace and take in the view of the sacred hill of Monte Albán at sunset.

Four blocks directly south of the Zócalo, **Hotel Villa Alta** (Miguel Cabrera 303, tel. 951/516-2444, US$21-34 d) has no-frills but clean budget rooms with private bathrooms and an enviable location. The main markets are just around the corner, the Zócalo a five-minute walk away, and the north side just beyond that. This is a great option for those planning an early morning trip south the following day, as the Líneas Unidas *suburban* (van) station is less than two blocks away, on the corner of Bustamante and Xóchitl.

I was pleasantly impressed by **Casa de Don Pablo Hostel** (Melchor Ocampo 412, tel. 951/516-8384, www.casadedonpablo.com. mx, US$11 dorm, US$25 d shared bathroom, US$32 d en suite), four blocks east of the Mercado Benito Juárez. It has a friendly, social vibe without being a full-fledged party hostel. The English-speaking staff are all smiles, and ready to help with any concerns or give travel advice. The dorm rooms are airy and full of sun, and the courtyard and terrace are perfect places for solo travelers to have a drink and meet other visitors.

US$50-100

Just one block south of the Zócalo, award-winning **Hotel Trébol** (Flores Magón 201, tel. 951/516-1256, www.hoteltrebol.com.mx, US$70 d no a/c, US$80 d with a/c) is an oasis of luxury in the hustle and bustle just outside the Mercado Benito Juárez. Bare red brick and dark wrought-iron furnishings lend the rooms an air of rustic class. A continental breakfast is included, and the on-site travel

agency can help with transportation or tour planning.

The **Riviera del Ángel** (Mina 518, tel. 951/516-6666, www.hotelrivieradelangel. com, US$55 d) must have been a paragon of luxury when it opened in the 1970s, but it's beginning to show its age. However, if you don't mind a few wrinkles (mismatched floor tiles, walls that could use fresh paint), you'll find your stay comfortable and convenient. The swimming pool is the biggest I've seen in the city, and the hotel operates super-cheap daily transportation to Monte Albán. Be aware that you'll find quiet inside, but just outside, this location is a windstorm of activity in the daytime.

Over US$100

A fellow guest described ★ **Hotel Boutique Casa Garay** (Miguel Cabrera 110, tel. 951/516-4322, www.hotelcasagaray.com, US$176 d) as a trip through time back to the Mexican Revolution. I responded that the best way I could describe it was as a monastery transmogrified into a hotel and decorated with my grandma's furniture. The hallways are domed with miniature vaulted ceilings, and images of the Virgen de Guadalupe and the Sacred Heart of Jesus adorn the walls. Opened in 2017, the hotel is a tribute to the Garay family, owners of the colonial house-turned-hotel, with each of the 10 rooms named after a family member. Book nerds and antiques lovers should ask for a quick tour of the private library of the family patriarch, Miguel Jiménez Garay, whose shelves are brimming with leather-bound tomes. Hotel staff do whatever they can to accommodate visitors. The aforementioned time traveler was so taken by the place that a bed was set up for him in the library.

Information and Services

TOURIST INFORMATION

Once in town, stop by the **Tourist Information Booths** (9am-6pm daily) in the Alameda de León and Calle Allende, in front of Santo Domingo. They're operated by the **Municipal Tourism Office** (Coordinación Municipal de Culturas, Turismo y Economía), whose main office (Matamoros 102, tel. 951/514-1461, 9am-6pm Mon.-Sat., 10am-2pm Sun.) is a block west of the Andador.

The office of the **State Secretary of Tourism** (SECTUR; Juárez 703, tel. 951/502-1200, www.oaxaca.travel, 9am-3pm Mon.-Fri.) is across from Parque El Llano, northeast of Santo Domingo. The likelihood that you'll need to visit this office is slim, and their hours make it about as difficult as possible. They offer lots of information on their Tourist Routes, such as the Ruta de las Artesanías (Crafts Route), Ruta del Mezcal (Mezcal Route), and Ruta Dominica (Dominican Church Route), but this information is more easily accessed on their website.

Tour Agencies and Guides

Many hotels and Spanish schools offer day tours of the city, so check with your hotel or school (if you're taking classes) to see what they offer.

El Andador (Vigil 509, tel. 951/205-9986, www.elandador.com.mx, 8am-8pm Mon.-Sat., 11am-8pm Sun.) operates some notably unique city tours. They have a chocolate-themed tour as well as a nighttime tour of local cantinas; each costs around US$19 and runs about three hours. El Andador stands out as the only LGBTQ-certified tourism agency in Oaxaca City. **Chimalli Travel** (M. Bravo 108, tel. 951/547-3656 or 951/501-2387, www.chimalli.travel, 9:30am-7pm Mon.-Fri., 9:30am-2pm Sat.) operates a two-hour walking tour (US$22) through the vibrant streets of the Centro Histórico.

Three companies run one-hour bus tours of the city that embark from Calle Morelos, just to the west of the Andador. Tours on the old-timey *tranvía* (streetcar) run by **La Verde Antequera** leave at 1pm, 3pm, 5pm, and 7pm daily for around US$3; just show up and hop on. Buses run by **Optimus Tours** (tel. 951/122-2896, www.optimuscar.net) leave at 2pm, 5pm, and 7pm daily, and cost US$3.50. Call **El Andador** (tel. 951/205-9986, www.elandador.com.mx) or stop by their booth at Morelos 701 (9am-8pm daily) to reserve a spot on their **Andabus**. They charge a bit more than the other companies (around US$5), but they are the only company offering tours in English. Tours run at 11am, 2pm, 5pm, and 8pm.

If you're really on a budget, take a general walking tour of the Centro with **Free Tour Oaxaca** (freetouroaxaca@gmail.com, www.freetouroaxaca.com), which meets up outside the Catedral de Nuestra Señora de la Asunción (also called the Catedral de Oaxaca) at 10am daily. There is no charge for this tour, which runs about two hours, but you must reserve online first. They also operate a street food tour (US$10) of the city and a mezcal-tasting tour (US$20).

CONSULATES AND IMMIGRATION

The **U.S. Consulate** (Alcalá 407, tel. 558/526-2561, toll-free U.S. tel. 844/528-6611, conagencyoaxaca@state.gov, 10am-3pm Mon.-Thurs.) is in the Plaza Santo Domingo, across from the famous church of the same name. Contact them if you lose your passport. The office's hours (which would make a bank teller jealous) make it highly likely that it will be closed in the case you have an emergency. In such an event, call the **U.S. Embassy in Mexico City**. During business hours (8:30am-5:30pm Mon.-Fri.), they can be reached at tel. 558/526-2561. For emergencies outside of business hours, call tel. 555/080-2000.

Canada does not have a consulate in Oaxaca, so Canadians will have to call the **Canadian Embassy in Mexico City** (tel. 01-55/5724-7900, mex@international.gc.ca). Citizens of the United Kingdom are in the same boat. They will have to call the **British Embassy in Mexico City** (tel. 01-55/1670-3200, mexico.consulate@fco.gov.uk). For information on embassies of other countries, visit www.embassypages.com.

HEALTH AND EMERGENCY SERVICES

The likelihood of personal safety problems in the Centro is very low. However, if you do find yourself in a dangerous or emergency situation, there are **Security Kiosks** (Módulos de Seguridad) outside Santo Domingo and the Alameda de León. There are officers at these two locations 24 hours a day, and 9am-6pm daily at the kiosk on Allende, also close to Santo Domingo. Officers of the **Municipal Police** (tel. 951/514-4525) and **Tourist Police** (who don white shirts reading Policía Tourística) have a strong presence in the Centro too. They are there to ensure general safety in tourist areas, but Oaxaca City is so safe for visitors that I've never seen them do much of anything beyond giving directions. As in many countries around the world, the **emergency telephone number** in Mexico is 911.

The cheapest option for things like stomach bugs and colds is the *consultorio médico* (doctor's office) at a pharmacy in the **Farmacias del Ahorro** chain. Consultations are free but require speaking Spanish with the doctor, so you'll need someone to translate if you don't. The branch with a *consultorio* is at the corner of Matamoros and Tinoco y Palacios (tel. 951/515-5000, 7am-11pm daily), and the doc is in 9am-2pm and 4pm-9pm Monday-Saturday.

For emergencies and serious conditions, there are highly qualified bilingual doctors at **Hospital Reforma** (Reforma 613, tel. 951/516-0989), on the block north of the Jardín Etnobotánico, and **Hospital Molina** (García Vigil 317, tel. 951/516-5468), a block west of the Andador at the corner of García Vigil and M. Bravo.

SEISMIC ALERT

As in many other parts of Mexico, Oaxaca City has an early alert system that sounds an alarm up to a minute before a quake. The **Alerta Sísmica** (Seismic Alert) is designed to be distinct from other urban noise, so if you haven't heard it (and don't speak Spanish), you won't recognize it. I highly recommend searching "*alerta sísmica México*" in YouTube and familiarizing yourself with the distinctly creepy tone before you come, so that you'll be ready to act if the earth begins to rattle. It's also prudent to ask about your hotel's *Punto de Reunión* (Meeting Point), usually marked by a green sign with four white arrows pointing to a central spot.

MONEY

There are a number of **ATMs** clustered around the Zócalo. **Banamex** has 24-hour ATMs at its branches on the corner of Hidalgo and Armenta y López (bank hrs 9am-4pm Mon.-Sat.), a block east of the northeast corner of the Zócalo, and on the corner of Morelos and Porfirio Díaz, two blocks north of the Alameda de León (tel. 951/514-0832, bank hrs 9am-4pm Mon.-Fri.). A stand-alone 24-hour Banamex ATM is a block north of the Zócalo on Valdivieso, across from the back of the Catedral de Oaxaca.

Banco Santander (tel. 951/513-9874, 9am-4pm Mon.-Fri., 9am-2pm Sat.) has a 24-hour ATM on Independencia, just north of the Alameda de León, and **Scotiabank** (tel. 951/501-5720, 8:30am-4pm Mon.-Fri., 10am-3pm Sat.) has an ATM on Independencia, just east of the corner with the Andador Alcalá. South of the Zócalo, **Bancomer** (toll-free Mex. tel. 800/226-2663, 8:30am-4pm Mon.-Fri.) has 24-hour ATMs across from the east entrance to the Mercado 20 de Noviembre.

I don't recommend exchanging money in

banks unless it's absolutely necessary. The lines are an aggravating lesson in patience, and the rate really won't be any better than what you'll find in the *casas de cambio* (currency exchanges), which are just to the northeast of the Zócalo. **Euro Dolar** (no phone, 8:30am-7pm Mon.-Sat., 9am-2pm Sun.) is on Valdivieso, across from the east wall of the Catedral de Oaxaca, as is **Centro Cambiario Metrópolis** (no phone, 8:30am-7pm Mon.-Sat., 10am-2:30pm Sun.). On the south side of Hidalgo, on the block to the east of the Zócalo, are two places that both simply say **Money Exchange.** The one closest to the Zócalo is open 8:30am-7:30pm daily, and the other, a few storefronts to the east, is open 8am-8pm daily.

LAUNDRY AND LUGGAGE STORAGE

Pricier hotels will offer on-site laundry services. However, if yours doesn't, there are many *lavanderías* (laundries) around the Centro, many of which are also *tintorerías* (dry cleaners). They all charge around US$5 a load and usually have clothes clean the next day. On the north side of the Centro, your options are **Azteca Lavandería** (Hidalgo 404, tel. 951/514-7951, 9am-7pm Mon.-Sat.); **Antequera Tintorería y Lavandería** (Murguía 408, tel. 951/516-5694, 8am-8pm Mon.-Sat.); and **Tintorería Mr. Klyn** (Reforma 703, tel. 951/139-1863, 8am-8pm Mon.-Fri., 8am-7pm Sat.).

South of the Zócalo, look for **Lavandería Hole** (Fiallo 413, tel. 951/516-4622, 8am-8pm Mon.-Fri., 8am-3pm Sat.) and **Lavanet** (Aldama 301-A, tel. 951/514-4269, 8:30am-8:30pm Mon.-Sat.), which is also an Internet café.

Most hotels will hold on to your luggage for a while after you check out at no extra cost if you stayed with them, and many will do so for nonguests for a small fee. Also, *suburban* (van) stations like **Atlántida** (corner of Bustamante and Zaragoza, tel. 951/390-5319, 7am-10pm Mon.-Sat., 8am-7pm Sun.) and **Líneas Unidas** (corner of Bustamante and Xólotl, tel. 951/516-2472 or 951/187-5511, 24 hrs daily) offer *guarda equipaje* (luggage storage) service for minimal fees.

Transportation

GETTING THERE

With more airlines adding direct flights from U.S. cities and highways being improved and expanded, it has never been easier to get to Oaxaca.

Air

The **Xoxocotlán International Airport** (code: OAX, tel. 951/511-5088, contactos@asur.com.mx) is about 7 km (4.3 mi) south of Oaxaca City.

United Airlines (local tel. 555/283-5500, toll-free Mex. tel. 800/900-5000), via the regional branch United Express, offers direct flights from Houston that take 2.5 hours; American Eagle, a similar subsidiary of **American Airlines** (local tel. 555/209-1400, toll-free Mex. tel. 800/904-6000), flies directly from Dallas/Fort Worth. Mexican airline **Volaris** (local tel. 551/102-8000, toll-free U.S. tel. 800/865-2747) has added a direct route from Los Angeles that gets to Oaxaca in 4 hours.

Aeromexico (Mex. tel. 555/133-4000, U.S. tel. 404/305-8200) and **Interjet** (toll-free Mex. tel. 800/011-2345, toll-free U.S tel. 866/285-9525) operate flights from many cities in the United States that connect in Mexico City. For flying from Oaxaca City to other destinations in Mexico, there are: **Viva Aerobus** (toll-free Mex. tel. 818/215-0150, toll-free U.S. tel. 888/935-9848), which flies to Monterrey; **TAR Aerolíneas** (tel. 552/629-5272, www.tarmexico.com), with routes to Guadalajara and Querétaro; and **Volaris** (local tel. 551/102-8000, toll-free

U.S. tel. 800/865-2747), which connects to many domestic destinations via Mexico City, Guadalajara, and Tijuana.

The regional airline **Aerotucán** (local tel. 951/502-0840, toll-free Mex. tel. 800/640-4148, www.aerotucan.com) operates flights to Puerto Escondido and Huatulco, on the Oaxacan coast, as well as flights to Tuxtla Gutiérrez, in neighboring Chiapas. The company's 10-14-passenger Cessna Grand Caravan planes are authorized to operate as air taxis, which means Aerotucán doesn't have to adhere to fixed flight schedules, allowing the company to be more flexible for clients. Flights are short, scenic, and safe.

Car

A number of highways, from wide, modern toll roads to winding, narrow strips of pavement barely two lanes wide and full of potholes, connect Oaxaca City to other destinations in the state, as well as to major cities in neighboring states. Average drive times to Oaxaca City are given in parentheses.

The fastest and safest way from Mexico City (6 hrs), 465 km (290 mi) from Oaxaca City, is via **Highway 150D,** a tollway, which leaves the capital via Calzada Ignacio Zaragoza and passes through Puebla City (4 hrs). About 75 km (47 mi) east of Puebla, take **Highway 135D** south until it meets up with **Highway 190** in the Valle de Etla, about 12 km (7.4 mi) northwest of Oaxaca City. This is a nice, scenic route, especially when it passes through the mountainous area on the border of Oaxaca and Puebla states, where weird, branchless forests of columnar cacti dominate the vistas. Be especially vigilant on mountain passes, as this stunning landscape also makes the road dangerous at times; rockslides aren't uncommon.

From the north, **Highway 135** connects Oaxaca City to Huautla de Jiménez (241 km/149 mi, 5 hrs) via Highway 182, and **Highway 175** winds through the Sierra Norte from Tuxtepec (218 km/135 mi, 4.5 hrs) and the neighboring state of Veracruz. I recommend extreme caution on this and other mountain "highways," as they are narrow, serpentine, and not in the best condition. The unnerving tendency of some Oaxacan drivers to take blind curves in the opposing lane adds another hazard to these roads. Landslides are possible in the rainy season, so check the weather. It is best to avoid these routes if storms are in the forecast.

Farther east, the mountains are traversed by **Highway 179,** also coming from Veracruz state. Both Tuxtla Gutiérrez (541 km/335 mi, 8 hrs), the largest city in the neighboring state of Chiapas to the east, and the Istmo de Tehuantepec (Juchitán; 278 km/175 mi, 5 hrs) are connected to Oaxaca City via **Highway 190.**

The main route from the coast is **Highway 175,** which connects with coastal **Highway 200** at Pochutla (239 km/148 mi, 5.5 hrs). After about 3.5 hours of winding through tropical and evergreen cloud forests, the highway stretches through 100 km (62 mi) of rugged desert landscapes; green fields of corn, maguey, and nopal cactus; and hazy vistas of blue mountains beyond, before arriving in Oaxaca City. This is the fastest route from the beaches at Mazunte, Zipolite, and Puerto Ángel, all about six hours away. The **Oaxaca El Zapote-Copalita Highway** zigzags through 47 km (29 mi) of jungle from the Huatulco airport (245 km/152 mi, 5.5 hrs) before meeting up with Highway 175 just north of Pluma Hidalgo (210 km/130 mi, 4.5 hrs).

Highway 131 is the quickest route from Puerto Escondido (251 km/155 mi, 6.5 hrs) and surrounding areas. From Pinotepa Nacional (336 km/210 mi, 8.5 hrs), scenic **Highway 125** squiggles north through La Mixteca until it meets up with the 135D toll road to Oaxaca. However, it's faster (7.5 hrs) to take Highway 200 east, connecting with Highway 131 via the **Río Grande-Juquila Highway** (turnoff in Río Grande O Piedra Parada).

A more leisurely route from Mexico City takes **Highway 95D** south, via Calzada de Tlalpan, to Cuernavaca and Morelos, and follows **Highway 160** and later Highway 190 to

Oaxaca City. There are toll roads at the beginning and end of this route (488 km/305 mi), which can run 8.5-11 hours, depending on traffic and conditions. It is best to do this route road-trip style, stopping for the night in Huajuapan de León, saving the last three hours of the drive for the next day.

A quick note on highway driving in Mexico: As a general rule for anywhere in the country, I recommend limiting your drive times to the daylight hours, especially on smaller, isolated highways like 125 and 160. Highway bandits are not uncommon; overnight buses are usually safe, but private automobiles are another story.

Bus

Oaxaca's main first-class bus station is the conveniently located **Terminal ADO** (5 de Mayo 900, Barrio de Jalatlaco, tel. 951/502-0560), in the northeast corner of the Centro. It's a quick 10-minute taxi ride (US$3) or a half-hour walk to the Zócalo. The main bus company here is **Autobuses de Oriente,** or ADO (toll-free Mex. tel. 818/354-3521, www. ado.com.mx), which operates the subsidiary companies **Ómnibus Cristobal Colón** (OCC) and **Autobuses Unidos** (AU), ADO's economy line, as well as the luxury brand **ADO Plantino.**

These three brands operate multiple daily buses to major cities outside the state, such as Mexico City (6 hrs); Puebla (5 hrs); Veracruz (7-8 hrs); Tuxtla Gutiérrez, Chiapas (10 hrs); and Acapulco, Guerrero (1 daily, 12 hrs). I recommend the smaller vans, called *suburbanes* or *camionetas,* for overland travel within the state, as larger buses take longer on curving mountain roads. In addition, *suburban* stations tend to be more strategically located in the Centro, cutting down on time spent in city traffic. However, ADO and its subsidiaries run all over the state, with daily trips to and from Pochutla (9.5 hrs), Huatulco (8 hrs), Puerto Escondido (11 hrs), Tuxtepec (5.5 hrs), Juchitán (5 hrs), and other destinations.

To get your bus tickets without trekking out to the terminal, stop by one of the **ADO ticket** booths (*puntos de venta*) in the Centro. There is one at Valdivieso 106 (7:30am-9:30pm daily) and another a block west of the Alameda de León (20 de Noviembre 103-D, 8am-10pm daily).

Van

The *suburban* (small, 12-15-passenger van) is the main type of interregional transportation in Oaxaca. They aren't the most comfortable trips, but they are very affordable. You can get anywhere in the state from the **Central de Autobuses de Segunda Clase** (on Calle Juárez Mara, just north of the Central de Abastos, tel. 951/516-5326). The great thing about this kind of travel is that it is so common here that companies run multiple routes daily, so you can basically show up and get on a van, usually within the hour.

You don't have to go all the way to the Segunda Clase station for most destinations. Six blocks south of the Zócalo, the companies **Atlántida** (corner of Bustamante and Zaragoza, tel. 951/390-5319, 7am-10pm Mon.-Sat., 8am-7pm Sun.) and **Líneas Unidas** (corner of Bustamante and Xólotl, tel. 951/516-2472 or 951/187-5511, 24 hrs daily) both go to the coast. From the north side of the Centro, **Transjuar** (Calzada Héroes de Chapultepec 801, Colonia Reforma, Oaxaca City, tel. 951/132-7227) *suburbanes* head north to Tuxtepec. On the west side of the Centro, companies like **Autotransportes Flechador del Sol** (to Nochixtlán; Periférico 408, Oaxaca City, tel. 951/220-9289), **Servicios Turísticos de Huajuapan** (Valerio Trujano 420, Oaxaca City, tel. 951/516-5759), and **Autotransportes de Tlaxiaco** (Trujano 505, Oaxaca City, tel. 951/516-4030) have routes to various locations in La Mixteca.

GETTING AROUND

Nothing in the Centro is really more than a half hour away on foot, which is why I highly recommend **walking** as much as possible. Everywhere you go, you turn a corner and . . . wow! So meander as much as possible.

To and from the Airport

Depending on traffic, the Oaxaca airport is only 20-30 minutes from the Centro. Many hotels offer transportation, either included in the reservation or at an extra fee. Consult your hotel to make arrangements before arriving.

You can get a **secure taxi** at the airport. *Colectivo* service, vans taking groups of 10-12 passengers, goes to the Centro for US$5 per person, and *privado* taxis of up to four people cost around US$17 per person. You can always rely on this service, as taxis wait until the last arrival of the night, even for delays.

When you depart, the cheapest way to get to the airport is via the buses run by **Transportación Terrestre** (Alameda de León 1-G, tel. 951/514-1071, 4:45am-6pm Mon.-Sat.). They run 12-passenger vans eight times a day from the Centro to the airport for US$5 per person (the same company runs the secure taxi and *colectivo* services from the airport). If you make reservations beforehand, they will pick you up at your hotel. The office can be a little difficult to see. It's in the building directly across from the Catedral de Oaxaca, tucked behind the small, narrow textile market. If you're in a group of three or four, it is cheaper to get a taxi from **Sitio Alameda** (tel. 951/516-2190 or 951/516-2685) on the north side of the Alameda; the charge is US$11 total for the trip to the airport.

Car

There are three car rental companies in the Oaxaca airport. Of the three, the only one that makes sure to have an attendant in the booth until the last flight arrives, even if it's delayed, is **Alamo** (tel. 951/503-3618, 5:30am-last arrival daily). With rates starting around US$65 a day (ranging to US$185), Alamo also has the cheapest rates of the three. **Hertz** (toll-free Mex. tel. 800/709-5000, 7am-11pm daily, US$90-680 per day) has the widest selection of vehicles, from compact cars and sedans to SUVs, sports cars, and luxury brands. The rates at **Europcar** (tel. 951/143-8340, 6am-10pm daily) run US$115-185 per day. (Note that these are the rack rates given at the rental counters for what you would pay to rent a car there without a reservation. Book online and well in advance to get better rates.)

Locally-owned **Optimus Car Rental** (Alcalá 100-A, tel. 951/514-1976, www.opti-muscar.net, 8:30am-9pm daily) is the only rental company in town that includes collision and theft insurance in its daily prices. Rates start around $80 per day for its fleet of new, clean, very well-maintained cars and SUVs. **Only Rent-A-Car** (5 de Mayo 215-A, toll-free Mex. tel. 800/227-6659, 8am-8pm daily) is another local option with more affordable rates than Optimus, but they don't include the insurance benefits.

Driving in Oaxaca is not for the timid. Drivers are in a hurry, and they'll let you know it. It is actually safer to be a somewhat aggressive driver yourself (When in Rome, right?). In addition to dealing with the pell-mell pace of traffic, you must be alert for speed bumps. These keep people from speeding too much but can be excessive on some roads. Many speed bumps are painted with yellow stripes and have a sign reading either *Tope* or *Reductor,* and many just pop up out of nowhere and toss everything and everyone in the car around like beans in a maraca.

Street parking in the Centro is free but scarce, and even scarcer the more central you get. However, if you don't mind walking, the more peripheral blocks usually have space. Many hotels offer on-site or valet parking included with reservations. Safer than the street, especially for overnight parking, are privately owned parking lots, usually marked with the word *Estacionamiento* (parking lot) or a large capital *E* inside a red circle. They charge about US$1 an hour, sometimes with discounted rates the longer your car stays in the lot. There is one (at least) on just about every block in the Centro. Ask if they close at night or if they are a 24-hour lot. You don't want to accidentally miss closing time and not be able to get your car out until morning.

Taxi

Taxis in Oaxaca City are safe and inexpensive.

Drivers don't use meters, but prices are surprisingly consistent. You shouldn't be charged more than US$3 to get anywhere within the Centro. It's a good idea to ask about the fare before getting in. That being said, I often forget and have never been excessively overcharged once I'm in the car. Taxis can be hailed on the street. The main companies (referred to as *sitios*) are **Multitaxi ADO** (tel. 951/516-0503 or 951/516-1572), **Sitio Antequera** (tel. 951/503-8434 or 951/515-4355), and **Sitio Reforma** (tel. 951/515-5638 or 951/518-7484). These are all yellow cabs. The maroon ones you'll see (mostly around the southern half of the Centro) are *colectivo* taxis that load up with as many passengers as possible on their way out to towns in the Valles Centrales and beyond.

Bicycle

Get around town in style on one of the refurbished vintage bikes from **Bicibella Oaxaca** (Alcalá 802, tel. 951/109-9727, 8am-8pm Mon.-Sat.). At just US$1 an hour, it's the cheapest way to get around the Centro aside from walking, and the hours only get cheaper the longer you rent the bike. Four hours cost US$2.50; 8 hours, US$4; and 12 hours, US$5. Make sure you bring an ID to leave as collateral—preferably a driver's license or school or military ID, as it's good to leave your passport locked away in your hotel. However, if your passport is your only ID, the folks at Bicibella are trustworthy. Don't worry about leaving it with them for a few hours.

Many hotels north of the Zócalo (**Los Amantes, Hotel Azul, City Centro,** and **Hotel Casa Nina,** among others) have bikes

for guests, either included in the price or to rent. Ask reception about this service. If you're not an experienced rider in urban settings, it's best to limit your pedaling to the northern half of the Centro, as the streets south of the Zócalo are congested, making it less safe for cyclists.

If you can deal with the sometimes manic traffic and want a good ride, take the **bike path to Tule,** the giant tree 11 km (6.8 mi) east of town. The ride takes about 30-45 minutes one-way, depending on your starting point. To get to the path from the Centro, take Guerrero east from the Zócalo until you cross Eduardo Vasconcelos. Follow the road as it turns to the right and changes names to Mariano Azuela, which will take you to the beginning of the bike path, in the median of Avenida Ferrocarril. However, be aware that the directionality of Azuela changes as you near the busy road, and cars are allowed to pull in off the busy Avenida Ferrocarril onto Azuela for a quick second before forking left to another road. The safest thing is to walk your bike around the corner and through the crosswalk to get to the path.

The friendly, English-speaking staff at **Mundo Ceiba** (Berriozabal 109, tel. 951/192-0419, www.mundoceiba.org, 8am-11pm Mon.-Sat., 9am-5pm Sun.) organizes nighttime social rides around the Centro every Wednesday, Friday, Saturday, and Sunday night 9pm-10:30pm. If you don't have a bike, you can rent one for US$4, and tandems go for US$7. Not very experienced in urban cycling? No problem. The point of the rides is to foster safe biking practices and culture in the city, and the staff at Mundo Ceiba is here to educate as well as have fun.

Valles Centrales

Some places cultivate tradition like a living, growing thing. In these three valleys that extend east, south, and northwest from Oaxaca City, it is alive and well. Buried in the soil of these rolling hills that almost burn green when the summer rains come, the roots of crafts, cuisines, rituals, and commerce—some going back thousands of years—still nurture the work of modern hands.

    The weavers of Teotitlán and other communities in the Valle de Tlacolula to the east have produced wool rugs embellished with Zapotec glyphs since the arrival of the Spanish (and their sheep) 500 years ago, and artists here today are still pushing the boundaries of what can be done with thread and loom. The bright, intricately painted wooden figures of fantastic animals called *alebrijes* have their roots in more recent

Highlights

Look for ★ to find recommended sights, activities, dining, and lodging.

★ **Monte Albán:** Take a quick day trip from the current regional capital to the ancient one, as these 2,500-year-old ruins of the seat of pre-Hispanic Zapotec culture and politics still dominate a hilltop just outside the city (page 103).

★ **Árbol del Tule:** You'll be waxing philosophical about the brevity of human life under the boughs of this colossal 2,000-year-old cypress, but the local guides specialize in a quirky tour that will get you laughing again in no time (page 110).

★ **Teotitlán del Valle:** Immerse yourself in the colors, textures, and stories of this quaint town whose people have dedicated themselves to making gorgeous rugs, tapestries, and other high-quality wool products for half a millennium (page 111).

★ **Mitla:** Visit the religious capital of the Zapotec civilization, or the "Place of the Dead," as

they called it, where the walls are adorned with unique, mortarless stone mosaics (page 119).

★ **Hierve El Agua:** These strange, towering "frozen waterfalls" might have you double-checking what planet you're on (page 122).

★ **Zaachila's Thursday Market:** It may technically be at the end of the Ruta de Artesanías (Crafts Route), but Zaachila is where you come to fill your belly, not your shopping bags—especially when the Thursday market fills the streets (page 126).

★ **San Bartolo Coyotepec:** Doña Rosa's technique of making black clay pottery has been attracting fascinated visitors to her hometown since she invented it in the 1950s (page 128).

★ **San Sebastián de las Grutas:** Perfect for an overnight trip from Oaxaca City, this cozy hideaway nestled in verdant hill country offers cave and subterranean river tours (page 134).

history. The art began less than a century ago, and the towns of Arrazola and San Martín Tilcajete in the Valle de Ocotlán have only been famous for making them since the late 1970s. And it is simply hard to describe the feeling you'll get standing over a 2,000-year-old kiln at the ruins at Atzompa, overlooking the Valle de Etla, when your next stop is the town of Santa María Atzompa, where you can buy ceramic coffee mugs in the green-glazed style that has made the town famous.

To see where it all began, visit the big sites, like Monte Albán and Mitla, but try to make it to the lesser-visited ones, like Yagul and Atzompa, as well. They are a wealth of information, and much less crowded. These ruined towns are where people from the surrounding areas used to gather to socialize and trade, a custom that is still alive today in towns like Zaachila, Ocotlán, and Tlacolula.

The past is so close here, you almost feel like you're trespassing through time to a place you didn't know you were allowed to visit. And the connection doesn't lie only in the man-made. The giant Moctezuma cypress called El Árbol del Tule sprouted over 2,000 years ago, when much of these valleys were under the waters of a great lake. At Hierve El Agua, you can go swimming atop "frozen waterfalls" that have been formed by "boiling" mineral springs for millennia.

You may come to the Valles Centrales to buy pretty pottery or a bottle of authentic mezcal, but after coming and experiencing this fascinating place for yourself, you might realize the most valuable things you take home with you are the stories. Come here to see. Come here to shop. Come here to eat. But, most of all, come here to learn.

PLANNING YOUR TIME

The traditional way to see the Valles Centrales is by staying in Oaxaca City and visiting destinations on day trips, for which you would need to devote at least five days of your trip in order to take in the highlights of this region. Tour agencies in Oaxaca City make this a very viable option, with tours that take in multiple sights a day, but it is also very possible by public transport.

It is becoming more popular for people to stay out in the valleys and explore them from towns like **Mitla, Teotitlán del Valle,** and **San Agustín Etla.** This is a great way to get to know a place better than a quick tour will allow, and I've included pertinent hotel information in places where you're more likely to stay.

You might plan your trips according to **market days** around the valleys. The markets in **Zaachila,** on Thursday, **Ocotlán,** on Friday, and **Tlacolula,** on Sunday, are the ones to see. It's best to make the market town your first stop on these days, as they have a better selection and are more lively in the morning.

Getting Around
PUBLIC TRANSIT

One thing I love most about Oaxaca is how easy and cheap it can be to get around. You can get anywhere in the valleys via **bus, taxi colectivo** (multiple passenger taxi), or **camioneta** (covered pickup truck) for US$5-10 a day. These types of transportation will stop if you wave them down just about anywhere on the highway. It may take more time than going by organized tour, but it's reliable, making it possible to get on and off whenever and wherever you feel like exploring. In theory, you only need to know place names to use this system, but it isn't always as simple as you'd think, so this might not be an option for those who speak no Spanish at all.

Another mode of public transport called the *suburban* (van) is also a very affordable option. (It's sometimes called *camioneta* as well—confusing, I know.) This is what you can catch at Oaxaca City's Central de Autobuses de Segunda Clase, on Calle Juárez Maza, just north of the Central de Abastos. To get here,

---

Previous: a cultivated field of *espadín* maguey; the hilltop pyramids at Monte Albán; the distinct embroidery style of San Antonino Castillo Velasco.

Valles Centrales

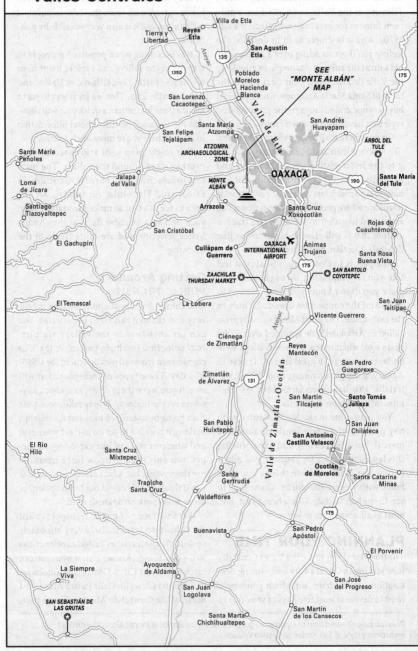

Villa de Etla

Reyes
Etla

Tierra y
Libertad

San Agustín
Etla

135

135D

Poblado
Morelos
Hacienda
Blanca

San Lorenzo
Cacaotepec

*SEE
"MONTE ALBÁN"
MAP*

175

Santa María
Atzompa

Valle de Etla

Atoyac

San Felipe
Tejalápam

**ATZOMPA
ARCHAEOLOGICAL
ZONE ★**

San Andrés
Huayapam

*ÁRBOL DEL
TULE*
⊛

Santa María
Peñoles

Jalapa
del Valle

**MONTE
ALBÁN** ⊛

OAXACA

190

**Santa María
del Tule**

Loma
de Jícara

Arrazola

Santiago
Tlazoyaltepec

San Cristóbal

El Gachupín

**Cuilápam de
Guerrero**

**OAXACA
INTERNATIONAL
AIRPORT** ✈

Santa Cruz
Xoxocotlán

Ánimas
Trujano

Rojas de
Cuauhtémoc

Santa Rosa
Buena Vista

175

*ZAACHILA'S
THURSDAY MARKET* ⊛

⊛ **SAN BARTOLO
COYOTEPEC**

El Temascal

La Lobera

Zaachila

San Juan
Teitipac

Vicente Guerrero

Atoyac

Ciénega
de Zimatlán

Reyes
Mantecón

San Pedro
Guegorexe

Zimatlán
de Álvarez

131

San Martín
Tilcajete

**Santo Tomás
Jalieza**

San Pablo
Huixtepec

San Antonino
Castillo Velasco

San Juan
Chilateca

El Río
Hilo

Santa Cruz
Mixtepec

Santa
Gertrudis

**Ocotlán
de Morelos**

Santa Catarina
Minas

Trapiche
Santa Cruz

Valdeflores

175

Buenavista

San Pedro
Apóstol

El Porvenir

La Siempre
Viva

Ayoquezco
de Aldama

San José
del Progreso

*SAN SEBASTIÁN DE
LAS GRUTAS* ⊛

San Juan
Logolava

San Martín
de los Cansecos

Santa Marta
Chichihualtepec

Valle de Zimatlán-Ocotlán

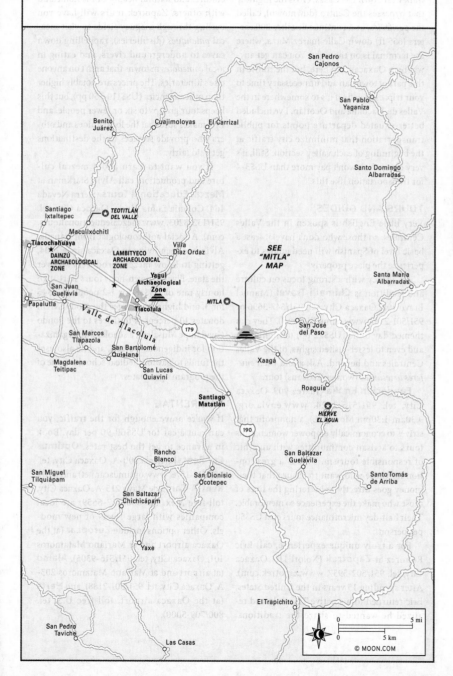

walk west down Las Casas, cross the highway that bypasses the Centro (downtown), called the *periférico*, and continue another 200 meters (655 ft) down Calle Juárez Maza, where the terminal is on the right. You can get anywhere in Oaxaca from here, but the traffic in this part of town can add unnecessary time to your trip, especially if it's to somewhere in the Valles de Tlacolula and Ocotlán. I've included better-situated departure points for public transportation that minimize city traffic at the beginning of each valley section. Still, it's very cheap. You won't pay more than US$3-4 for transportation like this.

TOURS AND GUIDES

Very little English is spoken in the Valles Centrales, so those who don't have at least a basic level of Spanish will need guides to experience the place properly.

An agency with a strong focus on culture and tradition is **Chimalli Travel** (Manuel Bravo 108, Oaxaca City, tel. 951/547-3656 or 951/501-2387, www.chimalli.travel). They run themed day tours (US$22 pp) to highlights, and even to lesser-visited sights, of the Valles Centrales and beyond. Ask about their *mujeres artesanías* (women artisans) tour.

Fundación En Vía (Juárez 909, Oaxaca City, tel. 951/515-2424, www.envia.org, 9:30am-1:30pm Mon.-Fri.), a nonprofit that strives to economically empower women, runs tours to artisan communities with an ethic of responsible tourism. This is a great option for those who want to ensure that their money goes directly to bettering the lives of those who make the experience so memorable. Their half-day microfinance tours cost US$50 per person.

For a truly unique experience, call Eric Ramírez at **Zapotrek** (Xolotl 110, Oaxaca City, tel. 951/502-5957, www.zapotrek.com). After spending 15 years in the United States, Eric returned to his native Tlacolula and realized he wanted to share the traditions,

culture, and natural beauty of his homeland with others. Zapotrek tours will have you cycling through maguey fields to visit mezcal *palenques* (distilleries), rappelling down caves to underground rivers, and eating in local *comedores* in towns that aren't on anyone else's itineraries. The prices are notably higher than other agencies (US$110-150 pp), but this keeps tour groups to six or fewer people, and Eric makes sure that the local guides and others who provide services in the destinations get paid fairly.

If you want to learn about mezcal culture and production, call Alvin Starkman at **Mezcal Educational Tours** (Sierra Nevada 164, Colonia Loma Linda, Oaxaca City, tel. 951/132-8203, www.mezcaleducationaltours.com). A social anthropologist from Canada, Alvin has been living in Oaxaca since 2004, getting to know mezcal producers all over the state. Five- to seven-hour tours start at an hourly rate of US$38 for 1-2 people, US$45 for 3, and higher the larger the group. Alvin donates 10 percent of tour fees to the Fondo Guadalupe Musalem, a scholarship organization for indigenous women, and he also uses the funds to pay for medical school for one of the program's graduates.

CAR RENTAL

If you're brave enough for the traffic, you can rent a car for US$60-90 per day. Book in advance to get the best rates. **Optimus Car Rental** (Alcalá 100-A, Oaxaca City, tel. 951/514-1976, www.optimuscar.net) and **Only Rent-A-Car** (5 de Mayo 215-A, Oaxaca City, toll-free Mex. tel. 800/227-6659) are local companies with large fleets of new models. Other options include **Europcar** (at the Oaxaca airport and at Mariano Matamoros 101, Oaxaca City, tel. 951/516-9305), **Alamo** (at airport and at Mariano Matamoros 203-A, Oaxaca City, tel. 951/501-2188), and **Hertz** (at the Oaxaca airport, toll-free U.S. tel. 800/709-5000).

Monte Albán and Vicinity

When the Zapotecs first arrived here over 2,500 years ago, they built their sophisticated capital, in alignment with their advanced knowledge of the stars, atop the tallest hill they could find in the crux of three great valleys, and looked out over what would be their domain for the next two millennia.

The ruins of Monte Albán, impressive as they are, are merely what we've found of this great capital's downtown district. Packed into the dirt of these hills just to the southwest of Oaxaca City, much of the city lies under modern-day construction. However, more recently discovered sites like Atzompa, only opened to the public in 2012, are shining new light on the extent of this extraordinary pre-Hispanic metropolis.

TOP EXPERIENCE

★ MONTE ALBÁN

The Zapotec name for the city they built at **Monte Albán** is Dani Baá, which means "Sacred Mountain," and from the views alone it's easy to see why. Distance paints the hills blue as sunlight pours into the Valles Centrales, no matter which direction you look.

It may look a bit rundown now, but Monte Albán is the earliest example of urban planning in the Americas, so it's fun to imagine it as the bustling, functional metropolis it once was. See the hordes of tourists as busy merchants or flagrantly dressed dignitaries or excited sports fans. Imagine the walls covered in the red stucco the Zapotecs were fond of finishing them with. Smell the smoke of copal sap drifting through the ancient hallways.

This place is 2,500 years old, and even with cameras clicking all over the ruins, it's not hard to see what Monte Albán's founders saw here. Walking this close to history has an electric feel to it, like you can hear the time humming in the stones, and two and a half

millennia somehow seem as close as memory among the work of such ancient human hands. This is where Oaxaca as we know it began, and a trip here is incomplete without seeing it.

History

Before the founding of Monte Albán, the hill on which the city was built was uninhabited. There were small settlements in the valleys below, at Mogote in Etla; Yegüi, what is now called Lambityeco in Tlacolula; and Tilcajete in Zimatlán-Ocotlán. These were chiefdoms with local sovereignty that were often in competition or at war with each other. The Monte Albán hill was a no-man's-land between the three settlements. Due to evidence of a steep population decline in Mogote at the time of the founding of Monte Albán, it is believed that its chiefs were the ones to decide to take advantage of the unpopulated hill, flatten its top, and found their capital city.

After its founding in 500 BC, Monte Albán quickly became the political and economic powerhouse of the region, and maintained that dominance until sometime between AD 750 and 900. It is one of the few settlements of its kind to show clear signs of the emergence of a state-style system of government. Much of its economy was based on tributes paid by the districts under its control, as well as the trade in beans, corn, squash, and other vegetables grown on the fertile hills of the Valles Centrales. In Monte Albán and other pre-Hispanic settlements, terraced fields were built into the hillsides, some of which are still in use today by neighboring communities.

Between 500 BC and 300 BC, the city's population rose to 5,200 inhabitants, and by the end of the Monte Albán I phase (500 BC-AD 100), that number had skyrocketed to 17,200. It ranked among the largest cities in Mesoamerica at the time. During

Monte Albán

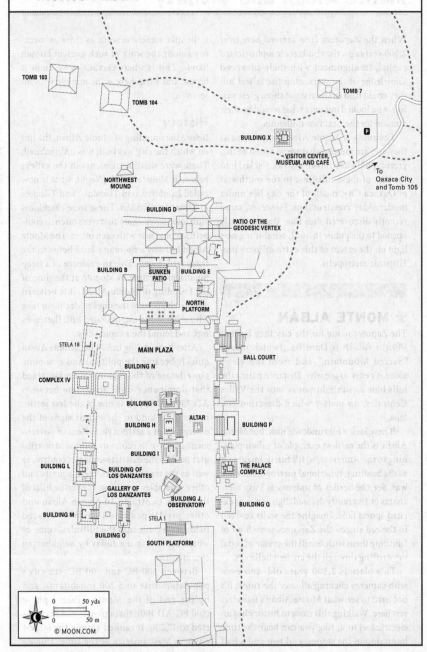

TOMB 103

TOMB 104

TOMB 7

BUILDING X

VISITOR CENTER, MUSEUM, AND CAFÉ

P

To Oaxaca City and Tomb 105

NORTHWEST MOUND

BUILDING D

PATIO OF THE GEODESIC VERTEX

BUILDING B

SUNKEN PATIO

BUILDING E

NORTH PLATFORM

STELA 18

MAIN PLAZA

BALL COURT

BUILDING N

COMPLEX IV

BUILDING G

BUILDING H

ALTAR

BUILDING P

BUILDING I

BUILDING L

BUILDING OF LOS DANZANTES

GALLERY OF LOS DANZANTES

BUILDING J, OBSERVATORY

THE PALACE COMPLEX

BUILDING M

BUILDING Q

BUILDING O

STELA 1

SOUTH PLATFORM

0   50 yds
0   50 m

© MOON.COM

the Monte Albán II phase (AD 100-300), the state expanded its domain to include areas in the valleys of Ejutla and Sola de Vega in the south, as well as in the highlands to the north. The city reached the height of its power and importance around the beginning of the Monte Albán III phase (AD 300-900), at its peak boasting a population of around 100,000 people in all areas under its sovereignty. Its importance in greater Mesoamerica is highlighted by evidence of connections with other pre-Hispanic cities, such as Teotihuacán, to the north of Mexico City, where archaeologists discovered a neighborhood that was inhabited by Zapotec people.

Monte Albán began its decline in power and influence sometime around AD 500, and by the year 900, the city had been completely abandoned for reasons that are still unclear. After its decline, settlements like Mitla and Yagul took over as centers of power.

In 1806, Belgian explorer Guillermo Dupaix stumbled across artifacts at the site and was the first to record descriptions of the Danzantes carvings. A number of small explorations were carried out in the 19th century, but large-scale excavation didn't happen until 1931, led by Mexican archaeologist Alfonso Caso. Over the next 18 years, Caso and his team uncovered and restored the majority of what can be seen at the site today. In 1933, Eulalia Guzmán, one of the first women to enter the field of archaeology in Mexico, aided Caso in the discovery of the gold artifacts in Tomb 7. In the late 1960s, American archaeologists Kent Flannery and Joyce Marcus began a two-decade study that focused on the socioeconomic development of the valley in the millennia leading up to what is called the Rosario phase (750-500 BC), which led to a better understanding of the founding of Monte Albán.

Exploring the Ruins

A thorough stroll around **Monte Albán** (tel. 951/516-7707, 8am-5pm daily, US$4) should take you about two hours. **Official guides** hanging around the entrance charge about US$14 per group for two-hour tours. The informational plaques have lots of information on the ruins, so choosing whether or not to take a tour can be left up to personal preference.

After entering the gate, you'll come to the northeast corner of the **Main Plaza,** the over two-million-square-foot courtyard walled in by tombs, palaces, and two enormous pyramidal platforms. The rectangular plaza was constructed to align perfectly with the north-south axis of the compass in order to make astronomical observations. The imposing structure to your right is the gigantic, multilevel **North Platform,** one of the oldest and most complex structures on the site. To your left you'll see the **Ball Court,** where the Zapotecs played their own version of the classic Mesoamerican ball game. The Zapotecs called the game either "Quibelagayo," which was the name of a deity related to the game, or "tiquija láchi," which is a description of the action of hitting the ball with the hip. However, despite the dozens of published academic studies on the game, no one has successfully discovered exactly how it was played.

Toward the southern end of the Main Plaza is the architectural oddball of the site, **Building J,** which stands out due to its shape and orientation. It is five-sided and resembles the shape of an arrowhead. Its walls are vertical, rather than pyramidal. Its stairway faces northwest, as opposed to those of the other structures, which face the cardinal points, and the "point" of the arrowhead faces southwest. Building J is believed to have been used as an observatory, as the Zapotecs' knowledge of astronomy was well advanced; however, definitive proof has yet to confirm this theory. The stones of the south wall of Building J are decorated with carved images of conquests of surrounding communities that date back to AD 100-200.

The 40-meter-wide (131-ft-wide) stairs behind you lead to the top of the humongous **South Platform,** on top of which you'll find two pyramid temples and the best views of the ruins and surrounding valleys in the site. The larger of the two pyramids is adorned with motifs from Teotihuacán, evidence of intermingling and influence between the two cultures.

It is absolutely necessary to visit the **Galería de los Danzantes** (Gallery of Dancers), at the southwest corner of the Main Plaza. The contortions of the portly figures were originally interpreted as dance moves; however, after further investigation, archaeologists concluded that these men aren't dancing. They're all dead. It is now believed that these images of flowing blood, disfigured faces, and mutilated genitals represent defeated warriors from other cities. The stones found here are actually in museums, but these replicas were designed to give visitors an accurate impression of their form and display as they were found.

Continuing north on the west side of the plaza, you'll come upon the 6-meter (20-ft) **Stela 18,** the tallest of its kind at Monte Albán, which is believed to have been an astronomical instrument. To the north of the North Platform, there are a number of tombs that are very interesting, though not as visually stunning as the rest of the city. You can climb down a couple of them and peer into the small spaces where Zapotec kings and priests were laid to rest. They're a great place to escape the crowds in the Main Plaza. Before heading back to the exit, make sure to stop by **Tomb 7,** one that was reused by Mixtecs after the decline of Monte Albán. It is here that archaeologists found the trove of gold, silver, alabaster, and jade that is now on display in the Museo de las Culturas, in the Santo Domingo Convent in Oaxaca City.

The neighboring ruins of Atzompa and El Gallo, on hills just to the north of Monte Albán, are also believed to have been considered within the city limits. The ruins at El Gallo aren't open to the public, but those at Atzompa were recently opened for visitors.

Visitors Center and Museum

The **Monte Albán Visitors Center** (tel. 951/516-7707, 8am-5pm daily) at the entrance to the park houses a **Cafetería** (8am-5pm daily, US$8-15) with a breezy terrace and food that is better than one expects from a tourist attraction such as this. There are also a jewelry store and a gift shop that is well-stocked with literature about the site, which are open the same hours as the site.

The **Monte Albán Museum** (8am-5pm daily, admission included in entrance fee), in the same building, is a necessary stop for anyone interested in learning more about what was found here. Unlike the placards among the ruins, there is no English here, so keep your guidebook handy. I've covered the salient exhibits here in a clockwise order from the entrance. Give yourself 30-45 minutes to fully take in what the museum has on display.

Just to your left as you enter, you'll see a gray clay funerary urn in the form of a woman wearing a jaguar headdress. Found during an excavation in 1995, the figure is believed to represent a traveling companion of the deceased with whom she was buried. It dates from AD 300-600.

The display on the other side of the entrance to the room for temporary exhibitions explains how the Zapotecs "domesticated" the hill, flattening some parts and filling in others to make the Main Plaza. It is known that **Zapotec architecture** was intentionally designed to align with the cardinal points, measurements based on the solar cycle, and even that of Venus; however, the exact symbolism of such urban planning is still a mystery. Simple houses were made of reeds, while the more elegant ones were made of stone and adobe, usually finished with red stucco. The dead were buried directly below their houses, so the majority of residences here included tombs or graves below the rooms.

The display in the following corner is of artifacts related to **daily life in Monte Albán,** such as grinding stones, sharpened pieces of flint used to carve and smooth wood, needles

---

1: Galería de los Danzantes at Monte Albán
2: Monte Albán's Stela 18, believed to be used to track the stars 3: ball court at Atzompa

and hole punches for weaving, as well as pots, pans, and various other containers used in cooking and other quotidian tasks. There are also objects believed to have been toys and musical instruments, such as whistles, flutes, and ocarinas. Many of these objects date from the first two phases of the city (500 BC-AD 300). Set in the floor between the two displays is a clay pot containing a **baby skeleton,** alongside a censer most likely used to burn copal sap during the burial. Despite this find (as well as another that is displayed across the room), child burials like this were rare in Monte Albán. The remains date from AD 600-900. Also in this corner is a display of the **Zapotec calendar and writing system,** possibly the first in Mesoamerica. The Zapotecs used glyphs to represent words; however, the repetition of glyphs in groupings of symbols suggests that they also used some form of syllabary, or set of characters representing syllables, that served the purpose of an alphabet.

The centerpiece of the large display of carved stones is called the **Half Moon Stone,** which was found in the northeast corner of the Main Plaza. Dating from around AD 800, it depicts a scene of an elderly person on a bed and another making offerings, surrounded by glyphs representing their calendrical and personal names. It is believed to be a scene of death or burial; however, the curse of uncertainty that afflicts the majority of our knowledge of the ancient inhabitants of Monte Albán is in these stones as well, and archaeologists do not know the precise meaning of this scene.

The glass displays in the next corner contain figures representing various gods, which were used for both religious and political purposes. The standout piece here is an urn representing the Zapotec god of rain and storms, **Cocijo,** whose name is synonymous with the word for "lightning bolt." It dates from AD 600-900. In the glass case on the floor beneath Cocijo lie the **skulls** of 18 children 6-12 years old found buried below a residence on the north side of the site. It is unknown if

their deaths were sacrificial, if they were decapitated, or if the skulls were moved from various other tombs to where they were ultimately found by archaeologists. They are believed to have lived in the first part of the third phase (AD 300-600).

In the last corner of the museum are the remains of people with signs of the practice of **bone mutilation.** Some children's skulls were deformed into tabular or conical shapes with the use of boards or bands. Others with holes in them show signs of what might have been surgeries to treat infections. Young people 20-25 years of age made incisions in their teeth in the same fashions that are found in many clay figures found at Monte Albán, and it was common practice to drill holes in their teeth to decorate them with stones like jade and magnetite.

The display with the map of the Valles Centrales covers the mystery of the **decline of Monte Albán.** Around AD 800, construction stopped and the population began to decline, both in the city as well as the surrounding valleys. One theory is that overexploitation of the environment and/or drought caused massive amounts of people to die of hunger, while another notes the possibility of the city's leaders losing sociopolitical control. The true reason, however, remains a mystery.

Getting There

The Monte Albán ruins are on a hill less than 5 km (3.1 mi) southwest of the Zócalo in Oaxaca City. The cheapest way to get here from Oaxaca City is by one of the buses that leave from the corner of Minas and García, just two blocks west of the Mercado 20 de Noviembre. Buses run by **Hotel Riviera del Ángel** (Mina 518, tel. 951/516-6175, round-trip ticket US$3) start at 8:30am and run every hour until 3:30pm. The trip takes about 45 minutes, and the last one leaves Monte Albán at 5pm. Hold onto your ticket. You'll need it for the return trip. Just across the street, **Viajes Turísticos Mitla** (Mina 501, tel. 951/516-6175, round-trip ticket US$3) runs the same schedule. **Monte Albán Tours** (Alcalá 100, tel. 951/226-2896, www.montealbantours.com) runs daily trips in vans that leave at 10am and return at 2pm for around US$16. All of these cover transport only; entrance fees are not included.

Drivers take Miguel Cabrera (which is called Flores Magón north of Aldama) south to the *periférico* and follow the Monte Albán signs across the Río Atoyac bridge. Take another right after the bridge and follow the road to the top of the hill. The road could probably use a few more signs, but it's not hard to stay on course. Just follow the tour buses. The drive takes about 30 minutes, depending on traffic.

ATZOMPA ARCHAEOLOGICAL ZONE

To get a more complete idea of life in Monte Albán, visit the recently excavated ruins at **Atzompa** (Cerro de la Campana, tel. 951/513-3346, 8am-5pm daily, free admission), which can be thought of as one of the first suburbs in the Americas. The suburb was founded during Monte Albán's peak, sometime around AD 700. At Monte Albán, you get a good impression of the life of the political and ideological lifestyle of its inhabitants, while Atzompa contains much more information on their daily lives.

Give yourself about an hour to explore the site. The **East House** is one of two residences of upper-class families found on the site, and eight other housing units were found here as well. Attached to the East House is the service area where food was prepared and other domestic tasks were carried out. The **Altar House** is another structure in which archaeologists found lots of evidence of daily activities. The ruins consist of square rooms around a central plaza, and a room at the back of the house was used as a pottery workshop.

The second **Ball Court** up the hill is the biggest of the six that are documented in the Monte Albán complex. There are two others in Atzompa, both on the properties of the aforementioned houses, which suggests they were for private use. The big one is believed to have been a public court, where the game was

both ritual and political propaganda used to bolster power.

Here you can also observe the origins of ancient traditions still alive today. At the top of the site, archaeologists discovered a kiln dating back thousands of years. It is quite simply incredible to stand over it and consider how you can head right down the hill to the town of Santa María Atzompa and buy the products of a tradition that began here over 2,000 years ago. The aisles of the **Santa María Atzompa artisans market** (Libertad 202, no phone, 9am-9pm daily) brim with the green-glazed pottery the town is now famous for.

Getting There

The Atzompa ruins are about 4 km (2.5 mi) north-northwest of Monte Albán. The easiest way to get to them from Monte Albán is by driving. A little less than a mile from the Monte Albán Visitors Center, take a left at the fork in the road, which will be the one you did not come in on if you followed my directions to Monte Albán. The turn at the bottom of the hill can be tricky, as the road feeds directly into the traffic going right on Ignacio Bernal, but you'll need to turn left. The safest thing to do is let the highway take you to the right and then pull a U-turn in the broad, three-way intersection just down the hill a ways. The sign to turn right is about 1 km (0.6 mi) in the other direction, and from there it's a scenic 10-minute drive to the top. To get to the artisans market, head back down the hill and take a left, back in the direction you came. Take another left at the intersection about 2 km (1.2 mi) down the road and follow the Atzompa Highway 4 km (2.5 mi), where you'll see the artisans market on the right.

Visiting the Atzompa ruins in public transport is a bit trickier. The site has only been open to the public since 2012, so it hasn't had much time to garner a reputation and draw the kinds of crowds Monte Albán does. The only option from Monte Albán is to negotiate a deal with a taxi driver to take you to the ruins and wait while you explore the site. The price will vary depending on the driver, but somewhere around US$16 is a fair price.

To visit the site from Oaxaca City, without seeing Monte Albán, your best bet is to organize transportation through an agency. It's not yet on the regular itineraries on offer, but agencies are willing to work with you. **Monte Albán Tours** (Alcalá 100, tel. 951/226-2896, www.montealbantours.com) can arrange a four-hour tour similar to its Monte Albán tour for the same price (US$16), which is transport only (no guide).

Valle de Tlacolula

Extending east from Oaxaca City, the Valle de Tlacolula is home to some of the state's greatest hits, like the intricately adorned ruins at Mitla and the "frozen waterfalls" of Hierve El Agua. The **Ruta de Mezcal (Mezcal Route)** is here, with its smoky capital Santiago Matatlán, as well as one of the region's oldest weekly markets in Tlacolula de Matamoros. And the 500-year-old tradition of wool weaving is alive and well (and evolving) in Teotitlán del Valle and neighboring towns in the valley.

The best way to explore this valley via public transport from Oaxaca City is by grabbing a bus or *taxi colectivo* at a stop at the northeast corner of the Centro, on the corner of Calle de los Derechos Humanos and Highway 190. The stop is just to the east of the baseball stadium, between it and the McDonald's. Check the vehicles' windshields for destinations. You can expect to spend around US$3-6 a day traveling the valley in *colectivos*, depending on where you go and how many stops you make.

SANTA MARÍA DEL TULE

The harlequin gardens and tidy lawns of the *zócalo* at **Santa María del Tule** set a charming foreground to the town's main attraction, a monumental *ahuehuete* (Nahuatl for the Montezuma cypress) that boasts the largest trunk diameter of any tree in the world. The only thing bigger than the tree is the imagination of the *niños guías* (child guides). Don't expect them to answer your lame grown-up questions about the tree's circumference or the year the church was built. These kids' specialty is pointing out the shapes they see in the whorls and gnarls of the trunk and branches. Personal favorite: Sleeping Baby Elephant.

Sights
★ **ÁRBOL DEL TULE**
According to what I got out of my young guide Jesualdo (whose favorite arboreal figure is the Lion's Mane) before he referred me to an informational plaque, this area was a big lake when **El Árbol del Tule** (no phone, 8am-8pm daily, US$0.50) sprouted on its shore over 2,000 years ago. Since then, it has grown to a diameter of 14 meters (46 ft). There's also an official measurement for the circumference, but the buttressed trunk is such an irregular shape that it makes more sense to say that it takes 30 children to encircle the colossal tree hand in hand. The guides have *niños guías* embroidered on their shirts and work for donations. Jesualdo knew the names of the shapes in five languages.

It's not the most impressive church in the area, but the 17th-century Templo de Santa María de la Asunción is a toothsome sight next to the ancient tree. It opens at 4pm, but don't worry if you miss it. The one you really want to see is right down the road.

Getting There
El Tule is about 11 km (7 mi) east of Oaxaca City. *Taxi colectivo* passengers should make sure their taxi stops in El Tule, about 20 minutes down the road. Taxis that go to towns beyond El Tule stay on the highway and skip the town completely. Drivers take Highway 190

east. The exit for El Tule is on the right about 5 km (3.1 mi) east of the Centro. The drive takes about 20-30 minutes, depending on traffic.

TLACOCHAHUAYA

Legend has it that a Zapotec warrior named Cochicahuala ("He who fights at night") founded **Tlacochahuaya** after a great victory. When the Spanish arrived, they oversaw the construction of the remarkably ornate **Templo y Ex Convento de San Jerónimo** (8am-6pm daily). You'll be asked to give a 10 peso (US$0.50) "cooperation," which supports the maintenance and restoration of the church and convent in back.

The mid-16th-century church houses a series of fine paintings depicting the revelation of the Virgen de Guadalupe to Juan Diego, the first indigenous saint in the Americas, but the real feast for the eyes is overhead. The vaulted ceiling is covered in a pattern of floral designs and baby angel faces that inspires true wonder. Don't leave without climbing the narrow spiral staircase to the balcony to see the still-functioning organ that is nearly as old as the church. It is definitely worth a quick half-hour stop on a trip to other destinations in the valley.

Getting There

Many tours include Tlacochahuaya in their itineraries, or it can easily be added to an independent trip to other sites in the valley. About 8 km (5 mi) east of El Tule, you'll see a sign for the town at a crossroads with a pedestrian bridge. *Mototaxis* charge US$0.25 for the ride into town from the *crucero* (crossroads). Drivers turn right. The town is about five minutes down the road.

★ TEOTITLÁN DEL VALLE

Although a few neighboring communities claim otherwise, **Teotitlán del Valle** is considered the birthplace of the nearly 500-year-old tradition of **wool weaving** that the Valle de Tlacolula is famous for. Zapotec people here have been weaving high-quality *tapetes*

(rugs), *tapices* (tapestries), and other wool products since Juan López Zárate, the state's first bishop, introduced European sheep to the region in the mid-16th century. Traditionally, the *tapetes* are decorated with Zapotec glyphs and other abstract designs; however, newer generations have begun to weave suns, hummingbirds, and other images into their rugs. Constantino Lazo, a local weaver who makes rugs for competitions, uses materials like thread, cotton, silk, and even feathers to work 3-D images into his pieces.

Some use synthetic dyes, but most weavers use natural ones in their rugs. Grinding the little scale insects called *cochinilla* (cochineal) that grow on nopal cactuses all over the valley produces the deep scarlets and other shades of red you'll see lining the walls of the *tapete* stores. Blue comes from fermenting, straining, then drying the pulp of the leaves of the indigo plant, which grows in the Istmo de Tehuantepec. Pomegranate rinds and *zacatlascal*, a parasitic plant that grows like spilled spaghetti on treetops, produce yellow, and materials like pecan shells and a moss called *musgo cuapascle* yield brown. It truly is extraordinary to see how these and other natural materials are combined to create any color on the spectrum the artist desires, and many *talleres* (textile workshops with stores) give demonstrations for voluntary tips.

Sights
TEMPLO DE LA PRECIOSA SANGRE DE CRISTO

Teotitlán's **Templo de la Preciosa Sangre de Cristo** was constructed in 1518 on the site of a Zapotec temple once dedicated to the feathered serpent god Quetzalcoatl. The church is rather homely, especially if your previous stop was Tlacochahuaya, but take a closer look and you'll see that some of the stones in the facade are from the original Zapotec temple, carved with images of Quetzalcoatl. The churchyard gets lively with food, fun, and dancing during its annual festival in July. The ruins of the original temple are down the stairs on the south side of the

churchyard and to the left, behind the municipal government offices.

COMMUNITY MUSEUM

The **Museo Comunitario Balaa Xtee Guech Gulal** (corner of Hidalgo and 20 de Noviembre, tel. 951/524-4463, 10am-6pm daily, US$0.50) may be small, but the "House (or Shadow) of the Old Town," as its name translates from the Zapotec, contains a wealth of information about Teotitlán and the surrounding valley. The first exhibit begins with a collection of Zapotec carved stonework depicting symbolic glyphs, jaguars, masked figures, and elaborately adorned gods.

The majority of the space, however, is dedicated to Teotitlán's long tradition of rug and tapestry weaving. The history and processes of the art are explained in detail. The last exhibit displays the history of arranged marriage traditions in Teotitlán, which included roaming groups of townsfolk armed with clubs, ready to clobber any man other than the groom caught chatting it up with the bride.

CENTRO CULTURAL COMUNITARIO

Inaugurated in August 2018, Teotitlán's **Centro Cultural Comunitario** (Community Cultural Center; next to artisan market south of churchyard, tel. 951/348-3607, 10am-6pm Tues.-Sun., US$2) houses a museum displaying rugs and explaining the town's weaving traditions. There is also an exhibit on the Danza de la Pluma (Dance of the Feather).

Festivals and Events

If your visit is in July, try to make it to Teotitlán on the first Wednesday of the month, when the town celebrates its **annual church festival** dedicated to the Holy Blood of Christ. You'll find local delights that aren't made during the rest of the year, like *tamales*

de amarillo (made with chicken and yellow *mole*) and a savory chicken soup flavored with cumin spices called *higadito*. Don't let the name of this soup fool you. Despite its similarity to the word for liver (*hígado*), there is no offal in the ingredients. It is made with chicken meat and eggs cooked casserole style and added to a rich broth.

During this and the **Lunes del Cerro** festivals (cultural heritage celebrations held on the last two Mondays in July), you'll be able to catch the **Danza de la Pluma** (Dance of the Feather), arguably Oaxaca's most visually stunning dance. Teotitlán claims to be the origin of the dance, though folks from Cuilapam de Guerrero tend to disagree.

Shopping
TEXTILE SHOPS

According to local weaver Manuel Lazo (Constantino's brother), 80 percent of Teotitlán's population works in weaving, and this is apparent almost as soon as you turn off the highway. Families all over town, especially along Benito Juárez and Hidalgo, sell their homemade *tapetes*, ponchos, and other fine wool products. The Bazán family converted part of their home into **Dulízùn Café** (Hidalgo 26, tel. 951/524-4021, 8am-8pm daily), where vivid and intricate rugs line the walls of the store and courtyard beyond. (*Dulízùn* is Zapotec for "Our House.") Ask Teresa for a demonstration of how they make the natural dyes (and leave a tip in the jar). Manuel sells his work here. If he's around, he'll tell you about his personal style.

Just down the street is **Shchintraalii** (Hidalgo 38, tel. 951/166-6209, 10:30am-7pm daily), run by the Martínez Hernández family. You'll probably meet one of Señora Antonia's sons or other family members to whom she has passed down her art.

Many tours that claim to visit Teotitlán don't actually bring clients into town, but merely stop at stores on the road from the highway, where customers are charged more than what they would pay in town in order to give a cut to the guides. This is a mistake, as

---

1: Árbol del Tule towering over surrounding buildings **2:** Tlacochahuaya's Templo y Ex Convento de San Jerónimo **3:** handwoven rugs in Teotitlán del Valle **4:** Teotitlán's Templo de la Preciosa Sangre de Cristo

Tejate: The Drink of the Gods

the pre-Hispanic drink *tejate*

Strolling through the markets, you're bound to see women behind large tubs of a strange-looking drink with white foam floating at the top. This is **tejate**, *"la bebida de los dioses"* (the drink of the gods), a pre-Hispanic drink that hails from **San Andrés Huayapam,** just north of Oaxaca City, and is still very popular in Oaxaca today. Don't let the odd look fool you. This stuff is delicious.

It is made from fermented cacao beans, toasted corn flour, seeds of the mamey fruit, and the flowers of a tree called *flor de cacao,* which literally translates to "cacao flower," but is actually a different tree entirely. These ingredients are ground to a thick paste, then mixed with cold water, usually by hand. The mixture is set aside, and after a while, the *flor de cacao* rises to the top, forming the weird-looking foam that you'll end up craving again and again after you try it.

San Andrés Huayapam, which is a quick and cheap 20-minute cab ride from downtown Oaxaca City, holds a *tejate* festival at the end of March. The Feria del Tejate y el Tamal (Tejate and Tamale Fair) is at the end of Guelaguetza season, usually in the beginning of August, in the Plaza de la Danza in Oaxaca City. The **Sunday Market** in **Tlacolula** and the **Benito Juárez market** in downtown **Oaxaca City** are great places to try this ancient drink, if you can't make it to the festivals.

the town is lovely enough to merit spending some time in, and the practice undercuts artists willing to ask a fair price for their work. Ask the tour company if they go into town before signing up. I recommend spending at least half a day in the stores on Benito Juárez and Hidalgo educating yourself on the processes, time, and work that go into making a rug. It can be easy to dismiss one as too expensive; however, seen in light of the fact that these products are the results of what can sometimes be three whole months of hard

work, the prices on the tags are actually great deals already.

Food and Accommodations

If you're already shopping at ★ **Dulízùn Café** (Hidalgo 26, tel. 951/524-4021, 8am-8pm daily), you might as well stay for lunch (US$2-3) in the courtyard. Octogenarian Señora Juana still grinds cacao by hand to make the chocolate you should order. Grab a shady table and have a plate of *mole* and a cup of Juana's famous chocolate. For a unique treat, ask for a *chocolate-atole,* a sweet mixture of hot chocolate and the corn-based drink *atole.* The verdant courtyard at **El Descanso** (B. Juárez 51, tel. 951/524-4152, 9am-6pm daily, US$5-10), where the Santiago family also has a rug gallery, is another great place for typical Oaxacan fare.

If you're looking for a serious caffeine kick, stop by **Café Vid** (Benito Juárez 47, tel. 951/327-1046, 7am-10pm Mon.-Sat., noon-10pm Sun., US$3-5) for espresso-based drinks. The café buys its organically grown coffee beans directly from the Sierra Mazateca, in the north of the state, which ensures the growers get paid a fair price for their product. They also serve baguettes and sandwiches. If you stay the night in town, check in to see if they're hosting live music.

Accommodations options in Teotitlán are limited. However, the town is gorgeous and the people warm, so if you have time, it's definitely worth staying a night at the **Casa de Huéspedes La Granada** (2 de Abril 23, tel. 951/524-4232, www.lasgranadasoaxaca.com, US$22-28), in the home of weaver Josefina Ruíz and family. The clean, quaint guest rooms are set around a colorful courtyard shaded by the large pomegranate trees that are the place's namesake (*granada* is Spanish for pomegranate). They offer **weaving workshops** and **cooking classes,** where guests can learn to prepare *mole,* salsas, chocolate from cacao, and a wide variety of other traditional foods. There is no sign outside. Just keep an eye out for the seafoam-green door on the north side of the street a half block west of Benito Juárez.

Getting There
Teotitlán is 29 km (18 mi) east of Oaxaca City, and many tours include it in their itineraries. The total drive time is 45 minutes. *Colectivos* stop at the corner by the baseball stadium in Oaxaca City all day long and also take about 45 minutes. Drivers (and passengers aboard *colectivos* bound for other destinations) should keep an eye out for the sign to Teotitlán del Valle about 18 km (11 mi) east of

El Tule. You shouldn't have to wait too long for a taxi (US$0.50) into town from the *crucero* (crossroads).

TLACOLULA
When the Zapotecs arrived in this valley in the 2nd century BC, they didn't live in what is now **Tlacolula de Matamoros.** They lived in Yagul, on a hilltop a couple miles east of town. The Spanish moved the population to the site of present-day Tlacolula in the 16th century. Some scholars believe the name Tlacolula comes from a Nahuatl name meaning "Within the Place Full of Sticks," others "Crooked Thing." The Zapotec name for Tlacolula is Guichiibaa, which means "The Town Close to Heaven."

Sunday Market
The market that sprawls through the streets of Tlacolula is the oldest of its kind in Oaxaca, almost in all of Mesoamerica. People from the surrounding communities in the valley and the mountains to the north have been coming here since the Zapotecs settled the region, and some practices, such as bartering, have survived to this day. The tarps spread out from the Mercado Municipal, covering most of downtown to shade the stalls of everything from produce to artisan crafts to household items to coffee "that smells like the mountains," as one woman likes to advertise. This is a great place to try *tejate,* the sweet, foamy drink made from cacao, nuts, and cacao flowers. There is a whole aisle dedicated to cacao in the main market, and many vendors in the street sell *tejate,* as well as one made with coconuts.

Goat/Lamb *Barbacoa* and Mezcal
Carnivores should visit Tlacolula whether they can make it to the Sunday Market or not. The gastronomic specialty here is *barbacoa de chivo y borrego,* goat and lamb slow-roasted up to eight hours in an earthen oven

The Slow-Roasted Flavors of *Barbacoa*

barbacoa stalls in the Tlacolula market

Foods like *mole*, *quesillo*, and *chapulines* (fried grasshoppers) are what usually come to mind when it comes to Oaxacan gastronomy, but with such a rich culinary tradition, it's no surprise that the Valles Centrales are full of mouthwatering *barbacoa*. Families in towns like Tlacolula, Zaachila, and Ocotlán have for generations perfected this technique of slow-roasting meat in ovens dug into the earth. It's not a meal unique to this part of Mexico, but it sure is delicious.

The process usually begins the day before cooking, when the goat or sheep (the primary meats used in *barbacoa* here, though some places specialize in pork and beef) is slaughtered, skinned, and bled. The organs are set aside for use in the *consomé* (stew), and sometimes *sangrita*, a blood soup prepared with offal and seasoned with onions, chiles, cumin, and *hierbabuena* (a type of mint).

For many families, cooking *barbacoa* is more than preparing a meal. It's spiritual. There are a few rituals to be performed before cooking. To avoid any *malas vibras* (bad vibes), points of maguey leaves in the form of a cross, or the meat of the *chile de árbol*, are placed in the oven before lighting the fire. *El mal del ojo* (The Evil Eye) is cast out by tossing the seeds and veins of the guajillo chile into the oven as well. And the cross is drawn over the pot of *consomé* ingredients before cooking, just in case a stranger stops by the house, possibly bringing bad vibes.

As early as 3am, it's time to prepare the oven, usually a brick-lined hole dug in the earth. A fire is lit in the bottom with wood from mesquite, laurel, and oak trees, and as the fire grows, more bricks are thrown into it to heat them up to cook the meat. After about two hours, the fire has died down to coals and the oven is ready. The bricks and coals are covered with a layer of avocado leaves, and then the meat is placed in the oven. The oven is covered with maguey leaves and dirt, which when dampened with water alerts the chefs to any leaks allowing heat out. The meat cooks in six to eight hours and is tender and flavorful by lunchtime.

When ordering *barbacoa*, you'll be asked questions like, "*Surtida o pura carne?*" or "*Roja o blanca?*" If that bit about offal doesn't sit well with you, stick to *pura carne* (just meat) or *blanca* (white meat). The other options, *surtida* (assortment) and *roja* (red meat), include the chewier stuff. You can order the meat in tacos, or in a steaming bowl of savory *consomé*. Toss on some crunchy cabbage, cilantro, lime, and salsa, and ¡Buen provecho! (Enjoy your meal!).

and served in a *consomé* (stew) made from the blood and offal. Head to the *barbacoa* stalls on the north side of the ★ **Mercado Municipal Martín González** (Galeana 2, no phone, 7am-7pm daily, US$3-5) to try it in tacos or in a stew. The smoky stalls are an organized chaos of vendors tending steaming pots of *consomé*, families squeezing in to eat, and guitar-toting musicians busking in the crowded aisles. If the group of rappers shows up, practice your Spanish listening for how they fit you and others at the tables into their rhymes.

A Oaxacan will tell you the best thing to settle all that grease in your stomach is a *trago* (drink) of **mezcal,** and Javier Pensamiento has just the thing at his shop just down the street from the Mercado Municipal, **Mezcal Pensamiento** (Juárez 9, tel. 951/436-4322, 9am-9pm daily). Javier and family specialize in mezcals made from wild agaves like *coyote*, *tepeztate*, and *cuishe*.

Zapotec Language Classes

Those interested in learning Tlacolula's dialect of Zapotec, called Disaa, should stop by the **Casa de Cultura de Tlacolula** (Palacio Municipal, tel. 951/241-9864, casadecultura. tlacolula@gmail.com, 9am-8pm Mon.-Fri., 10am-2pm Sat.-Sun., free admission), on the south side of the Parque Municipal. Here Miguel Hipólito Martínez teaches two-hour classes on Mondays and Fridays at 7pm, and on Saturdays at 9am. One month of classes costs only US$2.50, which is used to pay for supplies. Anyone is welcome. It's a great educational option for those spending a fair amount of time in the surrounding communities, even for those staying in Oaxaca City, as the drive really isn't much more than many daily commutes back home. The Casa de Cultura displays artwork by community youth and hosts occasional concerts by the local brass band.

Getting There

Tlacolula is 32 km (20 mi) east of Oaxaca City on Highway 190. Many tours go on Sunday for the market. Drivers keep an eye out for the sign that says Tlacolula Centro about five minutes after the Teotitlán crossroads. Take Zaragoza straight into town. Total drive time is about 50 minutes. *Colectivo* passengers wait a bit farther and get out at the stoplight just before the highway climbs a hill. This option takes about an hour. The Plaza Municipal is six blocks south down Juárez, and there are *mototaxis* (US$0.25) if you're not feeling the walk.

DAINZÚ AND LAMBITYECO ARCHAEOLOGICAL SITES

The lesser-visited ruins at Dainzú and Lambityeco may not be as impressive as some of their neighbors, but that actually works to their advantage, because they draw fewer visitors. If you're pressed for time, or aren't overly interested in the finer archaeological details of the Valle de Tlacolula, then you might do better focusing your attention elsewhere. However, they're both just off the highway, so it's worth stopping by, especially if you're driving.

You won't find tour guides at these sites, but there are informational plaques in both Spanish and English.

The Zapotecs named **Dainzú** (Hwy. 190, no phone, 8am-5pm daily, US$2.50) "the Hill of the Organ Cactus" for the tall, prickly, pipe-like succulents that mark the landscape. Founded around 700 BC, a couple centuries before the great capital Monte Albán, it was an important Zapotec settlement throughout the Classic Period (AD 250-900). The ruins, set in the west-facing slope of the hill, include religious and residential areas, tombs, bas-relief carvings, and a well-preserved ball court.

The ruins at **Lambityeco** (Hwy. 190, no phone, 8am-5pm daily, US$2.50) may be small, but what they lack in size, they make up for in accessibility, as they're right on the highway. They date from 700 BC-AD 750. Part of a larger settlement called Yegüi (Zapotec for "Small Hill"), Lambityeco was a major producer of salt in the region, at one point filling 90 percent of the demand in Oaxaca. Salt was produced here as recently as 1940 by running river water through the soil and evaporating it to extract the minerals. The name Lambityeco has something to do with this process, though its etymology is uncertain. Some scholars assert that it is a Zapotec term for "hollow hill," while others claim it is a compound of the Zapotec word for hill and the Spanish word *alambique*, or alembic, a distillation apparatus from days of old. The highlight here is the pair of impressively carved masks of Cocijo, the Zapotec god of rain, thunder, and lightning. They are large carvings on a mound at the southeast corner of the site.

Getting There

Not very many tours stop at these sites (but Zapotrek does!), so you'll probably be on your own if you want to see them.

The sign for Dainzú, about 10 km (6.2 mi) east of El Tule, is white (in contrast to the blue signage for towns). The road from the highway is rough, but fine for cars at slow speeds. *Colectivo* passengers will have a nice 15-minute walk to the ruins along the dirt road through the valley scrub. Keep an eye out for the sign about 10 minutes after leaving El Tule.

To get to Lambityeco, go back to the highway and flag down a passing *colectivo*. The ruins are 7.5 km (4.5 mi) east of Dainzú, right on the southern side of the highway, just after the turnoff to Teotitlán.

For information about tours, contact Eric Ramirez at **Zapotrek** (Xolotl 110, Oaxaca City, tel. 951/502-5957, www.zapotrek.com).

YAGUL

Founded sometime around 1500 BC, **Yagul** (Hwy. 190, no phone, 9am-5pm daily, US$4) was an important cultural and governmental hub in the region, especially after the decline of Monte Albán. The name is believed to mean "Old Tree." The city was built on top of (and

into) a steep cliff, resembling the civic planning of the great Zapotec capital to the west. Yagul remained an important and thriving urban area until the 16th century, when the Spaniards forced the Zapotecs out to form the current town of Tlacolula. Current residents of Tlacolula call the ruins Yugul, which means "Old Town."

You'll find structures similar to those at other sites like Monte Albán, such as a ball court, tombs, religious and residential buildings, and palatial patios, but what you won't see are the crowds. Yagul has the advantage of being a very interesting site that is slightly overshadowed by the grandeur of the region's most prominent ancient settlements. After the multitudes that flock to Monte Albán and Mitla, it can be a breath of fresh air to have a site that is (almost) as impressive (almost) all to yourself. The hill behind the main cluster of ruins is covered with trails and filled with more ruins. Up here you can peek into the entrance of **La Fortaleza** (The Fortress), an underground bunker in which citizens hid out during times of conflict. The views from up here are phenomenal, as well.

And these ruins aren't even the oldest traces of human life here. On the road from the highway is a small site called **Caballito Blanco** (Little White Horse), where nomadic groups of hunter-gatherers left paintings in caves and rock hollows over 7,000 years ago. You can spy one on a cliff wall to the right of the entrance from the highway.

Getting There

Some tours that go to Mitla or Hierve El Agua also include Yagul on their itineraries. The turnoff to the site is about 2 km (1.2 mi) east of Tlacolula. Drivers and *colectivo* passengers shouldn't have a hard time seeing the large sign on the left side of the highway about five minutes outside the town. If you're going via public transport, be ready for a 20-minute, partly uphill walk from the highway, as there are no taxis or *mototaxis* working the 1.5-km (1-mi) road to the ruins.

SANTIAGO MATATLÁN

Wood smoke from the numerous pit ovens around town licks the yellow walls of the houses of **Santiago Matatlán,** "The World Capital of Mezcal," as you pass under the welcome sign decorated with a copper still. This is an essential stop for any lover of Oaxaca's favorite spirit. Like other artisan towns, the majority of the population of Matatlán works with the local specialty, and *palenques* (distilleries) and *expendios de mezcal* (mezcal stores) are around every corner.

Sights

COMMUNITY MUSEUM

Your first stop should be the **Museo Comunitario Ta Guiil Reiñ** (Independencia, no phone, 9am-noon and 1pm-6pm daily, donations accepted), where you'll get a better idea of the mezcal culture in Matatlán. The ground floor has displays on local celebrations involving mezcal and the process of making the drink. Upstairs there is a sizable collection of artifacts found at a local archaeological site called El Palmillo, which dates from 200-300 BC.

MEZCAL DISTILLERY

Founded by Don Serafín Hernández, **El Rey Zapoteco** (Carretera Internacional Km 49, tel. 951/518-3020, www.elreyzapoteco.com.mx, 7am-7pm daily) is one of the most respected *palenques* in town. Mezcal is continually being made here, and the Hernández family offers tours of their *palenque*, demonstrations, and tastings. If you buy some mezcal, they'll show you around for free, but if not, it'll cost about US$3. They also have their world-famous mezcal for sale. They're by far not the only *palenque* in town, though, so take your time and visit a few to find one you like.

Getting There

Matatlán is located 47 km (29 mi) east of Oaxaca City. Total drive time is just over one hour. It is on many mezcal-themed tours run by agencies all over town. Drivers take Highway 190 east from the city and keep an eye out for the exit about 40 km (25 mi) from town. It is the same exit to go to Mitla, just hang right. *Colectivos* pick up passengers in the city at the corner stop by the baseball stadium. They take about 1.25 hours.

★ MITLA

Humans settled in **Mitla** sometime between AD 0 and 200. The Zapotecs call this place Lyobaam, which means "Place of the Dead." Both during and after the decline of Monte Albán, Mitla was the religious capital of the Zapotec civilization, and it flourished until the conquest in the 16th century.

The modern town of San Pablo Villa de Mitla (pop. 12,500) is built right on top of the ancient settlement. Some of the compounds can be seen in town, existing right next to residences and shops.

Exploring the Ruins

There are five architectural compounds, but the main cluster of ruins at the **Mitla Archaeological Zone** (Camino Nacional, tel. 951/502-1200, 8am-5pm daily, US$4) is where you'll find the unique, mortarless geometric mosaic stonework the site is famous for. You can view the walls and columns of the former administrative buildings now called the **North Group,** on top of which the **Templo de San Pablo Villa de Mitla** was constructed in the 17th century, without a ticket. They are just outside the ticket booth.

Buy a ticket and cross through the artisans market to enter the area called the **Columns Group,** a pair of open patios surrounded by structures elaborately adorned with Zapotec glyphs. At the top of the stairs in the patio to the north is the **Hall of Columns,** where six monolithic columns that once supported the roof still stand. A small passageway leads from this room to another small courtyard and a set of rooms, the walls of which are also covered in Mitla's distinct stonework. To get an

Mitla

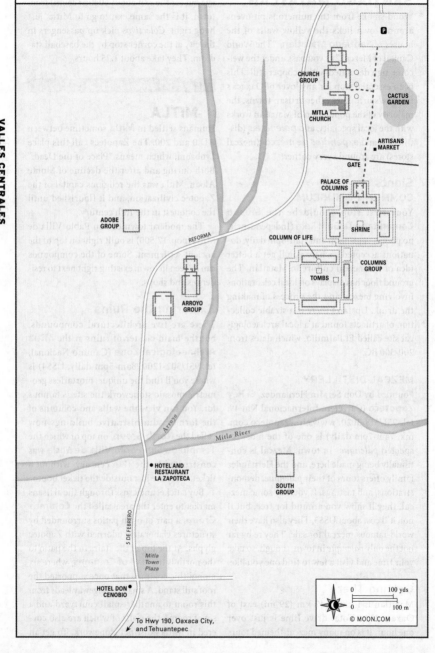

P

CHURCH GROUP

MITLA CHURCH

CACTUS GARDEN

ARTISANS MARKET

GATE

ADOBE GROUP

PALACE OF COLUMNS

SHRINE

REFORMA

COLUMN OF LIFE

COLUMNS GROUP

TOMBS

ARROYO GROUP

Arroyo

Mitla River

HOTEL AND RESTAURANT LA ZAPOTECA

SOUTH GROUP

5 DE FEBRERO

Mitla Town Plaza

HOTEL DON CENOBIO

To Hwy 190, Oaxaca City, and Tehuantepec

0   100 yds
0   100 m

© MOON.COM

idea of what it all looked like, try to imagine the floors and facades covered in red stucco. These were the palaces of high-ranking priests and other religious officials.

The patio just to the southwest of this one is home to what the Zapotecs named the place for: tombs. You can enter two of them, and you'll notice that here they decorated as lavishly for the dead as they did for the living. These tombs meant for high-ranking members of the priesthood also boast elaborate mosaics. Funerary tradition called for successive burials, in which the remains and offerings of previous burials were moved aside to make room for the newly departed.

Independent travelers can expect to spend about an hour in the Columns Group, and the other three compounds scattered around town can be seen in about a half hour by *mototaxi*. They are not as impressive as the Columns Group, but it is interesting to see them alongside modernity. The **Arroyo Group,** on 5 de Febrero on the way to the main site, is little more than the rocky walls of what were once the residences of high-ranking priests. The sign for the **Adobe Group,** also called the Calvary, reads "El Calvario" and is at the bottom of the last rise in the road to the site. It is a short, squat stone building at the top of a set of stairs that offers a nice view of the town and Columns Group below. Not much more than a large pile of rocks among the surrounding houses, the **South Group** is just to the south of the Mitla River, a block east of 5 de Febrero. The Adobe Group and South Group structures were used for religious ceremonies.

Shopping

Mitla's main draw is the ruins, but it is also a hub for artisans from the surrounding communities in the valley to sell their work. You won't miss the **artisan market** (8am-5pm daily), as you have to walk through it to get to the main ruins. The stalls are full of products from all over Oaxaca. Shops selling textiles, mezcal, and other Oaxacan products also line 5 de Febrero and Reforma, the main route to the archaeological zone.

Food

If you don't have time to explore the town, there are food stalls just outside the artisan market, where you can get tacos, *tlayudas* (large tortillas topped with meat and cheese), and other typical street food for around US$2-3. There are many cheap options in town, such as the *comida corrida* at the **Hotel La Zapoteca** (5 de Febrero 12, tel. 951/568-0026, 9am-8pm Mon.-Sat.), which will run you about US$3. Personal recommendation: *chile relleno de picadillo. Picadillo* is ground beef usually mixed with stuff like potatoes, but here they add a touch of sweet to the savory by tossing raisins into the mix.

The restaurant in the shady courtyard at the **Hotel Don Cenobio** (Juárez 3, tel. 951/568-0330, 8am-6pm daily, US$5-10) boasts a large menu of all kinds of Mexican food and is a comfortable escape from the midday heat. Your best bet for dinner is ★ **Doña Chica** (Morelos 41, tel. 951/568-0683, 10am-8pm daily, US$3-6), which serves up tasty *moles,* tacos dorados, *memelas* (tortillas topped with pork lard, salsas, cheese, and other ingredients), and more in a clean, casual setting among bamboo-lined walls and columns of bare green limestone. The service is impeccable, and the dining room stays nice and cool even in the heat of the day.

Accommodations

Mitla is another great town to consider spending a night in, conserving your energy to visit Hierve El Agua the following day, or to use as a base to explore the valley. There are many basic, affordable options, the best of which is **Hotel La Zapoteca** (5 de Febrero 12, tel. 951/568-0026, US$28). Nothing flashy here, but the rooms are clean and include TV and Wi-Fi. The hammocks on the patios are just what you need after a day of exploring.

For a bit more pizzazz at an excellent price, head to **Hotel Don Cenobio** (Juárez 3, tel. 951/568-0330, www.hoteldoncenobio.com, US$50 d, junior suite US$85 s or d, master suite US$100), which the current Don Cenobio built around the 90-year-old house of his grandfather. Part of the original adobe walls remain among the newly remodeled structure. The lush courtyard has a restaurant, pool, and a small playground for kids.

Getting There and Around

As it's one of Oaxaca's greatest hits, finding a tour that goes to Mitla is not a difficult task. It is usually included on itineraries that also stop at Hierve El Agua, Teotitlán, and other popular destinations.

Mitla is 47 km (29 mi) east of Oaxaca City on Highway 190. The drive takes a little over an hour. Drivers will find the exit to Highway 179 10 km (6.2 mi) east of Tlacolula, but don't get on 179. The signage is pretty clear. You'll take a left and cross over the highway onto the road that leads into town. If you don't want to deal with the traffic of the main drag to the ruins, keep an eye out for a sign that says "Zona Arqueológica" as you start to enter the town. Take a left and you'll follow a route that avoids the hustle and bustle. The main route is a little farther down the road, through the archway that says "Bienvenidos a Mitla" on the left.

If you're going directly to Mitla via *colectivo*, hail one at the corner by the baseball stadium in Oaxaca City. It'll get you there in about 1.25 hours. They'll drop you off at the archway. *Mototaxis* charge US$0.50 to get from the archway to the archaeological zone. *Camionetas* that go to Matatlán and Hierve El Agua stop at the archway. Hierve El Agua is a 30-45-minute *camioneta* ride from Mitla.

MOTOTAXI

It's not really common practice, since few people visit the three groups of ruins in town, but if you want to check them out, you can ask a *mototaxi* driver to take you around (though they are walkable). Something like US$5 should be fair for a quick half-hour tour of them. There is not much to see at these sites, and don't expect the driver to be a tour guide, but it doesn't take long, and it is interesting to see them right next to people's houses and businesses. From the highway, stop by the

South Group first, then the **Arroyo Group,** and finally the **Adobe Group.** Then just walk down the hill to see the main event.

TOP EXPERIENCE

★ HIERVE EL AGUA

Despite what its name (which translates as "The Water Boils") implies, it's not really boiling, but the water in the mineral springs at **Hierve El Agua** (no phone, 9am-6pm daily, US$1.50) sure looks like it is. For millennia, these springs have been gurgling up water laden with calcium carbonate and other mineral salts, which then flows over the edge of the cliffs, depositing the salts along the way. Slow as stalactites, these "petrified waterfalls" eventually grew to become the huge frozen water flows that spill down into the valley in uncanny formations.

The Springs

Make sure to bring your swimsuit—you can change into it in the restrooms (US$0.25) down by the pool. Coming down the hill from the food stands, you'll see the swimming pools of the *cascada chica* (little waterfall), where you can cool off in the heat of the afternoon. From here you can enjoy breathtaking views of the valley below, as well as the other "waterfall," known as the *cascada grande.* There are many springs bubbling to the surface here, trickling into the swimming pools and down the base of the formation.

Trails lead up and over another rise to the *cascada grande,* which does not have swimming pools, but is an excellent perch for photos. From here, trails lead down to the valley floor, where you can explore around the bases of the falls. When climbing back up from the *cascada grande,* you can get to the parking lot more easily by continuing to climb instead of taking the trail that leads back down to the *cascada chica.* This way you can avoid having

1: the ruins at Yagul from the hilltop fortress La Fortaleza **2:** Santiago Matatlán, the world capital of mezcal **3:** Mitla's Columns Group **4:** the swimming hole at Hierve El Agua

1

BIENVENIDOS A STGO. MATATLAN, OAX.
"CAPITAL MUNDIAL DEL MEZCAL"
H. AYUNTAMIENTO

2

3

4

to go back down and up to the side with the food stalls. The trails are moderately steep and require a bit of effort in the heat of the day.

Food and Accommodations

The **food stands** (9am-6pm daily, US$4-6) up above the falls all have cold beer and sodas to cool off in the heat, as well as quesadillas, tacos, *tlayudas*, and other street food favorites. Try a *piña loca*, an entire pineapple hollowed out, cut up, and served in the skin with orange juice, or, if you need the extra kick, a bit of mezcal.

You can have anything you want at **Comedor Alicia** (corner outside park entrance, tel. 951/105-9778, 7am-10pm daily, US$3-5), as long as you want sizzling *carnes asadas* accompanied by fresh guacamole and *salsa de molcajete* (roasted tomato and chile pepper salsa ground by hand in a volcanic rock mortar). Fans of the Woody Guthrie song will want to snap a picture of the sign a patron left years ago, on which the name of the restaurant is translated into English: Alice's Restaurant. If you stay the night at the springs, this will be your only breakfast and dinner option for when the food stands in the park aren't open.

Staying the night at Hierve El Agua is a rustic experience. The *cabañas ecoturísticas* (951/561-4189, US$12 pp) just to the north of the food stands come with spectacular views and almost all the bare necessities, and camping is also an option. They have private bathrooms, but bring your own towels, soap, and toilet paper, just in case. It costs about US$3 to pitch a tent.

Getting There

Like Monte Albán and Mitla, it's next to impossible not to find a tour to Hierve El Agua walking the streets of Oaxaca City. Most include it as the final stop on full-day tours that include sites like El Tule, Teotitlán del Valle, and Mitla. **Chimalli Travel Group** (Manuel Bravo 108, Oaxaca City, tel. 951/501-2387, www.chimalli. travel) runs such a tour for around US$22. However, to experience Hierve El Agua in a way that no other agency offers, call Eric Ramirez at **Zapotrek** (Xolotl 110, Oaxaca City, tel. 951/502-5957, www.zapotrek.com, US$150). Instead of driving to the springs, a local guide will accompany you on a four-hour hike through the valley, over ground that changes from bright yellow to orange to deep wine-red beneath your feet. The tour stops at a waterfall with springs and otherworldly rock formations like those at Hierve El Agua. And don't worry, you don't have to hike four hours back—the van meets you at the site to take you back to Oaxaca City.

Hierve El Agua is about 52 km (32 mi) southeast of Oaxaca City. Drivers take Highway 190 east from Oaxaca City. Take the Highway 179 exit about 39 km (24 mi) outside town. This route includes a toll (US$1.50), but it's worth it for the views. At kilometer marker 62, take a right and follow the signs. The drive takes about 1.75 hours. Public transport passengers can catch a *camioneta* from the main junction in Mitla; it takes 30-45 minutes and costs about US$2.50.

Valle de Zimatlán-Ocotlán

Home of the **Ruta de Artesanías (Crafts Route)**, the Valle de Zimatlán-Ocotlán extends south from Oaxaca City. It is rich with artisanal traditions both young and old, from *alebrijes*, which date back to the 1950s, to the various styles of *alfarería* (pottery) made here, which all have their roots in pre-Hispanic soil.

Public transport travelers can reach any of these destinations (except San Sebastián de las Grutas) from Oaxaca City's **Automorsa bus station**, six blocks south of the *zócalo*, at the corner of Bustamante and Xóchitl. Buses charge US$1-2 and leave every 8-10 minutes. You can get off these at any stop along the way, and then just wait for another one, or a *taxi colectivo*, by the side of the highway when you're ready to move on or return to the city. Make sure to confirm your destination with the driver before getting on, as there are two routes to take from here.

The **Oaxaca-Zimatlán Highway** and **Highway 175** are the two major highways running through this valley. Drivers access the Oaxaca-Zimatlán Highway by heading south on Miguel Cabrera and crossing the *periférico* and Río Atoyac bridge. For Highway 175, cross the *periférico* at Calle Armenta y López.

ARRAZOLA

The concept of *alebrijes*, the brightly painted figures of fantastic animals for which Oaxaca is renowned worldwide, actually began in Mexico City, where Pedro Linares made them out of papier-mâché in the mid-20th century. However, it is here in **San Antonio Arrazola** (pop. 1,100) where the art form took off. To pass the time while tending sheep, young Manuel Jiménez carved animals and other figures he saw in his dreams. Inspired by Linares's work, he began carving *alebrijes* out of wood, and the rest is history.

Shopping
ALEBRIJES

For the complete story of Manuel Jiménez (1919-2005) and his art, ask Manuel's son Isaías to show you around the small museum he made to his father's legacy at **El Tallador de Sueños** (Álvaro Obregón 1, tel. 951/517-1293, www.eltalladordesueños.com, 8am-8pm Mon.-Sat., 8am-4pm Sun., free admission). They also have pieces for sale and host demonstrations on the process of making *alebrijes*. The Jiménez family, however, aren't the only ones making *alebrijes* in Arrazola. People all over town have workshop/stores, so you can easily pass a pleasant couple of hours strolling the hilly streets in town, searching for the style that calls to you.

Getting There

To get to Arrazola on public transport from Oaxaca City, take a Zaachila-bound Automorsa bus from the stop at Bustamante and Xóchitl. You'll have to get off in Santa Cruz Xoxocotlán, about 20 minutes out of the city, and get a taxi to Arrazola at the crossroads (big green sign). From here, it's a quick 15-minute cab ride (US$2) to Arrazola.

Drivers cross the *periférico* at Miguel Cabrera, then cross the Río Atoyac bridge but steer clear of the walled-off right lane. After the bridge, turn left onto the Oaxaca-Zimatlán Highway. In about 3 km (1.9 mi), turn right at the sign for Arrazola in Santa Cruz Xoxocotlán. Follow the signs for the next 7 km (4.3 mi) to Arrazola. The drive takes about 40 minutes.

CUILAPAM DE GUERRERO

Originally a town of Mixtec origin called Sahayuco, meaning "The Foot of the Hill," Cuilapam (sometimes Cuilapan) de Guerrero is home to the **Ex Convento de Santiago Apóstol** (Vicente Guerrero, no phone,

9am-6pm daily, US$2.50), a masterpiece of Dominican architecture, despite being left unfinished. The long, roof-less chapel you see as you first enter the courtyard was meant to be covered, but costs became too much for the Spanish crown, and construction was halted in 1568. You can wander around the courtyard free of charge, but it is definitely worth paying to see inside. If it's not high season, there's a good chance you'll have the place mostly, if not all, to yourself. The quietness beneath the arches and vaulted ceilings is a great place to get away from it all and contemplate for a while, or not at all.

A visit to Cuilapam also brings you into contact with more recent Mexican history. This was where Mexico's second president Vicente Guerrero was killed in 1831 by firing squad during the political turmoil that followed the country's war for independence.

In the last week of July, Cuilapam holds its patron saint and **Lunes del Cerro** festivities, during which you can see performances of the **Danza de la Pluma** (Dance of the Feather). Cuilapam has a rivalry with Teotitlán del Valle over ownership of the dance's creation, and dancers here put their all into staking their claim.

Getting There

Cuilapam de Guerrero is about 10 km (6.2 mi) southwest of Oaxaca City. Zaachila-bound Automorsa buses stop in Cuilapam de Guerrero, just outside the Ex Convento. They take about 30-40 minutes from Oaxaca City. Drivers cross the *periférico* and Río Atoyac bridge at Miguel Cabrera and turn left (south) onto the Oaxaca-Zimatlán Highway. The turn to Cuilapam de Guerrero is 3 km (1.9 mi) down the road, in Santa Cruz Xoxocotlán. The town is 7 km (4.3 mi) down the road from here. The drive takes about 30 minutes.

ZAACHILA

Zaachila was the last political capital of the Zapotec civilization after the decline of Monte Albán. It was named after the dynasty that began here sometime around the 14th century.

Murals both here and in Mitla depict the divine lineage of the royal house of Zaachila.

What's left of this once great city can be seen at the **Zaachila Archaeological Zone** (Alarii 30, tel. 951/162-5065, 9am-6pm daily, US$3). You'll find the entrance just to the north of the bright-yellow church above the main square. Occupied from AD 1200-1521, it was one of the few inhabited Zapotec-Mixtec capitals when the Spanish arrived in Oaxaca. The Zapotecs and Mixtecs intermarried for political reasons. Much of the ruins have not been excavated, due to their locations beneath current residences, but you will be able to see a pair of tombs, one of which is decorated with human and animal representations of death. There are also a few aboveground platforms.

The hill where the ruins are located is the site where Zaachila holds its **Lunes del Cerro** festivities on the last two Mondays in July. At this lively festival, you can watch the stunning dance called the **Danza de los Zancudos** (Dance of the Stilted Ones), in which the participants dance on stilts over 2 meters (6.5 ft) tall. If you get a chance to see this cultural gem, don't pass it up.

★ Thursday Market

Zaachila is an essential stop for those who come to Oaxaca to eat. The town specializes in its own twists on regional favorites. It's worth coming to Zaachila any day of the week, but Thursday is the best day to come, when the tarps of the weekly *día de plaza* cover the downtown streets for blocks.

The goat and lamb *barbacoa* rivals that of Tlacolula, but the **barbacoa en rollo,** beef wrapped in avocado tree leaves and slow-roasted for eight hours or more, is Zaachila's claim to fame. It is only made on Thursdays. In the ★ **Mercado Municipal Alarii** (Plaza Municipal, no phone, 6am-6pm daily), you'll find a number of stalls like **Cholita,** where the 4th generation of the Martínez family still

---

1: a colorful *alebrije* hummingbird 2: Zaachila's Danza de los Zancudos 3: the Ex Convento de Santiago Apóstol in Cuilapam de Guerrero

serves this local delicacy. There's no place to sit. These are just stalls selling meat. But, it's barbecue. What else do you need? Just stand there and eat it right out of the big, fuzzy leaves of the *hoja de San Pablo* plant, the traditional wrappers used around here before plastic took over. Along the walls of the market you'll find women selling tortillas and salsas. You can take all the goodies out to the park and picnic.

Outside the market building, tarps cover the streets for blocks, shading vendors selling fresh fruits and vegetables, *tejate, aguas frescas* (fruit drinks), ice cream, folk art, and much, much more.

Goat/Lamb *Barbacoa* and Other Delicacies

While the *barbacoa en rollo* is a Thursday-only specialty, the **goat and lamb** *barbacoa* is available daily. On Thursdays, the goat and lamb *barbacoa* stands move to the west side of the Plaza Municipal, and the rest of the week you'll find them in the **Mercado Gastronómico** (Oaxaca-Zimatlán Hwy., no phone, 8am-7pm daily, US$2-4), to the west of the cemetery. Chocolate lovers will want to try a cup of *espuma,* literally "foam," a frothy, sweet cacao and corn-based drink unique to Zaachila. You can find it any day of the week at the Mercado Gastronómico.

Save room for dessert at one of the **ice cream stands** (9am-7pm daily, US$1-2) in the Plaza Municipal. Zaachila simply puts a little more TLC into its *nieves* (ice cream similar to shaved ice) than other places around here do, and the result is delicious. Personal favorite: *queso con zarzamora* (tangy white cheese with blackberries).

Getting There

Buses to Zaachila from the Automorsa stop in Oaxaca City take about 45 minutes to an hour. Drivers cross the *periférico* and Río Atoyac bridge at Miguel Cabrera and turn left (south) onto the Oaxaca-Zimatlán Highway. Zaachila is 11 km (7 mi) down the road. Stay on this highway, and in about 20 minutes, you'll see

the Mercado Gastronómico on your left. The drive takes about 30 minutes.

★ SAN BARTOLO COYOTEPEC

Of the various styles of pottery in the Valles Centrales, the most striking, and arguably most popular, is the *barro negro* (**black clay pottery**) of **San Bartolo Coyotepec.** It was here, in the 1950s, that Doña Rosa Real de Nieto pioneered the glossy black pottery style that is now found in shops all over town. Artists here don't use a potter's wheel, but stick to the traditional shaping method of a concave plate balanced and spun atop a convex one, spinning the piece with their hands.

Black clay pottery is primarily decorative, as the clay must be double-cooked in order to hold water, and a second cooking results in a dull-gray finish. Shops and markets all over town are full of vases, candleholders, figurines, skulls, and various other designs.

Sights

The **Museo Estatal de Arte Popular de Oaxaca** (Oaxaca State Folk Art Museum; Independencia, tel. 951/551-0036, museoartepopular@gmail.com, 10am-6pm Tues.-Sun., US$1), on the south side of the Community Park, has devoted one of its four exhibition rooms to black clay pottery. This permanent exhibit shows off the extremely detailed work of San Bartolo Coyotepec's most talented artists. There's more than vases on display here, and what can be done with this clay is truly remarkable. The other three rooms host temporary exhibits of art from other regions of Oaxaca. Keep an eye out for the work of artists or artisans you've met elsewhere.

Shopping
BLACK CLAY POTTERY

Your first stop should be to the place where the tradition began. At **Alfarería Doña Rosa** (Juárez 24, tel. 951/551-0011, 9am-6:30pm daily), the potter's grandchildren honor and continue her legacy. They offer demonstrations of Rosa's innovative technique, and their large stock of gleaming vases and figurines are for sale in the ample courtyard-turned-showroom.

The **Mercado de Artesanías de Barro Negro** (Juárez 37, no phone, 10:30am-8pm daily) is charming, but small. For a much broader selection from *alfareros* (potters) from all over town, take an hour strolling the rustic yellow booths of the **Plaza Artesanal de Barro Negro** (Iturbide 3, no phone, 10am-8pm daily). This market boasts the widest range of styles in one place in town, and has a nice, laid-back atmosphere that invites you to take your time and find just the piece you're looking for.

Getting There

San Bartolo Coyotepec is 13 km (8 mi) south of Oaxaca City, a quick 25-minute drive. It is a big hit on the tourist circuit, and there really isn't an agency in the city that doesn't stop here. Drivers cross the *periférico* at Calle Armenta y López and take Highway 175 south. The main artisans market and signs for Doña Rosa are very conspicuous. The turn for the Plaza Artesanal is a few hundred meters before this turn. Keep an eye out for the sign on the left side of the highway. The Automorsa buses that leave from the station on Bustamante and Xóchitl stop here on the way to Ocotlán; they take about 30 minutes.

SAN MARTÍN TILCAJETE

As the *alebrijes* craze spread in the 1980s, artists from the surrounding communities began to take up the craft. One such artist, Isidro Cruz, took what he'd learned in Arrazola to **San Martín Tilcajete** (pop. 1,800), and the art form took off. Now, like in Arrazola, the majority of the population works making and selling *alebrijes*, each with his or her own distinct style of carving and painting the figures.

Shopping
ALEBRIJES

It's easy to just wander around town for a couple hours, popping in and out of *alebrijes*

stores and chatting with the artists about their work. Stop by the **tourist information booth** in the Plaza Central to get more information on where to shop. To fully understand the time and work that go into making an *alebrije*, stop by the **Taller Jacobo & María Ángeles** (Callejón del Olvido 9, tel. 951/524-9027, www.jacoboymariaangeles.com, 8am-6pm daily), where award-winning sculptors Jacobo and María run a school where young people from the surrounding communities come to learn the necessary skills and patience. They offer short tours of the school free of charge, and a demonstration on making dyes and other stages in the process, which provides a clearer understanding of the work and time that goes into just one *alebrije*. Fun fact: The copal wood used to make *alebrijes* is so full of sap that the artist has to wait a full year for a sculpted piece to dry before painting.

In 2017, Mexico's National Institute of Anthropology and History (INAH) confirmed that up to 80 percent of copal species are endangered, but workshops like Jacobo and María's are working toward sustainability. They organize reforestation efforts, planting over 2,500 new copal trees annually.

Getting There

San Martín Tilcajete is located 26 km (16 mi) south of Oaxaca City. Drivers take Highway 175 south and turn right at the sign after about 35 minutes. The Automorsa bus takes 45 minutes. You can get a *mototaxi* (US$0.50) from the highway or walk into town; it's about 20 minutes on foot.

SANTO TOMÁS JALIEZA

Its Zapotec name means "Below the Church," the Spanish named it in honor of St. Thomas the Apostle, and now **Santo Tomás Jalieza** (pop. 3,600) informally goes by the nickname "La Ciudad de los Cinturones" (The City of Belts). Weavers here have been producing colorful cotton belts and other textile products decorated with pre-Hispanic glyphs distinct to the area for generations.

Días de Plaza: Weekly Markets

Of all the ancient traditions still practiced in Oaxaca, the *día de plaza* (weekly market), also called a *tianguis* (more so elsewhere in Mexico) or simply *mercado*, is definitely one of the oldest. Towns all over the state host weekly markets that occupy the blocks surrounding the Plaza Municipal, selling everything from fresh meat and produce to household items to handicrafts and other artisanal products.

This practice dates back to before the founding of Monte Albán, when subjects of what the Spanish later called *señoríos* (chiefdoms) met in the chief's town to pay tribute and trade with each other as well. The *día de plaza* in Tlacolula is one of Oaxaca's oldest continuously running weekly markets, and here, as well as in Zaachila, traditions run so deep that many people still barter, rather than shop.

Between the Valles Centrales and Oaxaca City, you could fill each day of the week with a new street market. Although similar in many ways, each market day has something special that makes it stand out. Vendors set up shop early, and things are usually in full swing by 8am. Make the market your first stop on these days to get the best selection and freshest food. They begin packing things up in mid- to late afternoon.

Sunday: Tlacolula
Renowned for its goat and lamb *barbacoa*, but also an excellent place to sample Oaxacan specialty drinks like *tejate* and mezcal.

Monday: Teotitlán del Valle
Artisans market where the wide diversity of styles of Teotitlán's expert weavers is on full display.

Tuesday: Santa Ana del Valle
Also an artisans market specializing in the wool products of local weavers with styles distinct from those in Teotitlán.

Wednesday: Villa de Etla
Market known for the quality of its *quesillo* (among other foods), a cheese that was accidentally invented by a forgetful teenager in neighboring Reyes Etla in the 1880s.

Shopping
EMBROIDERY
Belts are the specialty here, but you'll also find table runners, shawls, bags, bracelets, even backpacks and laptop cases. There are a number of shops in town, but most also sell in the small **artisans market** (no phone, 10am-6pm daily) in the Plaza Municipal, just across from the Templo de Santo Tomás. Weavers here yoke their long, skinny back looms to a corner of the market, hands moving to the rhythm of their voices as they chat.

Getting There
Santo Tomás Jalieza is 27 km (17 mi) south of Oaxaca City and just two minutes down the highway from the turnoff to Tilcajete. Drivers take Highway 175 south, turn left at the sign, and follow the paved road to the artisans market in the Plaza Municipal. The Automorsa bus takes about 50 minutes. You can get a *mototaxi* (US$0.50) from the highway or enjoy the 10-minute walk into town.

SAN ANTONINO CASTILLO VELASCO
You might be asked why you visited **San Antonino Castillo Velasco** (pop. 5,600), but you'll have fascinating ways to answer. This often-overlooked town is known regionally for its unique style of *huipil* (embroidered blouse), with designs inspired by local birds and flowers. The designs here are daintier than what you'll see on blouses made elsewhere in Oaxaca.

With its checkerboard domes and

the tarps of Zaachila's *día de plaza* market

Thursday: Zaachila
Home of the one-of-a-kind *barbacoa en rollo*, made from beef and cooked with avocado tree leaves, and also known for its *nieves* (artisanal ice cream).

Friday: Ocotlán de Morelos
Great place to shop for the embroidered blouses made in neighboring San Antonino Castillo Velasco, and home of La Cocina de Frida, where Beatriz Vázquez dresses up like Mexico's most iconic painter to serve clients.

Saturday: Oaxaca City (Central de Abastos)
Largest of its type in Oaxaca, and known for having products from all over the state.

pleasant pale-blue facade that in spots lets bare stone peek through, the 17th-century **Cuasiparroquia de San Antonino Obispo** (parish church dedicated to Anthony of Padua) in the town center is a fetching sight, so don't miss it on your way to go shopping and eating.

Shopping
TEXTILE SHOPS
Three blocks east of the church, Marta Serna runs **Aguja de Plata** (Macedonio Alcalá 32, tel. 951/539-6243, 8am-9pm daily), a small textile shop where she passes down the knowledge she learned from her mother to the next generation. She embroiders intricate and colorful floral designs on clothing for women, children, and even men, as well.

There are a few textile shops on the road leading in from the highway. Stop by **La Casa del Bordado** (The House of Embroidery; Castillo Velasco 12, tel. 951/571-0623, 9am-6pm daily) on your way in or out of town for more beautiful embroidered dresses, blouses, and men's shirts. The selection here is large and varied.

RED CLAY POTTERY
Potter José García Antonio contracted glaucoma in his 50s, and his vision began to fade. Within a few years, the artist, known regionally and internationally as **El Señor de las Sirenas** (The Mermaid Man) for his penchant for sculpting the mythical creatures, was completely blind. This, however, did not deter the man, who continues to work to this day,

imbuing the life he recorded in his mind while he still had his vision and imprinting those images in *barro rojo* (red clay). Alongside his wife and children, to whom he passed down the tradition, and who are taking it in their own unique directions, he sells his work at the **Taller Manos Que Ven** (Hands that See Workshop; Libertad 24, no phone, no official hours), also the family home. You'll notice the door by the statue of a lion above it.

FLORES INMORTALES

San Antonino Castillo Velasco is an important cultivator of decorative flowers in Oaxaca, and the most awe-inspiring blooms here are the *flores inmortales* (immortal flowers), which keep their form and colors up to 45 years after they are cut. The **Raymundo Sánchez family** (Independencia 57, 951/395-6535 or 951/196-8306, 10am-6pm Mon.-Sat.) creates gorgeous statues, figurines, and religious items with these colorful natural wonders. If you're lucky, you might be able to catch Liliana Sánchez Mateos at the southeast corner of the Mercado Benito Juárez in Oaxaca City, but you'll most likely have to make the trip to San Antonino to find this one-of-a-kind art.

Food

There are lots of tasty bites in the **Mercado Progreso,** just to the east of the main square, but if you've come all the way here, you've got to eat an *empanada de amarillo,* the town's specialty. And there's no better place to try them than ★ **Empanadas Carmelita** (Albino Zertuche 21, tel. 951/505-3427, 8am-4pm Tues.-Sun.), where the chef-owner takes her vocation seriously. Once, when I visited the day before the town's Feria de la Empanada, I asked her if she would be there, and she responded, "Every day is the Empanada Fair here." Distinct from other empanadas in Oaxaca, these are made with

pork and include cilantro and other herbs that jazz up the delicious *amarillo* sauce.

Getting There

The turnoff to San Antonino is 32 km (20 mi) south of Oaxaca City on Highway 175, just before you reach Ocotlán. The drive takes about an hour. If you arrive via Automorsa bus, which takes about an hour, there are *mototaxis* (US$0.50) that will take you into town from the highway. If you say you're going to visit El Señor de las Sirenas, they will know exactly where to go.

OCOTLÁN DE MORELOS

Friday is the day that tarps take over the central streets of **Ocotlán de Morelos,** about an hour south of Oaxaca City. Like the markets at Zaachila and Tlacolula, the **Friday Market** features phenomenal *barbacoa,* but for a truly unique meal, head to ★ **La Cocina de Frida** (Mercado Morelos, no phone, 9:30am-6pm daily, US$4-6). This stall inside the main market on the west side of the Plaza Principal is run by Beatriz Vázquez, a woman who bears a striking resemblance to Frida Kahlo. She dresses up as the famous painter and serves up shots of her homemade mezcal to satisfied clients. Her specialty is chiles rellenos, and her *mole estofado* (stewed *mole*) is rich and complex.

Church lovers must stop by the beautifully restored **Templo y Ex Convento de Santo Domingo,** just to the south of the Plaza Municipal. This 16th-century Dominican church was in drastic disrepair until the 1980s, when Ocotlán's most famous citizen, the painter Rodolfo Morales (1925-2001), restored it to the bright blue and white facade we see today. The interior is decorated with silver and gold from the neighboring town of Santa Catarina Minas. The shady church courtyard is a nice place to take food from the market and have a picnic.

Getting There

Ocotlán is located 33 km (20 mi) south of Oaxaca City on Highway 175. The drive takes

---

1: black clay pottery for sale in San Bartolo Coyotepec **2:** *barbacoa en rollo,* the signature dish of Zaachila **3:** the entrance to the caves at San Sebastián de las Grutas about an hour. Automorsa buses leave from the stop at Bustamante and Xóchitl every 10 minutes and take about an hour.

★ SAN SEBASTIÁN DE LAS GRUTAS

San Sebastián de las Grutas technically isn't in the Valle de Zimatlán-Ocotlán. It is tucked away in the rolling green foothills of the Sierra Madre del Sur mountain range that divides the Valles Centrales from the coast. The main attraction here is the system of **caves** (*grutas*) in a hill just to the west of town. This 400-meter (1,312-ft) cave has five rooms ranging 20-70 meters (66-230 ft) in height. The shapes of the countless stalactites and stalagmites have inspired names like "The Lovers," "The Rhinoceros Fossil," and "The Bell" (because of the sound it makes when struck). There is also an underground river that runs below the caves. During the rainy season (June-Sept.), it is too dangerous to explore, but at other times of the year, the **Centro Ecoturístico San Sebastián de las Grutas** (tel. 951/488-4601, www.sansebastiandelasgrutas.com, office open 24 hrs) runs tours that rappel down into this part of the cave system. They last about three hours and cost around US$10.

There is much more to do here than spelunk, though. The ecotourism center also offers cycling, hiking, and tours to pre-Hispanic tombs and mezcal *palenques* (distilleries). The nearby valley Sola de Vega is the cradle of mezcal made from *tobalá*, a wild species of maguey known as "El Rey de los Mezcales" (King of Mezcals).

Food and Accommodations

The ecotourism center has *cabañas ecoturísticas* with room for 5-8 people, which include hot water and Wi-Fi. The cost is US$11 per person. The *comedor* on-site is open 9am-9pm daily and has the usual fare of chiles rellenos, quesadillas, *huevos al gusto*, and so on. A meal here will run you US$3-4. Eating options in town can be quite limited, but there are a couple *comedores* here, as well. You can grab a *mototaxi* on the highway, or enjoy the 15-minute walk into town. It's a pretty sleepy little community, so your best option is to make sure you get to the *comedor* at the *cabañas* before it closes.

Getting to the Caves

The cheapest way to get to the caves from Oaxaca City is on a *suburban* (12-passenger van) from the Central de Autobuses Segunda Clase, on the west side of the Centro, by the Central de Abastos. They cost US$3, leave hourly, and take a little over two hours to get to the *cabañas*. The driver will drop you off at the turnoff just to the west of town, and the *cabañas* are a short, five-minute walk from the highway.

The caves are about 53 km (33 mi) southwest of Oaxaca City. Drivers take Highway 175 south from the city. The junction with Highway 131 is 15 km (9 mi) down the highway. From here, follow Highway 131 55 km (34 mi), until you see the sign to turn right. The town is another 12 km (7.5 mi) from this junction, and the caves and *cabañas* are about a half mile west of town. Total drive time is a little over two hours.

Valle de Etla

Extending northwest from Oaxaca City, the Valle de Etla is the smallest of the Valles Centrales. Although it draws the least attention from tourism agencies, it is also home to treasured Oaxacan traditions. The fortunate accident that gave the world *quesillo* happened

here toward the end of the 19th century. And Monte Albán is believed to have been founded by people formerly living in a settlement at San José El Mogote.

Any destination in the Valle de Etla can be reached from Oaxaca City by getting a *taxi colectivo* on Calle Valerio Trujano, seven blocks west of the *zócalo*, just on the other side of the *periférico*. It looks chaotic, and it is, but just ask a driver to help you find one for where you're going if you have any trouble. These taxis will get you anywhere in the valley and back for US$2-5 per day.

SAN AGUSTÍN ETLA AND VICINITY

Two freshwater springs keep water flowing through the river at San Agustín Etla year-round, making the town a leafy green oasis in the winter, when much of the surrounding landscape has turned brown for the season. Only a half hour from downtown Oaxaca, it's a great place to get away from the heat of the city and cool off at one of the local *balnearios,* public swimming pools that can often look like mini-waterparks.

San Agustín is the home of the **Centro de las Artes de San Agustín (CaSa)** (Independencia next to church, tel. 951/521-3043, www.casa.oaxaca.gob.mx, 9am-8pm daily, free admission), founded by the world-renowned Oaxacan visual artist Francisco

Toledo (1940-2019). In 2006, with the help of a grant from the Oaxacan government, Toledo bought and renovated the abandoned 19th-century textile mill on the north side of town, and turned it into a thriving arts and educational space. The center hosts temporary exhibits of art, photography, and video made in its many workshops, and the building itself is beautiful enough to warrant a visit.

CaSa offers a variety of cultural and artistic courses and workshops, from seminars on border issues to classes in painting, photography, theater, and other visual arts. Check their website for a list of available courses. There is no charge, but you must apply to enroll.

From CaSa, the signs that say "Taller de Papel" (Paper Workshop) will lead you down the hill to the **Vista Hermosa Paper Factory** (tel. 951/521-2394, 8am-4pm Mon.-Sat.). In the workshop just below the store, you can get a demonstration of how they make paper out of recycled materials, much of which was used in Toledo's own projects. The store sells notebooks, jewelry, kites, and other pieces of art designed by Toledo.

the Centro de Las Artes de San Agustín (CaSa)

TOP EXPERIENCE

LA MUERTEADA

On November 1, when other towns in Oaxaca are solemnly observing **Day of the Dead** rites in the cemeteries, the citizens of San Agustín Etla do the complete opposite with a raucous, ghoulish parade called **La Muerteada.** Locals don homemade costumes and gather at the fittingly gothic Iglesia de la Soledad Vista Hermosa, just next to the Centro de las Artes. Since its roots go back to the days of *haciendas* (large family-owned ranches), there is a classic list of characters representing members and ranch hands of the Ruiz Leyva family, who is said to have started the tradition. La Viuda (the widow) and El Muerto (her dead husband) are accompanied by El Viejo (the father of the deceased patriarch), the Butler, and others, who are corralled through the streets by the whip-wielding Chivero, or goatherd. This troupe from beyond the grave parades riotously through town until the sun comes up, when they return to the church full of mezcal and tamales, ready for another year of rest after dancing through the night.

Day of the Dead is a holiday meant to reflect on death and those that have gone before us, but La Muerteada takes the celebration to another level, truly rejoicing in the fact that the Grim Reaper hasn't visited us yet.

Food and Accommodations

The most reliable option in town is **Comedor Campestre** (Colón 1, tel. 951/290-9080, 8am-6:30pm daily, US$2-3). They serve the usual breakfast and lunch fare, but will also prepare vegetarian and vegan meals if you call ahead of time. Emelinda Bernal, at **Comedor Milagro** (Independencia 50, tel. 951/284-3147, 9am-6pm daily, US$2-3), serves a delicious *comida corrida*, as well as *tlayudas*, tamales, empanadas, and menudo on Sundays.

For something a little fancier, try the restaurant at **Casa María** (Independencia 64, tel. 951/521-3065, www.casamaria.mx, 9am-5pm and 7pm-9pm daily, US$5-8), where the dining room is decorated with sketches by Francisco Toledo. There is a set breakfast menu, and lunch and dinner menus change daily. Casa María is also a hotel with luxuriously rustic single and double rooms (US$42) and king-size rooms (US$49).

To save some dough without sacrificing aesthetics, try **Posada Villa Loohvana** (Independencia 11, tel. 951/521-2500, villa_loohvana@hotmail.com, US$22), in the home of polyglot Michelle Tommi. The large, white stucco house overlooks the green rolling hills of the Valle de Etla, and the sweet aroma of the *azucena* flowers (Madonna lily) permeates the terraced gardens at sunset. The house's four guestrooms are cozy yet spacious. Two have two double beds, and the other two have two twin beds; all have private bathrooms.

Amalia Cruz, at **El Rincón de San Agustín Etla** (Calle Reforma, tel. 951/521-2526, www.rincondesanagustin.jimdo.com) has a wide range of private bungalow options (US$30 d, US$35 with kitchen), and lots of space to pitch a tent (US$7). She also arranges hikes to a nearby lake and will fill the pond upon request if you need to cool off.

Getting There

Drivers take Highway 190 west from Oaxaca City. After about 14 km (8.7 mi), turn right onto the unnamed road just after the Instituto Euro Americano. Take the next left and follow the road lined with towering jacaranda trees another 3 km (1.9 mi) to San Agustín Etla. The drive takes about 30 minutes. Public transport passengers can get here from the *taxi colectivo* stop on Valerio Trujano in about half an hour (US$1.50).

El Andador (Vigil 509, Oaxaca City, tel. 951/205-9986, www.elandador.com.mx, 8am-8pm Mon.-Sat., 11am-8pm Sun.) runs a full-day tour that stops at the Centro de las Artes and other places in the Valle de Etla for about US$19.

REYES ETLA

As legend has it, sometime in the 1880s, a cheesemaker from **Reyes Etla** left his 14-year-old daughter in charge of the curds while he and his wife went into town for the day. Fortunately for us all, she forgot to tend to the cheese, and what her parents found when they got home looked strange, but tasted delicious. This classic teenage mishap was the birth of the sharp, stringy cheese Oaxaca is famous for, called *quesillo.*

If you're as crazy about this stuff as I am, you can learn more about how it's made at the **Dando Vida Cheese Factory** (Zapata 18, tel. 951/282-3965) on a Sunday. Simón Castellano and his wife host an hour-long demonstration on the process at 3pm, then serve chiles rellenos, *tlayudas*, quesadillas, and other classics with the cheese they just made in front of you. There is no charge for the demonstration, but there's lots of fresh *quesillo* for sale, and the fresh, home-cooked meal only costs US$2-4.

Can't make it on Sunday? Stop by the **Cremería Los Reyes Etla** (Constitución 3, tel. 951/571-4101, 8am-8pm daily) for freshly made *quesillo*, butter, cream, and other dairy products. Do yourself a favor and pick up a *cuarto* (0.25 kilo/0.5 lb.) or *medio* (0.5 kilo/1 lb.) of the *quesillo doble crema* (double cream). The **Mercado Municipal Porfirio Díaz** (Independencia, no phone, 7am-6pm daily) in neighboring **Villa de Etla** also has a number of booths selling locally made cheeses, and is the hub of the town's weekly **Wednesday Market.**

Getting There

Reyes Etla is just to the west of the larger town Villa de Etla, which is right on Highway 190, 20 km (12.4 mi) northwest of Oaxaca City. The drive from Oaxaca City takes about 40 minutes. The *taxis colectivos* that leave from the stop on Valerio Trujano also take about 40 minutes and cost about US$2.50.

Sierra Norte, El Papaloapan, and La Cañada

From vertiginous, pine-forested peaks

shrouded in almost constant cloud cover to hot, humid lowlands full of sugarcane and rubber tree fields, Oaxaca's northern regions call out to adventure-seekers. The altitude of the mountains combined with humid air from the Gulf of Mexico is the perfect combination for an ecosystem so varied that it earned Mexico a place on Conservation International's list of the world's 17 megadiverse countries. Plants we prize as rare and exotic in the United States are so common here that many locals thought it was funny how much I raved about them, since they see them every day.

Up in the Sierra Norte, an oak tree will be home to a half-dozen other plants, many of which you've likely never seen before. Entire

Highlights

Look for ★ to find recommended sights, activities, dining, and lodging.

★ **Cuajimoloyas:** This gateway town to the **Pueblos Mancomunados** has loads of hiking, mountain biking, and camping options, as well as culturally enriching workshops and Oaxaca's longest zip line (page 148).

★ **Parque Ecoturixtlán:** This ecotourism park is a great place to observe the megadiversity of the Sierra Norte (page 162).

★ **Balnearios Monte Flor and El Zuzul:** Come down from the chilly heights of the Sierra Norte to take a dip in this pair of crystal-clear swimming holes (page 170).

★ **Huautla de Jiménez:** Sprawled across a steep slope of the Sierra Mazateca, Huautla de Jiménez has much more to offer than the magic mushrooms that made it famous in the 1960s (page 175).

★ **Las Regaderas:** Spend an afternoon hiking down to this pair of 30-meter (98-ft) waterfalls pouring from cracks in the rocky hillside (page 179).

★ **Cañón del Sabino:** The sheer 600-meter (1,968-ft) walls of this spectacular canyon in the Cañada region are home to large flocks of green macaws, called flying emeralds by the locals (page 183).

forests are full of ghostly mosses or the bright flowers of bromeliads, so many that there's a good chance you'll witness bromeliads falling from branches they grew too big for. Hirsute ferns grow to 6-meter-tall (20-ft-tall) trees and cover entire mountainsides in what look like dark-green waterfalls. And you've probably never seen so many different orchids blooming in one place as you do in the Sierra Mazateca, at the western end of the range. It's not an exaggeration to say that something astonishing lies around nearly every bend in the highway.

The only reason so few tourists make it to El Papaloapan is because the region's coastline is in the neighboring state of Veracruz, but these tropical lowlands on the north side of the mountains are full of crystalline rivers that beg to be jumped into, and the seafood is as good as that of Oaxaca's Pacific coast.

The arid canyon country of La Cañada, to the west of the mountains, has been off the radar of foreign visitors for some time, but that should really change. Home to the Oaxacan half of the Tehuacán-Cuicatlán Biosphere Reserve, this region is home to sprawling cactus forests, stupefyingly deep canyons, and huge flocks of green macaws, not to mention some of the rarer recipes in the Oaxacan cookbook.

Lots of the places are out-of-the-way and therefore require a bit more effort than other parts of the state. However, as anyone who has driven these highways will tell you, the journey, as well as the destination, is worth it. If you're after adventure and adrenaline, head north from Oaxaca City.

HISTORY

Archaeological records suggest that the first inhabitants of Oaxaca's northern region were the Olmecs, who inhabited the coastal regions of what are now southeast Veracruz, west Tabasco, and the Papaloapan region of Oaxaca during the middle to late Preclassic

Mesoamerican Era (2000 BC-AD 250). Later, others came who now consider this rugged, diverse terrain to be their traditional homelands, such as the Cuicatecs and Mazatecs of La Cañada, the Chinantecs of the Papaloapan region, and the Ixcatecs and Mixe of the Sierra Norte.

Given that this area was a major thoroughfare for the Aztecs en route to the region of El Istmo de Tehuantepec, it makes sense that El Papaloapan was the first region in Oaxaca to which the Spanish traveled after they didn't find their city of gold in central Mexico. Founded in 1526, the first settlement of note during the colonial era was of Tuxtepec, then called La Villa de Medellín, in honor of the birthplace of Hernán Cortés. In 1765, a group of escaped African slaves from Córdoba, Veracruz, founded the town of Nuestra Señora de Guadalupe de los Morenos de Amapa, now part of the municipality of Tuxtepec.

Northern Oaxaca is also the birthplace of Mexico's most beloved (or most derided, depending on one's politics) historical figure. President and reform leader Benito Juárez (1806-1872) was born in San Pablo Guelatao, in the Sierra Norte, to Zapotec parents. The leader who would secularize Mexico (but not without a fight) was orphaned at the age of four and was raised by his grandparents in the chilly, smoky towns of northern Oaxaca. At the age of 12, still unable to read or write, and ignorant of the Spanish language, Juárez walked the 64 km (40 mi) to Oaxaca City, where he first enrolled at a seminary. He later transferred to the recently founded Institute of Sciences and Arts, ultimately earning a degree in law. And the rest is now highly mythologized history.

Although Oaxaca's tourist boom didn't really take off until the 1980s, the small mountain town of Huautla de Jiménez became popular among foreign visitors in the 1960s. After a 1957 article in *Life* magazine introduced Western science (and a generation of

---

Previous: the sea of clouds in the Sierra Mazateca; the defunct suspension bridge and waterfalls at Las Regaderas; Balneario Monte Flor.

Sierra Norte, El Papaloapan, and La Cañada

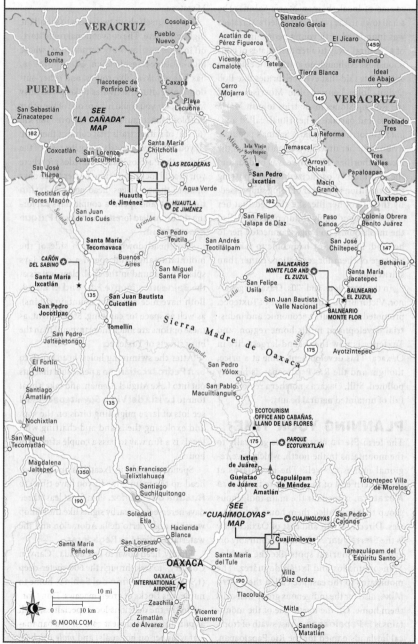

VERACRUZ

PUEBLA

Cosolapa
Salvador Gonzalo García
El Jícaro
1450
Pueblo Nuevo
Acatlán de Pérez Figueroa
Barahúnda
Loma Bonita
Vicente Camalote
Tetela
Tierra Blanca
Ideal de Abajo
Tlacotepec de Porfirio Díaz
Caxapa
Cerro Mojarra
145
VERACRUZ
San Sebastián Zinacatepec
Playa Lecuona
Poblado Tres
182
SEE "LA CAÑADA" MAP
La Reforma
Coxcatlán
Santa María Chilchotla
L. Miguel Alemán
Isla Viejo Soyltepec
Temascal
Tres Valles
San Lorenzo Cuaunecuíltitla
LAS REGADERAS
Arroyo Chical
Papaloapan
San José Tilapa
Agua Verde
San Pedro Ixcatlán
Macín Grande
Tuxtepec
Teotitlán de Flores Magón
Huautla de Jiménez
HUAUTLA DE JIMÉNEZ
San Juan de los Cués
San Felipe Jalapa de Díaz
Paso Canoa
Colonia Obrera Benito Juárez
Salado
Grande
San Pedro Teutila
182
San José Chiltepec
147
Santa María Tecomavaca
San Andrés Teotilálpam
Bethania
CAÑÓN DEL SABINO
Buenos Aires
San Miguel Santa Flor
BALNEARIOS MONTE FLOR AND EL ZUZUL
Santa María Jacatepec
Santa María Ixcatlán
San Felipe Usila
BALNEARIO EL ZUZUL
135
San Juan Bautista Cuicatlán
Usila
San Juan Bautista Valle Nacional
BALNEARIO MONTE FLOR
San Pedro Jocotipac
Tomellín
Sierra Madre de Oaxaca
Valle
San Pedro Jaltepetongo
Grande
175
Ayotzintepec
El Fortín Alto
San Pedro Yólox
Santiago Amatlán
San Pablo Macuiltianguis
Nochixtlan
135
ECOTOURISM OFFICE AND CABAÑAS, LLANO DE LAS FLORES
San Miguel Tecomatlán
PARQUE ECOTURIXTLÁN
Magdalena Jaltepec
135D
175
Ixtlán de Juárez
San Francisco Telixtlahuaca
Guelatao de Juárez
Capulálpam de Méndez
Totontepec Villa de Morelos
190
Santiago Suchilquitongo
Amatlán
Soledad Etla
CUAJIMOLOYAS
San Pedro Cajonos
Santa María Peñoles
Hacienda Blanca
SEE "CUAJIMOLOYAS" MAP
Cuajimoloyas
Tamazulápam del Espíritu Santo
San Lorenzo Cacaotepec
OAXACA
Santa María del Tule
Villa Díaz Ordaz
OAXACA INTERNATIONAL AIRPORT
190
Tlacolula
Mitla
Zaachila
Zimatlán de Álvarez
Vicente Guerrero
Santiago Matatlán

0   10 mi
0   10 km

© MOON.COM

U.S. and Canadian hippies seeking mystical experiences) to the hallucinogenic mushrooms of local shaman María Sabina, the small town in the peaks of the Sierra Mazateca was inundated with young people in search of a "natural" way to alter their states of consciousness. Although no journalistic evidence exists, it is said that even celebrities like Bob Dylan, John Lennon, Jim Morrison, and the Rolling Stones made trips to visit María Sabina and partake in her ritual, called a *velada*. Unfortunately, María Sabina's popularity brought her unwanted attention from the local authorities. Her house was raided, and the community ostracized her for putting their tradition in danger of being suppressed. By the end of her life, she claimed that her *"niños sagrados"* (holy children), as she called the mushrooms, no longer connected her to her god, for so many had come to take advantage of them for recreation, rather than spirituality.

In the late 1960s and '70s, Oaxaca's governor, Victor Bravo Ahuja, a native of Tuxtepec, promoted agricultural, economic, and industrial development in his home region, and Tuxtepec is now the second-largest city in Oaxaca. This development came at a price, though, and the Río Papaloapan is heavily polluted. Still, Oaxaca's northern regions are full of untainted natural beauty.

PLANNING YOUR TIME

The term **Sierra Norte** refers generally to the mountains in the north, which have regional names, as well. The mountains at the western end of the range are the **Sierra Mazateca,** named for the main indigenous group that has called them home for centuries. Directly north and east of Oaxaca City is the **Sierra Juárez,** home to admirably organized ecotourism spots like the Pueblos Mancomunados and Ixtlán de Juárez. The mountains to the east are called the **Sierra Mixe,** also for the indigenous group that calls them home. On the north side of the mountains is **El Papaloapan,** a vast swath of tropical lowlands named for the Río Papaloapan,

the region's largest river. **La Cañada** is the canyon country to the west of the Sierra Mazateca.

Give yourself about two weeks to see all the highlights here. The conventional route starts off in the **Pueblos Mancomunados,** whose high-altitude flagship town, **Cuajimoloyas,** has lots of hikes, bike routes, and other outdoor and cultural activities to keep you busy for days. Or you could hike to one of the other Pueblos Mancomunados via the over 100 km (62 mi) of nature trails that connect them all. (If you only have a few days to get a taste of the region, the Pueblos Mancomunados are where you should focus your time.) After three days or so in these villages, head north to **Ixtlán de Juárez** and spend a couple days exploring the bromeliad forests and caves in **Parque Ecoturixtlán.**

Now head down the north side of the mountain range and spend a couple days splashing around in the cool, clear waters at the **Balnearios Monte Flor and El Zuzul.** Both have nice *cabañas* (mountain cabins), as well as space for camping. Stay a night, as these options are much more tranquil than the busy streets of Tuxtepec.

After the swimming holes, head north to **San Pedro Ixcatlán,** on a peninsula that juts out into Lake Miguel Alemán, and take a boat tour to **La Isla del Viejo Soyaltepec.** You'll see lots of large migrating birds on the way, and exploring the island and chatting with locals is a fun way to pass a couple afternoon hours.

Spend the night in Ixcatlán's one hotel or head up the mountains (if you have time) to **Huautla de Jiménez.** Plan for at least three days here, seeing nearby sights like the hilltop worship area Cerro de la Adoración and the waterfalls called **Las Regaderas.**

Finally, head down to La Cañada, "Canyon Country," to trek through the 600-meter-deep (1,968-ft-deep) **Cañón del Sabino,** home to numerous flocks of green macaws. Don't forget to try the delicious local specialties, such as *pilte* (marinated meat cooked in a banana-leaf wrapper on hot coals) and *mole chichilo,* which gets its rich, smoky flavor from ground tortillas made of charred corn.

That should do it, though you'll probably see many things that will make you want to stay longer. If you really want to make this more adventurous route unique, try doing it backward.

Pueblos Mancomunados

TOP EXPERIENCE

Oaxaca's best example of community organizing for responsible ecotourism is the Pueblos Mancomunados (United Villages) in the cloud-covered peaks of the Sierra Norte. The town of Benito Juárez was the first to begin offering ecotourism services here in 1994, and the neighboring towns of Cuajimoloyas, Llano Grande, La Nevería, Latuvi, Amatlán, Lachatao, and Yavesía joined the organization four years later. (At the time of this writing, Yavesía was not offering ecotourism services, but they may organize again.) This excellent example of community organizing has benefited both the land and the people living on it by bringing new economic opportunities that promote sustainable treatment of the natural resources they depend on in order to be profitable.

Now over 100 km (62 mi) of two-track dirt roads and hiking trails snake up and down the piney slopes and steep valleys of cornfields and wildflower patches to connect all eight member communities of the organization. Local trails in each community offer even more hiking and mountain biking opportunities to visitors. Home to over 2,000 plant species, 400 bird species, 350 different types of butterflies, and six classes of wild mountain cats, this region is recognized by the World Wildlife Fund for its high biodiversity. Unfortunately, many of these plant and animal species are endangered, highlighting the need for responsible tourism on the parts of both organizers and visitors.

Peaks here reach as high as 3,330 meters (10,925 ft) above sea level, with minimum daytime temperatures averaging around 8-10°C (46-50°F) and nightly lows as cold as 1°C (34°F), so don't forget to bring warm clothes.

When the sun is out, however, you can expect temperatures as high as 28°C (82°F). The rainy season runs May-December, with the heaviest rains falling between July and September. The best time to visit is October-December, when the views are green and full of life. When the skies are clear, such heights receive intense sunlight, so pack sunscreen and a hat, as well as lighter clothing for daytime.

Access Fee

Once you get up here, you'll want to stay a night or two, but if you've only got a day to explore, you'll have to pay an **access fee** of US$3 to enter the Pueblos Mancomunados. You can arrange this beforehand or simply show up at the ecotourism office in the town you arrive in and pay the fee.

In each town you visit, you should plan to check in with the local ecotourism office; if you're in town for the day, you'll need to pay the access fee; if you're staying overnight, the fee is included in the price of the accommodations, for which you'll need to stop by the ecotourism office to check in anyway.

Local Guides

All tourism activities in the Pueblos Mancomunados are operated by **Expediciones Sierra Norte** (M. Bravo 210-A, Oaxaca City, tel. 951/514-8271 or 951/206-4531, www.sierranorte.org.mx, sierranorteoaxaca@gmail.com). You can organize trips with them beforehand or stop in at their offices in the towns. The *guías comunitarios* (community guides) are locals from the villages who know the mountain trails, including local flora and fauna, better than anyone. English-speaking guides are available. For shorter routes (8-13 km/5-8 mi), they charge around US$15 for groups of up to seven hikers. Longer routes (15-25 km/9-15.5 mi) cost around US$35 per group.

Trekking and Hiking

A hike through the Sierra Norte takes in sprawling vistas of sawtooth mountain ranges painted blue by distance; friendly farmers tending fields of corn, beans, and other crops; an array of orchids, wildflowers, ferns, bromeliads, and mosses; and whole choruses of crooning songbirds. In addition to the roads and trails that connect the Pueblos Mancomunados, each town has smaller hikes to *miradores* (lookout points), waterfalls, canyons, caves, and other impressive natural features. Most trails are marked, albeit sporadically and insufficiently; the recommended option for hikes here is to hire a guide. It is easy to take a wrong turn, and you don't want to get lost.

Besides the local hikes around each town, there are eight **Rutas de Naturaleza** (Nature Routes) that link them with hikes of about 7-20 km (4.3-12.4 mi). Linking Cuajimoloyas to Latuvi, the **Ruta Loma de Cucharilla** is named for the plant called *cucharilla* (little spoon), which grows in abundance along the route. Its spoon-shaped leaves are used to make decorations for religious celebrations in the region. This 15.7-km (9.8-mi) hike descends through pine and oak forests, past colorful meadows, babbling brooks, and the campgrounds north of Cuajimoloyas. Most of the hike is flat, but there are descents at the beginning and end, the latter of which is quite steep; good physical condition is required. The trailhead is at the signed gate on the ridge west of town. Total hiking time is around four hours.

The only route longer than this one is the **Ruta Yaa-Tini,** which links Llano Grande to Lachatao and Amatlán in the north. With a total length of 19.8 km (12.3 mi) and an elevation drop of nearly 1,100 meters (3,609 ft), this is the best hike for observing the Sierra Norte's spectacular range of the biodiversity. There is quite a bit of up and down, so

depending on your walking speed, this hike can take as long as five hours. Good physical condition is recommended.

Heading north from Llano Grande, the **Ruta Shoo Raa** will take you to Yavesía. Measuring a total of 14.7 km (9.1 miles), the first 8 km (5 mi) or so descend gently about 300 meters (984 ft). The second half of the hike is much steeper, descending all the way to 1,900 meters (6,234 ft) at Yavesía. This four-hour hike is another great opportunity to observe the changes in vegetation at various altitudes.

The **Ruta Camino Real** is believed to have been part of a much longer pre-Hispanic thoroughfare that connected the Zapotec settlements in the Sierra Norte and the Valles Centrales to villages in the Gulf Coast region of Mexico. In some parts, the original stones of the road are still intact. The Camino Real runs 11.9 km (7.4 mi) from Latuvi north to Lachatao and Amatlán, much of it along the banks of the Río Cara de León (Lion's Face River). With little elevation change, it's a relatively easy hike that takes about four hours.

The **Ruta Cipriano Cabrera** runs north 10.9 km (6.8 mi) from the pine forests of La Nevería to the warmer oak woods of Latuvi. After a slight ascent at the beginning, the quaint rural footpath descends almost 500 meters (1,640 ft) in just a few kilometers, offering stunning views of the surrounding landscape. Total hiking time is about 2.5-3 hours.

Running from Benito Juárez to La Nevería, the **Ruta Needa-Queta-Miru** is used by many local farmers to get to and from their fields. It's only 8.2 km (5.1 mi) long, and mostly downhill, but around the 6-km (3.7-mi) mark it begins to climb back up to La Nevería, so conserve your energy for the end. The easy walk, mostly through fields of beans and corn, takes about two hours.

The flattest route is the **Ruta Latzi-Hroo-Lii,** which runs along a high ridge between

1: a lookout point in the Pueblos Mancomunados
2: mountain biking in the Pueblos Mancomunados

Cuajimoloyas and Llano Grande. Since it doesn't change elevation much, the entire trail runs through forests of towering, moss-covered pine trees. This easy 8.2-km (5.1-mi) hike can be done in around two hours.

The shortest Ruta de Naturaleza, the **Ruta Needa-Yaa-Lagashxi,** leads west from Cuajimoloyas to Benito Juárez. This 6.6-km (4.1-mi) trail heads down the steep slopes west of Cuajimoloyas through farmland and pastures, bottoming out in a valley with a crystal-clear river. The trail ascends about halfway back up to reach Benito Juárez. As on the Ruta Needa-Queta-Miru, you'll probably meet local farmers heading to or from their fields or working in them. The walk takes about two hours.

Mountain Biking

There are miles and miles of double-track and single-track trails up in these mountains, and Expediciones Sierra Norte has all the gear you'll need, as well as highly trained and knowledgeable guides to show you the way. Cycling tours are charged by the group, not per person, and can include up to five cyclists. Easier routes cost US$21, and more technical rides run about US$36. Bike rentals without a guided tour cost US$15 per day. Call ahead to ensure the staff and equipment will be ready.

Four bike routes trace the contours of the varied topography of this high-altitude region. The **Circuito Taurino Mecinas Ceballos** has three sections that connect Benito Juárez, La Nevería, and Latuvi. The first is the shortest and least technical, running 7.7 km (4.8 mi) along the high ridge between Benito Juárez and La Nevería. After about 5 km (3.1 mi) of short climbs and descents, the rest of the trail slopes down to the terminus, which is only slightly lower in elevation than Benito Juárez. The ride takes a half hour to an hour, depending on your experience and condition.

From La Nevería, the second section climbs about 50 meters (164 ft) in about 0.5 km (0.3 mi), then descends steeply for 5 km (3 mi) before beginning a slight ascent the rest of the way to Latuvi. This is one of the more technical routes, as more than half of the 10.9-km (6.8-mi) trail is single-track, requiring a bit more experience than the first part. This leg takes 45 minutes or more.

The third section runs between Benito Juárez and Latuvi, descending from lofty pine forests that gradually fill with moss-covered oak trees in the lower elevations. The 12-km (7.4-mi) route drops about 600 meters (1,968 ft) on a two-track road. Be aware that, although they're infrequent, cars are allowed on roads like this. You can expect this leg to take 45 minutes to an hour.

Experienced riders who don't like pit stops can complete the circuit in a little over three hours. If you prefer a more casual pace and stops for sightseeing and meals, you can expect the trip to take up to twice as long.

The fourth and longest bike route here is the **Ruta Ka-Yezzi-Daa-Vii,** which runs 28 km (17 mi) north from Cuajimoloyas to the towns of Lachatao and Amatlán on the north side of the Pueblos Mancomunados. This is not for inexperienced riders. Starting from an elevation of 3,100 meters (10,171 ft), the trail descends, often steeply, a total of 900 meters (2,953 ft), and loose rocks and gravel cover some stretches. Also, vehicles are allowed on these roads. The one-way ride takes about three hours and is a great way to see various geographies and vegetation zones.

For a day-trip cycling tour from Oaxaca City, contact Eric Ramírez at **Zapotrek Tours** (Xolotl 110, Oaxaca City, tel. 951/502-5957, www.zapotrek.com, 9am-8pm Mon.-Fri., 2pm-6pm Sat.-Sun.). The one-day cycling tour (US$120) begins with an early morning breakfast in Cuajimoloyas. After you fill up on steaming cups of chocolate and plates of eggs, beans, and tortillas, the tour descends 1,500 meters (4,921 ft) down the rugged slopes of the Sierra Norte into the Valle de Tlacolula.

Comedores

The hatcheries serve mouthwatering trout, and you can find snack foods in the little corner shops called *misceláneas,* but most of your meals in the Pueblos Mancomunados will be in little home-style restaurants called *comedores.* They generally open from 8am-ish to 8pm-ish (emphasis on the *-ish*), and usually charge around US$3 for a set meal.

Although many *comedores* will have a whole list of dishes they potentially serve, the actual menu changes daily. It's customary to enter and ask what's available. The usual fare includes chiles rellenos, *moles,* quesadillas, beans, rice, and various *guisados* (meat stewing in a rich, flavorful sauce). Also, many folks prefer to save money and conserve energy by leaving the lights off if no one is dining inside. If you come upon a darkened *comedor,* just knock or enter and ask if they're serving food.

Accommodations

CABAÑAS

Cozy mountain cabins called *cabañas* (US$30 d) are the primary accommodations in the Pueblos Mancomunados. These brick structures are all run by Expediciones del Norte. Book ahead or inquire in the local ecotourism office when you arrive. They all include a private bathroom with hot water, comfy queen- or king-size beds, and fireplaces with a load of firewood for the chilly nights. All of these communities have *cabañas,* but my personal favorites are in Cuajimoloyas,

Latuvi, and Amatlán; they offer stunning views of the surrounding landscape. If you want to be more nestled in the woods, try Llano Grande or La Nevería.

Unique to Benito Juárez is the **Casa del Turista** (Tourist House; US$10 pp), a large, four-room cabin for up to 22 people with a glass roof over the living room that has a fantastic view of the stars as you fall asleep. The sky is so clear you can see the creamy splash of the Milky Way spill across the night sky. Aside from the bedrooms with dorm-style sleeping arrangements, the cabin has a loft-like second floor, multiple balconies, a beautiful green garden in front, and spectacular views of the valley below.

HOMESTAYS

La Nevería, Latuvi, and Amatlán offer **homestays** as an accommodations option. For just US$10 per person, you can stay a night in the home of a local family in order to get to know them better, learn more about quotidian life in the Sierra Norte, and practice your Spanish. The cost does not include food, but I highly recommend arranging to pay a little extra for the stay to include delicious, home-cooked meals. This, combined with a stint volunteering in the fields and greenhouses,

the hillside *cabañas* at Latuvi

is not only one of the best ways to improve your Spanish but also a perfect opportunity for those who desire that their tourism leave something more than money behind in the places they visit.

CAMPING

All of the Pueblos Mancomunados have **campgrounds** (US$5 pp), and many have more than one, giving you the option to stay closer to town or a bit farther away. If you're not traveling with one, you can rent a tent for another US$5. The only amenity at all of these campgrounds is a dry toilet, but some have access to fresh potable water. My personal favorites among the sites include those in **Llano Grande, La Nevería,** and the one outside of **Latuvi.** This last one is on the Camino Real trail, connecting it with Latuvi via a brisk half-hour to 45-minute walk. Large groups and families should consider the **Llano de Tarajeas** campgrounds, some 4.5 km (2.8 mi) north of Cuajimoloyas. On the Ruta Ka-Yezzi-Daa-Vii, which leads to Lachatao, the broad clearing has room for dozens of tents, and there is an on-site trout hatchery and *comedor,* as well as playground equipment for the kids.

Nighttime temperatures, especially in the higher-altitude communities, get pretty low, occasionally freezing. Make sure you bring the proper clothing and equipment to suit such temperatures. For warmer nighttime temperatures, camp in the towns at lower elevations (Latuvi, Lachatao, and Amatlán).

HOTEL

Across the street from the ecotourism office in Cuajimoloyas, **Hotel Yaa-Cuetzi** has simple rooms with twin or queen beds and lots of windows to take in the gorgeous views of the town below and the fog-shrouded peaks beyond. All have shared bathrooms. At US$10 per person each night, this is the cheapest option besides camping, and it keeps you in close range of all the delicious food in the *comedores.* It is the only hotel in the Pueblos Mancomunados. Book through Expediciones Sierra Norte, or inquire in the ecotourism office in Cuajimoloyas.

★ CUAJIMOLOYAS

I did not prepare well for my first trip to **Cuajimoloyas** (pop. 740), which I later discovered was named for how low the temperatures get up here. A plaque in town tells the story of Spanish conquistadores who, when they arrived here centuries ago, joked that it was so cold that "*el mole cuaja en la olla*" (the *mole* sets in the pot). The phrase was amalgamated to form the town's name. Only rarely does it get below freezing up here, but at 3,200 meters (10,499 ft) above sea level, it is one of the highest towns in the Pueblos Mancomunados. Squat concrete houses fill the small valley and are stacked up its steep slopes, with ribbons of gray woodsmoke rising from fires set for cooking or just to keep warm. At this altitude, you can expect temperatures in the high 20s Celsius (80s Fahrenheit) when the sun is out, and lows that flirt with the freezing point at night. Pack accordingly.

The **ecotourism office** (Centro Ecoturístico Yaa-Cuetzi; tel. 951/524-5024, cuaji_yaacuetzi@hotmail.com, 9am-8pm daily) is on the highway just as you enter town. The unnamed highway becomes Calle Oaxaca when it enters Cuajimoloyas. Stop here before you do anything to get information, reserve *cabañas* or campsites, or to pay the US$3 access fee (only if you're not paying for accommodations).

In the penultimate weekend of July, Cuajimoloyas hosts the **Feria Regional de Hongos Silvestres** (Regional Wild Mushroom Fair), a two-day festival of workshops, classes, and hikes focused on identifying, preparing, and consuming edible wild mushrooms. Cuajimoloyas bills itself as "the capital of wild mushrooms," as the surrounding mountainsides are the perfect habitat for a wide range of uncultivated fungi. This is not a magic mushroom festival. Some species that grow here have medicinal properties, but the majority are for plain old cooking and enjoying.

Cuajimoloyas

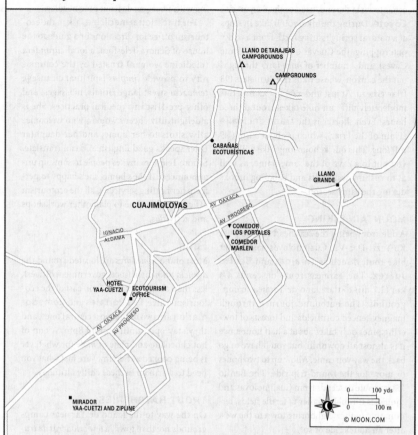

LLANO DE TARAJEAS
CAMPGROUNDS

CAMPGROUNDS

CABAÑAS
ECOTURÍSTICAS

LLANO
GRANDE

CUAJIMOLOYAS

AV. OAXACA

AV. PROGRESO

IGNACIO
ALDAMA

▼ COMEDOR
LOS PORTALES

▼ COMEDOR
MARLEN

HOTEL
YAA-CUETZI

ECOTOURISM
OFFICE

AV. OAXACA

AV. PROGRESO

■ MIRADOR
YAA-CUETZI AND ZIPLINE

0   100 yds

0   100 m

© MOON.COM

Sights and Recreation
MIRADOR YAA-CUETZI

It's recommended that you just take it easy the first day you get up here, to get adjusted to the high altitude. Try something easy like a short sunset hike up to the **Mirador Yaa-Cuetzi,** on a pointed crag on the west side of town. The walk from the ecotourism office takes about 20 minutes. Since you're up here, take the fun way down on the kilometer-long (0.6-mi-long) **zip line** (US$12), or *tirolesa*, that soars 100 meters (328 ft) above the smoky town below; make arrangements in the ecotourism office.

MIRADOR XI-NUDAA

Located 7 km (4.3 mi) northeast of town, at an altitude of 3,000 meters (9,842 ft), the **Mirador Xi-Nudaa** offers spectacular 360-degree views of dramatic alpine landscapes, pine and oak forests, winding valleys, and the neighboring villages of Benito Juárez and Latuvi. The cross on the peak commemorates the supposed appearance and tactical support of Saint Michael the Archangel at a battle here during the Mexican Revolution. The route begins at the landing side of the zip line, on the east side of town, and takes about four hours round-trip.

OTHER HIKES

For a shorter hike that won't leave you in another town at the end, head to the **Cañón del Coyote**. During the hike, you'll take in stops at a natural spring issuing forth from a rocky outcropping, the Cuevas del Coyote (Coyote Caves), and a number of *miradores* throughout the canyon, whose walls rise 30 meters (98 ft) overhead. At just under 6 km (3.7 mi), this moderately difficult hike takes around three hours. Even shorter is the **Llano del Fraile** (Plain of the Friar), which is about 3 km (1.9 mi) long. This quick, hour-long hike will take you out to a cave of the same name, as well as to rushing waterfalls and babbling brooks during the rainy season.

MOUNTAIN BIKING

Aside from being the trailhead for the Ruta Ka-Yezzi-Daa-Vii, Cuajimoloyas has shorter bike routes, such as **Tarajeas** and **Benito Juárez**. The Tarajeas route descends 4.4 km (2.7 mi) to the Llano de Tarajeas campgrounds. The outbound journey through maguey-fenced cornfields and forests of towering pines only takes about a half hour since it is almost all downhill, but you'll have to go back the way you came. Allow up to two hours or more for the round-trip ride. The Benito Juárez route descends from Cuajimoloyas and squiggles through a valley of fertile fields, terminating in the neighboring town to the west after an hour's ride or so.

ZIP LINE

The kilometer-long (0.6-mi-long) **zip line** over Cuajimoloyas is Oaxaca's longest. It stretches from the Mirador Yaa-Cuetzi on the south side of town and soars 100 meters (328 ft) to the north, offering a speedy, bird's-eye view of the smoky little village. Head to the ecotourism office to make arrangements and get equipment (US$12).

CULTURAL ACTIVITIES

The inhabitants of Cuajimoloyas invite guests to learn about their crafts and traditions. There are classes (US$11-25) on making *pan serrano* (artisanal "mountain" bread), medicinal and edible mushrooms, and basket weaving with fibers made from pine needles.

For **traditional medicine,** ask in the ecotourism office for directions or a guide to the house of Señora Telésfora, a local *curandera* (medicine woman) trusted by the community to provide *limpias* (spiritual cleanses), *temazcal* sweat lodge rituals, massages, and other pre-Hispanic medical practices. She is a delightfully cheery woman who welcomes all visitors to her home, and her daughter Ester speaks good English and can translate. Señora Telésfora invites people to show up unannounced. If she's home, she's happy to perform her healing services. Call the ecotourism office ahead of time to plan other workshops and activities.

Food

Most of the *comedores* are located around the *agencia municipal* (local government offices), less than about 0.8 km (0.5 mi) east of the ecotourism office. **Los Portales** and **Comedor Marlen** are two of the most central ones, and they stay open until around 8pm. A cup of hot chocolate and plate of *mole* (or whatever is being cooked at the time) are just what you need to warm up in these chilly altitudes.

TROUT HATCHERIES

On the way to the Llano de Tarajeas campgrounds north of town, a few *criaderos de truchas* (trout hatcheries) serve fresh trout in a variety of recipes, such as *al mojo de ajo* (in garlic), *enchipotlado* (in chipotle sauce), and *a la diabla* (in super spicy chile sauce). The closest one to Cuajimoloyas, **El Bocadito,** is about 3 km (1.9 mi) from town, and there is one in the Llano de Tarajeas campgrounds, about 4.5 km (2.8 mi) north of town.

Getting There

Cuajimoloyas is 56 km (35 mi) from Oaxaca City. Drivers head east from the city on Highway 190. At Tlacolula, take a left at the main intersection onto the road that leads to the town of Díaz Ordáz (you'll see a big green sign for it over the intersection). From there it's another 45 minutes through tightly coiled switchbacks that quickly get you up to the soaring heights of the Sierra Norte. The road is in mostly good condition; just drive with caution and hug the turns. Total drive time is about 1.5 hours.

You could take a *suburban* (shared van) from Oaxaca City's **Central de Autobuses de Segunda Clase** (Calle Juárez Mara, just north of the Central de Abastos, tel. 951/516-5326) to get up here in one shot, but the location of the second-class bus station makes it necessary to cross the whole city after getting out of the crazy traffic that buzzes around the Central de Abastos. This option is only viable for those already staying on the south side of the main plaza, the Zócalo. They charge about US$3 for the trip, but the traffic congestion around the terminal prolongs the trip to two hours or more. Vans leave hourly.

To opt out of this hectic city traffic, walk or take a taxi to the **bus and *colectivo* taxi stop** on the northeast side of the Centro, in between the baseball stadium and the McDonald's. Grab a *colectivo* (shared taxi van) bound for Tlacolula or beyond, and in Tlacolula, wait for a taxi, *suburban,* or *camioneta* (covered pickup truck) on the north side of the main intersection to take you the rest of the way. You shouldn't have to wait too long for a ride at these stops, so the journey shouldn't be much longer than 1.5 hours. In total, you'll spend US$2-3 to get up the mountain.

Expediciones Sierra Norte (tel. 951/514-8271 or 951/206-4531, www.sierranorte.org.mx, sierranorteoaxaca@gmail.com) offers transportation from Oaxaca City to the Pueblos Mancomunados, but it is a bit pricier than the public transport options, costing around US$30 for up to four people.

LLANO GRANDE

With an elevation just below that of Cuajimoloyas, **Llano Grande** (3,050 m/10,007 ft above sea level) is also one of the higher villages in the Pueblos Mancomunados. With a population of just 150 inhabitants, it is the smallest village in the cooperative. Because of its conscientious citizenry, it is one of the cleanest communities in Mexico. Most of the small town is tucked away in the tranquility of the surrounding woods.

The **ecotourism office** (tel. 951/524-5089 and 951/598-5086, adecordillera@hotmail.com, 9am-8pm daily) is on Calle Constitución, the first left upon entering town from the west. You'll see Comedor San Isidro first.

Sights and Recreation
CASCADA PINOVETE
Up in the high pine-oak forests north of Llano Grande, the **Cascada Pinovete** tumbles 30 meters (98 ft) down moss-covered stone to the riverbed below. At just 8 km (5 mi) round-trip, the easy hike out to the falls and back can be done in just over two hours, depending on how fast you make your way through the forest. With the sweet smell of pennyroyals and the songs of kingfishers and goldfinches permeating the clear mountain air, you might want to take your time.

OTHER HIKES
Other local hikes include the **Caminata El Amanecer** (Daybreak Hike), which begins around 4:30am. This 6.3-km (3.9-mi) hike takes about three hours round-trip and is a spectacular way to see the sunrise at nearly 3,350 meters (10,991 ft). The outbound leg climbs through dense pine forests until you reach the peak at sunrise, and the return home is an easy descent. Another route full of *miradores* with panoramic views and a wide range of flora and fauna is **La Sepultura,** a 9.5-km (5.9-mi) stroll through one of the highest regions of the Sierra Norte. The trail circles through the high-altitude pine forests north of town (no oaks this high up). It's a flat, easy hike that takes about three hours.

MOUNTAIN BIKING
Instead of walking, you could take a bike along the forested **Ruta Latzi-Hroo-Lii** (8

km/5 mi) west to Cuajimoloyas. With very little elevation change, it's an easy ride that takes just under an hour. You can rent the bike in Llano Grande and arrange to leave it at the ecotourism office in Cuajimoloyas, or just ride back to Llano Grande.

CULTURAL WORKSHOPS

Local cooks offer **cooking classes** (US$10 pp, three-person minimum) that feature regional specialties, as well as **workshops on making tortillas and artisanal breads** (US$23 per group of up to four people). Other cultural activities include bird-watching excursions, environmental education workshops, and classes about local legends and stories. Call ahead to give them time to prepare.

Food

There are three *comedores* in Llano Grande, the closest of which to the *cabañas* is **Comedor San Isidro** (US$3) at the corner of Calle Constitución and the highway, which is called Avenida Oaxaca in town. Owner and chef Andrea makes a phenomenal chile relleno, served with beans and rice. If she's made lentil soup when you visit, say yes. Right across the street, **Comedor Martínez** also serves delicious set meals.

Getting There

Llano Grande is 10 km (6.2 mi) down the highway east from Cuajimoloyas. If you wait for a *colectivo* (both taxis and trucks run this route) by the highway next to the Cuajimoloyas ecotourism office, it'll get you to Llano Grande in about 20 minutes (US$0.50). If you're not in a rush, why not walk it? The **Ruta Latzi-Hroo-Lii** is an easy 8-km (5-mi) walk that takes about 2.5 hours.

1: dense fog of the cloud forests of Cuajimoloyas
2: a reforestation workshop in the Pueblos Mancomunados

BENITO JUÁREZ

At 3,000 meters (9,842 ft) above sea level, **Benito Juárez** rounds out the trio of high-altitude towns in the Pueblos Mancomunados. At this altitude, deciduous trees like oak, fir, and strawberry trees begin to elbow in among the pines that dominate the higher peaks. The pine trees here grow up 30 meters (98 ft) tall during their life span of 250-300 years.

The **ecotourism office** (tel. 951/172-1581, ecoturismobenitojuarez@yahoo.com.mx, 9am-8pm daily) is in the center of town, just north of the basketball court and municipal government building. It is at the intersection of the road from Cuajimoloyas and the one that climbs up the mountains from Teotitlán del Valle. Make this your first stop upon arrival.

Sights and Recreation
MIRADOR AND SUSPENSION BRIDGE

From a peak northeast of the center of town, the view from the *mirador* stretches over the town's houses, basketball court, school, and governmental building, as well as miles and miles of green beyond. The one-way walk up the dirt road from town takes about 40 minutes. You'll find it by heading north from the ecotourism office and taking a right at the three forks in the road that you come across. From the *mirador*, a 150-meter-long (492-ft-long) long **suspension bridge** (*puente colgante*) stretches through the tops of the pine trees with their roots in the dirt of the gorge 30 meters (98 ft) below.

OTHER HIKES

Benito Juárez is the trailhead for the **Ruta Needa-Queta-Miru,** which heads west to La Nevería, and the **Ruta Needa-Yaa-Lagashxi**, which climbs up to Cuajimoloyas, to the east.

Staying local, you could hike out to the **Piedra Larga** (Long Rock), a vertiginous crag offering panoramic vistas east of town. At just under 3 km (1.9 mi) from town, the easy trek to the rock and back takes about two hours.

Or you could walk up to the *cascadas* north of town. The moderate hike takes about two hours round-trip, factoring in time to admire the 7-meter (23-ft) falls.

MOUNTAIN BIKING

From Benito Juárez, you could bike to either La Nevería (7.7 km/4.8 mi) or Latuvi (12 km/7.4 mi) via the **Circuito Taurino Mecinas Ceballos.** The section from Benito Juárez to La Nevería is the less technical and takes a half hour to an hour. The ride to Latuvi can be done in about an hour. Finish the whole circuit, and you'll be back in Benito Juárez in 3-5 hours, depending on your pace.

ZIP LINES

Up by the *mirador* and suspension bridge, a set of three **zip lines** stretches a total of 300 meters (984 ft) back and forth across the gorge. The tallest of the three is over 80 meters (262 ft) high. Inquire in the ecotourism office for operators and equipment. Zip-lining the set of three costs about US$10.

CULTURAL WORKSHOPS

Cultural activities (US$11-25) in Benito Juárez include medicinal mushroom production and preparation, cooking classes, and classes in making *pan serrano.* Unique to Benito Juárez is a trip to the farm of **Señor Eli** (US$25), a local farmer who invites visitors to spend a day with him and his family, learning the ins and outs of daily agrarian life in the Pueblos Mancomunados and preparing a traditional meal of *mole de gallina criolla* (creole hen *mole*). Guides from Expediciones Sierra Norte can translate. Always call ahead to plan cultural activities.

Food

In the small town center, **Comedor Alcatraz** and **Comedor Del Pueblo** (across the street from the ecotourism office) have you covered until around 8pm. There is also a **cafeteria** (8am-4pm daily, US$3) at the *mirador,* for lunch with a view.

TROUT HATCHERIES

From the ecotourism office, walk down the street past the basketball court and take a right. On the next corner is the **Comedor de Truchas Mi Ranchito** (My Little Ranch Trout Hatchery and Restaurant; tel. 951/953-9006, 8am-8pm daily, US$5), serving fresh trout hatched on-site. Try the *trucha al ajillo* (garlic trout).

the suspension bridge at Benito Juárez

Getting There

Drivers who aren't in a hurry can take the scenic route from Teotitlán del Valle, which is 29 km (18 mi) east of Oaxaca City via Highway 190. About a half hour after leaving the city, take the turnoff to Teotitlán del Valle and pass through town. This road, Avenida Benito Juárez, is unpaved north of Teotitlán, where it begins to wind up the southern slopes of the Sierra Norte. Benito Juárez is 20 km (12.4 mi) from Teotitlán, about an hour's drive up the mountain. From Cuajimoloyas, it's about 15 minutes away. Head south on Highway 17 2.5 km (1.5 mi) and take the signed turn to the right. Benito Juárez is another 3.5 km (2.2 mi) down the dirt road.

By public transport, the best way to get here from Oaxaca City is to arrive at Cuajimoloyas; from there you can organize transport at the ecotourism office. The trip costs about US$15, so it is more economical for groups of three or four. The best way to get around up here is on foot, so I recommend bringing only what you can carry in a backpack and taking the **Ruta Needa-Yaa-Lagashxi** from Cuajimoloyas to Benito Juárez on foot. The walk takes about two hours.

LA NEVERÍA

With a population of only 200 people, **La Nevería** (elevation 2,700 m/8,858 ft) is one of the smallest of the Pueblos Mancomunados. Set in the cradle of a small valley surrounded by oak- and pine-forested peaks, it gets its name (Ice House) from the intense cold that used to come with winters at the turn of the 20th century. The weather fostered the production of ice that was delivered on donkeys to the capital. Although the effects of climate change have caused average temperatures here and elsewhere in the Sierra Norte to rise, winter temperatures still flirt closely with freezing, so pack accordingly.

Follow the sign as you enter town to get to the **ecotourism office** (Hidalgo 1, tel. 951/507-5358, 9am-8pm daily). It's in the local government building next to the basketball court.

Recreation

HIKING

Ask in the ecotourism office about the **Recorrido de Plantas Medicinales** (Medicinal Plant Route), a guided tour (US$15, 4 hrs) through the forests north of town, which abound in orchids, bromeliads, and an array of plants used in traditional medicine in the Sierra Norte. Your guide will tell you the names of the plants, as well as how they are used to treat medical conditions.

There is also a hike to a waterfall on the **Río Las Guacamayas** (Macaw River) north of town, which is about 5 meters (16 ft) tall. The return to town passes through fields of beans, peas, mustard greens, and other crops; cultivated fields of big, bright calla lilies, gladiolas, geraniums, and daisies; and apple and hawthorn tree orchards. This easy 7-km (4.3-mi) hike takes about two hours. If you take the tour with the English-speaking guides from Expediciones Sierra Norte, the excursion includes a delicious meal in the community restaurant before the trek.

ZIP LINES AND OBSTACLE COURSE

For a bit of action and physical challenge, ask in the ecotourism office about the **zip line** and **obstacle course** (juegos de destreza). At 200 meters (656 ft) long, it's one of the shorter zip lines in the Pueblos Mancomunados, and it'll cost you only about US$6. The obstacle course, strung 3 meters (10 ft) up in the trees, costs about US$10.

CULTURAL WORKSHOPS AND VOLUNTEER OPPORTUNITIES

You'll find tortilla making and organic cooking classes, but what stands out in La Nevería are the agricultural tours and workshops. You can **tour the greenhouses** (US$15) where locals cultivate berros (watercress), an herb that is often served with tlayudas (large tortillas topped with meat and cheese) in other parts of the state. This tour also visits fields of maize and beans, as well as a reforestation area.

To gain a deeper knowledge of the farming and sustainability practices here, you can arrange to **volunteer with local farmers** in the fields and greenhouses. Locals will need to plan for this, so call ahead (it's easiest to call the Expediciones Sierra Norte office in Oaxaca City, tel. 951/514-8271 or 951/206-4531) and make sure everyone is ready upon your arrival.

Food
COMMUNITY RESTAURANT

Next to the *cabañas,* the *restaurante comunitario* (community restaurant) serves delicious regional recipes, the most notable of which are the *tortitas de berro* (US$3), a kind of fritter made with locally grown, organic watercress, served with beans, tortillas, and a fresh salad and salsa. The restaurant usually closes around 8pm, but it's always a good idea to let them know when you plan on eating dinner, to be sure they don't close earlier due to lack of diners.

Getting There

La Nevería is 8 km (5 mi) west of Benito Juárez. Drivers head south from the ecotourism office in Benito Juárez, past the basketball court, and follow the signage down the

unnamed dirt road to La Nevería. The drive takes a little over 20 minutes.

Get to La Nevería from Benito Juárez on foot via the **Ruta Needa-Queta-Miru.** The walk takes about two hours. You can also arrange transport in the ecotourism office in Benito Juárez (US$15 for up to four people).

LATUVI

At 2,400 meters (7,874 ft) above sea level, **Latuvi** ("rolled leaf" in Zapotec; pop. 1,150) is the gateway community to the even lower towns of Lachatao and Amatlán to the north. Spread along the top of a ridge descending from the higher elevations, the town is generally warmer and sunnier than the often cloud-veiled towns to the south. This is the southern trailhead for the famed Camino Real, a trail believed to be part of a longer pre-Hispanic commercial route that connected the Valles Centrales with communities near the Gulf of Mexico.

You'll find the **ecotourism office** (tel. 951/506-7903, lat_eco@hotmail.com, 9am-8pm daily) down the hill from the elementary school, on the second rise of paved road in town as you enter from the south.

the waterfall at Río Las Guacamayas, north of La Nevería

Sights and Recreation
EL MOLCAJETE

In the valley on the east side of town, the waters of the Río Cara de León (Lion's Face River) have perforated the rocks over millions of years to form the waterfalls called **El Molcajete,** named for the classic Mexican mortar and pestle. An English-speaking local guide (US$15 for up to seven people) can take you there, telling local history and legends, as well as explaining the various flora and fauna along the way. The tour can take 3-5 hours, depending on your preference, and it makes a stop at a *truchería* for a trout lunch. The toughest part of this moderately difficult 10-km (6.2-mi) hike is the uphill return to Latuvi, so conserve your energy for the end.

OTHER HIKES

You'll find the trailhead to the **Ruta Camino Real** to the right at the bottom of the hill from the ecotourism office. From here, the towns of Lachatao and Amatlán are about four hours away.

Locally, you can take the **Ruta El Manzanal** (Apple Orchard Route); the trailhead is to the left at the bottom of the aforementioned hill. Aside from the trail's namesake, you'll also pass through orchards of apricot trees and fields of corn, beans, and other crops until you reach the Río Guacamayas. Here, you can stop in at the *truchería* El Manzanal and enjoy a meal of fresh trout and locally grown veggies. A guided tour (US$15 for up to seven people) can be arranged in the ecotourism office.

The **Ruta Piedra del Corredor** (Runner's Stone Route) is a great hike for observing the various bromeliads, cacti, orchids, and other flowering plants that thrive in this region. It also passes through a forest called Las Canteras (The Quarries), where ghostly white mosses cover the oak trees.

MOUNTAIN BIKING

You can also take a bike on the **Ruta El Manzanal** or just pedal around the surrounding hills. Bike rentals at the ecotourism office cost about US$15 a day. Call ahead to arrange and ensure that the equipment is ready when you arrive.

CULTURAL WORKSHOPS

Local fruit farmers invite visitors to join them for a day in the fields. They offer **workshops** (US$20 for up to four people) on sustainable farming, fruit picking, and making jam. If you're going to be in town in the latter half of July, inquire about the exact dates of the **Feria de la Manzana** (Apple Fair), which hosts agricultural workshops, guided apple orchard tours, mountain biking excursions, live music, and lots and lots of delicious food.

Those interested in traditional alcoholic beverages should plan a visit with **Señora Julia,** a local producer of *tepache,* made from fermented pineapple rinds, and *pulque,* a fermented beverage made from maguey. She offers demonstrations (US$20 for up to four people) on the production processes and tastings of these low-alcohol drinks.

Latuvi is also a great place to do a *temazcal* (US$27), a traditional pre-Hispanic sweat bath. As with all cultural activities here, arrange everything with Expediciones Sierra Norte before your arrival.

Food

Across the street from the ecotourism office, **Comedor Doña Rosa** serves flavorful and healthy meals. Rosa likes to offer fresh fruit with her set meals (US$3), which were some of the best I had in the Pueblos Mancomunados. She usually closes up shop around 8pm.

TROUT HATCHERIES

Take just about any road down the eastern slope of the ridge from town and you'll find one of a number of *trucherías* that all serve delicious trout-based meals. They don't really have set hours. As long as the folks are up, they'll cook you a fish. Don't be unreasonably late, though. I was head over heels for the spicy *trucha a la diabla* (devil's trout) I had at **Cara de León** (Lion's Face) on my way out to see the waterfalls.

Getting There

Latuvi is 11 km (6.8 mi) north of Benito Juárez. Drivers head north from the ecotourism office and take Avenida Benito Juárez, the unmarked road that descends to the left at the first fork you see. Stick to this main road and you'll get here in about a half hour. Transportation arranged in the ecotourism office costs US$15 for up to four people.

Walk to Latuvi from Benito Juárez via the **Circuito Taurino Mecinas Ceballos** (12 km/7.4 mi), a relatively easy, mostly downhill walk that takes a little over two hours. With an elevation change of almost 600 meters (1,968 ft), it is a great way to observe the changes in vegetation at different altitudes in this part of the Sierra Norte. If your luggage permits, you could also rent a bike in Benito Juárez (US$15/day) to make the trip. Just make sure to arrange this ahead of time.

From La Nevería, walk the 10.9-km (6.8-mi) **Ruta Cipriano Cabrera,** which will get you to Latuvi in 2.5 hours or so, or take a bike down the second section of the **Circuito Taurino Mecinas Ceballos.**

LACHATAO

Lachatao definitely lives up to its name, which means "enchanted valley" or "enchanted plain" in Zapotec. At 2,200 meters (7,218 ft) above sea level, it is one of the lowest towns in the Pueblos Mancomunados. This quaint valley town stands out for its attractive, colonial-style cobblestone streets and colorfully painted adobe houses.

The **ecotourism office** (tel. 951/517-6058, ecoturlachatao@hotmail.com, 9am-8pm daily) is in a charming brick and adobe house to the south of the church in the center of town.

Sights

TEMPLO DE SANTA CATARINA DE ALEJANDRÍA

At the center of town, the baroque **Templo de Santa Catarina de Alejandría** was built

at the behest of Dominican friars in the 17th century. The gold-plated altarpieces and *retablos* depicting the martyrdom of Saint Catherine of Alexandria are in very good condition. The town celebrates its patron saint on November 25 with religious processions, music, and plenty of food.

COMMUNITY MUSEUM

To the left of the church facade, the **community museum** (*museo comunitario*; 9am-5pm, free admission) is the town's way of connecting with its history and sharing it with others. The museum divides the history of Lachatao into four stages, beginning with an exhibit of carved stone and other pre-Hispanic artifacts from the region. The next exhibit focuses on the colonial period, with a small collection of 16th-century religious paintings and baroque sculptures. A photo of Benito Juárez is the principal piece in the section concerning the Reform Era of the mid-19th century; turn-of-the-20th-century radios, wall telephones, sewing machines, and a cannon make up the final period represented in the museum, the Mexican Revolution. All signage is in Spanish.

EX-HACIENDA CINCO SEÑORES

The **Ex-Hacienda Cinco Señores** is another place in Lachatao to steep yourself in Mexican history. Built in 1750, it was once home to Faustino Díaz, father of infamous dictator and native Oaxacan Porfirio Díaz. Later, in the mid-19th century, hacienda owner Miguel Castro gave refuge to Margarita Maza de Juárez, wife of Benito Juárez, during his two-year exile to Cuba and New Orleans. And it finally ended up in the hands of Díaz's brother Felix in the last decades of that century. You'll have to book a tour (US$15 for up to four people) through the ecotourism office to visit. Book early to request an English-speaking guide. The tour will take you back to the village's colonial period, when it was a small but bustling mining community.

Recreation

HIKING

The local hike **Las Minas** has an interesting cultural theme to it. It takes you west of town, across the Río El Arco (Arch River) via a centuries-old limestone bridge, to the defunct mines La Escopeta (Shotgun) and El Águila (Eagle). Your guide (US$15 for up to four people) will discuss the history of gold and silver mining here, which dates as far back as pre-Hispanic times, and you can even enter one of the old mines. It's an interesting way to experience the history of the mining industry and to reflect on the ecological, economic, and social consequences of it and other businesses that exploit land and people for financial gain.

CULTURAL WORKSHOPS

The local *curandera* invites visitors to learn about the various medical uses of local plants, roots, and leaves—ancestral knowledge that dates back to pre-Hispanic times. She doesn't speak English, but guides (US$15 for up to four people) from the ecotourism office can translate. She also performs massages, *limpias,* and *temazcal* sweat baths (US$11-15). Her house is across the street from the ecotourism office.

Food

Your best food option in town is at the **community restaurant** in the western end of the museum building. A local specialty here is *mole chichilo,* a rich, dark *mole* of a soupier consistency than its six Oaxacan siblings. It gets its dark color from the mixture of smoked peppers such as *pasilla, guajillo,* and the rarer *chile chilhuacle,* as well as from its most interesting ingredient, charred and ground-up corn tortillas. It is usually served with pork and often with small balls of cornmeal called *chochoyotes. Comedores* don't always have everything on the menu, so if you're set on trying this dish, call ahead and have the folks at the ecotourism office make plans for the meal before your arrival.

Getting There

Get to Lachatao on foot from Latuvi in about four hours via the **Ruta Camino Real.** Get here from either Cuajimoloyas or Llano Grande via the **Ruta Yaa-Tini;** you'll find the turnoff to the Ruta Yaa-Tini about halfway (4 km/2.5 mi) between Cuajimoloyas and Llano Grande on the Ruta Latzi-Hroo-Lii. Plan ahead, however, as this route connecting the highest and lowest elevations in the Pueblos Mancomunados can take as long as five hours. Transport arranged by the ecotourism offices can cost up to US$32 for up to four people, so it is really an option for groups.

Experienced cyclists can take the **Ruta Ka-Yezzi-Daa-Vii** from either Cuajimoloyas or Llano Grande. Call ahead to arrange rentals (US$15/day) and/or a guide (US$36 for up to four people) with the ecotourism office in Oaxaca City or in your starting point to ensure everything is ready when you arrive.

From Oaxaca City, drivers take Highway 190 4 km (2.5 mi) east from the Centro and take a left onto Highway 175 at the Benito Juárez Monument. Head north 53 km (33 mi) until you see the turnoff to Amatlán and Lachatao, just before a bridge over the Río Yavesía. Lachatao is another 11 km (6.8 mi) down the unnamed dirt road, through distractingly beautiful vistas of green valleys, steep and rocky canyons, and picturesque hilltop chapels. Total drive time is just under two hours. You'll pass through Amatlán, and there's a good chance you'll get lost or be unsure of where to go in town, as there is little signage about which road to take to get to Lachatao. You can always ask a friendly local if you're headed in the right direction or not. Lachatao is 1.5 km (0.9 mi) south of Amatlán.

If you're driving from Latuvi, take Avenida Benito Juárez north until it hits Highway 175. Turn north onto the highway and make the turn at the river about 15 km (9.3 mi) up the road. This route takes about an hour.

AMATLÁN

The Nahuatl name **Amatlán** means "place of the *amate* tree," a type of ficus with alien-like roots that grow like tentacles sunk in earth or wrapped threateningly over huge boulders. The bark of this tree was used in pre-Hispanic times to make paper. The town's name in Zapotec, Yagaa-Tzi, means "yellow tree" in English, an allusion to the *encino amarillo*. This species of oak endemic to Mexico has yellowish hairs on the undersides of the leaves and is also abundant in and around town.

At 2,000 meters (6,562 ft) above sea level, Amatlán has the lowest elevation of the Pueblos Mancomunados, and it's no surprise that the names for the town are inspired by trees. Warmer temperatures at this altitude, combined with the humid air from the Gulf of Mexico, foster a broad variety of floral diversity, and orchids, bromeliads, mosses, and wild magueys thrive in this northernmost part of the Pueblos Mancomunados.

The **ecotourism office** (tel. 951/189-0453, ecoturismoamatlan@hotmail.com, 9am-8pm daily) is perched on a ridge on the north side of town, about 350 meters (1,148 ft) up the road from the church and government building.

Sights

Just down the street from the church is the **community museum** (*museo comunitario;* 9am-5pm, free admission), where you can learn the pre-Hispanic and colonial history of Amatlán, as well as the history of the formation of the Pueblos Mancomunados, which were officially delineated in 1961. Although the original is now in the National Anthropology Museum in Mexico City, you can see a copy of the 17th-century Códice San Lucas Yataú, a pictographic account of the pre-Hispanic history of the town, painted in oil on a piece of cloth.

Recreation

HIKING

As in Lachatao, gold and silver mining were once big business in Amatlán, and the **Ruta La Vida del Minero** (Life of the Miner Route) will take you back through that history. After passing through a verdant path of bromeliad-laden yellow oaks and patches of wild-growing medicinal plants, you'll stop at the Mirador Loma Amarilla (Yellow Hill Lookout Point), where you take in the view of the town and observe a natural spring that flows into the Río Papaloapan. Finally, you'll stop by an old mine that you can enter if you're on the guided tour (US$15 for up to seven people). The 200-meter (656-ft) tunnel still shows the open veins where miners extracted the precious metals over a century ago. This moderately difficult, 7-km (4.3-mi) hike takes about 2.5 hours.

An interesting trek offered here is a **guided nighttime hike** (US$15 for up to seven people) around town, in which you'll observe and identify the various bat species that call Amatlán home.

MOUNTAIN BIKING

You can also rent a bicycle (US$15/day) to explore the surrounding countryside and old architecture. On the south side of town, you can visit old haciendas like El Socorro (Help), which was built in 1827. Keep heading south until you find the trails that follow the banks of the Río El Arco. They're a good way to see the rich biodiversity of the region.

CULTURAL WORKSHOPS

Cultural workshops (US$10-23 for up to four people) available in Amatlán include cooking classes, embroidery demonstrations and classes with local women artisans, mushroom cultivation, organic farming, and artisanal bread-baking courses. Local *curanderas* offer massages, *limpias*, and *temazcal* sweat baths (US$27).

Food

Like nearby Lachatao, Amatlán is a great place to try *mole chichilo*, much rarer than the traditional *moles negro* (black), *amarillo* (yellow), and *coloradito* (red), which are also regional delights. Give them a try in the *comedor* next to the ecotourism office. As with other gastronomic and cultural services in the Pueblos Mancomunados, it's not guaranteed that the restaurant will be serving something like *mole chichilo* every day. If you are set on tasting it, which I highly recommend, call ahead and plan a meal or cooking class before you trek up the mountains.

Getting There

Amatlán is the northern terminus of the **Ruta Camino Real,** which will get you here on foot from Latuvi in about four hours, as well as the **Ruta Yaa-Tini,** which will get you here from Llano Grande or Cuajimoloyas in around five hours. The ecotourism cooperative will organize transport from the other villages for you, but it can cost as much as US$33 for up to four people, so it is more economical if you have a small group, if you don't want to travel on foot.

Drivers from Oaxaca City can take the same route via Highway 175 to get to both Amatlán and Lachatao. Take Highway 190 4 km (2.5 mi) east from the Centro and take a left onto Highway 175 at the Benito Juárez Monument. Head north 53 km (33 mi) until you see the turnoff to Amatlán and Lachatao, just before a bridge over the Río Yavesía. Amatlán is another 9.5 km (5.9 mi) down the unnamed dirt road, just before Lachatao. Total drive time is just under two hours.

If you're driving from Latuvi, take Avenida Benito Juárez north until it hits Highway 175. Turn north onto the highway and make the turn at the river about 15 km (9.3 mi) up the road. This route takes about an hour.

Sierra Juárez

The middle section of the Sierra Norte, which includes the Pueblos Mancomunados, is referred to regionally as the Sierra Juárez because it is home to the birthplace of legendary 19th-century president Benito Juárez. This route, up Highway 175 from Oaxaca City, is one of the most scenic routes in the whole state, with views that will have you rubbernecking around every curve. As you wind through tight tunnels of pine and oak trees, visibility is often limited to a mere couple of meters when dense clouds cloak the entire mountainside. The experience is made more surreal when the highway rises above the mantle of vapor, and the breathtaking phenomenon of thermal inversion pushes the wet air of the Gulf of Mexico down to lower elevations, filling the valley below with the spectacular *mar de nubes* (sea of clouds).

IXTLÁN DE JUÁREZ

In Nahuatl, the name Ixtlán means "place of the maguey fibers," and the town's Zapotec name, Laa Yetzi, means "thick leaf" or "maguey leaf." It later became **Ixtlán de Juárez** to honor Oaxaca's worthiest citizen, Benito Juárez, who was born in the small town of Guelatao, just 4 km (2.5 mi) down the road.

The forests around this part of the Sierra Norte are so biologically rich and diverse that they have earned Mexico a spot among the 17 megadiverse countries in the world, as identified by the U.S.-based nonprofit Conservation International. A trip to this part of Oaxaca feels like a visit to another world.

The office of the local ecotourism organization **Ecoturixtlán** (corner of 20 de Noviembre and Calzada de la Eternidad, tel. 951/553-6075, ecoturixtlan@hotmail.com, 7am-8pm daily) is one block south of the main square, just to the east of the church. They administer the nearby nature park and operate tours to cloud forests, *miradores*, and other sights around Ixtlán de Juárez.

Sights
TEMPLO DE SANTO TOMÁS APÓSTOL
Just across the street from the main square, you'll see a clock tower made of *cantera verde,*

or green (very green) limestone, in the courtyard outside the **Templo de Santo Tomás Apóstol.** This churrigueresque (a type of baroque architectural style) cathedral is lavishly adorned inside and out with finely detailed statues and flourishes in the facade, and large, elaborate, gold-plated altarpieces shining inside the dome-topped nave. Since it's across the street from the ecotourism office, you can quickly stop by to admire the architecture before leaving town to explore.

★ PARQUE ECOTURIXTLÁN

Just 5 km (3.1 mi) east of town, **Parque Ecoturixtlán** (tel. 951/553-6075, ecoturixtlan@hotmail.com, 9am-5pm daily) is the perfect alpine getaway, whether for just the afternoon (US$1 day access) or for a day or two with an overnight stay camping or in one of their *cabañas*. Don't miss both ends of the **Gruta El Arco,** a cave that cuts over 150 meters (492 ft) from one side of a mountain to the other and is home to a number of bat species as well as large gulps of swallows.

Head up the hill from the park office, past the family-size *cabañas*, to get to the *orquideario* (orchid garden), where park employees work to conserve these fantastical flowers. I was told that the best time of year to see them bloom in this part of the Sierra Norte is in April and May, but I still saw some bright yellow, octopus-faced blooms in November.

The park has numerous hiking trails and a bike route that wend through this impressively biodiverse region. It is easy to fill a day or two exploring the countryside. Aside from orchids, you'll find a variety of bromeliads, tree ferns, parlor palms, mosses, lichens, fungi, and many other examples of the region's 6,000 plant species.

Recreation
HIKING

For a shorter hike just outside of town, ask in the ecotourism office about the trip to the **Cerro de Cuachirindoo** (US$15 for up to four people, 3 hrs). This hike (8 km/5 mi round-trip) takes you up the hill north of town, stopping at a monument to the Zapotec warriors Juppa and Cuachirindoo, who fought valiantly against the Aztecs when they invaded Oaxaca just before the Spanish did. The tour then proceeds to a *mirador* that offers an impressive view of the town below. This tour can also be done in a vehicle (US$24 for up to four people, 1.5 hrs).

A trip to the **bosque mesófilo** (cloud forest) north of town is another unforgettable experience in nature. Often shrouded in dense clouds, the oak trees are dripping with wraithlike mosses that add to the forest's eerie, fantastical atmosphere. The tour, which takes seven hours on foot (US$25 for up to four people) or three hours in a car (US$29 for up to four people), is capped off by a visit to the **Mirador Shiaa Rua Via,** a lookout point 3,125 meters (10,253 ft) above sea level. From here, on a clear day you'll be able to see the Pico de Orizaba, Mexico's highest peak, over 200 km (124 mi) to the northwest in the state of Puebla. But don't worry: If there are clouds, there's a good chance you'll be above them, in awe of the Sierra Norte's *mar de nubes*.

Visitors to Parque Ecoturixtlán shouldn't leave without taking a tour to the **bosque de bromelias** (bromeliad forest), where these exotic, tree-climbing cousins of the pineapple are so abundant that you might witness one or two fall off of branches they outgrew. The 6-km (3.7-mi) walk takes about two hours and costs around US$10 for one person. Add another US$2.50 or so for each person in your group.

MOUNTAIN BIKING

Ecoturixtlán rents **mountain bikes** (US$5/hr) for use within the park. Besides the roads within the park, a bike path heads downhill from the park office and runs through the forests behind the *cabañas*, coming out on the road near the forest conservation area. At just over a half kilometer (0.3 mi), the trail is more of a jaunt than a serious ride, but the scenery is gorgeous and the other roads in the park provide enough track for a full afternoon of riding and exploring.

ZIP LINE

The **zip line** at Ecoturixtlán shoots 200 meters (656 ft) from a tower atop a hill above the western entrance to the caves, going through the treetops and over the obstacle course 29 meters (95 ft) below. A quick zip will cost you only US$3.

RAPELLING

Park staff also have all the equipment necessary to rappel down a 28-meter (92-ft) cliff within the park. Staff are well trained, and the equipment is all in good condition. A *bajada* (trip down) costs about US$6.

OBSTACLE COURSE

Test your balance and nerve on the park's **obstacle course** (*juegos de destreza*), built 3 meters (10 ft) up in the trees. Hop, hang, and swing your way from tree to tree, trying not to fall. But don't worry: The park has harnesses and helmets to make sure that one missed step isn't your last. A trip through the course costs US$2.50.

Food

If you're staying out in the *cabañas* in the ecotourism park, you can have breakfast or lunch at **Restaurante Los Duendes** (The Spirits [or Imps] Restaurant; 9am-5pm daily, US$3). However, for dinner, you'll have to head into town. If you don't have your own wheels, you can arrange transport with park staff in the office.

Ixtlán de Juárez has some rather mouthwatering options come mealtime. A must-eat here is ★ **Restaurante de la Calzada** (corner of Calzada La Eternidad and Francisco Villa, tel. 951/553-6225, 7am-5pm Mon.-Sat., 7am-1pm Sun., US$3), whose slogan says it all: *El Sazón de Mamá* (Mom's Flavor). Whether it's eggs for breakfast, a chile relleno for lunch, or a *tlayuda* for dinner, everything here has that special ingredient that only a mother can add to a recipe: love. And lots of it. The full flavor of the fresh, locally produced ingredients comes out in each dish, and the setting, in a quaintly decorated room and part

of the patio of the family home, is a pleasant place to enjoy such a meal. You'll find it on the Calzada La Eternidad, a block south from the church.

Later at night, you can count on **Taquería La Familia** (16 de Septiembre, no phone, 3pm-midnight daily, US$3) for some grade A *tacos al pastor* (made with seasoned pork flame-broiled on a vertical spit). If you're tired of tacos (crazy, I know, but it happens), try one of their baked potatoes topped with *al pastor* pork, *quesillo* (Oaxacan string cheese), and other fresh fixings like pineapple and *pico de gallo* (spicy garnish of tomatoes, onions, and chiles).

The taxi trip (US$3) out to ★ **Truchería Cuachirindoo** (tel. 951/157-7160, 9:30am-6pm daily, US$6), a trout hatchery 3.5 km (2.2 mi) north of town, is worth the trip. Their alfresco dining area perched on a hillside, a perfect position for being wowed by the sunset, is one of the most pleasant settings I found in the Sierra Norte. The trout cooked in aluminum foil with mushrooms and *quesillo* ranks high on my unofficial list of best meals in Oaxaca.

Accommodations
CABAÑAS

Parque Ecoturixtlán is home to the most luxurious *cabañas* (US$27 d) I've found in my multiple explorations of the Sierra Norte. The group of duplex-style *cabañas* down by the park office and restaurant are for one to two people, and each boasts a comfortable king-size bed, fireplace, bathroom with hot water (that works!), and shared patio space. White stones line the pathways between the structures, and ground lights fetchingly brighten the way after the sun goes down. Contact Ecoturixtlán to make reservations.

CAMPING

Parque Ecoturixtlán has three **campgrounds.** You can pitch a tent (US$2.50 pp) in the small field next to the obstacle course and small suspension bridge, though the other two sites are more inviting. You'll find

Best Camping in the Sierra Norte

Just about any town with an ecotourism sign in the Sierra Norte will allow you to pitch a tent somewhere close by, but not all campgrounds are created equal. Here is a handful of the most attractive spots to camp that I have come across in this beautiful part of Oaxaca.

Llano de Tarajeas (Cuajimoloyas), US$5

About 4 km (2.5 mi) down the mountain from Cuajimoloyas, this campground in a clearing in the pine forest is the perfect choice for large groups. Water from the nearby babbling brook is diverted to fill the tanks of the on-site trout hatchery, and the *comedor* will cook them up for you in delicious ways. There are also grills for cooking your own meals, playsets for the kids, dry toilets, and access to a number of great trails that wind through the Pueblos Mancomunados. Contact **Expediciones Sierra Norte** (M. Bravo 210-A, Oaxaca City, tel. 951/514-8271 or 951/206-4531, www.sierranorte.org.mx, sierranorteoaxaca@gmail.com) or stop by the ecotourism office in Cuajimoloyas to reserve a spot.

Parque Ecoturixtlán (Ixtlán de Juárez), US$2.50

Parque Ecoturixtlán, just outside of Ixtlán de Juárez, has three campgrounds, the best of which is in a clearing next to the river, a quick walk away from the eastern end of the Gruta El Arco, whose waters join the river next to the site. From here, trails lead in every direction through patches of bright red and purple wildflowers and stands of pines and oaks covered in bromeliads. Contact the **Ecoturixtlán office** (corner of 20 de Noviembre and Calzada de la Eternidad, Ixtlán de Juárez, tel. 951/553-6075, ecoturixtlan@hotmail.com, 7am-8pm daily) to make reservations.

Balneario Monte Flor, US$5

Although the *cabañas* here are some of the nicest and cutest I found roaming the north of Oaxaca, Balneario Monte Flor has lots of room in the shade of the ficus trees on the riverbank to post up for the night. Make sure to ask about a bathroom, and they'll leave the restaurant bathroom unlocked for you. There are no grills here, but the *balneario* (swimming hole) is right in the small town, which has *comedores* and taco stands. Call the **managers,** Rodolfo and

the second nestled among the towering pines below the official conservation zone about a half kilometer (0.3 mi) down the main road. Continue down this road to get to the prime camping real estate next to the river at the bottom of the gorge. All three have access to dry toilets. From here you'll have quick access to a number of trails leading into the surrounding forest, as well as the eastern opening of the Gruta El Arco, through which water flows to meet with the main river next to the campgrounds. Contact Ecoturixtlán to make reservations.

IN IXTLÁN

It's definitely not the same aesthetic experience as staying in the park, but the **Hotel La Soledad** (Hotel Solitude; Calle Francisco Javier Mina, tel. 951/553-6171, US$13 d) will save you some money and give you easier access to the food and services in town. The rooms are garishly lit and free of any frills beyond a TV set, but the hot water works and there's space for parking. From the church, walk west on Avenida Campos and take the second left to get here.

Getting There

From Oaxaca City, drivers take Highway 190 4 km (2.5 mi) east from the Centro and take a left onto Highway 175 at the Benito Juárez Monument. From here it's 59 km (37 mi) up this scenic and snaking road to Ixtlán. Total travel time from Oaxaca City is about 1.5 hours.

You can also get to Ixtlán from Oaxaca City via *colectivo* (US$2.50) from the Benito Juárez Monument. Look for the taxis from

a star-filled night in the Sierra Norte

Yolanda Inocente (tel. 283/132-4840), to reserve a spot, or just show up and ask around town for them if they aren't around.

Nindo-Da-Gé Caves, US$3

Spend the night with the open maw of the Nindo-Da-Gé cave system on one side and a breathtaking view of the Sierra Mazateca on the other at this campsite just a half hour from Huautla de Jiménez. You'll have to sacrifice services like a toilet, but if you don't have problems going au naturel, you'll have a pleasant evening in the outdoors. Contact Raúl Betanzas, owner of **El Rincón de la Trucha** (tel. 553/669-9396), to get information about camping here.

Sitio Laa-Yetzi. With frequent stops along the way, this mode of transportation takes around two hours.

CAPULÁLPAM DE MÉNDEZ

Probably the prettiest town in the Sierra Norte, **Capulálpam de Méndez** gleams on its perch on a sunny mountaintop 10 km (6.2 mi) east of Ixtlán de Juárez. The cobblestone streets and 16th-century Templo de San Mateo are built of luminous *cantera amarilla* (yellow limestone) that looks like bricks of hardened sunlight. The houses, hotels, and restaurants boast vividly painted adobe walls, wavy red clay roof tiles, and enough spectacular views of the valley below to earn it a designation as a Pueblo Mágico (Magic Town) by Mexico's secretary of tourism.

Capulálpam is more than just a pretty face, though. From hiking to climbing to cultural walking tours, there's lots more to do here than take in the view. Stop by the **ecotourism office** (tel. 951/539-2168 and 558/441-3285, contacto@turismocapulalpam.com, 8am-8pm daily) at the northwest corner of the charming main square, just behind the church.

Walking Tour

If the quaint, colorful architecture of Capulálpam enchants you, ask in the ecotourism office about a tour called **Descubriendo Capulálpam** (Discovering Capulálpam; US$6), a 2.5-hour stroll through town, during which you'll stop by the **Templo de San Mateo,** with its mix of baroque and neoclassical design, and enjoy a meal in the local market. Tours don't run regularly but

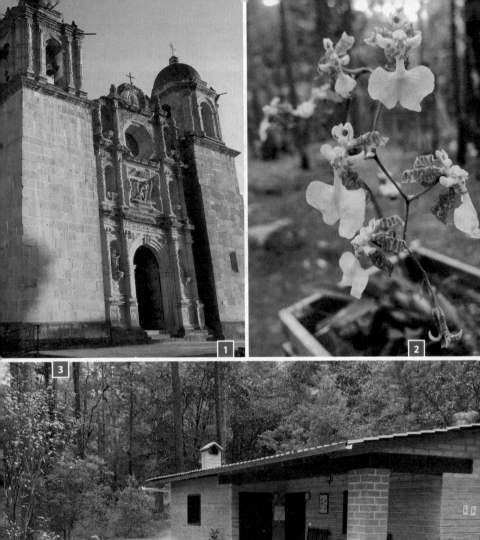

are offered on demand, so make sure to call ahead to make arrangements, especially if you need an English-speaking guide. You can inquire about *temazcal*, massages, and other pre-Hispanic treatments during the stop at the **traditional medicine hospital,** and search for souvenirs in the **Taller y Galería de Juguete y Arte** (Toy and Art Workshop and Gallery). The tour's final stop is at the **Mirador El Calvario,** from which you can take in a panoramic view of this gorgeous little town.

Recreation

For a bit more adrenaline, **rent a bike** (US$7/hr) from the ecotourism office and take a ride through the surrounding pine and oak forests. They have a three-hour **biking tour** (US$11) that ends up at a swimming hole, so don't forget to bring your swimsuit. Other ecotourism options include **zip-lining** (US$2.50), **rappelling** (US$4), **rock climbing** (US$6/hr), and **hiking** the many trails.

Food and Accommodations

In town, grab breakfast, lunch, or dinner at **Comedor San Mateo** (tel. 951/300-3658, 7am-10pm daily, US$2.50), one of many inside the Mercado Municipal, a market built in 2013 on Calle Miguel Méndez, a block and a half south of the main square. If they're making *mole coloradito* when you stop by, order it. In the afternoon, head north from the main square on Miguel Méndez four blocks to **El Verbo de Méndez Café** (Emiliano Zapata 3, tel. 951/539-2045, 4pm-10pm daily, US$3). They serve Oaxacan favorites, coffee grown in the Sierra Norte, sandwiches, and crepes. Try the crepe with cream cheese and locally produced caramelized quinces.

Restaurante Los Molinos (tel. 951/539-2168, 10am-6pm Mon.-Sat., 9am-6pm Sat.-Sun., US$6), tucked in a small gorge carved out by the river of the same name, is a great place to work up an appetite rappelling or climbing on the cliff behind the restaurant, and then satisfy it with a delicious grilled trout. There's also a playground on the banks of the river for the kids.

You'll find Los Molinos about a kilometer (0.6 mi) down the road past the *cabañas* (US$25) perched on a hilltop glade a kilometer (0.6 mi) north of town. Follow the ample signage on Miguel Méndez to get here. You can pick a cabin in the sunny clearing or one tucked into the shade of the pines beyond. It doesn't get as cold at night here as in the higher elevations, but all cabins include hot water and a fireplace. Book through the ecotourism office in town.

In town, stay on the charming main square at the peach-colored **Hotel Los Sabinos** (Hidalgo 4, tel. 951/539-2154, lossabinos2014@hotmail.com, US$20 d, US$27 king bed). It has nine comfortable rooms, as well as a terrace café and restaurant for dinner or evening drinks that has a view of the square in the yellow streetlights. Rooms with king beds have street-facing balconies.

Getting There

Drivers take the picturesque route from Oaxaca City up Highway 175 to Ixtlán de Juárez (about 1.5 hrs), where you'll head east on Avenida Campos or 16 de Septiembre. Capulálpam is 10 km (6.2 mi) east of Ixtlán, a curvy and enjoyable 20-minute drive through the pines.

You can also get to Capulálpam from Oaxaca City via *colectivo*. Grab one of these shared taxis (US$3.50) at the Benito Juárez Monument, at the junction of Highways 190 and 175. The ones that go to Capulálpam are green and white. The trip takes a little over two hours. These taxis take Calle Benito Juárez through Ixtlán until it terminates at Avenida Campos, and then turn right toward Capulálpam. If they've got an empty seat, they'll take you there for about US$1. A private taxi ride will cost you US$8-10.

1: the Templo de Santo Tomás Apóstol in Ixtlán de Juárez 2: orchids blooming in Parque Ecoturixtlán 3: the comfy and spacious *cabañas* at Parque Ecoturixtlán

GUELATAO DE JUÁREZ

There are a number of towns with "de Juárez" in their name to commemorate Benito Juárez, but Guelatao de Juárez is the only one that can call itself the birthplace of the renowned Mexican statesman. The town's first name has two meanings in Zapotec: "the place where hope abounds" and "embrace power." Locals like to simply call it *Laguna Encantada* (Enchanted Lagoon), in reference to the local pond where young shepherd Benito Juárez brought his sheep to drink.

Beyond its historical significance, Guelatao rivals Capulálpam in terms of charm, with cobblestone streets, a multitiered central plaza, and the aforementioned lagoon. Just a 10-minute drive from Ixtlán, and a half hour from Capulálpam, it is perfect for a quick day trip to brush up on Mexican history. The exhibition at the **Sala Homenaje a Juárez** (Room in Homage to Juárez; main square on Avenida Juárez, no phone, 10am-5pm Tues.-Sun., free admission) tells the story of the politician's life through a series of informational plaques (in Spanish) written in first person. On display are government documents dating back to the Reform Era in the mid-19th century, as well as a collection of woodcut prints that tell a visual story of the life of this man who changed the country forever.

After the museum, make sure to check out the **statue of Juárez** in the seated position in which he is usually depicted in statues in Mexico. He sits in the lowest level of the main square, to the north of the museum. The text above the fountain to the right of the statue is part of Juárez's most famous quotation. It reads: "Respect for the rights of others is peace." From here, head up the stairs on the east side of the plaza and stop by the **Laguna Encantada,** where Benito's humble beginnings as a shepherd are memorialized in a statue of the child with the sheep he brought here to drink from the enchanted waters of the pond.

Getting There

Guelatao de Juárez is 4 km (2.5 mi) south of Ixtlán de Juárez on Highway 175. Drivers have an easy 10-minute trip from the center of Ixtlán. If you're coming from Oaxaca City, you'll see the sign just before Ixtlán.

Take a private taxi (US$6) from the center of Ixtlán or wait for a southbound *colectivo* (US$0.50) on Highway 175 next to the gas station and entrance archway to Ixtlán. Keep an eye out for the Guelatao sign about five minutes down the road. The museum is just two blocks from the highway.

LLANO DE LAS FLORES

North of Ixtlán, Highway 175 climbs back up into chillier elevations, passing below, through, and above vast clouds that in the winter months collect in the valleys to form the *mar de nubes*. The day I visited **Llano de las Flores** (elevation 3,000 m/9,842 ft), fog shrouded the horses grazing in the fields just beyond the *cabañas*, lending a pleasantly spooky vibe to the whole scene. Despite its location right off the highway, the broad valley feels worlds away from roaring cargo trucks and speeding taxis.

Llano de las Flores is a much less-visited ecotourism spot in the Sierra Norte, so it's a good idea to call the **ecotourism office** (tel. 951/528-9086 and 951/528-9049 to plan activities before you arrive. Of course, there is that Sierra Norte ecotourism staple, the **zip line** (US$3), but this is one of the tallest in the region, a vertigo-inducing 180 meters (590 ft) high. However, as you'll notice when you enter the valley, the main attraction is **horseback riding** (US$7/hr). Guides will take you around to a number of local sites, such as a series of caves, a vine-strung tree locals call the *árbol de Tarzán* (Tarzan's tree), a wishing well, and finally, a *mirador* on the highest peak in the area. Only Spanish-speaking guides are available.

Llano de las Flores has six *cabañas* (US$22 d) with hot water and fireplaces for the foggy, chilly nights. There's also lots of room to set up a tent and **camp** for the

---

1: Capulálpam de Méndez's main plaza 2: the Laguna Encantada in Guelatao de Juárez

night, which will cost you about US$2.50 if you bring your own, and another US$5 if you need to rent a tent. Llano de las Flores is more informal than other ecotourism centers in the Sierra Norte, and you can set up camp anywhere you like. You can hide away in the thick pine forests at the valley's edge or sleep out with the horses in the middle of the field if you like. Make reservations through the ecotourism office before coming to ensure everything will be ready.

Getting There

Llano de las Flores is 24 km (15 mi) north of Ixtlán de Juárez on Highway 175. Public transport travelers take any Tuxtepec-bound *colectivo* from Ixtlán (US$1.50, easiest to flag one down on the highway at the gas station) and keep an eye out for one of the three blue signs for Llano de las Flores about a half hour up the road. All three lead to the ecotourism center. Drivers might take a little longer, due to the fantastic views and photo ops along the way. Take advantage of any turnouts you can find, as you don't see these kinds of panoramic vistas every day.

El Papaloapan

Cascades of gigantic ferns blanket the steep hillsides on the northern slopes of the Sierra Norte, as altitudes drop and you get closer to the hot, humid climate of the Gulf of Mexico. You won't be needing any of the warm clothing you brought for camping up in the mountains in **El Papaloapan,** a fertile tropical lowland with cane fields, rubber tree farms, and fruit tree orchards.

Agriculture, commerce, and industry, as opposed to tourism, move the economy of this most industrialized region of the state, but there are still a few gems for those determined to see a different side of Oaxaca.

★ BALNEARIOS MONTE FLOR AND EL ZUZUL

Highway 175 drops down from the mountains at the town of Valle Nacional and follows the curves of the river of the same name all the way to Tuxtepec. As soon as you get down here, you'll want to go swimming, and you won't have to wait long. Just 15 minutes (6 km/3.7 mi) north of Valle Nacional, you'll find the Edenic **Balneario Monte Flor,** a bend of crystal-clear water in the Río Valle Nacional under the shade of green ficus trees with undulating root systems dug into the riverbanks.

You can stop by for a dip (US$0.50) or choose to spend a night in one of the gorgeous riverside *cabañas* (tel. 283/132-4840, US$25 up to four people) and fall asleep to the relaxing sound of running water. Each of the eight *cabañas* set around the main lagoon has one full bed on the ground floor and two twin beds in the upper loft area, as well as comfy front porches from which to take in the paradisiacal scene beyond. A handful of highway *comedores* and taco stands around the main square just across the highway have you covered for food.

Monte Flor is also a beautiful place to camp for a night or two. For US$5 per person, you can stay under the dense canopy of the strangler fig trees with their tentacular roots dug in the ground like alien appendages. The river runs emerald green in the shade of the trees, offering a place to cool off in the heat of the day, as well as a calming soundtrack to fall asleep to. Bring your own equipment.

Another 10 minutes farther north on Highway 175, a freshwater spring bubbles to the surface at **Balneario El Zuzul** (tel. 283/101-7247, US$1 entrance fee). You'll see the turnoff 5 km (3.1 mi) from Monte Flor. The spring has been developed into a large swimming pool, from which the crystalline waters flow through a short canal into Rió

Valle Nacional. The dark-wood *cabañas* (US$25 d) on a hill above this canal are built on stilts to protect them from the regular floods of the rainy season, which sometimes reach the decks and leave the canal and grassy riverbanks caked in a layer of mud in the rainy season. This makes the spring months the best time to visit El Zuzul, especially if you're **camping** (US$3 pp), as the park staff have had time to clean any mud away. An on-site restaurant is opening in 2020, and there are *comedores* in **Vega del Sol,** the town in which the park is located.

Getting There

Take a Tuxtepec-bound *suburban* run by **Transjuar** (Calzada Héroes de Chapultepec 801, Colonia Reforma, Oaxaca City, tel. 951/132-7227) from Oaxaca City (US$8, 5 hours) or catch one on Highway 175 from Ixtlán (US$2.50, 3.5 hours). Running hourly, the vans pass by the gas station at the entrance to Ixtlán. Keep an eye out for the Monte Flor sign about 10 minutes after passing through Valle Nacional, a little over three hours from Ixtlán. The *balneario* is to your right, a two-minute walk from the highway. El Zuzul is another 10 minutes north on the highway. There should be taxis (US$1) here to take you to the

balneario, or you could do the 2.5-km (1.5-mi) trip on foot in about 30 minutes.

Drivers head north on Highway 175 from Ixtlán. The 133-km (82-mi) stretch of highway from Ixtlán to Monte Flor will have you slack-jawed the entire way, thanks to its abundance of phenomenal vistas, eerie cloud-covered patches, and slope after slope of gigantic tree ferns. For El Zuzul, continue past Monte Flor another 5 km (3.1 mi) until you see the signs for El Zuzul and Vega del Sol. Take a right and then your first left after crossing the bridge over the river. The signage is clear and abundant, making it easy to find the place.

TUXTEPEC

Although its name means "Hill of Rabbits," you won't find too many hills in **Tuxtepec.** Oaxaca's second-largest city, with an elevation of only 20 meters (66 ft) above sea level, is centered around a pronounced bend in the Río Papaloapan, which has become quite polluted as a result of the industry that has become the base of the region's economy. For someone on vacation, there is not much to do in Tuxtepec, but if you're exploring this far north in Oaxaca, there's a good chance you'll have to spend a night here.

Like many communities in El Papaloapan,

the turquoise waters of Balneario Monte Flor

Caldo de Piedra (Stone Soup)

El Papaloapan is home to one of the most interesting pre-Hispanic dishes from Oaxaca, the *caldo de piedra,* or stone soup, a recipe of the Chinantec peoples of Veracruz and northern Oaxaca. This seafood stew, made with shrimp, fish, tomatoes, cilantro, onions, dried chiles, and a potent herb called *epazote,* is prepared by tossing the raw ingredients in a bowl, and the cooking is done by fire-heated river rocks that are dropped into the broth, bringing the water to boil. The fish, shrimp, and fresh vegetables are ready to eat in about three minutes.

caldo de piedra

Caldo de piedra is traditionally made only by men, who serve the soup to the women. The meal is a way of giving mom a break and showing gratitude for the work she does for the family. Interestingly, however, a bowl is not part of the traditional preparation method. In the town of **San Felipe Usila,** the ingredients and broth are put in a bowl-shaped hollow in a rock, or a hole dug in the sand and lined with banana leaves. Because of this, anthropologists believe this recipe predates the use of ceramics in Mexico, which by some estimates dates as far back as 2300 BC. This makes *caldo de piedra* a contender for one of the oldest traditions in Oaxaca, and possibly in the Americas.

Usila is recognized as the *cuna,* or birthplace, of this intriguing soup, but the small village is very out-of-the-way, and as a result, it has no restaurants that serve the soup. However, the **Comedor Prehispánico Caldo de Piedra** (tel. 951/517-8318, www.caldodepiedra.com, 11am-6pm daily, US$6), founded in Usila by the Gachupín Velasco family in 1996, moved to the **Valles Centrales** in 1999. You'll find this location on Highway 190, 7 km (4.3 mi) west of Oaxaca City's Centro. It's just before Tule, but don't take the Tule exit. The restaurant is about a kilometer (0.6 mi) past the Tule exit.

César Gachupín Velasco was chosen by the town council of Usila as the "ambassador" of Chinantecan stone soup to the outside world, and he and his children are doing just that, having opened a location in downtown **Oaxaca City** called **Caldo de Piedra Cocina de Origen** (corner of 5 de Mayo and Murguía, Oaxaca City, tel. 951/517-8318, 8am-11pm Mon.-Sat., 10am-11pm Sun., US$6). Although a few higher-end restaurants in downtown Oaxaca had *caldo de piedra* on the menus for a while before this one opened in 2018, I put my trust in César and his family, who have dedicated their lives to conserving and promoting this fun and caring gastronomic tradition that dates back thousands of years.

Tuxtepec's patron saint is Saint John the Baptist, who is celebrated on July 24. May is another good month for festivals here. The **Fiestas de Mayo** (May Parties) begin with a carnival-style parade through town. During these and other national and local festivals, you're likely to see Tuxtepec's **Flor de Piña (Pineapple Flower) dance,** which is always a hit at the Guelaguetza, a festival that celebrates regional cultures.

Food and Accommodations

Enjoy a well-made Oaxacan *mole* or fresh seafood dish at **Restaurante El Legado** (Sebastián Ortiz 849, tel. 287/875-1359, 7am-11pm daily, US$6-8). The *empanadas especiales* (fried dumplings of plantains and ground beef) are a big hit. The service is impeccable, and some waiters speak English.

If you've worked up an appetite from all that hiking in the mountains, fill up on tacos, tostadas, fajitas, and fried plantains at the buffet at **La Cabaña** (5 de Mayo 1380, tel. 287/875-0410, 7am-8:30pm Mon.-Sat., 8am-4:30pm Sun., US$2.50). It's a sensible option for those staying at the adjacent **Hotel María de Lourdes** (tel. 287/875-0016, www.hmlourdes.com, US$15 d), which is a steal for the price. The 43 clean, comfy rooms are set around a charming inner courtyard and have air-conditioning, TVs, and Wi-Fi.

You'll feel a world away from Oaxaca's second-largest urban area at ★ **Hotel El Rancho** (Camacho 435, tel. 287/875-9500, www.hotelelranchotuxtepec.com, US$26 d, US$32 country room, US$35 suite), which puts a rustic touch on modern comfort. Inside the entrance, you'll see an old horse-drawn carriage covered in potted succulents, cacti, and tropical flowers. Distinctive among its 52 units are its "country rooms," with dark cedar finishing on the walls and support beams overhead; cut stone walls add a bucolic counterpoint to the luxurious suites. You might wake up in the morning thinking you're still in a cabin in the cloud-covered mountains.

Getting There

From Oaxaca City, get to Tuxtepec on a **Cuenca** or **AU bus** (US$10, 6 hrs) from the city's main bus station. Both lines make several trips daily. The trip is quicker in a *suburban* run by **Transjuar** (Calzada Héroes de Chapultepec 801, Colonia Reforma, Oaxaca City, tel. 951/132-7227, US$10, 5.5 hrs). Their base in Tuxtepec is at Melchor Ocampo 74 (tel. 287/875-1513).

However, it's highly unlikely that you'll make the trip directly from Oaxaca City, so if you're coming from the mountains, wait by the highway and flag down a passing Transjuar van or any other *colectivo* that passes by. Transjuar vans make a stop outside the gas station in Ixtlán de Juárez (US$4, 4.5 hrs).

Drivers take Highway 175 north from Ixtlán de Juárez, climbing and descending the vertiginous slopes of the Sierra Norte for a couple hours until the road finally bottoms out in the humid, tropical valley that snakes its way to Tuxtepec. The 155-km (96-mi) drive takes about 4.25 hours.

SAN PEDRO IXCATLÁN AND LA ISLA DEL VIEJO SOYALTEPEC

Created by a pair of dams in the 1970s, **Lake Miguel Alemán** covers 4,300 square km (1,660 sq mi) of lush valley and is home to a wide variety of tropical birds and freshwater fish, including catfish, bass, and tilapia. The small fishing village of **San Pedro Ixcatlán** is on a peninsula jutting into the lake from the southern shore. It's a good option for an afternoon meal en route to the Sierra Mazateca to the west, or a calm overnight respite for those who'd rather take their time.

Once an isolated hilltop town, **La Isla del Viejo Soyaltepec** became even more isolated when the waters of the reservoir cut it off from the surrounding landscape. Walk down the western slope of the peninsula from the church to find the *embarcadero* (boat dock), where you can hire a boat (US$30 for 3 hrs) to take you out to the island. During the half-hour trip, you'll see large flocks of ducks, cranes, herons, and other migrating birds that turn into a riot of wings and quacks when the noisy motorboat roars by. Almost always shrouded in clouds, the peak rising out of the lake north of Ixcatlán is called Cerro Rabón.

There is little to do on the island besides climb the steep path to the town at the top and greet the friendly locals. For a few decades after Soyaltepec's transformation into an island, the town mostly spoke Mazatec. However, the industry and tourism that have come as a result of the reservoir have brought Spanish to the island, and most folks are bilingual. You'll be hard-pressed to hear any English, though.

Overlooking the lake to the west of the island, the weathered **Iglesia de San Miguel Arcángel** is so old that locals couldn't tell me when the church was built. You'll only be able to see inside on Saturdays and Sundays, when locals gather for mass. Inside, the altar is much humbler than the gilded, hallucinatory retables in the churches in Oaxaca City. Surrounded by the usual pious cohort, Saint Michael slays his dragon inside a modest, concrete altar painted a pastel orange. Head through the grass-covered main streets of town and take a left to get to a rocky outcropping that serves as a *mirador;* it's at the far end of the soccer field. From here, you'll have a fantastic view of the lake below and an even larger, uninhabited island to the north. Keep your ears on alert for women artisans calling from their windows to sell *huipiles* (embroidered shirts) distinct to the region.

Food and Accommodations

Ixcatlán is a sleepy little town with not much going on besides school, work (primarily fishing), and church. I saw few restaurants during my visit, and only one was open: the **Comedor Familiar** (Calle Reforma, no phone, 9am-6pm daily, US$5), where you can enjoy a fresh grilled *mojarra* (tilapia) or ceviche (seafood salad of fish cured in lime juice). You won't miss the restaurant, which is on the main road into town. A few folks with grills set up along the main drag, Benito Juárez, selling tacos and *tlayudas,* and some homes had signs on front doors advertising homemade *tlayudas.*

Ixcatlán's one hotel is the quaint **Hotel Villa del Lago** (tel. 287/152-4847, US$14 fan, US$16 a/c), on Benito Juárez about a half kilometer (0.3 mi) north of the church. Rooms are basic but clean, and boast pleasant views of the lake and islands. There is also a swimming pool to cool off in the sweltering sun of El Papaloapan.

Getting There

From Tuxtepec, board a *camioneta* from behind the Pemex station at the Glorieta de la Piña, the junction of Highways 175 and 182. The base is a few storefronts down Highway 182 from the gas station. The sign reading San Pedro Ixcatlán is pretty conspicuous, making it easy to find, and the pickup trucks are white with a blue stripe. The 1.5-hour drive costs about US$2.

San Pedro Ixcatlán is about 60 km (37 mi) from Tuxtepec. Drivers take Highway 182 west from Tuxtepec and take the turnoff to San Pedro Ixcatlán in about 1.5 hours. The town is perched on a peninsula about 15 minutes from the highway. Or you might stop off for a meal at one of the *comedores* on either side of the **Puente Pescadito,** the bridge that spans the channel connecting the two reservoirs that constitute Lake Miguel Alemán. The bridge is on Highway 182, about 40 minutes from Tuxtepec.

La Cañada

With the rugged Sierra Mazateca on its eastern side, and a long arm of the Valle de Tehuacán-Cuicatlán to the west, **La Cañada** (Canyon Country) is a land of extremes. The valley may not boast the level of megadiversity of the mountains, where a single oak tree can be home to six or seven other colorful and rare plant species, but there is still an extraordinary abundance of life here. It boasts gullies teeming with succulents and massive colonies of green macaws, and is home to one of the highest concentrations of columnar cacti in the world. This lesser-visited region of Oaxaca truly deserves more attention from tourists, and not just those looking to get trippy in Huautla. Down in the valley there are lots of spectacular natural sites and ecotourism opportunities. It's a bit off the beaten tourist path in Oaxaca, but a visit to La Cañada doesn't disappoint. The variety in the natural setting, people, and food all follow the Oaxacan traditions of being completely unique and consistently awe-inspiring.

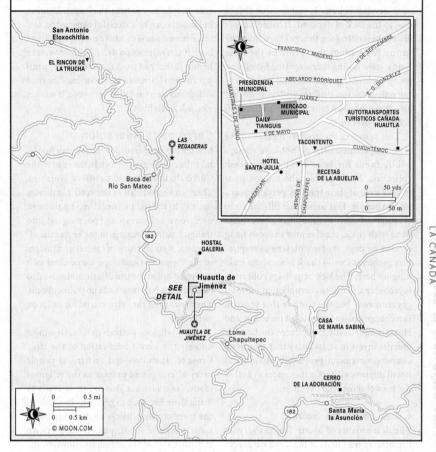

La Cañada

★ HUAUTLA DE JIMÉNEZ

Sprawled across a steep slope of the Sierra Mazateca, Huautla de Jiménez has been a destination for psychedelic thrill seekers since the 1960s, when hippies seeking a "natural" psychedelic experience (as opposed to LSD) came in droves to visit local *curandera* María Sabina. The Mazatecs had long used hallucinogenic mushrooms in their healing and spiritual ceremonies, but folk healer María Sabina was the first to openly share with the outside world the skills and knowledge passed down to her from her maternal grandparents.

Huautla was founded sometime between AD 1200 and 1375 by Mazatec people. The origin of the name Huautla ("Among the Eagles" in Nahuatl) comes from an ancient Mazatec legend of a pair of gigantic eagles that lived in the nearby caves and used to trouble the townsfolk.

Tourism is still driven primarily by María Sabina's magic mushrooms, still called *niños santos* (holy children) by the Mazatecs who carry on her tradition today. Despite the grandeur of these mountains and the extraordinary biodiversity in them, I was surprised to find that ecotourism was not very developed here. I imagine that this is due to the lack of demand. If more outsiders come looking for things other than the funny little fungi that grow in the cane fields—like taking tours, renting bikes, and going spelunking—the demand will lead to not only more fun stuff for visitors to do, but also more jobs and more money in the local economy overall.

This is one of the poorest regions in the state, and communities do not have enough public funds for basic services like trash collection. Many people who are too poor to take care of their trash by private means tend to burn it. This sometimes fills the air in Huautla and other communities where this is done with thick, acrid smoke that can hang around for days. People with serious respiratory problems should think twice about trekking up here. The lack of garbage collection is probably also due to corruption in the local governments, but the truth is that tourism can change a place for better or for worse, and Huautla has already experienced the latter. If tourists invest in an industry that requires a cleaner environment, people will respond, and it will improve visitors' experiences as well as the lives of those who live there.

Casa de María Sabina

The descendants of María Sabina carry on her healing traditions at the **Casa de María Sabina** (Carretera María Sabina, tel. 236/102-8567 and 236/108-6151), where she used to hold mushroom ceremonies with visitors. They have a small museum (US$1) dedicated to her life, which is mostly photos and paintings, and they also have some very rustic tin-sided *cabañas* (US$2.50 pp) and space for camping (US$2). Call or just stop in and see María's great-grandson Anselmo about accommodations, ceremonies, and other traditional medicine treatments.

The best way to get up here is to take a taxi (US$1.50), which all have pictures of mushrooms on them. All drivers will know exactly where you want to go. On foot, the 4-km (2.5-mi) walk takes a little over an hour and gets steeper as you near the house. Driving in Huautla can be a stressful experience, so I recommend a taxi or a hike even if you drove here. If you're intent on driving, however, take Benito Juárez east from the town center until it turns into Carretera María Sabina. The road switchbacks up the hill to her house. If you get lost, ask a neighbor.

Cerro de la Adoración

Just up the road from María Sabina's house, take the right leg of the fork in the road to the **Cerro de la Adoración** (Hill of Worship). There's a second fork in the road a little way up; stay to the right again, climbing through overgrown oak forests and popping out into tranquil, sunny clearings in the heat of the afternoon. A small group of crosses and images of the Virgen de Guadalupe are perched atop a pointed hill at the end of a thin, steep-sided ridge about a half-hour walk up the mountain. The views from the ridge extend for miles on either side.

Many religious festivals in Huautla—most notably the May 3 celebration of the Holy Cross of Huatulco—end up here, as people carry offerings and prayers to the religious icons. Goat farmers also use these trails to bring their livestock to graze in the shade of the trees on the hillside, so there are many trails to explore. A fun option is to head down the other side of the mountain, down to the neighborhood at the foot of the hill, and take a taxi back to town from there.

Food

Huautla's main plaza is covered in the tarps of a daily *tianguis* (outdoor market), where vendors sell fresh produce from the region, including all the delicious pineapples, papayas, and other tropical fruits from El Papaloapan. There's also prepared food like *tamales de mole,* which I recommend having Mexico City-style in a *torta* (bread-roll sandwich). You'll find more *fondas* (food stalls), produce, and butchers in the *mercado municipal,* in the building on the east side of the local government offices.

The name says it all (and the food backs it up) at ★ **Recetas de la Abuelita** (Granny's Recipes; corner of Cuauhtémoc and Niños Héroes, no phone, 8am-9pm Mon.-Sat., US$2.50). This quaint little *comedor* on the block just below the main square and *tianguis* has a number of regional specialties, such as the remarkably delicious *pilte*—chicken, pork, or beef marinated in chiles, onions, and herbs, and wrapped in banana and *hoja santa* leaves (or aluminum foil), then placed directly on red-hot coals to infuse the flavor.

Across the intersection from Recetas de la Abuelita, you'll find a small, sign-less, late-night taco place the proprietor told me she was calling **Tacontento** (corner of Cuauhtémoc and 5 de Febrero, no phone, 9pm-1am daily, US$2.50). She makes mouthwatering *tacos árabes*, which in other parts of the country means made with a pita-type bread, but here just means flour tortillas and parsley and dill in the *pico de gallo*. Get a *taco árabe especial,* which comes with melted *quesillo* and a slice of pineapple.

Accommodations

There are a couple of clean but basic hotels in the center of town, but since the rates are the same at ★ **Hostal Galería** (Mártires 3 de Junio, tel. 236/102-7252 and 222/349-8423, US$15 d), just a pleasant 10-minute walk from the Centro, you're going to want to stay here. Owner Inti García Flores has a beautiful plot of land just north of town that has the widest variety of orchids I've seen in one place, as well as a number of other incredible flowers, bromeliads, ferns, and trees. Inti, his wife, and two delightful children live in the upper story of the house, and they decked out the two bedrooms below (separate entrances) with two full beds, private baths with hot water, good working Internet, and tasteful lighting, antiques, Mexican memorabilia, and other fun curios. Guests can use the kitchen, and Inti has built a little *palapa* (thatched hut) on the hillside at the back of his property, where he invites visitors to read, do yoga, or just relax, take in the view, and listen to the wind in the sycamore trees.

Of course there's nothing wrong with a place like **Hotel Santa Julia** (Cuauhtémoc 12, tel. 236/387-0586, US$15 d), a block below the main plaza. It's just doesn't have any orchids shaped like octopuses. Rooms are clean and the hot water works, and the south-facing rooms have excellent views, especially when the steep valley below fills with clouds.

Getting There

Get to Huautla from Oaxaca City on a *suburban* run by **Autotransportes Turísticos Cañada-Huautla** (Trujano 600, Oaxaca City, tel. 951/188-9560, US$9). The very curvy trip takes about five hours. They make five trips daily (six on Sundays), beginning at 8:30am. Their base in Huautla (Cuauhtémoc 21, tel. 236/106-8555) is down the street from Hotel Santa Julia. *Camionetas* leave Tuxtepec regularly from the Glorieta de la Piña, the junction of Highways 175 and 182. The three-hour trip on these trucks is also very winding; it costs about US$3.

Drivers will have an amazing time driving through the Sierra Mazateca, but use caution. Landslides are not uncommon during the rainy season, so wait until the rain stops to drive. It's also a good idea not to drive after the sun goes down, as bands of carjackers are known to stop private vehicles late at night. Don't be in a rush when driving through the clouds, which can limit visibility to no more than a few feet in front of the car. Just go very slow and hug the yellow line.

Huautla is a 239-km (148-mi) drive from Oaxaca City. Take Highway 190 west and take Highway 135 (not 135D, the toll road that goes to Puebla) at Telixtlahuaca. From here it's 140 km (87 mi) on serpentine Highway 135 through canyon country to Teotilán de Flores Magón, where you'll turn east onto Highway 182. Total drive time is about five hours. If you're coming from Tuxtepec, you've only got 123 km (76 mi) to drive. Take Highway 182 west from Tuxtepec and stay on it for

about three hours, or maybe longer if you get snagged by a cloud and have to slow to a crawl for a while.

EXCURSIONS AROUND HUAUTLA

Just about anywhere you turn in these mountains, you're going to find something that inspires awe. Spend a day exploring nature's wonders both above and below ground at these spots within a half-hour's drive from Huautla.

★ Las Regaderas

At the western base of the peak on which Huautla is located, a pair of waterfalls called Las Regaderas (The Showers) flow out of the rock in the neighboring hill and fall 30 meters (98 ft) to the river below. The constant spray of the crashing waters has caused nature to begin reclaiming a long-defunct suspension bridge that used to give access to the base of the larger falls but now serves only for photo ops.

A taxi from Huautla will cost you about US$5. The falls can be thoroughly appreciated in 10 to 15 minutes, so just ask your driver to wait while you snap pictures. Make it more of an activity by hiking down to the falls. Inti García at Hostal Galería (tel. 236/102-7252 and 222/349-8423) will take you on a walk down through the lush oak forests to the falls that takes about two hours round-trip (US$10).

Drivers take a right onto Highway 182 after leaving from Huautla's main gateway. Zigzag down the road about 7 km (4.3 mi) until you see the sign for Santa María Chilchotla, just before the bridge. You'll see the falls on your left in about 0.8 km (0.5 mi).

Nindo-Da-Gé Caves

The neighboring town of San Antonio Eloxochitlán (eh-loh-sho-cheet-LAHN) is home to the Nindo-Da-Gé Caves, a large system consisting of 19 galleries (cave

passageways) full of stalactites and stalagmites. The first cavers to explore these galleries in 1898 and 1905 christened them names like Boca del Dragon (Dragon's Mouth), El Caracol (The Snail), Cuesta Infernal (Infernal Slope), and El Fortín (The Fort).

For safety reasons, you'll need a guide to explore the caves. Contact Raúl Betanzas, who owns El Rincón de la Trucha (tel. 553/669-9396, 10am-6pm daily, US$5), another fantastic trout hatchery restaurant in the Sierra Norte. He and his son Raúl Jr. can organize tours to the caves (US$15). You'll see the sign to the restaurant as you enter town. Ask about the comfy brick *cabaña* they were finishing up on the property at the time of this writing. Raúl's land goes far up the hillside, offering lots of trails to explore.

You can camp at the mouth of the caves, overlooking the valley below, for about US$3 per person. Out here, you'll be miles from people and services, and this is not a developed campground. You'll need to bring everything yourself and take it all with you when you go. Raúl also invites campers to pitch a tent (US$3) on a prominence behind his trout hatchery, which offers a pleasant view of San Antonio Eloxochitlán below.

The turnoff to Eloxochitlán is on Highway 182, just across the bridge from the turn to Las Regaderas. Take a *colectivo* from the bridge (US$1) or hire one for a private trip (US$5) if you don't want to wait for the taxi to fill up. If you're coming from Huautla, a taxi will cost about US$10. Drivers head west from Huautla on Highway 182, take this turn after the bridge, and drive another 15 minutes (6.5 km/4 mi) into town.

CUICATLÁN

The original inhabitants of Cuicatlán are believed to have migrated from the Toltec settlement of Tula, north of Mexico City, after its fall in AD 1150, but much of their history was destroyed during the conquest. The Cuicatecs named it Yabaham, which means "Earthen House." The Nahuatl name Cuicatlán means "Land of Poems."

1: cactuses in La Cañada 2: the skinny, precipitous ridge that leads to the Cerro de la Adoración 3: clouds rolling in to fill the valley below Huautla de Jiménez

María Sabina's Magic Mushrooms

In 1953 Robert Gordon Wasson, an amateur mycologist, writer, and then vice president of public relations at J.P. Morgan Bank, made his first of many trips in that decade to Huautla de Jiménez to visit, learn from, and partake in ceremonies with María Sabina. She allowed him to take notes and photos of the experiences under the condition that he not show them to the public at large. Then, as now, María's *niños santos* were illegal under Mexican federal law, but the practice was tolerated among indigenous Mazatecs in the region, due to their long tradition of using the fungus for medicinal and spiritual practices.

Wasson took samples of the mushrooms to Swiss scientist Albert Hoffman (known as the first to synthesize LSD), who isolated the hallucinogenic compounds in the fungi, psilocybin and psilocin, finally making them known to Western science. However, Wasson did not fully keep his promise, publishing the 1957 *Life* magazine piece "Seeking the Magic Mushroom" using altered place-names and personal names. He wrote that he visited one "Eva Méndez" in a remote village in the "Mixeteco mountains" as a way to skirt his responsibility to the deal he'd made with Sabina. The article was a huge success, and as the counterculture of the 1960s in the United States began to grow, hippies looking for a natural way to have a psychedelic experience came down in droves, flooding the town with tourism it was not prepared for. Rock stars of the day, including John Lennon, Bob Dylan, and Jim Morrison, are said to have visited María Sabina, as well.

The uncontrollable influx of visitors caused social tensions in the village. María and her family were shunned by others in town, who got so angry that they burned her house down. Her son was murdered. When the Mexican government caught on to why all these gringo freaks were trekking up the rugged Sierra Mazateca, the federal police blockaded the highway and did not allow foreigners to enter for a few years. Wasson claimed that he only wanted to "increase and refine our knowledge" of magic mushrooms, but the bank he was employed by was heavily invested in pharmaceuticals and experimental chemistry in the 1950s. It's likely he had ulterior motives for publishing the information, as well.

While an outsider may have viewed María Sabina as a drug dealer, in her mind she was performing a service to all who came to her for help. But she did not condone the use of magic mushrooms for mere diversion, which was what most foreign visitors were looking for. It is said that by the end of her life, she regretted having shared her gift with the outside world, due to all the problems it had created for her, her family, and her hometown. She also claimed that the *niños santos* had turned on her for sharing them with people who did not respect their spiritual power, and that by the end of her life they no longer caused any effect on her.

Despite the town's attitude toward her and her craft when she was alive, images of mushrooms

Cuicatlán is a good base for exploring the **Tehuacán-Cuicatlán Biosphere Reserve,** a 4,900-square-km (1,892-sq-mi) protected natural area with breathtaking topography and rich biodiversity in both plant and animal life. Shielded from rain by the Sierra Mazateca to the northeast and a ridge of mountains referred to as the Sierras Centrales de Oaxaca to the southwest, this arm of the Valle de Tehuacán-Cuicatlán is a hot, dry desert where 6-meter (20-ft) columnar and organ cacti thrive on the rugged hills lining the valley. This region is home to one of the world's greatest concentrations of columnar cacti.

Despite the area's aridity, the waters of the Río Cuicatlán allow for agriculture to thrive along its banks. Oranges, lemons, limes, papayas, beans, and especially chiles, which like the hot, dry weather, are all cultivated here, and the food is correspondingly delicious. On a walk through this area, you might see badgers, possums, snakes, iguanas, doves, and other desert-dwelling creatures.

Call or stop by the *presidencia municipal* (local government offices; tel. 236/372-2048) to get more information and to hire guides to local sights. It is actually a good idea to call beforehand for any ecotourism activities in

María Sabina's *niños santos* (holy children)

and the woman's visage are plastered all over town, and many people hail passing visitors from their homes to sell them mushrooms. (Consumption by visitors is tolerated by the authorities—with the stipulation that the mushrooms be collected, sold, and consumed within the community.) I did partake in a Mazatec ceremony with a local *curandera* who procured a batch of *niños santos* for the ritual. I was conflicted about how best to present this experience. How much credence do I really give to this ceremony and tradition, and how much of it is me looking for a psychedelic experience? How different am I from those thrill-seeking hippies who swarmed here in the 1960s, taking the tradition for granted and changing the community forever? What I do know is that the family could definitely use the money I gave them for the experience. It's a complex issue, to say the least, and ultimately you'll need to decide for yourself whether you want to participate in this kind of experience. As long as you are respectful of the people and traditions here, this kind of tourism can be done responsibly in a way that benefits both resident and visitor—and that is what tourism should do.

this part of Oaxaca. Tourism here is so slow that most offices don't keep regular hours, and people will need time to prepare activities and accommodations.

Sights
EL CHENTIL CAVE
Just a 30-minute walk from Cuicatlán, a cave called **El Chentil** is a natural gallery of *pinturas rupestres*, or ancient cave paintings. The paintings haven't been officially dated, but locals say they were chipped into the rocks as far back as 12,000 years ago. The easy hike to the cave is a great opportunity to observe local flora and fauna, and a local guide (US$7) can tell you what the paintings are believed to say about the origins of the Cuicatec people, if you speak Spanish (no English-speaking guides). Get here by taking Calle Mina east from the Hotel Real Sohiapam and making a U-turn onto Calle Juárez, which leads into the mountains east of town. The cave is a 5-10-minute drive from town.

MIRADOR CRUZ BLANCA
From the town's main square, head up the hill to the east (behind the church) to get to the **Mirador Cruz Blanca** (White Cross Lookout

Point), which offers a nice view of the center of town and the 17th-century Iglesia de San Juan Bautista. The walk up the hill takes about five minutes.

NEARBY COMMUNITIES

All within 1.5 hours of Cuicatlán, the communities of Tomellín, San Pedro Jocotipac, and Santa María Ixcatlán make great day trips from town. All lie in the rough, rugged, and absolutely beautiful canyon country to the west of Cuicatlán. Visiting these communities independently is not recommended, as the dirt roads that lead to them are all unnamed and very sporadically marked. Inquire about tours to these towns in the *presidencia municipal* in the center of Cuicatlán.

Tomellín, the closest town at only 30 minutes away, is believed to have been founded at the end of the 19th century by Chinese railroad workers who constructed the Ferrocarril Mexicano del Sur (Southern Mexican Railroad), which connected Oaxaca City to Puebla. Out here, you can wander the old tracks that passed by the Río Salado, through an enormous canyon full of trails and photo ops.

Artisans in **San Pedro Jocotipac** and **Santa María Ixcatlán** are renowned for the lovely *sombreros* (hats), *petates* (mats), *escobas* (brooms), and little figurines made of woven palm fronds. Both communities have lovely 18th-century Dominican churches. San Pedro Jocotipac, about an hour away from Cuicatlán, is at the southern end of the Cañón del Sabino (Cypress Canyon), home to vibrant green flocks of macaws. A little over two hours from Cuicatlán, Santa María Ixcatlán is known for the mezcal it makes from a wild species of maguey called *papalometl* that grows locally.

Food and Accommodations

Find delicious *comida corrida* (set menu) meals at any of the *comedores* around the main square, as well as in the market to the northeast of the square. To get a taste of the best of Cuicatecan gastronomy, head to ★ **Comedor La Abuelita** (Calzada de la

Juventud, tel. 236/374-0203, 7am-6pm daily, US$3) in the old railroad station across the highway from the main gateway into town. Doñas Delfina and Ofelia, the pair of *abuelitas* (grannies) who own the place, serve the traditional *moles, empanadas de amarillo,* chile rellenos, *memelitas* (corn tortillas with a sauce), and more that their grandmothers taught them long ago. Try anything they've made that day with the rare *chile chilhuacle* (a moderately spicy pepper) in it.

Tasty breakfasts and great tacos can be found in town at **Taquería El Borracho Loco** (The Crazy Drunk Taco Restaurant; Calle Hidalgo, tel. 951/362-3455, 7am-midnight daily, US$3). Rather than drunk, you're more likely to waddle away from this place a *glotón loco* (crazy glutton), leaving with *el mal del puerco* (the evil of being a pig) after one too many addictively delicious *gringas* (*taco al pastor* with melted cheese in a flour tortilla). You'll find it about two blocks north of Hotel Real Sochiapam.

Your best hotel option in town is **Hotel Real Sochiapam** (Hidalgo 50, tel. 236/374-0001, reservaciones@hotelrealsochiapam.com.mx, US$13 d), a few blocks south of the main square. The comfortable, airy rooms all have hot water and are cooled with fans. South-facing second-floor rooms have nice views of the valley. There is an on-site restaurant, and all rooms have a little rotating door for discreetly passing snacks and drinks ordered from reception. The hotel has ample parking space and a pleasant gazebo with tables and chairs for reading, writing, or just relaxing.

Getting There

Cuicatlán is 121 km (75 mi) northwest of Oaxaca City. Get here on a *suburban* run by **Transportes Turísticos Teoax** (Periférico 408, Oaxaca City, tel. 951/268-1192, US$4). Vans leave Oaxaca City hourly from early in the morning to 8pm (10pm on Sundays). The trip takes about 2.5 hours. Their base in Cuicatlán (tel. 236/374-0026) is on Calle Hidalgo, three blocks south of the main square. Bigger buses leave Oaxaca City from the **Terminal Periférico** (Periférico 1006, Oaxaca City, no phone, US$5) twice a day, arriving at the station in Cuicatlán, also on Calle Hidalgo, a block north of Hotel Real Sochiapam. The bus trip takes about three hours.

Drivers head west on Highway 190 from Oaxaca City. Stay on Highway 190 until you get to Telixtlahuaca, about 35 km (22 mi) from Oaxaca City, which takes about an hour. From here, turn right onto Highway 135 (do not confuse it with the toll road 135D) and follow this twisty stretch of desert road for another 1.5 hours to Cuicatlán. Cuicatlán is 85 km (53 mi) from Telixtlahuaca.

SANTA MARÍA TECOMAVACA

The small town of **Santa María Tecomavaca** is the gateway to the astounding landscapes of the Cañón de Sabinos (Cypress Canyon), with its towering, sheer rock walls and large flocks of green macaws. During the colonial period, the Spanish mispronounced the Nahuatl name Tecomahuaca, which means "where the possessors of the calabash tree live," adding the *v* with which it is pronounced today.

Local culinary specialties include *moles rojo y verde* (red and green moles), *tesmole* (a *mole*-like sauce made from *guajillo* and *chiltepec* chiles, pumpkin seeds, and *achiote*, a dark-red fruit), and *pipián,* another sauce with a base of roasted ground pumpkin seeds.

Ecotourism activities are administered by a committee in the local government's **Oficina de Bienes Comunales** (Office of Common Property; tel. 951/294-3360). The office is next to the basketball court in the main square, but call ahead to make sure those on the ecotourism committee have time to prepare for your arrival. If you have trouble getting in touch with this office, call the *presidencia municipal* (Tecomavaca main square, tel. 236/372-2048, 10am-4pm Mon.-Sat.). No English is spoken in these local government offices.

Sights
★ CAÑÓN DEL SABINO

Tecomavaca's main attraction is the awe-inspiring **Cañón del Sabino** (Cypress Canyon), where some of the cliff walls shoot up 600 meters (1,968 ft) from the canyon floor. The sides of these vertiginous crags are home to the nests of what locals call *esmeraldas voladoras* (flying emeralds), or *guacamayas verdes* (green macaws).

The best times to see them are in the early morning and late afternoon, as the colorful birds escape the midday heat in the cool nests they've made in the cliffs. You'll see entire flocks (at their largest between March and August) fly by with the spectacular view of the canyon in the background.

Since the canyon (about a half hour from Tecomavaca) is in the Tehuacán-Cuicatlán Biosphere Reserve, you'll have to hire a guide in town. To do this requires speaking Spanish, as committee members do not speak English. Call Leobardo in the Oficina de Bienes Comunales. The tour (US$25 for two people) is from 2pm to 8pm, and includes transport to the canyon from town and back.

Coming out here also requires patience. Tourism is not the primary activity of this and other areas in the valley, and cell phone service is spotty. Begin making arrangements well before you plan to come, as it may take a few calls just to get someone to pick up.

PUEBLO VIEJO ARCHAEOLOGICAL ZONE

An hour's walk from town, the ruins at the **Pueblo Viejo Archaeological Zone** are what is left of the original settlement of Tecomavaca. The ruins are just across the river to the west of town. There is much mystery behind who settled here first, but signs point to predecessors to the Mazatec people called Xicalancos, from the south of Veracruz and west of Tabasco. Even the date of origin of the settlement is unknown. Little more than a few stone foundations tufted with grass, the small site has yet to be fully explored by archaeologists, but the walk out here is gorgeous, with barrel and columnar cacti on full display. As with other ecotourism activities here, inquire first in the Oficina de Bienes Comunales, even if you're just going to head out to find them on your own.

RUTA DE LOS COMPADRES

September to December are the best months for seeing macaws along the **Ruta de los Compadres** (Route of the Buddies), a three-hour car trip through the deciduous forests of the lowlands. Various types of copal trees abound, one of which was the first species used to make *alebrijes* (painted carved wooden figurines) when they became popular in the 1970s. Another, called *lináloe,* was once used to make an aromatic essential oil for aromatherapies and perfumes. The tour costs US$17 for up to four people. Inquire in the Oficina de Bienes Comunales.

Recreation
RUTA DE LAS ECHEVERÍAS

This short hike is called the **Ruta de las Echeverías** for the profusion of the namesake succulents that grow in the area to the east of town. Their soft green rosettes and pink flower stalks are all over the place here. Just 2 km (1.2 mi) outside of town, this hike can be done in a couple of hours at a relaxed pace. A guided tour (Spanish only) costs about US$5. Inquire in the Oficina de Bienes Comunales about the tour, or to alert them to your presence and get info on where to find the trailhead east of town.

Getting There

AU buses leave Oaxaca City from the **Terminal Periférico** (Periférico 1006, Oaxaca City, no phone, US$7) multiple times a day. These buses make three stops daily in Cuicatlán, at 7:45am, 11am, and 10:50pm. The half-hour trip costs about US$2.50. The station in Cuicatlán is on Hidalgo, a block north of Hotel Real Sochiapam. From Huautla, board a Oaxaca-bound *suburban* run by **Autotransportes Turísticos Cañada-Huautla** (Cuauhtémoc 21, tel. 236/106-8555, US$7) and tell them you want to get off in Cuicatlán. They'll probably just drop you off on the highway, but it's only a 5-minute walk to the hotel, and 10 minutes to the main plaza.

Drivers take the same route to Cuicatlán. If you're coming from Oaxaca City, continue up Highway 135 another half hour to get to Tecomavaca, a total drive time of about two hours. From Huautla, the drive takes a little over two hours.

La Mixteca

Although the Mixtec tale of a warrior killing the sun with an arrow to conquer these mountainous lands is a myth, there is something to the blood-red color of the hillsides here at sunset. When it comes to tourism, La Mixteca (meeks-TEH-kah) has been presented to the world with a focus on its phenomenal human achievements, like the majestic Dominican architecture of the colonial churches and convents. But travel these lands zippered with rough, rocky hills and valleys and nature's hand might impress you even more.

The towering crags of the Apoala Valley will cause your imagination to run wild as you think of local myths about the gigantic two-headed eagles that are said to have once haunted their peaks. The colors in the aforementioned sunset appear in some places to have tie-dyed the

Highlights

Look for ★ to find recommended sights, activities, dining, and lodging.

★ **Monte Negro Archaeological Zone:** Take a scenic trip back thousands of years to the origins of Mixtec culture at these mountaintop ruins built of white limestone (page 193).

★ **Apoala:** This stunning valley is full of natural wonders like waterfalls, towering cliffs, and cramped caves, as well as a plethora of interesting cultural myths and fun legends to explore (page 195).

★ **Templo y Ex-Convento de Santo Domingo Yanhuitlán:** This 16th-century masterpiece of Dominican architecture dominates the surrounding landscape (page 200).

★ **Balneario Atonaltzin:** Cool off from the hot Mixteca sun in the gemstone-colored waters of this sulfur-spring-fed swimming hole outside of Tamazulapan (page 203).

★ **Templo y Ex-Convento de San Pedro y San Pablo:** The 16th-century cathedral and convent is home to Latin America's largest *capilla abierta*, the chapel where the local Mixtec people held religious ceremonies during the colonial era (page 206).

★ **Tlaxiaco's Saturday Market:** Tlaxiaco's main square is home to an open-air street market daily, but on Saturdays the commercial activity sprawls through the streets (page 208).

★ **Parque Natural Yosondúa:** The spectacular cascades of the Río Esmeralda tumble 100 meters (328 ft) to the canyon floor—and you can view them from a suspension bridge strung hundreds of feet above the rushing water (page 212).

★ **Cerro de las Minas Archaeological Zone:** Visit one of the oldest Mixtec settlements, perched on a hill north of the Heroic City of Huajuapan de León (page 216).

★ **Cañón El Boquerón:** Take a nice afternoon stroll along the walkway that cantilevers over the sides of the 400-meter (1,312-ft) cliffs that hem in La Mixteca's Bigmouth Canyon (page 220).

earth with their brilliance. In the hills around Yanhuitlán, Coixtlahuaca, and neighboring towns, the hues in the earth range from deep wine reds to vision-searing yellows to an eerie zombie-skin green.

That said, the work of human hands is nothing to disparage here. The monumental facades and *capillas abiertas* (open-air chapels) of the 16th-century cathedrals of La Mixteca's Dominican Route inspire awe, as well as curiosity about the history behind them.

A human endeavor that is perhaps even more impressive is La Mixteca's food. Out here you'll find lots of the original recipes that the avant-garde chefs in Oaxaca City are tinkering with. From mid-October to mid-November, a trip to Huajuapan de León for the goat meat-based *mole de caderas* is essential for anyone scouring Oaxaca for interesting flavors and spices. And the food—all the food—in Nochixtlán is so good that everyone should consider at least a day trip from Oaxaca City to try it.

Touring La Mixteca requires a bit more effort and patience than visiting more popular tourist destinations in Oaxaca. Very little English is spoken, and the advertised services don't always exist. However, the payoff for your senses is worth it. If you're looking to explore a place that's off the beaten path, La Mixteca, a few hours from Oaxaca City, is a world away from your wildest expectations.

HISTORY

Signs of human habitation dating back to 5000 BC can be found all over La Mixteca, such as the ancient paintings and rock carvings at Apoala and El Boquerón. However, it wasn't until the development of agriculture in the region, sometime around 3000 BC, that the pre-Hispanic Mixtec culture began to develop. Two thousand years later, the culture experienced an urban revolution, forming chiefdoms (what the Spanish called *señoríos*

when they arrived) and creating a vast trade network that extended north as far as Teotihuacán, north of Mexico City, and south as far as South America.

For millennia, La Mixteca was populated by small *señoríos* connected economically but not politically. This all changed when a *cacique* (chief) named Ocho Venado Garra de Jaguar (Eight Deer Jaguar Claw) founded Tututepec, or Yucudzáa in Mixtec, and set out on a military campaign to bring all regions of La Mixteca under his control. Thus the Mixtec empire united to defend itself against the incursion of the Aztecs, which took place just before that of the Spanish in the early 16th century.

The Mixtec empire flourished for centuries, becoming an economic powerhouse in the Post-Classic Era (AD 700-1521), mostly because of the region's production of cochineal dye, made from *cochinillas,* the little gray bugs that grow on the nopal cactus and turn red when ground with a mortar and pestle. The Mixtecs used the dye to add color to everything from textiles to the wood and stones of their buildings. When the Spanish arrived, they brought their global trade connections with them, and the industry boomed. La Mixteca became the world's largest producer of cochineal dye until the rise of synthetic dyes in the 19th century.

As in the rest of Mexico, the Spanish conquered La Mixteca with the cross and the sword, and the region now has the highest percentage of professed Catholics in the state of Oaxaca. Because of this history, La Mixteca is renowned for its abundance of stunning Dominican neoclassical architecture.

PLANNING YOUR TIME

To see all the sights in La Mixteca, you'll need around two weeks, especially if you're coming here to see awe-inspiring natural wonders and out-of-the-way archaeological zones. If you don't have time to see everything, pick

Previous: Teposcolula's Templo y Ex-Convento de San Pedro y San Pablo; La Cascada Cola de Caballo (Horsetail Falls) in Apoala; the suspension bridge and falls at the Parque Natural Yosondúa.

La Mixteca

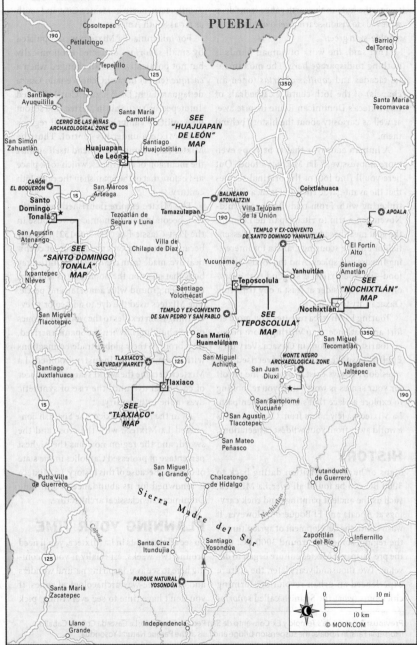

© MOON.COM

a few of your favorites and plan your route accordingly.

Start in **Nochixtlán,** taking a day to visit the mountaintop ruins at **Monte Negro,** and the next to trek out to **Apoala.** The sights in Apoala can be seen in a few hours, making this a possible day trip, but a long one that will involve getting up quite early and coming back late. I recommend spending the night in the *cabañas* (mountain cabins).

If you've come to see the churches, your best option for a base is Nochixtlán, from which all the must-see architectural wonders are within about an hour's drive. All churches in the **Dominican Route** section can be seen in two comfortable days of exploring. If you don't have time for them all, make sure to see Yanhuitlán's **Templo y Ex-Convento de Santo Domingo Yanhuitlán** and the gargantuan open-air chapel of Teposcolula's **Templo y Ex-Convento de San Pedro y San Pablo.**

If you don't have a full two weeks, I suggest you pick either Tlaxiaco or Huajuapan de León, depending on what you'd like to do after your time in and around Nochixtlán.

The hustle and bustle and delicious food of the **Saturday market in Tlaxiaco** are excellent reasons to head that way. The city is in constant *tianguis* (street market) mode, so if you want to see the rushing cascades at the **Parque Natural Yosondúa,** you can still get street-market food and fun. Like Apoala, Yosondúa is not easy to get to, so plan on staying the night there. Give yourself about three days to see the sights in and around Tlaxiaco.

On the way out to Huajuapan de León, you can stop off for a few hours in **Tamazulapan** to see the Parroquia de Santa María de la Natividad or take a dip in **Balneario Atonaltzin,** the local sulfur-spring-fed swimming hole. Give yourself a day in **Huajuapan de León,** taking a couple hours to walk to the ruins at **Cerro de las Minas.** The next day you could head down the highway to take the short hike through the **Cañón El Boquerón,** returning to Huajuapan in the evening, or spend a night in the small but lively little town of **Santo Domingo Tonalá,** where you should spend a tranquil hour or two in La Sabinera, the local park full of Montezuma cypress trees.

Nochixtlán and Vicinity

Although technically part of La Mixteca Alta (High Mixteca), this gateway to the region is more like a parti-colored middle ground between the heights of Tlaxiaco and the "Hot Country" of Huajuapan and the surrounding Mixteca Baja (Low Mixteca). Aside from the small but busy city of Nochixtlán, this area includes stunning natural and manmade wonders, such as the waterfalls and caves of Apoala and the white limestone mountaintop ruins of Monte Negro.

NOCHIXTLÁN

Nochixtlán (no-cheeks-TLAHN) is named for the scale insects used to make red dyes known as *nochiztli* in Nahuatl, *nduko* in Mixtec, and *grana* or *cochinilla* (cochineal)

in Spanish. According to local legend, Viejo Nochixtlán (Old Nochixtlán) was a Mixtec military outpost founded around AD 900, but this settlement was virtually wiped out in 1521 and 1522 by outbreaks of cholera, measles, and smallpox.

Officially named Asunción Nochixtlán, the current town (pop. 18,500) was founded in 1527 by conquistador Francisco de Orozco and 50 surviving Mixtec cochineal farmers, and the reputation it gained as "The Town of Merchants" during the conquest remains to this day. For such a compact city, Nochis (as locals affectionately call it) usually bustles with mercantile activity, from the lively Sunday *día de plaza,* to the hardworking market vendors of the *mercado municipal,* to

Nochixtlán

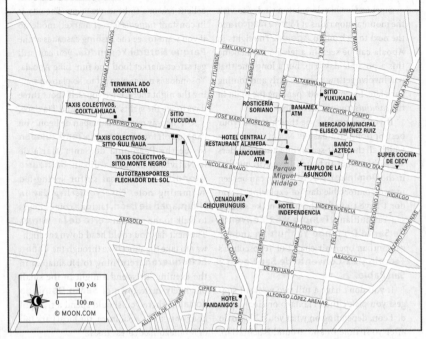

enterprising locals selling various wares off the hoods of their cars around Parque Miguel Hidalgo, the town's shady main square. Nochixtlán is full of mouthwatering morsels, both in the market stalls and in restaurants, so bring your appetite.

Sights
TEMPLO DE LA ASUNCIÓN
Dedicated to the Virgin Mary of the Assumption, the **Templo de la Asunción** is a great introduction to the religious architecture you're going to see in La Mixteca. Smaller and less ornate than the region's Dominican masterpieces, the church serves as an appetizer for the grandiose structures at Yanhuitlán and Teposcolula. The first mention of the church in the local registry dates back to 1581, and the facade and nave still date to that century, but the towers are not the originals. A pair of earthquakes in the first half of the 20th century toppled one

and then the other, but both were restored in the 1990s. The green wooden cross in front of the facade was atop the right tower before it came down in the quake. Inside, you'll find a comparatively small but lavish altar and gilded *retablo* (altarpiece, or retable), as well as colorfully decorated vaulted ceilings. The church and its interior are fetching, but if you are short on time and looking for truly impressive Dominican architecture, you won't regret skipping it.

Food
If you're in Nochis on a Sunday, the town's weekly market day, meander through the busy streets north of the *zócalo* (main square), where you'll find *barbacoa* (slow-cooked meat), tacos, quesadillas, empanadas, and more. Any other day of the week, you'll find the same kind of stuff in the **Mercado Municipal Eliseo Jiménez Ruiz,** just across Calle Porfirio Díaz from the Templo

de la Asunción. The stalls inside usually close around 6pm.

On the north side of the main square, you'll find ★ **Restaurant Alameda** (Porfirio Díaz 42, tel. 951/160-4402, 8am-7pm Mon.-Sat., US$3), festooned with brightly colored ribbons, woven handicrafts, and *papel picado* (stenciled paper decorations). The menu usually sticks to traditional Oaxacan breakfast and lunch dishes, with distinctive touches like thick, tasty salsas made from local seeds and chiles. They also roast their own cacao beans on an *anafre* (wood-fired grill) for the chocolate they serve with meals.

Even if the only thing you do here is eat a *tlayuda* (large tortilla topped with meat, veggies, and more) at ★ **Cenaduría Chiquirunguis** (Libertad 3, no phone, 3pm-11pm daily, US$3), your trip to Nochis will be worth the trip. It's a bold statement, but I believe their open-faced *tlayuda*, served with guacamole, radishes, cilantro, and sprigs of the strongly flavored herbs *pipiche, berroz,* and *epazote,* is the best I've had in the state so far. The Manzano family also put a lot of thought into the decorations. No generic paintings of lilies, religious figures, or faraway cities here: Bright Mexican colors, models of elaborate firework towers, a model *pozole* (hearty meat stew) stand, and much more delight the eyes as richly as the flavors in the food.

Nochis locals appear to be crazy for roasted chicken. A half-dozen *rosticerías* are within a two-minute walk of the main square. Most only serve food *para llevar* (to-go), but **Rosticería Soriano** (corner of Allende and Morelos, no phone, 9am-8pm daily, US$2-3) has indoor seating. These tasty chickens are sold whole or in halves or quarters, served with rice, tortillas, salsa, and other fixings. They also whip up delicious *tortas* (bread-roll sandwiches) and tostadas, the latter of which are gigantic. Both are great options for solo diners.

For tasty home-style meals, head to **Super Cocina de Cecy** (Porfirio Díaz 14, tel. 951/344-9154, 9am-9pm daily, US$3),

two blocks west of the *mercado.* Cecilia and her daughter Valeria change the menu daily, but everything they cook—such as the *verde* (pork in a green sauce similar to *mole verde*) I feasted on—is delicious. Best to come early, before menu items start to run out.

Accommodations

What ★ **Hotel Central** (Porfirio Díaz 42, tel. 951/522-0225, US$6-8 d, US$14 t) lacks in luxury, it makes up for in character. After passing through the colors and aromas of Restaurant Alameda, on the north side of Parque Hidalgo, you'll find the eight weathered rooms set around the central bathrooms that they share. The cheapest rooms don't include amenities like TVs, towels, or hot water (US$1 to light the boiler), but there's just something so satisfying about the old-fashioned signage and the disco lighting on the decorative *torito* (bull-shaped firework apparatus) hung in the courtyard—not to mention the room prices. Aside from a few cobwebs in the corners, the rooms and communal bathrooms are kept clean, and the family that runs the hotel is nice and friendly. And yes, there's Wi-Fi, kind of.

The next-closest option to the *zócalo* is **Hotel Independencia** (Independencia 6, tel. 951/522-0463, hotelindependencia@hotmail. com, US$13 d), where the street-facing rooms offer a nice view of the Templo de la Asunción. All rooms are decorated with a quirky yellow-and-white stripe or check pattern on the walls and ceilings, and have private bathrooms with hot water you don't have to ask for.

Drivers might want to opt for something like **Hotel Fandango's** (Roble 11, tel. 951/522-0545 or 951/164-4619, US$18) to avoid the congestion of downtown traffic, especially if you arrive on a Sunday, Nochixtlán's market day. Fandango's is almost a parody of modern design. The street-facing rooms have what can only be described as indoor balconies—little glass-enclosed breakfast nooks with curtains behind them—and yes, they'll bring breakfast to your room. If you want peace and quiet, double-check that

there isn't a concert scheduled during your stay (*fandango* means "dance party"). The hotel is five blocks south of the main square; it's a 10-minute, 750-meter (0.5-mi) walk to the town center.

Information and Services

Services in Nochixtlán are quite limited. This is not a tourist town, so there is no office or even a booth for tourist information. However, if you do have questions about something in town, you can try to find someone to help in the *presidencia municipal* (local government offices) on the south side of the main square. The **post office** (Progreso 1, no phone, 8am-4pm Mon.-Fri., 10am-2pm Sat.) is in the western corner of the same building.

Change money at the **Banco Azteca** (Porfirio Díaz 28, tel. 953/142-3775, www. bancoazteca.com.mx, 9am-9pm daily) in the Elektra department store. It has ATMs, as does **Bancomer** (Guerrero 4, tel. 800/226-2663, www.bancomer.com, 8:30am-4pm Mon.-Fri.) on the block west of the main square.

Hospital Básico Comunitario (Av. Carmen Zárate, tel. 951/522-0647, 24 hrs daily) has emergency services, but there is no English-speaking staff. The hospital is a little over a kilometer (0.6 mi) from the main square, about a 15-minute walk. Take Progreso south from the square until it meets Cristóbal Colón, continue south another half kilometer (0.3 mi), and then turn left onto Lázaro Cárdenas. You'll see the hospital from Colón. Taxi drivers know how to get you there.

Getting There

All your transportation options are on Calle Porfirio Díaz, three blocks west of the *zócalo*. The trip from Oaxaca City takes a little over an hour. First-class **Ómnibus Cristobal Colón** (OCC) buses (toll-free Mex. tel. 818/354-3521,

www.ado.com.mx, US$8) from the main bus station in Oaxaca City arrive at the **Terminal ADO** (Porfirio Díaz 78) in Nochixtlán.

To spend about a third of the first-class price, take a *suburban* (shared van) operated by **Autotransportes Flechador del Sol** (Periférico 408, Oaxaca City, tel. 951/292-9839, US$2.50). Vans leave for Nochis hourly. Get to their Oaxaca City terminal by walking west on Valerio Trujano until you get to the Periférico; then cross the street and take a right. It's on the third block north of Trujano. Their **terminal in Nochixtlán** (Porfirio Díaz, tel. 951/103-0360) is just east of the ADO station.

Drivers take Highway 190 west from Oaxaca City. In about a half hour (12 km/7.4 mi), you'll see the exit to Highway 135D, a toll road. From here it's another 65 km (40 mi) to the turnoff by the Pemex station, just after the overpass. Pull a U-turn through the dirt road by the gas station and take a left on Cristobal Colón. The center of Nochixtlán is about a mile down this road. The drive takes a little over an hour.

To get here from Huajuapan, take a Oaxaca-bound *suburban* from **Servicios Turísticos de Huajuapan** (Nuyoó 36, Huajuapan, tel. 953/530-5204, US$3). The trip takes about 1.75 hours. Vans leave Huajuapan hourly, sometimes more frequently if there are more passengers.

★ MONTE NEGRO ARCHAEOLOGICAL ZONE

About 1.5 hours southwest of Nochixtlán, you'll find the **Monte Negro Archaeological Zone**, a Mixtec settlement contemporaneous with Monte Albán. According to Mixtec legend, this is the famed site of the battle between El Flechador del Sol (The One Who Wounded the Sun with an Arrow) and the original inhabitant of La Mixteca, the Sun. The settlement he is said to have founded was Tilantongo, and ruins have been found beneath the church in the town of Santiago Tilantongo. The main archaeological zone of

---

1: Nochixtlán's Templo de la Asunción **2:** Hotel Central **3:** the colorful dining room at Cenaduría Chiquirunguis

The Warrior Who Wounded the Sun

the red hills of La Mixteca

Mixtec mythology locates the origin of their people in the Apoala Valley, where the four children of the spirits who separated darkness from light lived beneath the massive cliffs of the canyon walls. They decided to bring life to the world by summoning the waters of a great subterranean river to the surface from the depths of the earth. This was the River of Lineages, and it watered the Tree of Life. One of the four gods made a hole in the tree and copulated with it, and the tree soon gave birth to the first man and woman, the first two Ñuu Savi, or "People of the Rain."

As the population grew, the gods decided it was time to send out warriors to conquer the surrounding lands. The most ambitious of these climbed out of the valley to discover that the land he was sent to take over was inhabited by the Sun itself. Determined to complete the task he'd been sent to do, the warrior aimed his bow and arrow into the western sky and fired off a sally of darts at the Sun, which was injured and turned the sky red with its blood. This earned him the title El Flechador del Sol (The One Who Wounded the Sun with an Arrow), and on that battleground he founded the first Mixtec *señorío*, Tilantongo. From here he sent chiefs in all directions to found the *señoríos* of Coixtlahuaca, Tlaxiaco, and Tututepec. Mixtec codices, as interpreted by famed archaeologist Alfonso Caso (1896-1970), suggest that the founding of Tilantongo was in the year 692 BC. Spend an evening watching the sunset bleed over the red hills of La Mixteca, and this myth kind of starts to make sense.

Monte Negro, however, is atop a nearby hill to the south of town.

This is one of the oldest-known settlements in Oaxaca and is considered the first Mixtec settlement, probably founded sometime around 692 BC. Ancient Mixtecs formed the sides of the hill into terraces to build dwellings and facilitate agriculture, but not much remains of the original buildings. The most notable structures are the six white limestone columns atop the largest mound. The rest of the structures consist of low walls and foundations made of the same stone. The 1936 excavation led by Alfonso Caso, of Monte Albán fame, turned up artifacts from other cultures, such as a stone mask in the style of the central Mexico site of Teotihuacán, but it was unclear which phase of Monte Negro it pertained to. This and other finds suggest that the settlement may have been abandoned sometime around AD 300 and reoccupied later on, or at least used for ritualistic purposes.

There are no plaques or guides to give more historical information about the ruins, nor are they as impressive as Oaxaca's more famous pre-Hispanic leftovers, but the **scenic drive** out to them and the views from the ruins make every kilometer of the trip worthwhile. It's about a 1.5-hour drive from Nochixtlán through rough multicolored hills and broad expanses of valley fields and wildflower patches. The landscape on the way is truly awe-inspiring. All in all, an excursion to Monte Negro takes about four hours round-trip.

Getting There

Getting all the way out to Monte Negro is half the fun. Although a couple dozen people live way up by the ruins, there is no *colectivo* (shared taxi van) service that goes all the way out there. Your best (really, only) option is to hire a *colectivo* in Nochixtlán for a *viaje especial* (special trip). The driver will take you and as many other people fit into his car to Santiago Tilantongo, which takes a little over an hour. There are two taxi companies at the intersection of Porfirio Díaz and Cristóbal Colón two blocks west of Parque Hidalgo in Nochixtlán. If there aren't any taxis at **Sitio Monte Negro,** try the other company that drives out there, **Sitio Ñuu Ñaua.** Both are on the south side of the curve of Colón. The round-trip fare from Nochixtlán to the ruins should cost around US$15, though it may vary from driver to driver. Your driver will wait or explore the ruins with you, for which you'll need only 15-20 minutes.

Even if you have a car, you're better off letting someone in the know do the navigating here, so hire a taxi. It's difficult enough to get to Tilantongo, and from there, it's another 30 minutes through unmarked, pine-hemmed mountain roads to the ruins.

Be prepared to stop at the *presidencia municipal* of Tilantongo to pay around US$10 for permission and a guide (although these entry requirements are not always enforced).

★ APOALA

The legendary place of origin of the Mixtec people, **Apoala** is home to fantastic natural wonders including vertiginous canyons, circuitous caves, towering waterfalls, and what locals call *bosques fantasmas* (ghost forests), thickets of oak trees strung with wraithlike mosses that have a fun spookiness. According to Mixtec lore, this is the legendary cradle of the great civilization of the Ñuu Savi. It was here that the Mixtec gods are said to have summoned the waters of the River of Lineages, which watered the pair of trees that gave birth to the first Mixtecs.

Perched on a valley shelf about 1.5 hours north of Nochixtlán, **Santiago Apoala** is the small town used as a base for exploring the valley's canyons and waterfalls. It's a fun place to get away from the city and explore, especially if you want to do so on your own. Tourism has been developed insofar as it ostensibly exists, but beyond that, not so much. Don't trust signs like Wi-Fi Zone, for example. Guides are the same. There are people who will take money to walk you around the sights, but they are neither certified nor very knowledgeable about the area and its history. Still, if you need to disconnect and explore stunning natural areas, a day or two in Apoala is just the thing.

Sights and Recreation

The **ecotourism office** (corner of Independencia and Pino Suárez, tel. 555/151-9154, 7am-7pm daily) is staffed by gregarious locals who are nice but seem to know very little about the place. They will arrange a guide for you for about US$5 a person. You'll need about three hours to see the sights. I recommend hiring a guide only if you want to see La Cueva de la Serpiente Oscuro and the pre-Hispanic carvings, as they aren't very easy to find, but make sure to tell the office what you want to see.

LA CUEVA DE LA SERPIENTE OSCURO

La Cueva de la Serpiente Oscuro (Cave of the Dark Serpent), or Yavi Ko O Maa in Mixtec, lives up to its name. After entering through a slim crack in the canyon wall, you take narrow twists and turns down the serpent's gullet. A natural spring and wishing well lie deeper in the canyon. This experience is not for claustrophobes or people who have issues with creepy critters (like spiders and bats), but if these things don't bother you, crawl on in.

After 10-15 minutes of crawling, the cave opens up into two larger galleries, and ultimately an underground lagoon. Bring a coin to make a wish. Guides can provide flashlights, but if you have a headlamp, bring it in order to free up both hands. Also be aware that guides are not trained in first aid or other emergency procedures, so take each step carefully. They do, however, know the cave intimately, as they've been exploring it since childhood, so it's best to hire a guide to take you there (arrange through the ecotourism office).

LAS PEÑAS GEMELAS

Farther up the Río Apoala from the cave, past a narrow cut through 150-meter (492-ft) vertical canyon walls studded with cliff-hanging magueys, bromeliads, and moss-strewn trees, the valley opens up, and the brown earth turns to wine red where the trails snake through a green paradise of low shrubs, well-tended bean fields, and rainbow-colored wildflowers. By now you'll have noticed the 400-meter (1,312-ft) peaks called **Las Peñas Gemelas** (Twin Crags) in the background. Here the river flows through an even thinner cut through sheer rock walls shooting straight up from the canyon floor, and on either side of the narrow gorge, the pointed tops of the crags tower over the surrounding landscape.

The even taller cliff behind you is **La Peña Roja** (Red Crag). It measures a whopping 600 meters (1,968 ft) tall and is the subject of a fun local tall tale. It is said that sometime before the conquest, a large two-headed eagle lived on this peak and made itself a menace to a local shepherd's flock. The shepherd brought his concerns to the townsfolk, and together they killed the double-beaked beast. The legend still lives on in the imaginations of residents of Apoala, and a statue outside the *agencia municipal* commemorates the story. Although polycephaly has been observed in some animals, and the two-headed eagle is a common symbol in heraldry, no such bird has ever been scientifically recorded. Most Apoalans consider it no more than a fun story, but you never know.

You don't need a guide to get to Las Peñas Gemelas. From the *cabañas* on the west side of town, just continue west (upstream) through the canyon for about a half hour. The easy walk is mostly flat, along the banks of the river. There's lots of good exploring to be done out this way. Trails run up the sides of the valley to the bases of the cliffs, and you can always find your way with the aid of the river.

LAS CASCADAS COLA DE SERPIENTE AND COLA DE CABALLO

Just to the east of town, the valley shelf ends, giving way once again to steep, narrow canyon slopes. The Río Apoala winds through tight turns that twist like a snake, ergo the first falls, measuring 25 meters (82 ft), are called **La Cola de Serpiente** (The Snake's Tail). The second waterfall is called **La Cola de Caballo** because it looks like a horse's tail. It plummets 80 meters (262 ft) into a misty pool of emerald-green water. Both here and in **pools** farther downstream, there are great places to take a dip and cool off in the afternoon heat. You can swim in the pool into which the waters of the Cola de Caballo plunge, but the pools farther down are deeper and much more tranquil. They're just another minute or so down the trail. The largest is three meters (10 ft) deep.

1: columns at Monte Negro, one of Oaxaca's oldest settlements **2:** Las Peñas Gemelas (Twin Crags)

To get to the *cascadas* (waterfalls), head east (downstream) to the other side of town. Walk two blocks east from the corner on which the ecotourism office is located until you see a paved stone exit to the right that leads down to another dirt road. Loop around the cornfields and cross the little bridge to find the falls. You'll see La Cola de Serpiente winding alongside you to the left of the trail, and La Cola de Caballo is just another few minutes' walk down the trail. The walk from town to the falls takes about 20 minutes. Bring water and maybe a snack for the hike back up the stairs that descend alongside the rushing water.

ANCIENT ROCK CARVINGS AND PAINTINGS

The cliff with a cave at its base to the north of town is **La Peña del Diablo** (Devil's Crag), where you'll find interesting pre-Hispanic rock carvings. The carving called El Danzante (The Dancer) has been busy busting a move for an unknown number of centuries. There are also carvings representing the sun, moon, and a cornstalk. It is said that this was a ceremonial venue for rituals that thanked the gods for good harvests.

ROCK CLIMBING

Locals told me they occasionally see climbers come from elsewhere to scale the surrounding cliffs, which range from 150-600 meters (492-1,968 ft). It's not a sport they practice here, though, so they have no equipment or services for climbing. You'll have to bring your own gear.

Food

Food options in Apoala are quite limited. There is a *comedor* at the ecotourism office that has the usual *comedor* fare for around US$3. It is open 7am-7pm daily. Your only other option is **Restaurante El Centauro** (Calle Independencia, no phone, 8am-8pm daily, US$3), just a few steps down Independencia from the ecotourism office. You'll also find delicious comedor fare here, such as a simple but flavorful and spicy chile relleno.

A couple little *misceláneas* (corner stores) in town have eggs, veggies, and tortillas, as well as water and snack foods. They'll be able to help you out in a pinch if you're camping, but I recommend shopping for ingredients in the *mercado* in Nochixtlán before heading here.

Accommodations

With a view of the towering gray and orange canyon walls, and the sound of the Río Apoala chugging through its lane of *sabino* (cypress) trees, the **cabañas** (US$20 d) on the west side of town are a pleasant escape from the buzzing streets of Nochixtlán. They are basic but newly decorated and clean. Someone from the ecotourism office will come by around 6pm to light the boiler, which they leave running until morning. I recommend giving it about a half hour and then checking to see how well it works (you might just get a burst of steam and then cold water). If you absolutely need hot water, try to make it to the office to ask them to check it out before they close at 7pm. If not, just shower during the day, when it is warm out.

Tourism is so sparse here that you don't need to reserve a *cabaña* beforehand. Just show up at the ecotourism office in town to book one when you arrive.

CAMPING

In front of the *cabañas,* there is a small field where you can pitch a tent for about US$2.50 per night. You'll need to bring all your own equipment, but if you forgot a plate or a pan, just ask in the *comedor* at the ecotourism office; they might be able to lend you what you need. Bathrooms for campers are next to the *cabañas.*

Getting There

Apoala is so small, and tourism is so undeveloped, that the only way to get here by public transport is to pay for a *viaje especial* (special trip) in a taxi (US$15, one-way) from **Sitio Yukukadáa,** in a yellow house on Calle

2 de Abril two blocks north of the *mercado* in Nochixtlán. It's a pleasant 1.5-hour ride through rolling hills and ethereal *bosques fantasmas*. Make arrangements with your driver to come back to pick you up later. It's best to stay a night or two, but if you only stay for the day, make sure your driver knows you want him to return the same day before leaving Nochixtlán.

Santiago Apoala is about 44 km (27 mi) north of Nochixtlán. Drivers take Calle 5 de Mayo north from the *mercado* in Nochixtlán.

After about an hour, you'll get to San Miguel Chicagua. Follow the signs through town to get to the dirt road that leads to Apoala. When you start to see the edge of the canyon, keep an eye out for a large cross. Here, a *mirador* (lookout point) offers a stunning view of the valley and Santiago Apoala, with its corn and bean fields that hug the rim of the shelf of earth on which the town is located. The town is another 15 minutes or so down switchbacks that descend the steep slopes of the great valley.

The Dominican Route

After the arrival of Hernán Cortés in 1519, it didn't take long for the Spanish to turn up in La Mixteca. The Aztecs didn't have the treasure trove of gold the Spanish were looking for, so Moctezuma sent them in this direction to get rid of them. Although the first missionaries to arrive in the New World were Franciscans, the Spanish crown later chose Dominican friars to proselytize the indigenous peoples of this region due to the order's reputation for austerity and strict religious vows.

This, of course, was not a peaceful process. The Mixtec people the Spanish encountered saw their mission for what it was—a militant takeover masked by the pretty flourishes of baroque church facades—and they resisted the destruction of their temples and construction of Christian ones for decades.

Five hundred years later, the impressive architectural results of this conversion campaign dot the countryside of La Mixteca, making up what the Oaxacan secretary of tourism has designated the **Ruta Dominica (Dominican Route).** The most outstanding examples are in **Yanhuitlán, Coixtlahuaca, Tamazulapan,** and **Teposcolula.** The 16th-century structures have considerable artistic and historical value, but they should be appreciated for what they really were, which, as one resident of Coixtlahuaca described them

to me, were fortresses disguised as churches. This is not to say that the indigenous peoples of Mexico were always peaceful among themselves. They were constantly trekking around to conquer surrounding areas, and had it not been the Spanish who ultimately took over this part of the country, it would have been the Aztecs. Still, it is better to appreciate the full historical context when appreciating works of this kind.

These towns are quite close together and can be seen in a busy day, but I recommend using Nochixtlán as your base, both for its proximity to them as well as the plethora of delicious food options there. I've also included accommodations options in the pleasant town of Teposcolula, which has a bit more to see than the church.

Tours from Oaxaca City

The highlights of the Dominican Route can be seen in a day trip from Oaxaca City, but be prepared for a full day with the tour guides. **El Andador** (Vigil 509, Oaxaca City, tel. 951/205-9986, www.elandador.com.mx, 8am-8pm Mon.-Sat., 11am-8pm Sun.) runs a tour (US$19, 11 hrs) on Thursdays that takes in Yanhuitlán, Teposcolula, and Tamazulapan, ending the day at the Balneario Atonaltzin, a natural sulfur-spring swimming hole done up like a water park in miniature.

Chimalli Travel (M. Bravo 108, Oaxaca City, tel. 951/547-3656 or 951/501-2387, www. chimalli.travel, 9:30am-7pm Mon.-Fri., 9:30am-2pm Sat.) runs shorter tours (US$18, 8 hrs) daily that don't make it to Tamazulapan.

YANHUITLÁN

While it might be tempting to deem it a miracle that the Dominican friars were able to build such marvelous architectural wonders in this isolated area of New Spain, it's important (and historically accurate) to keep in mind that such feats were achieved by unwilling human hands, not a divine one. The Spanish town council in **Yanhuitlán** (New Land) donated land for a Dominican convent in 1529, but the friars weren't able to call it a permanent home until decades later due to multiple successful acts of resistance by the local Mixtec people, on whose temple ruins the Christian edifice was being constructed. The church and monastery here is a stunning masterpiece of colonial religious architecture that can still be appreciated (actually, should be) with the context of its autocratic history in mind.

Sights
★ TEMPLO Y EX-CONVENTO DE SANTO DOMINGO YANHUITLÁN

Set atop a low, flat hill in the center of town, the **Templo y Ex-Convento de Santo Domingo Yanhuitlán** commands attention from anywhere in the surrounding valley. Saints carved in pink limestone stand among the columns and flourishes of its towering facade. Big, stocky buttresses support its west-facing corners, and the musty stone hallways and flowered courtyards of the old convent are on the nave's east side.

The church's religious and political importance in the region was eclipsed only by the Santo Domingo church and convent in Oaxaca City. Formal construction finally began in 1550, when locals finally stopped resisting and gave in to the awesome political and physical force of the Catholic Church. The last stone was laid in 1575.

Despite a few modifications in the 18th century, many of the original sculptures and paintings remain intact, such as the altarpiece by Sevillian painter Andrés de la Concha. This gilded 10.9-meter (35.8-ft) altar is adorned with de la Concha's depictions of the life of Saint Dominic. The original designer and date of construction of the elaborate pipe organ in the balcony are unknown. Most likely built around 1700, the instrument shows signs of repairs over the centuries, such as a new keyboard installed in 1886. It was fully restored to working condition in 1998 in a collaborative effort by Mexican and French organ builders.

Part of the convent has been turned into a **regional museum** (9am-5pm Tues.-Sun., US$2.50), which houses lots of religious artwork and presents temporary exhibits. It also has an exact copy of the Yanhuitlán codex, a document dating from 1550 that depicts the history of Yanhuitlán and the intervention of the Spanish there in Mixtec glyphs and transcriptions of Mixtec phrases in Spanish characters. The original is in the Academy of Fine Arts in Puebla.

Getting There

Yanhuitlán is a quick, straight shot from Nochixtlán, 16 km (10 mi) northwest on Highway 190. Drivers will be glad for the paved road in good condition, passengers in the back of *camionetas* (covered pickup trucks used as vans) will appreciate the smooth 20-minute ride, and all will enjoy the sprawling views of the valley. The *camioneta* terminal in Nochixtlán is a block north of the *zócalo* on Calle Allende, just before the corner with Morelos. They charge about US$1 to get to Yanhuitlán.

From Oaxaca City, grab a Huajuapan-bound *suburban* at **Servicios Turísticos de Huajuapan** (Valerio Trujano 420, Oaxaca City, tel. 951/516-5759, US$4) and get off after about 1.5 hours in Santo Domingo Yanhuitlán,

---

1: the Templo y Ex-Convento de Santo Domingo Yanhuitlán **2:** Coixtlahuaca's Templo y Ex-Convento de San Juan Bautista **3:** the Parroquia de Santa María de la Natividad in Tamazulapan

about 20 minutes after Nochixtlán. The large pink church is striking against the green of the broad valley floor, so it's hard to miss.

COIXTLAHUACA

Coixtlahuaca (In the Field of Snakes) was founded around AD 37 by the Chocho people of La Mixteca Alta. It was an important commercial hub for the region in the centuries before the arrival of the Spanish, with a market that attracted both Mixtec and Chocho people from miles around. Coixtlahuaca is situated in gorgeous, multicolored hill country. The earth here holds all the hues you can think of, and a few others you never would have.

Sights
TEMPLO Y EX-CONVENTO DE SAN JUAN BAUTISTA

Because of Coixtlahuaca's strategic cultural and commercial position in the region, the Spanish decided to build the spectacular **Templo y Ex-Convento de San Juan Bautista,** which was completed in 1576. It sits atop a low, flat hill in a valley, commanding stunning views of the surrounding landscape, especially in the late afternoon when the west-facing church facade turns to gold in the light of the setting sun.

As with other indigenous peoples and most churches around here and in many parts of Mexico, the Chochos rightfully opposed the replacement of their temple with a Christian one and resisted for decades before finally giving in. Being obliged to build a temple to a god they did not serve, they took a few liberties with the design. They left signs of their displeasure with the deal in the bas-relief carvings of the facade and the archway of the open-air chapel, in which you'll see symbols such as moons with faces and the plumed serpent Quetzalcoatl. The stage-like open-air chapel to the side of the main nave was where the Chochos were forced to hold their masses, as they were not allowed inside to worship with the European believers.

The on-site **museum** is open 9am-5pm daily and is free to enter, but you'll have to pay about US$2.50 if you want to shoot video. The highlight inside is the *lienzo de Coixtlahuaca,* a 16th-century canvas map delineating the boundaries of the Coixtlahuaca chiefdom and the official recognition of Spanish authority over it. The main town is represented by a glyph of a snake, and the boundaries are delineated in a patched, jaguar-print perimeter.

Getting There

Coixtlahuaca is about 40 km (25 mi) north of Nochixtlán. From here, Highway 135D (toll) cuts straight through a firework-hued display of terra firma. Drivers will pay about US$2 for the toll road when they exit it. Take Porfirio Díaz west out of Nochixtlán and then take the unmarked turnoff to the right, at the top of a low hill about 1.6 km (1 mi) past the ADO station. The toll booth is about a half hour down the highway. Take a right after exiting and follow the road another 3.5 km (2.2 mi) into town. The total drive time is about 40 minutes.

Colectivo taxis leave from a car wash just to the west of the ADO station on Porfirio Díaz in Nochixtlán. They cost about US$3. If you hear the word *transbordar* (transfer), you'll have to get out at the toll booth and cross it on foot to change taxis, so that the drivers can avoid expensive tolls.

TAMAZULAPAN

In Nahuatl, **Tamazulapan** means "In the Water of the Toads," but don't worry. The crystal-clear water in the local swimming hole is toad-free. Boasting another fine example of Dominican architecture right on the highway, Tamazulapan is a nice place to stop for an afternoon on the way to Huajuapan de León.

Sights
PARROQUIA DE SANTA MARÍA DE LA NATIVIDAD

You should have no problem spotting the 16th-century **Parroquia de Santa María de la Natividad,** which stands out among the other church on this route for its paint job. The cochineal-red baroque embellishments of the facade contrast delightfully with the soft, buttery yellow of the bricks.

Inside, you'll find a towering altarpiece of gold and a number of paintings in which a phalanx of saints surrounds the Virgin Mary. This church is home to two 16th-century organs, a large stationary one and a smaller processional organ that was designed to be carried during ambulatory celebrations. It is the smallest organ in Oaxaca and one of only five of its kind in Mexico.

★ BALNEARIO ATONALTZIN

When the Mixtec sun gets to baking, folks from Tamazulapan head to **Balneario Atonaltzin** (Hwy. to Tepelmeme, km 2, tel. 953/540-0185, 9am-5pm daily, US$3), just north of town. The three swimming pools, one of which is Olympic size, are fed by sulfur springs that cycle water through them constantly, maintaining an average water temperature of about 26°C (79°F). A craggy slope of boulders borders one length of the large pool, and atop this sits a terrace where you can look out over the gemstone-hued waters while you enjoy a meal. Green gardens and *palapas* (thatched huts) provide shade around the pools.

The price above is only the entrance fee. You'll pay extra to rent tables, chairs, and other services; you also pay if you bring your own food. Might as well not worry about the picnic and enjoy the burgers, fries, nachos, and other snack-bar fare at the pool.

To get here, grab a *mototaxi* (US$1) at the northeast corner of the *zócalo* or walk the 2 km (1.2 mi) from town. Walk north on Calle Independencia from town, follow the curve and cross the river, and you're there. If you take a right onto the dirt road just after the bridge, you'll get to another spring called El Ojo de Agua Chico (Little Spring), where you can take a dip. It's about a half mile from the main road.

Food and Accommodations

The **Mercado Lázaro Cárdenas**, just north of the main square, is full of *fondas*

(food stalls) serving Mixtec delights, and **Restaurante Noemí** (Cristobal Colón 14, tel. 953/110-2692, 7am-11pm daily, US$3), a block west of the main square, is a good place to hunt for a rare *mole*. The menu at this *comedor*-style restaurant changes daily.

For coffee, head to **Café Portal** (Cristobal Colón, tel. 953/537-0272, 9am-10pm daily) in the arcade on the highway, next to the church. They source their coffee from the higher-altitude slopes around Tlaxiaco. From here, walk around the church, two blocks north, to **Oaxacanita Chocolate** (Plazuela Josefa Ortiz de Domingo 5, tel. 951/417-1778, www. oaxacanitachocolate.com, 10am-8pm Mon.-Fri.) for delicious chocolate made from cacao grown in La Mixteca. Although the Oaxacan chocolate recipe is unique to the state, the majority of raw cacao used to make it is sourced from Tabasco and Veracruz. Oaxacanita is special in bringing the whole production process to their corner of Oaxaca, creating jobs and supporting local artists with the proceeds. The room next to their chocolate bar is used to showcase the talents of local artists and artisans. Their cacao farm is a few hours away in the verdant hills around Tlaxiaco.

You can stay in town in a basic hotel like **Hotel Don Pedro** (Cristobal Colón 34, tel. 953/533-0736, US$13 d), but the *cabañas* at **Balneario Atonaltzin** (Hwy. to Tepelmeme, km 2, tel. 953/540-0185, US$31 4 people, US$52 6 people, US$78 12 people) will be more relaxing. Made of beautiful white limestone, the *cabañas* have hot water, TVs, coffee makers, and valley views. Plus, they're next to the spring-fed swimming pools.

Getting There

From Oaxaca City, grab a Huajuapan-bound *suburban* at **Servicios Turísticos de Huajuapan** (Valerio Trujano 420, Oaxaca City, tel. 951/516-5759, US$4) and get off at Tamazulapan's lovely Parque Central. Vans leave hourly, and the trip takes about 2.5 hours. From Nochixtlán, get a *colectivo* from **Sitio Yucudaa** (Calle Porfirio Díaz, Nochixtlán, tel. 951/105-9000 or

951/177-5943, US$2.50), just after the bridge on Calle Porfirio Díaz.

Drivers take Highway 190 northwest of Nochixtlán. Tamazulapan is 52 km (32 mi) down this highway. The hour-long drive speeds across low green valleys and twists through the variegated hills of La Mixteca Alta.

YUCUNAMA

If you've been paying attention to the toponyms in this part of Oaxaca, you might notice that Yucunama doesn't sound like the others, which are in Nahuatl, the language of the Aztecs. This is because Yucunama (Hill of Amole)— the name refers to a tuberous plant used to make soap—was never conquered by the Aztecs. The Spanish included Yucunama in the Teposcolula district when they arrived around 1520, but the Spanish viceroyalty endowed the settlement with political and territorial control in 1585, designating it an autonomous indigenous republic. The town is small and quaint, with cobblestone streets in the center, and the 16th-century Templo de San Pedro boasts a fetching façade plastered and painted white and red.

Archaeologists have found artifacts here that date back 2,000 years. These can be viewed in the small **archaeological museum** (9am-6pm daily, free admission) called Bee Ñuu (House of the People). Of note here is a copy of the **Codex Nuttall,** one of the principal pictographic documents relating the history and legends of the Mixtec people. Folded like an accordion, it details in full color the story of famed chief Ocho Venado (Eight Deer). You'll also see a 14th-century receipt for tribute payments printed on *amate* (paper made from the bark of the wild fig tree). If the museum isn't open, head to the *presidencia municipal* across the plaza and ask someone to open it for you.

Getting There

To get to Yucunama, head to the junction of Highways 190 and 125, 29 km (18 mi) northeast of Nochixtlán. Take the dirt road with a sign for Yucunama that leads west from the intersection. Drivers will enjoy the 20-minute ride through 9 km (5.6 mi) of low scrub- and pine-covered hills into town. At the junction, public transport passengers will find *colectivo* taxis that charge about US$3.50 for the ride into town. Get to the highway junction via a *colectivo* from Nochixtlán, which you'll find in front of a car wash just to the west of the ADO station on Porfirio Díaz. The drive takes about a half hour.

If you're headed to Teposcolula next, take the road that leads south out of town. Teposcolula is about 8 km (5 mi) south. A *colectivo* will charge you another US$3.50 for the trip.

TEPOSCOLULA

When the Spanish arrived in this part of La Mixteca in the 1520s, they found the Ñuu Savi living on a nearby hill called Yucundaa (Hill of the Ancient People). By 1550, Yucundaa was completely abandoned, and the Ñuu Savi were displaced by the Spanish to form the town now known as **Teposcolula** (which means "Next to the Twist of Copper," but as hard as I tried, I could not find the exact reason for such a name). For the next couple centuries, it was the most important trade hub in the region, with business connections that reached as far as Guatemala and even countries in South America.

As in other communities in the region, the people of Teposcolula resisted the invasion of their lands and traditions by the European colonizers, the most notable of which, the Danza de las Mascaritas (Dance of the Masked Ones), is still practiced today. The dance has its origins in the European courtier dances the Spanish brought to the town. The colonized native inhabitants made fun of the dance by caricatured, hammy movements. They donned outrageous masks and costumes so that the insult would fly under the radar of the people they were caricaturing.

Other interesting traditions here include the games *pelota Mixteca*, a Mixtec ball game similar to that of other pre-Hispanic cultures

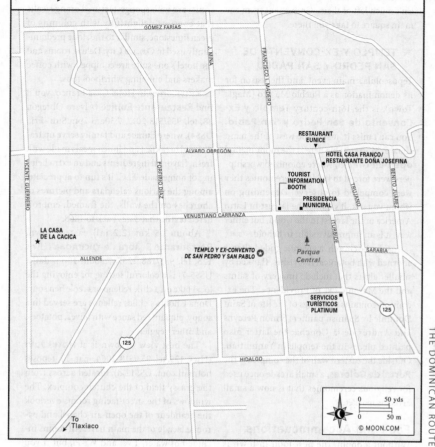

Teposcolula

GÓMEZ FARÍAS

J. MINA

FRANCISCO I. MADERO

RESTAURANT EUNICE

ÁLVARO OBREGÓN

HOTEL CASA FRANCO/
RESTAURANTE DOÑA JOSEFINA

TRUJANO

BENITO JUÁREZ

VICENTE GUERRERO

PORFIRIO DÍAZ

TOURIST
INFORMATION
BOOTH

PRESIDENCIA
MUNICIPAL

VENUSTIANO CARRANZA

LA CASA
DE LA CACICA

ITURBIDE

Parque
Central

SARABIA

ALLENDE

TEMPLO Y EX-CONVENTO
DE SAN PEDRO Y SAN PABLO

125

SERVICIOS
TURÍSTICOS
PLATINUM

125

HIDALGO

0   50 yds

0   50 m

© MOON.COM

To
Tlaxiaco

but played with a heavy rubber glove, and the *juego de batalla,* a game similar to hockey but played with a ball that is on fire. Experience these games, as well as riotous *calendas* (street parades), live music, regional foods, and more, at Teposcolula's nearly three-week-long **Feria Anual** (Annual Fair) from the end of February through the middle of March.

Sights

For such a small town, Teposcolula is packed with sights to see, such as **La Casa de la Cacica** (House of the Chief's Wife), which was constructed around 1560 and stands out for its fusion of Postclassic Mixtec and Spanish Renaissance architectural styles. Considered the last construction of the Mixtec *señorío,* the building now houses a children's library with copies of the Codex of Yanhuitlán, which contains interesting, colorful Mixtec glyphs.

Other sights to check out, if you have time, are **Tandaá** (The Wedding Place), a sacred hill with a natural spring where weddings were held in pre-Hispanic times, and **El Alarcón,** a well fed by nine natural springs that are said to all have different flavors. Stop by the **tourist information** booth at the west end of the Palacio Municipal for more information. You can also visit the ruins at **Yucundaa,** about 2 km (1.2 mi) southeast of town, although there isn't much left of them. Grab a taxi from the main square to take you there.

★ TEMPLO Y EX-CONVENTO DE SAN PEDRO Y SAN PABLO

Teposcolula's main event, and the reason for its denomination as a Pueblo Mágico (Magic Town), is the 16th-century **Templo y Ex-Convento de San Pedro y San Pablo.** You can't miss it, just to the west of the main square. Most notable here is the monumental **open-air chapel,** where colonized worshippers were forced to hold the ceremonies they were compelled to observe. Depending on whom you ask, it's either the largest in Latin America or the largest in the world, but either way, it is an impressive sight to behold.

Inside the church, a gigantic gilded altar is adorned with botanical flourishes, flanked by smaller altars that include imagery of saints and the Masonic Eye of Providence. The ex-convent contains paintings of the life of Saint Dominic by Spanish painters Simón Pereyns and Andrés de la Concha; the latter also painted pieces in the temple in Yanhuitlán. Outside the eastern wall of the complex is the **Portal de Dolores,** a small arcade once used for religious ceremonies that is now a small artisans market.

Food and Accommodations

Without a doubt, the best food in town is served in **Restaurante Doña Josefina** (Iturbide 20, tel. 953/552-7017, www. hotelcasafranco.com, 8:30am-7:30pm daily, US$5-7), where you can enjoy the chef's local take on *mole negro* in a room filled with 19th-century artifacts, pianos, documents, and family photos. They have three extensive menus for breakfast, lunch, and dinner, as well as a full bar. You'll find it in ★ **Hotel Casa Franco** (Iturbide 20, tel. 953/552-7017, www.hotelcasafranco.com, US$43 d, US$51 king bed, US$78 junior suite), a restored Independence-era villa that was home to Lieutenant Colonel Justo Franco, whose descendants opened the hotel in 2017. The 11 sleek, modern rooms are set around a lovely courtyard with sponge-textured orange walls that contrast delightfully with columns of green limestone, similar to the stone predominantly used in Oaxaca City. Deluxe rooms and the hotel's one suite are equipped with coffee makers and bubbling whirlpool tubs.

Kitty-corner to Hotel Casa Franco, you'll find **Restaurante Eunice** (Álvaro Obregón 28, tel. 953/518-2017, 7:30am-7pm Sun.-Fri., US$4), where Eunice and family serve up traditional breakfast and lunch meals made with fresh, flavorful ingredients and an extra helping of homemade TLC. It's fun to appreciate, among the various calendars and pictures of churches on the walls, the framed, embroidered textile that dates back to 1868.

About 3.5 km (2.2 mi) east of town, **Restaurante Señora de Yucundaa** (Hwy. 125, tel. 951/188-2257, 7:30am-10pm daily, US$5-7) is a colorful setting for enjoying the local take on a chile relleno or creole hen soup. Doña Cholita's chiles rellenos are served in a soupy, piquant red sauce with olives, potatoes, and other veggies.

The best view in town is at **Hotel Juvi** (Hwy. 125, tel. 953/518-2064, mat_10_tepos@ hotmail.com, US$12 d), located across from the grassy field of the church complex. The windows of the street-facing rooms overlook the grandeur of the open-air chapel and baroque facade of the main nave. All rooms include hot water, TVs, and Wi-Fi, but if you need Internet, check to see if it's working first.

Getting There

The cheapest way to get to Teposcolula from Nochixtlán is by *colectivo,* which you'll find outside a car wash on Calle Porfirio Díaz, just west of the main bus station. They'll take you to the junction of Highways 190 and 125, where *suburban* vans wait to take you the rest of the way. All in all, the trip takes about an hour and will cost you about US$3.

1: Teposcolula's Casa de la Cacica **2:** the open-air chapel in Teposcolula

To get here from Huajuapan de León, board a Tlaxiaco-bound *suburban* at **Servicios Turísticos Platinum** (Nuyoó 36-A, Huajuapan de León, tel. 953/503-4836, US$4, 1.5 hrs), a couple blocks north of the churchyard. Vans leave every half hour. If you're coming from Tlaxiaco, take the Huajuapan-bound **Platinum** *suburban* (Hidalgo 3, Tlaxiaco, tel. 953/552-0124, US$2, 1 hr) from their station on Calle Hidalgo, one block west of the Plaza de la Constitución. They also leave every half hour. Their station in Teposcolula is across from the southeast corner of the main square.

Drivers shouldn't have a hard time noticing the junction of Highways 190 and 125. Teposcolula is just 13 km (8.1 mi) from the junction, a 15-minute drive on Highway 125 through wildflower-strewn fields. From Nochixtlán, take Highway 190 29 km (18 mi) northeast until you see the junction. From Huajuapan, turn onto Highway 190 four blocks north of the main square and follow it for 63 km (39 mi) until you get to the junction.

If you're driving from Tlaxiaco, take Highway 190 north out of town. The 44-km (27-mi) drive through verdant, pine-covered peaks takes about an hour.

La Mixteca Alta

Although Nochixtlán and the towns of the Dominican Route are in the region called La Mixteca Alta (High Mixteca), it isn't until you head south from Teposcolula that the road begins to climb to mountainous altitudes. Lofty pine trees strung with spectral mosses rise over bright patches of wildflowers on the way to Tlaxiaco, the town of the perpetual street market. Tlaxiaco makes an excellent base from which to explore the surrounding attractions, such as the ruins at San Martín Huamelulpam and the rushing cascades and stunning vistas of Yosondúa.

TLAXIACO

In Nahuatl, **Tlaxiaco** (pop. 40,000) means "The Place Where It Rains over the Ball Court." Its name in Mixtec is Ndiji (Good View). Like Nochixtlán, the current Heroic City of Tlaxiaco did not exist before the conquest but was formed by moving the inhabitants of two nearby settlements after devastating outbreaks of fatal diseases. It earned its valiant name in a battle won here against the French during their Second Intervention in the 1860s.

Tlaxiaco today is the perfect place for anyone for whom one day a week just isn't enough *tianguis*. The **Plaza de la Constitución** and surrounding *callejones* (alleyways) are occupied by market stalls under the shade of their intricate network of tarps seven days a week. But the main event is on Saturday.

Sights
★ SATURDAY MARKET

Vendors begin arriving from the surrounding slopes and beyond on Friday night, claiming their spots and setting up beforehand to be ready for the early morning rush. Tlaxiaco's Saturday market is an overgrown version of the everyday street commerce around the Plaza de la Constitución, the tarps spreading to fill the neighboring streets to the south for blocks, including the garden in front of the 18th-century Templo de Santa María de la Asunción.

It's easy to spend hours winding through the narrow, congested aisles and alleyways, shopping, socializing, and eating. Although a few stalls sell gifts and souvenirs, this market is not aimed at tourists. Like other markets of this kind in Oaxaca, though, it is an excellent place to eat. Everywhere you turn there are tacos, tamales, mountains of *chicharrones* (fried pork rind), coconuts prepared with lime and chile served in the half shell, local raw honey, and much, much more. The selection

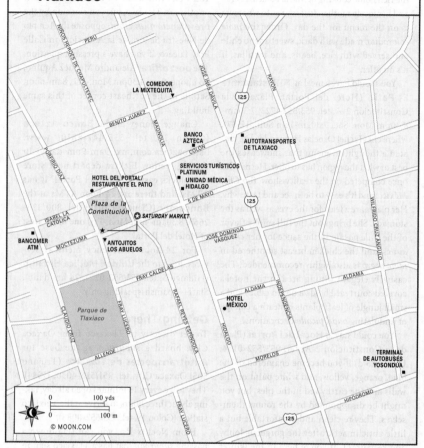

Tlaxiaco

Plaza de la Constitución

SATURDAY MARKET

COMEDOR LA MIXTEQUITA

BANCO AZTECA

AUTOTRANSPORTES DE TLAXIACO

SERVICIOS TURÍSTICOS PLATINUM

UNIDAD MÉDICA

HOTEL DEL PORTAL/ RESTAURANTE EL PATIO

BANCOMER ATM

ANTOJITOS LOS ABUELOS

Parque de Tlaxiaco

HOTEL MÉXICO

TERMINAL DE AUTOBUSES YOSONDÚA

0   100 yds
0   100 m
© MOON.COM

of fresh produce, meats, and dried chiles is impressively diverse. Other fun finds include broad selections of spices, herbs, barks, roots, seeds, and elixirs used in traditional medicines, as well as bags, shoes, artisanal soaps, and cool retro watches. Some unique locally produced artisanal products include *canastas* (reed baskets), *tenates* (smaller woven baskets with tops), and *petates* (woven reed mats), as well as belts, hats, and other accessories.

Food and Accommodations

Any day of the week, the *tianguis* is full of delicious, affordable food. Any night except

Saturday, stop by the food stall ★ **Antojitos Los Abuelos** (corner of Fray Lucero and 5 de Mayo, tel. 953/107-2952, 6pm-11:30pm Sun.-Fri., US$3) at the tarp intersection at the southwest corner of the Plaza de la Constitución. Sonya and Co. serve up fantastic *pozole*, tostadas, and *tlayudas* served with a side of *chapulines* (grasshoppers), pods of the *guaje* tree, and spicy slices of *chile de agua*. There are six stools to elbow into, or you can eat standing in the din of the market traffic.

For a more relaxed atmosphere at the same price, walk a block north of the main plaza to **Comedor La Mixtequita** (Benito Juárez

16, no phone, 8am-7pm Mon.-Sat., US$3) for the rich home cooking of María Palacios Pérez and her lovely mother. Just say yes to whatever is on the menu for the day. Order the *mole coloradito,* made with dark, sweet ancho chile and served with rice, beans, and tortillas, if it's on offer.

You should have a meal at ★ **Restaurante El Patio** (Hotel del Portal, Plaza de la Constitución 2-A, tel. 953/552-1723, 7:30am-8:30pm Mon.-Sat., 7:30am-1pm Sun., US$7), where chef Ixchel Ornelas Hernández has created a thoughtful menu that showcases the best of what the region has to offer. Hernández once competed on the reality show *Top Chef México,* and it's easy to both see and taste why. Her plates are a feast for the eyes as well as the stomach. She brings out the full smoky flavor of the *chile pasilla* in the sauce for her *chilaquiles,* and the chicken breast smothered in *mole negro* is also highly recommended. The casually elegant dining area in the hotel's covered courtyard holds a dozen tables and a small jungle of leafy plants beneath a canopy of undulating *papel picado* decorations.

You could stay at **Hotel del Portal** (Plaza de la Constitución 2-A, tel. 953/552-0154, US$22-25 d) if you become enamored of the blue, orange, yellow, and white paint on the walls and the earthy red in the tiles, but you might be disappointed by the rooms themselves. They're clean and comfortable but a little anticlimactic after the gorgeous lobby and restaurant. If you're here in the winter months, pay the couple dollars extra for a room with carpet. It keeps the room warmer.

Just around the corner from the market is **Hotel México** (Hidalgo 13, tel. 953/552-0086, US$16 shared bathroom, US$18 en suite), which is cash-only and also on a hot water schedule. The rooms are set around a courtyard with gardens of bougainvillea and other flowers and dark green fronds. Even the central parking area is colorful and pleasing, with columns and arches painted the colors of the sunset.

Information and Services

You won't find a tourist information booth or office in Tlaxiaco, but you can stop by the *presidencia municipal,* opposite the Templo de Nuestra Señora de la Asunción on Calle Fray Lucero, if you have a pressing question. The **post office** (Alejandro Méndez Aquino, no phone, 8am-4:30pm Mon.-Fri., 8am-noon Sat.) is in the northeast corner of this same building.

Change money at the **Banco Azteca** (Colón 13, tel. 555/447-8810, www. bancoazteca.com.mx, 9am-9pm daily) in the big, yellow Elektra department store two blocks east of Hotel del Portal. It has ATMs, and there are 24-hour ATMs at the **Bancomer** (Claudio Cruz 8, tel. 800/226-2663, 8:30am-4pm Mon.-Fri) one block west of Hotel del Portal.

For 24-hour emergency medical services, head to the **Unidad Médica Hidalgo** (Hidalgo 5, tel. 953/552-0221, 24 hrs daily). Staff is Spanish-speaking only.

Getting There

To get directly to Tlaxiaco from Oaxaca City, board a *suburban* at the base for **Autotransportes de Tlaxiaco** (Trujano 505, Oaxaca City, tel. 951/516-4030, US$4). They leave every 15 minutes or so all day, taking about three hours to arrive at the Tlaxiaco station (Colón 19, tel. 953/552-0088).

From Nochixtlán, you can flag down a passing *suburban* that has a Tlaxiaco sign in the windshield. Just wait by the road on Calle Porfirio Díaz. You can also take any *colectivo* that will get you to the junction of Highways 190 and 125, and from here grab a *suburban* headed for Tlaxiaco. You'll be charged around US$2.50 for the 1.75-hour trip.

To get here from Huajuapan, take a *suburban* run by **Servicios Turísticos Platinum** (Nuyoó 36-A, tel. 953/503-4836, US$6, 2.5 hrs). The vans go directly to Tlaxiaco (Hidalgo 3, tel. 953/552-1024), stopping in Tamazulapan

---

1: the mazelike alleys of Tlaxiaco's Saturday market **2:** the tarps of market vendors blanketing Tlaxiaco's Plaza de la Constitución

and Teposcolula on the way. Vans leave every half hour.

Drivers from Oaxaca City take Highway 190 west out of the city and take the left lanes to exit onto Highway 135D (toll) 11 km (6.8 mi) outside of the city. Stay on this highway another 69 km (43 mi) and exit onto Highway 190 just outside of Nochixtlán. Drivers from Nochixtlán head west on Porfirio Díaz to get on this highway. From this junction, continue 29 km (18 mi) until you reach the junction of Highways 190 and 125. Turn south onto Highway 125 and follow it for 57 km (35 mi) to reach Tlaxiaco. Total drive time from Oaxaca City is 2.75 hours, and 1.75 hours from Nochixtlán.

If you're driving from Huajuapan de León, turn onto Highway 190 four blocks north of the main square and follow it for 63 km (39 mi) until you get to the junction of Highways 190 and 125. Follow the same directions as above from the junction. Total drive time is 2.5 hours.

SAN MARTÍN HUAMELULPAM

The town of San Martín Huamelulpam was founded around 400 BC and became a political and economic center that may have been the largest Mesoamerican city at the time. Huamelulpam, its Nahuatl name, means "Hillock of Amaranth," which is derived from a pair of amaranth trees (*huautli* in Nahuatl) that grew into the shape of an *H* and lived that way for centuries. Its Mixtec name, Yucunindaba, means "Hill That Flew."

Just a half hour away from Tlaxiaco, it is perfect for a short day trip to the ruins of the old town and the small but interesting community museum.

Sights

YUCUNINDABA ARCHAEOLOGICAL ZONE

The town of Yucunindaba was a Mixtec *señorío* to which surrounding communities made tribute. The ruins date back to its founding in 400 BC. Its trade network extended north as far as Tehuacán in Puebla, and south all the way to the Pacific coast of Oaxaca. Many Zapotec urns were found here, showing that the Mixtecs also traded with Zapotec settlements to the east. Other discoveries were carved monoliths of a style found nowhere else in La Mixteca. You can view these and other artifacts at the **Museo Comunitario Hitalulu** (tel. 953/538-6085, 10am-5pm Tues.-Sun., free admission), next to the municipal government building at the center of town.

The ruins are just to the east of town. The largest of the structures is the **Church Group,** now little more than a few terraced structures and a couple damaged platforms. Many of the stones in this structure were used to build the present-day church on the hill.

Getting There

San Martín Huamelulpam is a half hour (21 km/13 mi) north of Tlaxiaco on Highway 125. Drive or grab a *suburban* bound for Oaxaca and tell them you want to get off at the Huamelulpam turnoff. Vans run by **Autotransportes de Tlaxiaco** (Colón 19, tel. 953/552-0088) leave every 15 minutes and will charge about US$1. From here you can walk the 1 km (0.6 mi) on foot, or flag down a passing taxi to take you into town.

★ PARQUE NATURAL YOSONDÚA

It isn't easy to get to, but the vertiginous waterfalls, breathtaking views, and endless exploring opportunities at the **Parque Natural Yosondúa** are definitely worth the trip. With lots of ecotourism activities such as hiking, mountain biking, and zip-lining, the park offers more than enough to fill a couple days with action, excitement, and discovery. There is a 15 peso (less than US$1) entrance fee for the park unless you stay in the *cabañas,* which I highly recommend you do.

Although there's little chance of accommodations or services being booked up, call ahead to check because it is such a trek to get to Yosondúa. Call Edilberto Martínez Sánchez (tel. 953/518-8057, or 951/212-2417 via WhatsApp), the park's head of communications, for information or to book tours, *cabañas,* or other services. (Edilberto does not speak English.)

Sights
LA CASCADA ESMERALDA

You'll hear the waters of **La Cascada Esmeralda** (Emerald Falls) rushing over the edge of the canyon as you begin to descend from the canyon rim toward the park entrance. From here, the waters of the river (also called Esmeralda) spill 100 meters (328 ft) to the canyon floor in a spectacular show of tiered splashdowns, for which there are numerous excellent viewing points.

SUSPENSION BRIDGE

The **park office/snack bar** (6am-5pm Mon.-Fri.) is perched on a ridge just to the left of the falls, and from here a 131-meter (430-ft) **suspension bridge** spans the width of the canyon, offering mesmerizing views no matter where you look. On one side, La Cascada Esmeralda surges down the canyon walls and through the forest hundreds of feet below, and on the other side, the canyon opens up to a panoramic view of the imposing ridges of the Sierra Sur. The distinctive peak in the distance that resembles El Cerro de la Silla (Saddle Hill) in Monterrey is called Yuku Yuu, which means "Hill of Stone" in the local Mixtec dialect.

Recreation
HIKING AND SWIMMING

The park has many marked and easy-to-follow trails, most of which descend into the canyon from the *cabañas* area, but there are also less frequently hiked trails that involve a bit more bushwhacking to satisfy your urge for adventure. No matter where you are along the slopes, you can orient yourself by the sound of rushing water. In calmer parts, the Río Esmeralda stalls in brilliant green pools that justify its luxurious name and offer paradisiacal settings for cooling off in the afternoon heat. But use your best judgment and stick to the calmer pools. The falls all through the canyon are quite strong and aren't really for splashing around in.

ZIP LINE

Also spanning the vertiginous heights of the canyon is a 300-meter (984-ft) zipline, in case the suspension bridge doesn't elicit enough adrenaline in you. You'll pay about US$5 a zip. Park attendant Miguel López speaks good English and will set everything up for you.

MOUNTAIN BIKING

Farther down the canyon, there are lots of great trails to explore on a mountain bike. Park staff will lend bikes at no extra charge, though this may change as they develop more formalized ecotourism options in the future. If you are set on pedaling around here, call ahead and let them know you want to bike, just to ensure they have the bikes up and running when you arrive. Bike trails aren't as easy to follow as the hiking trails, so get info at the park office or hire a guide to take you around.

TOURS

Edilberto Martínez Sánchez and the folks at the park offer four different hiking tours called *rutas* (routes), some of which venture beyond the boundaries of the park into the surrounding *rancherías* (rural neighborhoods). Other sights on these tours include caves, *pinturas rupestres* (cave paintings), lagoons and other waterfalls, and a ton of *miradores* with phenomenal vistas. Contact Edilberto for more information and to book tours.

Food and Accommodations

The one downside to staying in the park is that, aside from soda pop and Cheetos, there's nothing to eat here. Luckily, the nearby town of **Santiago Yosondúa,** about 10 minutes away in a taxi, has a few hotels and restaurants. Your most reliable option is **Restaurante El Manantial** (Nicolás Régules 8, tel. 953/618-8124, 7am-10pm daily, US$2), with a *comedor*-style rotating daily

menu of delicious home-cooked Oaxacan meals. From the Parque Central, head two blocks south to Nicolás Régules and take this east a block and a half. A handful of other *comedores* dot this street, but El Manantial is the most consistent.

A pair of hotels in town offer very cheap rooms, but not much cheaper than the *cabañas* in the park. The advantage here is being close to eateries. The cheaper is **Hotel California** (corner of Paz y Progreso and Aquiles Serdán, tel. 953/518-8161, US$7-9 d), and the slightly nicer (newer) **Hotel San Fernando** (corner of Benito Juárez and Flores Magón, tel. 953/518-8049, US$10 d, US$15 two beds). Both offer private bathrooms with hot water (ask them to turn on the boiler beforehand), but not much else. San Fernando has TVs, but neither has Wi-Fi. Your only Internet option in town is to buy a *ficha* (slip of paper with access info) at a store or pharmacy, which will give you a specified amount of Internet time.

CABAÑAS

Despite the food situation, the best place to stay is at one of the park's six wood and adobe *cabañas* (US$17-20 d). They're rustic, for sure, but they have solar-powered electricity and private bathrooms with hot water; all are surrounded by the lush, semiarid vegetation of the canyon. Unlike *cabañas* in other parts of the state, they don't have fireplaces, but these are less necessary here than at higher altitudes. It isn't likely that the *cabañas* will be booked up, but call beforehand and check since it's a trek to get here. To head into town to eat, ask Miguel at the park office to call you a taxi.

Getting There

This is the hard part. In Tlaxiaco, head to the **Terminal de Autobuses Yosondúa** but don't get on a bus (they go to Mexico City). You'll find the terminal on Calle Hipódromo, one block east of Calle Independencia. You can walk here from the Plaza de la Constitución by heading two blocks east on 5 de Mayo to Independencia, where you'll take a right. Walk four blocks south until you get to Calle Hipódromo. Take a left, walk one block, and cross the little bridge. You'll see the terminal on your left. Note: It's easier to just take a taxi.

At the ticket window, say you want to take a *taxi colectivo* to Santiago Yosondúa. The trip costs about US$5, takes about 1.75 hours, and is not comfortable; but as stated above, it is worth it. Taxis from Santiago Yosondúa to the park cost about US$3 and get you there in about 10 minutes.

Drivers don't have it much easier. I'm going to describe the long way from Tlaxiaco to Santiago Yosondúa, because the route the taxi drivers take is confusing. Take Calle Independencia south until you see the sign for Chalcatongo (you might have to ask for directions). Chalcatongo is 57 km (35 mi) from Tlaxiaco, and you should reach it in a little under two hours. Continue south from here 22 km (13.7 mi) until you get to Santiago Yosondúa, about 40 minutes down the road. From town, drive west on any road until you get to the unnamed dirt road that borders the west side of town. Take this road south; about 4 km (2.5 mi) outside of town, you'll see the sign for Parque Yosondúa. Turn right to descend into the canyon. The park office is about 130 meters (426 ft) down the road on your left.

1: La Cascada Esmeralda in Parque Natural Yosondúa **2:** Yosondúa's suspension bridge **3:** the colorful kiosk in Huajuapan's main square

La Mixteca Baja

The Mixtec name for La Mixteca Baja (Low Mixteca) is Ñuiñe (Nyoo-EE-nyeh), which means "Hot Country." As the name suggests, the climate of this lower region of La Mixteca is warmer than up in the pine forests of Tlaxiaco and Teposcolula. Out here are more stunning landscapes such as the 400-meter (1,312-ft) vertical walls of Cañón El Boquerón, as well as the ruins of Cerro de las Minas in Huajuapan de León and places to try more local culinary delicacies.

HUAJUAPAN DE LEÓN AND VICINITY

Although folks had already been living here for a couple thousand years, Huajuapan de León as we know it was founded in 1561. A group of brave locals who defended the town during the fight for Mexico's independence from Spain earned it the title "The Heroic City of Huajuapan de León" when it was officially designated a city in 1884. In Nahuatl, Huajuapan means "Place of Huaje Trees Next to the River," using an alternate spelling of the *guaje* tree for which the state is named. Its Mixtec name, Ñudee, means "Land of the Brave."

Huajuapan is the perfect base for exploring La Mixteca Baja. At its center is **Parque Independencia,** a virtual forest of a *zócalo* that is shaded by towering ficus and jacaranda trees, where speakers play classic and Latin rock in the evenings. A statue of town hero Antonio de León stands guard at its north side, watching over the Catedral de San Juan Bautista, a 17th-century neoclassical church built of rosy red limestone.

Sights
★ CERRO DE LAS MINAS ARCHAEOLOGICAL ZONE
The place now called **Cerro de las Minas** (Hill of Mines) was founded sometime around 400 BC by early Mixtec people known as the

Ñuu Yate, Mixtec for "The Ancient People." Its strategic location atop a hill surrounded by broad tracts of arable land made it the major economic, political, and sociocultural center for the surrounding communities, and within a couple centuries it reached a population of 1,000-2,000 inhabitants. In contrast to other pre-Hispanic sites in Oaxaca, which center around one large central plaza, Ñuiñe urban planning at Cerro de las Minas and other ancient settlements in La Mixteca included numerous smaller plazas with temples, tombs, and housing for the elite around them.

The most notable finds uncovered by archaeological excavations in the 1980s are the bas-relief Ñuiñe glyphs carved into limestone slabs. Generally consisting of a central glyph, most likely a person's name, surrounded by calendrical characters, this early Mixtec writing system is one of five documented Mesoamerican scripts. The best examples of these glyphs are on the walls inside Tomb 5.

It doesn't take more than a half hour or so to explore the ruins, but trails crisscross the hill, allowing for a bit of exploration among *guaje* trees and patches of bright wildflowers. The ruins' location atop the hill offers gorgeous 360-degree views of the surrounding landscape of La Mixteca Baja, which shines a vibrant green in the rainy season.

I was told at the **tourism kiosk** (in the Casa de Cultura, Calle Heroico Militar across from the southwest corner of the *zócalo*, no phone, 8am-10pm daily) that I should not go to the ruins alone, as there was the possibility of bandits hanging around the hill to ambush solo explorers. When I did exactly that, all I found were smiling grandmas and helpful old men who showed me the way to the ruins. I assume there is some truth to the warning, but as long as you go in the daytime, you shouldn't have any trouble. You can walk to the ruins in about 20 minutes by taking Calle Nuyoó north from the cathedral. When the road ends, take

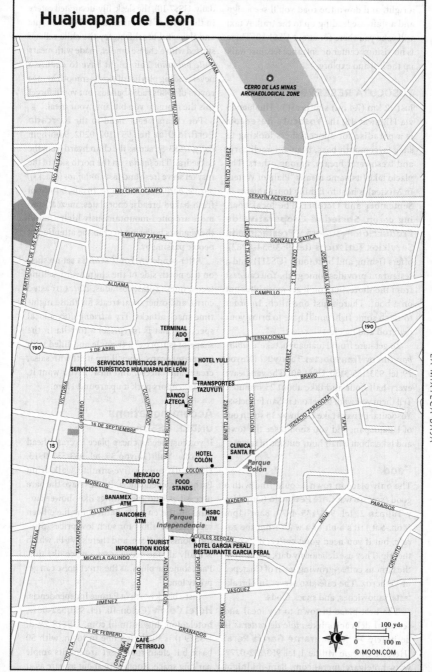

Huajuapan de León

CERRO DE LAS MINAS
ARCHAEOLOGICAL ZONE

YUCATAN

VALERIO TRUJANO

RIO BALSAS

MELCHOR OCAMPO

BENITO JUAREZ

SERAFÍN ACEVEDO

FRAY BARTOLOME DE LAS CASAS

EMILIANO ZAPATA

LERDO DE TEJADA

GONZÁLEZ GATICA

JOSE MARIA IGLESIAS

21 DE MARZO

ALDAMA

CAMPILLO

190

INTERNACIONAL

TERMINAL
ADO

190

2 DE ABRIL

RAMIREZ

BRAVO

SERVICIOS TURÍSTICOS PLATINUM/
SERVICIOS TURÍSTICOS HUAJUAPAN DE LEÓN

HOTEL YULI

VICTORIA

GUERRERO

CUAUHTEMOC

TRANSPORTES
TAZUYUTI

BANCO
AZTECA

BENITO JUAREZ

CONSTITUCIÓN

IGNACIO ZARAGOZA

TAPIA

16 DE SEPTIEMBRE

15

HOTEL
COLÓN

CLINICA
SANTA FE

Parque
Colón

GALEANA

MATAMOROS

MORELOS

ALLENDE

MERCADO
PORFIRIO DÍAZ

COLÓN

FOOD
STANDS

MADERO

PARAISOS

BANAMEX
ATM

BANCOMER
ATM

Parque
Independencia

HSBC
ATM

MINA

CIRCUITO

MICAELA GALINDO

TOURIST
INFORMATION KIOSK

AQUILES SERDÁN

HOTEL GARCIA PERAL/
RESTAURANTE GARCIA PERAL

ANTONIO DE LEÓN

HIDALGO

PORFIRIO DÍAZ

VASQUEZ

JIMÉNEZ

REFORMA

5 DE FEBRERO

GRANADOS

CAFÉ
PETIRROJO

ORQUIDEA
XITLALINA

VIOLETA

0   100 yds
0   100 m

© MOON.COM

LA MIXTECA
LA MIXTECA BAJA

a right, and down the road you'll see a sign and a staircase leading up to the trail. A taxi will take you there for about US$1.50. There is no visitors center or entrance fee. Just walk up the hill and explore.

YOSOCUTA RESERVOIR

Just 12 km (7.4 mi) southeast of Huajuapan via Highway 15, the **Yosocuta Reservoir** is a paradise for sport fishers looking to snag largemouth bass, tilapia, Israeli carp, and freshwater bream, among others. The placid lake (its name means "Plain of Water" in Mixtec) is host to fishing tournaments in September and October. The local boating co-op, **Sociedad Cooperativa de Producción Pesquera y Prestación de Servicios Turísticos** (tel. 953/534-8082), offers fishing and boat tours (US$11), and a restaurant provides some grub. You can cast from the shore, but you'll get more bites out on a boat. There's just one hitch: In order to catch some fish, you'll have to bring your own rod and tackle.

To get here from Huajuapan, take a *suburban* run by **Transportes Tazuyuti** (Nuyoó 29, tel. 953/155-3180, US$1.50). The vans leave every half hour and take about 25 minutes. Tell them you want to get out in San Francisco Yosocuta. Drivers take Highway 15 south out of Huajuapan, and you should see the town and lake about a half hour outside of town.

Food

The only place in town I could find with a good espresso was **Café Petirrojo** (Orquídea y Tulipán 2, tel. 953/135-4172, 8am-11pm Mon.-Sat.). It's a bit of a walk from the *zócalo,* but if you need good coffee, it's worth the trip. They use deliciously dark beans from the famous coffee-growing town of Coatepec in Veracruz. The café also serves full breakfasts, sandwiches, and snack foods.

The best place in town to try local and seasonal delicacies like *mole de caderas* is definitely ★ **Restaurante García Peral** (Heroico Colegio Militar 1, tel. 953/532-0777, www.hotelgarciaperal.com, 8am-midnight

daily, US$7-10), the sleek, lily-decorated eatery in the hotel of the same name. For a unique and flavorful breakfast, try the chile relleno stuffed with a cheese omelet, made with meaty *chile poblano.* You might have to endure a never-ending playlist of sickly-smooth lounge covers of 1980s radio ballads, but you'll forget this the moment you bite into your meal.

For cheaper eats, head to the **Mercado Porfirio Díaz** (tel. 953/102-0202, 9am-6pm daily, US$3-5), across the churchyard from the cathedral. The *fondas* on the north side of the market serve fresh and tasty *antojitos* (snacks), *pozole, barbacoa,* and more. Inside, booths of fresh-baked breads, chocolates, mezcal, and more are piled mountainously high around the vendors hollering to grab the attention of people passing by.

After sundown, **food stands** set up shop on the north side of the churchyard, selling tacos, quesadillas, tostadas, *elotes* (roasted corn), and other local treats for those nighttime snack attacks. Try a *triangulito,* a local specialty that is (surprise) a tortilla in the shape of (surprise) a triangle and filled with (surprise) beans. They'll top it off with salsa, cream and cheese, and meat if you want it. These vendors pack it up around 11pm.

Accommodations
UNDER US$25

If you just need a cheap place to crash, head to **Hotel Yuli** (Nuyoó 35, tel. 953/532-0913, US$11 d), only a five-minute walk from Parque Independencia. Rooms have the bare necessities, and even things like shower curtains in the en suite bathrooms have been sacrificed to allow for such low prices. Still, the rooms are clean, and there's Wi-Fi, which is really all one needs from a place like this. Pack some earplugs, as the street noise can get pretty loud.

Just a block north of Parque Independencia, **Hotel Colón** (Colón 10, tel. 953/532-0817, hotelcolon_hj@hotmail.com, US$18-29 d, US$29 t) is the best value in town, with 50 basic but clean rooms set around its ample parking space. Rooms are about as bare as at

Mole de Caderas: A Seasonal Delicacy

Mid-October to mid-November is the time to visit Hua-juapan if you're coming to eat. This is the season for the regional delicacy *mole de caderas,* a spicy goat-meat stew made with *guajillo,* serrano, and *costeño* chiles, to-matoes, avocado tree leaves, onions, cilantro, and a type of corn endemic to the region. The origins of this dish are generally acknowledged to be from Tehuacán, Puebla, 120 km (74 mi) north of Huajuapan, but you don't have to truck all the way up there to try it.

The tradition dates back to the 16th century, when Mexico was a Spanish viceroyalty of New Spain. Goats are fattened for a year on grasses and wildflowers, and the slaughter begins in October. Traditionally, knives were used to slaughter the animals, but this was seen as barbaric by animal rights organizations, and now the kill-ing is done quickly and painlessly with bolt pistols. The care and diet the goats are given during the year yield what some consider to be the best goat meat in Mexico.

mole de caderas

As a barbecue-loving Texan, I knew this dish was going to be good when I saw that it was messy enough to war-rant wearing a bib. Cuts of hip bone and spine stick up from the piquant broth, and the meat pulls right off of them. Still, the bib is necessary, as is a stack of napkins. I was told that the wood block provided was for breaking bones to get to the marrow, but I couldn't get the slippery things to crack. No matter, the dish is plentiful and delicious without it. Fresh limes and diced onions add a fresh, classically Mexican touch to this unique and hearty meal from La Mixteca.

Other regional specialties during these months are *ubres al ajillo* (goat udder cooked in garlic), *cabrito al pastor* (goat meat seasoned with *achiote,* red chiles, and other spices), and *mole de chito,* which is similar to *mole de caderas* but made with dried, salted goat meat (*chito*).

Hotel Yuli, but this place has TVs, parking, and a fresher, more open look.

US$25-50

Drivers who don't want to deal with the congested traffic of the Centro should con-sider staying at **Hotel Boutique Ñuu, Xua** (Eucaliptos 4, tel. 953/532-5070, www.nuuxua. com.mx, US$50 d), whose name means "New Town" in Mixtec. Just two blocks west of Highway 190 on the east side of town, it of-fers easy access when arriving and leaving. The 1.5-km (1-mi) walk to the Centro takes around 20 minutes. Ñuu, Xua artistically combines modern luxury with ancient tradi-tion, with white stucco juxtaposed with red stone walls that resemble the ruins atop the hill to the north of town. Inside, the rooms are

furnished in a sleek, contemporary style that tastefully accents the bare bricks in the walls. Amenities include parking, air-conditioning, TVs, and Wi-Fi. The on-site restaurant is an-other good place for *mole de caderas* when it's in season, and the tables in the courtyard next to the grand staircase leading to the second-floor rooms are perfect for a romantic alfresco dinner.

OVER US$50

Hotel García Peral (Heroico Colegio Militar 1, tel. 953/532-0777, www.hotelgarciaperal. com, US$47 d, US$52 d with a/c, US$69 suite) has been in business since 1945, but that doesn't mean they rest on their laurels. They are constantly adapting to new services and technology, most recently by using solar power to generate electricity. Aside from its excellent location at the southeast corner of the zócalo, the hotel boasts a gym, swimming pool, and lush garden areas for relaxation. Locals hail the on-site restaurant as the best food in town.

Information and Services

For information on the ruins and other local attractions, stop by the **tourism kiosk** (in the Casa de Cultura, Calle Heroico Militar across from the southwest corner of the zócalo, no phone, 8am-10pm daily) on the south side of the main square.

For medical services and emergencies, **Clínica Santa Fe** (Benito Juárez 2, tel. 953/532-0902, 24 hrs daily) has round-the-clock emergency care. Doctors only speak Spanish.

The **post office** (5 de Febrero 16, no phone, 8am-5pm Mon.-Fri., 8am-noon) is a few blocks south of the main square. From its southwest corner, walk south on Antonio de León until it curves to the right and becomes 5 de Febrero. The post office is a block and a half down the street on the left.

Getting There

To get to Huajuapan from Oaxaca City by bus, you have limited choices. Autobuses SUR runs two daily routes from **Terminal Periférico** (Periférico 1006, Oaxaca City, no phone, US$9) in the southwest corner of the Centro, about three blocks south of the Centro de Abastos, but they leave at 5am and 11pm. This means you'll either have to get up super early or arrive super late, as the trip takes about three hours. The **ADO Terminal in Huajuapan** is on the corner of Calle Nuyoó and Highway 190, three blocks north of the churchyard.

Your best option from Oaxaca City is to take a suburban run by **Servicios Turísticos de Huajuapan** (Valerio Trujano 420, Oaxaca City, tel. 951/516-5759, US$6). Vans run every 1.25 hours, beginning around 4am. They will take you to their **terminal in Huajuapan** (Nuyoó 36, tel. 953/530-5204), a couple blocks

north of the main square. From Nochixtlán, you'll have to take a taxi to the gas station west of town on Highway 190 and hop on one of these suburbanes. The trip from here takes about 1.5 hours and will cost around US$4.

Drivers from Oaxaca City take Highway 190 west out of the city and take the left lanes to exit onto Highway 135D (toll) 11 km (6.8 mi) outside of the city. Stay on this highway another 69 km (43 mi) and exit onto Highway 190 just outside of Nochixtlán. Drivers from Nochixtlán head west on Porfirio Díaz to get on this highway. Huajuapan is 91 km (57 mi) down Highway 190 from this junction. Total drive time from Oaxaca City is 2.5 hours, and 1.5 hours from Nochixtlán.

SANTO DOMINGO TONALÁ

The small farming town of **Santo Domingo Tonalá** is the perfect escape from the busy streets of Huajuapan de León. Mototaxis cruise the town's broad, palm-lined avenues, ferrying residents around the tranquil, traffic-free couple dozen blocks that make up town. Even the short hike through the canyon north of town is a rather laid-back activity.

Tonalá is Nahuatl for "The Place Where It Gets Hot," but don't worry. If you need to cool off, you can find some shade in the jungly churchyard in front of the 16th-century neo-classical **Iglesia de Santo Domingo,** or among the massive ahuehuete (Montezuma cypress) trees in **La Sabinera,** a small park two blocks east of the zócalo. The largest of these trees is at the far west end of the park, with a diameter of 4.5 meters (14.8 ft) and a girth of 15 meters (49 ft).

★ Cañón El Boquerón

You'll pass the entrance to the **Cañon El Boquerón** (Bigmouth Canyon) when you cross the bridge over the Río Salado on your way into town. Decreed a protected area in 2008, this awe-inspiring gorge is home to hundreds of species of flora and fauna, although you're not likely to see many animals besides lizards, weird caterpillars, and a spectrum

Santo Domingo Tonalá

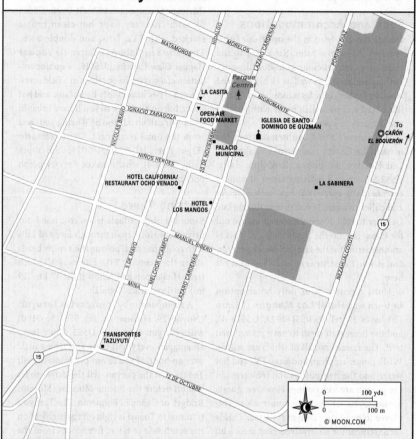

MATAMOROS

MORELOS

HIDALGO

LÁZARO CÁRDENAS

PORFIRIO DÍAZ

IGNACIO ZARAGOZA

NICOLÁS BRAVO

NIÑOS HEROES

Parque
Central

LA CASITA

OPEN-AIR
FOOD MARKET

NIGROMANTE

IGLESIA DE SANTO
DOMINGO DE GUZMÁN

To
CAÑÓN
EL BOQUERÓN

20 DE NOVIEMBRE

PALACIO
MUNICIPAL

HOTEL CALIFORNIA/
RESTAURANT OCHO VENADO

LA SABINERA

HOTEL
LOS MANGOS

15

MANUEL RIBERO

5 DE MAYO

MELCHOR OCAMPO

LÁZARO CÁRDENAS

NEZAHUALCÓYOTL

MINA

TRANSPORTES
TAZUYUTI

15

12 DE OCTUBRE

0   100 yds
0   100 m

© MOON.COM

of colorful butterflies on the trail. Much of the walking path is cantilevered over the river below, hugging the sheer canyon walls that tower more than 400 meters (1,312 ft) above the canyon floor. Other stretches of the trail run under lines of jacaranda trees, which are stunning in spring when their leafless branches are ablaze with pinkish-purple blossoms that fall to the ground like snow on an alien planet.

It takes only about an hour to walk the flat, easy 2-km (1.2-mi) trail, but since there's little else to do, you might make a leisurely afternoon of it with a picnic or just chilling out on

the riverbank. To get here from Tonalá, grab a *colectivo* bound for Huajuapan on the highway (about US$0.50) or hitch a ride. The bridge is about 4 km (2.5 mi) north of town; you'll find the entrance to the trail on the north side of the bridge.

As in many other parts of La Mixteca, tourism is loosely organized here, but if you want an informed **local guide** who can tell you about the plant and animal species that inhabit the canyon, ask for Artemio Cruz in the veterinarian pharmacy/popsicle shop next to Hotel Los Mangos. Artemio knows everything there is to do in and around town, and will help you get to appreciate the place, but he only speaks Spanish.

Food and Accommodations

During the day, head to the **open-air food market** (9am-6pm Mon.-Sat.) next to the main plaza for delicious *antojitos* like quesadillas and tacos, as well as richly flavored *moles* and other *guisados* (sauce-based dishes) like *chileajo*, a pork dish made with *guajillo* and *chicoxtle* peppers.

Just across Calle Cuauhtémoc from the market, **La Casita** (corner of Cuauhtémoc and Hidalgo, no phone, 8am-9pm daily, US$2.50) serves a rotating menu of *comida corrida* (daily special) dishes, such as *moles* and chiles rellenos. If you're here during late October to mid-November, keep an eye out for *huaxmole* on the menu outside. This is another name for the famed *mole de caderas*, and it won't cost an arm and a leg to try it here.

Until recently, your only hotel option in town was **Hotel Los Mangos** (Lázaro Cárdenas 27, tel. 953/531-0023, US$13 d), and the hotel staff seem to have gotten used to it. The rooms, not all of which are within Wi-Fi range, are clean and have TVs and hot water, and the rose bushes and fruit trees in the garden are welcoming. However, guests are not given their keys and must ask an employee to open the room every time. This is inconvenient for all involved (and feels a bit patronizing).

On the block to the west of Los Mangos, Alí Martínez and family run **Hotel California** (Melchor Ocampo, tel. 953/531-0026, US$13 d), with five very basic but clean rooms stocked with TVs, fans, and double beds. They also run **Cabañas Garra de Jaguar** (Jaguar Claw Cabañas; US$18), a quaint collection of also very basic cabins in a field south of town. They have comfy beds, fans, and hot water, but no kitchens, so you'll have to eat in town—or call up Alí and he'll bring you food from the hotel restaurant, **Ocho Venado** (Eight Deer; tel. 953/531-0026, 7am-10pm daily, US$2-4), which makes a pretty bomb pork burrito.

Getting There

Santo Domingo Tonalá is a scenic one-hour drive from Huajuapan through forested hills with columnar cacti poking their spiny heads above the treetops. Take Highway 15 south from Huajuapan and follow it for 47 km (29 mi) until you reach Tonalá.

A *suburban* run by **Transportes Tazuyuti** (Nuyoó 29, Huajuapan, tel. 953/155-3180) will cost you a bit over US$2. They leave Huajuapan every half hour and take a little over an hour. If you're not planning to visit Tonalá, just the canyon, tell the driver to let you off before the Puente Morelos (Morelos Bridge), or Cañón El Boquerón. The Tazuyuti terminal in Tonalá is right off the highway on the south side of town, five blocks from the *zócalo*.

Pacific Coast and the Sierra Sur

The towering cloud-forested peaks of the Sierra Madre del Sur run the entire coast of Oaxaca, terminating in the Istmo de Tehuantepec to the east, and to the west running through the state of Guerrero and on into southern Michoacán. On the sierra's northern rim, which abuts the semiarid deserts of the Valles Centrales, giant magueys thrive in the abundance of moisture, shooting their flower stalks over 12 meters (40 ft) into the mountain air, brilliant tufts of yellow and orange flowers at their tips. Night-black caterpillars with pink and gold fireworks for hair crawl the pine needle carpet of the forest floor. Sometimes the valleys fill with a sea of clouds, and the sunset drenches it in the full array of colors available. I half-jokingly believe that this is

Highlights

Look for ★ to find recommended sights, activities, dining, and lodging.

© MOON.COM

★ **San José del Pacífico:** This foggy mountain town, a popular destination for hippies seeking psychedelic experiences since the 1970s, has its head in the clouds, in more ways than one (page 229).

★ **Pluma Hidalgo:** Site of the first coffee farm in Oaxaca, Pluma Hidalgo is where all the caffeine-fueled magic started and is a mandatory pilgrimage destination for anyone who lives by the mantra, ". . . but first, coffee" (page 232).

★ **Mazunte:** Oaxaca's premier "hippie beach" is the ideal spot to do as little as possible—but if you want to do more than nothing, the Mexican Turtle Center in town and crocodile hatchery at neighboring Ventanilla offer exciting and informational ecotours (page 239).

★ **La Crucecita:** Founded originally to make room for tourism on the bays, this vibrant little town at the heart of Bahías de Huatulco has enough delicious restaurants, quality handicrafts stores, and affordable hotels to attract visitors as well (page 254).

★ **Las Cascadas Mágicas and Finca La Gloria:** Spend the day sipping shade-grown coffee and swimming in the cool, clear water of the Copalita River in the sultry jungle north of Huatulco (page 269).

★ **Playa Zicatela:** Home of the world-renowned "Mexican Pipeline," this beach offers top-tier surfing, international wave riding competitions, and out-of-this-world sunsets (page 273).

★ **Playas Manzanillo, Puerto Angelito, and Carrizalillo:** The sapphire water that laps the fine sands of these protected coves is perfect for snorkeling and splashing around (page 274).

★ **Laguna de Manialtepec:** This lagoon just a half hour from Puerto Escondido is home to countless species of migratory birds, as well as bioluminescent phytoplankton that glow in the water (page 289).

★ **Parque Nacional Lagunas de Chacahua:** Take a boat tour through the mangrove forests of the park's seven coastal lagoons, where crocodiles lurk. Fortunately for surfers, the crocs stay away from the 16 km (10 mi) of beach on Isla Chacahua (page 289).

the exact place Dr. Seuss was telling me about in *Oh, The Places You'll Go.*

The mountains grow increasingly more tropical as they near the coast, often referred to as "La Costa Chica" (The Little Coast), a toponym that also includes the shores of neighboring Guerrero. With 595 km (370 mi) of coastline, Oaxaca has a beach for everyone....

Playa Zicatela in Puerto Escondido offers the best surfing in the country. Only experienced surfers should tackle the world-class beach break here—but the calmer point break at Punta Zicatela, farther down the beach, is perfect for learning the ropes.

The beaches of Mazunte, San Agustinillo, and Zipolite are popular destinations for hippies, nudists, yoga retreaters, and sea turtles alike. Seven of the world's eight sea turtle species swim to Oaxaca's shores to lay eggs, and Mazunte, home of the Centro Mexicano de la Tortuga (Mexican Turtle Center), is a great place to learn about these incredible and endangered animals, and even observe them in the wild.

Billed as the "Cancún of the Oaxacan coast" when it was planned by the federal government in the 1980s, Bahías de Huatulco has everything from virgin beaches to five-star, all-inclusive resorts to the ebullient and colorful La Crucecita, the pint-sized urban heartbeat of the place. Huatulco is the kind of place where you can live in the lap of luxury one night, and the next pitch a tent at the campground right next door. With nine bays, a national park, 2,000-year-old ruins, more surfing, and waterfalls all within reach, Huatulco, like the rest of the gorgeous Oaxacan coast, truly does have something for everyone.

PLANNING YOUR TIME

The Oaxacan coast is the kind of place where you meet people who came for a week six years ago and never left. How does one plan a stay in paradise? Give yourself at least a week, and start in the heavens. When you get all the way up to towns like **San José del Pacífico,** you're going to want to stay longer, so you might as well just plan for it. Stay a night or two in the foggy heights of San José, catching your breath at soaring vistas everywhere you turn and sampling the plethora of delectable organic and artisanal products like blackberry pie, coffee, and mezcal cooked high up in the mountains. Oh, and *hongos,* magic mushrooms that have been used by the summit-dwelling locals for centuries. Spend a couple nights here, or head to nearby **San Mateo Río Hondo** for the second. Coffee pilgrims absolutely must visit **Pluma Hidalgo,** the town that started the coffee craze in Oaxaca and still produces world-class *café de altura,* coffee grown in tropical conditions at just under a mile above sea level.

If you've only got one week in this region, I recommend choosing one of the three major tourist centers on the coast according to what you want to do and spending the rest of your week there. **Puerto Escondido** is Mexico's top surfing destination, where the monstrous beach break at Zicatela has world-class riding year-round. The beaches from **Puerto Ángel** west to **Mazunte,** Oaxaca's de facto "hippie beaches," grow increasingly more so as you move west from Puerto Ángel, and have a few surfing and ecotourism opportunities, but beach bumming is the primary activity here. And **Bahías de Huatulco** has all that and more (except the nudism and professional-grade surfing). The rest of your week can be a combination of beach bumming and excursions to local attractions.

In Puerto Escondido, your day-trip options include adventure tours in the wildlife-rich **Lagunas de Chacahua** and **Laguna de Manialtepec,** or cultural excursions to towns like **Santa Catarina Juquila.** Over on the hippie beaches, take a boat ride through a croc-filled swamp at **La Ventanilla,** or learn

---

Previous: beach *palapas* in Puerto Escondido; Mazunte's Playa Rinconcito; Las Cascadas Mágicas.

Pacific Coast and the Sierra Sur

GUERRERO

Xochistlahuaca
Ometepec
San Pedro Amuzgos
Santa María Zacatepec
La Reforma
San Juan Cacahuatepec
Santiago Llano Grande
Cuajinicuilapa
Mancuernas
Pinotepa Nacional
San Andrés Huaxpaltepec
Santiago Jamiltepec
Laguna de Corralero
SIERRA MADRE DEL SUR
San Miguel Panixtlahuaca
EL PEDIMENTO
Santa Catarina Juquila
Verde
San José del Progreso
Parque Nacional Lagunas de Chacahua
Río Grande
Chacahua
PARQUE NACIONAL LAGUNAS DE CHACAHUA
LAGUNA DE MANIALTEPEC
Bajos de Chila
SEE "PARQUE NACIONAL LAGUNAS DE CHACAHUA" MAP

PACIFIC OCEAN

0   10 mi
0   10 km
© MOON.COM

to free dive in Puerto Ángel. In Huatulco, take a trip out to the **Cascadas Mágicas,** a jungle cataract that tumbles into a pool of refreshing turquoise water; wander the recently discovered pre-Hispanic ruins at the **Parque Eco-Arqueológico Copalita;** or speed through the dense jungle of **Parque Nacional Huatulco** on a mountain bike. If you have more time and want to do it all, I recommend spending at least three days each

in Puerto Escondido, Mazunte, and Bahías de Huatulco.

High season on the coast corresponds with major national holidays. To get your accommodations of choice, book at least a month in advance of the Christmas holiday and Semana Santa, the two weeks leading up to Easter. The coast is also very busy in the months of July and August, when school is out for summer vacation.

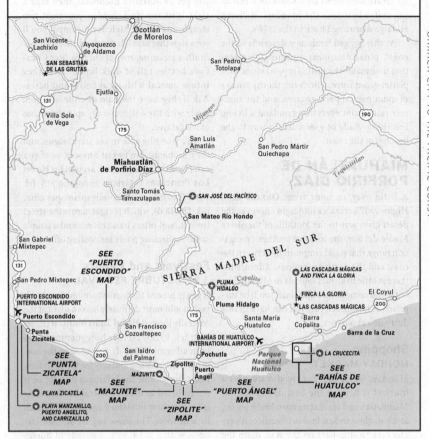

Oaxaca City to the Pacific Coast

Highway 175 will get you to the coast in less than six hours from Oaxaca City, but I don't recommend doing it all in one go. Artisanal mezcal aficionados will want to consider a quick stop in Miahuatlán to try the moonshine-grade infusions the little *expendios* (shops) sell out of old Coca-Cola bottles. Up in the cloud forests of the Sierra Madre del Sur, little towns like San José del Pacífico and San Mateo Río Hondo have cozy *cabañas* (cabins) sprinkled all over the peaks, offering

breathtaking views and other mind-boggling experiences.

Moving south, the middle strip of the sierra climbs even higher into thick pine forests where day turns to night in an instant, at the whim of the swift billows of clouds that scud over the peaks and reduce visibility to nada. Farther south, these altitudes meet the sultry air of the coast, and banana, almond, gigantic fig, and other tropical trees sprout wherever they can between the pines. The altitude, humidity, and combination of hot and cold air create the perfect conditions for cultivating coffee beans, as the founders of Pluma Hidalgo discovered back in the 1870s.

As this rugged landscape descends to the coast, pines disappear and jungle vegetation dominates the hills. Tropical vines with platter-sized leaves climb the thorny trunks of monumental *pochote* trees, and the summer rains paint everything on land a living, breathing shade of green all the way to the beaches of the coast.

MIAHUATLÁN DE PORFIRIO DÍAZ

A little over an hour from Oaxaca City, Highway 175 crinkles into tight curves as the desert gives way to the foothills of the Sierra Madre del Sur, the massive southern mountain range that stands imposingly between the coast and the northern regions. Admittedly, there is little to attract tourists to Miahuatlán, but if you come at the right time, you'll be surprised at how much fun you can have in this dusty desert outpost.

Shopping
MONDAY MARKET

Monday, when the weekly *día de plaza market* is held, is the best day to stop in Miahuatlán and see it at its most lively. Seeing as it's so close to San José del Pacífico, it's really easy to stop here on the way, roam the tarpaulin-shaded central streets, chow down on some tacos or *empanadas de amarillo*, grab a bag of fresh fruit for the road, and still make it to San José by sunset.

MEZCAL

Mezcal producers here are very well respected by those in the know, and on Mondays, their homemade, unregulated spirits are sold throughout the chaotic market. There's a little **nameless *expendio***—barely more than an open door—that is also open every other day of the week except Sunday a few blocks from the *zócalo,* or main square (which is a block south of the Líneas Unidas station). From the

zócalo, walk east on Juárez two blocks until you get to Mariano Escobedo, then take a right. Walk two blocks, and on your right, two storefronts before Melchor Ocampo, you'll see a sign that says "Expendio de Mezcal" beneath a gleaming row of old two-liter Coca-Cola bottles full of dark liquid. Here they infuse mezcal with local fruits and herbs. Ask if they have the *palo de chile* infusion, made with the enigmatically spicy branches of a local tree.

You won't be able to see street signs, and they probably don't exist anyway, so if you can't find the *expendio,* ask around for **Hotel Los Príncipes** (Mariano Escobedo 315, tel. 951/572-0790, www.hotellosprincipes.com.mx, US$18 d), which is right across the street from it, and offers basic rooms and a couple small swimming pools for cooling off.

Festivals and Events
3 DE OCTUBRE FESTIVAL

If you're headed to the coast around October 3, you should most definitely book a night at the centrally located **Hotel Juan Manuel** (Rojas 202, tel. 951/572-1152, hoteljuanmanuel@hotmail.com, US$13 d), just around the corner from the *zócalo,* and stay for the festivities. Before he became the infamous dictator he is remembered as today, General Porfirio Díaz led a battalion to victory against the French here in 1866. The show begins in the afternoon with a *cabalgata,* a parade of horses through the Centro. Then at night the mezcal comes out, and a riotous party ensues in the *zócalo.* Wear clothes you don't mind getting wet or possibly stained. Kids and teenagers shoot soapy, sometimes colored water at each other from plastic bottles, and break confetti eggs over each other's heads.

Don't forget to keep a few coins in your pockets, too. Around the *zócalo,* people have set up bamboo cages, and throughout the melee, young folks grab unsuspecting revelers and drag them inside. If you're caught, you'll have to pay a few pesos to make bail. This is truly a unique festival you don't want to miss if you have the chance.

Magic Mushrooms

For centuries, the inhabitants of the northern peaks of the Sierra Sur have used *hongos* (literally, "fungus," but in this context, "magic mushrooms") in spiritual ceremonies and to commune with nature. To this day, residents of San José del Pacífico and neighboring communities begin taking mushrooms as early as age six, and tourists looking for a different kind of trip have been coming here since the 1970s.

Just about every *cabaña* hotel in San José will ask you if you're interested in buying mushrooms when you check in—some even advertise conspicuously. Although the mushrooms are technically illegal under Mexican federal law, authorities consider the practice to be an essential part of cultural life here, and since trade remains hyper-local, the sale and use of them is overlooked. The authorities also tolerate consumption by visitors but stipulate that the mushrooms must be collected, sold, and consumed within the community.

From July to October, fresh mushrooms are available, in *familias*, clusters of 4-6 small mushrooms, or the tall, broad-capped *maestro*. At the end of the rainy season, people conserve them in honey, and supplies usually last for a month or two after that. Some places will prepare them in a tea. The *hongos* of San José are considered to be quite strong. Some visitors eat only half of what they're sold to see how it affects them before taking the rest—everyone has a different response and level of tolerance.

Getting There

Miahuatlán is 105 km (65 mi) south of Oaxaca City, a two-hour drive or *suburban* ride. *Suburban* vans leave Oaxaca City from the **Líneas Unidas** (US$3.50) stop on the corner of Bustamante and Xólotl every hour or two. It's super easy to just show up and hop on one within the hour. Drivers take Highway 175 south from Oaxaca City. About halfway there, you'll have to go through Ocotlán, which can be confusing, but usually there is enough traffic to make the way obvious. Miahuatlán is a little over an hour down the highway from Ocotlán.

TOP EXPERIENCE

★ SAN JOSÉ DEL PACÍFICO

Perched atop the first row of the sierra's towering peaks, the smoky *cabañas* of San José del Pacífico (elevation 2,500 m/8,202 ft), appear about an hour after you begin the ascent. During the rainy season (June-September), night and day here are mercurial concepts that don't stick to the rest of the world's circadian rhythms. Clouds regularly scud through the valley, blotting out the spectacular views and shrouding the early afternoon in a false twilight. If you're lucky, you'll see the famous *mar de nubes*, an effect that science calls a temperature inversion, when the valley below is filled with a "sea" of clouds.

This mountain town has its head in the clouds in more ways than one—it's been a popular destination for hippies since the 1970s due to the locals' use of psychedelic mushrooms. But even if you have no interest in magic mushrooms, the views, coffee, and blackberries in San José are also excellent reasons to come. And there are trails everywhere—through tunnels of fragrant pines and harlequin patches of wildflowers—perfect for strolling and taking in the beautiful scenery.

Food

Roasted in-house, the espresso at ★ **Café Express** (Hwy. 175, tel. 951/596-7329, 6:30am-10pm daily) is dark as night and has sharp teeth, but doesn't bite so hard as to overtake the fruity, smoky undertones the plants pull from the high-altitude soils here. They also serve large, fresh, and inexpensive baguette sandwiches and a phenomenal *pay de zarzamora* (blackberry pie).

For breakfast, grab a steaming cup of *café*

de olla and a plate of *huevos al comal* (eggs fried on a ceramic griddle called a *comal*) at **Comedor La Morenita** (Hwy. 175, no phone, 7am-4pm daily, US$2-3), just to the south of La Montaña, the store where the vans stop. A few other *comedores* (family-run restaurants) line this part of the highway as well.

For dinner, you absolutely must eat at ★ **La Taberna de los Duendes** (Hwy. 175, tel. 951/169-2672, 2pm-10pm daily, US$8-20), an Italian restaurant that serves incredible pastas, salads, steaks, steamed trout, sausages, cheese plates, and more. If it's available, grab the table in the little lookout nook that offers a panoramic view of the pine-forested valley below. They also have a good selection of mezcal infusions. Los Duendes buys *espadín* maguey hearts from Miahuatlán and distills them into homemade mezcal up here in the mountains. They sometimes host live ska and reggae music. Stop by and ask about upcoming shows, or check their Facebook page for event listings.

Accommodations

About 4 km (2.5 mi) north of San José, a steep cobblestone road leads down to the aptly named **Refugio Terraza de la Tierra** (Hwy. 175, no phone, www.terrazadelatierra.com, thomaskokdk@gmail.com, US$27 d, US$34 t, US$44 four-person *cabaña*). The name means "Earth's Terrace Refuge," and once you see the view, you'll know why. No cell service, Wi-Fi only in the restaurant, and the soothing sound of trickling water from the system of small canals around the *cabañas* make this the perfect refuge from the real world, which we all need every now and then. The on-site restaurant serves only vegetarian food.

Just north of town, **La Puesta del Sol** (Hwy. 175, tel. 951/190-8256, www.sanjosedelpacifico.com, US$21 d, US$31 *cabaña*) has hotel-style rooms, as well as *cabañas* made of beautiful blonde pine and situated along the slope so as not to leave a bad seat in the house for a view of the sunset. All rooms have hot water in the showers and

potable water in the taps (it's delicious), and *cabañas* include fireplaces, which are key for the chilly, high-altitude nights up here. Only about a half a mile north of town, it's a pleasant 10-15-minute walk into town along the highway.

★ **Cabañas La Cumbre** (Camino al Cerro La Postema, tel. 951/126-3993, US$8-15 shared bathroom, US$18 en suite) offers pretty, wood-paneled *cabañas*, giving visitors the chance to stay on the hill with the best view in town. Prices are quite low, making it one of the best values up here in the clouds. They offer guided hikes and *temazcal*, and the on-site restaurant is open 8am-10pm daily; they also sell *hongos* (magic mushrooms).

On the hill just below La Cumbre, **Sueño Atrapado** (Trapped Dream; Camino al Cerro La Postema, tel. 951/281-2399 or 951/323-1496, diamante_negro57@hotmail.com, US$5 dorm, US$8-13 d, US$31 *cabaña*) doesn't have as spectacular a view as its neighbor, but is still an excellent value. Amenities include Wi-Fi access and a communal kitchen, and the *cabañas* have fireplaces.

Getting There

San José del Pacífico is 136 km (84 mi) south of Oaxaca City on Highway 175. The drive takes a little less than three hours in a private car, and closer to three in one of the *suburban* vans run by **Líneas Unidas** (Bustamante 601, Oaxaca City, tel. 951/516-2472). Vans leave Oaxaca every 15-30 minutes and cost about US$5.

To get here from Miahuatlán, flag down a passing *suburban* (US$1.50) on the highway, or take a *camioneta* run by **Servicio Mixto Suchixtepec,** which costs about US$1. Their base is on Calle Álamos, two and a half blocks south of the *zócalo*. Look for the orange walls and blue gate across from the elementary school. San José is 35 km (22 mi) south of Miahuatlán via Highway 175. The drive up the northern slopes of the Sierra Sur takes about 50 minutes.

Temazcal: Indigenous Sweat Lodge

When the Spanish arrived in Mesoamerica, they found the little adobe huts used for *temazcal*, a pre-Hispanic spiritual and medicinal sweat bath, just about everywhere they went. The Aztecs called it *temazcalli*, a contraction of the Nahuatl words *temas* (bath) and *calli* (house). Despite the conquistadors' attempts to quash the practice, it has survived to this day under the name *temazcal*, and gained popularity in Oaxaca as tourism grew.

Traditionally, a *temazcal* was performed in part to worship Temazcalteci, "the grandmother of baths." The ceremony involved elements of ancient Aztec cosmology, and the process is more or less the same today. The fire for heating the stones is lit on the east side of the hut, representing the sun, and the small south-facing opening in the hut is known as "the pathway of the dead." As the ancient doctrine states, to enter a *temazcal* is to return to the womb, and to exit afterward is a form of spiritual rebirth.

Spiritual beliefs aside, *temazcal* has a physical effect on the body, and this medicinal aspect has always been as important as the metaphysical. A healer called a *temazcalera* (usually a woman) selects herbs used in the vapor according to what ails the patient. She controls the heat during the sweat bath and can even give traditional massages to treat specific ailments, such as sciatica. After the bath, the patient is wrapped in a blanket and told to lie on the floor, usually in a separate room, to cool down. This cooldown is essential to the process, allowing the bather to recoup the energy lost in the process. *Temazcal* is said to relieve conditions such as rheumatism, arthritis, muscle and nerve pain, and even assuage the pain of childbirth.

There is much talk about the removal of toxins through the sweat, but it's questionable that extreme sweating does anything for you that your kidneys don't already do. Still, there is something to the "rebirth" aspect of it. After overheating and cooling off in the chilly mountain air, you'll feel renewed and ready to continue your journey.

SAN MATEO RÍO HONDO

Near San José del Pacífico, **San Mateo Río Hondo** is much more representative of a normal south Oaxacan mountain town. Although they're available, you won't find signs for magic mushrooms on every corner, like in San José—just wood and brick houses up and down the slopes, and the bright-orange Plaza Municipal standing out against the background of green.

Food and Accommodations

The small terrace at **Las Amapolas** (Escotel 2, tel. 951/488-7906, 8am-7pm Mon.-Sat., 8am-5pm Sun., US$2-3), just up the road from the bright-orange Ayuntamiento Municipal (local government offices) is the best place in town to enjoy a chocolate and take in the view of the town. Oaxaca mountain villages like these have a central speaker system from which local announcements and music are broadcast, so you might have a bit of *banda* music echoing through the valley as

soundtrack to your lunch. Their robust *mole coloradito* is just the thing for when the clouds blow in and it gets chilly.

There are only a couple hotel options in San Mateo. You'll find them on a lofty hillside on the east side of town. Blanca Astudillo runs **La Casa de la Abuela** (Privada Ixcotel, tel. 958/118-4145, US$11-13), a small collection of *cabañas* painted with colorful murals and with balconies overlooking picturesque San Mateo. The on-site restaurant (8am-10pm Mon.-Sat., US$3-5) serves tasty wood oven-baked pizzas and other Italian and Mexican dishes.

Right next door, **Posada Yegoyoxi** (Calle Ixcotel, no phone, www.yegoyoxi.com, posadayegoyoxi@gmail.com, US$11 d) has bright orange and yellow brick *cabañas* that seem to have almost grown out of the forest like the flowers and vines that thrive around them. Yegoyoxi (which means "River of Sand" in Zapotec) is a leader in responsible ecotourism in Oaxaca, having been the first establishment of its kind in the state to install composting toilets all the way back in 1987.

Getting There
WALKING
The most enjoyable way to get to San Mateo is on foot from San José. If you're not loaded down with luggage, take the road that climbs the hill just to the north of the main cluster of cafés and *cabañas* on the highway in San José. Take your first right at the local government building. From here, walk about 2 km (1.2 mi), or about half an hour, on the paved road until you see a sign to turn right onto a dirt road that says "San Mateo Río Hondo." From here, it's another 30-45-minute walk through tunnels of fragrant pine trees and dizzyingly high mountain vistas to the east side of San Mateo. The road is paved as it descends into town and terminates at its intersection with Calle Ixcotel. From here, the center of town is to the right, another 10 minutes downhill. To get to the *cabañas*, turn left and walk 100 meters (328 ft), where you'll see the turnoff to Privada Ixcotel.

CAR AND PUBLIC TRANSPORT
From San José, board a *suburban* or *camioneta* headed south and tell the driver you want to get off at the Zapotitlán stop, about 10 km (6.2 mi) down Highway 175. This should take about 15 minutes in a private car; it's a few minutes longer in public transport if the driver stops to let people on or off. From here, drive or grab a *taxi colectivo* or *camioneta* to take you the last 9 km (5.6 mi) to town. Taxi and truck drivers will drop you off near the hotels for a minimal extra charge, or you can foot it up the steep hill from the Centro in about 15 minutes. The trip will take 30-45 minutes, depending on how long you have to wait for the transfer, and should cost about US$3 in total.

★ PLUMA HIDALGO
Coffee grown in Pluma Hidalgo can be found in cafés all over the state, especially along the coast, but my fellow caffeine addicts should seriously consider making a pilgrimage to the mountaintop town on the misty southern slopes of the Sierra Madre del Sur. This, as they say, is where all the magic happens.

One of the local peaks is named Cerro de la Pluma (Hill of the Feather), either because it was in the habit of forming plume-shaped clouds at its peak when the town was founded, or because of the feathers that floated down from abandoned eagle nests when the raptors were more common there, depending on who you ask. The town's first name was derived from that. Its second name pays homage to Father Miguel Hidalgo, who famously kicked off the revolution in 1810 with a rousing speech remembered as the *Grito de Dolores* (Shout of Dolores) in the town of Dolores, Guanajuato, whose current second name also honors the insurgent priest.

Coffee from Pluma is referred to as *café de altura*, literally "coffee of heights," and it's exactly this altitude (Pluma averages around 1,300 m/4,265 ft above sea level) combined with the hot, humid tropical air that comes in from the coast that gives it its distinct full body and rich flavor. Some coffee is grown as high as 1,500 meters (4,921 ft) above sea level.

Pluma is a quiet, workaday town at present, but residents are opening businesses and making strides to attract more tourism. There are a few cafés in town where you can taste the local coffee, or you can tour a nearby *finca* (coffee plantation).

Sights
CAFÉS
There are a couple of coffee shops right around the main square.

The espresso at **La Bóveda** (Pluma Hidalgo *zócalo*, tel. 958/103-8245, rosilaboveda@ gmail.com, 9am-11pm daily) is worth the trip to Pluma, as is the view of the verdant slopes of the Sierra Sur from the **lookout point** on

---

1: the horse procession at Miahuatlán's 3 de Octubre festival 2: San José del Pacífico 3: the cloudy slopes around Pluma Hidalgo, perfect for growing coffee

the basketball court on the other side of the municipal government building on the west side of the *zócalo.*

Next door to La Bóveda, **Café Cerro de la Pluma** (Pluma Hidalgo *zócalo,* tel. 951/282-0405 or 951/115-1573, cafe_cerrodelapluma@hotmail.com, 9am-2pm and 4pm-10pm daily), the coffee shop of local *finca* Cerro de la Pluma, has a small selection of locally produced mezcals in addition to phenomenal cups of joe.

You'll also find the Black Gold of Pluma at **Café Origen Mágico** (Guerrero 2, tel. 958/525-8057, 7am-11pm daily), to the south of the church, Iglesia Ave María. The café boasts a flowery terrace with a spectacular view of mountains below.

FINCAS (COFFEE PLANTATIONS)

To get a taste of what it's like to grow and process coffee in Pluma, contact Damián Ramírez or his sister Concepción of **Cerro de la Pluma,** whose café (Pluma Hidalgo *zócalo,* tel. 951/282-0405 or 951/115-1573, cafe_cerrodelapluma@hotmail.com, 9am-2pm and 4pm-10pm daily) in town is right next to La Bóveda. The Ramírez family's *finca* (coffee plantation) is situated over 1,500 meters (4,921 ft) above sea level, and everything from sowing to harvesting to drying and roasting is done using artisanal methods. Their customizable tours, or *rutas* (routes) as they call them, can include trips to waterfalls, *finca* tours, hikes, coffee tasting, samplings of local gastronomy, and more.

Tours range US$17-27 for the day, depending on the season and activities you want to do. The Ramírez family is more focused on spreading knowledge and awareness of coffee culture and production in Pluma than making a profit, so if you're interested in learning more, Damián will throw in a rustic night out on their plantation at no extra cost. They need at least a couple days to prepare, so call or write them in advance.

If roughing it isn't your preferred way of seeing a coffee farm, book a room at ★ **Finca Don Gabriel** (Colonia José Palogrande,

Pluma Hidalgo, tel. 958/583-9444 or 958/108-0763, www.fincadongabriel.com, US$24-45 d, US$45 t), about a mile south of town. The bright-orange hotel-quality *cabañas,* with private bathrooms and hammocks strung on the porches, offer sprawling views of the southern slopes of the Sierra Sur as they descend to the sea. You can easily see the ocean from here. There is a small coffee museum, playground, and swimming pool on the grounds. The on-site restaurant, open 8am-6pm daily, is good enough to draw locals from Pluma for weekend dinners of traditional Oaxacan fare. There's also a spa that offers massages, facials, *temazcal,* and other beauty and relaxation treatments.

For activities, they offer tours of the plantation grounds for US$16 per person, with discounts for groups. There's also lots of hiking in the surrounding hills, as well as a *tiorlesa* (zip line), which costs about US$5 a zip.

Food and Accommodations

A couple *comedores* around the *zócalo* serve traditional Oaxacan dishes until the late evening. **Comedor La Flor del Café** (corner of Matamoros and Allende, tel. 958/525-8108, 8am-8pm daily, US$2-4) is next to Café Origen Mágico, south of the church, and **Comedor Raquel** (Pluma Hidalgo *zócalo,* tel. 958/525-8081, 8am-9:30pm daily, US$2-4), on the west side of the *zócalo,* stays open a little later.

If you're charmed into staying a night in town, the seafoam-green **Posada Isabel** (behind the Iglesia Ave María, tel. 958/525-8113, US$18) has clean private rooms with hot water, TV, internet, and gorgeous views of the valley to the south. The harlequin shades of sunset are best viewed from the second-floor room with big bay windows on three sides, so snag it if it's available.

Getting There and Away

Suburban vans run by **Huatulco 2000** (Hidalgo 208, Oaxaca City, tel. 951/516-3154, US$11) leave Oaxaca City every two hours beginning at 7am. The trip takes about five

Oaxacan Coffee

Native to east Africa, coffee first arrived in Mexico around 1796, making its way from Cuba to the ports of Veracruz on merchant ships. It later came to the state of Michoacán from Mocha, Arabia (present-day Yemen) in 1823, and in 1847, coffea (the name of the shrub) seeds made their way from Guatemala to Oaxaca's neighbor to the east, Chiapas.

In the mid-19th century, the production of synthetic dyes began to have a negative effect on the demand for Oaxacan cochineal, the scale insect that grows on the nopal cactus, used to make red dyes. This forced bug farmers from Miahuatlán to seek economic opportunity elsewhere. Illustrious Oaxacan statesman Don Matías Romero suggested they take a trip to Veracruz to learn about coffea cultivation and look for favorable places to grow it in the Sierra Sur.

They didn't have to look far. The shrub thrives all over these mountains, but it found its Shangri-La on the southern slopes, where the high altitudes and wet tropical air create the ideal conditions for growing a bean that produces a dark, muscular coffee with a not unpleasant bite of acidity that is usually blunted with *piloncillo* (Mexican brown sugar) in the traditional *café de olla*, made in a big clay pot (*olla*). The enterprising *miahuatecos* founded Pluma Hidalgo in the mid-1870s, and it didn't take long for word of the plant's potential to spread. Soon *fincas de café* (coffee plantations) were producing beans on slopes all along the mountainous coast.

the black gold of Pluma Hidalgo

We also have coffee to thank for the popular port towns of Puerto Ángel and Puerto Escondido, as both were established specifically to ship coffee beans. Since then, coffee has come to be grown in every region of Oaxaca save the low, dry Valles Centrales. Other popular growing regions are La Mixteca Alta and the Mixe region of the Sierra Norte.

hours. But you'll most likely be catching one of these on the main drag in San José de Pacífico. From here, the trip is a little over two hours and costs about US$6.

Drivers should keep an eye out for the junction at a sharp turn in the road on Highway 175 about 1.5 hours (61 km/38 mi) south of San José del Pacífico. From here, drive the last 9 km (5.6 mi) of the El Zapote-Copalita Highway to the vertiginously steep entrance to the town. Take a right at the top of the hill to get to the Centro.

To get to the **Puerto Ángel-Mazunte** beaches or **Puerto Escondido,** take a *colectivo* (US$1.50) back to Highway 175. From here, flag a passing *suburban* (US$2) to take you down to Pochutla and transfer from there.

To get to **Bahías de Huatulco** (not to be confused with Santa María Huatulco), hop on a *suburban* run by **Huatulco 2000** (US$3). They come through town every two hours, making a stop outside Café Origen Mágico.

Puerto Ángel and Vicinity

The string of beaches from **Puerto Ángel** west to Mazunte are unofficially known as Oaxaca's "hippie beaches." Here you won't find many luxury hotel options, but rather an abundance and wide variety of the predominant form of lodging: the *cabaña*. The main activity on this part of the coast is good old-fashioned beach bumming, and sights like the crocodile hatchery in La Ventanilla and turtle center in Mazunte offer fun, educational ecotourism opportunities.

Puerto Ángel was founded in 1850 at the behest of Benito Juárez, who saw the need for a port somewhere along the isolated coastline to ship lumber and all that delicious coffee grown in the clouds and shade of the southern slopes of the Sierra Madre del Sur. Puerto Ángel's time as a busy port was short-lived, however, as the railroad connection built in Salina Cruz in El Istmo a few decades later became the primary shipping point for products that had formerly been loaded onto ships at the dock on Puerto Ángel's Playa Principal.

As with other parts of the coast, tourism began to take over as the primary economic opportunity along these shores after the construction of Coastal Highway 200 in the 1960s, but despite its growing popularity with visitors both foreign and domestic, Puerto Ángel and its neighboring beaches have retained the essence of the isolation that has characterized this part of Oaxaca since before Benito put that dock there. If you're looking for an escape, this is where you want to come.

Getting Oriented

From Pochutla to the north of Puerto Ángel, Highway 175 crosses the coastal highway and winds south through tight, jungled curves toward the sea. Along this stretch of highway you'll find the turnoffs to the isolated beaches of **Playa La Boquilla** and **Playa Estacahuite. Puerto Ángel** is 10 km (6.2 mi) south of the junction with Highway 200,

and here Highway 175 turns west and runs along the coast, passing through the small beach towns of **Zipolite** (4 km/2.5 mi from Puerto Ángel), **San Agustinillo** (8 km/5 mi), and **Mazunte** (9.5 km/5.9 mi), which grow increasingly more "hippie" as you move west, before curving back north to meet up once again with Highway 200. **La Ventanilla** is 3 km (1.9 mi) west of Mazunte.

Getting Around

Travel between these beaches is cheap and easy. Anytime you want to head up or down the coast, just wait along the main road (Hwy. 175) for a *camioneta* to come along. The trucks charge US$1 or less, depending on where you're going.

A little more expensive, but much more fun, is renting a **scooter** from the unnamed scooter rental place in Mazunte, operated by the owners of the ice cream shop **La Garrafita** (tel. 958/119-0161, 9am-10pm daily), on the main road by the broad, open square a couple hundred meters west of the turtle center. They charge about US$27 for 24 hours, and give discounts if you rent one for multiple days. The scooters guzzle gas, so you'll most likely need to fill up at **Refaccionaría López** (Hwy. 175 in Zipolite, no phone, 8am-10pm Mon.-Fri., 9am-10pm Sat.-Sun.), a small mechanic shop on the east side of the soccer field in Zipolite. It's difficult to spot, so if you're headed west and see the soccer field, pull a U-turn and look for the shop in the little storefront to the right of the public library.

BEACHES AND SIGHTS
Playa La Boquilla

The first beach as you head south from Pochutla is **Playa La Boquilla,** a petite splash of sand with only enough room for one hotel at the bottom of a very steep and bumpy decline from the mountainous terrain above. You'll see the sign for the turnoff about 5.5 km

Puerto Ángel

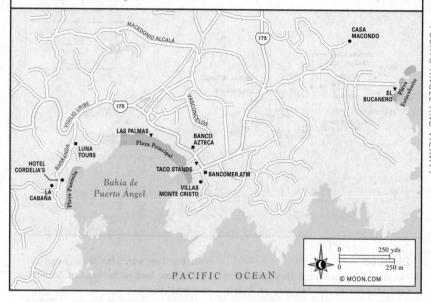

(3.4 mi) south of the junction with Highway 200. From here, the dirt road, heavily rutted during the rainy season, climbs over a sylvan ridge before descending somewhat perilously to the miniature paradise below. If you're having second thoughts about trying the road on a scooter, I can assure you that it's doable, as the trio of eager young Oaxacan surfers who were piled onto one showed me after I chickened out and turned mine around to leave before making it to the beach. *¡Sí, se puede!* (Yes, you can!)

Playa Estacahuite

Tucked away in a sheltered cove to the east of Puerto Ángel, the waters at **Playa Estacahuite** are turquoise, tranquil, and oh-so-inviting. The soft, fine sand of the beach is split in two by a rocky outcropping that extends into the gentle waves. Rock formations farther out in the small bay offer good snorkeling opportunities. The turnoff to Estacahuite is at the north edge of Puerto Ángel.

Playas Principal and Panteón

They may not be as Instagramable as the pair of aforementioned beaches, but Playas Principal and Panteón, in Puerto Ángel's main bay, have their own charm. The dock on **Playa Principal** gets lively toward sundown, as fishermen line up shoulder to shoulder to toss their lines out into the bay, local families relax in the sand after the workday is done, and youngsters practice their penalty shots between two sticks stuck in the sand.

Across the pint-sized bay, and connected to the main beach via a cobblestone path that skirts the rocky cliff between the two, **Playa Panteón** (Graveyard Beach) also has boats bobbing in the water and pulled up onto the sand, but fewer of them, making it the better choice for swimming. But don't let the currently charming little Playa Panteón fool you. It has a rather spooky past. Its name comes from the fact that human bones were found in the sand when the modern development was put in. The remains were moved to the graveyard farther inland.

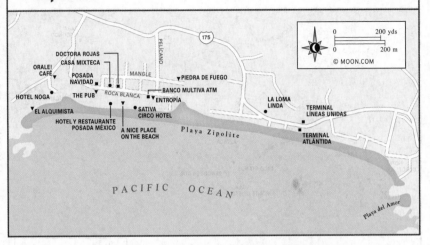

Zipolite

The most developed beach (though nowhere near as done up as Huatulco or Puerto Escondido) along this stretch of coastline is **Playa Zipolite,** known as the place where your birthday suit is acceptable beachwear, if that's what you're into. Although nudism is allowed all along the beach (most hotels and restaurants ask that you cover up when you come in from the sand), it's not necessarily the norm. In Zapotec, the name means "Beach of the Dead," as legend has it that early inhabitants used to offer their dead to the sea here.

The street behind the beachfront establishments, referred to as **El Adoquín,** is lined with bars and restaurants that get pretty lively during high season in July and August, which is a bit of a change of character for the beach. According to Horacio, a hotel owner who was reading Huxley's *Point Counter Point* when I greeted him, Zipolite isn't as hippie as it used to be. Horacio used to rent hammocks hung in the jungle for next to nothing, but he told me that recently people visiting Zipolite are looking for nicer rooms with air-conditioning and other amenities, so if you're looking to escape, you're better off looking elsewhere along the coast. But if you want a fun, social, au naturel kind of time, look no further that Zipolite's windswept shores.

At the eastern edge of Zipolite you'll find **Playa del Amor,** a secluded notch of golden sand stashed away among large igneous boulders. It's perfect for more private enjoyment of hanging out in only what God gave you.

San Agustinillo

Between Zipolite and Mazunte, **Playa San Agustinillo** has the best of both worlds. Not as active or naked as Zipolite, but neither as mellow as Mazunte, this broad, open sea beach is perfect for those who like to surf or bodyboard but also sometimes just want to splash around in some gentle waves. The west end of the beach curves out into the sea, and the rocky outcropping at sand's end creates a miniature bay that forms small but surfable waves when the ocean gets a little rowdy. At other times, the blue-green waters chill out and become perfect for snorkeling or just lazily cooling off in the afternoon heat.

The hilly terrain here snuggles up right next to the beach, forcing the main road to curve as closely as possible to the shore. Because of this, all the accommodations here are either right on the beach or just across the street from it, meaning you'll never have a long walk to the waves in San Agustinillo.

TOP EXPERIENCE

★ Mazunte

Oaxaca's beach bumming capital is **Mazunte**. There is no better place along the coast for doing absolutely nothing, and there's lots of space to do it in. The larger **Playa Mazunte** is just one of the beaches here, but most of the (in)action is on **Playa Rinconcito**, just over the rocks on the west side of the beach, around which the majority of the town's bars, restaurants, and *cabañas* are located. Over the hill to the west of the main town, **Playa Mermejita** is good for watching a sunset, but swimming isn't allowed due to the roughness of the water, so the beach is usually empty.

PUNTA COMETA

In between Playas Rinconcito and Mermejita juts the rocky headland called **La Punta Cometa**, probably the best place to watch a sunset in Oaxaca. Also called the Cerro Sagrado (Sacred Hill) of the coast, La Punta is the southernmost patch of earth in Oaxaca.

To get out to the point, take the road that climbs the hill to Playa Mermejita from Calle Rinconcito in the main town. At the top, you can follow the signs that lead you through the forested area out to the cactus-covered rocks of the promontory, or continue down the hill to Mermejita, where you'll climb up the hill at the east end of the beach. At the bottom of the south-facing cliffs there is a little tide pool with a small opening to the sea. Locals call this "the jacuzzi" for the rambunctious nature of the water that is agitated by the waves splashing through the opening in the rocks, similar to a bubbling hot tub. It is more or less safe to wade around or swim in—just steer clear of the breach in the rocks, as the water can pull you out to the open sea beyond.

CENTRO MEXICANO DE LA TORTUGA

Before the growth of tourism here, the main economic activity in Mazunte was sea turtle hunting. The facilities at the **Centro Mexicano de la Tortuga** (Hwy. 175, tel. 958/584-3376, www.centromexicanodelatortuga.org, 10am-4:30pm Wed.-Sat., 10am-2:30pm Sun., US$2) were originally a sea turtle slaughterhouse and processing plant. However, as development along the coast caused the human population to grow, populations of sea turtles began to decline. The tide began to slowly change in the 1970s, when Oaxacan fishing company Pesquera Industrial Oaxaca decided to take action. The company bought the slaughterhouse and founded the conservation center.

The collection of sea turtle eggs was banned in Mexico in 1971, but the ordinance had little effect in the real world, and sea turtle nests continued to disappear from Oaxaca's shores until 1990, when the Mexican federal government fully banned the turtle meat and eggs trade. Although things aren't perfect (turtles still get caught in drift nets to this day, sometimes by the hundreds), the turtle center's habitat conservation and baby turtle release programs have had a positive effect on the marine animal's population.

The small on-site museum provides information about the various species that visit Mazunte, as well as the steps the center is taking to conserve them and their habitat. Most of the signage is in Spanish, but visitors have the option to view the informational video in English. Also on-site is an aquarium that houses around 500 sea and freshwater turtles, many of which are rescues being prepared for release back into the wild. Kids especially love the baby sea turtle tanks.

Playa La Ventanilla

A little over a mile from Mazunte, **Playa La Ventanilla** is a long expanse of wave-battered sand, fully open to the gusts and swells of the powerful Pacific Ocean. But no big deal. You

Mazunte and San Agustinillo

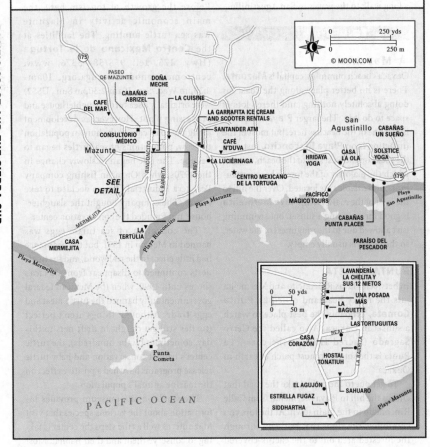

0 250 yds
0 250 m
© MOON.COM

175

PASEO DE MAZUNTE

DOÑA MECHE

CAFÉ DEL MAR

CABAÑAS ABRIZEL

LA CUISINE

LA GARRAFITA ICE CREAM AND SCOOTER RENTALS

SANTANDER ATM

CONSULTORIO MÉDICO

CAFÉ N'DUVA

Mazunte

LA LUCIÉRNAGA

San Agustinillo

CABAÑAS UN SUEÑO

HRIDAYA YOGA

CASA LA OLA

SOLSTICE YOGA

SEE DETAIL

CENTRO MEXICANO DE LA TORTUGA

175

Playa San Agustinillo

PACÍFICO MÁGICO TOURS

Playa Mazunte

RINCONCITO

LA BARRITA

CAREY

MERMEJITA

CABAÑAS PUNTA PLACER

LA TERTÚLIA

Playa Rinconcito

PARAÍSO DEL PESCADOR

CASA MERMEJITA

Playa Mermejita

Punta Cometa

PACIFIC OCEAN

LAVANDERÍA LA CHELITA Y SUS 12 NIETOS

0 50 yds
0 50 m

RINCONCITO

UNA POSADA MÁS

LA BAGUETTE

REAL

LAS TORTUGUITAS

CASA CORAZÓN

LA BARRITA

HOSTAL TONATIUH

EL AGUJÓN

SAHUARO

ESTRELLA FUGAZ

SIDDHARTHA

Playa Mazunte

don't come here to swim. On an island in the mangrove swamps behind the beach is a crocodile hatchery that works to conserve the habitat and maintain populations of the scaly reptiles. You'll also see loads of migratory seabirds, deer, and iguanas on the little island, and the hatchery has other animals, like monkeys. There's a good chance you'll see crocs in the wild, too. The beach is called La Ventanilla (The Window) for the portal-shaped rock formation at the beach's east end, which can be clearly seen from the lookout point on La Punta Cometa.

RECREATION

Mangrove and Crocodile Tours

In La Ventanilla, the **Sociedad Cooperativa Servicios Ecoturísticos de la Ventanilla** (Cooperative Society of Ecotourism Services of La Ventanilla; Playa La Ventanilla, tel. 249/596-0410 or 958/585-9111, www. laventanilla.com.mx, 8am-5pm daily) offers **boat tours** of the mangrove swamps and visits to the **crocodile hatchery** and *coco-drilario* (crocodile farm) on the small island in the lagoon, as well as **nighttime walks** to observe nesting sea turtles and baby turtle releases. The boat tour (Spanish only) and visit to the island hatchery costs a little over US$5 (half for kids 6-12 years old; children under 6 get in free) and takes about two hours. Nighttime turtle monitoring tours cost US$14. They also have rustic *cabañas* for US$40 a night, and they offer group discounts.

The ecotourism cooperative offices are a quick 10-minute drive from Mazunte. Getting there is easy, even without a car. Just board a westbound *camioneta* anywhere along the main road and keep an eye out for the sign at the turnoff about 2.2 km (1.4 mi) west of Mazunte, about five minutes after leaving the town. The trip from Puerto Ángel takes a little over half an hour. The walk from the main road to the ecotourism cooperative offices takes about 15 minutes; the offices are on the left-hand side of the road.

TOP EXPERIENCE

Surfing and Swimming

If you're coming to the Oaxacan coast primarily to surf, you're better off hitting the waves of Puerto Escondido or Barra de la Cruz than these beaches here, but there's still some wave riding fun to be had here. The beach break off Zipolite is pretty reliable, and surfing is sometimes possible in the miniature bay at the west end of San Agustinillo. Bring your own board, as there aren't board rental services here.

The swimming is great on any of these beaches, especially those in coves or bays. Zipolite and San Agustinillo are both unprotected from the open ocean and have very strong undertows that often take swimmers out to sea; swim with extreme caution on these beaches. If you are not a strong swimmer, Playas La Boquilla, Estacahuite, Principal, and Panteón are your best bet. The water at Playas Mazunte and Rinconcito is generally calm, but can also get rowdy if the sea gets in a mood. Swimming is not allowed on Playas Mermejita and Ventanilla.

Snorkeling

For scuba diving on the Oaxacan coast, you'll have to look to Huatulco or Puerto Escondido, but there are a few good snorkeling spots to be found among the hippie beaches. The best snorkeling is on **Playa Estacahuite,** which has calm, clear waters and lots of rocks for marine critters to hide in. You can rent equipment from the *palapas* on the beach.

Unless you're a guest at Bahía de la Luna, the hotel on **Playa La Boquilla,** you'll need to bring your own equipment to snorkel at that beach. Like Estacahuite to the south, La Boquilla's waters are calm, crystal clear, and full of rocks to peek around.

For snorkeling tours, call Aaron Vásquez at **Luna Tours** (corner of road to Playa Panteón and public beach parking, tel. 958/117-7538 or 958/106-6062, www.lunatours.wordpress.com). He's a Puerto Ángel native who has lived here since before tourism reached these shores. Aaron, a free diver who dives down as far as 25 meters (82 ft) below the surface without a tank, knows every nook and cranny of the local reefs, and will take you on a 3-4-hour snorkel tour (US$11) where you'll see lobsters, octopuses, crabs, and a wide variety of reef fish. Aaron says that they also regularly see dolphins, whales, turtles, manta rays, and an array of marine bird species. Aaron's not really an office kind of guy—you're more likely to find him wandering the beach, but unless he's in the water, he's always got his phone handy.

Fishing

In addition to snorkeling tours, Aaron at **Luna Tours** (tel. 958/117-7538 or 958/106-6062, www.lunatours.wordpress.com) also runs artisanal fishing tours (US$54-80 for up to 8 people). Tours run 2-3 hours and can be scheduled in the early morning (6am) or afternoon (4:30pm). It varies season to season, but you're likely to snag tuna, marlin, bonito, sea bass, and mahimahi, among others. They provide equipment traditionally used on the coast, or you can bring your own gear.

In San Agustinillo, call up **Pacífico Mágico Tours** (in Restaurante Alejandra on the main road, tel. 958/587-9224 or

The Endangered Sea Turtles of the Oaxacan Coast

a baby albino sea turtle

Inhabitants of the Oaxacan coast have been subsisting on the meat and eggs of sea turtles, iguanas, armadillos, and other exotic species since they first got here a few millennia ago, and some still do. For the longest time, there weren't enough people living here to have a negative effect on the populations of the wildlife they consumed. It was not until fairly recently, with the proliferation of coffee production in the 19th century and commercial fishing in the second half of the 20th, that the need for conservation arose.

A ban entered into force in 1990 that criminalized the collection, trade, and consumption of turtle eggs in Mexico, but authorities turn a blind eye in some communities that have stubbornly held onto the culinary tradition. The eggs have been used as a reserve food to get through tough times when other food sources are scarce. Boiled eggs are said to keep for up to a year buried in the cool, damp sand near the dishwashing area of a bungalow kitchen.

Still, most people along the coast, even if they remember the days when trucks carried loads of turtle meat up and down the dirt roads of the coast, understand their importance to the local ecosystem and economy, and do not eat them. Many beaches on this coast are popular nesting grounds, most notably La Ventanilla, La Escobilla, and Mazunte, home of the Centro Mexicano de la Tortuga (Mexican Turtle Center). On these beaches, you can witness a baby sea turtle release, or, as I was amazed to see one moonlit night in Mazunte, a turtle mother laying her eggs in the sand just 9 meters (30 ft) from where I was sitting with friends.

So while seven of the world's eight sea turtle species choose Oaxacan beaches for their nests, this is all the more reason to protect them from the threat we present to them. Come down, learn about conservation, and take that valuable information with you when you leave. Just don't eat them.

958/118-2710), which comes highly recommended by both locals and tourists alike. Sportfishing tours cost around US$11 per hour per person.

Yoga

Up on the hill between Mazunte and San Agustinillo, **Hridaya Yoga** (tel. 958/100-8958, www.hridaya-yoga.com) offers hatha yoga classes in English 8:30am-10:45am Monday-Saturday. They also offer very affordable month-long yoga retreats that start at US$335 for the course only, and you can choose to add meal plans and accommodations.

In San Agustinillo, Brigitte Longueville runs **Solstice Yoga** (in Cabañas Las 3 Marías on the main road, no phone, www.solstice-mexico.com, info@solstice-mexico.com, US$5.50), where she also teaches hatha yoga, giving instructions in both English and Spanish. Check her website for the class schedule and retreat information.

In Zipolite, **La Loma Linda** (Hwy. 175 east of Adoquín area, no phone, www.lalomalinda.com, info@lalomalinda.com, about US$5) has a 1.5-hour restorative yoga class in English every morning at 9am.

ENTERTAINMENT AND EVENTS
Nightlife

Nightlife on these beaches is about as chilled out as you'd expect from the vibe they have in the daylight. You'll find the liveliest bar scene in the Adoquín neighborhood of **Zipolite**, along Avenida Roca Blanca. The bar at **A Nice Place On The Beach** (Avenida Roca Blanca, tel. 958/584-3195, aniceplaceonthebeach@outlook.com, 7:30am-1:30am daily) is, well, a nice, casual place on the beach for drinks both before and after the sun goes down. Popular among sundried foreign beach bums and friendly locals alike, A Nice Place is one of the few places in Zipolite that still gets lively during the lazy low season.

At the western end of El Adoquín, the eponymous owner of **Ron's Place** (Avenida

Roca Blanca, tel. 222/873-5697, 7pm-1am Tues.-Sun.) is renowned for the friendly, easygoing vibe at the bar he opened here in 2016. Over on the east end of Roca Blanca, restaurant and bar **Entropía** (Avenida Roca Blanca, no phone, 5pm-midnight Tues.-Sun.) has a good selection of mezcals, wines, cocktails, and more. The regular DJ sets and live music, ranging from blues to cumbia to gypsy swing, usually get folks on their feet to dance.

In **Mazunte,** the restaurant **Sahuaro** (Calle Barrita, tel. 958/100-8694, noon-11pm daily) has movie nights every Thursday at 8pm, and occasionally hosts mezcal tastings featuring local producers. For mezcal, grab one in the very laid-back setting at mezcal shop **Las Tortuguitas** (Calle Rinconcito, no phone, 9am-2pm and 6pm-10pm Thurs.-Tues.), on Calle Rinconcito across from the turn to Playa Mermejita. Right next door to each other are the softly lit restaurants **Estrella Fugaz** (Andador Rinconcito, tel. 958/113-2895, 7am-11:30pm daily), which has a wide selection of mezcals, and **Siddhartha** (Andador Rinconcito, no phone, 8am-11pm daily), which serves the only frozen mojito (made with mezcal) in Mazunte; they both generally tend to play chilled-out house music, but sometimes host live music duos playing classic reggae songs.

Festivals and Events

The biggest festival on this stretch of coastline is the **International Jazz Festival of Mazunte,** held in mid-November. Not strictly a jazz event (a recent headliner was Oaxacan favorite Lila Downs, who sings everything from *ranchera* ballads to songs in her native Mixtec), this three-evening festival usually includes genres such as rock, reggae, afrobeat, *trova*, and more. Mazunte is also home to a one-day **Spring Equinox Festival** that includes various types of healing rituals and dancing in the square on the main road.

The **San Agustinillo Eco Fest** is a four-day event with conferences on ecology, fishing excursions, photography exhibitions, whale watching, concerts, and more. It is held in mid-March, the time of year that migrating humpback whales pass by Oaxaca's shores.

On the first weekend in February, Zipolite plays host to the **Zipolite Nudist Festival,** a three-day, stitch-free celebration of what your momma gave you that includes traditional dances, music, yoga, theater, *calendas* (street parades), and more.

FOOD
Puerto Ángel

There are a number of great *palapa* restaurants on the beaches in Puerto Ángel. On the Playa Principal, **Las Palmas** (Playa Principal, tel. 958/584-3140, 8am-6pm daily, US$7-9) serves fresh fish, shrimp, and other seafood caught daily. The fish fillet stuffed with cheese is delicious. Portions are big here, and the location on the beach is perfect for watching the action of the fishermen on the dock in the evening.

Over on Playa Panteón, the restaurant at **Hotel Cordelia's** (Playa Panteón, tel. 958/584-3021 or 958/106-0420, www.hotelcordelias.com, 7:30am-10pm daily, US$7-9) has been serving fresh, delicious coastal Oaxacan seafood since 1972. Steamed lobster, shrimp cocktails, and *pescado a la talla* (red snapper grilled with *chile guajillo*) are just a few of the plates Cordelia's has perfected in their decades of service.

For something quick and cheap, hit up the **taco stands** that set up on the main road behind the Playa Principal around 4pm or 5pm in the afternoon. You'll find fried fish, as well as pork, beef, and chicken tacos for around US$2.

Playa Estacahuite

Only a trio of *palapa* restaurants can be found on Playa Estacahuite, and your most reliable option is **El Bucanero** (The Buccaneer; Playa Estacahuite, no phone, 9am-9pm Mon.-Sat., US$8-11). As is the norm for this type of restaurant, the fish is fresh, the portions big, and the view breathtaking. If you're staying on Playa Estacahuite, Puerto Ángel is only 15 minutes away on foot, so you've got options.

Zipolite

At ★ **Piedra de Fuego** (Firestone; Calle Mangle, tel. 958/113-9935 or 958/100-9234, 3pm-11pm daily, US$4-8), husband-and-wife team Horacio and Isabel serve up an array of delicious seafood dishes, such as their mountainous plate of *camarones a la diabla* (shrimp sautéed in devilishly spicy red salsa). Due to its somewhat secluded location at the east end of Calle Mangle, Piedra de Fuego can be easy to overlook, but you're doing yourself a disservice if you pass it by. Set on a patio beneath the second floor of their house, the tables are kept cool by the breeze blowing through.

Hotel y Restaurante Posada México (Avenida Roca Blanca, tel. 958/584-3194, 8am-2pm and 6pm-10:30pm Thurs.-Mon., 8am-2pm Tues., US$5-9) not only has a primo location right on the main beach, they also bake fresh croissants and other pastries daily to accompany their traditional Mexican and Italian breakfasts. After the early afternoon siesta, Posada México reopens to serve wood-oven pizzas, pastas, and other specialties from both Italy and Mexico. Happy-hour specials include two-for-one drinks and complimentary snacks.

Tucked away in a secluded cove at the west end of the beach, **El Alquimista** (Calle Shambala, tel. 958/587-8961, www.el-alquimista.com, 8am-11pm daily, US$8-13) has a massive menu of pizzas, pastas, salads, seafood, and other Mexican and international specialties, such as *bistec a la pimiento* (thin beef steak in black pepper sauce) or grilled chicken breast served in a cream of mushroom sauce. It's a great option if you're craving something different from the *palapa*-style seafood available on just about every beach on the coast.

On the road toward El Alquimista, you'll see **Orale! Café** (Calle Shambala, tel. 958/117-7129, oralecafe@hotmail.com, 8am-3pm Thurs.-Mon., US$2-4) peeking out from the tropical foliage. Aside from super-cheap breakfast options, you'll find baguette and bagel sandwiches made with fresh, healthy ingredients, as well as fresh juices, *aguas de sabor* (fruit drinks), and rich, organic, locally sourced coffee.

Mazunte and San Agustinillo
CAFÉS AND BREAKFAST

At the far west end of Mazunte, one of the first businesses you'll see coming in on the road from the highway is **Café del Mar** (tel. 958/107-9942, 8am-4pm Tues.-Sun., US$4), with good coffee and a wide selection of vegan burgers and other animal-free options. Antique radios on the second-floor terrace pay decorative homage to the café's musical preference, jazz, which they play all day.

Continuing down the main road, just across from the turtle center, is **Cafe N'duva** (Hwy. 175, tel. 954/133-8748, 7:30am-5pm), its walls adorned with photos of famous Mexican actors and musicians. N'duva serves rich, dark coffee from Pluma Hidalgo, and you'll also find Oaxacan chocolate, *mole*, and locally produced roasted peanuts on its shelves. They have a few tables to sit and sip your cup of joe. On the road to Playa Rinconcito, **La Baguette** (Calle Rinconcito, tel. 958/111-3529, 7am-10pm daily) serves super-strong Italian-style moka pot coffee to accompany the fresh bread (both sweet and savory) baked in-house daily. There are a few stools to sit at, but most orders here are to-go.

You'll find cheap, tasty, traditional Mexican breakfasts at any of the restaurants along the main drag between Calles Rinconcito and Barrita. On Calle Rinconcito, **Doña Meche** (Calle Rinconcito, tel. 958/109-8712, www.comedorlostraviesos.blogspot.com, 8am-11pm daily, US$5) has full breakfasts that include coffee or tea, fruit or juice, and a main dish of eggs cooked how you like them.

Down on Playa Rinconcito, stop by **La Tertulia** (Playa Rinconcito, tel. 958/113-8292, 10am-8pm daily) for a coffee or cold beer and a game of chess, with the lull of the waves for a relaxing soundtrack. They also serve up fresh ceviche and grilled tuna, pork ribs, and other delights.

FUSION

Right on the pedestrian walkway at Playa Rinconcito, with a terrace overlooking the beach, **Siddhartha** (Andador Rinconcito, no phone, 8am-11pm daily, US$7-10) has an inventive menu of pastas, sandwiches, and seafood, as well as a wide selection of mezcals that they use to make their famous frozen mojitos. A standout dish is the shrimp guajillo pasta, which really brings out the subtle flavor of this delectable pepper.

Hidden from the beach by the hill that separates the Mazunte and Rinconcito beaches, **Sahuaro** (Calle Barrita, tel. 958/100-8694, noon-11pm daily, US$3-5) serves up delectable Baja-style fish and shrimp tacos, as well as *yakimeshi* (Japanese fried rice), burgers, and other snack-attack favorites, as well as numerous veggie options. Thursdays are movie nights, and if it's your birthday, you can eat free as long as you bring at least one other person to celebrate.

Farther up Calle Barrita, almost to the main road, **La Cuisine** (Calle Barrita, tel. 958/107-1836, 7pm-11pm Tues.-Sat., US$8-11) is the brainchild of French chef Jean Michel Thomas. This Franco-Mexican kitchen changes out the menu daily, depending on what's in season and what's in Jean Michel's head at the time. The big, *palapa*-covered restaurant has a pleasant, minimalist vibe, creating a dining experience that straddles the line between casual and fine, creating the perfect environment for a gourmet dinner you can enjoy with no shoes on.

ACCOMMODATIONS
Playa La Boquilla

The only accommodations option on this compact beach, ★ **Bahía de la Luna** (Playa La Boquilla, tel. 958/589-5020, www.bahiadelaluna.com, US$65 d, US$155 five-person *cabaña*) managed to squeeze in 12 luxurious *cabañas* on the beach and up the hillside, not one of which has a disappointing view. A stay at one of the *cabañas* here is definitely worth the precipitous ride in, as owners Laila and Jorge have you covered for everything from activities to lounging to dining. The accommodation's restaurant is the only dining option at Playa La Boquilla, but it's excellent. Originally from Switzerland, Jorge mixes his roots with the bountiful and delicious ingredients available to him in Oaxaca, and the coffee he serves, grown on his own *finca* in the hills, is phenomenal. For activities, they lend snorkel equipment and kayaks to guests free of charge, and there are lots of trails in the surrounding hills for hiking. They will organize taxi trips to get you to and from the airport, or wherever you're headed next.

Playa Estacahuite

Two of the three studios at **Casa Macondo** (hill above the beach, tel. 958/587-5081, www.casa-macondo.com, US$30-35 studio, US$50-75 apartment) have fully stocked kitchenettes, as do the two apartments, and all have their own private terrace or semi-private patio space. All this is packed into a big, mango-colored house up the hill from the beach, with hammocks hanging wherever they'll fit and an ocean-view swimming pool out front. No air-conditioning here, this is a fans-and-mosquito-net kind of place, but the sea breeze keeps everything nice and cool at night.

Puerto Ángel

On the east side of the Bahía Principal, **Villas Monte Cristo** (Privada de Bravo 13, tel. 958/584-3100, www.hotelesdepuertoangel.com/villamontecristopuertoangel.html, US$16 d, US$54 bungalow) has four private rooms and three bungalows stacked on the low, verdant hillside overlooking the bay. Some have fans and some are cooled with air-conditioning. The swimming pool glints in the sunlight, surrounded by tropical flowers and palm trees waving in the sea breeze, and the on-site restaurant, complete with hammocks and lazy lounge chairs, offers phenomenal views of the sunset behind the bay.

On the other side of the bay, ★ **La Cabaña** (Playa Panteón, tel. 958/584-3105 or 958/584-3448, www.lacabanapuertoangel.

com, US$35 d) is a beautiful bright-orange house overlooking the beach. Lounge in the sun on the ocean-view terrace, or cool off in the swimming pool, spying the jungle-green hillside through the brick archways. All rooms have hot water (not always a guarantee down here), TV, Wi-Fi, and fans. Air-conditioning will cost you another US$8. The rooftop *palapa* restaurant serves breakfast and *antojitos* (snacks), but catch it early, as it's only open 8am-1pm.

Aside from its perfect location on Playa Panteón, La Cabaña accepts pets, offers on-site laundry service (about US$1/kilo), and will even change out dollars for you. Extra services include outings to neighboring beaches, sportfishing tours, and whale-watching excursions.

Zipolite
UNDER US$25

During high season, **Sativa Circo Hotel** (Avenida Roca Blanca, tel. 958/584-3475, US$14 shared bathroom, US$16 en suite) regularly transforms from hotel into the "big top" (*circo* means circus). Jugglers, acrobats, fire dancers, contortionists, and other experts in the carnival arts come to showcase their unique talents, and entry is usually free even for non-guests. Sativa also regularly hosts live afrobeat and jazz music, as well as workshops in African and belly dancing. If you've brought your tent along, you can set it up on their grounds for around US$5. The rooms themselves are basic but comfy and clean—though with all the festivities and the hotel's excellent location on the beach, you'll only be in there to sleep.

US$50-100

★ **Casa Mixteca** (Avenida Roca Blanca, tel. 958/688-5514, zipolitecasaoaxaca@gmail.com, US$45 suite, US$51 bungalow, US$59 penthouse) has a strong focus on aesthetics. The

1: the gemstone waters of Playa Panteón
2: Zipolite's main drag, Avenida Roca Blanca
3: Playa Principal

verdant tropical plants of the meticulously tended interior garden strike a pleasing contrast with the vibrant orange of the courtyard walls, which are adorned with handwoven artisanal baskets and textiles. The upper bungalows and penthouse are reached via a bridge that spans the courtyard below. Hammocks hang inside the bungalows as well as on their private terraces, and the interior design is both comfortable and visually pleasing. The overall effect is one of relaxation and the simple enjoyment of the tasteful interaction of colors and textures.

Stay in a tree house just steps away from the ocean at **Hotel Noga** (Calle Shambala, tel. 954/138-9368, www.hnoga.com, US$83-93). These beautiful wooden bungalows are nestled in the dense green foliage of the mangroves, connected via catwalks raised above the forest floor. All rooms come with a refrigerator, air-conditioning, a safe, and TV, as well as hammocks on the terrace for relaxing in the shade. The on-site restaurant/bar (8am-11pm), set in a leafy nook on the beach, serves everything from delicious breakfasts to fresh seafood dinners.

San Agustinillo
UNDER US$50

The rooms and large terrace at **Paraíso del Pescador** (The Fisherman's Paradise; Hwy. 175, tel. 958/589-9517, US$27 d) look right out over the golden expanse of Playa San Agustinillo. This is a hotel-style paradise, unlike the more popular *cabañas* elsewhere along the beach, but it's an excellent value. Most rooms have that aforementioned phenomenal view, private bathrooms, and fans, or air-conditioning for another US$5.

US$50-100

The 16 units right on the beach at **Cabañas Un Sueño** (A Dream; Hwy. 175, tel. 958/113-8749, www.unsueno.com, US$62-87) are covered in brilliant white stucco and adorned with naturally finished wooden doors and window shutters, with comfy hammocks hung between the palm trees out front and a

half dozen or so more strung beneath a *palapa* on the beach. Un Sueño is a popular choice for couples realizing their dreams of a tropical paradise wedding. Ceiling fans and the sea breeze keep the bungalows cool at night.

A couple hundred feet to the west of Paraíso del Pescador, **Cabañas Punta Placer** (Hwy. 175, tel. 958/109-0164, www.puntaplacer.com, US$65 d, US$75 t, US$80 family-size apartment) has four stone, wood, and stucco *cabañas* divided into eight luxurious yet simple units (no air-conditioning). You'll find no corners here. Everything, from the bathroom counters to the windows to the arches over the beds and the shape of the *cabañas* themselves, has curved edges, a design feature meant to foster rest, relaxation, and escape from the hustle and bustle of modern life.

OVER US$100

The apogee of luxury in San Agustinillo is **Casa La Ola** (Hwy. 175, tel. 553/103-6257, www.casalaola.mx, US$96 d, US$140 junior suite, US$166 suite), on the hillside just as the road rises on the way to Mazunte. La Ola's motto is "Life as it should be," and when you have a spectacular view of the beach below from the comfort of your own private hillside terrace, it's hard to argue otherwise. The tasteful simplicity of the white and natural wood inside the hotel's 15 units is touched off with sparks of color by local handicrafts, such as intricately embroidered textiles and brightly painted *alebrijes* (painted carved wooden figures), and fresh-cut tropical flowers.

All units have air-conditioning, safe boxes, private bathrooms, and hot water, and a complimentary continental breakfast is served 8am-noon. The public areas include a swimming pool and lots of comfy chairs in *palapa* shade for reading, enjoying the view, or a leisurely afternoon siesta.

Mazunte
UNDER US$25

Some of Mazunte's most interesting and economical *cabañas* are found hidden away in the mangrove forest just behind the rocky hill that separates Playas Mazunte and Rinconcito. From Calle Palma Real, which runs east to west between Calles Barrita and Rinconcito, follow the raised wooden walkway through the mangrove trees to ★ **Casa Corazón** (Calle Palma Real, tel. 958/109-7397 or 558/527-7893, US$16-37), a small cluster of *cabañas* raised on stilts above the swampy ground below. The fairy lights hung in the trees along the way, and the constant and surprisingly loud rustle of crabs in the grasses and mud below, create a truly surreal experience. The bamboo and palm frond *cabañas* have only mosquito netting for walls, allowing maximum ventilation, which will be necessary in the heat of the swamp. It may be a rugged setting, but Casa Corazón has modern amenities like Wi-Fi, a communal kitchen, and a dry toilet in the shared bathroom, so that the hotel and its guests have as little impact as possible on the environment.

You'll find the entrance to **Hostal Tonatiuh** (Calle Barrita, tel. 958/107-3220, www.posadamazunte.wixsite.com/hostaltonatiuh, US$14) at the southern end of Calle Barrita, just before it turns right to meet up with Calle Rinconcito. Similar to Casa Corazón in style, though notedly more rustic, Tonatiuh has four simple bamboo cabins raised on stilts and connected via a creaky raised wooden walkway. All mosquito netting (so necessary in this setting) is tight and regularly maintained, keeping guests safe from the little winged demons come bedtime. The shared bathrooms here are also equipped with eco-friendly dry toilets.

A couple of personal favorites here in Mazunte are **El Agujón** (Andador Rinconcito, no phone, elagujonmazunte@gmail.com, US$13-16), with bare-necessities *cabañas* on the hill just above Playa Rinconcito, and **Cabañas Abrizel** (Calle Rinconcito, tel. 958/119-5794, US$13) on Calle Rinconcito, closer to the highway. The *cabañas* they rent are nothing special, with fans, mosquito nets, and private bathrooms, but the owners (Yesenia and Ariel at El Agujón, and Manuel at Abrizel) are very friendly and accommodating. Despite the lack of frills, both make for a very pleasant stay.

New to the Mazunte hotel game, and with what looks like a bright future ahead of it, is **La Luciérnaga** (on dirt road west of turtle center, tel. 958/111-3681, www.laluciernagamazunt. wixsite.com/la-luciernaga, US$8 dorm, US$22 d, US$5 camping pp), behind Playa Mazunte. Buddies Arturo and Armando, both natives of Oaxaca's neighbor to the north, Veracruz, are bringing a little life back to this side of Mazunte with their lively, social hostel that has options ranging from camping to private rooms. Colorful murals adorn the walls, and screens on the windows and doors eliminate the need for nets over the beds.

US$25-50

Una Posada Más (Calle Rinconcito, tel. 958/119-4504, www.unaposadamas.com, US$25 d, US$32 t) literally means One More Inn, but it has a more flippant connotation in Spanish, making a more accurate translation something like "Just Another Inn." But on passing through the bougainvillea-framed entrance, you'll see that this isn't just another hotel. The seven airy rooms of the inn overlook a small, jungly courtyard strung with hammocks in the shade of giant tropical fronds. It's like sneaking away from one paradise to another. All the rooms, which can accommodate 2-6 people, have private bathrooms, mosquito nets, and Wi-Fi access.

OVER US$50

On the east-facing slope of the hill that separates Playas Rinconcito and Mermejita, the *cabañas* at ★ **Casa Mermejita** (Camino a Playa Mermejita, tel. 958/106-0700 or 958/109-4106, www.casamermejita.com, US$65-105) boast stunning design both inside and out. The six unique *cabañas*, named for their geometric shapes, include king-sized beds, fans, and mosquito nets (air-conditioning isn't necessary up here on the hill). The bathroom sinks and tubs are fetching solid concrete installations stocked with soaps and shampoos from the local natural cosmetics shop. The triangular infinity pool offers a stunning view of the riotous waves of Mermejita below, which provide a soothing soundtrack that will lull you to sleep come bedtime.

INFORMATION AND SERVICES
Laundry Services

In Mazunte, head to **La Chelita y Sus 12 Nietos** (Chelita and Her 12 Grandkids; Calle Rinconcito, no phone, 7am-9pm daily) where, according to the sign, they "wash clothes with love." Chelita charges about US$3 per dozen pieces of clothing, so wait till you get close to 12 dirty garments before stopping by.

In Zipolite, take your clothes to the *lavandería* in **Posada Navidad** (Christmas Inn; Avenida Roca Blanca, tel. 958/584-3358, 8am-5pm daily); in Puerto Ángel, the folks at **La Cabaña** (Playa Panteón, tel. 958/584-3105 or 958/584-3448, www.lacabanapuertoangel.com, 8am-6pm daily) will charge you a little under US$1 per kilo.

Medical Services

In Mazunte, the *consultorio medico* (doctor's office; Hwy. 175, tel. 669/262-3649, 8am-10pm daily) next to the natural cosmetics shop charges about US$5 for a doctor's visit. You can call the number listed anytime for emergencies. In Zipolite, call or stop by the office of **Doctora Rojas** (Avenida Roca Blanca, tel. 221/266-4947, 9am-9pm daily), across from Posada México.

The closest hospital to these beaches is the **Hospital General San Pedro Pochutla** (Calle del Hospital 4, tel. 958/584-0236, 24 hrs daily), up in Pochutla. This is your best option for serious emergencies. Calle del Hospital is 600 meters (about 0.3 mi) north of the junction of Highways 175 and 200. After you turn right, you'll see the hospital on your left about 50 meters (165 ft) down the street.

Banks and Money Exchange

Your banking and money exchange options on Oaxaca's hippie beaches are quite limited.

In Mazunte, there's a **Santander ATM** on the main road next to the scooter rental/ice cream shop La Garrafita. In Zipolite, there's a **Banco Multiva ATM** on El Adoquín.

In Puerto Ángel, you'll find a **Bancomer ATM** in the municipal government building at the center of town, where the highway turns away from the Playa Principal to wind north toward Pochutla. You can change out dollars at **Banco Azteca** (Hwy. 175, toll-free Mex. tel. 800/040-7777, 8am-8pm daily), inside the Elektra appliance store on the main road behind the Playa Principal.

In Pochutla, you'll find a **Scotiabank ATM** and a **Bancomer ATM** on the main road from the mountains, as well as a **Santander ATM** on Calle Constitución, From the Bancomer ATM, take Calle Allende one block west and turn left onto Calle Constitución, where you'll see the machine a half a block down on your left.

TRANSPORTATION
Air

If flying directly to the coast, your best bet location-wise is the airport in **Huatulco,** about 28 km (17 mi) east, just under an hour away from Puerto Ángel. You could also fly into **Puerto Escondido,** 73 km (45 mi) west down Coastal Highway 200, but the trip to Puerto Ángel from here takes 1.5 hours or longer. However, flights from Mexico City to Puerto Escondido tend to be cheaper than to Huatulco, so it might be worth the extra ground travel time. Check both airports to see which will be best for your trip.

Van

If you're going directly to Oaxaca City from the coast, or vice versa, both **Líneas Unidas** (Hwy. 175, tel. 958/119-6666, 7 trips daily, US$13) and **Atlántida** (Hwy. 175, tel. 958/117-8911, 4 trips daily, US$12) have recently set up terminals in Zipolite. You'll find them on the main road, where it curves toward the beach just to the east of the Adoquín area. Be warned that it's a long, windy trip (6-7 hrs), so stopping over for a night in the mountains in San

José del Pacífico, San Mateo Río Hondo, or Pluma Hidalgo is recommended.

Car

Puerto Ángel is at the final southernmost curve of Highway 175, which connects it to Oaxaca City 250 km (155 mi) north via Pochutla. North of Pochutla, the highway zigzags through the low tropical foothills of the Sierra Madre del Sur and quickly climbs up the foggy, forested slopes of this awe-inspiring mountain range. The road is basically switchbacks the first four hours (150 km/93 mi), until it reaches the other side of the mountain range about an hour after passing through San José del Pacífico. The total driving time between Oaxaca City and Puerto Ángel is just under six hours. Driving through these mountains is a breathtaking experience that should really be broken up into two days or more with a stop in one of the quaint mountain towns.

Ten kilometers (6.2 mi) north of Puerto Ángel, Highway 175 meets up with Coastal Highway 200. From this junction, it's a curvy 45-minute drive east to La Crucecita and Bahías de Huatulco (42 km/26 mi), and three hours out to Salina Cruz (180 km/112 mi).

Puerto Escondido is 72 km (45 mi) west of this junction. The mostly straight drive over rolling coastal hills takes about 1.25 hours.

Just be extremely cautious and aware of your surroundings on all these highways in the mountains and on the coast. Take curves at a sensible speed and hug the outer line as much as possible, as it's quite common for hasty drivers here to cut corners to save time, sometimes intruding a little into the oncoming lane.

Traveling via Pochutla

The town of **San Pedro Pochutla** spreads out laterally from the last few kilometers of Highway 175 north of its junction with Coastal Highway 200, before Highway 175 begins to snake its way up the sierra. Its status as a major commercial and transportation hub in the region keeps the central streets abuzz with activity. Aside from watching the gulps of swallows that fly around the town's central **Parque de las Golondrinas** (Park of the Sparrows) around sunset, there's little else to do here but leave.

TO AND FROM OAXACA CITY

Since the "direct" (they still make a couple stops along the way) trips from Oaxaca City started up rather recently, the vast majority of vans run by **Líneas Unidas** (Lázaro Cárdenas 94, tel. 958/584-1322) and **Atlántida** (Lázaro Cárdenas 88, tel. 958/117-8911) terminate in Pochutla. The trip between Oaxaca City and Pochutla is six hours, for which these companies charge around US$11. Vans run every hour or so.

TO PUERTO ÁNGEL

Taxis line the block of Lázaro Cárdenas with all the bus and van terminals. They are the best option for getting to Puerto Ángel, charging US$2-3 dollars on average. Don't worry about getting scammed. It's common practice here to agree on a price before setting out, and taxi drivers by and large are honest, hard-working people.

TO MAZUNTE AND SAN AGUSTINILLO

Rather than follow Highway 175 south through Puerto Ángel, the quickest way to get to the western hippie beaches from Pochutla is via the covered pickup trucks called *camionetas*. They take Coastal Highway 200 14 km (8.7 mi) west to the junction with the terminus of Highway 175, where they turn left and take Highway 175 south to the coast. Mazunte is another 15 minutes (7 km/4.3 mi) from the junction, then the highway turns east and follows the coast to the other beaches. The total trip from Pochutla to Mazunte takes about 30-45 minutes and will only run you a little over US$1.

The *camionetas* leave from the corner of Calles Matamoros and Galeana, just beyond the tiny **Capilla del Niño Jesús** (Chapel of the Baby Jesus) on Calle Jamaica. They don't really have a schedule, but rather leave when enough passengers to make it worth their while hop on, so you can show up and just wait, but never for very long. They run all day until the sun goes down.

TO HUATULCO

To get to Huatulco, take an *urbano* bus run by **Transportes Rápidos de Pochutla** (across from Líneas Unidas on Lázaro Cárdenas, tel. 958/584-0159, US$2). The drivers live up to the company's name, getting you there in just under an hour. Buses leave every 10 minutes 5am-8:30pm daily.

TO PUERTO ESCONDIDO

For buses to Puerto Escondido, walk up to Calle Hidalgo and take a right. A couple hundred feet down the street on your right, you'll see the terminal for **Transportes Delfines** (Calle Hidalgo, no phone), which charges about US$3 for the trip, which takes 1.5 hours, sometimes longer. Buses leave the terminal every seven minutes until around 8pm.

Bahías de Huatulco and Vicinity

Huatulco means "The Place Where Wood is Venerated," due to the mysterious presence of a cross with peculiar physical properties. It's unknown exactly when Huatulco was founded, or who did so, or who put the cross on these shores some 1,500 years before the arrival of Christian conquistadors.

Documents in the Ex Convento de Santo Domingo in Oaxaca City claim that Hernán Cortés conquered Huatulco on January 8, 1539, but this is most likely a case of stolen credit. According to a geographical account of the area carried out in 1579, elderly Huatulco residents who had been around at the time said the deed was done by Pedro de Alvarado, known to indigenous people in Mexico at the time as Tonatiuh (Nahuatl for Sun), due to his bright-blond hair and beard. No matter. Whoever did the actual trouncing was shocked to find that the people who lived on these shores had been venerating a wooden cross for centuries before their arrival. The Spanish were told it was brought to the native *huatulqueños* by a bearded man in a white robe. And there you have miracle number one.

Miracle number two came in 1587, when English pirate Thomas Cavendish, who was in a bad mood after not finding Huatulco to be the gilded city he'd been hunting, ordered his men to burn the small coastal village to the ground. When the cross didn't burn with everything else, Cavendish and his men tried everything from saws to hatchets to tying the thing to their boat and trying to wrench it from the ground, but to no avail. In 1612, the stubborn cross finally let itself be moved, and it was taken to Oaxaca City, where it was broken down into smaller crosses. Three of these now reside elsewhere, one in the main cathedral in Oaxaca City, one in Mexico City, and one in the Vatican. The fourth was sent back home, where it now resides in the charming alfresco Capilla de la Santa Cruz de Huatulco (Chapel of the Holy Cross of Huatulco), right on the beach in Santa Cruz.

The history of Huatulco as we know it begins in the 1980s, when the Mexican federal government expropriated the nine bays of Huatulco to create what was hoped to be the "Cancún of Oaxaca." To accommodate the residents that the project displaced, the town of La Crucecita was created, and grants were disbursed for people to start businesses and secure housing. According to locals, the project has been good for the people of Huatulco, and folks are generally happy with how the arrangement has worked out. The clean streets, active residents, thriving businesses, and finger-licking-good food of La Crucecita attest to that. With numerous beaches, campgrounds next door to five-star resorts, and a wide range of cultural and

Bahías de Huatulco

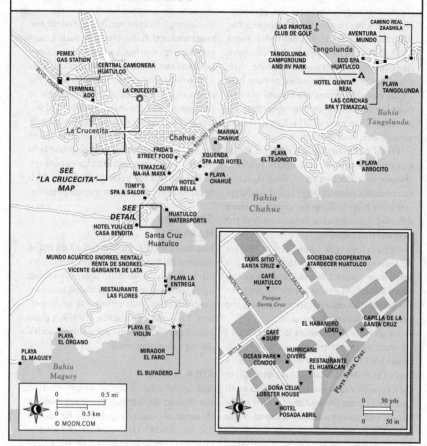

recreational activities, Huatulco has something for everyone.

Getting Oriented

The town of **La Crucecita** is the central urban nucleus of Bahías de Huatulco. It is located about a mile northwest of **Bahía Chahué**, which is accessed via the broad Boulevard Chahué, its median beautified with well-manicured lawns and pedestrian walkways. Huatulco's eight other bays are east and west of Chahué.

Just to the west of Bahía Chahué is **Bahía de Santa Cruz**, where many hotels and

tourism agencies are located, as well as a long dock where cruise ships come to port throughout the week. The neighborhood of **Santa Cruz Huatulco** is home to a pleasant, shady central square, a small marina, and a tourist market stocked with water toys and other beach items.

West from Santa Cruz, the other bays are **Bahías Órgano, Maguey, Cacaluta, Chachacual,** and **San Agustín,** all within the borders of **Parque Nacional Huatulco.**

The bays to the east of Chahué are **Bahía Tangolunda** and **Bahía Conejos.** They are home to the fancier Huatulco resorts.

Getting Around

The easiest way to get around Bahías de Huatulco is by **private taxi**. They are cheap, efficient, and trustworthy. Companies like **Sitio Santa Cruz** (tel. 958/587-0888) charge US$1.50-4 anywhere among the main bays. As is custom for taxi sites down here, their prices are posted to the public at their base on the east side of the central plaza in Santa Cruz Huatulco, and you can expect to never pay more than around US$10 to anywhere around here, even the airport.

Travel between Santa Cruz and Bahía Conejos along Boulevard Benito Juárez is cheaper via *colectivo* travel. Both taxis and vans run this route all day. They won't charge you more than US$1 to get anywhere along this road. Just wait a few minutes and hail the next one that passes by.

Drivers can get anywhere in Bahías de Huatulco in less than 15 minutes. The main bays (Santa Cruz to Conejos) are all along Boulevard Benito Juárez. To get to La Crucecita, turn onto Boulevard Chahué, just east of the bay of the same name.

To get from La Crucecita to Santa Cruz, I recommend the scenic route: on foot via the broad, well-lit pedestrian walkway Camino a Santa Cruz; the walk takes 20 minutes. Get to the Crucecita end by taking Bugambilia south two blocks from the southeast corner of the zócalo and taking a left on Colorín. Walk three blocks until Colorín ends, and you'll see the walkway on your right. It traverses a low slope between two hills and terminates at the northeast end of Santa Cruz.

★ LA CRUCECITA

La Crucecita has a much more "Mexican" feel to it than the hotel areas on the beaches, with delicious restaurants, colorful markets and crafts stores, and a profusion of charming low- to mid-range accommodations options, all set around a shady *zócalo* with attendant church.

Forget about the luxury down on the beaches. La Crucecita is where all the life is. The Centro, little more than a couple dozen blocks surrounding the *zócalo*, is a hive of activity, even during low season when other places on the coast are hearing crickets.

Although its excellent dining and accommodations options have recently made it more popular with tourists, La Crucecita is a town built and run by hardworking Mexican folks who aren't going to take the seeds out of the chiles to make the salsa more palatable to foreigners. With the calm, jewel-colored waters of Playa Santa Cruz a 20-minute walk across a pedestrian walkway over the hill to the south of the Centro, and cheap taxi fares to almost anywhere in Huatulco's nine bays, La Crucecita is the perfect base from which to explore this resplendent tropical paradise.

Shopping
MARKET

Renovated in 2018, the **Mercado 3 de Mayo** (Guamuchil 208, no phone, 8am-8pm daily), just to the east of the main square, is a much more spacious and well-ventilated home for the plethora of stalls selling folk art, souvenirs, toys, and much more. It's also a great place to grab a shrimp cocktail or smoothie during a shopping break.

FOLK ART

Just to the east of the *zócalo*, you'll find the **Museo de Artesanías Oaxaqueñas** (Museum of Oaxacan Handicrafts; Flamboyán 216, tel. 958/587-1513, www.travelbymexico. com/oaxa/museodeartesanias, 9am-9pm daily, free admission), which is more store than museum. Still, staff members are very knowledgeable of the products they sell, and can give you a short, museum-like tour, informing you of the origins, artists, and processes behind the pieces as you shop.

A block east and one block south of the museum, the **Mercado de Artesanías, Gastronomía, y Mezcal: Reliquias de Oaxaca** (Relics of Oaxaca Handicraft, Gastronomy, and Mezcal Market; corner of Carrizal and Chacah, tel. 958/587-2534, compras_arte@hotmail.com, 9am-9pm daily) is a mouthful to say and an eyeful when you

La Crucecita

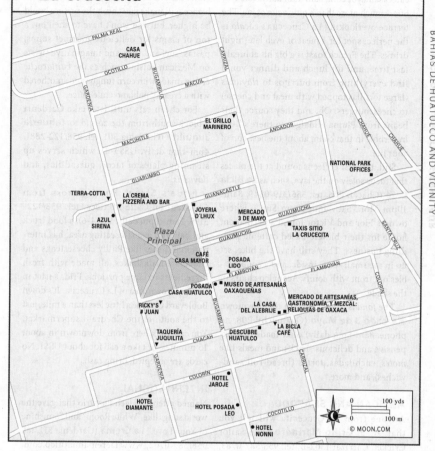

go in. Fitting for such a prolix name, the selection is wide and varied, except for the mezcal. The only brand is the store's namesake, La Reliquia.

You'll also find good, locally produced mezcal at **Casa Chahue** (Bugambilias 1202, tel. 958/123-2462, www.mezcalchahue.com, 8am-11pm daily). They've got a wide selection of mezcals, from young to aged five years, as well as an indigenous topical remedy for rheumatism, arthritis, and muscular pain they call Nep Viguú. This stuff isn't for drinking, as it contains scorpion venom at the bottom of the bottle.

Lots of silver stores like **Joyería D'Lhux** (Bugambilias 703, tel. 958/688-1883, 9:30am-9:30pm daily) dot the streets of La Crucecita around the *zócalo*. For *alebrijes* (painted carved wooden figures), head to **La Casa del Alebrije** (Chacah 303, tel. 958/100-1812, 9am-10pm daily). They have a wide selection, ship worldwide, and take orders for custom pieces.

Food
CAFÉS, BAKERIES, AND *ANTOJITOS*
The sign claims they'll serve you the best coffee of your life, but **Café Casa Mayor**

(Bugambilia 601, tel. 958/597-1881, www. cafecasamayor.com, 8am-1am daily, US$4-6) offers much more than a quick cup of joe. The terrace overlooking La Crucecita's *zócalo* is the perfect spot for a meal or even late-night drinks. The French toast is a big hit at breakfast time, and for lunch and dinner you'll find everything from burritos to *tlayudas* (large tortillas topped with meat and cheese) to cheeseburgers. Oh, and they source their beans from Pluma Hidalgo, so there's little hyperbole in that claim about the best cup of your life.

Still, the best coffee is found at the places that focus solely on the java, such as **La Bicla Café** (Chacah 206, tel. 556/319-0849, 8am-10pm Mon.-Sat., 4pm-10pm Sun.), where owners Flor and Victor found a permanent home for their bicycle-based caffeine peddling business. They still have the bike, set up in the small space inside, and a couple tables out front with comfy Acapulco chairs in the shade.

The *fondas* (food stalls) in the downtown **Mercado 3 de Mayo** (Guamuchil 208, no phone, 8am-8pm daily) offer loads of inexpensive and delicious snacks and meals like *moles*, enchiladas, *tortas* (bread-roll sandwiches), and more.

MEXICAN AND SEAFOOD

Anyone from La Crucecita will tell you that ★ **El Grillo Marinero** (The Sailor Cricket; Carrizal 1302-B, tel. 958/587-0783, elgrillomarinero@hotmail.com, 1pm-8pm daily, US$7-10) serves some of the best *mariscos* (seafood) in town. But pay attention to their hours. A funny quirk about La Crucecita is that seafood is for lunch only, and restaurants like this tend to close early. Try the *sopa de mariscos* (seafood soup), a hearty, spicy bowl packed full of shrimp, octopus, and fish. The breezy *palapa*-style restaurant is usually packed with locals grabbing the catch of the day.

The finest dining to be had in La Crucecita is at **Terra-Cotta** (Gardenia 902, tel. 958/587-1135, www.misiondelosarcos.website,

8am-11pm daily, US$9-13), the restaurant at Hotel Misión de los Arcos. The upscale ambience will make you think the prices should be higher, but you won't have to shell out a ton of clams for delicious gourmet soups, pastas, surf and turf, and imaginative twists on Mexican cuisine, such as the *cuitlacoche* crepes, made with corn fungus and smothered with a creamy poblano chile sauce.

For cheap eats until late, take Gardenia a block south from the *zócalo* to **Taquería Juquilita** (Gardenia 501, tel. 958/122-2881, 4pm-1am daily, US$3-4), which serves up steaming plates of tacos, quesadillas, and *tlayudas*.

Frida's Street Food (across from Chedraui on Calle Mixteca, tel. 958/122-5199, 2pm-10pm daily, US$4-6), a food truck and bar with a small seating area, has international dishes like Philly cheesesteaks and chocolate milkshakes, all made with fresh ingredients in large portions. Frida's isn't in the downtown area of La Crucecita. It's down Boulevard Chahué a little less than a mile, just to the south of the Chedraui supermarket. You can walk here from downtown in about 15 minutes, or take a cab for about US$1. No cards are accepted; bring cash.

INTERNATIONAL

Named after the legendary trio that gave the world songs like "White Room" and "Sunshine of Your Love," **La Crema** (Gardenia 311, tel. 958/587-0702, www.lacremahuatulco.com, 7pm-2am daily, US$6-9) is a hip, rock-and-roll-themed bar and pizzeria that is almost always busy. Try the La Crema Special, a pie topped with mushrooms, ham, pepperoni, green peppers, and sour cream. For dessert? More pizza! The banana pizzas are made with cinnamon and coconut cream. It's on the northwest corner of the *zócalo*.

Just across the *zócalo* from La Crema, **Ricky's # Juan** (Flamboyán 308, tel. 958/585-0416, 8am-2am daily, US$8-11) is a great place

---

1: sunny view from the balcony of Hotel Posada Leo in La Crucecita **2:** a delicious plate of *camarones* (shrimp) *a la mexicana*

to stop for a drink or enjoy a Mexican-style shawarma or plate of chicken wings while you watch the hockey game with Huatulco's Canadian crowd. Ricky, the restaurant's owner, has a reputation for being friendly and knowledgeable of the area, and will probably sit down and chat with you for a while.

Accommodations

A quick cab ride or pleasant half-hour walk from the beach in Santa Cruz, lively little Crucecita has a number of affordable accommodations options perfect for budget travelers, or for those looking for something more traditionally Mexican than the options close to the beach.

UNDER US$25

The five basic rooms at **Posada Lido** (Flamboyán 209, tel. 958/100-4869 or 958/587-0810, US$16 d) have few bells and whistles, but the price is right for budget travelers, and the location is perfect. A block east of the *zócalo*, Lido is just steps away from fantastic restaurants, bars, cafés, handicraft stores, and more. All rooms have private bathrooms, one has a fully stocked kitchenette, and the air-conditioning can be turned on for an extra US$8-10 per night.

Just across the street, **Posada Casa Huatulco** (Flamboyán 214, tel. 958/587-0211, casahuatulcomar@hotmail.com, US$24 d) is another unbeatable value in downtown Crucecita. Rooms come with private bathrooms, TV, Wi-Fi, and air-conditioning. The entrance to the hotel is in a little storefront next to the Museo de Artesanías Oaxaqueñas, but the reception is a couple doors to the left in Restaurante El Patio.

US$25-50

Two blocks south of the *zócalo* on Bugambilia, **Hotel Jaroje** (Colorín 304, tel. 958/116-8698, www.hotelhuatulco.com.mx, US$27 d) has 14 double rooms, with either two queen beds or one king bed, with air-conditioning, TV, and Wi-Fi. The price almost doubles during high season, but you can get a 15 percent discount if you reserve online or through WhatsApp at the number listed.

Crossing the small canal next to Hotel Jaroje, you'll find a pair of hotels run by amiable Leonora Carmona. The smaller, more homey of the two, **Hotel Posada Leo** (Bugambilia 302, tel. 958/587-2601, posadaleo_hux@hotmail.com, US$25 d) has six double rooms with air-conditioning, TV, Wi-Fi, and hot water. **Hotel Nonni** (Bugambilia 203, tel. 958/587-0372, hotelnonni@gmail.com, US$29-32 d, US$45 t) has a few more options for larger groups. The rooms are bigger and slightly fancier, and the triple, with one king and two queen beds, sleeps up to six guests.

Three blocks south of the *zócalo*, the slender ★ **Hotel Diamante** (Colorín 404, tel. 958/587-2200 or 958/115-2266, www.travelbymexico.com/oaxa/diamante, US$21-43 d, US$75 t, US$95 suite) is a little odd, but in the best way. The narrowness of the building led to a refreshingly unique interior design: skinny, high-ceilinged rooms that fit up to four king-size beds. The rooms still manage to feel airy with this clever use of limited space. All rooms include air-conditioning, TV, and Wi-Fi, and most have a mini-fridge and coffeemaker. Another interesting and fun design feature is the ample public spaces, such as the street-facing balconies on the open-air stairwell landings, and long benches built into the walls of the hallways. The rooftop pool is similarly unique, with its pyramid-shaped design and pleasant view of La Crucecita.

At the northwest corner of the *zócalo*, **Azul Sirena** (Calle Gardenia, tel. 958/587-0113, www.azulsirena.com.mx, US$47 d, US$85 villa) is a villa-style construction of white stucco with sky-blue cornices and window frames. The hotel's standard rooms are set around a fetching central courtyard with green grass and a stone fountain; most rooms have small balconies with nice views of the church or central plaza. The two-bedroom villas around the swimming pool in back of the hotel can accommodate up to six people and have kitchenettes. All rooms have Wi-Fi, TV, and air-conditioning.

Getting There

AIR

The small size of the **Huatulco airport** (Aeropuerto Internacional Bahías de Huatulco; HUX, tel. 958/581-9004) makes it easy to get in and out, and the white stucco terminals topped with thatched *palapa*-style roofs will get you in the coastal mood the minute you arrive.

Highway 200 connects the airport with the major destinations along the coast. The airport is located about 18 km (11 mi) west of La Crucecita, only a 15-minute drive. The popular surfing destination Barra de la Cruz, 40 km (25 mi) east, is a 45-minute drive down the coast. To Puerto Ángel, 38 km (24 mi) to the west, the drive takes about 50 minutes. Puerto Escondido, 100 km (62 mi) west, is about two hours down the highway.

Mexican airlines **Interjet** (toll-free U.S. tel. 866/285-9525, www.interjet.com) and **Volaris** (tel. 551/102-8000, toll-free U.S. tel. 855/865-2747, www.volaris.com) both run daily flights that connect Huatulco to various U.S. destinations via Mexico City. Canadian airlines **Air Canada** (toll-free U.S./Can. tel. 888/247-2262, www.aircanada.com) and **West Jet** (toll-free U.S. tel. 888/937-8538, toll-free Can. tel. 888/937-8538, toll-free Mex. tel. 855/269-2979, www.westjet.com) both have direct flights between Huatulco and Toronto, and connect Huatulco to many Canadian and U.S. cities.

Aeromexico (tel. 555/133-4000, www.aeromexico.com) runs two daily flights between Huatulco and Mexico City, and, along with Interjet and Volaris, connect Huatulco to other major cities in Mexico. To fly within Oaxaca, book a flight with **Aerotucán** (tel. 951/502-0840, toll-free Mex. tel. 800/640-4148, www.aerotucan.com), whose fleet of small Cessna planes have air taxi privileges, making the company very flexible with scheduling.

For money matters, there is a *casa de cambio* in the arrivals hallway, as you leave baggage claim. If you need to change money upon arrival, make sure to do it before you exit the hallway to the parking lot, as you will not be allowed to reenter. To withdraw money, exit the arrivals *palapa* and turn right to head to the ticketing building, where you'll find **ATMs** for Banamex, Santander, and Bancomer.

A small, open-air **food court** between the departures and ticketing *palapas* serves burgers, sandwiches, and other food, as well as coffee and alcoholic drinks.

Taxis from the **official taxi stand** outside the arrivals terminal charge around US$22 to get to La Crucecita, but you'll be charged about half that if you walk the 450 meters (1,475 ft) out to the highway and get a cab from **Sitio Fraccionamiento El Zapote** (tel. 958/589-3337 or 958/587-8126, info@taxihuatulco.com), which has an official stop in front of the gas station across the highway from the airport road. To save even more, flag down an eastbound *taxi colectivo* or *urbano* at this spot on the highway. These modes of transport only charge a little over US$1 to La Crucecita from here.

BUS

The **Terminal ADO** (Blvd. Chahué, tel. 958/108-6041, www.ado.com.mx) is on Boulevard Chahué, just north of downtown Crucecita. ADO routes connect Huatulco to Oaxaca City (7-8 hrs, US$11-24), Puerto Escondido (2.5 hrs, US$4-10), and Mexico City (14-17 hrs, US$30-63). Heading east, ADO buses go to Salina Cruz (2.5 hrs, US$10), Tehuantepec (3 hrs, US$10-14), Juchitán (4 hrs, US$12-17), and Tuxtla Gutiérrez, Chiapas (9 hrs, US$31).

From Pochutla, the *urbanos* of **Transportes Rápidos de Pochutla** (across from Líneas Unidas on Lázaro Cárdenas, Pochutla, tel. 958/584-0159) only cost about US$2 for the speedy trip to La Crucecita, which takes just under an hour. Buses leave every 10 minutes 5am-8:30pm daily. The terminus in La Crucecita is the **Central**

Camionera on Calle Carpinteros, northwest of the ADO station.

CAR

Coastal Highway 200 connects Huatulco to the rest of the Oaxacan coast and beyond. To the west of Huatulco, the *crucero* (crossroads) with Highway 175 is about 42 km (26 mi) from La Crucecita through tight switchbacks in the tropical foothills; it's a 45-minute drive. From this junction, Puerto Ángel is 10 km (6.2 mi) south on Highway 175. Total drive time to Puerto Ángel is just over an hour. Puerto Escondido is another 72 km (45 mi) west down Highway 200 from the junction, two hours from La Crucecita.

If you're coming from Oaxaca City (262 km/160 mi; 6 hrs) or San José del Pacífico (124 km/77 mi; 3 hrs), it's faster to take the El Zapote-Copalita Highway through Santa María Huatulco. The junction with Highway 175 is 62 km (38 mi) south of San José. From here, follow the highway 44 km (27 mi) to the junction with Highway 200. La Crucecita is 16 km (10 mi) east down Highway 200.

You can rent a car in the airport terminal at **Alamo** (arrivals terminal, tel. 958/581-9134 or 951/160-3057, 8am-6pm, US$52-130 per day), but you'll save money by renting from local company **Los Tres Reyes** (next to gas station across the highway from airport road, tel. 958/109-8147 or 958/105-1376, www.losreyescarrent.com, 7am-8pm daily, US$42-105 per day). If you rent ahead of time, they can come into the airport to meet you with your rental.

WEST SIDE

Only two of Huatulco's western beaches, Santa Cruz and La Entrega, have any kind of development on them. The others (El Violín, El Maguey, and Cacaluta) are in the officially protected coastline of Huatulco National Park and are great places to escape all the hubbub without having to travel too far.

Sights

The lazy waves of Playa Santa Cruz softly splash the foundation of the **Capilla de la Santa Cruz** (Chapel of the Holy Cross of Huatulco) all day long. This open-air chapel is dedicated to venerating Huatulco's piece of the mysterious, indestructible cross put on this beach by a mysterious, bearded man in a white robe some 2,000 years ago. The chapel is closed in the evenings, but you can always sneak a peek, since it has no walls.

On your way to Playa La Entrega, stop at the **Mirador El Faro** (Lighthouse Lookout) to get a spectacular view of the coastline in both directions and the open sea to the south. If the waves are right, you should be able to see (and hear) **El Bufadero,** a rock formation that causes water to shoot up 10 meters (33 ft) or more into the air. It's called El Bufadero, or The Snorter, because it makes a loud sound like someone raucously snorting. Ask your taxi driver to make a stop at the lookout. If you're in a car, keep an eye out for the lighthouse about 3 km (1.9 mi) after turning off Boulevard Benito Juárez west of Santa Cruz.

Beaches

The pint-sized waves of **Playa Santa Cruz** rarely get more than ankle-high. A dock jutting over 300 meters (984 ft) into the bay at the beach's east end separates the public beach from the small marina on the other side. *Palapa* restaurants line the beach, with the exception of the spot occupied by the chapel, providing shade, seafood, and cold beer and coconuts for tourists and local families alike. The beach is near the center of Santa Cruz Huatulco.

Just south of Santa Cruz, **Playa La Entrega** is a miniature paradise of still turquoise waters, with a small dock on one end and a few *palapas* and snorkel equipment rental shacks along the short strip of sand. Reefs just 70 meters (230 ft) from the beach offer lots of opportunities to see tropical fish and other coral-dwelling sea life. To get to La Entrega, follow Boulevard Benito Juárez west past Santa Cruz. You'll quickly see the sign to turn left to La Entrega.

Playas El Violín, El Maguey, and Cacaluta

are all within the boundaries of **Parque Nacional Huatulco.** Get to **Playa El Violín** via the same road that goes to La Entrega. To get to **Playa El Maguey,** take Benito Juárez west, staying to the right, rather than turning left to get to La Entrega. It's easiest to just take a taxi.

Playa Cacaluta is a very steep slope of sand that, not far into the waves, drops sharply into open ocean. It can be spooky to watch as the waters receding down the beach sometimes fall off the edge before the next wave arrives. Swim with extreme caution here, as there are no lifeguards on duty. To get here from the road, you'll have to walk the last 0.5 km (0.3 mi) through the jungle. Just ask the taxi driver to take you to the entrance to the trail. The most fun way to get out here, though, is on a bicycle, but be aware that there are quite a few hills. It's also easy to get lost on the trails in the national park, so hiring a cycling guide is recommended.

Recreation
SWIMMING, SNORKELING, AND SCUBA DIVING

The best **swimming** is on Playas Santa Cruz and La Entrega. Both are in tight bays that protect them from the brute force of the Pacific.

For **snorkeling,** head to Playa La Entrega. In a *palapa* at the end of the beach opposite the dock, you'll find **Renta de Snorkel Vicente Garganta de Lata** (Playa La Entrega, tel. 958/106-5211, vicente_gargantadelata@ hotmail.com, 8am-6pm daily). Both Vicente and **Mundo Acuático** (Playa La Entrega, tel. 958/100-4729), just next door, charge about US$5 for goggles, snorkel, and fins. They also have lockers to stow your valuables while you snorkel around the reefs.

The best time of year for **scuba diving** in Huatulco is in September and October, at the tail end of the rainy season. In the shopping center by the beach in Santa Cruz, you'll find the offices of **Hurricane Divers** (Playa Santa Cruz, tel. 958/587-1107, www.hurricanedivers. com, 9am-6pm Mon.-Fri., 9am-4pm Sat.), a very well-respected dive center that offers everything from fun dives to all levels of PADI certifications. Contact the dive center for pricing.

ADVENTURE AND BOAT TOURS

Just to the west of the central square in Santa Cruz, **Sociedad Cooperativa Atardecer Huatulco** (Calle Mitla, tel. 958/100-4042 or 958/688-1890, www.atardecerhuatulco.com) is a local co-op that operates sportfishing and boat tours that include snorkeling and take you to many of Huatulco's beaches, as well as sights like El Bufadero. Contact the co-op directly for pricing.

The office of agro-ecological reserve **Hagia Sofia** (Mitla 402-7, tel. 958/587-0871, www.hagiasofia.mx, 9am-2pm and 4pm-7pm Mon.-Sat.) is in central Santa Cruz, but all the adventure is out in the tropical foothills of the Sierra Madre del Sur, about 35 km (22 mi) northwest of Santa Cruz. On 130 hectares (320 acres) ranging 260-309 meters (850-1,014 ft) above sea level, the reserve is the perfect venue to observe the wide spectrum of Oaxaca's polychromatic flora. You'll also see rainbows of butterfly and bird species as you hike out to a small waterfall for a swim. Their daylong tours include transportation, breakfast, and lunch, and cost around US$85.

I can't recommend highly enough going on a bicycle tour through the jungle of Huatulco National Park with Miguel, Lalo, and the guys at **Descubre Huatulco** (Chacah 210, La Crucecita, tel. 958/119-7325 or 958/587-2195, www.descubrehuatulco.com, 8am-8pm daily). They took me out to Playa Cacaluta via dirt (sometimes rocky) roads through the thick jungle of the national park. The bilingual guides are very knowledgeable of these trails and the plants and wildlife found here. On the aptly nicknamed "Mil Ojos" (Thousand Eyes) trail, I was thankful I had their guidance as well as wheels, as I could clearly see the literally thousands of eyes of all the wolf spiders on the trail and in the jungle beyond. The tour costs about US$29 with rental included, and bikes alone cost US$13 for a 12-hour rental.

SURFING AND STAND-UP PADDLEBOARDING

The calm waters of Santa Cruz are perfect for paddleboarding, and there is good surfing on nearby beaches. **Café Surf** (in shopping center next to the Teatro del Mar, tel. 958/105-1806, www.huatulcosurftrip.com, 6:30am-6pm daily) rents equipment and offers lessons and tours, but they specialize in fully planned surfing trips that include two lessons a day, English-speaking instructors, all necessary transportation, and accommodations in the Ocean Park Condos in the same building as the office.

JET SKIS

Rent Jet Skis in Santa Cruz, across the marina from the beach, at **Huatulco Watersports** (next to Pemex gas station at the end of Calle Tehuantepec, tel. 958/106-1185, www.huatulcowatersports.com, 8am-6pm daily). You can rent one by the hour (US$80), which can be a fun way to get out to see Playa La Entrega, but you can't explore much farther than that. To see more of the coast, consider taking one of their bilingual tours. The three-hour snorkeling tour (US$175) visits four bays and includes hotel pickup and all the equipment.

SPAS AND *TEMAZCAL*

Hidden away on a little corner street on the west side of the big intersection of Boulevards Juárez and Chahué, just east of Santa Cruz, **Temazcal Na-Há Maya** (Vialidad 14, tel. 958/585-8185, www.nahamaya.com, 7am-10:30pm daily) offers 30-60-minute massages for US$18-47, as well as *temazcal* (US$11) and various packages that include aromatherapy, hydrotherapy, music therapy, and more.

In Hotel Castillo Huatulco, on Benito Juárez in Santa Cruz, **Tomy's Spa & Salon** (tel. 958/107-6133, tomy_s_spa@hotmail.com,

8am-10pm daily) offers shiatsu, Swiss, craniofacial, and other massage techniques and relaxation therapies.

Food

SANTA CRUZ HUATULCO

Housed in the gazebo in the central plaza, **Café Huatulco** (Parque Santa Cruz, tel. 958/587-1228, 8am-11:30pm daily, US$2-4) serves rich, shade-grown coffee cultivated in the tropical heights a few hours north. They also have a decent menu of enchiladas, sandwiches, cakes, and more.

Over by the water, offering classic Mexican seafood dishes, **Restaurante El Huayacán** (Playa Santa Cruz, tel. 958/587-2651, 7am-10pm daily, US$6-8) will serve you a cold coconut and shrimp cocktail at a table in the shade of its namesake tree on the beach. Now that I think of it, I don't think they normally serve coconuts, but my waiter Benito ran off in search of one for me, which attests to the quality of service here.

Down at the other end of the row of *palapas*, **Doña Celia Lobster House** (Playa Santa Cruz, tel. 958/583-4876, www.restaurantdonacelia.com.mx, 8am-11pm daily, US$6-9) is a great place to try its titular specialty, or a *piña rellena* (stuffed pineapple), loaded with shrimp, octopus, fish, veggies, and melted manchego cheese.

Right next to the Capilla de la Santa Cruz, **El Habanero Loko** (Playa Santa Cruz, tel. 958/587-2000, 7am-11pm daily, US$6-8) offers pizzas baked in a wood-fired clay oven, and also has an extensive menu of seafood and other international dishes. The quoted hours are pretty flexible. The Crazy Habanero will stay open as long as there are people who want to drink beer, so if you're looking for some nightlife during the quiet low season, you're likely to find some drinking buddies here.

PLAYA LA ENTREGA

The only other beach with restaurants on this side of Bahías de Huatulco is La Entrega, on which a handful of breezy *palapas* like **Las Flores** (Playa La Entrega, no phone, 8am-6pm

1: the open-air Capilla de la Santa Cruz 2: view from the Mirador El Faro, near Playa La Entrega 3: Playa Santa Cruz 4: Playa La Entrega daily, US$6-8) serve more or less the same delicious Oaxacan coastal fare. Most of them close around sunset.

Accommodations
SANTA CRUZ HUATULCO

A five-minute walk from the beach, **Hotel Yuu-Lee Casa Bendita** (Huatulco Salvaje, tel. 958/100-4951, US$26-40) has a particular allure to it, especially for mezcal enthusiasts. This small, basic hotel is owned by Casa Chahué Mezcal (whose store is in La Crucecita), and the hotel staff can put you in contact with the owners to arrange a visit to their *palenque* (distillery) about 30 minutes from Santa Cruz. All rooms have air-conditioning, TV, and Wi-Fi.

There isn't a hotel directly on Playa Santa Cruz, but the medium-sized **Hotel Posada de Abril** (Cerrada de Montealbán, tel. 958/587-2380 or 958/587-2260, www.posadadeabrilhuatulco.com, US$47 d) is just 50 short meters (165 ft) from it. And there's a pool, in case the walk is too much. All 27 units have air-conditioning, TV, and Wi-Fi access.

Perfect for longer stays, **Ocean Park Condos** (Mitla 402, tel. 958/587-0440 or U.S. tel. 770/658-2113, www.oceanparkcondominiumshuatulco.com, rebeca@propiedadesideal.com, US$100-150 daily, US$1,000 monthly) has all the comforts of home, and then some. All units are either studio apartments or full 1-2-bedroom condos, all have kitchenettes and balconies, and most have a washer and dryer. Manager Rebeca Anaya, a polyglot who speaks English, Spanish, and French, lives on the grounds and is available 24/7 to help with anything that may come up for her guests.

CAMPING AND TRAILER PARKS

To camp on one of the building-free beaches in **Parque Nacional Huatulco,** get a permit from the **park office** (corner of Guamuchil and Blvd. Chahué, tel. 958/587-0849, 9am-2pm and 4pm-6pm Mon.-Fri.), which is three blocks east of the *zócalo* on Calle Guamuchil in La Crucecita.

Getting Around

Taxis to anywhere in the Bahías de Huatulco (except Bahía San Agustín) won't charge more than US$4 from Santa Cruz. The stand for **Sitio Santa Cruz** (tel. 958/587-0888) is on the east side of Parque Santa Cruz.

EAST SIDE

The bays on Huatulco's east side cater more to luxury travelers. Here you'll find five-star all-inclusive resorts and a golf course, but you'll also find a campground and trailer park, as well as economical activities that will draw you here even if just for the day.

Sights
PARQUE ECO-ARQUEOLÓGICO COPALITA

What we know is that someone lived at the mouth of the Copalita River about 2,500 years ago—we just don't know who, exactly. The ruins they left behind are at **Parque Eco-Arqueológico Copalita** (Blvd. Benito Juárez, tel. 958/587-1410, parquecopalita@fonatur.gob.mx, 8am-5pm daily, US$4), 11 km (7 mi) east of Santa Cruz. In the decades since their discovery in 1996, researchers have gleaned that these temples, ball court, and ancient lighthouse were constructed sometime around 500 BC by people originating from the Gulf Coast region of Mesoamerica, in the modern states of Veracruz and Tamaulipas.

It's likely that the original inhabitants were Mixes or Chontales, who were among the first to settle in this region. The Aztecs, whose own plans for conquest in Oaxaca were foiled by the arrival of the Spanish, were the last to live here before it was consequentially abandoned in the 1520s.

Although not as impressive as other Oaxacan pre-Hispanic sites, the ruins at Copalita have interesting features, such as the patches of original white stucco found on the Pirámide del Serpiente (Pyramid of

1: the ball court at the Parque Eco-Arqueológico Copalita **2:** a surfer riding the dependable point break at Barra de la Cruz **3:** rope swing at Las Cascadas Mágicas

the Serpent). The grand pyramid of the old Templo Mayor (Main Temple) rises over 20 meters (66 ft) from the jungle floor. The other half of the park is an ecological reserve where you may see lots of birds and butterflies, but little other wildlife.

You can explore the trails of the park on your own, which takes about two hours, or hire a bilingual guide for around US$25. Either way, be prepared for a lot of walking. Take bug spray and sufficient water for a couple sweaty hours in the jungle. There is also a small museum on-site with mostly ceramic artifacts from all over Oaxaca.

Taxis charge about US$4 from Santa Cruz, and a *colectivo* heading east on Boulevard Benito Juárez will get you there for around US$1.

Beaches

Playa Chahué is a little less than 400 meters (1,312 ft) of brilliant yellow sand with a slight gradation that sometimes causes red-flag swimming conditions. It is home to a few mid- to high-range resorts and spas, and a jetty at the east side of the beach separates it from the Chahué Marina, where you can dock a boat.

Four and a half kilometers (about 3 mi) east of Playa Chahué, **Playa Tangolunda** is a beach of extremes in terms of spending the night. You could do so in the lap of luxury in one of the five-star resorts, or rough it at the camping and trailer park area. **Playa Arrocito,** in between Chahué and Tangolunda (you'll see the sign about half-way in between), has a couple *palapa* restaurants, but little else. One of the three beaches in **Bahía Conejos** has been appropriated by the all-inclusive resort Secrets, but the two to the east have nothing on them. Ask your taxi driver to show you the entrances to the short trails to get down to them, about five minutes past Tangolunda.

There is some okay surfing off the rocks at **Playa La Bocana,** one hill west of Parque Copalita, but you'll have to bring your own board. You'll see the turnoff about three minutes after the Secrets resort. La Bocana

is just the curled western end of a beach that stretches east to the mouth of the Copalita River and continues for nearly a mile beyond. It's nice to head to this beach after walking around Parque Copalita and stop for some refreshments like fish tacos and cold soft drinks.

Recreation
SWIMMING

Swimming is possible on Chahué and Tangolunda, but the water can get pretty rough. Pay attention to the water condition flags.

ADVENTURE AND BOAT TOURS

Aventura Mundo (Adventure World; Benito Juárez 25-1, tel. 958/581-0197, www. aventuramundo.net, 9am-7pm daily), at the east end of the shopping center in Bahía Tangolunda, has you covered for all your ecotourism and adventure sports desires. The Aventura experience includes bike tours, hiking, ATV excursions, Jet Skis, kayaking, snorkeling, surf lessons, and more.

BOAT LAUNCHING

Marina Chahué (tel. 958/587-2652, 9am-2:30pm and 4pm-6pm Mon.-Fri., 9am-1pm Sat.-Sun.), located in the bay of the same name, has over 80 slips for seafaring vessels of 27-60 feet, two for boats up to 100 feet, and 11 spots to dock all your mega yachts. Slip rates are about US$0.50 per foot if you rent daily, and about US$8 per foot monthly. Water and electricity are extra.

GOLF

Las Parotas Club de Golf (Blvd. Tangolunda, tel. 958/581-0171, www.lasparotasgolf.com, US$140) is located in Bahía Tangolunda. It has 18 holes of championship-level fairways and greens, the last few of which are right on the beach.

SPAS AND *TEMAZCAL*

Eco Spa Huatulco (across from Las Parotas golf course on Benito Juárez, tel. 958/581-0025, www.ecoyspa.com), in Bahía

Tangolunda, provides massages, facials, body treatments, and other relaxation therapies.

Also in Tangolunda, just a quick jaunt east down Benito Juárez from Eco Spa, **Las Conchas** (Blvd. Benito Juárez, tel. 958/119-3666, 8am-8:30pm daily) offers *temazcal* in addition to massages and other relaxation therapies.

HORSEBACK RIDING

Rancho Caballo de Mar (Blvd. Benito Juárez, tel. 958/131-8137, 9am-5pm daily) runs horseback riding tours from its small ranch on the banks of the Copalita River. Tours trot along shady jungle roads, ford shallow rivers, and take you right out onto the sand of the beach. Owner María is very knowledgeable of local flora and fauna.

Accommodations

CHAHUÉ

Primarily a spa, **Xquenda Spa and Hotel** (Bahía Chahué, tel. 958/583-4448 or 554/738-6263, US$50-76) has two hotel rooms and a suite, all with very comfy beds, private terraces, ocean views, air-conditioning, hammocks, and soft yellow lighting, all of which comes together to create an environment in which stress is unable to thrive. Other perks include two pools, a *temazcal* sweat lodge, a gym and tennis court, and palm trees whispering quiet things in the sea breeze.

A popular destination for weddings, **Hotel Quinta Bella** (Bahía Chahué, tel. 958/587-2466, www.quintabellahuatulco.com, US$78-94) is a modern, family-oriented resort right on Playa Chahué. Aside from the multiple pools for all guests, most rooms include a small splash pool on the private balcony.

TANGOLUNDA

Huatulco's *zona hotelera* is where you'll find classy luxury resorts like ★ **Camino Real Zaashila** (Benito Juárez 5, tel. 958/583-0300, www.caminoreal.com, US$150-220), whose primary concept is harmony between nature and the man-made. Broad-leafed tropical vines climb the white stucco

of the contemporary architectural design by renowned Mexican architect Javier Sordo Madaleno.

The laundry list of amenities includes a gym, spa, tennis court, restaurant, bar, and beach store all on-site. Taxi and room service are 24 hours. There is a large public pool and a beach club, and many of the luxury suites have their own private plunge pool right outside the back door.

The 27 banana-yellow bungalows of ★ **Hotel Quinta Real** (Benito Juárez 2, tel. 958/581-0428, www.quintareal.com, US$200-400 suites) stagger down a lush hillside to the golden beach below. All suites have private balconies with breathtaking views of the turquoise waters and hazy islands out in the bay. They are tastefully designed with pastel-colored, locally woven textiles that complement the color of faded sun on the bungalow walls.

At the bottom of this sprawl of luxury, the tables of the bar are set above and around the swimming pools that make tiered steps down the hill, like the rest of the architecture. Dotted along the walkways that zigzag up and down the hillside are informational plaques about the tropical birds you might see here or in the marshy low ground below.

CAMPING AND TRAILER PARKS

Sandwiched between the extravagance of the Quinta Real and the last few holes of the golf course, you'll find the **Tangolunda Campground and RV Park** (no contact information), where for less than US$3 per person you can pitch a tent or park an RV. The only services provided are bathrooms and showers; there are no water or electricity hookups for trailers. Camping is allowed on the beach, as well as in the area back behind the swamp. The 50 or so spots are first-come, first-served. If you don't see an attendant, just post up and someone will eventually come to you.

Getting Around

Taxis charge no more than US$3 for travel

between these bays, US$1 or so more to get out to the horseback riding ranch. *Colectivo* taxis that zip up and down Benito Juárez will cost US$1 or less along this stretch of the road.

BARRA DE LA CRUZ

The sleepy surfer's paradise of **Barra de la Cruz** is only a half-hour drive from Tangolunda.

TOP EXPERIENCE

Surfing

The beach's west end curls like a claw out into the Pacific Ocean, and the clusters of igneous boulders on the point form the swells coming from the open ocean into one of the most reliable point breaks on the Oaxacan coast. Once it hits the point, this regular right-hander breaks slowly down the crest of the wave, allowing surfers to cut back and forth on it for a long time before splashing down.

The best time of year to surf in Barra de la Cruz is between April and September, when swells are most consistent. The beach is open 7am-8pm daily, and access costs about US$1.50, which you'll be asked to pay at a roadside hut before descending to the beach.

Food and Accommodations

Down on the beach, a small, ramshackle *palapa* **restaurant** (no phone, 9am-5pm daily, US$3-5) serves breakfast as well as ceviche, *yakimeshi*, shrimp cocktails, and more. Beers are served until "six o'clock," but it's probably more like "when it's too dark to surf."

Up in the town scattered along the road in from the highway, **Pizzería El Dragón** (tel. 958/587-0702, 6pm-midnight daily, US$5-8) is owned by employees of La Crema bar and pizzeria in La Crucecita. La Crema has a long history of providing financial assistance to employees to start their own micro-enterprises, and El Dragón, along with the *cabañas* (US$16-32) on the property, is La Crema's flagship project. You'll find it 300

meters (984 ft) down the dirt road, around the corner from Cabañas Pepe.

The majority of accommodations in Barra de la Cruz are rustic wood cabins along the main road to the beach. About a mile up the road from the beach, **Cabañas Pepe** (main road, Barra de la Cruz, tel. 958/589-2592, c_pepecastillo@hotmail.com, US$13) has a small collection of basic *cabañas* that have everything you need after a long day of surfing: bed, fan, shared bathrooms, hammock outside, Ping-Pong, and cold beer. Just down the road, **Cabañas La Joya** (main road, Barra de la Cruz, no phone, US$11) has similar crash pads, also with shared bathrooms, as well as space for camping (US$3 pp). Most *cabaña* hotels here double as surf shops.

Getting There

A **private taxi** from Huatulco to Barra de la Cruz will cost about US$13. You can call dispatch at **Sitio La Crucecita** (tel. 958/587-1616 or 958/144-4092) to schedule a trip, or just hail a taxi on the street. All taxi companies here have the same fares. This is the best option, as they'll take you directly to the *cabañas* in town.

Alternatively, you could take *colectivos* to get out there. Your best bet is to catch one on Benito Juárez east of the intersection with Boulevard Chahué in Bahía Chahué, some of which go all the way out to Barra de la Cruz. It's possible you'll have to get off on Highway 200 before reaching Barra de la Cruz, in which case you just post up on the side of the road and wait for another to come by. If the *colectivo* doesn't go into Barra de la Cruz, you'll have to walk or hitch a ride the 2.5 km (1.5 mi) into town. All in all, you shouldn't pay more than US$2-3 for the whole trip.

To drive here, take Boulevard Benito Juárez east from anywhere in Bahías de Huatulco until it terminates at Highway 200. Take Highway 200 east for 14 km (8.7 miles), until you see the turn for Barra de la Cruz. From here, the beach is 4 km (2.5 mi) down the dirt road through town. Total drive time from Tangolunda is about 30-40 minutes.

★ LAS CASCADAS MÁGICAS AND FINCA LA GLORIA

The Copalita River snakes down from its source high up in the misty mountaintops of the Sierra Madre del Sur through hill after hill of the superabundant tropical vegetation before finally emptying into the Pacific at a mile-wide beach next to the ruins at Parque Copalita. Sixteen kilometers (10 mi) inland, at **Las Cascadas Mágicas** (Magic Waterfalls), its contents tumble down a pile of boulders in a magical rush of white water that pools like liquid gemstones in a small clearing in the jungle. A swim in the cool water is exactly what you'll need in the sweltering tropical afternoon, and if you've been lugging a backpack around Oaxaca for a while, your shoulders could definitely use a brisk massage under the cataracts.

Just over 1 km (0.6 mi) from the Cascadas is **Finca La Gloria Coffee** (Llano Grande, tel. 958/587-0697), where robust arabica beans are grown in the sultry shade of the jungle canopy. Established early on in the coffee industry boom of the 19th century, La Gloria is one of the oldest coffee farms along the coast. Most of the tours from Huatulco to the Cascadas include a coffee tasting here, and you can also just show up and grab a cup of joe.

Getting There and Away

Getting out to the waterfall is not easy, so I recommend taking a tour to do it. The daylong tour run by the bilingual guides at **Descubre Huatulco** (Chacah 210, La Crucecita, tel. 958/119-7325 or 958/587-2195, www.descubrehuatulco.com, 8am-8pm daily) costs about US$26 and includes transportation to and from the falls, an afternoon meal, and a tour of the *finca* with a coffee production demonstration and tasting. Seeing as a private taxi will cost you close to the same amount, this is your best option for getting out there. The tour leaves at 10am and gets back to La Crucecita around 4pm.

If you have your own car, be aware that the dirt road is deeply rutted in parts and is not recommended (though not impossible) for sedans and other low cars. Take Highway 200 west from La Crucecita about 10 km (6.2 mi) until you see the sign for the turnoff on the right-hand side of the road. From here, follow the scant signage and trust your best judgment the slow rest of the way. The falls are another 30.5 km (19 mi) into the jungle. The drive takes about 1.5 hours.

Puerto Escondido and Vicinity

It may be the beer-tipping sailors and plethora of dubious-looking hideout hotels, but Puerto Escondido can give off a bit of a seedy vibe, despite the vegan restaurants and no-smoking sections in the areas that cater to foreign tourists. Therefore, I was not surprised to find a swashbuckling pirate story when I looked into the town's history. While the name may translate to Hidden Port, it has nothing to do with the visibility of the harbor. Legend has it that 16th-century pirate Andrew Drake, supposed brother to sea captain and slave trader Sir Francis Drake, pulled into the uninhabited bay to rest and hide from Spanish authorities after having kidnapped a Mixtec girl from Huatulco a few weeks earlier. While anchored in the bay, the girl escaped from her cabin and swam to shore. Search as they might, Drake and his men never found the girl on that or subsequent stops, during which time they came to call the bay Bahía de la Escondida (Bay of the Hiding Girl).

In beginning of the 20th century, the sleepy little costal village, then known as Punta Escondida, was woken up by the same stuff that wakes most of us up each morning: coffee. As more and more farmers began to cultivate the plant in the shade of the humid

Puerto Escondido

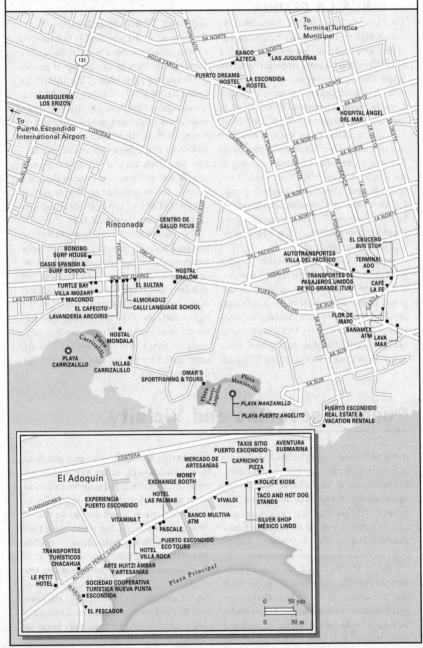

To
Terminal Turística
Municipal

9A NORTE

4A PONIENTE

AGUA ZARCA

8A NORTE

BANCO
AZTECA

LAS JUQUILEÑAS

131

PUERTO DREAMS
HOSTEL

LA ESCONDIDA
HOSTEL

7A NORTE

MARISQUERIA
LOS ERIZOS

CAMINO REAL

6A NORTE

To
Puerto Escondido
International Airport

COSTERA

HOSPITAL ÁNGEL
DEL MAR

5A NORTE

3A OESTE

4A PONIENTE

3A PONIENTE

2A PONIENTE

5A NORTE

AYOTAXACA

4A NORTE

1A OESTE

GUELAGA

2A NORTE

1A PONIENTE

3A NORTE

1A NORTE

2A NORTE

CENTRO DE
SALUD FICUS

CARRIZALILLO

Rinconada

FOCAS

ORCAS

DEL PACIFICO

EL CRUCERO
BUS STOP

BONOBO
SURF HOUSE

AUTOTRANSPORTES
VILLA DEL PACÍFICO

TERMINAL
ADO

OASIS SPANISH &
SURF SCHOOL

BENITO JUAREZ

HOSTAL
SHALOM

HIDALGO

TRANSPORTES DE
PASAJEROS UNIDOS
DE RÍO GRANDE (TUR)

CAFÉ
LA FE

TURTLE BAY

EL SULTAN

PUERTO ANGELITO

2A SUR

GASGA

VILLA MOZART
Y MACONDO

ALMORADUZ

LAS TORTUGAS

EL CAFECITO

CALLI LANGUAGE SCHOOL

FLOR DE
MAYO

LAVANDERÍA ARCOIRIS

BANAMEX
ATM

3A PONIENTE

LAVA
MAX

HOSTAL
MONDALA

Playa
Carrizalillo

4A SUR

PLAYA
CARRIZALILLO

VILLAS
CARRIZALILLO

OMAR'S
SPORTFISHING & TOURS

Playa
Manzanillo

5A SUR

Playa
Puerto Angelito

PLAYA MANZANILLO

PLAYA PUERTO ANGELITO

PUERTO ESCONDIDO
REAL ESTATE &
VACATION RENTALS

TAXIS SITIO
PUERTO ESCONDIDO

AVENTURA
SUBMARINA

COSTERA

MERCADO DE
ARTESANÍAS

CAPRICHO'S
PIZZA

El Adoquín

MONEY
EXCHANGE BOOTH

POLICE KIOSK

FUNDADORES

EXPERIENCIA
PUERTO ESCONDIDO

HOTEL
LAS PALMAS

VIVALDI

TACO AND HOT DOG
STANDS

VITAMINA T

BANCO MULTIVA
ATM

SILVER SHOP
MÉXICO LINDO

PASCALE

ALFONSO PÉREZ GASGA

PUERTO ESCONDIDO
ECO TOURS

TRANSPORTES
TURÍSTICOS
CHACAHUA

HOTEL
VILLA ROCA

LE PETIT
HOTEL

ARTE HUITZI ÁMBAR
Y ARTESANÍAS

MARINA

SOCIEDAD COOPERATIVA
TURÍSTICA NUEVA PUNTA
ESCONDIDA

Playa Principal

EL PESCADOR

0   50 yds

0   50 m

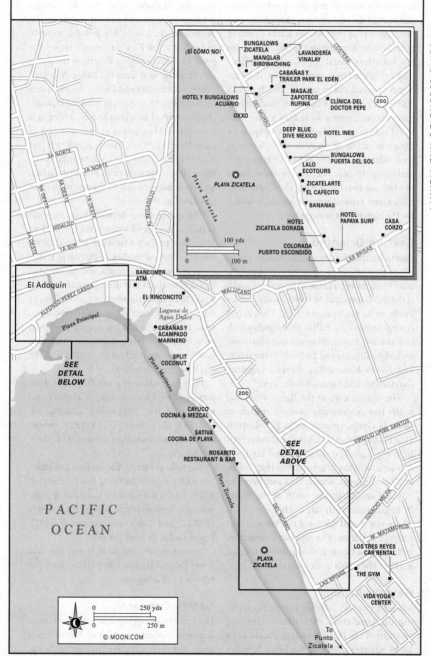

Detail Above:

- ¡SÍ CÓMO NO!
- BUNGALOWS ZICATELA
- MANGLAR BIRDWACHING
- LAVANDERÍA VINALAY
- CABAÑAS Y TRAILER PARK EL EDÉN
- HOTEL Y BUNGALOWS ACUARIO
- MASAJE ZAPOTECO RUFINA
- CLÍNICA DEL DOCTOR PEPE
- OXXO
- DEEP BLUE DIVE MEXICO
- HOTEL INES
- BUNGALOWS PUERTA DEL SOL
- LALO ECOTOURS
- ZICATELARTE
- EL CAFECITO
- BANANAS
- HOTEL PAPAYA SURF
- CASA CORZO
- HOTEL ZICATELA DORADA
- COLORADA PUERTO ESCONDIDO

COSTERA
DEL MORRO
200
LAS BRISAS

⊛ PLAYA ZICATELA

0   100 yds
0   100 m

Lower / Left Detail:

El Adoquín

ALFONSO PÉREZ GASGA

Playa Principal

SEE DETAIL BELOW

BANCOMER ATM

EL RINCONCITO

MALUCANO

Laguna de Agua Dulce

CABAÑAS Y ACAMPADO MARINERO

SPLIT COCONUT

Playa Marinero

200

COSTERA

CAYUCO COCINA & MEZCAL

SATIVA COCINA DE PLAYA

ROSARITO RESTAURANT & BAR

SEE DETAIL ABOVE

VIRGILIO URIBE SANTOS

Playa Zicatela

PACIFIC OCEAN

DEL MORRO

IGNACIO MEJÍA

M. MATAMOROS

⊛ PLAYA ZICATELA

LOS TRES REYES CAR RENTAL

THE GYM

LAS BRISAS

VIDA YOGA CENTER

3A NORTE
2A NORTE
5A OESTE
7A OESTE
HIDALGO
1A OESTE
1A SUR
AL REGADILLO

0   250 yds
0   250 m

© MOON.COM

To Punto Zicatela

southern slopes of the Sierra Madre del Sur, the need for a port to ship their product arose, and in 1928 the port of Puerto Escondido was established. For decades, problems sourcing potable water kept the local population quite low, but after Coastal Highway 200 was constructed in the 1960s, surfers from California began to notice the monstrous beach breaks off Playa Zicatela, and the rest is modern history. Puerto Escondido is now known the world over as one of the best surfing spots on the globe, attracting novice to professional wave riders and hosting annual international surf competitions. Puerto also draws loads of Mexican tourists during the Christmas, Easter, and school summer holidays, which are the high tourist seasons here.

Getting Oriented

Puerto Escondido stretches across 15 km (9 mi) of coastline, encompassing eight beaches, from Playa Bacocho to the west, curving south at the Bahía Principal, to Punta Zicatela, or La Punta, at its southeastern limit. The central coastal point is the **Bahía Principal,** which contains the Playas Principal and Marinero, with Playa Zicatela and La Punta to the south, and Playas Manzanillo, Puerto Angelito, Carrizalillo, and Bacocho to the west.

The tourist area of the Bahía Principal is the last cobblestone-covered stretch of Avenida Gasga, referred to as **El Adoquín** (The Paving Stone), which is closed to car traffic every night 5pm-6am. Coastal Highway 200 separates the beaches from the Centro and town proper, which fans out over the sylvan foothills to the north of the Bahía Principal; this north side of Highway 200 is where you'll find the town market and municipal bus station. The highway intersection with Avenida Gasga (called Avenida Oaxaca north of Hwy. 200) is the local *crucero.*

Getting Around

Many of Puerto's beaches are within walking distance from each other. Heading south from the Playa Principal, Zicatela is a 10-15-minute walk along the beach between

the wave-battered stones of Playa Marinero and the Mirador Romance de Verano (Summer Romance Lookout Point) at the north end of Zicatela. It's possible to walk to La Punta, but Zicatela's length makes it a good 45-minute trip on foot from the *mirador.* Heading west from the Bahía Principal, Playas Manzanillo and Puerto Angelito can be reached in 15 minutes by walking through the residential neighborhoods. There is a stairway to Manzanillo at the west end of Calle Cuarta (4ª) Sur. Puerto Angelito is just west of Manzanillo. Playa Carrizalillo is another 20-minute walk from Puerto Angelito, and Playa Bacocho is a 30-minute walk from Carrizalillo.

The quickest way between beaches is via taxi. The green-and-white taxis operated by **Sitio Puerto Escondido** (tel. 954/582-0990, 954/582-0876, or 954/128-1620) charge US$2-5, depending on your origin and destination. Quick note about taxi directions: If you take a taxi to El Adoquín when it is closed to car traffic at night, your driver will ask you if you want to go to the marina, on the west side, or to the *puente* (bridge) side, in which case you'll be dropped off on the east side of the street, by the police kiosk.

Or you could rent a car from **Los Tres Reyes** (The Three Kings; in airport and on Coastal Hwy. 200 above Zicatela, tel. 954/582-3335 or 954/134-9235, www. lostresreyescarrent.com) for around US$60-180 per day.

The folks at **Puerto Escondido Ecotours** (on Adoquín next to Hotel Las Palmas, tel. 954/103-1177, www.puertoescondidoecotours. com.mx, 7am-midnight daily) rent scooters (US$27) and 250cc motorcycles (US$37). Prices are for 24-hour periods.

Numerous *colectivo* taxis, buses, and vans travel Coastal Highway 200 all day long, for trips out to the lagoons.

Safety Concerns

Until recently, muggings and petty thefts were common at night and in lesser-visited beach areas. But these days, Puerto Escondido has upped its police presence with 24-hour kiosks and beach vigilance, which has caused crimes of this type to drop significantly. That isn't to say it no longer happens at all, but just be aware of your surroundings and keep your wits about you, and you should be fine. Personal thefts are more likely during the hustle and bustle of high season.

Your biggest safety concern in Puerto, however, isn't on land. The undertows on many of the beaches are extremely powerful and should be taken seriously. Anyone who is not an experienced surfer should steer clear of the water at Playa Zicatela completely. I've been told that the water off La Punta is okay for experienced swimmers, but even here the undertow can be a formidable force. Playa Bacocho is also not recommended for novice swimmers.

BEACHES

Playas Principal and Marinero

With its calm waters, the **Playa Principal** is the biggest of the swimmable beaches in Puerto, so it is easier to find a spot here than in Carrizalillo or Manzanilla. You'll have to share the bay with the flotilla of fishing and tour boats that constantly come to shore carrying anglers, scuba divers, and snorkelers, but there's usually enough room for everyone.

The cluster of beachfront restaurants that face the Bahía Principal have their main entrances on the cobblestone-paved stretch of the Avenida Pérez Gasga called **El Adoquín,** which means "paving stone." To simplify things, this area can be thought of as the "locals' beach," as the Playa Principal is usually crowded with weekenders from Mexico City or families from Puerto taking advantage of the beautiful coastline just blocks from their homes in their free time.

A small lagoon separates the Playa Principal from the smaller **Playa Marinero,** which really looks like the same beach. At low tide, you can cross the lagoon on foot to get to Playa Marinero and Zicatela to the south. The rocky outcroppings at the beach's southern point are called Los Marineros for their supposed resemblance to the ocean-weathered faces of hardened sailors.

★ Playa Zicatela

Puerto's pride and joy, **Playa Zicatela** (Place of Big Thorns) is known the world over as one of the best surfing spots on the planet, and definitely the best in Mexico. At 3 km (1.9 mi) long and averaging about 60 m (197 ft) wide, Zicatela is a broad, flat giant whose shallow waters curl the massive Pacific swells into waves that reach up to 6 m (20 ft) high. Because of this, anyone who is not an experienced surfer should stay out of the water, but there's lots of room for Frisbee, volleyball, and other beach sports, and there's a collection of *palapa* restaurants that are perfect for watching the surfers while enjoying a cold coconut or fresh seafood. Despite the numerous warning signs on the beach and general knowledge that Zicatela is not for splashing around, lifeguards still regularly pull floundering swimmers out of the waves, so take heed and be safe here. Puerto boasts nine beaches of varying sizes and currents, so if you want to go swimming, or want to learn how to surf, there are many other options close by.

Punta Zicatela (La Punta)

Beginning surfers should start out on the calmer waves off the beach at **Punta Zicatela,** at the southern end of Playa Zicatela. This southern tip of Zicatela tapers back out into the sea, creating a smaller "lefthander" point break that peels slowly and consistently off the rocky barb of land. Since the waters are slightly calmer than the raging beach breaks to the north, swimming is okay here, but I still only recommend it for experienced swimmers.

The vibe in the streets along the beach seems to take its cue from the surf, with a much more laid-back atmosphere than the rest of Puerto. The main drag on this end of the beach is the last few long, skinny blocks of Calle Alejandro Cárdenas, with its central point at the intersection with Calle Héroes Oaxaqueños, where taxis will most likely

Punta Zicatela

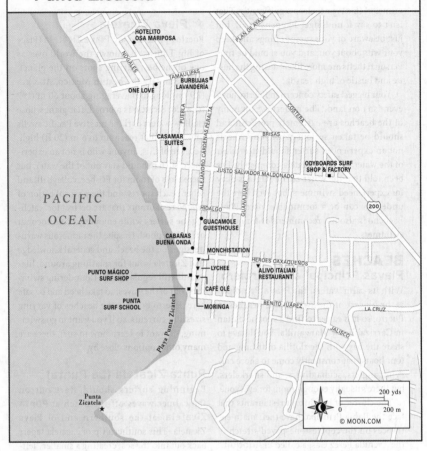

drop you off if you tell them to take you to "La Punta." This area has grown in popularity in recent years, attracting people from all over the world who have set up tasty Italian, Thai, fusion, and specialty-diet restaurants that cater to the international tourist set.

★ Playas Manzanillo, Puerto Angelito, and Carrizalillo

Luckily, for those of us who don't hang ten, Puerto Escondido isn't all gnarly waves. A pair of small coves to the west of the Bahía Principal boast calm, clear waters where you can splash around without worry. Just 1 km

(0.6 mi) west of El Adoquín is the pair of pint-sized beaches, **Playa Manzanillo** and **Playa Puerto Angelito.** Separated by a small, rocky outcropping and lookout point, these beaches are simply gorgeous, with mesmerizingly clear waters and a smattering of *palapa* restaurants on each. If the boats bug you, stay on Manzanillo, which is for swimmers only, but if you're looking for activities, head across the rocks to Puerto Angelito for fishing excursions, snorkeling, and banana boats. Both beaches are a quick 15-minute walk from El Adoquín. A stairway at the west end of Calle Cuarta Sur leads down to Manzanillo, and

Camino A Puerto Angelito (Road to Puerto Angelito) leads exactly where its name says.

Another 0.5 km (0.3 mi) west, a steep stone staircase leads down to **Playa Carrizalillo,** a compact stretch of sand tucked into the rocky coastline. The view from the top of the stairs is spectacular, especially as the afternoon sun goes down over the western point of the bay. At the west end of the beach, there is a little foot trail that leads to a tiny, hidden "lovers' beach."

The residential and tourist area above Carrizalillo is called **Rinconada,** where many new hotels, hostels, restaurants, and surf/Spanish schools have popped up in recent years. These are mostly concentrated in the outlet mall lining the southern side of Calle Benito Juárez, with a few new hostels in the blocks just to the north.

Playa Bacocho

About 1.5 km (1 mi) west of Carrizalillo, Puerto Escondido's westernmost beach is long, windy **Playa Bacocho.** Save a pair of resorts, the majority of Bacocho's soft, fine sand is undeveloped, so it's a good idea to bring your own parasol or other shade. Bacocho is usually less crowded than Puerto's other beaches, especially during low season, so you shouldn't have any trouble finding a place to post up. The temperament of the water, however, is somewhat similar to Zicatela's, with massive waves and an undertow that should not be underestimated. If you're an experienced swimmer and can get out past the breakers, there's some good stuff to be seen with a snorkel around the rocks that poke up out of the surf about 100 meters (328 ft) offshore.

Until recently, Bacocho had a bit of a shady reputation, with frequent petty thefts and muggings, but crimes like these have all but disappeared since the police began 24-hour vigilance of this stretch of shoreline. Many of the rocky nooks on the beach enclose perfect little camping spots, but do so at your own risk. Around-the-clock surveillance still doesn't fully guarantee safety.

RECREATION AND ACTIVITIES

Surfing

The best surfing in the entire country is at **Playa Zicatela,** where a long sandbar forms massive tubular beach breaks in the mornings and evenings. You need to be an experienced surfer to ride the towering waves, which can reach up to 6 meters (20 ft) in height, so Zicatela is not the place to learn to ride. The waves farther down the beach, at **Punta Zicatela,** are usually calmer, but sometimes take after their big brothers up the shore and get too hairy for learners. The gentle but ridable reef breaks at the entrance of the bay that shelters **Playa Carrizalillo** are the best waves on which to learn the ropes.

For classes at Carrizalillo, head to **Oasis Spanish and Surf School** (Benito Juárez 6, tel. 954/582-1445, www.spanishandsurflessonsmexico.com, 8am-6pm Mon.-Fri., 8am-4pm Sat.), where the team of expert instructors led by "Mexi-Pipe Warrior" Roger Ramírez have been teaching newbies to hang ten since 2006. Part of the first generation of professional Mexican surfers, Roger has been riding Puerto's waves his entire life and has won numerous international competitions. He also shapes the custom boards used by his students at his workshop in Rinconada. Weeklong packages of accommodations, surf lessons, and Spanish lessons start at US$420.

If you want to learn down on La Punta, you can schedule anything from daily classes to two-week intensive courses at **Experiencia Puerto Escondido** (corner of Héroes Oaxaqueños and Nuevo Leon, tel. 954/582-1818, www.experienciamexico.mx, 8am-3pm Mon.-Fri.), which also offers Spanish classes and volunteer opportunities through its campus on El Adoquín (Andador Revolución 21). Or if you want to just show up and get started, head to the southernmost corner of Calle Alejandro Cárdenas, where the guys at **Punta Surf School** (no phone, 8am-5pm

The World-Famous Mexican Pipeline

world-class surfer and Puerto Escondido resident Carlos "Coco" Nogales

With regards to tourism in Puerto Escondido, the monstrous break off Playa Zicatela is what started it all. As opposed to many other beaches along the Oaxacan coast, which can get pretty steep, Zicatela is broad and flat, and a long sandbar that stretches down to La Punta forms the swell into gigantic beach break waves that can tower up to 6 meters (20 ft) over the surfers who ride them. Nicknamed the "Mexican Pipeline" due to its similarity to the Banzai Pipeline of Oahu's North Shore, these huge, tubular waves draw amateur and professional surfers from all over the world and play host to a number of international competitions, usually held in November.

Zicatela's giants first caught the eyes of longboard surfers from California in the 1950s, but their bulky boards, perfect for the mellow southern Cali point breaks, were too unwieldy for Puerto's powerful waves. Surfing didn't become a popular activity here in Puerto Escondido until a couple decades later, during what is known as the shortboard revolution, when legendary American surfer Gerry Lopez (b. 1948) pioneered the faster and more difficult technique of riding tube-shaped waves, for which he earned the sobriquet "Mr. Pipeline." After the rise in popularity of this surfing style, and the construction of Coastal Highway 200, tourism began to grow like a tropical vine in Puerto Escondido.

Zicatela also fostered the skills of local surfers who went on to become national and international champions, such as Roger Ramírez, who runs Oasis Surf School and still shapes custom boards in Rinconada, and Ody Ordaz, who founded Odyboards Surf Shop and Factory in La Punta. And it continues to do so. Puerto native Jhony Corzo, for example, won the International Surfing Association (ISA) 2017 World Surfing Games in Biarritz, France, at just 18 years old. And Carlos "Coco" Nogales, although he was born in Mexico City, went from orphaned and selling gum on the streets of the capital to being a world-class surfer who knows the breaks in Puerto so well, he may as well be a native.

November is the time of year to come see the best of the best tackle Zicatela's unforgiving tubes. This month sees big-time international competitions like the Surf Open League's annual event on Playa Zicatela, which hosted Latin America's first ever Big-Wave Heat for women in 2018.

daily) offer two-hour, first-come, first-served lessons for US$28.

SURF SHOPS AND RENTALS

On Avenida del Morro, the main drag of Zicatela, head to **Colorada Puerto Escondido** (corner of del Morro and Las Brisas, tel. 954/101-8548, 9am-10pm daily) for boards, gear, repairs, and rentals (US$13/day).

Farther south, in La Punta, get quick repairs done at **Punto Mágico Surf Shop** (Calle Alejandro Cárdenas, tel. 954/118-6782, 9am-6pm daily). You can also rent a board for US$13 per day. It's on the main drag, half a block south of the intersection with Héroes Oaxaqueños. Closer to the highway, you'll find **Odyboards Surf Shop and Factory** (corner of Justo Salvador and Aguascalientes, tel. 954/101-1058, www.odyboards.com, 10am-5pm Mon.-Fri., 10am-1pm Sat.). Two-time national surf champion Ody Ordaz moved back to his hometown in 2005 to open what is now Puerto's largest surfboard factory.

In Rinconada, above Playa Carrizalillo, head to **Oasis Surf Shop** (Benito Juárez 6, tel. 954/582-1445, www.spanishand surflessonsmexico.com, 8am-6pm Mon.-Fri., 8am-4pm Sat.), founded by "Mexi-Pipe Warrior" Roger Ramírez and his wife, Soledad Fernández.

Head to the base of the stairs at Playa Carrizalillo to **rent a surfboard** (US$12/day). A group of crusty-haired local surfers hang out there from sunup to sundown and won't let you past them without letting you know they rent boards. They also offer lessons for around US$12 per hour.

Snorkeling and Scuba Diving

As you might expect, the calmer beaches like Manzanillo, Puerto Angelito, and Carrizalillo are the best places to *echarle un vistazo* (have a look) at what's going on under the surface. Many of the *palapa* restaurants on these beaches rent snorkeling equipment and offer tours for around US$25-30, and many hostels and hotels lend goggles, snorkels, and flippers to guests free of charge, so it never hurts to ask at reception before heading to the beach.

Puerto's dive sites are almost exclusively igneous rock formations and shallow-water reefs, where you'll see a wide variety of tropical fish, such as trigger, parrot, angel, and butterfly fish, puffers, groupers, and various species of moray eels. Winter is the best time to dive in Puerto, November-February. During these months, although the water is cooler than the rest of the year (72-75°F), it's very likely you'll see humpback whales, giant manta rays, and, with a little luck, whale sharks. The water begins to warm up in May and still has good visibility until September, which, along with October, is the worst part of the year to dive.

There are a couple of dive centers in Puerto that have maintained admirable reputations for safety and quality for years. Since 2003, Italian Master Scuba Diver Trainer Lorenzo Biny has run **Deep Blue Dive School** (in Hotel Ines on Playa Zicatela, tel. 954/127-8306, www.deepbluedivemexico.com, 9:30am-2pm and 6pm-8pm Mon.-Sat.), offering everything from snorkel tours (US$30) to fun dives (US$55-85) to certification courses (US$220-420). Lorenzo and his crew of Divemasters always adhere to PADI safety regulations, ensuring the best-quality experience beneath the waves. **Aventura Submarina** (Gasga 609, tel. 954/544-4862, bravoescondido@gmail.com, 9am-6pm daily) is also well regarded, and offers fun dives for around US$75 and three-day open water certification courses for US$385.

Sportfishing

Fishing is Puerto's forte, and you can trust just about anyone with a boat to know where they're biting. The waters off Puerto's shores are full of black and blue marlin, albacore tuna, dorado (mahimahi), red snapper, sea bass, Mexican needlefish, and many other edible species.

Highly regarded for their knowledge and skill, Rodolfo and the guys at **Sociedad Cooperativa Turística Nueva Punta Escondida** (tel. 954/102-4090, www.tomzap.

com/pe-coop.html, US$30/hour, 4-hr min.) operate out of the restaurant El Pescador, at the west end of Playa Principal, where your fresh catch is grilled after you come back to shore. Rodolfo has sailed all over the world, and has never seen a coastline with more sea turtles than Oaxaca's, which is why he likes to include a lot of information about turtle conservation on his fishing and dolphin-, whale-, and turtle-watching tours.

Another very well-respected sportfishing agency in town is **Omar's Sportfishing** (Playa Puerto Angelito, tel. 954/559-4406, www.omarsportfishing.com, 9am-3pm daily). Born and raised in Puerto Escondido, Captain Omar Ramírez has a lifetime of fishing experience and nearly three decades of experience operating fishing tours. The agency will send a taxi to your hotel to pick you up bright and early for the trip. Omar's fishing charters run US$255 for half-day tours and US$410 for the full day.

Ecotourism

The Oaxacan coast isn't only popular with humans. The Chacahua and Manialtepec lagoons, to the west of Puerto, are important stopovers on the migratory routes of herons, ibis, storks, roseate spoonbills, and many other species of avian nomads. **Manglar Birdwatching** (Avenida del Morro next to Bungalows Zicatela, tel. 954/118-6713, 954/108-2641, or 954/559-2431, 9am-8pm daily) focuses primarily on bird-watching tours (US$36 pp) and also offers surf lessons, coffee plantation tours, baby sea turtle releases, and other ecotourism activities. They also have an office on El Adoquín next to Restaurante Los Crotos.

One of the most popular ecotours around Puerto is the quick trip to see and swim among the bioluminescent plankton of Laguna de Manialtepec, about a half hour away from Puerto. **Lalo Ecotours** (in Rockaway shopping center on Zicatela, tel. 954/582-1611 or 954/588-9164, www.lalo-ecotours.com, 9am-8pm daily) runs evening tours out to Manialtepec (US$25 pp) for the

bioluminescence, as well as in the mornings and afternoons for kayaking and bird-watching (US$60 pp). Horseback riding, baby sea turtle releases, and waterfall and boat tours are also on the menu (US$25-75).

Yoga and Meditation

The majority of yoga classes in Puerto are in Zicatela and out in La Punta. In Zicatela, **Casa Corzo** (half a block west of the beach on Calle Las Brisas, tel. 954/101-3525) has ocean-view yoga classes at 8am and 5pm Mon.-Sat., and **Vida Yoga Center** (Vista Hermosa 4, tel. 954/114-7675, www.vidayogacenter.com), in Casa Mandala Apartments, offers hatha yoga classes every weekday morning. To get to Vida Yoga, walk south on del Morro from the corner with Las Brisas about 240 m (790 ft) until you get to the first actual street, which is Calle Las Palmas. Walk east until the street ends at Vista Hermosa and take a right. Vida Yoga is about halfway down the block on your right.

In La Punta, one block north of Héroes Oaxaqueños on Calle Alejandro Cárdenas, **Guacamole Guesthouse** (tel. 556/144-6961) hosts classes by donation under their rooftop *palapa* every morning. The "hippy chic" hostel **One Love** (two blocks from the beach on Calle Tamaulipas, tel. 954/129-8582) has classes throughout the week as well. Check their website for the schedule, which is also posted outside the hostel.

Massage

With little more than a sign that says "Massages," **La Tierra de las Especias** (Gasga 405, tel. 954/540-5222, 9am-8pm daily) can be a little difficult to find, but it's worth the search. It's right next to the Banamex on the corner of Gasga and Andador Unión. Here, Sang Sisouphanthong and his wife, Sandra, give massages that are a sort of fusion of shiatsu and other Asian massage practices, as well as facials. They also sell essential oils and homemade soaps.

On Zicatela, Rufina of **Masaje Zapoteco Rufina** (Andador Las Olas, 954/588-4804 or 954/113-3524) has magic in her strong, bony hands. She will lighten her touch upon request, but the sharp pressure of her Zapotec massage technique might be just what your shoulders and feet need if you're lugging around a backpack full of gear.

Spanish Schools

For Spanish classes on the Bahía Principal, contact **Experiencia Puerto Escondido** (Andador Revolución 21, tel. 954/582-1818, www.experienciamexico.mx, 8am-5pm Mon.-Fri.), which doesn't stop at language learning. They also offer accommodations, homestays, surf lessons in La Punta, and volunteer opportunities at local orphanages, farms, schools, and wildlife conservation centers. Spanish lesson packages run US$200-270, and US$285-390 when combined with surf lessons.

In Rinconada, **Calli Language School** (Benito Juárez 13 and 14, tel. 954/103-9190, www.callilanguageschool.com) offers weekly packages (US$77-130/week), 60-90-day long-term courses (US$450-615), and immersive courses (US$353-890) that include surf lessons, lagoon and whale-watching tours, and other cultural experiences.

The Puerto Escondido branch of Oaxaca City-based **Spanish Immersion School** (corner of Puebla and Tlaxcala in La Punta, www.spanishschoolinmexico.com, oaxacaimmersion@gmail.com) will have you chatting away *en español* in no time. Classes run US$180-280 per week.

SHOPPING
Gifts and Souvenirs

The storefronts and sidewalks—and, at night, the middle of the street—of El Adoquín are stocked full of handicrafts from the coast and the state at large. Garishly bright inflatables, buckets, and swimsuits clutter the *artesanías* shops, many of which focus on textiles from weavers in Puerto Escondido and other coastal communities. The **Mercado de Artesanías** (El Adoquín, no phone, 10am-10pm daily) is at the east end of El Adoquín, just before the corner with Andador Azucenas. Just across the street, **Silver Shop Mexico Lindo** (El Adoquín, tel. 954/124-6817, 9am-10pm daily) and a few others sell fine, handcrafted silver jewelry and other decorative pieces. Businesses like these, as well as the vendors in the street, generally stay open as long as there are people out and about.

Down at the west end of El Adoquín, **Arte Huitzi Ámbar & Artesanías** (Gasga next to Hotel Villa Roca, tel. 954/101-5005, 11am-11pm daily) has a great selection of beautiful

money exchange and folk art stores on El Adoquín

amber jewelry, as well as silver and other artisanal products from Oaxaca.

In Zicatela, head to **Zicatelarte** (in Rockaway shopping center, tel. 954/108-4041 or 954/126-5004, 9am-10pm daily) for more unique silver and precious stone jewelry. In 2011, owners and silversmiths Cristina Fragapane and Alan González took their custom gem and jewelry business from the streets to this little beachfront store, where they make custom silver pieces and also have lots of rare stones and fossils for sale.

FOOD
El Adoquín
RESTAURANTS

Your most reliable option on El Adoquín is dependable **Vitamina T** (across street and to the west of Hotel Las Palmas, tel. 954/104-2034, 7am-2:30am daily, US$4-7). The service is usually friendly and speedy (except for when it's super busy), and the *tlayudas* are nice and unwieldy, just like they should be. They also serve tacos, *pozole*, seafood, salads, and more.

Every restaurant in this part of town serves fantastic seafood, and **El Pescador** (north end of Playa Principal, tel. 954/582-1678, 9am-9pm daily, US$4-8) is no exception. Run by the fishermen of the Sociedad Cooperativa Turística Nueva Punta Escondida, everything on the menu is fresh out of the sea. Savor a shrimp cocktail on their breezy terrace that looks out over Playas Principal and Marinero.

For dinner, there is no better place on El Adoquín than **Pascale** (Gasga 612, tel. 954/103-0668, 6pm-11pm daily, US$12-17), where the wooden deck dining area offers a broad, boat-speckled view of Playa Principal. The specialty here is grilled surf and turf, like seared tuna and perfectly cooked flank steak. Follow these up with a homemade crème brûlée or chocolate mousse. Bringing bug spray is a good idea.

BREAKFAST AND SNACKS

Most restaurants along El Adoquín serve breakfast at tourist prices (US$3-4), but there are cheaper options if you look for them.

Hidden near the top of Andador Unión, to the west of El Adoquín, **Flor de Mayo** (Andador Unión, no phone, 7am-5pm Mon.-Sat. low season, 7am-10pm Mon.-Sat. high season, US$2.50 breakfast, US$3.50 *comida corrida*) charges about half of what the tourist places charge for breakfast, fruit, and coffee. Look for the sandwich board that reads *Comida Corrida* near the top of the alleyway stairs.

Head to **Café La Fe** (Gasga 106, tel. 954/104-4595, 7am-9pm Mon.-Sat.) for top-notch espresso. They buy their coffee from Mixe growers in the Sierra Norte, a region that produces beans with a sharp bite that flirts with acidity without slipping into bitterness. You'll see the café to your right from the top of Andador Unión.

For late-night snacks, hit up the **taco and hotdog stands** on Andador Azucenas. They set up around sundown and usually stay open until the drinking crowd goes home. There's also pizza by the slice at the street counter at **Capricho's Pizza** (Gasga 609, tel. 954/101-5462, 11am-2am daily).

Playa Zicatela

A favorite among Zicatela's foreign-born residents, **Split Coconut** (Avenida del Morro, tel. 954/104-2689, 2pm-11pm Wed.-Mon., US$4-9) serves up tasty barbecue ribs, pork, steaks, and pulled pork sandwiches. Also on the menu are burgers, burritos, and cheap, cheap drinks. You'll find it on the north curve of Avenida del Morro, at the entrance to the access road to Playa Marinero.

Another great place for barbecue is **The Gym** (a block from the beach on Las Brisas, no phone, 4pm-11pm daily, US$5-10), run by amiable Miguel Ángel Ramírez and his lovely mother. Fish-and-chips and the catch of the day are also favorites of the local and tourist crowd that fills the place. Miguel has been grilling in Zicatela for years, but has moved quite a bit, so if he's not in this location by the time you arrive, just ask around.

Any one of the *palapa* restaurants along the beach is an excellent choice for a sunset dinner. They generally serve similar menus of seafood and traditional Mexican dishes, such as shrimp cocktails and *filete a la diabla* (fish fillet in super-spicy salsa). The comfortable beach house atmosphere at **Rosarito Restaurant and Bar** (Avenida del Morro, tel. 954/582-2500, restaurant.rosarito@gmail.com, 7am-2am daily, US$4-9), with its hammock areas, couches, and wooden boardwalk through the sand, is a great place for everything from breakfast to a sunset dinner to late-night beers and cocktails.

Words like "fusion" and "gastronomical workshop" are red flags for me, but I was pleasantly surprised by a couple places on the beach that are too cool for the word "restaurant." Try the *tiritas de pescado* (strips of fish fillet cured in lime juice with onions and chiles) at **Cayuco Cocina & Mezcal** (Avendia del Morro, tel. 954/104-2078, 11am-10pm Tues.-Sun., US$9-16), at the north end of the beach, or the octopus tacos at **Sativa Cocina de Playa** (Avenida del Morro, tel. 954/582-4384, www.sativapuerto.com, 9am-11pm Wed.-Mon., US$10-13). Sativa also has lots of vegetarian options and signature cocktails, and brunch is served daily (until 2pm Sun. for late risers).

Established in 1983 by the Conti family, originally from Verona, Italy, **Bananas** (Avenida del Morro, tel. 954/582-0005, 8:30am-12:30am daily, US$8-13) has been serving quality Italian classics in Puerto Escondido for decades. The open-air dining area catches the sea breeze just right in the evenings, the service is impeccable, the lasagna is cheesy and tasty, and there's a pool table to boot.

A favorite of locals and visitors alike, **El Cafecito** (Avenida del Morro, tel. 954/582-0516, elcafecitozicatela@hotmail.com, 6am-11pm daily, US$5-8) is almost always busy, and is the only place to get a good espresso on the Zicatela strip. Food offerings include tacos, enchiladas, Mexican breakfasts, and international staples like cheeseburgers and club sandwiches. It's a great choice if you get bothered by cigarette smoke in other alfresco restaurants, as all the street-side tables are

non-smoking. If you want to light up, you'll be sequestered in the tables in the pleasant garden patio in back.

Satisfy your late-night munchies with a slice of pizza from either of the two locations of **¡Sí como no!** (Yes, of course!; Avenida del Morro, no phone, 5pm-5am daily, US$1.50). The location at the south end of the beach closes during low season, but the one across from Casa Babylon stays open year-round.

Punta Zicatela (La Punta)
RESTAURANTS

Lots of great restaurants line Calle Alejandro Cárdenas, the main drag of La Punta, offering a wide range of cuisines and dietary options. ★ **Lychee** (Alejandro Cárdenas, tel. 954/134-5718, lycheetasacv@gmail.com, 5pm-11pm daily, US$6-8) serves up some of the best pad thai in Mexico as well as a number of other Thai favorites, like green curry, tom yum soup, and spring rolls. The catch of the day is also a big hit. Fenced off from the street and neighboring buildings by thick, green vegetation, the restaurant is more tropical garden than building, with polished log tables and chairs (even a tree house) set in the sand around the bar and open kitchen.

Six short blocks from the beach, you'll find ★ **Alivo** (corner of Héroes Oaxaqueños and Colima, tel. 954/135-3811, 2pm-10:30pm Tues.-Sun., US$8), where founders Giorgio and Alex have been serving delectable Italian dishes from their native Italy since 2015. Candlelit when the sun goes down, the humble yet stylish all-wood interior creates an intimate setting for a glass of Italian wine and a plate of gnocchi gorgonzola or lasagna Bolognese. The coffee, sourced from Pluma Hidalgo, is made Italian style: strong, foamy on top, and full of flavor.

You'll find burritos, stir-fries, baguettes, and more on the menu at **Monchistation** (corner of Alejandro Cárdenas and Héroes Oaxaqueños, tel. 954/152-9863, monchistation@gmail.com, 8am-11pm daily, US$3-5). They serve a nice espresso and have a good selection of vegan options, and sometimes have live reggae music. They also rent surfboards and offer surfing lessons. Bonus points for the all-day breakfast.

BREAKFAST AND SNACKS

Just to the south of Lychee, **Café Olé** (Alejandro Cárdenas, tel. 954/123-0473 or 954/124-6297, www.frutasyverdurasmexico. com, 8am-10pm daily, US$3-5) is part of the hostel/restaurant/café/organic grocery complex called Frutas y Verduras. Aside from fantastic coffee, they also serve crepes, pastries, omelets, and paninis. The organic grocery store **Moringa** (Alejandro Cárdenas, tel. 954/120-4616, 8am-9pm daily) is at the south end of the block.

For cheap, tasty eats, hit up one of the *comedores* that stay open late on Héroes Oaxaqueños.

Rinconada

Trusty **El Cafecito** (Benito Juárez 1, tel. 954/582-3465, elcafecitocarmens@hotmail. com, 6am-11pm daily, US$5-8) has you covered here in Rinconada when other places close for low season. For something new and unique, try the *almendradas* (enchiladas made with an almond-based sauce).

Heavily influenced by the gastronomy of California, talented chef Alejandro Hernández Aquino runs the open kitchen at ★ **Turtle Bay** (Benito Juárez 9, tel. 954/147-7469, www. turtlebay.com.mx, noon-midnight Tues.-Sun., US$7-14), where he applies the North American coastal culinary style to his extensive knowledge of the ingredients and recipes of Oaxaca. Shrimp and octopus tostadas and *aguachile* (raw shrimp in super-spicy green salsa) share menu space with jalapeño burgers, rib-eye sandwiches, and mahimahi cooked in chardonnay. Speaking of chardonnay, their dark wood wine shelves along the walls boast the widest selection in Puerto, and Alejandro and his knowledgeable staff know just what to pair with whatever you order from the rich, inventive menu. The humble tables and chairs of the same polished wood create a date-night ambience while keeping things comfy.

Kebabs, shawarmas, falafel, hummus, tabbouleh, and other Mediterranean delights are served up daily at **El Sultán** (corner of Benito Juárez and Pargos, tel. 954/582-0512, 10am-10pm daily, US$3). They also serve fresh juices and flavorful coffees from both Mexico and abroad. Try the piquant and "muddy" Israeli coffee, spiced with cardamom and served with the fine grounds in the cup, like Turkish coffee.

At the vanguard of Puerto's gastronomical culture are chefs Quetzalcóatl Zurita and Shalxaly Macías of ★ **Almoraduz** (Benito Juárez 11, tel. 954/582-3109, www.almoraduz. com.mx, 1:30pm-10pm Mon.-Sat., 6pm-10pm Sun., US$20-27 entrées), whose menu changes constantly, according to what is in season. They call their restaurant a *cocina de autor* (author's kitchen), and like good writers, they never seem to be content with what has been done before (even in their own kitchen). They say to "write what you know," and the chefs are doing just that. They don't aim to reinvent Oaxacan cookery by searching outside the state, but rather search for novel flavors in new arrangements of what is grown, caught, foraged, or made here at home. Tasting menus (US$42, US$60 with drinks) include dishes like corn soup with *istmeño* cheese and *chile costeño* and grilled octopus drizzled with a balsamic agave honey. Try the churro stuffed with Oaxacan chocolate cream and served with mamey ice cream for dessert. The small but tasteful location adds a touch of class to Rinconada's main drag.

Centro

The Centro is a bit out of the way for folks staying on the beach, but it is home to a few eateries that you'll regret leaving Puerto without visiting.

At ★ **Las Juquileñas** (Octava Norte, tel. 954/582-1231, 7am-5pm daily), a small army of waitresses donning white scarves on their heads keep the colorful communal tables piled high with delicious local specialties while bright *papel picado* flags flutter overhead. Try an *empanada de amarillo* and an *embarrada* (literally, muddied tortilla, but it means with sauce) with cheese and *mole*, and wash it all down with the restaurant's signature *agua de cacahuate*, a delicious *agua fresca* made with peanuts. Seriously, don't not eat here. This is one of the best restaurants in the state.

Marisquería Los Erizos (Hwy. 200 just west of junction with Hwy. 131, tel. 954/107-1376, noon-8pm Tue.-Sun., US$5-7) is a favorite with locals craving ceviche, Baja-style shrimp tacos, or the local specialty *tiritas de pescado* (tangy lime-cured strips of fish). Other seasonal treats include clams, oysters, and fresh salty seaweeds to top off their towering shrimp cocktails.

ACCOMMODATIONS

From rustic jungle cabins to luxury villas, Puerto Escondido has enough accommodations options to suit any budget or taste.

The prices listed below are for low season, since that is the vast majority of the year here. During high season, you can expect prices to be 25-50 percent higher, and some even double. Contact hotels directly if you're visiting around the Christmas or Easter holidays.

Playa Principal and El Adoquín
UNDER US$25

A pair of *cabaña* and camping areas hidden back in the sultry jungle around the Laguna Agua Dulce, in between Playas Principal and Marinero, just might be your cheapest option on the beaches of Puerto. The *cabañas* at **El Rinconcito** (tel. 954/113-0997, US$5 d shared bathroom, US$11 d en suite) are set around a tranquil, grassy social area with a communal fridge and barbecue for grilling up the fresh marlin steaks you can buy direct from the fishermen on the beach. **Cabañas y Acampado Marinero** (tel. 954/107-1716, US$2 pp camping, US$11-13 *cabañas*) has secluded areas among the palm trees to pitch tents, in addition to the dozen affordable *cabañas*. To get here from Highway 200, get off the highway on the east side of the lagoon

bridge. Take the road down the hill to reach El Rinconcito, on the south side of the highway, just below the bridge. Continue down the cobblestone street to the beach, where you'll see Cabañas Marinero on the right.

★ **Hotel Las Palmas** (across from amphitheater in middle of El Adoquín, no phone, US$14 d, US$19 t) may look like it hasn't been renovated since the 1980s, and that may well be true, but the rooms are surprisingly cozy and very clean. Aside from its primo location right on the Playa Principal, the best part about Las Palmas is that the quoted prices include air-conditioning, and you can expect to spend about US$5-8 less if you want to sweat out the night with just a fan. It's your best option if you need to beat the heat on a budget. Other amenities include parking, TV, and Wi-Fi that really works. No reservations; this is a first-come, first-served kind of place.

US$50-100

The bright-orange **Le Petit Hotel** (Andador Soledad 379, tel. 954/582-3178, ptithotelpesc@hotmail.com, US$50 d, US$70 suite) spreads out up the hillside from a little nook of an entrance on the east end of El Adoquín. The multitiered courtyard area, decorated with murals, tile mosaics, and fountains, has a small swimming pool. They allow pets during low season, but they ask that they be well-trained and housebroken. You can expect to pay a little less if you don't need air-conditioning.

Rather than maintaining a restaurant or swimming pool, **Hotel Villa Roca** (Gasga 602, tel. 954/582-3525 or 954/118-9485, villaroca1@hotmail.com, US$54 d, US$70 t, US$80 suite) focuses its efforts on maintaining its seven charming and comfortable rooms, all of which boast their own private balconies. There is a marked difference between Villa Roca and others that don't regularly update their facilities. It is exceptionally clean, and the constant upkeep makes the lovely boutique hotel look young for its age.

Playa Zicatela
UNDER US$50

At the southern end of the Zicatela strip, **Hotel Papaya Surf** (Avenida del Morro, tel. 954/582-1168, www.papayasurf.com.mx, US$37 d) is as orange as its delicious namesake, and is the perfect place to crash after a day of surfing and a night of partying. The rooms are set around a cozy courtyard with cacti, palms, and papaya trees and have all the bare necessities: queen size beds, fans, air-conditioning (for an extra US$5), small patio areas (some strung with hammocks), and Wi-Fi.

★ **Bungalows Puerta del Sol** (Avenida del Morro, tel. 954/582-2922, www.bungalowspuertadelsol.com, US$35 d with fan, US$50 d with a/c) feels like a close-knit neighborhood in miniature. Two-story white bungalows with green trim flank the narrow cobblestone street that opens onto Avenida del Morro. The broad leaves of almond trees provide shade around the swimming pool. Double rooms have king-size beds, and other rooms have combinations of queen or king beds to accommodate up to five people. This is a great option for those with a car, as there is room for parking. The communal kitchen is large and well-stocked, and there's enough room at the tables for up to 14 hungry surfers.

Hotel y Bungalows Acuario (Avenida del Morro 501, tel. 954/582-0357 or 954/582-1027, www.hotelybungalowsacuario.com, US$36 cabaña, US$40 d, US$60 bungalow) is one of the best values in Zicatela during low season, as they offer discounts of 15-20 percent off their usual prices. Tucked away in the jungled grounds behind the crimson, palapa-topped facade are simple cabañas with fans, standard hotel rooms with air-conditioning, and deluxe bungalows and cabañas with ocean views, kitchenettes, and other luxurious amenities.

US$50-100

Casual and comfortable **Hotel Ines** (Avenida del Morro, tel. 954/582-0792 or 954/582-0416, www.hotelines.com, US$57 d, US$95 suite) has options for everyone from groups of surfers to vacationing families. The 45 units built around the large pool and restaurant area, surrounded by tropical fronds and towering palm trees, run the spectrum from simple (but clean, spacious, and fetching) hotel rooms to cabañas to deluxe suites with broad, private ocean-view terraces hung with hammocks.

Add a little luxury to your beach bum vacation with a room at ★ **Bungalows Zicatela** (Avenida del Morro, tel. 954/582-0798, www.bungalowszicatela.com, US$77 d, US$83 bungalow). All rooms have air-conditioning, TV, Wi-Fi, and en suite bathrooms, and the bungalows include a fully stocked kitchenette. They maximize lounging and relaxation space with two on-site, multitiered swimming pools, and Caña Brava, the on-site restaurant, serves mouthwatering seafood and Mexican and international dishes. All rooms have balconies and great views, whether it be of the Pacific or the gorgeous whitewashed interior courtyard. Other amenities include surf classes at La Punta, laundry services, private parking, medical services, in-room massages, and much more.

Punta Zicatela (La Punta)
UNDER US$50

Right on the main drag, **Cabañas Buena Onda** (Alejandro Cárdenas north of corner with Héroes Oaxaqueños, tel. 954/582-1663, US$8 dorm, US$19 cabaña) appears to have grown out of the jungle like a vine, but none of the vegetation was here when the first cabañas were built and the first palms planted in 1999. The cabañas are now nestled in dense foliage. There are also four- and six-bed dorm rooms, as well as a couple spaces to pitch a tent. All rooms, including cabañas, share the bathrooms, and there is a kitchen on-site that guests can use 8:30am-10:30pm.

Close to the beach is the backpacker favorite **Hotelito Osa Mariposa** (Privada de Cancún, tel. 954/131-0660, info@osamariposa.com, US$5-8 dorm, US$14 d). Despite the rustic, definitely budget-level look to the sylvan cluster of cabañas, Osa

Mariposa is clean and tidy, and the staff are super friendly and helpful. An on-site restaurant serves healthy, tasty, all-vegetarian food.

US$25-50

Delightfully trimmed in avocado green, **Guacamole Guesthouse** (Alejandro Cárdenas, one block north of Héroes Oaxaqueños, tel. 556/144-6961, www.guesthousepuertoescondido.com, US$32 d) has an intimate, home-like feel to it. No dorm beds here, only private rooms with en suite bathrooms, and great ocean views from the hammocks on the rooftop *palapa*. They host yoga classes (by donation) up here every morning, and guests receive a discount on meals at Monchistation, right down the street.

The folks behind ★ **One Love** (two blocks from the beach on Calle Tamaulipas, tel. 954/129-8582, www.hostalpuertoescondido.com, US$33 dorm, US$40 d, US$65 suite) asked themselves a simple question when conceiving the idea for their hostel: What if a hostel doesn't have to be dirty? With this revolutionary idea in mind, they set about building a "hippy chic" luxury hostel that offers everything from dorms to master suite bungalows with views of the ocean. Although the bungalows are named after Jimi Hendrix, Jim Morrison, the Bobs Dylan and Marley, and a hit parade of other 1960s rock 'n' roll greats, this is not a party hostel. Yoga is offered daily, and the vibe is respectful and laid-back. The on-site restaurant serves a fusion of French, Italian, and Mexican dishes, as well as Mexipipe Beer, its proprietary craft beer label, and is renowned among both travelers and locals for its value and quality.

Rinconada

UNDER US$25

If you want to stay close to Playa Carrizalillo, your cheapest options are **Hostal Mondala** (top of stairs to Carrizalillo, tel. 954/131-2454, www.guiapuertoescondido.com/mondala, US$5 dorm, US$19 *cabaña*) and **Hostal Shalom** (easternmost end of Benito Juárez, tel. 954/582-3234, US$5 dorm, US$19 *cabaña*).

Both are known as fun, social hostels, but they are infamous for their uncleanliness.

A step up on the hostel list is ★ **Bonobo Surf House** (Barriletes 7, tel. 954/146-1037, www.bonobosurfhouse.com, US$11 dorm, US$27-38 d), two blocks north of the shopping and dining strip on Benito Juárez. The rooms fill up three floors of a tall, bright-orange building with a view of the Pacific on one side and a homey courtyard and swimming pool on the other. Each floor with dorms has a communal kitchen, and the top-floor master suite with an ocean-view terrace includes a fully stocked private kitchenette. Bonobo fosters a very friendly, family-style vibe by organizing weekly social events like barbecue nights and volleyball games.

US$50-100

Upon entering the sandy tropical garden that is home to the *cabañas* at ★ **Villa Mozart y Macondo** (Las Tortugas 77, tel. 954/104-2295 or 954/113-0849, www.hotelmozartymacondo.com, US$55-70), you'll be confronted with the possibility that this place may be just as prone to fantastical occurrences as the fictional Colombian town from which it takes half of its name. Large wooden statues stand among the tropical ferns and flowers, ready to groan to life at any moment. With only four little fetching bungalows, Mozart y Macondo is intimate and secluded, despite its proximity to the commerce on Benito Juárez. This gay-friendly, adults-only hotel is for the lovers; it's not an option for families (no kids or pets) or groups of surfers (max. 2 people per bungalow).

OVER US$100

Perched atop the cliffs overlooking the gorgeous turquoise and green waters of Playa Carrizalillo below, there isn't a bad view from any of the 12 whitewashed deluxe villas at **Villas Carrizalillo** (Avenida Carrizalillo, tel. 954/582-1735, www.villascarrizalillo.com, US$155-190 villa), all but two of which come equipped with fully stocked kitchenettes. Villas range in size from one bedroom for two people, to large three-bedroom, two-bath units for up to six people. Despite its beauty, comfort, amenities, and the phenomenal surf and turf on the menu at the on-site restaurant Espadín, the superlative feature at Villas Carrizalillo is the private beach access that descends through the forested hillside to the sandy bank below.

Apartments and Long-Term Rentals

Originally begun as private vacation apartments for the owner's family, **Casamar Suites** (Puebla 407, tel. 954/582-2593, www.casamarsuites.com) has grown into a complex of 15 fully stocked and furnished apartments decorated with hand-painted ceramic tiles from Puebla and furniture and other interior design features by local carpenters and artisans. Although they're also rented out nightly (US$105-140), Casamar welcomes longer stays, offering weekly and monthly discounts. Recreational and relaxation facilities and amenities include the swimming pool and meticulously tended garden, Ping-Pong tables, movie nights, communal cookouts, massages, reflexology, and yoga classes.

For vacation rentals elsewhere in Puerto, contact Nancy Radmin at **Puerto Escondido Real Estate and Vacation Rentals** (Camino de la Luz and Calle Tercera Poniente, tel. 954/582-3130, www.puertorealestate.com), whose website has a lengthy list of available rental properties in town.

Trailer Parks and Camping

For camping spots hidden away in the middle of all the action, head to **Cabañas y Acampado Marinero** (Calle Marinero, tel. 954/107-1716), where you can pitch a tent right in the sand between a pair of windblown palm trees for only US$2 per person. *Cabaña* guests and campers share bathrooms. From the beach, head toward the jungle on the east side of the lagoon, where you'll find them at the end of the cobblestone road to the highway. From Highway 200, get off on the east side of the Regadío bridge and take Calle Marinero

down to the beach, where the campground will be on your right.

Down on La Punta, you can pitch a tent in the dense jungled area inside **Cabañas Buena Onda** (Alejandro Cárdenas north of corner with Héroes Oaxaqueños, tel. 954/582-1663) for around US$5 per person. It's more expensive than up on Playa Marinero, but it's a better option if you're here to learn to surf. Over by Playa Carrizalillo, you can camp at **Hostal Mondala** (top of stairs to Carrizalillo, tel. 954/131-2454, www.guiapuertoescondido.com/mondala) for about US$3 per person. Both places have shared bathrooms.

For trailer travelers, Puerto Escondido offers few options compared with years past. The only still-viable option at the time of writing was **Cabañas y Trailer Park El Edén** (Avenida del Morro, tel. 954/122-0037, edenlocales_zicatela@outlook.com), which has six spaces with water, drainage, and electricity access for about US$6 per person.

INFORMATION AND SERVICES

Banks and Money Exchange

Banks, ATMs, and *casas de cambio* in Puerto Escondido are mostly located in El Adoquín and along Coastal Highway 200, with a pair of options in Zicatela. If you're staying out in La Punta, you'll have to come to town to withdraw or change money, so be aware of that before you get in the taxi.

Around El Adoquín, there is a **Banamex** (Gasga 314, 9am-4pm Mon.-Fri., ATM 24 hrs) on Gasga, where the road curves and climbs the hill on the west side of the main drag on the corner with Andador Unión. At the other end of El Adoquín, you'll find a **Bancomer ATM** in the Azul Plaza shopping center at the east end of the street. There is also a **Banco Multiva ATM** to the left of the ice cream shop next to Hotel Las Palmas. Change dollars at the **Money Exchange Booth** (10am-9pm Mon.-Sat.) a little farther east and across El Adoquín. In the Centro, you can change dollars at **Banco Azteca** (across from Benito Juárez market on Calle Octava Norte, toll-free

Mex. tel. 800/040-7777, www.bancoazteca.com.mx, 9am-9pm daily), inside the Elektra appliance store.

Laundry Services

Most *lavanderías* in Puerto charge a little under US$1 per kilo. If you're staying on El Adoquín, drop your dirty rags off at **Lava Max** (Gasga 405, tel. 954/540-9441, 8am-8pm Mon.-Sat., 8am-6pm Sun.). It's a few storefronts down the hill from the Banamex.

In Zicatela, head to **Lavandería Vinalay** (Andador Gaviotas, tel. 954/137-3443, 9am-10pm daily), just a ways down Andador Gaviotas, by Bungalows Zicatela. Down in La Punta, **Burbujas Lavandería** (Alejandro Cárdenas, tel. 954/124-9172, 9am-6pm Mon.-Sat.) has you covered. They're closer to the highway, on the block between Calles Tamaulipas and Tlaxcala.

In Rinconada, **Lavandería Arcoiris** (east end of Benito Juárez, tel. 954/110-9284, 9am-9pm daily) offers delivery service, as well as alterations and mending.

Medical Services

For emergencies, your best bet is the private **Hospital Ángel del Mar** (corner of Sexta Norte and Primera Oriente in the Centro, tel. 954/104-2270 or 954/582-1026, www.hospitalangeldelmar.com.mx). It is seven blocks north of the *crucero,* and one block east of Avenida Oaxaca.

The government-run **Centro de Salud** (Health Center; Calle Puerto Vallarta, tel. 954/582-2360) that was over by El Adoquín has moved 1 km (0.6 mi) west to the Los Ficus neighborhood. They accept regular doctor visits 8am-8pm daily, and emergencies 24 hours.

If you get injured surfing on Zicatela, your closest option is the **Clinica del Doctor Pepe** (top of Andador Las Olas, tel. 954/582-0016), who claims to be *the* Zicatela doctor. Just like his location and clientele, Dr. Pepe is about as laid-back as a physician can get, but people from all over the region know him and come to him for medical attention. He has

a couple of scary-looking but harmless dogs running around the grounds, so if that deters you, it's best to head to one of the other two options.

GETTING THERE
Air

A little over a mile from Playa Bacocho, the **Puerto Escondido International Airport** (PXM; tel. 954/582-2023 or 954/582-2024) is a quick 5-20-minute drive from anywhere you're going in town. The small terminal has a couple snack bars and a bar and grill. There is also a Banco Multiva ATM and a small *artesanías* shop.

The only car rental agency with a booth in the airport is **Los Tres Reyes** (tel. 954/582-3335 or 954/134-9235, www.lostresreyescarrent.com), which has a wide selection of cars for around US$60-160 a day. If you drive a car to the airport and stay longer than 10 minutes, make sure to pay for parking at the booth inside before leaving.

Secure taxis from the airport charge US$13-16 per person for up to four people, and US$16-21 for 6-7, to anywhere in town. If you're not too weighed down with luggage, you can foot it the five-minute, 0.5-km (0.3-mi) walk to the highway and grab a taxi that shouldn't charge more than US$2-5 to anywhere in town.

Flights run by **Interjet** (toll-free U.S. tel. 866/285-9525, toll-free Mex. tel. 800/011-2345, www.interjet.com) connect through Mexico City to 10 major U.S cities. The Mexican low-cost airline **Viva Aerobus** (toll-free U.S. tel. 888/935-9848, toll-free Mex. tel. 818/215-0150, www.vivaaerobus.com) connects to Houston, Las Vegas, and Los Angeles via Mexico City, Guadalajara, and its hub in Monterrey.

Based in Mexico City, **Aeromar** (toll-free U.S. tel. 844/237-6629, toll-free Mex. tel. 800/237-6627, www.aeromar.com) operates super-cheap flights between Puerto and the nation's capital, which connect to other major cities elsewhere in the country, and even McAllen, Texas. Especially during low season, check for flights to Mexico City before buying bus tickets, since flights cost only slightly more than bus trips, which take 17-19 hours.

For air travel within Oaxaca, check out regional airline **Aerotucán** (tel. 951/502-0840, toll-free Mex. tel. 800/640-4148, www.aerotucan.com), whose scenic flight over the Sierra Sur to Oaxaca City in a small Cessna is said to be a visually stunning trip.

Bus

The **ADO bus station** (tel. 954/582-1073, www.ado.com.mx) is centrally located on the coastal highway, just to the west of the *crucero* (crossroads). From here, there are regular trips to Oaxaca City (11 hrs, US$14-27), Huatulco (2.5 hrs, US$4-10), Tehuantepec (6 hrs, US$18), Mexico City (17-19 hrs, US$34-50), Tuxtla Gutiérrez in Chiapas (11-12 hrs, US$29-40), and numerous other destinations in the south of Mexico. The shops, restaurants, and hotels of El Adoquín are a 5-10-minute walk from the station, and taxis charge US$2-4 to other destinations in Puerto.

For shorter travel along the coast, your most economical option is to board an *urbano* (local/regional bus) at the *crucero*, or flag one down anywhere along the highway. This is your best option for getting out to the Lagunas de Manialtepec and Chacahua to the west, and Mazunte and Puerto Ángel to the east. They pass by every 20-30 minutes and charge a maximum of US$3, depending on your destination.

Second-class buses leave from the **Terminal Turística Municipal** (tel. 954/582-3893), about a mile north of the *crucero* on Avenida Oaxaca, but with all the *suburban* options along the highway, it really doesn't make logistical sense to schlep through downtown Puerto traffic to get all the way there.

Van

From the *crucero* west along the highway, a couple *suburban* companies run routes to destinations all over Oaxaca. About 140 m (460 ft) west of the ADO station, **Autotransportes Villa Del Pacífico** (Hwy. 200 between Hidalgo and Calle Primera Norte, tel. 954/132-5643) leaves for Oaxaca City (US$12) hourly on the half hour 3:30am-11pm daily. The trip takes about seven hours.

To get out to the *lagunas*, Jamiltepec, or Pinotepa Nacional, grab a *suburban* from **Transportes de Pasajeros Unidos de Rio Grande,** or **TUR** (corner of Hwy. 200 and Calle Primera Poniente, tel. 954/582-2605, www.puertoshops.com/tur.html, transtur01@hotmail.com), whose terminal is just to the west of the ADO station on the coastal highway. Vans leave every half hour or so all day and cost US$2.50-8, depending on your destination.

Car

West from Puerto Escondido, Coastal Highway 200 winds through verdant palm, papaya, and pineapple orchards out to Pinotepa Nacional (141 km/87 mi, 2.75 hrs), and on into the neighboring state of Guerrero to Acapulco (391 km/240 mi, 7 hrs) and Zihuatanejo (641 km/395 mi, 11 hrs).

To the east, Highway 200 will take you to the turnoff to Mazunte (57 km/35 mi, 1 hr), where you'll turn right at the Oxxo onto Highway 175 and drive another 11 minutes (7 km/4.3 mi) to get to Mazunte. Playas San Agustinillo, Zipolite, and Puerto Ángel are farther down this highway. The drive from Puerto to the Pochutla junction of Highway 175 (70 km/43 mi) takes a little over an hour, and Puerto Ángel (8 km/5 mi from *crucero*) is another 15 minutes from here. Total drive time to Huatulco (113 km/70 mi) is about two hours.

The most direct route from Puerto to Oaxaca City (257 km/160 mi, 6.5 hrs) is via Highway 131, which climbs over 7,000 feet through lush mountain terrain before rolling through the hills of the Sola de Vega district, and finally flattens out through the valleys to Oaxaca City. The only official place to gas up in between is in Sola de Vega, but mechanics in Oaxaca often sell gasoline if you're in a pinch. It's best to just fill up in Puerto before heading out.

Taxi Colectivo

As with anywhere in Oaxaca, you can always flag down a *taxi colectivo* along the highway to reach regional destinations for next to nothing, but it's not really recommended for anything more than a day trip with light luggage. Space for both people and cargo is limited, and the ride can get pretty uncomfortable when the car gets packed.

West of Puerto Escondido

Lagoons full of crocodiles, bioluminescent plankton, and dozens of bird species lie to the west of Puerto Escondido, along with towns rich in traditions. I know it's hard to leave the beach once you've gotten in the zone, but this area of the coast has much to offer, from bird-watching tours to visiting Santa Catarina Juquila, a place of pilgrimage. Or you could just take your board and that beach laziness with you to Chacahua and rent a *cabaña* for an indeterminate amount of time.

★ LAGUNA DE MANIALTEPEC

Less than a half-hour drive from Puerto Escondido, **Laguna de Manialtepec** is a haven for an outrageous variety of migratory fowl, such as pelicans, roseate spoonbills, parrots, wattled jacanas, falcons, and herons in all kinds of colors. Most nights of the year, you can also see and swim among the glowing schools of phytoplankton that light up the water of the lagoon.

Tours

Two tour companies based in Puerto Escondido, **Lalo Ecotours** (in Rockaway shopping center on Zicatela, Puerto Escondido, tel. 954/582-1611 or 954/588-9164, 9am-8pm daily, US$25-75) and **Manglar Birdwatching** (Avenida del Morro, Puerto Escondido, tel. 954/118-6713, 954/108-2641, or 954/559-2431, 9am-8pm daily, US$36), run tours out to Laguna de Manialtepec, and they also have offices in Manialtepec. Manglar focuses mainly on bird-watching tours, while Lalo Ecotours offers an array of options, including morning and afternoon tours for

kayaking and bird-watching and evening tours for the bioluminescence.

But if you get to Manialtepec all by yourself, stop by **La Puesta del Sol** (east end of the lagoon, tel. 954/124-7001, ulisesr532@ gmail.com, 8am-6pm daily), where Elvira and family run sunset boat tours that include bird-watching, a trip to the undeveloped beach Playa Puerto Suelo, and bioluminescence. Tours cost about US$100 for up to five people. They also rent kayaks for US$5-11 per hour.

Accommodations

Hotel options are pretty limited around the lagoon, but luckily the **Best Night Hotel La Laguna** (Hwy. 200 km 124, tel. 954/582-1997, aldeabacochopuerto@hotmail.com, US$38 d, US$53 king size) has 18 clean, comfortable rooms with air-conditioning, TV, and Wi-Fi, as well as a swimming pool. It may not have much competition, but the hotel isn't lying with that name.

Getting There

Getting out to Laguna de Manialtepec is really easy. In Puerto Escondido, board a *suburban* at **TUR** (corner of Hwy. 200 and Calle Primera Poniente, tel. 954/582-2605, www.puertoshops.com/tur.html, transtur01@hotmail.com), just to the west of the ADO station. They leave every half hour or so and charge about US$2.50 for the 25-minute ride.

★ PARQUE NACIONAL LAGUNAS DE CHACAHUA

The **Parque Nacional Lagunas de Chacahua** comprises 55 square miles of lush

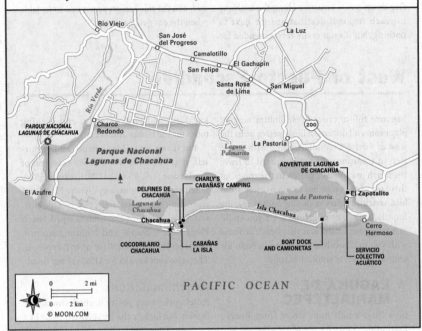

Parque Nacional Lagunas de Chacahua

tropical vegetation and mangrove forests and seven salty lagoons. Tens of thousands of migratory birds call this a temporary home, and some, just like some of us, become so enamored of the place that they never leave. You'll see many pelicans, herons, and other birds that also stop by Manialtepec. The town of **Chacahua,** on Isla Chacahua, has a few *cabañas* and *palapa* restaurants that will tempt you to stop migrating as well.

Sights
ZAPOTALITO AND LAGUNA PASTORIA

The easiest access to the lagoons is at **El Zapotalito,** a small village on the eastern side of **Laguna Pastoria,** the largest of the lagoons. From here, you can get to Isla Chacahua by boat, either *colectivo* style or on a tour that takes you around to some of the numerous mangrove islands in the lagoon.

ISLA CHACAHUA

Long, skinny **Isla Chacahua** separates Laguna Pastoria from the open ocean. Only the western tip of its 10 miles of pristine coastline is developed, with several *cabaña* hotels and *palapa* restaurants offering economic beds and grub to beach loungers and surfers alike. The waters of the little strait that leads from Laguna Chacahua to the sea are calm and crystal blue, perfect for taking a dip. Private boat owners will take you across the channel for about US$1.

COCODRILARIO CHACAHUA (CROCODILE HATCHERY)

Just across the channel from Isla Chacahua is the **Cocodrilario Chacahua,** run by the Secretary of the Environment and Natural Resources (SEMNARAT). The conservation center houses hundreds of caimans and river and swamp crocodiles, a few of which measure as much as 10-12 feet long. They are crammed into close quarters, the majority of which are enclosed by nothing more than chain-link fences. Local children are in charge of maintaining the grounds and provide brief tours by donation. Visiting this center is bittersweet, because it appears as though it has met its goal of crocodile conservation, which was its purpose when it was founded in 1968, but now that the species are plentiful in the wild, there are too many in the lagoons to release crocs hatched here; the place seems more like a poorly-cared-for zoo than conservation center.

So visit here at your own moral risk. And possibly physical risk as well. The chain-link fences all bulge out from the inside at the bottoms, and though the crocs supposedly never get out, many of the fences somewhat ominously show signs of repair.

Recreation

TOP EXPERIENCE

SURFING

There is a long, slow, right-breaking wave just off the westernmost side of the beach on Isla Chacahua, where all the *cabañas* are located. You can haul your board down the jetty and hop right in. At the time of writing, there were no surf shops in town, so make sure all your gear is good to go before you leave Puerto Escondido. There's also a short but fun beach break on the mainland, just across the channel from the beach on Isla Chacahua.

BOAT EXCURSIONS

The best boat tours leave from Zapotalito. **Adventure Lagunas de Chacahua** (tel. 954/114-8539, 7am-10pm daily) will take you around the numerous islands of red and white mangrove forests before dropping you off on the east end of Isla Chacahua. Guides (Spanish only) are very knowledgeable of local bird species, and if you're lucky, you might see a crocodile. Tours take about three hours and cost about US$55 in low season, possibly more during high season.

Food and Accommodations

Friendly and helpful Juana at ★ **Delfines de Chacahua** (west end of the beach, tel. 954/160-0818 or 954/131-5740, US$16-27) has 19 simple *cabañas* with fans, mosquito nets, and private bathrooms, both on the beach and tucked back on the lagoon side of the island. Juana also rents hammocks for US$1.50 per night—many places along the Oaxacan coast used to do this, but the practice has largely gone out of fashion. Aside from costing next to nothing, spending the night swaying in the sea breeze is a unique and fun experience.

At the westernmost end of the beach, **Cabañas La Isla** (tel. 954/130-5168, US$38-43) have a few *cabañas* with private bathrooms and views of both the beach and the crystalline channel on the other side. Offerings at the adjoining *palapa* restaurant include delicious shrimp cocktails and fish. The *miscelania* (convenience store) just up the road that runs parallel to the channel has fruit, snacks, beer, and a few other necessities, as well as a variable schedule.

CAMPING

Just about any of the *palapa* places will let you pitch a tent if they've got the space for about US$2.50 per person. Juana at **Delfines de Chacahua** (west end of the beach, tel. 954/160-0818 or 954/131-5740) charges this much for camping, as does Charly at **Charly's Cabañas y Camping** (east end of developed section of the beach, tel. 954/132-3860, charlychacahua@gmail.com), which has the most camping space available and also rents hammocks. All have shared bathrooms.

Getting There

TUR vans from Puerto Escondido (corner of Hwy. 200 and Calle Primera Poniente, tel. 954/582-2605, www.puertoshops.com/tur.html, transtur01@hotmail.com) charge about US$3 for the trip out to the turnoff to Zapotalito, which runs just a little over an hour. From here, *colectivo* taxis wait to fill up before setting out on the five-minute ride to

Zapotalito, and charge a little over US$1 per person.

You have a couple of options for the last leg of the journey. The long way is via the highly recommended tour by **Adventure Lagunas de Chacahua** (tel. 954/114-8539, 7am-10pm daily), which gets you to the beach in about three hours, after wending through the various islets and narrow mangrove canals of Lagunas Pastoria and Chacahua. This route will run you about US$55 per boat, so this option is better for groups of three or more.

To get there the cheap, *colectivo* way, continue down the main road, up over the small rise about 300 meters (984 ft), until you see a sign on your right that reads **"Servicio Colectivo Acuatico."** Boats from here charge about US$2 to take you to the east end of Isla Chacahua, where you'll board a *camioneta* that also charges about US$2 to take you the rest of the way overland. The whole journey takes about an hour.

SANTA CATARINA JUQUILA

Founded in 1272 by inhabitants of La Mixteca, **Santa Catarina Juquila** is a place of pilgrimage for many Oaxacans, as it is one of many sites to have reportedly played host to a miracle. People come from far and wide to pay their respects to the pint-sized **Virgen de Juquila,** often affectionately referred to in the diminutive "La Juquilita" for its small stature. The wooden figure in her triangular robe is only 30 cm tall (just under a foot) and 15 cm wide. In Náhuatl, Juquila means "The Place of the Beautiful Legume," but its original name, Xiquilla, means "The Place Where Blue Amaranth Abounds."

Juquila's status as an important religious center in the region goes all the way back to the year 1526, when the town was under the Spanish vassalage of Tututepec. Town folklore tells of a Spanish priest from the state of Santa Catarina named Brother Jordán, who had been serving in the neighboring village of Amialtepec. When it was time for Jordán

to leave his post, he gave the local farmer who had given him room and board during his stay a little figurine of the Virgen de la Purísima Concepción (Virgin of the Immaculate Conception), which had been made in Spain. The farmer, who Jordán had proselytized, placed the virgin in a little hut in Amialtepec, and she came to be revered by the local Chatino people.

The miracle happened over a century later in 1633, when a slash-and-burn fire in the fields got out of control and burned the huts of Amialtepec to the ground, including the one housing the relic. When the flames died down, the people returned and were shocked to see the little wooden statue still standing among the ashes. Friars in the larger town of Santa Catarina Juquila felt she deserved a better home than middle-of-nowhere Amialtepec, so La Juquilita was moved to her current home in 1719.

To this day, devout Oaxacans from all over the state leave their homes on foot in November to make the pilgrimage to venerate the blessed virgin on December 8, the town's main festival in celebration of her honor.

Sights
SANTUARIO DE NUESTRA SEÑORA DE JUQUILA
Constructed in the mid-18th century, the **Santuario de Nuestra Señora de Juquila** is a brilliant white masterpiece of neoclassical architecture that is a stunning sight to see when lit up at night. The simple but intricate geometrical designs of the facade, once a burgundy red, are now outlined in gold.

The neoclassicism is apparent inside as well, with large, gold-lined columns along the blank white walls of the cross-shaped, dome-topped nave. A unique feature of this church is that there are no pews. You'll find La Juquilita above the altar at the back of the church, clothed in her unique triangle-shaped, gold

---

1: a sunny day at Laguna de Manialtepec 2: dance of Las Chilenas from Pinotepa Nacional 3: inlet between the sea and Laguna de Chacahua

embroidered silk robe, and surrounded by flowers brought to her by the faithful.

EL PEDIMENTO

No one really knows how the tradition started, but pilgrims to Juquila also usually make a stop and leave an offering at **El Pedimento,** a hilltop chapel east of town. Pilgrims bring offerings for the life-sized Virgen de Juquila outside the chapel, usually little figurines made out of clay, to accompany their *pedimentos* (petitions) to the virgin. You'll see the sign for it about 7 km (4.3 mi) east of town on the north side of the road. It's 30 minutes from the junction with Highway 131, and about 25 minutes from Juquila.

Festivals and Events

Friday is Santa Catarina Juquila's *día de plaza,* or market day, when farmers and vendors from the neighboring communities set up shop in the downtown streets.

Pilgrims begin arriving in late November and early December, leaving offerings and lighting candles for the virgin, attending daily early morning masses, and leading religious processions through the streets. From then the celebration grows into a riot of fireworks, music, food, parades, and religious ceremonies until December 8, the day of the **Fiesta de la Virgen de Juquila.** Her sanctuary brims with flowers during the festivities, adding a harlequin touch to the austere interior. And since the day to honor the Virgen de Guadalupe, the patron saint of Mexico, is December 12, the fun usually continues until then.

Getting There and Away

Getting to Juquila can be a bit hairy. By public transport from Puerto Escondido, your fastest route is to take an *urbano* from the *crucero* in Puerto or a *suburban* from the **TUR station** (corner of Hwy. 200 and Calle Primera Poniente, tel. 954/582-2605, www. puertoshops.com/tur.html, transtur01@ hotmail.com) west on Highway 200 to Rio Grande. From here, grab a *taxi colectivo* from

the *crucero* for the trip north to Juquila. All in all, this can take three hours or more. If you take this route, you'll need to get a *colectivo* going east to Highway 131 when you leave Juquila in order to stop by El Pedimento. This trip should cost around US$4-5.

Alternatively, you could get in a *suburban* destined for Oaxaca at **Autotransportes Villa Del Pacífico** (Hwy. 200 between Hidalgo and Calle Primera Norte, tel. 954/132-5643) and tell the driver to drop you off at the turnoff to Juquila from Highway 131. Grab a *colectivo* from here, and you can stop by El Pedimento on the way into town. This route also costs around US$4-5.

To make things easier, consider calling the guys at **Transportadora Turística Chacahua** (three storefronts east of Le Petit Hotel on Gasga, tel. 954/588-4592 or 954/101-1337, transportadorachacahua@gmail.com, 8am-11pm daily), who will take care of the transportation and take you to all the necessary sights. The tour costs around US$100 for 2-4 people, and runs 7am-5pm.

Drivers take Highway 200 west from Puerto Escondido. In 50 km (31 mi), turn onto the Rio Grande-Santa Catarina Juquila Highway at Rio Grande. Follow this road 48 km (30 mi) to Santa Catarina Juquila. The drive takes about 2.25 hours.

SANTIAGO JAMILTEPEC

Admittedly, there is little to do in the tiny town of **Santiago Jamiltepec,** but it has its quirks, so it could be a fun, short stop on your way out to Pinotepa Nacional. The block-like masonic architecture of the 17th-century **Parroquia de Santiago Apóstol** stands out among the baroque and neoclassical styles much more popular in Oaxaca. Across from the church you'll see the *relojes del sol y de la luna,* a pair of dials (one a sundial, the other a moondial), both adorned with masonic symbolism. Don't miss the Mixtec statues in the nearby park.

Festivals and Events

The main festival in Jamiltepec is the **Fiesta**

de la Virgen de los Remedios, held on February 15. Although nowhere near as grandiose a celebration as the one for La Juquilita, the party is thrown to celebrate an even tinier virgin (Jamiltepec's measures only 12 cm, or about 5 inches, tall), and it is a culturally enriching and rollicking good time, with fireworks, food, *calendas* (street parades), dancing, and the like for nine days leading up to the main event.

Getting There and Away

Grab a *suburban* from the **TUR station** (corner of Hwy. 200 and Calle Primera Poniente, tel. 954/582-2605, www.puertoshops.com/tur.html, transtur01@hotmail.com) in Puerto Escondido. From here it's a straight shot 109 km (68 mi) west on Highway 200 to Jamiltepec. The trip takes about two hours and costs around US$5.

PINOTEPA NACIONAL

It's a ways out there, but the trip to Pinotepa Nacional is worth it if you can make it during a festival. If you went to the Guelaguetza in Oaxaca City, you most likely saw *los sones y chilenas de Pinotepa Nacional,* a dance and musical genre from the Costa Chica region of Oaxaca and Guerrero that has its roots thousands of miles away in South America. Chilean sailors first brought the genre they called *la cueca* to Oaxaca's shores in 1822, and it later gained more popularity as sparkly-eyed prospectors from Chile stopped in Oaxacan ports on their way to California during the gold rush.

Pinotepa's signature dance is a tale of seduction told by up to 15 couples, the steps slowly bringing each couple closer and closer together. The cadence of the music, sensual tension in the dance steps, and long, flowing skirts of the women, dyed vibrant colors and trimmed with horizontal layers of lace, all combine to create a truly hypnotizing experience.

Festivals and Events

Fiestas in Pinotepa are called *mayordomías,* which denotes both the parties and the "stewardship" system used in many Oaxacan communities to organize and fund them. The person in charge of everything from changing out the flowers in the church altars all year to making sure the fireworks go off for the finale is called the *mayordomo* (steward). Each year, the *mayordomo* (or *mayordoma*) chooses the following year's master of ceremonies.

Mayordomías are thrown for various saints and virgins year-round, but Pinotepa's biggest one is the **Semana Santa** (Holy Week) holiday leading up to El Día de Pascua (Easter Sunday). This weeklong festival of solemn religious observances, lively dances, and community building honors Tatchu, the local Mixtec name for Jesus Christ, as well as Our Lady of Solitude. Another lively *mayordomía* to try and catch in Pinotepa is **La Fiesta Patronal en honor a Santiago Apóstol,** when the town venerates its patron saint James, son of Zebedee, or as he's called in the local Mixtec dialect, Tata Santiagu. It is held on June 25.

Getting There and Away

Pinotepa is 140 km (87 mi) west of Puerto Escondido on Coastal Highway 200, a 2.5-hour drive. **TUR** vans (corner of Hwy. 200 and Calle Primera Poniente, tel. 954/582-2605, www.puertoshops.com/tur.html, transtur01@hotmail.com) from Puerto Escondido charge about US$7.50 for the three-hour trip. Vans leave every half hour.

Istmo de Tehuantepec

My bus pulled into Tehuantepec just after midnight on January 1. People on just about every block between the bus station and my hotel in the Centro had lit little fires for igniting the barrage of fireworks they launched into the air to blast in the New Year. Everywhere I looked from the roof of my hotel, small explosions bloomed in the night sky like the flowers on *huipiles,* the embroidered blouses for which the region is well-known and widely respected.

I really couldn't recall having seen so many people shoot off bottle rockets and Roman candles in such high density, but it didn't surprise me. The citizens of El Istmo are as renowned for their indomitable spirit and energy for the fiesta as they are for those captivatingly colorful embroidery styles. These people know how to party.

Highlights

Look for ★ to find recommended sights, activities, dining, and lodging.

★ **La Tehuana:** This seven-meter (23-ft) stainless steel statue has commemorated the strong, enterprising women of Tehuantepec since its installation in 2008 (page 303).

★ **Mercado Jesús Carranza:** Participate in Tehuantepec's matriarchal economy in this bustling downtown marketplace (page 303).

★ **Casa Museo Shunashi:** The 17th-century home of the Villalobos family is also a museum where you can learn about the rich, riotous, and rebellious culture of El Istmo (page 303).

★ **Juchitán Plaza and Market:** Whether filled with concert stages or temporary market stalls, Juchitán's main plaza and market are always alive with sound and color—and the indomitable Juchiteco spirit (page 308).

★ **Springs North of Juchitán:** The spring-fed pools of these *balnearios* (swimming holes) north of Juchitán are close enough for a relaxing day trip but are still worlds away from the commerce-crazy streets of the bustling city (page 314).

★ **Surfing Salina Cruz:** The coast between here and Huatulco is home to over 20 world-class point and beach breaks, as well as other types of waves, and the pros at a handful of locally owned surf camps can show you where they all are (page 317).

El Mezquite

Aguas Calientes la Mata • Mazahua

Santiago Laollaga

Ixtepec

★ **Springs North of Juchitán**

Asunción Ixtaltepec

★ **Juchitán Plaza and Market**

★ **La Tehuana**

Juchitán

★ **Mercado Jesús Carranza**

★ **Casa Museo Shunashi**

Santa María Xadani

Tehuantepec

Laguna Superior

Salina Cruz

Salinas del Marqués

★ **Surfing Salina Cruz**

Gulf of Tehuantepec

0   5 mi
0   5 km

© MOON.COM

They even have their own word for it: *vela*. A typical *vela* in Juchitán or Tehuantepec is three nonstop days and nights of drinking, eating, and dancing to the regional musical style known as *el son istmeño*. Even the preparations—as early as six months before the fiesta—are turned into celebrations. Add the calendar of *velas* to that of the national and statewide festivities, and your chances of catching a raucous party are pretty good no matter what time of year you come.

Here at the isthmus, the funnel of mainland Mexico thins out to just over 214 km (133 mi). Sparsely populated, misty mountains cover the north of Oaxaca's chunk of it, but most folks live in the windswept, semiarid lowlands between these low peaks and the Pacific coast. Natural springs dot the dusty landscape, crystalline oases in this sporadically soaked region, which experiences freak droughts even when the rest of the state is getting drenched.

To visit El Istmo is to experience a culture and society wholly its own. Women run the economy, as they have for centuries. Seamstresses here weave four distinct *trajes típicos* (traditional embroidered dresses). Cooks have found even more delicious things to do with corn tortillas, such as the fried but chewy *garnachas* and the crispy *totopos,* riddled with finger-poked holes and served with seafood. The *muxes,* men raised as women from childhood who often dress the part and take on traditionally female roles in the home and society, are considered a third gender here, fully accepted in Istmeño culture. Citizens are so prepared to defend their land and traditions that they have been known to burn their cities to the ground rather than let outsiders take them. The people of El Istmo are willing to protect and celebrate their culture at any cost.

HISTORY

El Istmo was originally inhabited by the Mixe and Zoque peoples in the north, and the Huave people south of them to the coast. Archaeological findings at Laguna Zope, a pre-Hispanic site about 2 km (1.2 mi) east of Juchitán, suggest that the Zapotecs came along as far back as 1500 BC. Laguna Zope remained a small, economically self-sufficient settlement until around 1100 BC, when it expanded to become one of the largest Mesoamerican communities of its time—in terms of area, not population. Unknown causes forced the community to relocate closer to the nearby river sometime between AD 300 and 600, and more communities began to pop up in the surrounding tropical lowlands and along the shores of the lagoons on the coast, where people dedicated themselves to fishing.

The most notable pre-Hispanic historical event in the Istmo occurred in the Zapotec town of Guiengola, about 14 km (8.7 mi) north of the contemporary city of Tehuantepec. In the 1490s, the Mexica (also referred to as the Aztecs) began a colonization campaign in Oaxaca, seeking to extend their territory to demand tributes. The Zapotec king Cosijoeza of the kingdom of Zaachila, the founder of Guiengola, ordered the killing of the realm's Mexica children, who were accused of being spies. In response, Ahuizotl, the Aztec emperor in 1497, launched a fierce military campaign that took Huaxyacac (now Oaxaca) and then Mitla before it began to spread through the Istmo. Cosijoeza fended off this incursion by making an alliance with the Mixtecs, led by King Dzahuindanda, who supplied 24,000 warriors to Cosijoeza's army of 36,000.

Ahuizotl did not give up, though. Later that year, he mounted another offensive, this time on Guiengola. After a seven-month-long battle, the Aztec king chose diplomacy over continued militarism and proposed a treaty with the Zapotec king. His daughter Xilabela was part of the terms, and she married Cosijoeza

Previous: the otherworldly dunes off Salina Cruz's Playa Azul; the bright colors of the Juchitán market; the sweet-smelling blooms of the *flor de mayo* tree.

Istmo de Tehuantepec

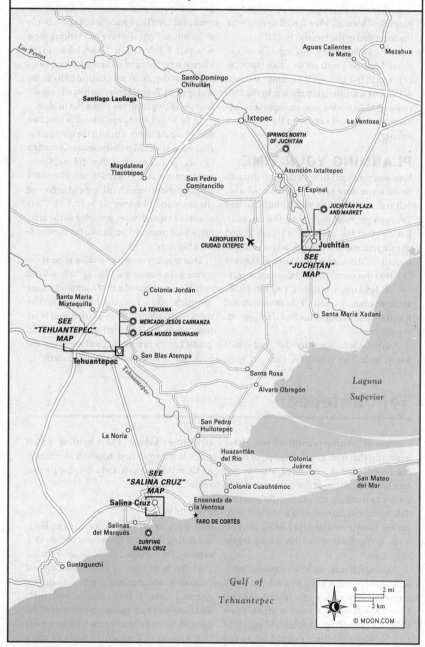

© MOON.COM

to seal the deal. Peace in the kingdom of Zaachila did not last long, however: A few decades later the Zapotecs, like all indigenous peoples of Mexico, were forced to deal with the incursion of the Spanish in 1521.

In the 19th century, this region was considered for the construction of an interoceanic canal, but the much narrower Isthmus of Panama was ultimately chosen. In the 20th century, El Istmo became an important economic center, most notably in the petroleum industry.

PLANNING YOUR TIME

How you plan your time in El Istmo depends on what you want to do. Most attractions are cultural, such as the *velas* in Juchitán and Tehuantepec, and depend on the calendar. Luckily, it is full of them, so there's a good chance your trip will coincide with a *vela*. The majority of the *velas* are in April and May, but El Istmo has plenty of multiday ragers year-round. January, September, and December are festive months, and all the other national holidays, such as Day of the Dead, are also celebrated here.

A typical *vela* is a three-day (and night) party fueled by countless cases of beer, mountains of food, and exciting dances and parades. If you come for one, plan for an extra day and spend an afternoon relaxing in the springs at **Laollaga** and **Tlacotepec,** north of Juchitán. Even if you're not visiting for a *vela,* plan 2-3 days in **Juchitán,** taking in the vibrant street life and escaping to the springs on the last day. Because of its proximity to the springs and Tehuantepec, Juchitán is a good base for taking in all the Istmo has to offer.

In **Tehuantepec,** you'll need at least two days to see the sights, a third if the tasty *garnachas* outside the **Mercado Jesús Carranza** impress you as much as they did me. Spend an afternoon at the **Casa Museo Shunashi** learning about the rich culture and history of the town and El Istmo. As in Juchitán, it is possible to spend hours shopping in the market, whose commerce spills into the surrounding alleyways.

Due to safety concerns and for general enjoyment, I recommend visiting **Salina Cruz** only if you've booked a **surf camp** trip, most of which have a five-night minimum. The town itself offers little to tourists and is far from where you'll be surfing. The surf camp guides know where all the good waves are, and packages include transportation to them.

Tehuantepec

Citizens of Tehuantepec will tell you, rather haughtily, that their city is the *cuna,* or birthplace, of all that is considered Istmeño culture today. Whether or not these proprietary claims to tradition are historically accurate, Tehuantepec is currently the best place to experience and learn about the history, art, customs, and gastronomy of this unique region of Oaxaca.

Although it may not be as rebellious today as it has been in the past, Tehuantepec is still a raucous firecracker of a town—one that knows how to party. A sense of mystery pervades the crumbling colonial buildings of the Centro, with its defunct railroad tracks and rich history hidden behind bustling market stalls. What you'll find, however, are friendly locals, delicious meals, and a festive spirit that refuses to quit.

History

Ever since its days as the last Zapotec holdout during the Aztec invasion of the late 15th century, Tehuantepec, like Juchitán down the road, has been ready to defend itself against incursions and exploitation by unwelcome guests. In March 1660, citizens both male and female rose up against the officials of the Spanish viceroyalty after the *cacique* (chief) of the village of Tequisistlán died as a result

Tehuantepec

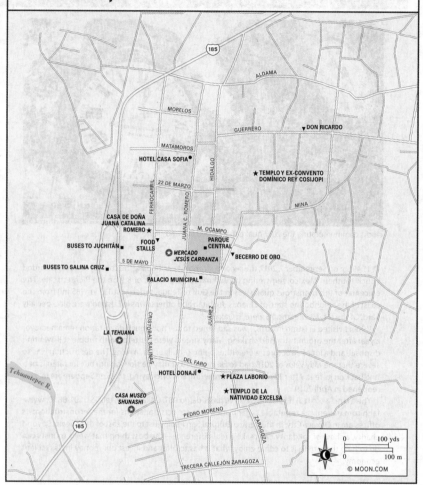

of a beating he received for not fulfilling his tribute duties. The insurgents occupied and governed Tehuantepec for 14 months, demanding an official pardon for those involved in the uprising; the legitimization of the local officials they had put in place; an end to the *repartimiento* system, which obliged indigenous populations to work for no pay; and a governor who would be fair in matters of trade and "of benevolent condition."

The citizens were overjoyed when Spanish judge Juan Francisco Montemayor came to town with orders from the crown to meet the rebels' demands. The jubilee was short-lived, however, as Montemayor and his Spanish cohorts had no intentions of honoring the royal decree. He imprisoned the local officials that had been elected by the insurgents, killed some of them, and reinstated Spanish viceregal power in El Istmo.

A couple centuries later, during the Reform Era of the 1850s, the *istmeños* got fed up with

The 2017 Earthquake

clocks commemorating the 2017 quake that rattled El Istmo

At 11:49pm on September 7, 2017, the second-strongest earthquake the country has ever recorded struck southern Mexico, registering an estimated magnitude of 8.2 on the Richter scale. The epicenter of this monstrous quake was in the Gulf of Tehuantepec, just 137 km (85 mi) from the coast of the neighboring state of Chiapas. Juchitán and other towns in El Istmo were hit especially hard. Of the total 98 deaths, 78 were in Oaxaca.

When I visited El Istmo in 2018, I was saddened to see how much devastation remained over a year after the ground stopped shaking. Many streets were cluttered with rubble still awaiting disposal, and a lot of structures were either being rebuilt or lay in ruins. The destruction was so severe that the May *velas* of 2018 had to be canceled. It may be slow going, but Juchitán is getting back on its feet. After 19 months of hammering and bricklaying, the 5 de Septiembre market reopened in April 2019.

The **Fundación Alfredo Harp Helú** (Hidalgo 907, Oaxaca City, tel. 951/501-8800, www. fahh.com.mx/en) is a reputable organization that collects donations for the reconstruction; its offices are in Oaxaca City, in the Centro Cultural San Pablo, just to the east of the Zócalo. Beyond charity, a show of solidarity can make a real difference—the best thing that we as tourists can do to help the region is to come enjoy what it has to offer and invest our money in its resilient economy.

another unfulfilled promise, this time from the federal and state governments, the latter of which was led by Oaxaca's own Benito Juárez (who later became president of Mexico). Despite his famous adage that "respect for the rights of others is peace," Juárez did not come through with his promise to redistribute land to indigenous peoples. Instead, he opened the door to more privatization of land and resources. The resistance to this move intensified into a full-fledged movement for a secession of El Istmo from Oaxaca, with local musician and politician Máximo Ramón Ortiz acting as governor of what he considered to be a sovereign Istmo de Tehuantepec. The secession, however, was never acknowledged by Juárez's state government or the federal government.

Getting Oriented

The Río Tehuantepec splits town into two parts, with the Centro to the north. Just north of the bridge, Highway 185 divides into two roads with a large median between them, where buses running between Juchitán and Salina Cruz make stops every 10 minutes or so.

Tehuantepec's charming **Parque Central** is two blocks east of this median, with the municipal government building on its south side. Across the gazebo from this building, you'll find a statue of one of the city's most illustrious citizens, Juana Catalina Romero (1837-1915), honored for her economic support of the defense against the intervention of the French in the 1860s, as well as for her work developing public education in her hometown. To the east of the gazebo, two clocks memorialize the earthquake that rocked southern and central Mexico on September 7, 2017. The clock on the left tells the current time; the other marks the hour the quake struck, 11:49pm.

The block west of the Parque Central is home to the **Mercado Jesús Carranza,** on the west side of which the old train tracks run through town. To the north, the tarps of more market vendors cover the old tracks. Follow them south, where the tracks have been turned into a nice public space with a playground and exercise equipment, to arrive at the old train bridge. A well-lit walkway has recently been installed along the riverbank in this part of town, a great place for a late afternoon stroll to walk off all those greasy *garnachas.*

SIGHTS
★ *La Tehuana*

On a highway median to the west of the Centro, the *Monumento a la Mujer Tehuana* stands seven meters (23 ft) tall and overlooks the broad banks of the Río Tehuantepec, welcoming visitors to town as they cross the bridge. Installed in 2008 by Mexico City artist Miguel Hernández Urban and endearingly referred to as *La Tehuana* (the woman from Tehuantepec), the stainless steel statue depicts a woman in the traditional Tehuantepec gala dress, the fanciest and most elaborate of the region's many styles of embroidered dresses. Urban, who died in 2017, built the statue to honor the courage of the women of Tehuantepec, who have always fought alongside the men to defend their homes and customs during various incursions, rebellions, and other conflicts here.

★ Mercado Jesús Carranza

On the block west of the Parque Central, the **Mercado Jesús Carranza** (6am-10pm daily) is a hive of commercial activity. Inside the building, you'll find lots of embroidered *huipiles,* purses, skirts, and other textiles ablaze with the vivid flowers unique to the Istmo de Tehuantepec. The only prepared food inside is from a couple of juice bars and *refresquerías,* little snack bars serving mostly *tortas* (Mexican sandwiches).

The alley on the west side of the market has more food stalls. Don't leave Tehuantepec without eating *garnachas* here. It's no surprise that the market building isn't big enough to hold all the commerce of Tehuantepec's enterprising citizenry. The *callejón* (alleyway) to the north is covered with tarps, under which vendors sell everything from housewares to *huipiles* to fresh ground coffee from the Sierra Mixe, the part of the Sierra Norte closest to El Istmo.

★ Casa Museo Shunashi

The gorgeous riverside home of José Manuel Villalobos and family is also the **Casa Museo Shunashi** (Callejón del Faro 1, tel. 971/161-1425 or 971/185-0222, noon-5pm daily, admission by donation, US$3-5 recommended), the perfect place to learn about the culture and food unique to the Istmo. The whitewashed 17th-century house is as sturdy as it is pretty, having withstood who knows how many quakes since it was built. It's also full of artifacts from the colonial period, including a pair of ancient wooden looms.

José himself is a wealth of information on the history and traditions of his hometown. He gave me a quick demonstration when I showed up unannounced, but he said that

Matriarchy in El Istmo and Frida Kahlo

Mexico is well known for its patriarchal culture, but El Istmo is one place where gender roles follow their own set of guidelines. Although political power is still the domain of men, women run the economy here. Trade is considered a woman's birthright, and just about every *istmeña* has her hand in buying and selling something to a certain degree. In a family of fisherfolk, for example, dad will be responsible for getting the fish out of the saltwater lagoons south of town, but it's mom's job to get the catch to market. You'll see women doing jobs like driving taxis and *mototaxis* in El Istmo, vocations generally reserved for men in other parts of the state.

Iconic Mexican painter Frida Kahlo was known for dressing in the traditional *trajes* of El Istmo. She is remembered for having said *"Mi vestido soy yo"* (I am what I wear); for Frida, as with women from El Istmo, the clothing represented more than looking good. Although for security reasons the practice isn't as common as in the past, part of the traditional *traje de gala* includes clunky necklaces of gold coins and other gold ornaments, which represent the economic dominance of women in the society and households. It's not surprising that such colorful traditions would be attractive to a painter, but Frida also identified with this matriarchal power of El Istmo.

Although some researchers have claimed that the arrival of the petroleum industry in El Istmo has presented a challenge to the matriarchal economic dominance here, women still control commerce in the markets and homes. They also take over the dance floor during the *velas*, creating mesmerizing mosaics of colors and movements, while the much less flashily dressed men sit alongside and watch.

more detailed cultural presentations need prep time, so book at least a week in advance. He'll arrange a whole show with dancers in traditional dresses, a meal of regional foods, historical presentations, and more. For groups of 12 or more, the price should come out to around US$25 per person. No English is spoken.

Finding the museum can be a little tricky. Head south down Cristóbal Salinas from the railroad track park and take a right on Callejón del Faro. It is the last house on the right. There is no sign, and if you haven't booked a demonstration, there's a good chance it won't be open. Look for the cord hanging by the door up the stairs and ring the bell.

Templo y Ex-Convento Domínico Rey Cosijopi

The beautiful 16th-century **Templo y Ex-Convento Domínico Rey Cosijopi** has housed Tehuantepec's Casa de Cultura since 1973, but it was severely damaged by the 2017 earthquake. Currently undergoing repairs, it's not expected to reopen until 2021 at the earliest. You'll reach it by taking Calle Hidalgo north from the main square for two blocks. Take a right on Guerrero, then your next right. The entrance is at the end of this alley.

Dedicated to Saint Dominic, the church and convent were constructed from 1544 to 1550 with funds provided by King Cosijopi, Tehuantepec's last Zapotec monarch, who had converted to Catholicism. Of course, the conversion was also to Spanish colonialism and its characteristic *tequio* (forced labor). Cosijopi compelled his loyal subjects from communities all over El Istmo to come to Tehuantepec and build the church. In the 19th century, the edifice was used as barracks, and it later functioned as a prison until 1975.

Plaza Laborio

The pint-size **Plaza Laborio** and adjacent **Templo de la Natividad Excelsa** are among the numerous structures in El Istmo damaged by the 2017 quake. The church's right tower

1: dancers from Tehuantepec in their *trajes de gala* (party dresses) **2:** *La Tehuana* statue **3:** Casa Museo Shunashi **4:** late-night street tacos in Tehuantepec

Garnachas: An Istmeño Specialty

Just when you think Mexico has done everything there is to do with corn tortillas, you visit El Istmo and find more nuance in the country's vast gastronomic canon referred to as *antojitos*, or snack foods. Like tostadas, *sopes, huaraches*, and tacos, **garnachas** are a tortilla-based *antojito* topped with meat and a garnish, but the subtle differences create flavors and textures wholly distinct from those of the others.

The main difference is in the preparation of the tortilla itself. *Garnachas* use small, stout corn tortillas, usually thicker than taco tortillas, and instead of being heated in an oven or on a *comal* (traditional ceramic griddle), they are lightly fried in oil, which gives them a crunchy texture while still conserving the malleable nature of the tortilla. The meat commonly used is either a dry, shredded beef or something like *picadillo* (ground beef with diced potatoes). Instead of diced onions and cilantro, the garnish is a vinegary coleslaw made from cabbage that adds a delightful tang to the spice of the salsa.

garnachas from El Istmo

The best *garnachas* I found were in the **food stalls** outside the Mercado Jesús Carranza in **Tehuantepec.** Do not leave town without trying them.

was already leaning before the quake hit, but repairs were made, and a new wooden playground for the kids was installed in the plaza. You'll find the church two blocks south of the main square, down Calle Juárez. You'll see the park on your left, and the church facade is on the next block to the east, on Calle Porfirio Díaz.

FOOD

Your first meal should be *garnachas* at one of the ★ **food stalls** in the alley on the west side of the Mercado Jesús Carranza. I recommend the first stall from Calle Benito Juárez, with a sign that reads Ruta Gastronómica de Tehuantepec, an organization that promotes local eateries. They make *garnachas* with *picadillo*, *queso Istmeño* (the local crumbly *queso fresco*, a kind of cheese), and a side of tangy coleslaw to pile on top of them—which is more manageable if you do so after applying salsa and lime. The little tortillas are fried perfectly, giving them the flavor and texture distinct to this Istmeño specialty. The stall is generally

open from early morning until the late afternoon, and a meal will cost around US$3.

Don Ricardo (Guerrero 17, tel. 971/137-4173, noon-midnight daily, US$6) functions as a breezy, stylish restaurant by day and a hip, fully stocked bar at night. The restaurant-bar is in the courtyard of a 200-year-old home and has murals by local artists. The food is a bit hipper than the traditional stuff in the market. Try the delicious, healthy fish tacos.

The best late-night tacos are at **El Becerro de Oro** (The Golden Bull Calf; no phone, 5pm-2am daily, US$2.50), a bright-red street taqueria on the east side of the Plaza Central. They've got *chorizo* (spicy pork sausage), *cecina* (pork cutlet), *carne asada* (grilled beef), and *cabeza* (head); the last is exactly what it sounds like. Give it a try. It's good!

ACCOMMODATIONS

The rooms at **Hotel Donají** (Josefa Ortíz de Domínguez 10, tel. 971/715-0064, www.hoteldonaji.com, US$18 d) might be insufficiently lit, but the natural light filling the covered central courtyard makes up for it. Strands of green ivy hang from the mezzanine, over the restaurant (Café Yizu; 8am-11pm daily, US$4) that serves delicious Mexican staples and often hosts music, one-act plays, and other cultural events. Book early if you're coming for a *vela*, as it fills up quickly due to its central location.

Two blocks north of the main square, **Hotel Casa Sofia** (Romero 20, tel. 971/713-7747, US$25 king bed, US$33 two full beds) enchants with its gold columns and white-walled hallways trimmed with the radiant floral patterns distinct to Tehuantepec. The 15 rooms themselves aren't as colorful, but they are comfortable, albeit a bit quirky—the walls facing the hallway aren't walls, but rather floor-to-ceiling windows and glass doors that make up the side of the room facing the hallway (there are curtains). The air-conditioning in the rooms is necessary, as they can get stuffy without it. The Internet works well, and credit cards are accepted.

INFORMATION AND SERVICES

For tourist information, head to the *presidencia municipal* (Cinco de Mayo, no phone, 9am-6pm Mon.-Fri.). There is no official information office, but the friendly staff will be available to help.

The **Hospital General de Tehuantepec** (Calle Universitario, tel. 971/715-0197, 24 hrs daily) has doctors on call around the clock in case of emergencies. No English is spoken.

GETTING THERE
Bus

For travel within El Istmo, board one of the rickety buses that stop at the **bus stop on the median** in Highway 185 just to the west of the Centro. Northbound buses get you to Juchitán in about a half hour and cost a little over US$1. The southbound ones go to Salina Cruz. They take a little bit longer and cost a few more pesos. Buses leave every 15-20 minutes.

For longer distances, head to the **Terminal ADO** on the highway north of the Centro. Take a taxi there for about US$2. Since Tehuantepec is a major stop on the route between Oaxaca City and the neighboring state of Chiapas, buses run day and night. Buses from Oaxaca City (US$11-20) leave from the main ADO station (Cinco de Mayo 900, Barrio de Jalatlaco, Oaxaca City, tel. 951/502-0560) on Highway 190 and take a little under five hours. To the east, in the state of Chiapas, the ADO routes run to Tuxtla Gutiérrez (US$12-21, 5.5 hrs) and San Cristóbal de las Casas (US$13-27, 7 hrs). If you're on a budget and heading to Chiapas next, you can save yourself a night of hotel expenses and sleep on the night bus.

Car

Drivers from Oaxaca City head east on Highway 190. In about an hour, just before Mitla, stay on Highway 190 by taking the turnoff to Tehuantepec. You'll wind 251 km (156 mi) through the dry, scenic hill country for about 3.5 hours. If you're coming from the coast, take Highway 200 east to Salina Cruz. From here, head north on Highway 185 to Tehuantepec. The 18-km (11-mi) trip from Salina Cruz takes about a half hour. As with highways anywhere in Mexico, keep your long-distance driving confined to daylight hours.

GETTING AROUND

Everything to see in Tehuantepec is in the cluster of downtown blocks around the main square. All the sights listed here are within easy walking distance of the main square. To save a little time and effort, hop on one of the town's unique *motocarros*. Similar to the *mototaxis* found elsewhere in the state, these souped-up flatbed tricycles will putt-putt you anywhere around the Centro for US$1 or less.

The Legacy of Juana Catalina Romero

Born to a Zapotec mother and creole Spanish father, the illustrious Doña Juana Catalina Romero (1837-1915) was the exemplary *tehuana*. Historical accounts describe her as an enterprising, industrious, and beautiful young woman who bet money on games of billiards and rolled cigarettes in tobacco leaves to sell to the soldiers quartered in the convent/barracks in town.

As a businesswoman, Juana Cata, as she was affectionately called, was the owner of a successful, award-winning sugar company. The silver and gold medals her company earned at World's Fairs in St. Louis, Missouri (1904), and London (1908) made her the first Mexican woman to receive international renown for her own industrial achievements.

Locally, Juana Cata is revered for her work in education in Tehuantepec, providing counsel and economic support for public schools in her hometown. She is also credited as the person who came up with the celebratory customs of Tehuantepec, such as the dresses worn by both men and women during certain parties. We have Doña Juana Cata to thank for all those colorful dresses and fun festivities in Tehuantepec and all over El Istmo.

monument to Doña Juana Catalina Romero

At the age of 19, she met a young Oaxacan soldier named Porfirio Díaz, and the two are said to have had a long amorous affair. She would later provide him with monetary assistance for military campaigns, as well as sanctuary when he was on the run from the French. Díaz went on to become president (some say dictator) of Mexico for more than 30 years. It is said that Díaz had the train tracks run by her house in the Centro so that he could pop in whenever he came through town. It's unfortunate but not surprising that despite her role as the mother of Tehuantepec culture and education, this aspect of Juana Cata's life has come to dominate popular remembrance of this intelligent, creative go-getter.

The French-style mansion the unmarried Juana Cata lived in until her death in 1915 is across the train tracks from the northwest corner of the market. It's strange that the home of such an important person has not been fixed up and turned into a museum, but as it stands today, you'll have a hard time even getting a glimpse of it through the outdoor market stalls that currently surround it. It appears to be abandoned at this point, but if you do want to view it, it is the white, French-style mansion with faded blue awnings over the windows and a wrought-iron fence around the yard.

Juchitán and Vicinity

Juchitán (hoo-chee-TAHN) means "Place of Flowers" in Nahuatl, which seems fitting given the big, bright blooms embroidered on the *huipiles* made here and elsewhere in the Istmo (though folks from Tehuantepec will tell you they thought of them first and Juchitán copied them). The two cities have historically had a rivalry fueled by claims to cultural and political power, one that at times has escalated to violence. Despite who started which tradition, Istmeño culture, music, art, and party ethic are just as vibrant here as they are in Tehuantepec, and bustling, business-oriented Juchitán is an excellent place to experience them.

SIGHTS

★ Juchitán Plaza and Market

The **Mercado Municipal 5 de Septiembre**

Juchitán

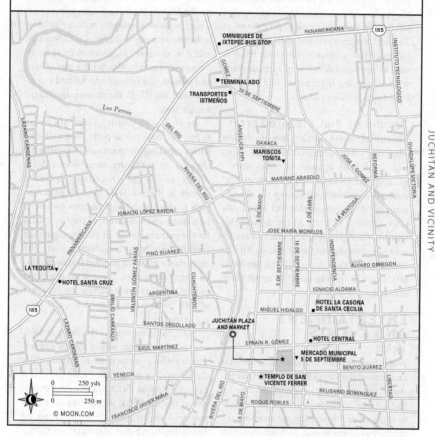

(no phone, 8am-8pm daily) was rebuilt after the 2017 earthquake and inaugurated in April 2019, but due to a disagreement with the electricity commission, market vendors still haven't moved in. At the time of publication, the main square was a labyrinth of steamy food stalls; tunnels of vivid, kaleidoscopic textiles; vendors of housewares; and pungent, meat-strung aisles of the *carniceros* (butchers). Here you might see exotic foods such as sea turtle eggs, iguana, and armadillo—these are traditional sources of protein in this part of Oaxaca and have been a staple of the Istmeño diet since the place was first inhabited. (I would try these types of dishes only

if I were invited into someone's home, and I recommend other visitors do the same, if they want to try them at all. Modern conservation efforts strive to control the consumption of these endangered species.)

In Juchitán's main square, **Parque Benito Juárez,** you'll see a bust of Benito Juárez on the park's east side, and one of his wife, Margarita Maza, on the opposite (west) side of the plaza. (If the stalls are still there, you can turn finding the busts into a fun scavenger hunt.) On the north side, a statue of Juárez and a majestic eagle honor an 1866 battle hard fought against the French, when Juchitecos banded together to defend their town from the imperial invasion. For a snack unique to Juchitán, head to the plaza's east side when the market closes, around 6pm. Here women sell the pre-Hispanic drink **bupu** ("foam" in Zapotec), a super-sweet and frothy corn-based beverage flavored with chocolate. Enjoy it with a tasty *tamal de cambray,* a tamale made with surprising ingredients like chicken, boiled eggs, raisins, and nuts.

Templo de San Vicente Ferrer

The charming 19th-century **Templo de San Vicente Ferrer,** dedicated to Juchitán's patron saint, is no stranger to *sismos* (earthquakes), unfortunately. The September 2017 quake did extensive damage to the church, bringing down repairs that had been made after a tremor in 1955. At the time of this writing, the right tower and much of the facade were missing, but the Fundación Alfredo Harp Helú (of the Centro Cultural San Pablo in Oaxaca City) was working to get them restored.

ENTERTAINMENT AND EVENTS
Velas

People from El Istmo are renowned state-wide and around the nation for their ability to celebrate, which is saying something in a country like Mexico. Nightlong parties aren't unique to this part of the country, but nowhere else are they as common as in Juchitán and other Istmeño communities.

In El Istmo, these all-nighters are called **velas,** most likely a cheeky abbreviation of the word *velada* (evening party). These ragers, however, are much more than social evenings. Fueled by excessive amounts of beer (mezcal isn't as popular here in El Istmo), *velas* are scheduled to last all through the night, for multiple nights in a row. When the dishes from one have been washed and put back in the cupboard, it's usually time to start another.

The *velas* are generally organized by occupational or social guilds called *gremios.* So one will be thrown by the fisherfolk, the next by firework manufacturers, then *muxes,* and so on. *Velas* often honor a patron saint of a particular *barrio* (district). Like parties elsewhere in Oaxaca, *velas* are overseen by *mayordomos,* a couple in charge of the festivities, and it is customary for guests to bring an offering to the couple. Men bring a case of beer, and women give *botanas* (snacks) and a monetary offering (US$5-10 recommended) to the female host.

As on a good journey, much of the fun is had en route to the party. Preparations, such as making the tamales and candles for the shindig, are festive, social events. Main events include the mesmerizing dances of women in their colorful *trajes de gala;* raucous parades with floats and processions of horsemen and bulls; and, of course, a mass for the patron saint. Even the cleanup on the final day has been turned into a party, the main dance of which is called *lavada de ollas* (cleaning of the pots). Some of the events are public, some are private, and some are a mix of both. Some events are in homes, and some are in the street.

Essential to the *velas* is the **son istmeño,** or traditional music played for the dances. The unofficial anthem of El Istmo is "La Zandunga," a song penned by musician Máximo Ramón Ortíz, the onetime governor of the unofficial (depending on whom you ask) sovereign state of El Istmo de Tehuantepec when it attempted to secede from the state of Oaxaca in the mid-19th century.

The main *vela* season is in May, during the **Fiestas de Mayo,** with the first *velas* beginning at the end of April. There are also important *velas* in September and January. To get the full experience, consider booking an all-inclusive package with **Hotel Santa Cruz** (Carretera Transístmica, km 818, tel. 971/712-1326 and 971/712-0707, reservaciones@hotelsantacruzjuchitan.com), which includes everything from accommodations to breakfast to clothing rentals to cases of beer and other offerings for the *mayordomos.*

Third Gender: The *Muxes* of El Istmo

muxe Nelson Morales

One night in Tehuantepec, I returned to my hotel to find a one-person show underway in the courtyard restaurant. The tables were full, the audience enraptured by a tragic tale of ennui, of lost love and disenchantment with city life. Clad in a pink-and-white traditional *traje de costura* (sewing dress), the performer was a **muxe** (MOO-sheh), a nonbinary gender fully accepted in the culture and society of El Istmo.

Most, but not necessarily all, *muxes* are homosexual men raised as females who follow the rigid gender norms that govern economic life in El Istmo. Much of the literature about *muxes* claims that they choose the identity themselves at an early age, but the choice is usually made by the parents, who assign the role to their firstborn son. *Muxes* are expected to care for their aging parents later in life. Many, but not all, consider the role to be a great honor. Others view it more as a burden than a privilege, a life they never asked for.

Still, the majority of *muxes* enjoy an esteemed social position in Istmeño society, and other big life choices are theirs to make, such as who to love and marry. Some *muxes* partner with men and play the female role in the household, while others marry women and raise children with them. It is not as common, but some women also take on this gender role reversal. Called *marimachas*, they take on traditionally male attributes and mannerisms in both social and private life, and are accepted in Istmeño society.

Hotel Santa Cruz (Carretera Transístmica, km 818, tel. 971/712-1326 and 971/712-0707, reservaciones@hotelsantacruzjuchitan.com), in Juchitán, encourages LGBT travelers and others interested in this unique practice to come to Juchitán and learn more about *muxe* culture. They offer packages that include accommodations and immersive cultural activities that provide fun learning opportunities. The experiences are organized by locals who know the culture and want to share it in a respectful (rather than exoticized or othering) manner.

FOOD

The ★ **Mercado Municipal 5 de Septiembre** (no phone, 8am-8pm daily), just to the east of Parque Benito Juárez, is where you'll find the tastiest food. From fresh produce and seafood to tacos to *garnachas*, the best of Juchitán's gastronomic offerings are here. The market was rebuilt after the 2017 quake; the new structure was inaugurated in April 2019.

Try a *coctel de mariscos* (seafood cocktail) at a little stall called **Mariscos Toñita** (5 de Septiembre 123, no phone, 9:30am-5:30pm daily, US$5). Toñita prepares her delicious cocktails differently than they're made elsewhere in the state, with more lime juice and less ketchup. Now, don't get confused—despite the market's name being Mercado Municipal 5 de Septiembre, it is not on the street called 5 de Septiembre, and this seafood stall is not in the market. The stall is six blocks north of the Parque Benito Juárez on Calle 5 de Septiembre, which runs along the park's west side.

You won't see a sign for **La Banqueta** (The Sidewalk; corner of 16 de Septiembre and Mariano Abasolo, no phone, 7:30pm-midnight daily, US$2.50-6); just look for the sidewalk rising four feet high from street level at the northwest corner of the intersection (don't worry—there are steps). In this unassuming family home, you'll find deliciously greasy *garnachas* and the unique local delicacy *pollo garnachero*, chicken fried in the *garnacha* oil, served with fried potatoes, tomatoes, and onions and topped with tangy pickled cabbage.

Due to its proximity to the fishing villages on the lagoons, Juchitán is renowned for its fish dishes, the best of which are at ★ **La Tequita** (Ruiz 181, no phone, 9am-5:30pm daily, US$7); the specialty is *pescado al horno* (oven-baked fish). The *palapa*-style (thatched hut-style) restaurant gets pretty lively at lunchtime, when folks chow down on fried sea bass (*robalo*) and *camarones a la diabla* (devilishly spicy shrimp). All meals come with a free appetizer of steamed crabs and *totopos*, fun corn tostadas with holes in them. The *aderezo* (dressing) is chipotle mayo, a staple with seafood in Oaxaca, but La Tequita does it best in Juchitán. The fruits of the sea are not considered a dinner meal in this part of the world, and seafood restaurants close even earlier here than on the coast. Be sure you get there for lunch at the latest.

ACCOMMODATIONS
Under US$25

Just down the street from the Parque Benito Juárez, **Hotel Central** (Gómez 30, tel. 971/712-2019, www.hotelcentral.com.mx, US$20 d, US$28 t) is your best budget option. All 18 rooms include air-conditioning, TVs, and Wi-Fi, and are spotlessly clean. Staff are friendly and helpful, and there are computers with Internet connections and printers in the lobby.

US$25-50

Hotel La Casona de Santa Cecilia (corner of Hidalgo and 2 de Abril, tel. 971/281-0871 and 971/281-0063, US$30 d) came out of the 2017 quake mostly unscathed, and the minor damage has been fixed. It's unfortunate that structural soundness has become a positive feature for hotels and other buildings here, but it's true. Beyond this, not much is special about the hotel, but the rooms are clean and comfy, with air-conditioning units, TVs, and private bathrooms.

Opened in late 2018, ★ **Hotel Santa Cruz** (Carretera Transístmica, km 818, tel. 971/712-1326 and 971/712-0707, reservaciones@hotelsantacruzjuchitan.com, US$40 d, breakfast included) is the most luxurious accommodations option in Juchitán. All rooms have air-conditioning units, TVs, private bathrooms, and coffee makers for that morning jolt. Aside from its sleek, minimalist four-star design, the hotel offers affordable all-inclusive packages that immerse guests in the raucous parties known as *velas*. The packages include

1: spicy crabs, *totopos,* and chipotle mayo at La Tequita in Juchitán **2:** a system of canals twisting through Santiago Laollaga **3:** decorations at a *vela* in El Istmo

traditional dresses for women; embroidery and Istmeño music demonstrations; a case of beer; round-trip travel from Oaxaca City, Huatulco, or the Ixtepec airport; and much more. Aside from being invited into someone's home during a *vela*, this is the best way to experience Juchitán's fiesta culture.

INFORMATION AND SERVICES

The **tourism office** (tel. 971/717-8898, 9am-6pm Mon.-Sat.) is in the recently reconstructed *palacio municipal* on the east side of the main square. Juchitán's tourism director, Tomás, is a friendly guy who is ready to help in any way he can.

For medical emergencies, head to **Clínica Hospital Sinaí** (16 de Septiembre 87, tel. 971/711-1342, 24 hrs daily), five blocks north of the main square. No English is spoken.

GETTING THERE

Bus

The **Terminal ADO** (16 de Septiembre, tel. 971/711-1022) connects Juchitán to Oaxaca City (US$14-18), a 5.5-hour trip. Buses coming and going between Oaxaca City and Tuxtla Gutiérrez, Chiapas, run all night long, so this is a good option for night bus travelers. Leave at midnight or later, and wake up in Juchitán. Buses from Oaxaca City leave from the main **ADO station** on Highway 190. ADO buses will also get you here from Tehuantepec (US$3.50, 30 minutes), Salina Cruz (US$2-5, 1.25 hrs), Huatulco (US$12-16, 4 hrs), and Puerto Escondido (US$20, 6.5 hrs). If you're continuing on to Chiapas, Tuxtla Gutiérrez (US$14-18) is about five hours away, and San Cristóbal de las Casas (US$24) is six hours away. Buses leave Juchitán for Chiapas seven times daily, beginning at midnight.

For traveling within the Istmo, it's cheaper and easier to take the local buses run by **Autotransportes Istmeños** (16 de Septiembre 5, tel. 971/711-4300), which leave from the corner of 16 de Septiembre and Callejón Angélica Pipi every five minutes or so. The trip to Tehuantepec takes a half hour

and costs about US$1.50. The fare to Salina Cruz, a little over an hour away, costs about US$2. Buses run 4:30am-10pm daily.

Air

The airport here is called the **Aeropuerto de Ciudad Ixtepec,** but it's actually closer to Juchitán. If you're coming from Oaxaca City, it'll be much, much cheaper to take the bus, but Aeromar has daily flights if you're in a hurry. It makes more sense to fly from Mexico City; the flight takes less than two hours and is usually pretty affordable (US$120-160) if you book early. Taxis from the airport to the Centro of Juchitán cost about US$14.

Car

From Tehuantepec, head north from the statue *La Tehuana* and stay on Highway 185. Juchitán is a straight shot 28 km (17 mi) across the tropical plain, about a half hour away from Tehuantepec.

GETTING AROUND

If your feet get too tired to carry you around town any longer, you'll have no problem hailing a *mototaxi* on the street. It shouldn't cost you more than US$1 to get anywhere you need to go in town.

★ SPRINGS NORTH OF JUCHITÁN

For such a small city, the streets of Juchitán can get pretty hectic, especially during celebrations (which is when you want to come). Luckily, a couple of natural springs north of Juchitán are great for a day trip to beat the heat and enjoy a moment away from the busy city.

Santiago Laollaga

A spring outside of **Santiago Laollaga** flows through a stream lined with spider-legged cypress trees to fill the local *balneario* (8am-8pm daily, US$0.50) in town, but the swimming pools are filled only occasionally; your best chance is on the weekends. Most days, the water is allowed to flow through the pools and into the creeks that run through town, where women wash clothes standing waist-deep in the crystal-clear water and children splash around alongside them. All this water allows some folks to have thick green lawns in their gardens, as well as hibiscus and bougainvillea bushes.

To get to the *balneario*, take Calle Oaxaca west until it terminates at Calle Raúl Enrique Palomec, where you'll take a left. At the bottom of the hill, turn right and follow the road beside the canal another 100 meters (328 ft) to the pools. If the *balneario* isn't full when you visit, you can take a *mototaxi* (US$0.50) to the *ojo de agua* (spring) outside of town. It's a small natural swimming hole that hasn't been developed into swimming pools, but there are a couple of *palapas* selling drinks and snack food. Do not confuse this *ojo de agua* with the one in Tlacotepec, about 15 minutes south of Laollaga. If you just say *ojo de agua*, your *mototaxi* driver will take you to the one here in Laollaga.

Laollaga isn't far from Juchitán, but you'll have to make a bus transfer in Ixtepec, about 40 minutes north. Take a bus run by **Omnibuses de Ixtepec** (US$1); these buses leave every few minutes or so from the north side of the three-way highway intersection (all roads are somehow Highway 185) in Juchitán, just north of the ADO bus station. Once in Ixtepec, get off at the second stop next to the railroad tracks, cross them, and walk two blocks up Calle Guadalupe Victoria to the corner with Isabel la Católica. White buses with a red stripe line up around this block, which has a white-and-yellow apartment complex with a green-and-white fence; the buses (US$1) leave every 15 minutes or so. Laollaga is another half hour's ride. To get back to Ixtepec,

take a *taxi colectivo* (US$1) from the main intersection in town, where there are signs for the *balneario* and *ojo de agua*.

Drivers take Highway 185 north from Juchitán, and in a little over a half hour (17 km/10.6 mi), you'll reach Ixtepec. Take a left on Calle Galeana, four blocks after crossing over the train tracks. Follow this through town for 1.25 km (0.8 mi) and turn right on Calle Cuauhtémoc. In 400 meters (0.2 mi), take a left onto Highway 49. Laollaga is 14 km (8.7 mi) down this highway. The whole 33-km (20-mi) trip takes about an hour.

Ojo de Agua de Tlacotepec

The much larger *balneario* at the **Ojo de Agua de Tlacotepec** (8am-8pm daily, US$0.75) is definitely worth the extra bit of transportation. Water just as clear as that in Laollaga fills the large pools and canals, teenagers plunge from the branches of the ficus trees by the water's edge, and mango and palm trees provide shade and tropical pizzazz. You can depend on this one, unlike the *balneario* in Laollaga, to be open every day, and there's a snack bar for those midday munchies.

To get here, take a *mototaxi* from Laollaga, an enjoyable jaunt through the countryside with green foothills in the distance. Arrange with your driver to come back in a couple hours to pick you up. The trip only takes about 15 minutes and will cost around US$2.50 round-trip.

If you drove from Juchitán, stop by Laollaga first. From the main intersection in town, take Avenida Tehuantepec south and follow it through cane fields and cornfields for 5.5 km (3.4 mi) to the Tlacotepec spring. You'll make it there in about 10 minutes, a little faster than in a *mototaxi*.

Salina Cruz and Vicinity

Oaxaca's third-largest city, Salina Cruz is home to a large oil refinery, and the air in town is more often than not permeated with the funk of crude oil. Despite the pollution, the beaches around Salina Cruz boast some of the best surfing on Mexico's Pacific coast. The locally owned surf camps provide the best accommodations options in the area, and their guides can show you where all the good waves are.

When you're not riding the waves, you can admire the otherworldly effect of the strong winds on the dunes—they blow the soft sand up and over the crests in ghost-like strands—and on the patches of rocks that look like they'd fit right in on Mars. However, if you're not a surfer and want to do some beach lounging, swimming, and exploring, any of the other destinations along the coast will suit you better.

History

The first inhabitants of Salina Cruz were of Chontal, Huave, and Zoque origin, and they were later displaced by Zapotecs and Mixtecs who expanded into the region beginning sometime around 1500 BC. Much of the archaeological evidence here and elsewhere in El Istmo shows signs of Olmec influence, as well. The inhabitants of Salina Cruz had been harvesting salt in the *salinas* (salterns) in the bay to the west of town for generations when Hernán Cortés arrived in this part of Oaxaca in 1527.

Various legends explain the name of the city. The most popular (and most likely) says that the Catholic missionaries sent here found, as they did in most places they went to proselytize, a population hostile to their presence and religion. In an attempt to fool the Zapotecs, they placed a *cruz* (cross) in the middle of a saltern and claimed it had miraculously appeared there when the sun rose. The ruse ultimately worked well enough for

the name to stick, but skepticism is evident in the legend—stories of magically appearing crosses elsewhere in Oaxaca seem to accept the supernatural at face value, but Salina Cruz's lore is the only one that includes the possibility of a reasonable explanation for the "miracle."

The salt wasn't Salina Cruz's only attraction for Cortés. The nearby beach he and the other Spaniards dubbed La Ventosa for its windy disposition was perfect for the shipyard he built there. Here the Spanish constructed the ships they used to explore the Pacific coast.

The port of Salina Cruz opened in 1872 at the behest of President Benito Juárez, who had made the official declaration the previous year. Later in the century, when the Ferrocarril Transístmico (Trans-Isthmus Railroad) was constructed, Salina Cruz was connected with Puerto Mexico (now Coatzacoalcos, Veracruz) on the Gulf of Mexico, and the town continued to grow in population and in importance to the Mexican economy.

In the 1970s, the national petroleum company Pemex built a large oil refinery in the bay to the west of town. The installation brought great economic prosperity, employing thousands of people. Unfortunately, the economic benefits have come with negative effects to the environment. In addition to air pollution, spills inevitably and regularly occur, taking a toll on the local sea turtle population and leaving large splotches of shiny black oil on the beaches.

Getting Oriented

The city of Salina Cruz is situated around the port, with the Centro built in a grid pattern to the north of the docks. Parque Independencia, the town's main square, is five blocks north and one block east of the port of entry. There are many restaurants, food stalls, convenience stores, banks, and other services around

Salina Cruz

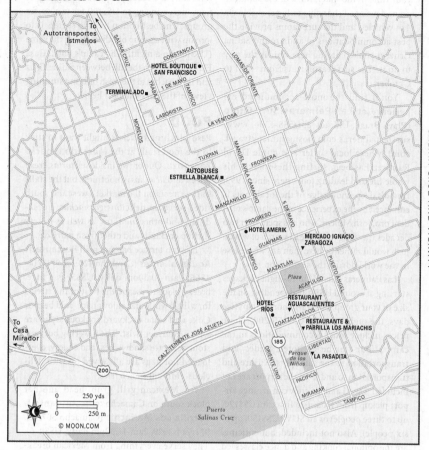

Parque Independencia, but it's unlikely you'll be spending much time in town. That's because Santa Cruz's main tourist attractions are the waves up and down the coast from here.

Playa La Ventosa is to the east of town, only 10-15 minutes away by taxi or bus, and offers good surfing. Two bays to the west offer more fun for surfers and swimmers (locals swim here, but I don't recommend it if there's oil on the beach). **Playa Las Escolleras** is a 5-km (3.1-mi) stretch of soft, windswept sand; the craggy point called **Punta Conejo** at its western end separates it from **Playa Brasil** and **Playa Azul**. The large **salterns** from

which Salina Cruz takes its name are just behind the beach at Playa Las Escolleras.

TOP EXPERIENCE

★ SURFING

The rugged coastline between Salina Cruz and Huatulco, 100 km (62 mi) to the west, is home to over two dozen surf spots, among which surfers of all skill sets will find the perfect wave to ride. From powerful point and beach breaks to jetty and other natural wedge waves, this stretch of coast is basically a buffet for surfers. A number of well-established surf camps offer all-inclusive tours that maximize your time in the water. Most of the spots are on undeveloped shoreline only accessible via 4x4 vehicles, and the surf camps provide the best accommodations in and around Salina Cruz; if you're coming here, this is the way to do it. The surf season runs from April to October.

You'll find the most accumulated experience at **Las Palmeras Surf Camp** (Playa Brasil, U.S. tel. 831/588-1306, www.surflaspalmeras.com, josh@mulcoytravel.com), where local surfer and guide David Ramírez has been surfing these waves his whole life and leading tours here since 1992. David's deep knowledge of the local spots is enhanced by the experience of the camp's resident pro, Josh Mulcoy, who has spent over two decades traveling the globe in search of waves. Josh would rather be here than anywhere else in the world during the surf season.

Las Palmeras offers 5- to 10-night packages starting at around US$900, depending on the size of your group. For stays shorter than five days, the nightly rate is US$175-200. These prices include food, accommodations in the camp's four-star beach hotel, guides, and transportation to the surf spots. Airfare and transportation to and from the airport are not included. David and his crew can arrange airport pickup from Huatulco in a car (US$120, up to three people) or an SUV (US$150, up to six people). Also not included, but enticing, are the optional cooking and dance classes led by camp manager and native of Tehuantepec Karla Gutiérrez.

Another well-respected and experienced camp is **Salina Cruz Surf Camp** (Calle Monte Bello, tel. 971/107-0918, U.S. tel. 714/916-9663, www.salinacruzsurfcamp.com, surfingmexico@me.com), where local surfer César Ramírez and his crew of guides have been taking both amateur and pro riders to the area's best spots since the camp opened in 2000. Like those offered by Las Palmeras, Salina Cruz Surf Camp tours include food, accommodations, and travel to and from surf spots. The nightly rate is slightly cheaper, but

here they have a five-night minimum. Nightly rates start at US$150 per person in a group of four, increasing up to US$190 for two-surfer groups. The best option for solo surfers is to join up with a group of others doing the same (US$160 pp a night). The camp's hotel, Casa El Mirador, is on the hill between Salina Cruz and the beaches to the west, offering stunning views of the bays and port below.

FOOD

Peso-pinching travelers might want to stick to the food stalls at the **Mercado Ignacio Zaragoza.** One or two inside sell *tortas,* fresh juices, and *licuados* (smoothies), but the stalls in the streets on the market's west and south sides serve up delicious *garnachas,* quesadillas, and other *antojitos,* as well as hearty shrimp cocktails and other fresh *mariscos.*

The fun terrace bar and grill **Restaurant Aguascalientes** (Camacho 420, tel. 971/714-3866, 9am-10:30pm daily, US$5) is a nice, breezy place to escape the heat of the streets for a little while and enjoy an ice-cold beer or Coke and some backyard cookout-style fare with a gourmet twist. The towering burgers, stout baguette sandwiches, and cheesy, overloaded hot dogs are all served up with delicious, thin-cut french fries.

For Mexican grill grub, head another block south on Camacho to **Restaurante & Parrilla Los Mariachis** (Camacho 507, tel. 971/714-3529, 7am-11:30pm daily, US$4-6). They serve everything from Mexican breakfast favorites like *chilaquiles* and *huevos rancheros* to tacos, *tortas, tlayudas, garnachas, pozole,* and more, but the specialty here is the *parrillada,* a colossal plate of grilled meat and veggies served with a mountain of tortillas. It's basically a mini taco buffet at your table. Bring your friends.

Since you're this close to the ocean, you'll most likely have a hankering for fried fish or some spicy shrimp. Satisfy the craving at ★ **La Pasadita** (Camacho 603, tel.

1: Playas Brasil and Azul, west of Salina Cruz
2: surfing Salina Cruz

971/714-2848, 7am-10pm daily, US$6), one more block south on Camacho. The large, breezy dining area has a casual, family-style feel, with the usual paintings of waterfalls and lilies hung on the avocado-colored walls. For something unique, try the bacon-wrapped crab cakes. They also have mountainous seafood *parrilladas*, hearty and flavorful seafood stews, and tangy ceviches and shrimp cocktails. Portions are large, so make sure to bring your appetite.

ACCOMMODATIONS

If you've come to Salina Cruz, you've most likely booked a trip with one of the camps, and if so, there is little need to come to town. Take precautions and be aware of your surroundings in town, as robberies and other crimes are not uncommon. These hotel options are more contingency plans than recommendations, as I do not recommend staying in Salina Cruz proper.

Under US$25

A block away from Parque Independencia, **Hotel Ríos** (Tampico 405, tel. 971/714-0337, US$11 s, US$13 d) is a roof over your head and little else, but it's got what counts. The very basic rooms, on three stories set around a small, sunny, unadorned courtyard, are weathered, but they're kept spick-and-span. What's more, they don't have the musty funk that is usual in hotels in this price range here. There is no Internet, TVs, or air-conditioning, and only cash is accepted.

US$25-50

The extra security and comfort are well worth the extra cost at **Hotel Amerik** (Progreso 24, tel. 971/720-2663, www.hotelamerik.mx, US$28 d, US$34 king bed), pronounced "America." The 22 comfortable rooms have TVs, air-conditioning, Internet access, and all that other good stuff Hotel Ríos doesn't mess with, but don't blindly trust the photos on their website. The hotel is not on the beach and does not have a swimming pool glistening in the sun. It does, however, have a great

restaurant, which comes in handy if you don't want to head out into the street.

Since I recommend staying in Salina Cruz proper only as a contingency plan, your best option is **Hotel Boutique San Francisco** (Camacho 705, tel. 971/714-0796 and 971/720-3052, US$38 d, US$46 king bed), up near the ADO station. Catering to traveling business folk, it has rooms comfortably decorated with dark-wood furnishings, as well as services like fast, dependable Wi-Fi, TVs, air-conditioning, safes, hair dryers, and more. It's an especially convenient option for those taking an ADO bus, as the station is two blocks away.

INFORMATION AND SERVICES

Should you require tourist information in town, head to the *auditorio municipal* (no phone, 9am-6pm Mon.-Fri.) at the corner of Avenida Tampico and Calle Pacífico. Ask the security guard to direct you to the tourism office when you enter.

The best emergency medical services in town are at the **Hospital General con Especialidades** (Camino a San Antonio Monterrey, tel. 971/281-3232, 24 hrs daily). It is 8 km (5 mi) north of town, up Highway 185. Take a right at the Nissan dealership, and you'll see the hospital about 400 meters (0.2 mi) down the road on your left. Taxis in town should know how to get here, but if not, tell the driver about the Nissan dealership. No English is spoken.

GETTING THERE
Bus

For travel within El Istmo, the cheapest option is a bus run by **Autotransportes Istmeños** (Avenida Tampico, tel. 971/711-1751). Their base is north of the Centro, on Avenida Tampico, just before the road meets up with the highway. There is an Oxxo convenience store next to it. A cab from the center of town will cost you about US$1.50. These buses charge a little over US$1 to Tehuantepec (30 minutes), and a little over US$2 to Juchitán (1 hr). Buses leave every 15-20 minutes.

If you're headed elsewhere in Oaxaca or Mexico, take a bus from the **Terminal ADO** (Primero de Mayo 32, tel. 971/714-1441). Buses to Oaxaca City (US$11-18, 5.5 hrs) leave daily and nightly every 3-5 hours. Buses leave even more frequently for destinations along the coast. Huatulco (US$12) is a little under three hours away, and Puerto Escondido (US$18) is about 5.5 hours away. If you're going to Puerto Ángel or one of the neighboring beaches, you'll have to take a bus to Pochutla (US$14), which takes about four hours, and get to the beach from there.

ADO buses will also get you to Chiapas. Tuxtla Gutiérrez (US$16-21) is about six hours from Salina Cruz, and the trip to San Cristóbal de las Casas (US$28) takes 7-8 hours. These routes also make stops in Tehuantepec (US$3, 30 minutes) and Juchitán (US$5, 1 hr), but the extra comfort makes the trip more expensive than the bouncier, hotter Autotransportes Istmeños buses.

Slightly cheaper and with similar schedules (sometimes exactly the same as ADO) are the **Autobuses Estrella Blanca,** whose station is on the corner of Tampico and Frontera. ADO buses are generally more comfortable (and often smell better), but if a price or schedule doesn't work for you, check with Estrella Blanca.

Car

Both highways that lead to Salina Cruz are in very good condition. If you're driving from Oaxaca City, take Highway 190 to Tehuantepec, turn south on Highway 185, and continue for another half hour or so to town. The 266-km (165-mi) drive takes about five hours total. From anywhere along the coast, take Highway 200 (which locals refer to as *la costera*) east to reach Salina Cruz.

Salina Cruz is 254 km (160 mi) from Puerto Escondido, a four-hour drive. Between Puerto Escondido and Pochutla, Highway 200 is mostly straight, cutting through coastal plains full of papaya and pineapple fields. Between Pochutla and Huatulco, the rough foothills of the Sierra Madre del Sur run all the way to

the sea, making the road very curvy. These foothills continue east of Huatulco for a while. The hills then begin to give way to more extensive coastal plains, creating bays bounded by rocky points that crinkle the highway again, in between long, straight stretches of road.

GETTING AROUND

With the heat, the odor, and safety concerns, it's best to take a taxi for any distances longer than four or five blocks, especially at night. Take taxis to any of the bus stations from the Centro.

PLAYA LA VENTOSA

The winds of **Playa La Ventosa** (Windy Beach) promised adventure when Cortés ordered his shipyard to be built here. As he expected, those winds took his vessels far up and down the Pacific coast. These days, those winds promise adventure for kite surfers looking to catch some air. The gusty conditions are caused by the Venturi effect, the same amplifying effect that occurs between two buildings on a windy day. The mountains on either side of El Istmo funnel the strong Atlantic winds from the north, increasing their speed on their way out over the Pacific. Most of the year, wind speeds here average 20 to 35 knots (23-40 mph), but they calm down a little bit between August and October.

Sights and Recreation

Atop the rocky southern point of the bay, a modern lighthouse stands next to the **Faro de Cortés** (Lighthouse of Cortés). It was constructed at the conquistador's behest in 1529 and remained in use until 1596. Aside from taking in a bit of Mexican history, the easy, 30-minute hike up to the lighthouse offers stunning views of the bay and open ocean.

If you're looking to **kite surf,** you'll have to bring your own equipment. At the time of this writing, no one local had decided to take advantage of this type of tourism here or elsewhere in Salina Cruz. (The beach at Punta Conejo, to the west of town, also seems gusty

322

enough to fill a kitesurfing sail; bring your own equipment.)

Unfortunately, when something goes wrong at the refinery, La Ventosa suffers from the same petroleum pollution as the beaches to the west of Salina Cruz.

Getting There and Away

Playa La Ventosa is 6 km (3.7 mi) east of Salina Cruz. Get to La Ventosa in a taxi for about

US$5, or take one of the buses that read "La Ventosa" from Avenida Tampico, where it turns to an east-west street by the container docks. Drivers head east on Tampico and take a left at the fork, remaining on the main road—it changes names to Bahía La Ventosa. The beach is another 10 minutes or so along this road, which climbs up and over the hill between Salina Cruz and La Ventosa and past the refinery.

Background

The Landscape

Oaxaca's rich, vibrant culture has as much to do with the rugged landscape as it does with the people living on it. The rim of mountains surrounding the Valles Centrales has made access to certain areas difficult for centuries, creating pockets of isolation in which human life developed into traditions, recipes, and languages wholly unique from anywhere else in the world. It wasn't until the latter half of the 20th century that highways and other modern development began to connect Oaxaca's more out-of-the-way places with each other and the rest of Mexico.

The bright, broad color spectrum of Oaxaca's traditions comes as no surprise when considering the fireworks-colored earth of La Mixteca, the brilliant blooms of the orchids in the Sierra Mazateca, the pinks and greens in the limestone bricks of the old churches, and the indigo plant, cochineal insects, pomegranate rinds, pecan shells, mosses, and other sources of natural dyes. Oaxacans are deeply rooted in the land they call home, and everything from ecotourism to parties to clothes to the food on the table to the toponym itself is a reflection of that link with this diverse and fertile part of Mexico.

GEOGRAPHY

At 93,757 square km (36,200 sq mi), Oaxaca is the fifth-largest state in Mexico. The rugged ranges that hem in the Valles Centrales are the southernmost curves of the two great chains in Mexico, the Sierra Madre Oriental and the Sierra Madre Occidental, which stretch over a thousand miles to the north, all the way to the border with the United States.

In Oaxaca, these mountains are referred to as the Sierra Madre de Oaxaca, in the north (or, more casually, the Sierra Norte or Sierra Juárez), and the Sierra Madre del Sur, in the south. Together they constitute 36 percent of the state's landmass and boast 20 summits higher than 3,000 meters (9,843 ft).

Inside this nest of craggy peaks, Oaxaca City and the surrounding Valles Centrales have an average elevation of 1,500 meters (4,921 ft). To the west, La Mixteca ranges 1,200-2,300 meters (3,937-7,546 ft) above sea level, dividing it nominally into the High Mixteca (La Mixteca Alta) and the Low Mixteca (La Mixteca Baja).

To the north of La Mixteca, the canyon country called La Cañada abuts the foothills of the western part of the Sierra Norte, known regionally as the Sierra Mazateca for the people who have called it home for generations. Peaks here don't get as high as in the Sierra Juárez and Sierra Mixe (also named for the local indigenous people) to the east, but these mountains are just as rough and rich in biodiversity.

The lofty heights of the Sierra Norte give way to the broad, tropical lowlands of Oaxaca's northernmost region named after Oaxaca's largest river, El Papaloapan. Average altitudes here are only 10-20 meters (33-66 ft) above sea level. Oaxaca's easternmost region, El Istmo de Tehuantepec, is also mostly tropical lowlands and short, squat hills.

Most of Oaxaca's Pacific Coast is rough and rocky, as the Sierra Madre del Sur lines the vast majority of it, in some places tumbling all the way into the sea. The Sierra Madre del Sur is home to the Cerro Nube (Cloud Peak), Oaxaca's highest, and the tallest non-volcanic summit in Mexico, with an altitude of 3,750 meters (12,303 ft) above sea level.

CLIMATE

Although over half of Oaxaca's landmass has a hot, tropical humid or subhumid climate, the mountains and seasonal rains keep average temperatures within moderate ranges. This rough terrain creates a number of different climate zones. Nearly half of Oaxaca is a hot, subhumid climate zone, which is found on the coast and in El Istmo to the east. Seasonal rains averaging 79-99 cm (31-39 in) annually turn the hills green May-October, but by January the lack of moisture turns them brown until April. Average temperatures here range 22-35°C (72-95°F) year-round. Just about any day of the year, you can expect temperatures on the coast to climb into the 90s by mid-afternoon.

The tropical region of El Papaloapan, in the north of the state, receives an average of 206 cm (81 in) of rain during the same months. Average temperatures range from 21.5°C (71°F) in January to 28.5°C (83°F) in May. Temperatures can get into the 90s here in the hot months, but highs usually range

---

in the 80s. The humidity might make it feel warmer, though.

In Oaxaca City and the Valles Centrales, you'll find a hot, semiarid climate where average temperatures range from 17.5°C (64°F) in January to 23°C (73°F) in May. Highs in the hot months get into the upper 80s. The rainy season here is also April or May-October, but these desert areas only receive about 68.5 cm (27 in) of rain per year.

Don't let all this heat fool you, though. If you plan on staying up in the higher altitudes of the mountains, you'll need to plan for colder, often wetter weather. In Cuajimoloyas and other towns at and above 3,000 meters (9,843 ft), the lows average 8-12°C (46-54°F) throughout the year, and in the winter months it can even freeze at night. Still, when the sun is out, it gets hot up here. Average highs run 20-25°C (68-77°F) in April and May, and it can get as hot as 28°C (82°F) at the hottest time of day.

ENVIRONMENTAL ISSUES

The main environmental problem Oaxaca faces is pollution due to industry, agriculture, and government corruption. Salina Cruz is home to one of Mexico's biggest oil refineries, which has negatively affected the local environment and wildlife, with numerous oil spills taking a toll on the sea turtle population.

Although lots of Oaxaca may seem empty, the reality in many areas is that human activity has had a negative effect on the environment. Much natural vegetation has been lost to agriculture and animal husbandry. Many subsistence farmers in Oaxaca still practice slash-and-burn agriculture, which often gets out of control and leads to destructive wildfires.

Fires started to burn trash have also contributed to deforestation, but that practice's main effect is on the air quality. Data released by the National Institute for Statistics and Geography (INEGI) in 2017 indicated that 73 percent of Oaxacan municipalities burn somewhere between 30 and 100 percent of their garbage. This is a result of the destructive and unfortunately almost ubiquitous government corruption here and elsewhere in Mexico.

Plants and Animals

Oaxaca is partly to thank for Mexico ranking among the 17 countries designated by Conservation International (CI) as megadiverse. With 707 species, Mexico tops the world list of reptilian biodiversity. The country also boasts 438 mammalian species (second on the list), 290 amphibian species (fourth), and 26,000 different species of flowers, the fourth highest on the floral diversity list.

Unfortunately, Mexico could someday be kicked out of its privileged place in the biological categorization of countries. The aforementioned lists aren't the only ones Mexico tends to rank highly in. In the 2000s, it has regularly appeared in the top five countries with the fastest rates of deforestation in the world.

VEGETATION ZONES
Semiarid Scrub

Visitors to Oaxaca City and the Valles Centrales will be familiar with this type of vegetation zone. The Valle de Tehuacán-Cuicatlán, in La Cañada, also has this type of ecosystem. Found at altitudes between 1,400 and 1,700 meters (4,595-5,575 ft) above sea level, the mountains that hem in these deserts keep out the majority of the wet air from the Gulf of Mexico to the north and the Pacific Ocean to the south. These parts of Oaxaca average only about 33 cm (13 in) of rain annually.

Trees here tend to be short scrubs, such as the **guaje** (*Leucaena leucocephala*), from which Oaxaca derives its name. The little seeds are edible, and you might be served a pod of them with a *tlayuda* or plate of tacos. Taller trees here include jacarandas (*Jacaranda mimosifolia*), which fill with lilac-colored blooms at the beginning of spring, and Montezuma cypress (*Taxodium mucronatum*), which prefer the wet earth of riverbanks and creek beds. Although the monumental Árbol del Tule is no longer close to a body of water, it started out next to a great lake that filled parts of the Valles Centrales when it sprouted over 2,000 years ago. In Oaxaca, people call this cypress *sabino* or *ahuehuete*.

The plantlife that dominates this ecosystem by far is shrubs, grasses, and succulents. Morning glory plants are common in this ecosystem. Of the 10 species that grow here, one of the most common is the *cazahuate* (*Ipomoea paucifora*), which spreads its fetching white blooms in November and December.

Cactuses that thrive here include the emblematic nopal (*Opuntia ficus-indica*), various parts of which are staples in the Mexican diet. The broad, flat leaves are eaten grilled on tacos, fried with eggs, beef, or other ingredients, or fresh in chunky salsas that the cactus turns slimy and a little sweet. The super-sweet prickly pears, called *tuna* in Spanish, range from green to yellow to red to a deep wine purple, and are eaten fresh or used to make *aguas de sabor* (fruit drinks). Like great, green candelabra towering as high as 7 meters (23 ft) over the critters on the desert floor, the *garambullo blanco* (*Myrtillocactus schenckii*) is also common in this vegetation zone, especially in the Valle de Tehuacán-Cuicatlán. This valley is also home to one of the highest concentrations of ceroid, or columnar cactus (of the *Pachycereus* genus), in the world.

Other non-cactus succulents common here include various types of yucca, such as Joshua trees (*Yucca brevifolia*) and *Yucca mixtecana*, but the Valles Centrales are known for having the perfect conditions for a variety of agave species, called maguey here in Oaxaca. Many of these species are used to make mezcal.

Pine-Oak Forest

The majority of forested land in Oaxaca is covered in lush pine-oak forests, which you'll find in both the Sierra Norte and Sierra Sur at altitudes starting around 2,000 meters (6,562 ft). Oaks prefer lower, drier elevations, and gradually mix with pines as the altitude rises. By the time you get to 3,000 meters (9,843 ft) above sea level, it's too cold for the oaks, and pines and sacred firs (*Abies religiosa*), here called *oyamel*, cover the slopes. Much of these forests are considered cloud forests, as giant clouds often sweep in and shroud the peaks in a dense fog.

The mountains of Oaxaca are home to more than 10 species of pine, the more common of which are Mexican white pine, Chiapas white pine, and Montezuma pine. The most common oak tree is the yellow oak, but you'll also see the netleaf oak. The latter is sometimes called *encino chicharron* (pork rind oak), as some locals see a similarity between its leaves and the crunchy pigskin snacks Mexicans love so much.

In many parts of Oaxaca's pine-oak forests, especially in the Sierra Norte, oaks are often covered in a number of other plants, such as mosses, ferns, agaves, bromeliads, orchids, and other various wildflowers. Spend enough time in these forests and you'll hear them falling from branches they grow too big for. Ixtlán de Juárez is a good place to go to see these kinds of plants. The oaks of the *bosque mesófilo* (mesophyll, or cloud forest) west of the city are usually shrouded in mist, and their branches are covered with spectral mosses. North of the Parque Ecoturixtlán, the *bosque de bromelias* (bromeliad forest) is likewise full of bromeliads and other epiphytes. The Sierra Mazateca, in the northwest of the state, has the perfect conditions for various species of orchids to bloom at the same time.

Tropical Deciduous Forest

These color-changing tropical forests of primarily short trees and scrubs cover the foothills along the coast, as well as parts of El

The Maguey Plant: Emblem of Oaxaca

The importance of the maguey plant to Oaxacan people can be summed up in the common adage *"Para todo mal, un mezcal, para todo bien, también"* (For all the bad, mezcal, and for all the good, as well). This succulent, generally called agave elsewhere in Mexico, is vital to the Oaxacan cultural identity and livelihood.

Aside from alcoholic drinks (mezcal isn't the only one), maguey plants have been used here for thousands of years to create various necessities. The fibers of the plant, called ixtle, come with their own needle, and can be used to make cords, ropes, bags, hammocks, paper, and more. Some people place a pair of maguey leaf points in the form of a cross in the earthen oven before they cook *barbacoa* as a way to ward off malign spirits. In the mountains, farmers use a species that grows up to 2.5 meters (8.2 ft) as fences to delineate the boundaries of their fields.

the maguey, one of the most important plants to Oaxacans

Less popular than mezcal, the alcoholic beverage *pulque* is also made from certain types of maguey. This is made by fermenting the sap of the maguey heart, which is called *aguamiel* (honey water), collected by boring a hole in the *piña* (heart) and collecting it in a gourd. The *aguamiel* can also be drunk. It is very sweet and does not contain alcohol.

Despite these various uses, say the word "maguey" to a Oaxacan, and you can bet that the first thing that comes to mind is mezcal. Types of mezcals depend on the species of maguey used to make them. The most common type is made from the *espadín* maguey (*Agave angustifolia*), with swordlike, hazy-blue leaves. One called *cuishe, madre cuish,* or *tobaziche* is made from an endemic species to Oaxaca called *Agave karwinskii*. This one grows in long, skinny stalks, yielding more tubular *piñas* than its cousins that stay closer to the ground. Tobalá (*Agave potatorum*), a wild species common around Sola de Vega, is another in-demand type for mezcal. Popularity in the 1980s and 1990s took a heavy toll on the populations of this wild species, and farmers began to look for ways to cultivate it. The cultivated plant is now common in mezcal-producing towns. Other types of maguey commonly used for mezcal include *coyote* (*Agave americana*), *arroqueño* (*Agave americana oaxacensis*), *jabalí* (*Agave convallis*), and *tepextate* or *tepextate* (*Agave marmorata*).

To this day, botanists continue to discover new species of maguey in Oaxaca. Scientists in the Institute of Biology at the National Autonomous University of Mexico (UNAM) found four new species in 2017, bringing the total for the 35 years preceding 2018 to 44 previously undiscovered species.

Istmo. They'll be burning a brilliant green if you visit during the rainy season, but come January, that vivacious luster will have faded to brown until the rains come back. But just because the green is gone doesn't mean things look dreary. The **bougainvilleas,** *flor de mayo,* **passion flowers,** and other vibrant blossoms keep the place colorful year-round.

The more common scrub trees in these forests are *rosa amarilla,* **Pacific Coast mahogany,** and **Mexican plumeria,** or, as it is more commonly called here, *flor de mayo* (May flower). The taller trees with trunks covered in large thorns and what looks more like green skin than bark are called *pochotes* here in Oaxaca, in English known as the **silk cotton** or **Kapok trees.** The Aztecs named **Pochutla,** just north of Puerto Ángel, "place of the *pochotes.*"

Savanna and Mangrove Forests

Along much of the coast, the rocky, forested foothills of the Sierra Madre del Sur tumble straight into the sea, but in some places between the hills, you can find broad, flat grasslands speckled with palm trees. These savannas are mostly found around the Lagunas de Chacahua and in between Huatulco and Salina Cruz, where the mountains become much sparser. This is one of Oaxaca's ecosystems on which agriculture has taken its toll, as much has been converted to fields or grazing pastures.

Common palms here include many types of **fan palms,** with broad fan-shaped leaves, and of course an array of **coconut palm** species. These types of trees are some of the most useful in the state. The fruit is eaten, the trunks and leaves are used to build all the *palapas* on the beaches, and mats, baskets, hats, and a laundry list of other useful items are produced with materials from palms.

Around the Lagunas de Chacahua and La Ventanilla you'll find mangrove swamps. The two most common mangrove trees here are the **red mangrove** and **white mangrove.**

Tropical Evergreen Forest

Highway 175, which squiggles its way through the Sierra Norte from Oaxaca City to Tuxtepec, gets a bit tricky about half an hour before you reach Valle Nacional. Once it dips below 1,500 meters (4,921 ft) above sea level, the forest is wet enough, either by rain or being enveloped in thick fog, for plants to sport healthy green leaves year-round. Not only are the curves tight, there's a good chance rain has made the road slick and limited visibility, and entire slopes like green waterfalls of gigantic ferns are so impressive as to be a potentially dangerous distraction.

These **tree ferns** thrive in the tropical evergreen forests that blanket the northern slopes of the Sierra Norte, growing up to 6 meters (20 ft) or taller. Their leaf stalks grow up to 1.2 meters long (4 ft) and 0.9 meter wide

(3 ft), and the new fronds slowly uncurl from the top like thick, hairy tails.

The **rubber tree,** called *palo de hule* (rubber stick) in these parts, is among the taller trees here, growing up to 50 meters (164 ft) tall. **Coffee trees** thrive in this environment too. And growing on all the trees are thick vines and the holey-leafed climber plant **ceriman,** or as it's called around here, *piñanona.* It has a marvelous scientific name: *Monstera deliciosa.*

Also growing on lots of trees in this forest is a species of the very alien-like **strangler fig,** which sprouts from a notch in another tree and slowly grows around it, eventually killing it and taking the place it once held in the earth. Another type of **fig tree** common here, called *amate,* has thick, twisted, tendon-like roots dug into the ground.

Flowers in these forests are equally as otherworldly. The famed **bird of paradise** grows here. There are also lots of species of **heliconia** in these forests, whose flowers resemble those of the bird of paradise, but grow in strings of alternating blooms that get so heavy they fall over and hang from the plant like the tail of a creature born of imagination.

Tropical Rainforest

The lowlands to the north of the Sierra Norte are covered in dense tropical rainforest. The abundant rain, high humidity, and warm temperatures here make plantlife extremely competitive, making it difficult to pick out a type of tree that dominates, such as the pines and oaks in the higher altitudes. A number of **fig** species thrive here, as well as **mahogany** trees. Also important to this type of ecosystem are **sapodillas,** which bear the fruit *zapote,* and their cousin in the genus, *Manilkara chicle,* which bears a natural chewing gum called *chicle.*

A number of other fruit-bearing trees also thrive here, such as **mango, banana, papaya,** and **coconut palms,** and lots of land is used in the cultivation of these fruits. Other cultivated plants here include **rubber trees, sugarcane,** and **pineapples.**

The tropical rainforest is so important to Oaxacans (and the rest of us) because this is the favorite rooting grounds of the **cacao tree.** Smaller than the figs and mahoganies, the cacao trees are found beneath the canopy with their branches full of yellow pods about 25 cm (10 in) long, which are full of the beans from which chocolate is produced. "Father of modern taxonomy" Carl Linnaeus (1707-1778) liked chocolate so much, the nomenclature he gave it means "food of the gods." The rest of us ended up calling it what the Aztecs called it, more or less. Their word for chocolate, *xocolatl,* means "bitter water." So we can all be thankful for the tropical rainforests of Oaxaca and elsewhere in southern Mexico. Without them, we'd have no candy bars.

BIRDS

Birds are the most common type of wildlife you'll see in Oaxaca, and there are a lot to see. With 741 known species in the state, Oaxaca is home to two-thirds of the country's bird species. Some to look out for in the Valles Centrales are the **vermillion flycatcher, gray-breasted woodpecker,** and **ocellated thrasher.** Birds like the **bridled sparrow, Oaxaca sparrow,** and **white-throated towhee** forage for food among the cacti and shrubs of the desert.

The pine-oak forests of the mountains are home to **mockingbirds, red warblers, mountain trogons,** and various types of **hummingbirds.** Populations of the **dwarf jay,** found only in the state of Oaxaca, are low enough to almost put them on the endangered species list.

Hundreds of bird species call the tropical deciduous forests of the Sierra Sur foothills and Pacific Coast home. Some that stand out are the **golden-cheeked woodpecker, orange-breasted bunting, russet-crowned motmot,** and **white-throated magpie-jay.** Bird-watching is a popular tourist activity on the coast.

A wide array of colorful and unusual birds inhabit the tropical evergreen forests and tropical rainforests of the Sierra Norte and El Papaloapan. In the evergreen forest, you'll see and hear the **white-winged tanager, gartered trogon, Lesson's marmot, band-backed wren, red-legged honeycreeper, emerald-chinned hummingbird,** and many, many more. Among the hundreds of species known to live in the Oaxacan rainforest, some rather spectacular ones include the **olive-throated parakeet, keel-billed toucan, red-throated ant tanager,** and **Amazon kingfisher.**

Parrots, Parakeets, and Macaws

You'll mostly find parrots and macaws along the pacific coast. They enjoy the subhumid foothills of the Sierra Sur. They also like parts of the Sierra Norte, and a large population of green **military macaws** inhabits the Cañón del Sabino, in the Valle de Tehuacán-Cuicatlán in the northwest of the state. Parakeets, part of the same family as parrots, are also very common in Oaxaca. The **olive-throated parakeet** is found in the northern slopes of the Sierra Norte and the tropical lowlands beyond. **Green** and **Pacific parakeets** are abundant in the coastal regions, and many people have them as pets, despite laws that prohibit the practice. **The orange-fronted parakeet, white-fronted parrot,** and **yellow-headed parrot** are also common in this region.

Seabirds

Oaxaca's Pacific Coast is an ornithologist's utopia. The Lagunas de Manialtepec and Chacahua are the best places to go bird-watching in this region. They are home, either temporarily or permanently, to dozens of species, including fantastic-looking birds like the **roseatte spoonbill, blue heron,** and **yellow-crowned night heron.** Other birds that either live here or stop by on their migrations are **American white pelicans, brown pelicans, royal terns, wood storks, tricolored herons, bare-throated tiger herons, red-billed tropicbirds, brown boobies,** and many, many more.

The Lagunas de Manialtepec and Chacahua are huge avian migration stopovers, where these types of birds are so numerous that you'll likely see normally solitary ones like cranes and herons actually hanging out in groups.

REPTILES AND AMPHIBIANS

While Mexico tops the worldwide list of diversity of reptile and amphibian species, Oaxaca tops the nationwide list. Mexican scientists have identified at least 245 reptilian species and 133 amphibian species in the state.

The dry Valles Centrales region isn't the best place for amphibians, but it is perfect for the over 60 species of reptiles that call it home. Take a hike through the Valle de Tlacolula, and you're most likely to see lizards like **Sack's giant whiptail lizard** and the **eastern spiny lizard.** You might see a snake, but your chances are much less likely. The **Oaxacan coral snake** is endemic to this region. Amphibians do live here, though. The **Mexican tree frog, southern highland tree frog,** and **giant toad** are a few of the species that like the foothills and wetter areas.

On a hike through the pine-oak forests of the mountains, you might see an **emerald spiny lizard** or a **southern crevice spiny lizard.** You probably won't, but if you do see the Oaxacan subspecies of the **pygmy rattlesnake,** steer clear. Like all rattlesnakes, they're poisonous, but unlike other rattlesnakes, they aren't as inclined to give you a warning before they bite. Near streams, you might see a **shiny peeping frog** or a **Cochran's false brook salamander.**

In the forests on the Pacific Coast, check the trees for **green iguanas** and the rocks for **spiny-tailed iguanas.** These forests are also home to the **brown basilisk lizard,** which uses its webbed feet to run across the surface of water. The lagoons at Chacahua and La Ventanilla are home to **caimans** and **swamp** and **river crocodiles.** In the rainy season, **Mexican giant tree frogs** hop down

from the branches to breed in ponds and still pools. You might also see a **marbled toad.**

The brown basilisk also walks on water in the higher-elevation tropical evergreen forest, and the **red coffee snake, Mexican jumping pit viper,** and **greater scaly anole** call this type of forest home as well. Down in the rainforest, dozens of lizard species thrive, as well as the **Central American crocodile** and the **Central American boa.** The classic lime-green **red-eyed tree frog** lives down here, too. The **Mexican burrowing caecilian,** an amphibian that looks like an overgrown earthworm, burrows under the plant debris of the jungle floor.

SEA LIFE
Fish

The waters of the Pacific Coast of Oaxaca are equally rich in fish species. At the dinner table, you'll see *huachinango* (red snapper), *róbalo* (sea bass), *pez vela* (sailfish), *lisa* (mullet), *atún amarilla* (yellowfin tuna), *dorado* (dolphin fish), and **marlin** (pronounced mar-LEEN in Spanish). Other fish that swim these waters include **angelfish, bonito, barracuda, stingrays, swordfish, triggerfish, spadefish, yellowtail, parrotfish, mackerel, pufferfish,** and many more.

More than a few species of *tiburón* (shark) like to call these waters home, but don't worry. They are not known to attack humans. These include the **angel shark, scalloped hammerhead shark, whitetip shark,** and **blacktip shark.**

Sea Turtles

Four of the world's seven sea turtle species come to the Oaxacan coast to lay their eggs. The most abundant is the **olive ridley** (*golfina*), whose favorite nesting beach in the world by far is La Escobilla in Puerto Escondido. Thousands of them crawl up the

1: white mangrove trees in the Lagunas de Chacahua **2:** brown pelicans in Puerto Escondido **3:** one of the many species of bromeliad that thrive in the Sierra Norte **4:** a crocodile in La Ventanilla

beach June-September to lay eggs, a spectacular event the locals call the *arribazón* (great arrival). This is how La Escobilla earned the nickname Playa Tortuguera (Turtle Beach).

Green sea turtles (*tortuga verde* or *blanca*) and **hawksbills** (*tortuga carey*) also come here to nest, as well as the gigantic **leatherbacks** (*tortuga laud,* also called *garapacho* and *machincuepo* in some areas), which can reach a length of 2.5 meters (8.2 ft). Other popular nesting sites along the coast include Mazunte, La Ventanilla, and Playa Morro Ayuta, near San Pedro Hamelula. The name Mazunte is actually derived from a Nahuatl word meaning "Please lay eggs!"

Despite their endangered status, sea turtles are so abundant on the Oaxacan coast that you may not have to go looking for them to find one. (Once, on the way back to my *cabaña* after a late-night dip in Mazunte, I serendipitously crossed paths with a huge leatherback mom diligently digging a hole in the sand with her platter-sized flippers.) Only what is considered subsistence foraging or fishing for sea turtles or their eggs is allowed in Mexico. Commercial fishing has been outlawed since 1990. Unfortunately, poaching is still common, but organizations along the coast, such as the Centro Mexicano de la Tortuga (National Mexican Turtle Center) in Mazunte work to conserve the habitats and nesting grounds they have been using for millions of years.

INSECTS AND ARACHNIDS

There are lots of creepy crawlers in Oaxaca. Insects run the gamut from houseflies to mosquitoes to tropical and exotic species like **rhinoceros beetles** and **footlong stick-bugs.** Chiapas has the highest rate of **butterfly** biodiversity in Mexico, but Oaxaca, especially in the Sierra Madre del Sur, has the highest number of endemic species, such as the *mariposa esperanza Oaxaqueña* (Oaxacan hope butterfly). The cute little yellow ones that are regular companions on hikes through the pine-oak forests are called **cloudless sulfur butterflies** (*mariposa azufre*). Some rather spectacular-looking ones to keep an eye out for are the kites, such as the **Mexican kite swallowtail,** or as it's called here, *cometa cebra* (zebra kite), with white and sky-blue wings with black stripes and pointy, tail-like wingtips.

One of the most common spiders you'll see in Oaxaca are **wolf spiders.** (Since wolf spiders and tarantulas are both hairy, people call them both *tarántulas*.) If you don't want to know exactly how numerous these guys are, don't wear a headlamp at night in the forests along the coast. Also common here are spiders of the *Selenops* genus. These flat, crab-looking spiders were the first in which scientists observed the ability to glide and somewhat steer themselves when falling in order to land on branches. They like the dry desert and foothills of the Valles Centrales. Other common desert spiders here include **black widows** (check your shoes) and the aforementioned **tarantulas,** which can grow to be bigger than your hand. If you don't want to see firsthand just how big spiders can get in Oaxaca, do not enter the Cueva de la Serpiente Oscuro (Cave of the Dark Serpent) in Apoala. Some of the stranger species here include **spined micrathena** (*araña espinosa*), which has a bulbous, oversized abdomen with ten spines, and the **golden orb-weavers** (*araña seda dorada*), whose silk has a yellow pigment that shines gold in the right light. They like arid regions as well.

MAMMALS

The richest areas of mammal biodiversity are the Sierra Norte, followed by El Istmo and the Sierra Sur. Human activity such as agriculture, logging, and development have encroached on the natural habitats of mammals, and they have learned to avoid us. Aside from **squirrels, rabbits, bats,** and the possible **deer,** there is little chance you'll be able to observe very many mammals in the wild in Oaxaca.

Pumas, Jaguars, and *El Tigrillo*

You may not see the **pumas, jaguars, ocelots, lynxes,** and other wild cats when hiking through the mountains, but you can bet they see you. These cats are masters at stealth, and will almost always avoid you altogether.

The *tigrillo,* a smaller wildcat native to forests from here to Brazil, has spotted fur similar to that of a jaguar. The **jaguarundi** is another small wildcat endemic to Mexico and Central and South America, with monotone gray, red, or black fur. The *tigrillo* is considered a vulnerable species, but populations of jaguarundis in the Amazon Basin are large enough for the species to not worry conservationists.

Monkeys

What would a jungle be without monkeys? The tropical rainforest of El Papaloapan is home to the **black-handed spider monkey,** one of the largest monkey species in the Americas. Spider monkeys have prehensile tails and hooked fingers that they use to swing from branch to branch with ease. As more and more of El Papaloapan gets claimed for human use, the less room there is for the spider monkeys. The species is considered endangered.

Black howler monkeys are sometimes spotted in the rainforests of El Papaloapan, but they tend to mostly hang out in those in the states of Veracruz and Tabasco, closer to the Gulf Coast. Unlike their neighbors the spider monkeys, howler populations are large enough for them not to appear on the endangered species list.

Armadillos, *Tamandúas,* Coatis, and *Cacomixtles*

Armadillos are common in many parts of Oaxaca. Of the 20 armadillo species in the Americas, the **nine-banded armadillo,** found in Oaxaca and elsewhere in Mexico, is the only species whose populations are on the rise. It is one of only two species that lives outside of South America. Armadillo is a part of the traditional diet in El Istmo. One of its cousins, the anteaters called *tamandúas,* also live in Oaxaca, preferring the southeast-facing part of the coast east of Mazunte.

Raccoons have a couple of cousins that call Oaxaca home. The ring-tailed *cacomixtle* prefers the tropical humid and subhumid forests in the north and on the coast. Its name comes from the Nahuatl, meaning "half lion." The other cousin, the **white-nosed coati,** has a larger habitat in Oaxaca, as coatis venture deeper into the pine-oak forests of the mountains than *cacomixtles.*

Bats

There are at least 82 species of **bats** in Oaxaca, and they have found homes all over the state. One species in Oaxaca is endangered, and 16 others are either under special protection or considered threatened.

Vampire bats like the semiarid foothills around the Valles Centrales and La Mixteca, as well as the muggier regions of the coast and El Papaloapan. Cases are rare, but vampire bats here and elsewhere in the world are known to bite people and spread rabies. Other rarer bats in Oaxaca include the **Aztec fruit-eating bat, Parnell's mustached bat,** and **Salvin's big-eyed bat.** Oaxaca is at the southern tip of the habitat of the funny-looking **Townsend's big-eared bat,** which, well, has big ears.

History

PRE-HISPANIC OAXACA

The earliest known evidence of crop domesticating in the Americas were found in the Guilá Naquitz cave outside Mitla in the 1960s. Paleobotanists date the *cucurbita* (type of squash native to Mesoamerica) seeds found here as far back as 8000 BC. Beans and *teocintle* (predecessor to maize) didn't become domesticated until 4,000 years after squash, so the presence of those seeds in these caves has led archaeologists to conjecture that the caves hosted a succession of seasonal residents over the millennia. The evidence suggests that Oaxaca might be the epicenter of agriculture in the New World.

Marcus Winter, U.S. archaeologist and author of *Oaxaca: The Archaeological Record* (1989) has broken down the history of Oaxaca into four stages. The seeds from Guilá Naquitz date back to the Agricultural Phase (9500-1500 BC). As agriculture ensured more dependable food supplies, the hunter-gatherers began to prefer to stay put, forming villages and building the foundations for the great societies to come.

The Village Era

Winter dates the Village Stage of Oaxacan history from 1500 BC to AD 500. These peoples had quite a bit more time on their hands, now that they did not have to hunt or migrate as much in search of food. Small villages formed, and people began forming the customs and traditions that would go on to define their cultural identities in the phases to come.

The most important site from this era is San José Mogote, just north of Monte Albán, in the Valle de Etla. This is the first known Zapotec settlement, and it was here that they began to create some of the cultural characteristics of their descendants. The layout of the constructions leads archaeologists to believe that the residents of San José Mogote were already performing impressive astronomical calculations, and the hieroglyphic inscriptions found here make the Zapotecs one of the primary candidates for the earliest writing system in the Americas.

Monte Albán

Winter's third phase, the Urban Stage (AD 500-750), begins with the founding of the greatest of pre-Hispanic Zapotec cities, Monte Albán. By this time, the Aztecs had founded Teotihuacán, in the Valley of Mexico, and the Maya were taking care of business in Tikal, in Guatemala. Evidence of influence from both cultures has been found in Monte Albán.

Citizens of Monte Albán continued to study astronomy and develop their writing system, and by AD 200, the city was an economic and political powerhouse in the region, being known as the capital of the Zapotec empire and reaching a peak population estimated by some to be as high as 100,000 people around AD 600. More recently discovered evidence at Atzompa, atop a hill just north of Monte Albán and considered to have been under its jurisdiction, has led researchers to conject that Monte Albán was the first example of suburbia in the Americas.

The Zapotec religious center Mitla, in the Valle de Tlacolula, came along a few centuries after the founding of Monte Albán. Mitla was home to Zapotec high priests, and was the final resting place for many important political and religious figures. All of its names have to do with passing on. In Nahuatl and Mixtec, its names mean "Place of the Dead," and the Zapotec word for it means "Place of Rest."

Archaeologists believe that sometime around AD 500 Monte Albán's importance in the region began to decline, and by the year 900, the city was completely abandoned. The

---

1: monument to Benito Juárez 2: view of the Valles Centrales from a wall at Monte Albán

1

2

reason or reasons remain a mystery to this day. Mitla and the nearby city of **Yagul** became the important Zapotec centers. This period represents the beginning of the fourth and final stage of Winter's pre-Hispanic Oaxacan history, the **City-State Stage** (AD 750-1521).

Oaxaca's second most powerful group at this time, the Mixtecs, had founded their important centers, such as **Monte Negro** and **Yucuita,** around the same time as Monte Albán, and invaded Zapotec territory in 1325, occupying Mitla and bringing life back to Monte Albán. In the early 1490s, the Aztecs invaded Oaxaca, setting up a military outpost on the **Cerro del Fortín,** the hill just to the northwest of the Centro of Oaxaca City, and giving the place the name we know it by today, named after the abundance of *guaje* trees they found there. The Aztecs' colonial aspirations were short-lived, as the arrival of the Spanish three decades later thwarted the designs they had on Oaxaca.

THE CONQUEST

Spanish conquistador **Hernán Cortés** (1485-1547) made his first landing in Mexico in Cozumel, an island off the Caribbean Coast, in 1519. Pop history will have you believe that the Aztecs were a gullible people, easily duped into believing that Cortés was the reincarnation of their plumed serpent god **Quetzalcoatl,** making them fearful and more inclined to welcome the outsiders. This notion was actually propagated by the Spanish themselves in the 1540s as a way to justify what they had done in the New World. The word Quetzalcoatl was also the Toltec term for high priests and other elites. **Moctezuma II,** the Aztec emperor at the time of the arrival of the Spanish, did not think that Cortés and his men were gods, but rather the descendants of **Ce Ácatl Topiltzin Quetzalcóatl,** a Toltec king who had been exiled by the Aztecs in 987, and that they had come back to reclaim power in the region. Well aware of these fears before his arrival in Tenochtitlán, Cortés used them to his advantage, claiming that **King Charles of Spain** (1500-1558) was indeed divine, and

that the conquistadors had been sent to bring the true word of god back to the Aztecs.

By 1521, European diseases introduced by the Spanish had helped them conquer Tenochititlán and other important Aztec cities and towns, and Cortés began to go after the rest of the Aztec empire. Outbreaks of smallpox in 1520, 1531, and 1545 would go on to kill over five million Mexicans before it finally ran its course. More recent research points to climatic causes for later epidemics in that century, revising the history in a way that takes a bit of the heat off the Spanish for these outbreaks. Survivors of the initial outbreaks of smallpox would have passed the immunities down to subsequent generations by then. However, even if the epidemics of the late 16th century were in fact blood-hemorrhaging fever caused by rats after severe periods of drought, as the theory proposes, the initial smallpox epidemics caused by the Spanish presence in Mexico still had devastating effects on the native populations.

Into Oaxaca

Their first excursions into Oaxaca were into La Mixteca, led by **Francisco de Orozco y Tovar,** first taking towns like Yucundaa, which was subsequently relocated to form the town of **Teposcolula.** Conquistador **Pedro de Alvarado** also played a hand in the colonization of Oaxaca, as he passed through the region on his way to conquer Guatemala. The town of **Huaxyacac,** now Oaxaca City, fell to the Spanish in 1521, marking the beginning of a new era for Oaxaca. The diocese of **Antequera** was established in Oaxaca City in 1535, and subsequent dioceses eventually popped up in Tehuantepec (1891), Huajuapan de León (1902), and Puerto Escondido (2003), as well as a territorial prelature in Huautla de Jiménez (1972).

COLONIAL OAXACA

Due to the number of different indigenous peoples in Oaxaca, the Spanish found a variety of welcomes, or lack thereof. As in many parts of Mexico, many populations resisted little and were easier to convert and colonize, but some put up a pretty fierce fight. For decades, the people of **Yanhuitlán,** in La Mixteca, which is currently renowned for the quality of the Dominican architecture there, resisted the construction of the Christian temples on the foundations of their own, as well as the fact that they were the ones being forced to build them. Many towns today are not in the same location as the pre-Hispanic towns of the same names, as many were moved after smallpox and other diseases took root in them. This also served political purposes, and was done even when not made necessary by disease. The system called *congregación* (congregation) displaced indigenous communities, forcing them to live under the administrative stipulations imposed by the colonizers.

The *Encomienda* System

The Spanish adapted the tributary system of *señoríos* (chiefdoms) already in place in Oaxaca and elsewhere in Mexico to fit their imperial needs. Part of this system was the concept of *tequio,* or unremunerated communal labor that benefited the society as a whole and paid tribute to the ruling class. Although pre-Hispanic peoples did colonize each other, *tequio* was a common social and economic system in many indigenous societies before the conquest, and it was more like community service than slavery. Precolonial economies and infrastructure, such as the canals of Tenochtitlán, were built under this system. The feudal Spanish system called *la encomienda* corrupted this native social structure by redirecting the benefits of that labor to the conquistadors and the Spanish crown.

This system granted an *encomendero,* usually a conquistador who had earned the privilege by fighting in expansionist battles, with native villages, whose welfare, religious instruction, and, most importantly, economy, were now his responsibility. The products of farm work, construction, and other activities previously meant to benefit the community itself were now the property of the Spanish

conquistadors and their European king. Not surprisingly, *encomenderos* focused more on the economy aspect of the job than that of the welfare of the people under their care, and rampant abuse led King Charles to enact the *Leyes Nuevas* (New Laws) of 1542, which attempted to revise the system.

The *encomienda* system was replaced by one intended to abolish slavery in the New World and reduce abuse, called the *repartimiento.* Under the New Laws, no *indio* (indigenous person) was allowed to be considered property, and limits were put on work schedules and conditions. Still, the Spanish crown had trouble enforcing the laws from the other side of the pond, and the *repartimiento* didn't end up looking much different from its predecessor. Abuse and economic exploitation continued for centuries, as did local uprisings in Oaxaca and elsewhere in Mexico. One of the most successful uprisings occurred in 1660 in Tehuantepec, when the citizens rebelled against Spanish officials and held the city for over a year after the savage beating of a local *cacique* (chief). After 14 months, they thought they'd struck a deal with the Spanish, who later double-crossed the rebels, killing the insurgent leaders and reinstating viceroyal control.

The Caste System and Population Decline

Disease and overwork killed millions of people in Mexico during the colonial period. It is estimated that in 1500, the indigenous population of Mexico was anywhere from 15 to 25 million people, around 2 million of those in Oaxaca. By the mid-17th century, those numbers had dropped to 1.3 million and 150,000, respectively. Because of this, the Spanish began to bring slaves from Africa to make up for the lost labor and save their economy. Critical to the colonial economy was the red dye cochineal, of which Oaxaca was Mexico's, and for a while the world's, largest producer.

Colonial Mexican society was broken down into three distinct social groups: the *peninsulares* or *blancos,* white people born in Spain who moved to Mexico; the *indios,* indigenous

La Pintura de Castas
(The Caste Paintings)

Painters like **Andrés de Islas** (active 1753-1775) and Oaxacan-born **Miguel Cabrera** (1695-1768) seemed to have a lot of fun with the **caste system,** each producing a series of 16 paintings depicting families of different races and their offspring. Each had text explaining the caste, for example, *"De Español e India, Mestiza"* (From a Spanish man and an indigenous woman, a mestizo child). The names get a little silly, and that seemed to be the point. The paintings were very popular, both in New Spain and on the Iberian Peninsula, and they were even sold on little cards like souvenirs.

Cabrera's series was released in 1763, that of Andrés de Islas in 1774, and an anonymous painter produced a third series around the same time. It is ironic that Cabrera dedicated a whole series to ultra-specific socio-racial rankings based on birth, as he himself was an orphan and never knew his parents. Only the first five castes on each list are the same, and the rest seemed to be made up by each individual artist, or perhaps the differences were regional. Aside from being weirdly obsessive about categorizing people as such, the text in the paintings further dehumanizes non-Spanish and non-white people with its grammar. The words for the mother and father are grammatically rendered as describing the people represented, whereas all of their children are grammatically female, since the product of said union is not a person but *la casta* (caste), a measurement of social value.

The following list includes the first five castes that all three series have in common. They go on to include some pretty shocking names in light of proper modern understandings of race, such as *Coyote* and *Loba* (Wolf), as well as the enigmatic *Tente en el aire* (Hold yourself in the air) and the flat-out rude *No te entiendo* (I don't understand you). Now, I'm no geneticist, but it looks like they made a mistake only three steps in.

Father	Mother	Caste
Spanish	Indigenous	Mestiza
Spanish	Mestiza	Castiza
Spanish	Castiza	Spanish
Spanish	Black	Mulata
Spanish	Mulata	Morisca (literally, Moorish)

Mexicans; and the *negros*, slaves brought from Africa. The subsequent Spanish generations born in Mexico were called *criollos*, and were a notch down from the *peninsulares* in the social hierarchy. There was much discord between these two groups, as the *criollos*, who considered themselves to be fully Spanish, were often denied the perks they felt their skin color earned them, like *encomiendas*. From the intermixing of these groups, the Spanish created a **caste system** that was more than racial classification, but was also a form of economic control. Tributes were based on a people's caste, with the larger sums unsurprisingly falling to the lower levels.

One positive effect of the colonial period was that the Spanish introduced new products for the indigenous Oaxacans to put their creativity to, such as cows, horses, goats, pigs, sheep, chickens, and crops like rice, garlic, and onions. Many of the highly prized Oaxacan foods and artisanal crafts wouldn't exist without these materials.

MEXICAN
INDEPENDENCE

At the beginning of the 19th century, Spain was experiencing political instability and started to see its power wane. The incompetence of King Charles IV allowed his wife,

María Luisa, to do the governing along with her lover, Manuel de Godoy, whom she appointed as prime minister. Godoy got the country embroiled in the French Revolution, leading Napoleon Bonaparte to invade Madrid in 1808. He forced Charles, then his son Ferdinand VII, to abdicate from the throne, then tossed them in jail and named his brother Joseph as King of Spain. This created a power vacuum in New Spain, as the *peninsulares* supported backing the new king, while the *criollos* did not.

Conspiratorial Book Clubs

Luckily for the *criollos*, they had a majority in the Mexico City Council, and they chose to refuse to acknowledge Joseph, instead forming a junta that would govern in the name of King Ferdinand VII. This power spread from the capital to the provinces, and a *criollo*-controlled junta of municipalities was also established. *Criollos* all over New Spain began attending "literary clubs" that were merely a front for conspiratorial meetings, where the main word whispered was "*revolución*." Their intentions were not to make an independent Mexico for the people, but rather for themselves. They wanted what the *peninsulares* hadn't let them have for a long time.

Spanish captain **Ignacio Allende** (1769-1811) sympathized with the *criollos* and their movement for independence, and in 1810 he headed the Literary and Social Club of Querétaro. Allende knew the movement needed the support of high-ranking religious and political officials in New Spain, so he appealed to a priest from Dolores, Guanajuato, named **Miguel Hidalgo** (1753-1811), who was friends with a few powerful bishops. The plan was for Hidalgo to lead the movement, while Allende would take care of the coup, which they planned for the first of December in San Juan de los Lagos, Jalisco, where many *peninsulares* attended the annual festival for the Virgen de Guadalupe. But word got out, and on September 13, Spanish authorities arrested many involved. For those that hadn't been caught, the time was now or never.

The *Grito de Dolores* and Rise of the Insurgency

Father Hidalgo was at home in Dolores when word of the arrests got to him. Early in the morning on the September 16, he gave a rousing call-to-arms that has gone down in Mexican history as the *Grito de Dolores* (Shout of Dolores), which lit the fire in the people that grew into the **Mexican War for Independence** (1810-1821). The exact words of his speech are unknown, and various accounts exist, but they all run along the lines of "Death to the bad government! Long live the Holy Virgin of Guadalupe! Long live King Ferdinand!"

The message was later altered to fit various political agendas, and phrases such as "Death to the *gachupines*!" (*gachupín* was a derogatory term for *peninsulares* in colonial Mexico) and "Long live Spanish America!" were said to have been shouted by him as well. The most important of these subsequent additions is "*¡Viva México!*" (Long live Mexico!), which is still shouted in cities and towns all over the country every Independence Day, kind of. The first celebration of the *Grito de Dolores* was on September 16, 1812, and the festivities continued as such until 1840, when the fireworks and chants were moved to the night before. Hidalgo had made his speech at five in the morning, a good time to start a revolution, but a terrible time for a party.

Back in 1810, Hidalgo went around Guanajuato state, amassing a growing army of indigenous citizens who ransacked the houses of the rich and killed as many *gachupines* as they could find. They took the capital of the state, and by the time they were ready to move on Mexico City, Hidalgo's army had grown to over 80,000 strong. Despite their numbers, the insurgents were no match for the military expertise of the only 6,000 Spanish soldiers, and they were forced to retreat. Hidalgo was captured in March 1811. He was defrocked and executed by firing squad. As a warning to other insurgents, his head and those of three of his officers were hung outside the granary in Guanajuato where he and 20,000 angry peasants had overtaken the Spanish forces the previous year.

Ten Years of War

The next ten years in Mexico were volatile and bloody. In Oaxaca, the royalists had control of the capital, suppressing an 1811 insurrection in the city led by **Felipe Tinioco** and **José Palacios**, but the insurgents had traction elsewhere in the state. A mule driver turned insurgent soldier named **Valerio Trujano** (1676-1812) led rebel forces in La Mixteca, holding out in Huajuapan de León. Oaxaca City finally fell to the rebels in 1812, led by **José María Morelos** (1765-1815). After taking Oaxaca, Morelos marched to Huajuapan, where he and his men helped Trujano fight off the royalist troops besieging the city.

Despite his early victories, Morelos was captured and executed in 1815, and his place at the head of the insurgency was taken by **Vicente Guerrero** (1782-1831). He was so successful in leading the insurgents that the royal government offered him amnesty to capitulate, but he refused. Royalist general **Agustín de Iturbide** (1783-1824) was sent to take on Guerrero's rebel forces, but seeing that the tide was turning, he did so himself, and the two wrote up the **Plan de Iguala** on Februrary 24, 1821. This revolutionary proclamation announced the official independence of Mexico from Spain and guaranteed "Religion, Independence, and Union" in the country. On August 24 of that year, the Plan de Iguala was ratified by the signing of the Treaty of Córdoba in Veracruz, settling the matter once and for all, kind of.

Emperor Iturbide and the Constitution of 1824

The insurgents had achieved their goal of ousting the royalists from power, but once they had it, they found themselves faced with a new problem. The peasants and farmers who had won the fight with sheer determination and ingenuity had no experience running governments. Ironically, they ended up getting another sovereign who had his own interests and desires at heart, rather than equality and independence. In the political instability that followed the war, Iturbide was elected emperor of Mexico. His sovereignty was short-lived, however, and two year later, he abdicated power after former allies turned against him.

Mexico's first constitution was signed in 1824, officially forming the Estados Unidos Mexicanos (United Mexican States). Oaxacan had been a government department since the end of the war, but that year, the department wrote up its own constitution and was granted statehood. This year also saw the founding of the Institute of Sciences and Arts of Oaxaca, which would go on to educate two of the most important figures in Mexican history.

Santa Anna and War with the United States

The rest of the decade was plagued by political instability, a number of failed coups, and more plots. Renowned military leader **Antonio López de Santa Anna** (1794-1876), who had crossed over to the side of the insurgents when Iturbide did so, was declared president by the congress. His reputation in Mexico was pretty good at the time, as he had led a number of successful operations, such as the Spanish invasion of Tampico in Veracruz, and had founded villages in the state for displaced citizens.

That good standing in the Mexican collective memory when down the drain when Santa Anna lost Texas to the United States. The province was very sparsely settled by Mexicans, and few others wanted to help out with peopling the rugged land, prompting Mexico to sell land for next to nothing to U.S. citizens willing to come work it. After a series of bloody battles, including the ill-planned and unforgettable one at San Antonio's Alamo mission, the Texas settlers and *Tejanos* (Mexicans from Texas) won the state's independence from Mexico. Santa Anna never recognized Texas independence, and disputes over the territory led to the Mexican-American War (1846-1848). As part of the

Treaty of Guadalupe Hidalgo, which brought an end to the conflict, Mexico lost the states now called Colorado, New Mexico, Arizona, Utah, Nevada, and California.

Santa Anna hopped in and out of the president's office 11 times between 1833 and 1855. By the time he was done, Mexico had lost over half of its territory to the United States, whether by insurrection, treaties, or transactions. To this day, Santa Anna is known as the guy who gave the Lone Star State to the *gringos*. Some have been far too eager to demonize him and call him a villain, but the reality is that, despite his obviously keen military mind, he made a few too many fundamental blunders that ended up costing him and his country a great deal.

REFORM, CIVIL WAR, AND FRENCH INVASION

While Santa Anna dealt disastrously with the United States, **Benito Juárez** (1806-1872) was doing good things in the Oaxacan governor's office. During his tenure from 1848 to 1852, he greatly improved the state's infrastructure and revived the economy by attracting foreign investment. After a Santa Anna-imposed two-year exile spent working in a cigar factory in New Orleans, Juárez returned to Mexico. He and other liberals wrote the Plan of Ayutla, which forced Santa Anna to step down and called for a new constitution to be written. The formation of the provisional government under liberal strong-arm Juan Álvarez marked the beginning of the period known as the Reform.

Juárez went to work as the provisional government's Minister of Justice, but what he did there would put into question his status as a man of the people. He drafted the Juárez Law, which restricted the jurisdiction of the church and military and declared all citizens equal before the law, but part of the limitations on the church included large divestments of church-owned land. The idea was to redistribute lands among the people, but as it worked out, the only ones with means to buy the land were elites with money, defeating

the purpose of the law. Juárez's legacy went on to be altered and used to fit various political agendas in the ensuing centuries, making him into a spotless, sometimes almost godlike figure in the formation of the country as it is known today. More recent scrutiny of his time in power has called into question these myths, noting the effects of the Reform Laws, leading some to jokingly call him Mexico's first dictator. However, this sentiment is merely the other extreme of deeming him a historical superhero. He was merely human, and his overall track record suggests that his intentions were always good, even when the results weren't what was planned.

The Reform Law sowed even more discord between liberals and conservatives, and the latter organized an uprising in 1858 that lasted for three years. When the liberals finally won out in 1861, Juárez assumed the presidency.

Juárez and Maximillian

Unfortunately, his term was short-lived. In 1862, Napoleon wanted more for France and invaded Mexico with an army of 60,000 men. After all the fighting of the previous half century, Mexicans weren't ready to go gently into that good night, and put up a few good fights. The most famous was the Battle of Puebla on May 5, 1862, led by Oaxacan **Porfirio Díaz** (1830-1915), the battle that is the origin of the 5 de Mayo celebration in the United States, whether revelers know it or not. The holiday was first celebrated on May 5, 1863, by residents of Puebla who had moved to California.

Despite Díaz's best efforts on the battlefield, the French took a number of state capitals, including Oaxaca, and ultimately Mexico City by 1864. Austrian archduke **Maximillian** and his wife Carlota were instated as emperor and empress of the Second Mexican Empire. The United States continued to recognize Juárez as the president, and he fled to the mountains to set up a government-in-exile. Pressure from the United States caused the French to begin pulling out of Mexico in 1866, and by the next year, the Mexican army had taken back

Mexico City. Juárez ordered Maximillian's execution by firing squad on June 19, 1867.

Juárez was reelected with little opposition that year, but fellow Oaxaqueño Porfirio Díaz started talking trash, claiming Juárez had violated the constitution. Juárez continued his attempts at reform, but Díaz would not relent. A tough, stressful life had taken its toll on Juárez, and he died of a heart attack in the National Palace in Mexico City on July 18, 1872.

THE PORFIRIATO

After Juárez's death, the office of president was assumed by the Supreme Court chief justice Sebastián Lerdo de Tejada. Díaz opposed Lerdo de Tejada's appointment as well, and when the liberal announced he was running for reelection in 1876, Díaz picked up the refrain he'd shouted during Juárez's term: ¡No reelección! (No reelection!). He issued the Plan of Tuxtepec Díaz in 1876, sparking a nationwide revolt against the Lerdo administration.

When he finally made it to the presidency in 1877, Díaz began to change his perspective on reelection, and he ended up serving seven presidential terms over 31 years. Díaz's main goal was to bring peace to the country, no matter the cost. He created a provincial police force call the rurales, who were ordered to be as ruthless with bandits as Díaz's soldiers were with the French. Even low-level crimes were often punished with a bullet in the back.

Still, despite his heavy hand (or, as Díaz would say, because of it), peace finally did come to Mexico. He attracted foreign investments in the railroad and other industries, and the economy prospered. The British-built Ferrocarril Mexicano del Sur (Southern Mexican Railroad), which connected Oaxaca City with the nation's capital, was inaugurated in 1892. The economic stability and peace came to be known as the Pax Porfiriana.

Such progress came at loggerheads with the communal landownership common in Oaxaca, and many communities only pretended to accept privatization. This conflict was very prevalent in the coffee boom on the coast. Many communally owned indigenous lands were appropriated during this time in order to establish coffee plantations. In the north, around the town of Valle Nacional, tobacco cultivation became popular, and both indigenous people from the region and elsewhere were brought in to work the fields. Exploitation, malnutrition, and abuse was rampant in the business. Overall, however, peace flourished in the nation.

At the end of the 19th century, a worldwide surplus of coffee caused prices for the beans to plummet, and sowed even more dissatisfaction with the Díaz regime. At the end of the first decade of that century, Díaz's former position of opposing reelection came back to bite him on the behind.

THE MEXICAN REVOLUTION

In 1909, Díaz saw a formidable electoral opponent in acting National Anti-reelectionist Party president **Francisco I. Madero** (1873-1913), who began to stir up trouble for Díaz. In December of that year, after releasing a manifesto directed toward Oaxacans, Madero came to Oaxaca City, where he planned a mutiny. The mob gathered on the Cerro del Fortín, prompting the city leadership to send in police. Luckily, things didn't get violent. The protestors moved their function to a private residence and began sowing the seeds of revolution.

Although Díaz tried to suppress this and similar movements in La Mixteca, La Cañada, El Istmo, and on the coast, the stage was set, and his nephew, **Felix Díaz** (1868-1945), was ultimately ousted as governor of Oaxaca. Discontent was rife among the poor populations of Mexico, and two firebrand rebels would soon bring back the chaos Díaz had worked so violently to control.

Villa and Zapata

While Oaxacans were revolting in the south, farmhands, cattle rustlers, miners, and other poor workers joined the cause of **Francisco "Pancho" Villa** (1878-1923), who was leading

Porfirio Díaz: National Villain, Local Hero

The Battle of Puebla was Díaz's main military claim to fame, but the citizens of Miahuatlán de Porfirio Díaz remember him for chasing the French out of their town on October 3, 1866. Although the Imperial troops outnumbered them by almost double, Díaz knew the terrain better than the foreign generals and used this to his advantage. He posted riflemen in a ravine and a group of armed *Miahuatecos* in a field of maguey opposite. He then climbed a hill and made himself visible, attracting the French forces, who were ambushed by the flanks he'd hidden. When all was shot and done, Díaz's men had killed 70 French soldiers and taken 400 prisoner. The casualties on his side only totaled 59 dead and 14 wounded.

Many Mexicans villainize Díaz for what he did during the Porfiriato, but to this day, *Miahuatecos* celebrate his victory every October 3 with a *cabalgata* (cavalcade of horses), foam and confetti fights, and lots and lots of tacos and mezcal. One interesting aspect of this party is the practice of setting bamboo cages around the *zócalo*. Throughout the night, distracted partiers get nabbed and locked up in these *jaulas*. The jailers charge a coin or two for freedom. The 3 de Octubre festival is something you won't experience elsewhere, so if you're around Miahuatlán at this time, don't miss out. Oh, and wear clothes you don't mind getting wet, stained, or otherwise altered.

them around Chihuahua, attacking *rurales* and wealthy landowners.

Also at the same time, in the state of Morelos, just south of Mexico City, **Emiliano Zapata** (1879-1919) was rounding up loyal indigenous followers under the slogan *¡Tierra y Libertad!* (Land and Liberty!). He and his indigenous army violently retook ancestral lands from the wealthy *hacendados* who had bought it up during the Reform, eventually taking the capital, Cuernavaca.

Madero, who had been in exile in the United States, saw the turning tide and crossed back over the Rio Grande to join in. Díaz's troops began deserting the federal army in droves, and Díaz resigned on May 25, 1911. He went into exile in Paris, France, where he died four years later. When Madero's deputy, General Victoriano Huerta, escorted Díaz to the ship that would take him to Europe, he said to the ousted dictator, "Madero has unleashed a tiger. We'll see if he can control it."

The Mexican Civil War

By 1912, the beast that Madero had created turned against him. Zapata and his followers wanted to see a faster redistribution of lands, but Madero was taking his time. His army in

Mexico City turned against him, and Huerta ordered both his resignation on February 18, 1913, and his execution four days later.

War raged on in Mexico. In Oaxaca, liberals and conservatives duked it out. By now, Villa and Zapata, along with revolutionary generals **Álvaro Obregón** (1880-1928) and **Venustiano Carranza** (1859-1920), were a group known as the "Big Four," but Oaxaca's revolutionary leaders weren't on board. They denounced the Big Four and proclaimed Oaxaca a sovereign republic, denying outside revolutionaries entry into the state.

For three more years, the struggle ground on across the nation, with various insurgent factions vying for control. In 1917, Carranza had majority power in the country, and he called a convention in Querétaro to write up a new constitution. The Constitution of 1917 harkened back to the redistributive policies of the Reform-Era Constitution of 1857. It reformed labor laws, limited the presidential term to one four-year term (which would later be changed to a six-year term in 1927), and prioritized public over private landownership. Still, it would take another three years for the fighting to calm down. It has been amended since, but this is the constitution that governs Mexico to this day.

Obregón Brings Stability

In 1920, Álvaro Obregón found himself president of a country battered and bruised by 10 years of bloody civil war. He and the rest of the country badly wanted peace. Pancho Villa and another insurgent officer, Lucio Blanco, made his job difficult the first few years, but after Blanco's murdered body washed up on the banks of the Rio Grande in Nuevo Laredo in 1922, and Villa was executed in 1923, he was finally able to effect change. He instituted land and labor reforms, and built over 1,000 rural schools and 2,000 public libraries around the country.

Oaxacan governor Manuel García Vigil followed suit, writing up the constitution the state still uses today. It included tax reforms that were not popular among wealthy landowners in the state.

Obregón was succeeded by Plutarco Elias Calles in 1924. He continued to balance the budget, improve infrastructure, and organize health services like vaccination programs. Despite leaning far enough to the left as to quarrel with the United States over the petroleum industry, Calles eventually turned conservative. He stepped down, and Obregón hopped back in, but the term was short-lived, as Obregón was assassinated two weeks after the election. The next three presidents were mere puppets of Calles, who called the shots off-stage.

THE REIGN OF THE PRI

In 1929, Calles formed the political party that would rule over Mexican politics for the rest of the century. The **Partido Revolucionario Institucional** (Institutional Revolutionary Party, PRI) was originally formed of workers, the rural poor, and the middle class, but the party moved closer to the right, becoming known as a corrupt party for the rich by the end of the century.

Lázaro Cárdenas, a True People's President

Previously governor of Michoacán, **Lázaro Cárdenas** (1895-1970) did much to create a government that served the people. During his term, he reverted 49 million acres of land to public ownership, improved education, and enacted more labor reform. He even cut his own salary in half, and turned the opulent Chapultepec Castle, previously the residency of the president, into a museum. However, he is most remembered as the president who nationalized Mexico's petroleum industry.

The foreign oil companies he expropriated put up a fuss, but he eventually compensated them, and they quieted down. Cárdenas created the national oil company, Petróleos Mexicanos (Pemex) in 1938. Mexico's oil business would stay in the hands of the government until the dawn of the 21st century.

Manuel Ávila Camacho

Successor to Cárdenas was **Manuel Ávila Camacho** (1897-1955), who did much to improve relations with the United States. He was the first Mexican president to meet a U.S. president on Mexican soil, when Roosevelt visited him in Monterrey in April 1943. During World War II, his economy sent raw materials north of the border, and the United States sent manufactured consumer goods south.

Political Unrest in Oaxaca

New taxes designed to be used to modernize agriculture in the state began to cause political trouble in the 1940s and 1950s. A coalition of farmers, merchants, students, and others organized uprisings across the state in protest. One student protest resulted in the deaths of two students at the hands of police, and Oaxaca City erupted in protests by various groups. President **Miguel Alemán** (1900-1983) sent the federal army into the state to control the situation, but this was just the beginning.

Political Activism in the 1960s and 1970s

Women voted in Mexico for the first time in 1958, helping to elect **Adolfo López Mateos** (1908-1969). A leftist, he redistributed farmland to the tune of 40 million acres, constructed thousands of new schools and stocked them with millions of new textbooks, and set a minimum of at least 60 percent of gross domestic product for car manufacturing. He also nationalized the country's power companies and founded the National Museum of Anthropology upon leaving the presidency in 1964.

Despite also being from the PRI, his successor, **Gustavo Díaz Ordaz** (1911-1979), had much different political ideals than Mateos. His authoritarian style of leadership didn't fly with liberals, especially students. The disagreements came to a head in 1968, when student activists from the National Autonomous University of Mexico gathered in the Plaza de las Tres Culturas (Plaza of the Three Cultures), in the Tlatelolco neighborhood of Mexico City 10 days before the Summer Olympics were to be held there. Government forces massacred up to 400 people that day in order to suppress the protests. Although the government told media outlets that the students began firing first, documents released in 2000 make it all but certain that there were federal snipers in the buildings around the square.

Students in Oaxaca were also fired up, and they teamed up with unions to form a coalition based on their indigenous Zapotec heritage. They organized boycotts, strikes, protests, and marches, and some more-radical factions applied terroristic tactics with explosives. Their efforts ended up forcing the government to improve working conditions in rural areas. The success was especially seen in Juchitán, which in 1980 voted leftists into the local government offices, making it one of very few towns in the country to not be governed by the PRI. The turbulent climate in the state also caused Mexico City to respond by sending more funds and resources Oaxaca's way, which improved the highways and health and education services and connected many small rural towns to the electrical grid for the first time.

The *Maquiladora* Industry

During this time, the United States and Mexico continued to exchange goods and develop their trade relations further. The most significant development was the creation of the *maquiladora* industry. These duty-free factories built in Mexican towns along the border allow U.S. companies to take advantage of cheap labor without having to provide the kinds of salaries, working conditions, and infrastructure they would north of the border. This industry, which produces many of the separate parts of "American-made" automobiles, which are then assembled in the United States, is notoriously corrupt and exploitative. *Maquiladora* workers all along the border work in unsafe conditions, are underpaid, and are often forced into debt slavery disguised as home ownership.

Oil Boom and the Inevitable Bust

In 1972, colossal oil reserves were found in the Gulf of Mexico, bringing about rapid economic growth in the 1970s. Oaxaca saw the results of this boom in construction of the trans-isthmus pipeline and one of the country's biggest refineries in Salina Cruz. The business grew the small coastal town into the state's current third-largest city.

But, of course, all the infrastructure to suck that oil out of the ground had to come from somewhere. Mexico had turned to the United States for that loan, but in the 1980s, when interest payments were due, the global market was glutted with oil and the barrel price plummeted. Mexico's oil industry couldn't pay its debt, and the peso collapsed, sending inflation sky-high. Try as he might, President Miguel de la Madrid was unable to curb inflation, and in 1988 one U.S. dollar was worth 2,500 Mexican pesos. As they always do, the macroeconomic games of the rich hit the poor hardest, worsening the already extreme poverty in Oaxaca, Chiapas, and other poor areas of the country.

NAFTA

The PRI candidate to win the presidency in 1988 was Carlos Salinas de Gortari, who broadened the trade landscape with the

United States and Canada by signing the North American Free Trade Agreement, or NAFTA, on January 1, 1994. All of a sudden, U.S. products flooded the Mexican market, and Mexican farms kept U.S. supermarkets stocked with fresh fruits and veggies year-round. The most notable effect of NAFTA was the reduction in prices for these agricultural products. The price of corn, for example, plummeted, putting thousands of poor Mexican farmers out of work. As a result, many began to seek the means to support their families north of the border.

The Zapatistas

The signing of NAFTA didn't go over well in the state of Chiapas. On the day of its signing, a guerilla army of indigenous citizens who called themselves the **Ejército Zapatista de Liberación Nacional** (Zapatista Army of National Liberation, EZLN), or the Zapatistas, for short, stormed and occupied a number of towns in the state, and took one of its former governors hostage.

The movement inspired communities in Oaxaca to organize to ensure their rights, as well. Many formed communal work programs designed to foster local economies by keeping money in the community. The Zapatistas' activity has waned since, but they continue to declare war on the Mexican state to this day, and the repercussions of their struggle can be seen in the indigenous community-organizing seen in Oaxaca and elsewhere in Mexico.

Another Peso Crisis

Luis Donaldo Colosio (1950-1994) was the PRI's first candidate for the 1994 elections, but he was assassinated. Instead of destroying the party, the assassination elicited grief across the country and from his would-be opponents. **Ernesto Zedillo** (b. 1951) took his place on the PRI stump and won, ensuring the PRI's grip on Mexican politics for the rest of the century.

Zedillo didn't have long to celebrate, though, for the peso collapsed again by the time he took office, devaluing by half by January 1995. U.S. president Bill Clinton put together a massive loan package that gave the Mexican economy a lifeline, but did not stop inflation from soaring and causing Mexico's poor to once again have to worry about putting food on the table.

This caused more guerilla activity in Oaxaca, Chiapas, and Guerrero. One guerilla army, the **Ejército Popular Revolucionario** (Popular Revolutionary Army, EPR), coordinated attacks in Guerrero, Puebla, Guanajuato, Tabasco, Mexico City, and Oaxaca. On August 28, 1996, EPR soldiers attacked Tlaxiaco first, and others attacked Huatulco two hours later. As a result of these attacks, the Mexican naval officers watching for turtle poachers at Playa Escobilla, in Puerto Escondido, were called away to address the threat in Huatulco. The word quickly spread, and poachers flocked to the beach, killing thousands of olive ridley turtles.

Zedillo saved his reputation by commissioning over a billion U.S. dollars on public works and infrastructure projects. The economy began to recover, and inflation began to fall by 1998. Mexico repaid the debt it owed the United States, and the peso returned to stable values.

The political climate began to change as well. For the first time in Mexican history, primary elections were held in 1998, putting the choice of candidate in the hands of the people, rather than the political parties themselves. Non-PRI candidates began winning more elections, and the party saw its grip on the nation's government slacking.

21ST-CENTURY OAXACA

The PRI's luck did indeed change when the country elected **Vicente Fox** (b. 1942) as president. A member of the **Partido Acción Nacional** (National Action Party, PAN), Fox was the first non-PRI president in 71 years. Fox was a right-wing populist and neoliberal businessman who had already had a profound effect on Mexico before becoming president. During the 1970s he had been the president and CEO of Coca-Cola in Mexico, and the

The Disappeared: Mexico's *Desaparecidos*

The Iguala 43 (sometimes Ayotzinapa 43) were a group of students from the Rural Teachers' College in Ayotzinapa, Guerrero, whose disappearance and presumed murders shocked the country in 2014. The politically active students of these left-leaning schools, called *escuelas normales*, were known to commandeer passenger buses for transportation to and from their rallies and protests. It was more or less tolerated by the bus companies, who could usually count on the students to bring them back.

On September 26, the group from Ayotzinapa went to the town of Iguala to nab the buses they were planning to use to drive to Mexico City in October for protests, as well as disrupt a party thrown to celebrate the public works of María de los Ángeles Pineda, wife of the mayor of Iguala. Pineda had been widely accused of being connected to organized crime in Guerrero, one of Mexico's most active states for gang activity. Investigations revealed that in order to save her fiesta from embarrassment, she ordered the municipal police to stop them at any cost.

The details that follow are uncertain, but what is known is that those 43 young men haven't been seen again, and it is generally accepted that they have been murdered. The movement that has grown out of this tragedy to denounce those involved, from the governor of Iguala and his wife to then-president Peña Nieto, uses the slogans *"Nos faltan 43"* (We're missing 43) and *"¡Vivos los llevaron, vivos los queremos!"* (They took them alive, and we want them back alive).

This kind of state violence is unfortunately not uncommon in Mexico. In January 2019, the National Search Commission reported that its National Registry of Missing and Disappeared Persons had grown to include over 40,000 people. In Oaxaca City, there is a good chance you'll see people from one or more of the state's indigenous peoples outside the state government palace, on the south side of the Zócalo, protesting the disappearances of friends and loved ones. If you speak some Spanish, take a little time to ask them about their experiences, and maybe buy something they're selling. It is shocking that the international community has not taken notice. There is power in knowing, and more outside attention on this problem could possibly open the doors to change.

---

soda's sales skyrocketed under his leadership. Now Mexico is the largest consumer of Coca-Cola in the world.

Despite his wealth and status, Fox struck a chord with poor and indigenous communities. He had campaigned heavily in poor barrios and rural villages, and one of his first acts in office was to visit indigenous leaders in Chiapas, where he significantly scaled down the federal military presence. He also presented Congress with a bill of rights for indigenous people. The Zapatistas visited Mexico City and spoke to Congress with their faces hidden behind their black masks, and the two sides worked out a plan for indigenous rights, despite the complaints by some Zapatista leaders that it wasn't enough.

Fox also went after government corruption, signing the country's first freedom of information act and founding a transparency committee to investigate cases of administrative unscrupulousness.

The 2006 Oaxacan Teachers Revolts

In May 2006, Oaxacan members of the **Sindicato Nacional de Trabajadores de la Educación** (National Education Workers Union, SNTE) organized their 25th annual strike for better conditions and funding for rural schools. Unofficial tallies counted as many as 80,000 teachers occupying the Centro in Oaxaca City. During the strike, protestors also took up the cause of demanding the resignation of PRI governor Ulises Ruiz Ortiz, who many accused of rigging the 2004 election. In response, Ortiz sent in 3,000 federal police to disperse the protestors on the morning of June 14, and violence ensued, but luckily there were no deaths.

Protestors responded by forming the **Asamblea Popular de los Pueblos de Oaxaca** (Popular Assembly of the Peoples of Oaxaca, APPO), which went on to boycott the Guelaguetza celebrations in July, ultimately forcing the government to cancel the festival by blocking access to the Auditorio Guelaguetza with burned buses and trash. The first deaths in the conflict came in August, when people later identified as plainclothes police officers and members of organizations supporting the PRI began to raid APPO-controlled radio stations. Ortiz fled to Mexico City for a few months. He would later be arrested for embezzlement in 2014.

Teachers still strike each year in May and June, and protests have grown violent in recent years, with highway blockades, burned buses, and clashes between police and protestors. It is not necessarily dangerous for tourists, but the last two weeks in May and the first two in June really aren't the best time to plan trips here.

Calderón and the Drug War

The 2006 presidential election was so close as to require a recount. The country was split right down the middle between the more conservative PAN candidate **Felipe Calderón** (b. 1962) and the leftist former mayor of Mexico City **Andrés Manuel López Obrador** (b. 1953), or as he's known colloquially, AMLO. The recount came up Calderón, and for weeks Obrador pulled strings in Congress to obstruct Calderón at every turn, going so far as to make him unable to deliver the state of the union address his first year. But Obrador's tactics backfired on him, and public opinion was adamantly against him.

Unlike his predecessor, who had a rather laissez-faire attitude toward drug trafficking in the country, Calderón decided to amp up military action against narcotraffickers, but with disastrous consequences. His first year saw the escalation of drug-related violence, and put Mexico in the international spotlight for the number of murders, femicides, disappearances, mass graves, and other atrocities

that happened as a result. Cities like Acapulco and Ciudad Juárez regularly appear on most dangerous lists, and Mexico is considered the world's most dangerous country for journalists. The worst years were between 2008 and 2012, but the scourge of drug violence still plagues much of Mexico.

The PRI Makes a Comeback

The 2012 presidential elections saw the return of the PRI with the election of **Enrique Peña Nieto** (b. 1966), or as he was called, EPN (eh-peh-EH-ne). Again, his biggest opponent was López Obrador, who staged over a month of protests in the city after Nieto was named the winner. Widespread allegations of fraud plagued his campaign. In one instance, it was widely reported that EPN had bought the votes of millions of people by offering them gift cards to the Soriana chain of supermarkets. When the voters went to use them, they found that all the funds on the cards had been cancelled.

It was apparent from the beginning of his presidency that EPN, with his wax-figure smile and telenovela-star wife, was going to be a pretty face and little more. His approval rating went from 50 percent when he took office to a meager 12 percent by the last year of his term. The angry refrain *¡Fuera Peña!* (Out Peña!) was shouted at protests throughout his presidency.

AMLO Makes a Comeback

The third time was the charm for López Obrador, who ran again in 2018. After the unpopular presidency of Peña Nieto, he didn't have to worry too much about the PRI, or anyone else, for that matter. He won the vote by a landslide, taking in over 53 percent of the popular vote.

Like liberal presidents before him, López Obrador took a pay cut of 60 percent. He also declined to live in the presidential residence called *Los Pinos* (The Pines) in Chapultepec Park in Mexico City, opting to continue living in his personal home and opening up *Los Pinos* as a public cultural center. One of his first acts in office was to create a truth commission to investigate the disappearance and presumed murders of the Iguala 43, a group of teachers' college students who were attacked by state police in Guerrero during Peña Nieto's administration.

Government and Economy

ORGANIZATION

Before the conquest, the regions of Oaxaca were divided into *señoríos*, chiefdoms in which a ruling *cacique* (chief) held sovereignty over a group of tributary towns. In many places, the Spanish uprooted the indigenous populations from the original seats of their *señoríos*, due either to disease wiping out the native population or to impose their political organization. Still, the organization of the *señoríos* at the time of the arrival of the Spanish dictate the borders of Oaxaca's districts and municipalities.

The Spanish saw some of the fiercest resistance to their presence in Mexico in the peoples of Oaxaca, the majority of whom fought against colonization for decades. Some churches in La Mixteca took decades to complete, as many Mixtec tribes organized uprisings in response to the forced labor imposed on them. People all over Oaxaca fought hard to preserve their customs and ways of life, and modern Oaxaca now boasts more municipalities (*municipios*) than any other Mexican state, with a grand total of 570.

These municipalities are grouped into larger administrative branches called districts (*distritos*). Many of the state's municipalities and districts were poorly delineated until the 1990 census. Since then, satellite imagery has helped better define the borders of the government entities woven through Oaxaca's rough geography.

In 1950, the federal government applied the traditional regional divisions in Oaxaca to its official political map in order to both improve administrative functions and preserve the cultural identity of the people here. You might hear talk of the seven regions of Oaxaca, the traditional number, but today they are considered to add up to eight, after the Sierra Region was divided into the **Sierra Norte** and **Sierra Sur.** The other six regions in the state are the **Valles Centrales, La Costa, La Mixteca, La Cañada, El Papaloapan,** and **El Istmo de Tehuantepec.**

At the state level, the governor holds the office of the executive branch. A unicameral legislative branch makes statewide laws, and the judiciary branch consists of seven judges who preside over the supreme court.

POLITICAL PARTIES

Mexico's three dominant political parties are the Institutional Revolutionary Party (PRI), the National Action Party (PAN), and the Party of the Democratic Revolution (PRD). Since the Revolution, the PRI has been the party to occupy the governor's seat in Oaxaca, from its first iterations as the Party of the Mexican Revolution (PRM) and the National Revolutionary Party (PNR) to the political powerhouse it eventually became in the latter half of the 20th century.

The PRI's political dominance has led scholars to label the party as a "state party," basically a government monopoly or de facto party-based autocracy. Despite the insurrectionist connotations of its name, the PRI became a conservative juggernaut, holding power at the federal and many state levels uninterrupted from the Revolution all the way through to the end of the 20th century. At the federal level, the PRI's grip was finally wrested from the presidential office with the election of Vicente Fox (b. 1942), a member of the PAN, in the year 2000.

In Oaxaca, the PRI lost gubernatorial power in 2010, when Gabino Cué Monteagudo (b. 1966), of the more recently formed

Citizen's Movement, a self-described social-democratic party, was elected to power, but the change didn't last. In 2016, PRI candidate Alejandro Murat Hinojosa (b. 1975) was elected governor, bringing the state once again under PRI control. His term ends in 2022.

THE OAXACAN ECONOMY

According to Mexico's National Council for the Evaluation of Social Development (CONEVAL), Oaxaca has the fourth-highest poverty rate in the nation. Although its population comprises 3.3 percent of Mexico's population, it only contributes 1.5 percent of the country's GDP. This gap between Oaxacans and economic opportunities at home has driven many to migrate north to the United States in search of ways to support their families.

Agriculture is the main economic option for most of Oaxaca's poor rural communities. Much of it is subsistence, and the majority is for consumption within the state, such as corn, chiles, and beans. Tropical fruits such as pineapples, mangoes, and coconuts are also grown, as well as sugarcane. Mining and oil production are other significant industries here.

Much of Oaxaca's economy has its roots in its pre-Hispanic culture. The weekly markets known as *tianguis* or *día de plaza* (market day) come from traditions based in the tributary systems of the *señoríos* of the Zapotecs, Mixtecs, and other indigenous groups here. The Sunday Market in Tlacolula is one of the oldest continuously running markets in Mexico, and ergo, the Americas. Commerce among Oaxacans is vital to the economy all over the state, and in El Istmo, it's all run by women.

Tourism

The largest chunk (68.5 percent) of Oaxaca's economic activity is categorized in the tertiary sector, or service industry. Tourism is a vital part of the state's economy, intrinsically linked with all the primary economic activities here: real estate and property rentals (17.2 percent), construction (11.6 percent), retail (9.9 percent), educational services (7.9 percent), and wholesale (7.5 percent). Because so many foods and artisanal products in Oaxaca are sourced from within the state, you can be sure that just about any purchase you make puts money into the local economy.

People and Culture

Evidence of advanced cultures date back over 2,000 years in Oaxaca, but cave paintings at places like Yagul and Apoala reveal signs of human habitation here as far back as 6,000 years ago. Half a millennium ago, these pre-Hispanic cultures combined their rich indigenous traditions with the new customs and goods introduced by the Spanish to create a land teeming with art, craftworkers' products, festivals, dances, and recipes wholly unique from anywhere else in the world.

DEMOGRAPHY AND DIVERSITY

Nearly 70 percent of Oaxaca's population has its roots in one of the state's 17 distinct indigenous groups, making it the state with the highest percentage of indigenous peoples in Mexico.

The geographic isolation caused by Oaxaca's mountainous terrain also led to cultural and linguistic isolation, creating practices unique to a certain region, or even to one small town, some of which survive to this day. One of the most striking examples of this is the *caldo de piedra* (stone soup) of San Felipe Usila, in El Papaloapan. Since it is traditionally served in a bowl-shaped hollow in a boulder or in the sand next to the river, anthropologists believe this recipe to predate the making of ceramics in Mexico, which is estimated to have begun as far back as 2300 BC.

The Immigration Issue

Immigration from Latin America has become a contentious topic in the 21st century, but, as with the majority of news stories, it is often discussed in a contextual vacuum, rarely taking into account the historical events that caused it. Yes, many Mexicans came to the United States in search of work in the 1990s and early 2000s, but this surge was due to NAFTA's effect on corn prices in Mexico, making the cultivation of it unsustainable for poor farmers all over the country. If the United States is at least partially at fault for such an occurrence, do its citizens not have the responsibility to deal with the consequences of their actions? Do the people of Mexico and other Latin American countries affected by U.S. policies not have the right to seek the country's help when it has made life for them so difficult?

U.S. citizens really need look no further than their hometowns to realize that their economy needs these people. And the United States has known this for a long time. During World War II, U.S. farmers were worried about labor shortages, so the United States implemented the Bracero Program (from the Spanish word *brazo*, for "arm") in 1942. Although it definitely was not perfect, as much abuse and mistreatment was reported, it still offered a legal way for Mexican laborers to work temporarily in the United States and return to their families in Mexico when the season was over.

U.S. farmers got the labor they needed, but they still took advantage of their workers. It took the brilliant organizational minds and sheer determination of César Chávez (1927-1993) and Dolores Huerta (b. 1930), of the United Farm Workers of America (UFW), to force farmers to treat their workers more fairly, including paying them the wages they were owed. With their slogans "*¡Sí, se puede!*" (Yes, we can!) and "*¡Huelga!*" (Strike!), as well as hunger strikes and intentional arrests, they organized one of the most successful boycotts in U.S. history, ultimately forcing the grape farmers of Delano, California, to come to the table, negotiate, and attempt to run legitimate businesses.

The Bracero Program ended in 1964, but not the U.S. economy's need for cheap labor. The creation of the *maquiladora* industry in 1989, by which foreign companies can take advantage of cheap labor and tax breaks in Mexican towns along the border, is evidence enough of this fact. Furthermore, much is said about the people coming to the United States to work, but the discussion rarely focuses on the willingness of U.S. employers to hire them. The common anti-immigrant trope in the early 2000s was that they were taking jobs that could be done by American workers. This one lost traction due to the fact that the majority of U.S. citizens, including the ones who claimed to believe it, widely recognize that they really don't want to do those jobs anyway.

Anti-immigrant fear-mongering in the second decade of the 2000s turned toward the claim that immigrants are a drain on public funds. With what I see when I cross the border, all the technology and personnel, the trucks, vans, ATVs, drones, guns, fences, "detention centers," and everything else involved with border security, that argument falls flat. Why is it preferable to buy bullets rather than food?

Every region in the state has created its own cultural identity, each with its own dances, music, traditional vestments, recipes, ingredients, and more that represent it. If you study up on the embroidery styles of the various regions, for example, you'll be able to identify the region, sometimes the specific town, that a person wearing them calls home. This rich cultural diversity really is what makes getting to know Oaxaca so much fun. Around just about every corner, you'll find something new.

INDIGENOUS CULTURES

This section covers 17 indigenous cultures, including the Tacuates, who speak a dialect of Mixtec but are a different ethnic group.

The annual festivals known as the **Guelaguetza,** or sometimes **Los Lunes del Cerro** (Mondays on the Hill) revel in the vibrancy and diversity of Oaxaca's indigenous traditions with folk dance extravaganzas and colorful processions. The official Guelaguetza is held in Oaxaca City on the last two Mondays of July, but communities all over the state have their own Guelaguetza or Los Lunes del Cerro at other times of the year. One of the most popular is in Zaachila and is also held in July.

Zapotecs

The Zapotecs didn't name themselves as such. The Spanish word *zapoteco* comes from the exonym the Aztecs gave them during their colonization campaign just before Cortés and company arrived in Mexico. The Aztecs called them *tzapotēcah*, which means "inhabitants of the land of the *zapote*," for the region's abundance of the *zapote* fruit, a type of persimmon.

Most Zapotecs call themselves "The People of the Clouds" in their various dialects. Those of the Valles Centrales call themselves Ben Zaa; those of El Istmo, Binni Zaa; and those of the Sierra Norte, Bene Xhon. The Zapotecs of the Sierra Sur call themselves Mén Diiste, which means "People of the Old Language."

With over 400,000 speakers in Oaxaca, Zapotecs make up the largest indigenous group in the state. Although many people will identify as Zapotec, they will identify more strongly with the region from which they hail.

Their heartland is the Valles Centrales, where you'll find the remains of their greatest pre-Hispanic urban centers, such as Monte Albán, Mitla, and Yagul. Along with the Mixtecs, they put up the strongest resistance to the Aztec invasion of the late 15th century, ultimately putting the kibosh on it and reaching a peace treaty after a lengthy battle at Guiengola, near present-day Tehuantepec, in El Istmo.

Zapotecs had a polytheistic religion, which, like many Mesoamerican religions, had gods that represented natural forces. The most important god was Cocijo, whose name means "lightning bolt." Similar to the Aztec god Tlaloc, Cocijo's domain was the lightning, thunder, and, most importantly, rain, and was also credited with having created the world. In ceramics and other artwork found at pre-Hispanic Zapotec sites, he is represented as a short, squat deity with a porcine nose and a forked snake's tongue curled over his chin. His headdress features traditional Zapotec glyphs. You can see statues of him in the museum at Monte Albán and large stone masks of his face at Lambityeco, in the Valle de Tlacolula.

The Zapotecs were one of the first Mesoamerican peoples to have a writing system, but aside from a few details about calendric symbols, linguists are still unable to decipher the true nature and meaning of their pictographic characters. Instead of left to right, Zapotec glyphs are read from top to bottom, and the language is believed to have been less phonetic than the more developed script of the Classic Maya, but this is speculation and has not been confirmed.

It could easily be said that the Zapotec *huipiles* (embroidered blouses) of El Istmo are the most popular in Oaxaca. Technically part of a full *traje de gala* (party dress), they feature big, brightly colored flowers on a background of black velvet. Other traditional dresses of El Istmo include the geometrically intricate *traje de costura* (sewing suit) and the much less elaborate *traje de luto* (mourning dress). Zapotec embroidery from other parts of the state tends to also feature flowers, though with different designs, as well as other inspirations from nature, such as birds, foxes, and other animals, including people. Some feature monochrome embroidery on a white cotton fabric, while others, such as the much smaller and more delicate stitching of San Antonino Castillo Velasco, in the Valles Centrales, are as multicolored as the flower fields outside the town.

Zapotec communities tend to have a communal political organization, and many in the Sierra Norte have abolished the practice of private landownership altogether, instead preferring to work the land together and benefit the community as a whole. Unlike the majority of indigenous peoples across the Americas, Zapotecs have played a pivotal political role in Mexico. Benito Juárez (1806-1872), born in Guelatao, in the Sierra Norte, served as governor of Oaxaca and president of Mexico multiple times during his turbulent career.

Women in Zapotec society are traditionally in charge of a household's economy and finances, especially in El Istmo. While the male head of household may be in charge of working the fields, animal husbandry, or fishing, his wife manages the process of getting the goods to market. Nontraditional gender roles have been taken a step further in El Istmo, where the *muxes* (MOO-shehs), a third gender of men raised to take on the roles of women, are widely accepted in society there.

Mixtecs

With around 267,000 speakers, the Mixtecs are the second-largest indigenous group in Oaxaca, accounting for just over 22 percent of the indigenous population. Like the Zapotecs, Mixtecs did not choose that name for themselves. The Aztecs called them the *mixtecah*, which means (possibly to the chagrin of the Zapotecs) "People of the Clouds," and they weren't far off. The Mixtecs called themselves the Ñuu Savi, or one of its dialectical variations, which means "People of the Rain."

Because of the similarity in their languages and names for themselves, it is widely believed that Zapotecs and Mixtecs were once the same people, and that their languages began to diversify sometime around 4400 BC in the Valle

de Tehuacán, which now straddles the border of Puebla and Oaxaca. Their heartland is called La Mixteca, which is in the western part of Oaxaca, and includes the neighboring parts of Guerrero and Puebla. It is divided into highlands (La Mixteca Alta), lowlands (La Mixteca Baja), and the coast (La Mixteca de la Costa).

According to Mixtec legend, their people were conceived from trees along a river summoned up from the depths of the earth by the gods, and they conquered their land, La Mixteca, with the help of El Flechador del Sol (The One Who Wounded the Sun with an Arrow), a mythical warrior who made the western sun bleed red when he aimed his dart skyward. When you see the red hillsides of La Mixteca at sunset, the myth kind of starts to make sense.

Mixtec codices tell of a great ruler named Eight-Deer Jaguar Claw, who is now remembered as the great unifier of the previously disparate Mixtec *señoríos* (chiefdoms). Born in AD 1063 in Tilantongo, Eight-Deer left town at the age of 18 with the specific purpose to create his own dynasty. He moved south, toward the coast, where he took advantage of political instability and the region's agricultural resources, valuable to those in the highlands,

dance from La Mixteca called Jarabe Mixteco

and founded the *señorío* of Tututepec. In 1098, he returned to his hometown of Tilantongo to become the *cacique* there. Using a series of military campaigns and politically motivated marriages, he ruled over and unified the *señoríos* of Tututepec, in La Mixteca de la Costa; Tilantongo, in La Mixteca Alta; and Teozacualco, in La Mixteca Baja.

Mixtecs are known for their economy. Many pre-Hispanic towns in La Mixteca were large regional trading hubs that connected commerce with civilizations all over the Americas, even as far south as Peru. La Mixteca was once the largest global producer of the cactus-dwelling scale insects called *cochinilla* (cochineal), which was used for red dyes before the invention of synthetic ones in the 19th century. They were also renowned for their skills as goldsmiths, and many of the intricately filigreed pieces found in Monte Albán and Zaachila are believed to have been of Mixtec design.

Traditional Mixtec clothing varies widely, depending on region, and often features images of birds, scorpions, deer, winged horses, or people, but geometrical designs are just as prominent. Common, but not ubiquitous, among the various Mixtec embroidery styles are elaborately designed collars. One style from Pinotepa Nacional, for example, features embroidery only along the collar.

More recently, Mixtecs have been known for their ability to stick together even after migrating thousands of miles. Mixtecs are estimated to be the largest indigenous immigrant population in the United States, and have been organizing migration while maintaining social and familial bonds since the 1980s, despite the challenges presented by diaspora. Because of this, academic researchers have applied labels such as "transnational" and "transborder" to the Mixtec community. Residents of Santiago Yosondúa, in La Mixteca, told me that all the new, colorful houses I saw on the hillside were not there just a few years ago. More and more people were able to come back home and start anew after spending time working in the United States, providing a better life for their families.

Mazatecs

The western slopes of the Sierra Norte (part of the La Cañada region), parts of El Papaloapan, and the bordering areas of Puebla and Veracruz, are home to the Mazatecs. Like Zapotec and Mixtec, Mazatec is an exonym that comes from the Nahuatl, the language of the Aztecs, meaning "People of the Deer." Their endonym for themselves is Ha Shuta Enima, which means "Humble People of Traditions Who Work in the Mountains." Their homeland is one of the most biodiverse areas in Oaxaca, and the world. Farmers here cultivate some of the rarest chiles in Mexico, some of which face the threat of extinction.

Mazatecs make up the third-largest indigenous group in Oaxaca, with around 180,000 speakers of the language, or about 15 percent of the indigenous population. Mazatec identity lies primarily in knowledge of their oral language, which currently has 10 distinct regional dialects, some of which are mutually unintelligible. Despite this lack of semantic understanding between dialects, speaking one of them still identifies one as pertaining to the group and its customs. The Mazatec language is considered to be a branch of the Popolcan linguistic tree, along with the Ixcatec, Chocholtec, and Popolcan tongues.

Mazatec embroidery is quite fond of the colors blue and pink, such as those of Huautla de Jiménez, which often feature floral and avian designs, like peacocks, and blue and pink ribbons woven through. Also quite popular are the two-tone blouses from towns like San Bartolomé Ayautla and San Felipe Jalapa de Díaz. These feature large embroidered designs of birds and flowers that cover the majority of the shirt and are generally of one hue that stands out against the color of the fabric.

Because of their isolation on the steep slopes and ravines of the northern Oaxacan mountains, many Mazatec communities have preserved ancient traditions and languages. With up to 40 percent of the

Mazatec-speaking population speaking little or no Spanish at all, they are considered among the least Hispanicized indigenous peoples in Oaxaca. This lack of interaction with the Mazatec community reached a critical point in the mid-19th century, when the Río Papaloapan was dammed to create Lake Miguel Alemán, which forced over 22,000 Mazatec people to migrate elsewhere, as their homes were now underwater.

One tradition that has lasted and garnered much global attention is the use of hallucinogenic mushrooms in traditional medicinal and spiritual practices. The *curandera* (shaman and medicine woman) María Sabina garnered worldwide notoriety for herself and her hometown of Huautla de Jiménez when she openly welcomed outsiders to participate in her traditional ceremonies. Like the filling of Lake Miguel Alemán at the foot of the mountains, this event changed Mazatec life in Huautla de Jiménez forever, and hallucinogenic experiences are now the main tourist attraction here.

Chinantecs

Inhabitants of the northern foothills of the Sierra Norte and the hot, humid tropical lowlands of El Papaloapan, the Chinantecs call themselves Tsa Ju Jmí, which means "People of the Ancient Word." They call their traditional homeland La Chinantla, which includes the towns of Valle Nacional, San Felipe Usila, San Pedro Sochiapam, and other small communities tucked away in the sultry ravines of the foothills. With just over 107,000 speakers of one of the tonal languages called Chinantec (linguists have a hard time fully classifying them as dialects), Chinantecs are the fifth-largest indigenous group in Oaxaca.

Like their Mazatec neighbors, Chinantec weavers are fond of using ribbons to decorate their *huipiles*. Whereas other regions tend to find inspiration for their designs in nature, Chinantec *huipiles* are a reflection of their religion, much of which has to do with cosmogony and elemental opposites—night and day, animal and human, good and bad, body and soul. Common design motifs include a sun and moon, two-headed eagles, plumed serpents, and traditional Chinantec *grecas*, geometric patterns used to represent various elements, such as the four cardinal directions or concepts like protection or punishment. Although the majority of Chinantecs are now Catholic, much of their old religion has been syncretized into that of those who conquered them centuries ago.

Around AD 999, a Chinantec king named Quiana founded a *señorío* (chiefdom) in La Chinantla, but internal conflicts caused a rift in the sovereignty he established, and La Chinantla was subsequently divided into two *señoríos*, La Chinantla Grande, comprised of the tropical lowlands to the east, and La Chinantla Pichinche, in the rough, hilly west. Around 1300, part of the population of La Chinantla Pichinche seceded and formed its own *señorío* based in Usila. In the mid-15th century, the Aztecs established an outpost at Tuxtepec, and from there led campaigns to conquer the Chinantecs and other native inhabitants of northern Oaxaca.

When the Spanish arrived, they began to enforce their policy of *congregación*, which involved displacing indigenous populations and forcing them to live in communities organized by the conquistadors. After decades of paying tribute to the Aztecs, the Chinantecs had had enough of colonization, and many put the past behind them and united once again to rise up against the Spanish. The first of these uprisings was in the town of Tepetotutla in 1530. Despite their resistance to the colonizers, the Spanish eventually won out, forcing Chinantecs to work on tobacco, sugarcane, and fruit plantations and cattle ranches for the next three centuries.

Like the Mazatecs to the west, the Chinantecs once again faced displacement in the 20th century, when the Cerro de Oro Dam was built in the 1970s and 1980s. This reservoir, now connected to the Miguel Alemán reservoir, displaced over 26,000 people. That being said, both reservoirs paved the way to the industrialization of El Papaloapan, bringing jobs, schools, and agriculture and connecting once remote communities to the outside world. Today the Chinantec heartland is Oaxaca's biggest industrial center, producing pineapples, bananas, mangoes, and other tropical fruits, as well as sugar, paper, and other important products.

Mixes and Zoques

Although they are distinct, the languages of the Mixes and Zoques are considered to be part of the same linguistic family. With about 115,000 speakers, Mixes make up 9.5 percent of Oaxaca's indigenous population. Zoque speakers make up a much smaller percentage, with only about 11,000 native speakers. Some linguists have theorized that the Mixe-Zoque peoples came from the Olmecs of the Gulf Coast, but others claim that evidence traces their origins as far south as Peru.

According to Mixe legend, they migrated to their lands under the leadership of a great king named Condoy, who settled them in the lands around the sacred, cloud-covered Cerro Cempoaltépetl (sem-poh-ahl-TEH-peh-tl), which in Nahuatl means "20 Winds Mountain." It is believed that the Mixes once occupied an area much larger than their current homeland in the eastern Sierra Norte (known as the Sierra Mixe) and northern part of El Istmo, but much of their territory was lost due to the imperial forces of the neighboring Zapotecs, Mixtecs, Zoques, and Popolocas, as well as the Aztecs and Spanish. The political turbulence of Mexican independence also had a hand in shrinking the boundaries of Mixe domain.

Little archaeological evidence exists in the Sierra Mixe, but it is known that the pre-Hispanic and colonial-era Mixes were fierce defenders of the land their legendary king bequeathed them. Neither the Zaachila of the Zapotecs, Ahuitzotl of the Aztecs, or Cortés of the Spanish conquistadors were able to subdue the Mixe completely. After two failed attempts to put them under his thumb, Hernán Cortés mentioned the tenacity of the Mixes and Zapotecs in a letter to the King of Spain,

writing that his men failed "because of the roughness of the terrain, and because the warriors are very fierce and well-armed."

Figuring he'd catch more bees with honey, Cortés turned to religion to further Spanish dominance, finally reaching a peace agreement in 1555, when Dominican friars began proselytizing and building in the region. Despite the success of the conquest's spiritual element here and elsewhere in Oaxaca, the Mixe pride themselves on never having been conquered by outside forces. Like many other indigenous peoples in Mexico, their brand of Catholicism is heavily syncretized with elements of their native spiritual beliefs. Deities such as Poj 'Enee (Thunder Wind), the Mixe rain god, and Naaxwiiñ (Earth Surface), a fertility goddess, are in their pantheon alongside Jesus Christ, the Virgin Mary, and the host of saints.

The Zoques did not have the same luck against invaders. In pre-Hispanic times, the Zoques occupied much of Chiapas, part of Tabasco, and the northern part of El Istmo, in Oaxaca. They are believed to be descendants of the Olmecs. Until the end of the 15th century, they maintained peaceful social and economic ties with the Aztecs, but in 1494, Aztec emperor Ahuitzotl wanted more and invaded the Selva Zoque (Zoque Jungle). They were unable to defend themselves as fiercely as the Mixes, and were quickly subjected to pay tributes to the Mexica empire. Cortés also found success in colonizing the Zoques. His dispatch to the region, led by conquistador Luis Marín, divided the Zoque land up into *encomiendas* and promptly put the people to work for the Spanish crown.

In the early 20th century, Mixe towns were still run like chiefdoms, with *caciques* (chiefs) in the towns of Cacalotepec, Ayutla, and Zacatepec, but were not united politically. Each belonged to different neighboring administrative districts. In the 1920s, the *cacique* of Zacatepec, Manuel Rodríguez, began to get a taste for non-Mixe comforts and luxuries, like fancy dress, riches, even emigration, but his son Luis, however, was not on board. In 1926, Luis ran his father out of town and usurped his position as *cacique* of Zacatepec. This was only the beginning of Luis Rodríguez's devious, power-hungry political career.

Twelve years later, when the Oaxacan legislature was persuaded by President Lázaro Cárdenas to give the Mixe their own administrative district in Oaxaca in honor of their bravery on the battlefield against the French in 1865, the three Mixe seats of power began to fight over which would be named the capital. Luis Rodríguez used violence to grab power over the Mixe communities, and even hired his godson to shoot his main rival, Daniel Martínez, *cacique* of Ayutla. Most likely in an attempt to cover his tracks, Rodríguez then banished his godson to Mexico City, but the scorned hitman instead returned to the villages, organizing an uprising that proved to be the bloodiest battle of the conflict. Even at war, Luis Rodríguez liked to have a good time, and during a patronal festival reportedly ate too much *barbacoa*, for which he was transported to Oaxaca City, where he died of an embolism.

However, aside from bloodshed, his legacy also included the formation of the Association of Progressive Town Councils of the Sierra Mixe, which collected data on the communities that could be taken to the state and federal governments to request funding for schools, clinics, and other services.

Today, Mixes are known as the producers of the rare *chile pasilla mixe*, sometimes called *chile pasilla oaxaqueño*. *Pasilla* is the dried form of a chile called *chilaca*, but the cloudy alpine conditions of the Sierra Mixe make it impossible for the chiles to air dry completely. To finish the drying process, Mixe growers smoke the chiles in adobe huts. The *pasilla mixe* is one of the Oaxacan chiles you will have an extremely hard time finding outside the state. Mixe embroidery sometimes features floral or anthropomorphic designs, but tends to stick to finely stitched geometric patterns. Zoque *huipiles* tend to be less elaborate, usually white cotton blouses with hand-stitched embroidery along the collar. Zoque weavers also work with wool and silk.

Chatinos

Chatinos make up a little over 4 percent of Oaxaca's population, with about 50,700 speakers. The low, tropical foothills around Santa Catarina Juquila and neighboring communities in this small slice of the coast are where the Chatinos call home. Like many native Oaxacans, the majority of Chatinos work in agriculture, primarily on coffee plantations. If you have trouble pronouncing their name for themselves, Qne-a Tnya-e, or one of its dialectical variations, don't worry. In all of its forms, it means something like "People of the Language that Takes Some Work."

Chatinos have a number of linguistic and cultural commonalities with the Zapotecs. Their language is considered to be in the same branch as that of the Zapotecs. Linguistic evidence linking the Chatinos to the Zapotecs is very scant, but points to language divergence from the Zapotecs anywhere between 4000 BC and AD 200. They began to break cultural and political ties with their linguistic descendants toward the end of that period.

Much of what is known about the Chatinos is found in the codices of the Mixtec people. It is written that they made an alliance with the kingdom of Mixtec unifier Eight-Deer Jaguar Claw during his reign in the 11th century. The Chatino were still tributaries to the Mixtec kingdom when Spanish conquistador Pedro de Alvarado arrived in Tututepec in 1522. The foreign diseases brought by the European explorers had devastating consequences for the Chatinos, who are estimated to have numbered as many as 250,000 before the conquest. By 1544, a pair of voracious epidemics had shrunk that number to as low as 35,000 people.

The Spanish put the Chatinos to work in fields, basically appropriating the tribute system already in place, but redirecting its benefits from the Mixtec to the Spanish crown. Many farmers began producing cochineal, which was then New Spain's second most valuable export, outshined only by silver. The Spanish exploited Chatino labor and goods through a system of credit and inflated prices euphemistically called *repartimientos de comercio* (commercial distribution).

Like the Mixtecs and Zapotecs, who also relied on cochineal, the Chatinos had to find other sources of income when synthetic dyes took over the market in the 19th century. After the Miahuatecos (Zapotecs from Miahuatlán) brought the coffee plant to the Sierra Sur, many Chatinos also began to plant the crop in the shady, tropical hillsides they called home. This brought more money to the people, but also led to more privatization of the land, and this, along with the repartition of landholdings of the Reform Era, caused many Chatinos to lose the rights to the land they had lived on for generations. This economic subjugation continued into the 20th century, and by the 1980s, subsistence and coffee farmers began to leave their previous crops behind to focus on one much more profitable, marijuana. Despite the hundreds of hectares devoted to marijuana cultivation here and elsewhere in Oaxaca, the state has seen relatively less violence related to narcotrafficking than neighboring Guerrero and states in the north.

Chatino *huipiles* are white cotton blouses with crocheted designs of flowers and/or birds along the collar, shoulders, and upper chest, with a sternum-shaped strip of crochet down the middle. Chatino artisans also work with ceramics, and weave the fibers of the maguey plant, called ixtle, into ropes, strings, nets, and hammocks.

Chatino religion is based on an equilibrium between human society, the natural world, and the divine, which they see as intrinsically linked. Many of their traditional gods, mostly based in nature and natural forces, have been syncretized with Catholic saints and deities. The most famous celebration in the region is the patronal festival for the Virgin of Juquila, held in Santa Catarina Juquila on December 8.

Triques

The Triques, or Triqui in Spanish, occupy a small 500-square-km (193-sq-mi) patch of mountains in La Mixteca, in the districts of Tlaxiaco, Putla, and Juxtlahuaca. With just over 18,000 speakers, Triques make up 1.5 percent of Oaxaca's population. Their territory spans the slopes delineating the High and Low Mixteca, ranging 800-2,500 meters (2,625-8,202 ft) above sea level. The biggest Trique settlements are San Martín Itunyuoso, Santo Domingo del Estado, and San Juan Copala. A few theories speculate different origins of the Spanish name Triqui, but their own name for themselves, in its various dialects, means "Native Person."

According to their oral tradition, the descendants of the Trique hailed from Monte Albán and were forced to roam the Mixteca after being banished for disobeying a royal decree. They kept moving south, but were forced to stop around Putla and vicinity due to mosquitoes, rains, and other unforgiving natural barriers to settlement. The Mixtecs of Tlachquiauhco, modern-day Tlaxiaco, subjugated them and forced them to pay tribute, and when the Aztecs arrived, both Mixtecs and Triques were made tributaries to the outside regime.

With the Triques and Mixtecs, the Spanish had more luck with the word than the sword, but the Catholic religion didn't take root immediately. Communities such as Copala fiercely resisted the imposition of new beliefs. Their lot didn't improve much with independence, either. Triques remained under the yolk of the ruling class's various modes of labor exploitation, and rebelled in 1843. After five years of fighting, their leaders were captured and the uprising quelled. Triques lost more land to privatization after the introduction of coffee to this part of Oaxaca.

The Triques' struggle for land and civil rights continues to this day. In 1956, a struggle between Triques and government forces left a number of soldiers dead, and the federal government responded by bombing and firing machine gun rounds on the indigenous residents of Copala. Since then, Triques have organized to demand an end to oppression. Throughout the majority of my time writing this book, a group of Trique women were camped outside the Palacio de Gobierno in Oaxaca City, demanding justice for the disappearance of their husbands and illegal appropriation of ancestral lands.

One controversial pre-Hispanic practice that survives in Trique culture to this day is that of "bride price," money paid by a potential groom to a bride's family for her hand in marriage. Trique brides traditionally marry very young, sometimes as young as 13 or 14 years old. Like the practice of eating sea turtle eggs in some parts of the coast, this custom has been judged by outsiders as being outdated or immoral, but proponents note that the bride and groom always know each other beforehand, and everyone involved gives consent to the marriage.

Triques are known for their distinct red, full-body *huipiles* with horizontal stripes embellished with geometric designs and ribbons woven vertically the full length of the dress. Some will have multicolored ribbons hanging from the collar. Girls learn the art of weaving from a young age. Trique artisans also make ceramics, hats, baskets, mats, and other products for personal and commercial use.

Amuzgos and Tacuates

The Amuzgos and Tacuates occupy small patches of land in La Mixteca de la Costa, or what is also referred to as La Costa Chica (Small Coast), which spans the Oaxacan border with Guerrero. Only about 8,000 of the total 58,000 Amuzgo speakers live in Oaxaca. Their name comes from the Nahuatl word *amoxco*, which the prevailing theory states as meaning "place of books," most likely because the main pre-Hispanic Amuzgo settlement was once a large regional administrative center.

The true origin of the Amuzgos is unknown, but their linguistic link with Mixtecs leads researchers to infer that they were once the same people. The town of Xochistlahuaca,

in Guerrero, was the Amuzgo capital in AD 1100, when the Mixtecs conquered and subjected them to tributaries. Later, when the Aztecs made their way to La Mixteca, the Amuzgos rebelled against their new colonizers, but uprisings in 1497, 1504, and 1507 were suppressed by the Aztecs.

The colonization by the Spanish had devastating consequences on the Amuzgos. Disease, state violence, and overwork nearly eradicated their populations completely, their numbers dwindling to a mere 200 people by 1582. As indigenous populations declined in Mexico, the Spanish brought slaves from Africa, primarily to the port of Veracruz. Many slaves who escaped settled in areas along La Costa Chica, pushing the Amuzgo even farther inland than the Mixtecs and Spanish had.

The construction of highways in the 20th century opened up Amuzgo communities to the outside world, which opened up economic opportunities to the previously isolated inhabitants. Many opened transportation businesses, while others took their chance at immigration, many choosing to try their luck in the United States.

Numbering only about 3,300 people, the Tacuates inhabit a tiny patch of La Mixteca de la Costa east of Amuzgo land, in the towns of Santa María Zacatepec and Santiago Ixtayutla. Fond of snakes themselves, the Aztecs must have taken a liking to the Tacuates, calling them the same name they called themselves: Snake Men. The Tacuates are believed to have originated from Ixtayutla, but according to their legend, a giant eagle forced the original population to split, which formed the town of Zacatepec. The mythical eagle is not unique Tacuate lore. Legends of giant, sometimes two-headed eagles also appear in the oral traditions and artisanry of the Mazatecs, Mixtecs, and Chinantecs.

Although their language is considered a Mixtec dialect from Zacatepec, the Tacuates do not consider themselves Mixtec. Their language, which they call Tu'un Va'a, is at most only about 60 percent mutually intelligible with Mixtec dialects in neighboring towns.

Amuzgos and Tacuates share a style of *huipil* that is a blouse or full-length dress, usually white, but sometimes blue, black, or other colors, with two vertical stripes and rows of intricate, colorful floral embroidery. Tacuate women also wear *huipiles* that feature brightly colored animals embroidered on the chest and back.

Huaves

A little under 17,000 Huaves inhabit the large sandspits between the lagoons of El Istmo and the Gulf of Tehuantepec, principally in the communities of San Mateo del Mar, San Dionisio del Mar, Santa María del Mar, and San Francisco del Mar. Although they shared El Istmo with the Mixes and Zoques, before the arrival of the Zapotecs, the Huave language is considered an isolate, totally unrelated to other languages. Linguists have attempted to demonstrate connections to the Mixe-Zoque and Mayan families, but none of these theories have panned out.

Around AD 1300, the Aztecs came through El Istmo to open up a trade route to the Soconusco region in Chiapas, and the Zapotecs came on their heels to take advantage of the instability they left in their wake. This pushed the Huave as close to the coast as possible. The name Huave is actually a rather derogatory Zapotec exonym meaning "People Who Rot in the Humidity." During the colonial era, disease almost wiped them out completely, until toward the end of the 16th century, the Huave only numbered around 100 people.

Due to their precarious location between the sea and the lagoons, Huaves have learned to live with the water and other elements, earning them the nickname Mareños (Sea People). Year-round, they deal with fierce winds, either from the north or the south. Rains are scarce, but when they do come, they can cause deadly flooding. When they don't come for too long, the lagoons dry up. Their lives are intricately linked with the sea, and they are known as excellent fishermen. The pre-Hispanic Zapotecs basically viewed them

as a cash cow, knowing that the Huave needed the corn, beans, and other fruits of the land, and would therefore keep their markets brimming with fresh seafood. The Spanish likewise took their pound of flesh in fish and shrimp.

Considering there is little else to do on the sandspit, the Huave continue fishing to this day. Census data shows that their numbers are growing, and toward the end of the 20th century, they even founded new communities, such as Cuauhtémoc and Benito Juárez, in between San Mateo del Mar and Salina Cruz.

Cuicatecs

Numbering just under 11,000, the Cuicatecs live on about 8,400 square km (3,243 sq mi) in the Cañada region, in the state's semiarid northwest. Their name in Nahuatl means "People of Song." The Cuicatec language is in the same family as Mixtec, and, like La Mixteca, their heartland is divided into the lowlands of the canyon country and the highlands to the west.

Little is known about the origins of the Cuicatecs, due to the Spanish having destroyed their codices, maps, and other texts, but archaeological findings in the region suggest that they are the descendants of the Toltec refugees fleeing the fall of Tula in 1064. When the Spanish arrived in this part of Oaxaca around 1526, the Cuicatecs had been weakened by Mixtec and Aztec incursions on their land, and were in no condition to put up a fight. The majority of Cuicatecs fled to the mountains west of present-day San Juan Bautista Cuicatlán, and now most live in mountain towns like Concepción Pápalo and San Juan Tepeuxila.

Dominican friars had a hard time with the Cuicatecs, and much of the naturalism of their native religion remains to this day. Their principal deity Sá Iko, now associated Jesus Christ, inhabits their sacred mountain, Cerro Cheve. Practices such as sacrificing livestock for favorable weather conditions are also still quite common. Cuicatecs are so fond of doing things their own way, that only one of the nine communities in which they live is governed by the official party system, whereas the others do so according to their ancestral customs.

Cuicatec land is very fertile, and many devote themselves to farming—cultivating beans, corn, chiles, squash, mangoes, oranges, apricots, and nuts. Coffee is grown in the highlands. This is the only region in Oaxaca, and the world, where the rare chile pepper *chile chilhuacle* is grown.

Chontals

According to the Documentation of Endangered Languages Archive (DOBES), the speakers of one of the two extant variations of Oaxacan Chontal number less than 5,000, and fluent first-language speakers are much fewer, and aging. They inhabit a chunk of the coast and foothills of the Sierra Sur measuring only 870 square km (336 sq mi), between Huatulco and Salina Cruz. This land is divided by name and by dialect into highlands and lowlands. The citizens of Santiago Astata and San Pedro Huamelula, closer to the coast, are called *costeños*. Chontals that live in towns like Magdalena Tequisistlán, Santa María Ecatepec, and San Carlos Yautepec, up in the hills, are called *serranos* (of the mountains).

Linguists have traced the genealogy of the Chontal language to that of the Hokan peoples of Arizona, California, and Baja California, as well as to the Jicaquean languages of Honduras. The Chontals of Oaxaca, however, are not related to the Chontals of Tabasco, who speak a language in the Mayan family. The word *chontal* is an Aztec exonym for a foreign people. The *costeño* dialect of Oaxacan Chontal, sometimes called Huameluteco, is more endangered than its *serrano* version. The DOBES Archives estimate that there are only around 1,100 speakers of *costeño* Chontal, and all 100 or so of those who are fluent first-language speakers are over 70 years old. The Chontal of the highlands is sometimes called Tequistlateco, but linguists view this as erroneous. The true Tequistlateco, once spoken in Tequisistlán and considered a third dialect of Chontal, is now extinct.

Chontals are primarily subsistence farmers, depending on the rains that fall June-September to water their fields of corn, beans, squash, soursop, avocado, mamey, nache, and guava. Coffee is also grown on the shady hillsides in the Chontal highlands, which reach altitudes around 700 meters (2,297 ft) above sea level.

Nahuas

Nahuatl is the most widely spoken pre-Hispanic language in Mexico, but in Oaxaca, there are only a couple small enclaves of people who speak the language of the Aztecs. Perhaps the colonial endeavors of the Aztecs at the end of the 15th century had insufficient time to root the language in Oaxaca before the arrival of the Spanish, or maybe the language found too much resistance among the headstrong native Oaxacans, but Nahuatl is now one of the lesser-spoken indigenous tongues in the state.

The largest population of Nahuatl speakers is in the northwest corner of the state, on the border with Veracruz. Around 13,000 native Nahuatl speakers live primarily in the towns of Santiago Texcalcingo, Santa María Teopoxco, Capultitlán, Vigastepec, and San Bernandino. This community is bordered to the north, east, and south by Mazatec-speaking towns, like Huautla de Jiménez.

Nahuatl is also spoken by a small group of people in and around Tuxtepec, in the northeast corner of El Papaloapan. However, the language is at risk of dying out in the area, and in 2018, a group of teachers and concerned citizens of Tuxtepec began offering courses in Nahuatl to keep it alive in this part of Oaxaca.

Chocholtecs, Ixcatecs, and Popolocas

The Chocholtecs, Ixcatecs, and Popolocas live in the northwest of Oaxaca, in La Mixteca and the Valle de Tehuacán-Cuicatlán. According to the 2015 census, the most at-risk of these three languages is Ixcatec, spoken primarily, if not solely, by just under 150 people in Santa María Ixcatlán, about two hours through the rough canyon country west of Cuicatlán.

Ixcatlán is a Nahuatl term meaning "place of cotton." When attempting to put Ixcatec on the family tree, linguists initially tried to relate it to Zapotec and Mixtec, but the final conclusion shows that it is more closely related to the tongues of the Chocholtecs and Popolocas.

Numbers of Chocholtec speakers are also quite meager. Also called Chochos, Chochones, or sometimes Chuchnones, in Spanish, only about 730 native speakers of the language live in San Juan Bautista Coixtlahuaca and other nearby villages in La Mixteca Alta. Their traditional land has historically been quite isolated and not easy to live on. The first highway came through Chocholtec territory in 1945, and the main Chocholtec towns weren't connected to the electrical grid until 1967. Because of the poor quality of the soil and general lack of resources in their region, many Chocholtecs have turned to migration in order to survive. Oaxaca City and Huajuapan de León are popular destinations within Oaxaca for finding work, but many choose to make the perilous journey to the United States in search of a better life.

The largest of these three groups is the Popolocas, who inhabit the Valle de Tehuacán-Cuicatlán that straddles the border with Puebla, but only a fraction of them live in Oaxaca. Like the Chontals, the Popolocas get their name from a pejorative word (*popoluca*) the Aztecs used for foreigners who didn't speak a version of Nahuatl, the connotation of which implies stammering or stupidity. Linguists believe that the Chochos and Popolocas were once the same people, but that their languages and cultures began to diverge sometime around the 11th century. Only a small slice of Popoluca territory is in Oaxaca, primarily in the municipality of Santiago Chazumba.

AFRO-MEXICANS OF LA COSTA CHICA

The Afro-Mexicans of La Costa Chica constitute a significant ethnic group in the state, one which is often overlooked culturally and politically.

Before President Vicente Guerrero (1782-1831), an Afro-Mexican himself, abolished slavery in 1829, escaped slaves from places like Veracruz fled to isolated spots along La Costa Chica of Oaxaca and Guerrero, and many others joined them once they were freed. In Oaxaca, they primarily inhabit the Lagunas de Chacahua, west of Puerto Escondido, but census data shows they also live in communities in La Cañada, El Papaloapan, El Istmo, and elsewhere along the coast.

When disease began to whittle down indigenous populations in Mexico, which the Spanish relied on for cheap or free labor, they began to bring slaves from Western Sudan in Africa, as well as from islands in the Caribbean, most of whom disembarked in Veracruz. They have historically had difficulty figuring into the Mexican identity, for they have never been quite populous, and are neither considered indigenous nor mestizo, which specifically means a mix of Spanish and American Indian.

The Afro-Mexicans of Oaxaca speak Spanish and celebrate the same holidays as elsewhere in Mexico, but they have retained elements of their African roots, which they combine with Mexican traditions. The Danza de los Diablos (Dance of the Devils), which they perform during Day of the Dead celebrations, has a clear African influence.

LANGUAGE

Spanish is the primary language spoken in Oaxaca, but it is by far not the only one. Oaxaca is the most linguistically diverse state in Mexico. About a third of the population speaks one of the 16 indigenous languages endemic to Oaxaca.

English is usually spoken at hotels, hostels, and restaurants that cater to foreign tourists in places like Oaxaca City, Huatulco, and Puerto Escondido. Still, it is a good idea to learn as much Spanish as possible, at least some basic phrases, before visiting. Mexican people are generally very helpful and patient with

Spanish language learners, often grateful for the effort and offering friendly corrections.

Indigenous Languages

Among the 31 Mexican states, Oaxaca has the most indigenous languages with 16, as well as the highest number and highest percentage of speakers of a language other than Spanish. Around 1.2 million Oaxacans speak an indigenous language, accounting for 34 percent of the entire population. Of these, 14 percent, or around 163,000, speak no Spanish at all. Many have a number of variant dialects, some of which are mutually unintelligible, despite being from the same mother tongue. Zapotec, for example, has 62 different linguistic varieties.

Speakers of **Zapotec** and **Mixtec** make up over half of the indigenous population in Oaxaca. These, along with many others in Oaxaca, belong to the Otomanguean language family, the branches of which include languages as far north as San Luis Potosí and as far south as Nicaragua. The Oto- is derived from the language Otomi, spoken in the states of Mexico, Querétaro, Hidalgo, and Guanajuato. The languages that comprise the Manguean branch of this family tree, which were once spoken in Central America, are now extinct. The other indigenous Oaxacan languages that are from the Otomanguean language family are **Chatino, Mazatec, Popoloca, Chocholtec, Ixcatec, Amuzgo, Cuicatec, Trique,** and **Chinantec.**

Mixe and **Zoque,** spoken in El Istmo and the Sierra Mixe (easternmost ranges of the Sierra Norte), are part of their own language family. Speakers of these languages also live in the states of Chiapas, Veracruz, and Tabasco. Linguists have counted 12 languages and 11 dialects within this language family. **Huave,** also spoken on El Istmo, is considered a language isolate, and has no genealogical connections to any other language.

The two mutually unintelligible languages called **Chontal** are believed to be part of language family trees with roots as far away as Cailfornia and Honduras. The Aztecs brought their language **Nahuatl,** part of the Uto-Aztecan language family, to Oaxaca through trade and colonization, and a small percentage of Oaxacans still speak it, primarily in the Sierra Mazateca.

RELIGION

According to Mexico's National Institute for Statistics and Geography (INEGI), 81 percent of Oaxacans profess to be Catholic. However, the religion brought by the Spanish didn't fully supplant the old beliefs, so much of the Catholicism practiced in Oaxaca, especially in rural areas, is heavily syncretized and acculturated with elements from pre-Hispanic faiths. Jesus took over for supreme beings that inhabited sacred mountains, and saints took the places of gods representing the sun, moon, rain, and other natural elements. Religions with oral traditions or dances depicting a god decapitating a snake, for example, could replace their god with Saint Michael the Archangel, who is often depicted as slaying a dragon.

Syncretism is most notable in celebrations like Day of the Dead, practiced by many pre-Hispanic cultures, most notably the Aztecs. The Zapotecs of El Istmo call their ceremony for honoring the dead Xanduu 'Yaa. The pre-Hispanic ceremonies were made to coincide with the Catholic All Saints' Day, resulting in the modern Day of the Dead holiday.

INEGI reports that there are a total of 17 religions practiced in Oaxaca, but the second-largest religious affiliation in Oaxaca actually isn't a religion at all. Just under 170,000 people in Oaxaca claim to not be a member of any specified faith. A number of Protestant faiths, such as Pentecostal, Jehovah's Witnesses, and Seventh-day Adventists, are next on the list. Also counted were Judaism, Islam, indigenous religions, and spiritualism.

VISUAL ARTS

Oaxaca has produced some of Mexico's most famous visual artists. Historically, the most notable is **Rufino Tamayo** (1899-1991), born in Oaxaca City. His parents died when he

Indigenous Languages of Oaxaca

According to the 2015 inter-census survey done by Mexico's National Institute for Statistics and Geography (INEGI), a total of 1,171,878 people five years and older speak an indigenous language in Oaxaca. Below is the breakdown by language.

Language	Population	Percentage of Total Oaxacans	Important Centers in Oaxaca
Zapotec	405,583	10.2%	Tlacolula, Pochutla, Juchitán
Mixtec	266,767	6.7%	Huajuapan de León, Tlaxiaco, Jamiltepec
Mazatec	179,856	4.5%	Huautla de Jiménez, Jalapa de Díaz
Mixe	114,673	2.8%	Santiago Zacatepec, San Pablo y San Pedro Ayutla
Chinantec	107,431	2.7%	Valle Nacional, San Lucas Ojitlán
Chatino	50,679	1.3%	Juquila, Santos Reyes Nopala
Trique	18,106	0.45%	Santo Domingo del Estado, San Juan Copala
Huave	16,899	0.42%	San Mateo del Mar, San Dionisio del Mar
Nahuatl	13,278	0.33%	Santiago Texcalcingo, Tuxtepec
Cuicatec	10,863	0.27%	Cuicatlán, Concepción Pápalo
Amuzgo	8,359	0.21%	San Pedro Amuzgos
Zoque	7,136	0.17%	Santa María Chimalapa, San Miguel Chimalapa
Chontal	5,064	0.12%	San Pedro Huamelula, Magdalena Tequisistlán
Chocholtec	735	0.018%	Coixtlahuaca
Ixcatec	145	0.0037%	Santa María Ixcatlán
Popoloca	144	0.0036%	Santiago Chazumba

was young, and he moved to Mexico City to live under the guardianship of his aunt, who worked as a fruit vendor in the markets there. This may have been where Tamayo obtained his artistic fondness for watermelons, a subject he painted often and for which he is remembered. In Mexico City, he worked and studied cubism and surrealism with another Oaxacan important to the arts, **José Vasconcelos** (1882-1959), a philosopher, writer, and politician known as the *caudillo cultural* (cultural leader) of the Mexican Revolution.

Although Tamayo was contemporary with and is remembered alongside Mexico's great painters of the Revolution, such as Diego Rivera (1886-1957), José Clemente Orozco (1883-1949), and David Alfaro Siqueiros (1896-1974), Tamayo did not have the same view of the Revolution as they did. Whereas Rivera, Orozco, and Siqueiros believed the Revolution was necessary for the future of their country, Tamayo was convinced it would only harm it. His painting *Niños jugando con fuego* (Children Playing with Fire, 1947) represents a pair of children being burned by the fire they started, an obvious metaphor for his opinion of the Revolution.

Tamayo's controversial attitudes toward the Revolution and the branch of Mexican art meant to support it led him to move to New York in 1926, but not before creating a buzz with a solo exhibition in Mexico City. When he returned in 1929, his work was met with much applause, and the media took notice. Tamayo began working with woodcuts, etchings, and lithographs, and even developed a new printmaking technique called Mixografía, which resulted in prints with a three-dimensional texture. Tamayo's printmaking legacy lives on today in the numerous graphic arts galleries that have popped up in Oaxaca in recent years.

Also part of the legacy Tamayo left to his native Oaxaca is his rich collection of pre-Hispanic art, which is now on display in the **Museo de Arte Prehispánico de México Rufino Tamayo,** in Oaxaca City. With pieces chosen for their artistic, rather than their archaeological value, the collection truly demonstrates the creative ability of the indigenous peoples of Mexico. Some pieces still have the original paint from centuries ago.

Born in Ocotlán de Morelos, **Rodolfo Morales** (1925-2001) was another Oaxacan painter of Zapotec origins who reached worldwide recognition. He is remembered for his surrealist, oneiric canvases and collages that often depict the Zapotec women of his birthplace. It wasn't until he was 50 years old that he gained mainstream recognition, when his work at a solo exhibition in Cuernavaca caught Tamayo's keen artistic eye. Morales was introduced to the larger art world via the connections Tamayo had with galleries and critics all over the world.

The fame brought Morales some money, which he used to spruce up his hometown of Ocotlán, about an hour south of Oaxaca City. There, he founded the Rodolfo Morales Cultural Foundation, which dedicated itself to restoring the old buildings in town. The pretty, sky-blue Templo y Ex Convento de Santo Domingo, now home to the town's municipal government offices, was the foundation's most important project. At the end of his life, Morales and fellow Oaxacan painter Francisco Toledo were considered Mexico's greatest living artists.

Like Tamayo and Morales, **Francisco Toledo** (1940-2019) was a world-famous graphic artist of Zapotec origins. As a young painter and sculptor, Toledo studied in the School of Fine Arts of Oaxaca, as well as the National Institute of Fine Arts (INBA) in Mexico City, where he studied under famous Colombian painter Guillermo Silva Santamaría (1921-2007).

Toledo's favorite subject was the natural world, especially the elements that normally give us the willies. Spiders, scorpions, cockroaches, crocodiles, and other creepy crawlers feature prominently in his tessellations, prints, and jewelry. One of his signature techniques was using lasers to cut materials like leather, gold plating, or X-ray film into visual representations of stylized bugs and beasts. One of his

Francisco Toledo: Pioneer and Patron of Oaxacan Art

Born in Juchitán, world-renowned artist Francisco Toledo (1940-2019) was a feverishly active player in the cultural, political, and artistic scenes in Oaxaca. In 1982, he founded the publisher Ediciones Toledo, which published books about Mexican history and culture with a focus on Oaxaca. His most famous project was **IAGO**, the Instituto de Artes Gráficas de Oaxaca (Graphic Arts Institute of Oaxaca). Located in a gorgeous 18th-century house across from the Santo Domingo church in Oaxaca City, which the Toledo family donated to the National Institute of Fine Arts, IAGO has one of Latin America's most extensive graphic arts libraries and hosts temporary exhibits of both new and established Mexican artists. An on-site gift shop sells Toledo's famous work. As a cultural activist, he campaigned to block the opening of a McDonald's in Oaxaca City's Centro to protect the city's gastronomical heritage. In 2006, he founded the **Centro de Artes de San Agustín (CaSa)**, a cultural and artistic center in San Agustín Etla that offers workshops in painting, writing, dance, filmmaking, and many other artistic pursuits free of charge to those accepted. Toledo was still very active in the arts scene in Oaxaca up until his death in 2019.

most famous works that demonstrated Toledo's ability to turn the repugnant into something aesthetically refined is his *Los cuadernos de la mierda* (The Shit Notebooks), which features 1,745 images of people, animals, and skeletons defecating. Drawn during Toledo's second stay in Paris from 1985 to 1987, the images are meant to explore the pre-Hispanic views toward this quotidian act that all of us have in common, no matter our wealth or social status. In Mexico, artists can pay certain taxes using their work, and Toledo did so with these images, possibly commenting on what he thought of taxation in his country.

The second decade of the 2000s saw a resurgence in the practice of **printmaking**, popularized by Oaxacan artists like Tamayo and Toledo. Now over a dozen printmaking workshops and galleries dot the map of the Centro in Oaxaca City, the majority of them located on Calle Porfirio Díaz, west of Santo Domingo. Artists in these galleries use xylography (woodcut), lithography, etching, engraving, and other techniques to create beautiful images representing political ideas or Oaxaca's wealth of cultural symbols. If you're really head-over-heels for this type of art, pick up a **Pasaporte Gráfico** (Graphic Passport) at one of the galleries and take it around to all included. If you get a stamp from each one, you get a discount at any of them.

MUSIC

Oaxaca's tireless creativity is heard in its music, as well. The conquest brought new instruments for people to tinker with, and people in regions all over the state have come up with their own genres of music, some of which take influences from music as far away as South America. The marimba, for example, re-created in the Americas by slaves brought from Africa, is very popular in Oaxaca, especially in Oaxaca City.

In La Costa Chica, an area of the coastline straddling the border with Guerrero, the popular music is called **La Chilena,** which combines music brought by Chilean sailors in the 19th century with traditional Mexican music. It is popular in Pinotepa Nacional and other towns on the coast, and is usually what accompanies their dancers in the Guelaguetza and other festivities.

Another popular Oaxacan music genre is the *son istmeño,* literally "Sound of the Isthmus." *Son* is a Spanish word used for various regional types of folk music, the most well-known of which is the Son Cubano, from Cuba. The *son istmeño* is traditionally played with a trio of guitars: a normal six-string, a smaller six-string called a *requinto*, and a 10-string guitar called a *bajoquinto*. This genre from El Istmo de Tehuantepec contributed one of the most

Oaxacan Brass Bands

The music you're most likely to hear in Oaxaca is the traditional Oaxacan brass band called *Tambora Oaxaqueña,* literally "Oaxacan Bass Drum." These groups of 15-20 musicians provide the lively accompaniment for the parades called *comparsas* and *calendas,* which are thrown to celebrate everything from major holidays to college graduations, so your chances of seeing and dancing in one in Oaxaca City are pretty good just about any time of year. The songs these bands play have much in common with Balkan music, at one moment slow, introspective, and somewhat gloomy, and in the next exploding with energy and celebratory rhythms and melodies.

When I first moved to Oaxaca, I would hear this exuberant music and head out to the street to see what all the commotion was about. To my surprise, I didn't find the party I was expecting, but a funeral. To me, it seemed the perfect way to conduct such a ceremony, expressing both the pain of loss and the joy of the memory the person left behind.

---

popular standards in Latin American music, called "La Llorona" (The Weeping Woman). Its poignant melody and hypnotizing pace have captivated musicians and listeners all over Latin America since its popularization by Oaxacan poet Andrés Henestrosa (1906-2008) in the 1940s.

The song has been part of the *son istmeño* since the mid-19th century, and refers to the tradition of *la llorona,* a woman always searching for her lost children. This legend is said to come from the Aztec goddess of birth and motherhood, Cihuacóatl (see-wah-CO-at-l), who abandoned her son Mixcoatl at a crossroads and returned often in search of him, only to find a sacrificial knife. The legend became a metaphor for the conquest, and the traditional lyrics include the lines "Cover me with your shawl, Llorona, because I'm dying of the cold."

The song has been sung in El Istmo since the 1850s, but Henestrosa and others later added a number of verses that turned it into a tragic love story meant to represent the tumultuous Mexican Revolution. Mexican singer Susana Harp (b. 1968) has recorded it five times without repeating a verse. The most popular version was sung by Chavela Vargas (1919-2012), who was born in Costa Rica, but found fame and fortune singing in Mexico. The song has become a sort of rite of passage or badge of honor for Spanish-language singers, and has been interpreted by Mexican stars like Eugenia León (b. 1956), Natalia Lafourcade (b. 1984), and Oaxacan singer of Mixtec origin Lila Downs (b. 1968).

Lila Downs was born in Tlaxiaco to a Mixtec mother and an American father. Taking influences from both cultures, Downs's music runs a wide range of styles, genres, and languages. She is fluent Mixtec and often sings songs in the language, as well as Zapotec. She tours all over the world, but also sings at many events in Oaxaca, like the Guelaguetza, the Mazunte Jazz Festival, and the Zipolite Nudist Festival. Lila has also lent her money, talent, and celebrity to the Fondo Guadalupe Musalem, which promotes and supports education for young women in Oaxaca's rural and indigenous communities.

Oaxaca is also home to **Álvaro Carrillo** (1921-1969), who also contributed a song now considered a standard in Latin music—his "Sabor a mí" (Taste of Me). Popularized by the Latin romantic trio Los Panchos in 1959, the song has gone on to be sung by a number of famous Mexican singers, including Lila Downs, Luis Miguel (b. 1970), Javier Solís (1931-1966), José José (b. 1948), and even the U.S. Latin rock band Los Lobos.

The Oaxaca City native **Macedonio Alcalá** (1831-1869) may not have gained the worldwide recognition as the previously mentioned artists, but he might be the most important to Oaxacans themselves. He was the composer of the waltz "Dios nunca muere" (God Never Dies, 1868), the de facto anthem of Oaxaca. The popular pedestrian walkway and downtown theater in Oaxaca City are named in his honor.

DANCE

Dance has been deeply rooted in Oaxacan culture for millennia. The indigenous peoples of this land used dance to tell religious tales and allegories. When the Spanish arrived, many stories were kept alive via the dances, which were ostensibly changed to represent Christian elements. Some, like the **Danza de las Mascaritas** (Dance of the Masked Ones) of Teposcolula, in La Mixteca, were actually created to surreptitiously mock the dances brought by the conquistadors.

Dances are the main attraction at the **Guelaguetza,** or **Los Lunes del Cerro** (Mondays on the Hill), as it is sometimes called. The first dance is usually an homage to **Centéotl** (sen-TEH-oh-tl), the goddess of corn, which is then followed by dances from the invited delegations from all over the state. Dances represent the language, culture, food, and enterprise of a certain region. Tuxtepec, in the El Papaloapan region

where lots of pineapples are grown, is known for its consistently crowd-pleasing **Flor de Piña** (Pineapple Flower). The star dance of Zaachila, in the Valles Centrales, is called the **Danza de los Zancudos** (Dance of the Stilted Ones), in which the dancers perform atop tall stilts, some over 2 meters (6.5 ft) tall.

One of Oaxaca's most famous dances is the **Danza de la Pluma** (Dance of the Feather). Citizens of both Cuilapam de Guerrero and Zaachila claim the dance as originally from their respective towns, but now it is also performed by dancers from various towns in the Valles Centrales, such as Teotitlán del Valle and Zimatlán de Álvarez. Like the Danza de las Mascaritas, this one is a product of the conquest, owing as much to its indigenous influences as to its Spanish ones. According to those from Guerrero, who seem to have more evidence than others, the dance was invented by Dominican friars and Mixtec Christian converts to represent the triumph of Catholicism over the pagan religions of the Aztecs and other indigenous peoples of Mexico.

Folk Art and Craftwork

TEXTILES AND CLOTHING

Hand-woven wool rugs, called *tapetes,* are one of the most popular artisanal products in Oaxaca, especially in the Valles Centrales, where the main centers of production are **Teotitlán del Valle** and **Santa Ana del Valle.** Weavers here use wool from La Mixteca, which is regarded as the softest in the state.

The Spanish brought the sheep and looms, and the folks here used dying techniques they'd been practicing for generations, transferring the kaleidoscope of colors found in the land to their woven works. The most popular and profitable (for a while) of these dyes was made from grinding up the scale insects called *cochinilla* (cochineal) to create a deep

red. Farmers on the coast cultivated the plant that is fermented and filtered to make indigo for the blues. They found brown in the pecan shells and yellow in the pomegranate rinds and tree-climbing mosses, and using various techniques and ingredients, they produced all the colors of the rainbow.

At first sight, the prices that weavers ask for their rugs can seem expensive, but when taking into account the time and skill that goes into creating a rug, as well as the quality of the product you're getting, the prices start to look like a steal. Weaving one rug can take an artist up to three months or more, depending

1: the Flor de Piña, a relatively recent Chinantec and Mazatec dance 2: red clay pottery 3: intricate glyphs painted on an *alebrije* 4: harvesting cochineal to make a natural red dye

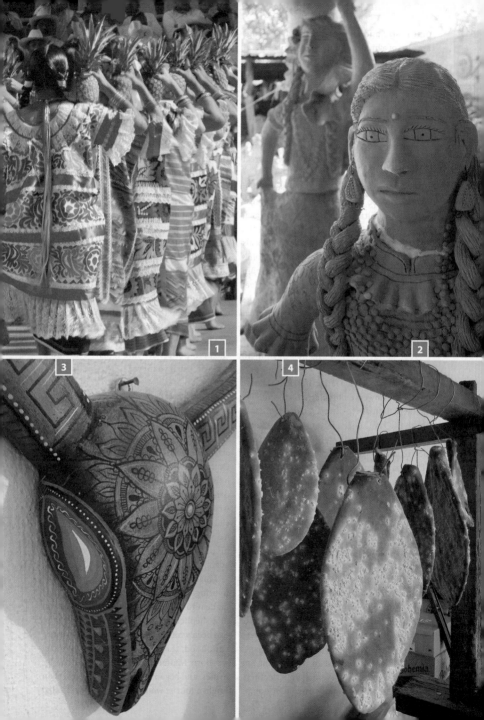

on the size and style of a piece. These rugs are also of a higher quality than similar mass-produced textiles, generally boasting thread counts twice as thick as rugs woven elsewhere. Weavers in Teotitlán del Valle and Santa Ana del Valle are happy and eager to share their knowledge with others, so when shopping for *tapetes,* take your time and get a demonstration or two. You'll appreciate more the product you end up buying, and will have a great story to go with it.

Embroidered blouses and dresses called *huipiles* (wee-PEEL-ehs) not only express a person's culture and origins in Oaxaca, they are now big business, being one of the most popular products for tourists and locals alike in the state. The most popular *huipiles* come from **Tehuantepec** and **Juchitán,** in El Istmo de Tehuantepec. These black velvet garments emblazoned with the fiery colors of bright tropical flowers are so popular that they could be considered the de facto emblem of Oaxaca.

Just about every indigenous group in Oaxaca has its own style of *huipil,* giving garment shoppers a wide range of styles to choose from. The flowers embroidered on the *huipiles* made in **San Antonino Castillo Velasco,** south of Oaxaca City, for example, are much smaller than those from El Istmo, with finer details and images of people and birds, as well. If you pay attention to detail, you'll be able to spot where the piece was made just by the colors and stitching.

POTTERY

Pottery (*alfarería* in Spanish) is probably the oldest and most dynamic craft practiced in Oaxaca. In Atzompa, for example, you can observe the remains of a 1,300-year-old kiln once used by the suburbanites of Monte Albán, then head down the hill to **Santa María Atzompa,** where the modern descendants of this tradition work day in and day out to keep it alive. The style currently popular in Santa María Atzompa is glazed an eye-catching forest green that highlights small imperfections, making each piece totally unique. Atzompa

is also known for decorative white and earth-toned pieces, as well as clay jewelry and other decorative articles adorned with extremely intricate filigree-style floral patterns.

In the 1950s, a potter from **San Bartolo Coyotepec** named Doña Rosa came up with a technique of polishing the clay before firing it in the kiln, which produces a shimmery black finish to the decorative pieces. Her distinct style was an immediate hit among tourists, and now her children and grandchildren, as well as many others in town, carry on her tradition of *barro negro* **(black clay pottery).** One quirk of the process is that a second baking, required to make pieces watertight, corrupts the shiny finish, so *barro negro* products are generally decorative only.

José García, the blind potter of **San Antonino Castillo Velasco,** creates unglazed *barro rojo* **(red clay pottery)** pieces, opting to keep the tone earthy and subdued.

Whether it's a decorative piece for a gift, or a new set of mugs for the kitchen cabinets, Oaxacan potters are sure to have something that will catch your eye.

ALEBRIJES

Although the origins of *alebrijes,* the psychedelically painted wooden statues of fantastic animals you'll find at just about any artisans market in the state, aren't completely Oaxacan, the figurines have come to be symbols for the creative impulse of the place. The concept came from a Mexico City-based artist named Pedro Linares (1906-1992), who claimed to have seen the fanciful creatures in a dream when he became ill at 30 years old. In his dream, the creatures shouted over and over again the word "¡alebrijes!"

Linares used wire frames and papier-mâché to bring his visions to life, but when the idea made it to Oaxaca and grabbed the attention of a shepherd named Manuel Jiménez, who had been whittling figurines out of wood since childhood, the *alebrije* as we know it today was born. Manuel initially didn't paint his figurines, and began to do so at the request of an English tourist who told the artist he wanted

Bargaining

A classic element of a trip to Mexico is the concept of bargaining (*regateo*) with vendors in the markets. I'm going to come right out and say I do not do it, and I really don't recommend it either, at least not how it is often done by tourists. The argument could be made that our conception of indigenous art as "artisan handicrafts," and not the communal art that it truly is, has much to do with foreigners' ideas of what an artist's work is worth. As I usually see it, bargaining by foreign tourists comes off as an often rude deprecation of the value of the product.

This is not to say that there aren't places in Mexico where vendors try to charge tourists the highest prices they can, but Oaxaca in general isn't one of them. A rug from Teotitlán, for example, may have taken as long as three months to make, so keep this in mind when considering how much an artist is asking for his or her work.

I myself can count on one hand the times I feel like I've been overcharged for something in Oaxaca, and never has it been so outrageous that I felt bamboozled. Most people charge a fair price for their work, and it is only fair to pay them well for something you really like.

After a few discussions with market vendors, I've discovered a bargaining method that is fair for both client and vendor. Instead of asking for a lower price for one item, propose that you'll buy more than one if you're given a discount per item. For example, say you really like that *alebrije* with the owl's head on a monkey's body, but you want to haggle down from the 500 pesos (US$25) he is asking for it. Surely there must be another one on the vendor's table that a friend or family member would like. Propose you take two and pay 700 or 800 pesos (US$35 or US$40) for the two of them. This shows that you respect the artist's work, and the majority of vendors will accept such a deal.

some color on them. The process took root in Manuel's hometown of **Arrazola,** and later in nearby **San Martín Tilcajete,** and artists have been developing new carving and painting styles ever since.

Now it's just about impossible to find an artisans market or handicrafts store in Oaxaca that doesn't have a shelf loaded with *alebrijes.* Shopping for them can be a fun and personal experience. For many artists, *alebrijes* came to represent the indigenous concept of *tonas y nahuales,* animals that represent and protect a person based on their date of birth. The *tona* is the animal based on the Zapotec calendar, and the *nahua* is based on one's specific day and year of birth. Some *talleres* (workshops) will find what animals are yours based on your birthday, and you can then seek out one that combines the two, or get one commissioned.

CANASTAS, TENATES, AND PETATES

Oaxacan artisans use reeds, palm fronds, plastic bands, maguey fibers, and other materials to make beautiful *canastas* (baskets),

tenates (different style of baskets), *petates* (woven mats), and a number of other useful products, as well as decorative items. The most useful of these to visitors to the state are things like shopping bags, but you could also get a cool laundry basket or floor mat for the kitchen or patio.

You'll find that many of these products are named based on their usage. For example, a *panera* is a bread basket (*pan* is bread in Spanish), a *frutero* is a basket for holding fruits, and a *florero* is one for flowers. You'll also find *canastas* (small baskets) and *canastos* (bigger ones, usually with a lid). Artisans in towns like **Etla, Ocotlán,** and **Tlacolula** are famous for their products made with *carrizo verde* (green reed). Out in **La Mixteca,** craftworkers use palm fronds to create beautiful *tapetes* and *petates* (mats), *bolsas* (bags), *sombreros* (hats), *sopladores* (hand fans for stoking the cooking fire), and more.

Historically, the town of **Santo Domingo Xagacía** (sha-gah-SEE-ah), in the Sierra Norte, is the biggest producer of goods made with ixtle, the fiber of the maguey plant, but there are ixtle weavers in a number of other Oaxacan communities. You'll have a good chance of finding these products at the Sunday Market in **Tlacolula,** but places like **Ixtlán de Juárez** (which takes its name from the fiber), **Teposcolula, Nochixtlán,** and **Miahuatlán** also make things with ixtle. The fiber is known for its durability and pliability.

JEWELRY

Fine jewelry is another artisanal product that has its roots in pre-Hispanic Oaxacan culture. When archaeologist Alfonso Caso (1896-1970) and his team excavated Tomb 7 at Monte Albán, they found a treasure trove of gold jewelry fit for a movie scene. Among the riches were intricately filigreed earrings, rings, necklaces, chest plates, and little bells, as well as decorative or symbolic representations of birds, fish, and deities, like gods of happiness and light. One popular jewelry store has dedicated itself to purveying replicas of these pieces. **Oro de Monte Albán** has four stores in downtown Oaxaca, as well as one in the visitors center at the Monte Albán archaeological site.

Down on the coast, you'll find lots of jewelry made with *ámbar* (amber), as well as a cornucopia of hand-woven hippie trinkets, like bracelets, anklets, necklaces, earrings, and charms. Areas like **El Adoquín** in **Puerto Escondido** and **La Crucecita** in **Bahías de Huatulco** are great places to go shopping for silver jewelry.

LEATHER GOODS AND KNIVES

The craft of *talabartería* (leatherworking) is popular in **Oaxaca City.** Markets here are stocked to the brim with leather jackets, purses, coin purses, backpacks, hats, belts, wallets, shoes, and many other fine goods made from animal hide. Artisans in places like **Ocotlán de Morelos** and **Miahuatlán de Porfirio Díaz** are known for the fabrication of *sombreros de panza de burro,* wide-brimmed sunhats made from the bellies of donkeys.

Oaxaca City and Ocotlán are also home to makers of fine blades, such as **machetes, swords, knives, daggers,** and **silverware.** Many are more for showing that using, adorned with acid-etched images of Oaxacan landscapes and local proverbs.

Essentials

Transportation

GETTING THERE
Air

If you're coming straight to Oaxaca, your best travel option will be to fly directly here. U.S. and Canadian airlines in recent years have begun to add more direct flights to Oaxaca City, Puerto Escondido, and Huatulco. This has made the trip easier and quicker for citizens of these countries, as well as those from others who connect via those countries. Visit September-October and January-March to get the best deals on flights.

FROM THE UNITED STATES AND CANADA

Many airlines have either connecting or direct flights between Oaxaca City and major U.S. and Canadian cities, such as **Dallas, Houston, Austin, San Antonio, Albuquerque, Phoenix, Los Angeles, San Francisco, Chicago, Atlanta, New York, Miami, Toronto,** and **Vancouver.** If you're coming from Southern California or close by, check for flights from **Tijuana.** It might be cheaper to fly domestically, and since 2015, flyers have been able to cross from San Diego directly to the Tijuana airport via the Cross Border Xpress international bridge.

For **nonstop flights to Oaxaca City,** you'll have to fly out of **Houston,** with **United Airlines** (toll-free U.S. and Canada tel. 800/260-1952, toll-free UK tel. 0800/028-5003, www.united.com); **Dallas,** with **American Airlines** (toll-free U.S. and Canada tel. 800/433-7300, UK tel. 0207/660-2300, www.aa.com); or **Los Angeles** or **Tijuana,** with **Volaris** (toll-free U.S. tel. 855/865-2747, Mex. tel. 551/102-8000, www.volaris.com).

The only other Oaxacan city with direct flights from the United States and Canada is **Huatulco.** Canadian airline **Westjet** (toll-free U.S. and Canada tel. 888/937-8538, toll-free UK tel. 0800/279-7072, www.westjet.com) has direct flights from **Toronto, Vancouver,** and **Calgary.** Volaris flies directly from Chicago, and Minnesota-based **Sun Country Airlines** (U.S. tel. 651/905-2737, www.suncountry.com) has direct flights from **Minneapolis.** At the time of writing, they were only scheduled on Fridays.

Other major airlines with flights that connect via one of these cities, or **Mexico City,** include **Aeromexico** (toll-free U.S. and Canada tel. 800/237-6639, toll-free UK tel. 0800/977-5533, Mex. tel. 555/133-4000, www.aeromexico.com), **Interjet** (toll-free U.S. tel. 866/285-9525, toll-free Canada tel.

844/874-4053, international tel. +52 998/881-6836, www.interjet.com), and **Delta Airlines** (toll-free U.S. and Canada tel. 800/221-1212, UK tel. 0207/660-0767).

FROM EUROPE, LATIN AMERICA, AUSTRALASIA, AND ASIA

To get to Oaxaca from elsewhere in the world, your quickest option is to fly **Aeromexico** and connect via **Mexico City.** In **Europe,** Aeromexico flies directly to **London, Paris, Madrid, Amsterdam, Frankfurt, Munich,** and **Rome.** In **Latin America,** Aeromexico has direct flights to Mexico City from major cities in **Cuba, the Dominican Republic, Belize, Guatemala, El Salvador, Honduras** (San Pedro Sula), **Nicaragua, Costa Rica, Panama, Colombia, Ecuador, Peru, Chile, Argentina,** and **Brazil** (Sao Paulo). The only city in **Asia** with which Aeromexico offers nonstop flights to the capital is **Tokyo.**

Visitors from **Australia** and **New Zealand** have a long flight itinerary ahead of them. Aeromexico does not fly to Australasia, so you will have to fly one of the U.S. airlines (**United, Delta,** or **American Airlines**) and connect either through one of the cities with direct flights to Oaxaca, or have one more stop in Mexico City.

Bus

Bus travel is the primary mode of long-distance transport in Mexico. Unlike the United States, where bus passengers are at the mercy and whim of one company, Mexico boasts over 50 major long-distance bus companies. With such a large, varied, and competitive market, you can generally expect to walk into a bus station almost anywhere in the country and board a bus in an hour or two.

The bus company that reigns supreme in Oaxaca is Autobuses del Oriente (Buses of the East), or **ADO** (Mex. tel. 555/784-4652, www.ado.com.mx) and its subsidiaries Autobuses

---

Previous: *motocarros,* an urban transport unique to Tehuantepec.

Unidos (United Buses), or **AU, Estrella de Oro** (Gold Star), Omnibuses Cristóbal Colón, or **OCC**, which, unlike its namesake, Christopher Columbus, actually knows where it's going. You can view schedules and buy tickets for all of these companies on ADO's website. If you're coming from Mexico City, Puebla, Chiapas, Veracruz, or even as far east as Quintana Roo, on the Caribbean Coast, ADO and its daughter companies will be your main bus options.

Anywhere in Mexico, use the website for **ClickBus** (Mex. tel. 554/744-0276, www. clickbus.com) to check bus schedules and travel times for any company and destination. I've never had any luck with getting my U.S. credit or debit card to work to pay on this and many other Mexican websites. The best thing to do is use the website to check schedules, then go purchase a ticket in person.

It takes a long time, but you can take a bus from U.S. destinations to Mexico City. **Greyhound** (toll-free U.S. tel. 800/231-2222, outside U.S. tel. 214/849-8100, www. greyhound.com) has a few bus stations in the north of Mexico, but they have partnered with many Mexican bus lines, making it possible to plan and pay for an entire trip from anywhere in the United States, and some destinations in Canada, to just about anywhere in Mexico on their website. However, be aware that with so many players in the game, you never know when a bus line won't put you on another bus, or won't be able to, if you miss a bus due to your late arrival from the previous leg of your journey.

My personal recommendation for bus travel from the United States to Mexico is the Mexican-owned **Turimex Internacional** (toll-free U.S. tel. 800/733-7330, toll-free Mex. tel. 818/151-5253, www.turimex.com), whose website can be read in both English and Spanish. In the United States, you can board a Turimex bus in the states of **Texas, Oklahoma, Illinois, Michigan, Louisiana, Missouri, Arkansas, Mississippi, Tennessee, Alabama, Georgia,** and the **Carolinas.** Turimex destinations in Mexico

are in mostly northern states, such as **Nuevo León, Coahuila,** and **Durango,** but they do go as far south as **Zacatecas, Jalisco,** and **Mexico City,** usually with no bus transfers in Mexico.

Patience is more than a virtue on trips like this—it's a requirement. To give you an idea of how much time these long-distance bus trips take, the one-way trip from Central Texas to Oaxaca is often a full two days travel, including the border crossing and transfer in Mexico City. During busy holiday seasons, especially Christmas, it can take up to 12 hours or more to cross the border in a bus.

Car or RV

To see Mexico and Oaxaca at your own pace, you might consider **driving to Oaxaca.** This option requires quite a bit more money than taking public transport in Mexico, as you will have to factor in **expenses** such as **gas, insurance, permits, parking,** and **tolls.**

MEXICAN CAR INSURANCE

All vehicles in Mexico, foreign and domestic, are required to have an insurance policy issued by a Mexican company. One of the most experienced is **Sanborn's Mexico Auto Insurance** (2009 S. 10th St., McAllen, TX 78503, toll-free U.S. tel. 800/222-0158, www. sanborns.com). Their tourist insurance includes civil liability, physical damage and theft, roadside and legal assistance, medical coverage, and more. They also insure motorcycles and other street-legal recreational vehicles. You can also get quotes and buy insurance at **Mexpro.com** (toll-free U.S. tel. 855/639-7761).

Quotes vary, depending on your type of car and the amount of coverage you want. Get a quote for your vehicle on these companies' websites.

GAS

U.S., Canadian, and Australian drivers in Mexico will find higher gas prices in Mexico than they are used to back home. At the time of this writing, Mexico was in the long process of privatizing its petroleum industry, and ushering in a new president, which caused some instability in the market and gas prices to fluctuate. U.S. drivers in Mexico can expect to spend a dollar or more per gallon, but gas is sold by the liter here. Keep your phone handy for conversions. There are approximately 3.785 liters in a gallon. Multiply this by the prices you see, then convert the pesos to U.S. dollars to get a better idea of how much you're going to spend on gas.

Drivers accustomed to gas prices in the United Kingdom and New Zealand can most likely expect to pay considerably less than they would for a liter back home. For up-to-date listings on gas prices in Mexico, check the website **GasolinaMX.com**, which reports daily average prices both state- and nationwide. You can even choose specific communities and find the updated prices at the *gasolineras* (gas stations) there. This will be your best resource in getting an idea of how much of your budget you will need to devote to fuel expenses. To get an idea of how they will compare to gas prices back home, check the website **GlobalPetrolPrices.com**. Buying gas in Mexico will be much more expensive than taking public transport here, so take this into account when planning your budget.

TOLLS

Tolls are going to be another not insignificant expense if you drive to Oaxaca. For safety, time, and general comfort reasons, toll roads (indicated with a capital D after the highway number) are worth taking, but tolls at Mexican expressways on average tend to be higher per kilometer than many countries. To get an idea of how much they cost, the total amount of tolls on the six-hour drive from Mexico City to Oaxaca City was around US$24 at the time of this writing.

The main inconvenience of toll roads here is that they bottleneck traffic and cause long waits. Have games, music, audiobooks, or some other way to pass the time, just in case you get stuck in standstill traffic. **Pro tip:**

Although it can be difficult to find change for larger bills even (especially) in chain convenience stores in Mexico, toll booth operators almost always have exact change in order to keep traffic moving. Take advantage of this and get those cumbersome 500-peso notes changed out at the toll booths, and you won't have to worry as much about this unfortunately frequent problem in Mexico.

PARKING TICKETS

One procedure in Oaxaca and other parts of Mexico to be aware of is that **officers will remove your front license plate** when they give you a parking ticket, to ensure that you pay the fine before moving your car. After paying your fine (*multa*, also the word for the paper ticket), make sure to ask where you retrieve your license plate (*placa*). Keep all paperwork, *por si las moscas* (just in case).

THE GREEN ANGELS

Since the 1960s, **Los Ángeles Verdes (The Green Angels)** have provided free information and roadside assistance to tourists driving on Mexican highways. If you need assistance on a main highway, dial 078 to be connected with a representative and ask for help. Both Spanish- and English-speaking representatives are available.

If you don't have a cell phone with Mexican service, you can flag down a passing vehicle and ask them to call you some help, but I recommend having phone service if you are going to be driving to Oaxaca. If your phone will not accept SIM cards from other carriers, it might be best to just **buy a cell phone** to use in case of emergency. You can get an old button phone as cheap as US$25-30 at a cell phone distributor.

HIGHWAY ROUTES FROM THE U.S. BORDER
Central Route

If you're driving from **Texas**, I recommend taking the **central route**, for which the best place to cross is in Laredo, Texas, at the southern end of I-35. From here, take Highway 85 (part of which you have the option to take a toll road) to **Monterrey,** where you should see the **Barrio Antiguo** neighborhood and go for a stroll in the **Parque Fundidora.** There are also tons of great opportunities for outdoor activities within an hour or so of the city, from rock climbing or hiking at **El Potrero Chico** to skiing at the **Bosques de Monterreal** mountain resort.

From Monterrey, take Highway 40 toward Saltillo, and get on 57D (toll), which will turn into the free federal highway of the same number, and take it to **San Luís Potosí.** Spend the evening strolling its gorgeous colonial downtown streets.

From San Luís, you could reach **Mexico City** in about six hours via Highway 57 and its tolled stretches. If you've got another day available in your itinerary, though, you could head east on Highway 70 until you get to Highway 85, where you'll turn south to stop over in **Xilitla,** renowned for its location in the stunning natural area called **La Huasteca Potosina.** Alternatively, you could take Highway 57 toward **Guanajuato,** making a quick stop in **Dolores Hidalgo** to shout "*¡Viva México!*" on the same church steps where Don Miguel Hidalgo famously sparked the Mexican Revolution with his inspiring speech, now called *El Grito de Dolores.* Spend the night in colorful Guanajuato, maybe taking part in a *callejonada,* in which musicians from the local university sing songs and crack jokes as they guide you through the city's cobblestone streets.

From Mexico City, take Highway 150 and its tolled stretches to **Puebla.** About an hour outside of Puebla, take the exit for tolled Highway 135D, which will take you through **La Mixteca** to meet up with the free (*libre*) 135, about a half hour from **Oaxaca City.**

Eastern and Alternate Central Routes

Alternate routes from Texas include the **eastern route,** for which you'll cross the border in **McAllen** or **Brownsville** and drive through the states of **Tamaulipas** and **Veracruz** en route to Oaxaca. However, be aware that these states are unfortunately quite dangerous, especially Tamaulipas. Aside from security concerns, the central route will be more fun. Extreme caution is also advised for crossing from **El Paso** into **Juárez,** via which route you can stop in the cities of **Chihuahua, Durango, Zacatecas,** and **Guanajuato** on your way to **Mexico City.**

Pacific Routes

If you're driving the **Pacific route** from **California** or **Arizona,** be aware that the states of **Sonora** and **Sinaloa** are also high-risk states, due to the amount of drug trafficking in them. As with anywhere in Mexico, be sure to keep your driving confined to the daylight hours. From Nogales, Arizona, take Highway 15 south to either **Hermosillo** or **Guaymas,** on the coast, depending on how early you start out. Try to make your next stop down Highway 15 **Mazatlán,** in Sinaloa, where you should stay a night on the beach at **La Isla de la Piedra** (Stone Island), which is home to a handful of *palapas* and restaurants, then nothing but palm trees as far as you can see down the shore. If you can't make it all the way to Mazatlán, stop for the night in the coastal town of **Los Mochis.**

Next, continue down the coast on Highway 15 to the major tourist destination of **Puerto Vallarta,** where you can take treks through the same jungly areas where they filmed the original *Predator* movie. From here, the Oaxacan coast is another two or three days of driving straight down Highway 200. On your way, you can make stops in towns like **Manzanillo, Zihuatanejo,** and **Acapulco,** before finally reaching **Puerto Escondido.**

Alternatively, instead of continuing on the coast to Oaxaca, you could stay on Highway 15 at **Tepic,** just before Puerto Vallarta, and see **Guadalajara** on the way to **Mexico City,** then reach Oaxaca from there. If you do go this route, don't miss **Guanajuato** on the way to the capital.

If you start off in California, you might consider avoiding the state of Sonora altogether, and drive down **Baja California**

Highway Routes from U.S. Border to Oaxaca

The projected total travel days in this chart have been estimated by considering driving by day and staying one night in the suggested stops. Of course, you'll miss a lot on the way if you just drive and sleep, so make sure to factor in time for fun along the way. If you're driving to Oaxaca, you're obviously not pressed for time, so enjoy the trip.

Route	Via	Km (Miles)	Hours at the Wheel	Travel Days
Eastern	Matamoros or Reynosa-Tampico, Veracruz-Oaxaca City	1,421 km (883 mi)	20 hrs	3 days
Central	Nuevo Laredo-Monterrey, San Luís Potosí-Xilitla or Guanajuato, Mexico City-Oaxaca City	1,740-2,021 km (1,081-1,256 mi)	22-26 hrs	4-5 days
Alternate Central	Ciudad Juárez-Chihuahua, Durango-Zacatecas, Guanajuato-Mexico City, Oaxaca City	2,393 km (1,487 mi)	30 hrs	5-6 days
Pacific	Nogales-Guaymas, Los Mochis-Mazatlán, Puerto Vallarta-Manzanillo, Zihuatanejo-Acapulco, Puerto Escondido	2,981 km (1,852 mi)	44 hrs	8 days
Pacific-Mexico City	Nogales-Mazatlán, Tepic-Guadalajara, Guanajuato-Mexico City, Oaxaca City	2,723 km (1,692 mi)	33 hrs	7 days
Baja California-Pacific	Tijuana-San Felipe, La Paz-Mazatlán, Puerto Vallarta-Manzanillo, Zihuatanejo-Acapulco, Puerto Escondido	3,987 km (2,477 mi)	62 hrs	8-9 days

to **La Paz,** where you can **take a ferry to Mazatlán** (www.bajaferries.com) and continue driving from there. The ferry takes around 13 hours, longer if there are delays, which are unfortunately frequent. Still, it's faster than driving back up the peninsula. Rates for vehicles start at around US$200 for a standard car. You'll save a little bit on the ferry price if you go to their other destination, Topolobampo, but it is north of Mazatlán, so you'll have to factor in gas expenses to see if it'll save you money. Get more detailed information at the website **DiscoverBaja.com,** which is in English and works better than the ferry company's official site. Total drive time from Tijuana to La Paz is over 18 hours, so you should break it up with a stay in a town along the way, like the popular beach destination **San Felipe.**

GETTING AROUND
Air

There are airports in **Oaxaca City, Puerto Escondido, Huatulco,** and **Ixtepec** (actually closer to Juchitán), but since this is the least common way for people to move around inside Oaxaca, any flight itinerary with large airlines will have you connecting via Mexico City or elsewhere.

However, Oaxaca-owned **Aerotucán** (Emilio Carranza 303, Colonia Reforma, Oaxaca City, tel. 951/502-0840, toll-free Mex. tel. 800/640-4148, www.aerotucan.com, 8am-8pm Mon.-Fri., 8am-6pm Sat.) offers flights between these cities. For a one-way flight from Oaxaca City to Puerto Escondido, you can expect to pay around US$135, to Huatulco, US$85-130, and to Ixtepec, US$90-150. All Aerotucán flights go between Oaxaca City, meaning you can't fly between airports on the coast, or to Ixtepec from there. It is definitely a unique way to see the magnitude and magnificence of the Sierra Madre del Sur.

Aside from their main office in Oaxaca City, you'll also find Aerotucán offices in the airports, as well as one in La Crucecita, **Huatulco** (Carrizal 603-H, tel. 958/587-2427, 11:30am-3pm Mon.-Sat.). The office is inside Plaza Madero, two blocks east of the main square.

Car
ROAD SYSTEM

To travel between regions in Oaxaca, you'll take a paved *carretera federal* **(federal highway),** which will be designated with a police badge-shaped symbol with the word Mexico at the top and the number of the highway below. Speed limits on these roads range 60-90 kilometers per hour (40-55 mph), and are lower in curvy stretches. It is not uncommon for drivers here to go well over the speed limit.

Conditions on these roads range from severely potholed to nice and smooth to nonexistent in cases of landslides in the mountains. Since they are so important to trade, they are usually repaired quickly. Check for construction (*construcción*), landslides (*derrumbes*), and other road conditions on the website **Retio** (www.ret.io, in Spanish) if you're planning on driving through mountains during the rainy season, and pay attention to the weather forecast. Do not drive in the mountains during a rainstorm. For driving anywhere in the state, use that site to check for roadblocks (*bloqueos*) and other driving conditions.

Toll roads in Oaxaca, and elsewhere in Mexico, are designated with a **capital D** after the number of the highway route they cover. At highway intersections where you must choose to get on the toll road or not, you will see the words *cuota* (toll) and *libre* (freeway), as well as the capital D, to distinguish the roads. Pay attention to the speed limits as you approach the *caseta de cobro* (toll booth). The maximum speed limit on toll roads is 110 kilometers per hour (about 70 mph).

Road conditions in towns and cities also range from nice paved roads to fields of potholes to heavily rutted dirt roads, as well as many speed bumps. Many roads in the mountains are nice, two-track dirt roads with space to pass a car in the opposite direction. Be aware that you'll potentially be sharing these roads with cyclists, hikers, and locals and their livestock, who use them to get to their fields or commute between villages.

CAR RENTAL

Although you can get anywhere in Oaxaca in public transport, you might consider renting a car to save time or have more freedom to explore. It can really come in handy in places with lesser-developed tourism sectors, such as La Mixteca and La Cañada, to get to those really out-of-the-way places.

You can expect to spend around US$60-90 per day to rent a car. Depending on what you want or need, prices can get as high as US$185 per day. Unless you are certain you will be going to very rugged terrain, you shouldn't need something like a 4x4, but get something with a good amount of clearance, just to avoid having to worry at every speed bump.

Your valid driver's license issued in your home country is valid for driving a rental car in Mexico. Your rental will include the necessary insurance to legally drive in Mexico, but you might want to consider getting the extra collision and theft coverage. At the time of this writing, only one agency in Oaxaca (**Optimus Car Rental,** in Oaxaca City) included collision and theft in their daily price.

Bus

The thing about traveling on a large, first-class, or similarly sized bus within Oaxaca is that the places that are far enough away to warrant bus travel are often at the other end of skinny, very curvy roads, which slow down large vehicles. For example, an ADO bus from Oaxaca City to Puerto Escondido can take as long as 11 or 12 hours, whereas in a 12-15-passenger van called a *suburban,* you could make it to Pochutla in about 6 hours, then reach Puerto Escondido in just under 2 hours on a local bus from there. Or make it more fun, and break up the trip with a stop-over in the mountains.

In addition to time, you'll save money by traveling in vans. The one advantage of the larger buses is that they are much more

Speed Bumps

Oaxaca's main method for speed regulation is the **speed bump.** They are everywhere, even on highways when passing through populated areas. In many cases, you'll see a sign that reads *tope* or *reductor,* and in some places they'll be painted yellow. Rather frequently, they'll have neither and jump right out of the road if you're not looking out for them. To avoid damage to your car or your rental, always be on the lookout for *topes.*

comfortable than the smaller *suburbanes,* which do not accommodate tall people well. Within Oaxaca, you'll most likely be taking advantage of smaller bus companies, such as Estrella Blanca, SUR, and AU.

Suburban

The main mode of interurban transport in Oaxaca is the 12-15-passenger van called a *suburban.* These are your cheapest, fastest, and most widely available option. You'll see them and their stations (*bases*) everywhere. Prices generally range from about US$3 for a two-hour trip to US$10-12 for a six-hour trip. *Suburban* trips longer than six hours are rare in Oaxaca, unless there are unexpected hold-ups, such as a roadblock, accident, or construction.

Suburban passengers should be aware that one way these companies offer you such savings on time and money is by the drivers usually being in quite a hurry. They drive fast and pass a lot, even on mountain roads and in other situations with limited visibility. I've never been in an accident in one of these, but a quick search of Oaxacan news reports reveals that they do happen. Use your seatbelt, if there is one.

Taxi Colectivo and Camioneta

For shorter trips between towns within a region, you'll either have one or both of these

Safe Driving in Mexico

Rule number one: Do not drive on highways at night here in Oaxaca, or elsewhere in Mexico. I was warned specifically about highways in the northern parts of the state, in El Istmo to the east, and parts of La Mixteca in the west. It is not uncommon for highway bandits to wait for private automobiles to come along a secluded stretch of darkened highway and pull a rope across to stop drivers and rob them. Night buses are generally safe. I've taken countless night buses in Mexico and have never had a problem like this.

Be very cautious in mountainous areas, and don't drive during rainstorms. I drove through the Sierra Norte three weeks after a hurricane in the Gulf drenched the region with days of hard rains, and saw numerous large landslides that occurred as a result. If you're driving through the mountains and there is a big storm, just wait it out. You never know when a disaster like this will occur, so better safe than sorry.

On two-lane highways with shoulders, it is common for slower vehicles to ride the shoulder to allow faster ones to pass. This sometimes leads to some tight squeezes, when both lanes are jockeying for room. Be aware of this and practice caution. If you're not sure about a pass, don't do it, even if the driver behind you alerts you to his or her frustration.

Road blockages are also common in Oaxaca. They are mostly due to agrarian disputes between neighboring farm communities over land rights, and aren't directed toward tourists. They do sometimes get violent, however, so if you're caught in one, just be patient, or try to find another route to get to your destination. Never get involved with these types of disputes. Also, pay attention to the news to see if there is a blockage on the road you plan to take. A good source is the Spanish-language website **Retio** (https://ret.io/r/MX/OAX/cat/bloqueos), which has up-to-date information on roadblocks and other traffic and crime events in Oaxaca and elsewhere in Mexico.

options. *Taxis colectivos* are small, five-passenger sedans that follow a more-or-less fixed route. On just about any highway in the state, you can depend on these to be running their routes from early in the morning, some as early as 4am, until just after the sun goes down. Do not be on the highway trying to flag down a *taxi colectivo*, or for any reason, at night. Although they are nominally five-passenger cars, drivers often squeeze in six or seven to make the trip as profitable as it can be, so don't expect comfort, but with fares rarely over US$2, you can't really complain.

Camionetas are the same collective travel concept, but with covered pickup trucks with benches in the bed to accommodate more people and cargo. They often have ample seating in the cab, if you're not into riding in the back. Fares for *camionetas* are usually similar to *taxis colectivos*.

Cycling

Although it is definitely not developed and widespread enough to say Oaxaca has a "cycling culture" when it comes to highways and other busy roads, traveling Oaxaca on a bicycle is definitely doable. I have cycled through the Sierra Madre del Sur on Highway 175, and seen others doing it, as well.

At the time of this writing, billboards were set up on Highway 190 east of Oaxaca City to promote awareness of cyclists on this busy stretch of pavement, and you'll probably see a few on it if you head out to the Valle de Tlacolula.

Seasoned bike tourers probably already have accounts, but it is worth mentioning the online cycling community **WarmShowers. com,** where you can find fellow cyclists who can offer you a place to stay on your tour. There are hosts in a number of communities in Oaxaca.

Hitchhiking

I myself have both hitchhiked and picked up hitchhikers in Oaxaca. Everyone I have met this way has been friendly and polite. This doesn't mean it is 100 percent safe, but as long as you take the same precautions as you would when hitchhiking back home, you should be fine. You really don't want to be thumbing it at night anywhere, but I must reiterate the fact that you shouldn't be on the highways at night in Oaxaca or elsewhere in Mexico. Keep your rides confined to the daytime. I usually offer to pay a little for gas.

Visas and Officialdom

PASSPORTS AND TOURIST VISAS

Visitors from the United States, Canada, the United Kingdom, Australia, New Zealand, and dozens of other countries do not require a visa to enter Mexico for tourism purposes. This means that as long as your passport is valid for at least three months after the time you plan to depart, all you have to do is show up at a port of entry and present your passport to an immigration official.

Citizens of these countries are allowed to stay in Mexico up to 180 days for unremunerated activities. On your flight, or in the immigration office at the border, you will be given a bilingual Forma Migratoria Múltiple (FMM), on which you will state your purpose for visiting (check Tourism) and request the amount of time you plan to stay. If you're making a long trip, simply write 180 days, but if your trip is shorter (say, only a week long), I recommend requesting an extra week or so, just in case. You never know when you'll lose your passport, or miss a flight, and have to stay longer. You'll also need to write the address of your hotel or person you're visiting, so have your accommodations information ready when filling out the form. You don't need to show proof of hotel reservations, but you will need the address, so if you haven't booked a room, have the guidebook handy and write the address of the place you plan to stay.

If you fly to Oaxaca, or anywhere in Mexico, the fee for this card is included in your plane ticket. If you are crossing at the border, the form costs around US$20. Those traveling with children should note that Mexican law requires children under 18 to also have their own tourist card, so make sure everyone in the family has a valid passport.

REPLACING A LOST TOURIST CARD

You will be given a part of the form that the immigration official will tear off for you. Do not lose this small piece of paper. (I use a leather passport cover that has a little pocket that fits the document perfectly—this way I know that the form is always with my passport.)

If this card is lost, stolen, or damaged beyond legibility, you will need to get it replaced before you leave. This is a tedious bureaucratic process, so avoid it at all costs. It is a good idea to make a copy of all your travel documentation (passport, tourist card, plane ticket, etc.) once you arrive, in order to make the process as easy as possible. You will need to go to the immigration offices at one of the airports in Oaxaca City, Puerto Escondido, or Huatulco with your passport and any other information that shows when you arrived in Mexico, such as your plane ticket.

The fee for replacing a lost tourist card is around US$40. If you are not close to an airport when you lose your card, and do not have too much time before you leave, it might be best to just sacrifice your last day to replacing your card. Again, this process could take a long time, so if you do it the day of your flight, make sure to get to the airport at least five hours before departure to ensure you don't miss your flight.

CROSSING AT THE BORDER

Crossing at the border can sometimes be a lengthy process, but it is considerably shorter if you cross the bridge on foot. If you're on a bus that crosses the border, you could end up waiting as long as 12 hours to enter the country. Visitors entering Mexico for longer than 72 hours or farther than the "border zone" (about 35 km/22 mi from the border) must pay for a tourist permit, so this includes you, visitor to Oaxaca.

If on a bus, you will be told to get off after crossing into Mexico and go to the immigration office. Here you will present your passport and receive your tourist card, but you will not pay the fee here. You will be given an invoice that you must take to a bank and pay at any time during your stay. If you enter on foot, with plans of taking a bus from a border town, it is your responsibility to go to the immigration office and take care of this. Entering Mexico farther south than the border zone will result in a fine if you get caught.

CUSTOMS

The customs process when entering Mexico from the United States, United Kingdom, European Union, Australia, and New Zealand is easy and streamlined. As long as you do not have the usual prohibited items (firearms, drugs, etc.), you should have no problem when entering the country. Things like food items could cause your bags to be searched and make the process take longer. For an extensive list of what you can and can't bring into Mexico, visit the **Foreign Relations Secretariat** website (https://consulmex.sre.gob.mx/reinounido); the list can be found with the information on entry requirements for foreign nationals.

After collecting your luggage from the baggage claim, you'll most likely pass through a gate where you're required to press a button to see if your bags will be inspected more closely. Get a green light, and you're good to go. Get a red one, and you'll have to wait a bit longer for them to search your luggage. Note that travelers flying in from a Central or South American country might be searched more thoroughly.

The general **duty-free limits on goods** brought from Mexico by country are as follows: **United States,** US$800; **Canada,** C$200; **United Kingdom,** £390; **Australia,** A$900; **New Zealand,** NZ$700.

The **duty-free limits on alcohol** by country are as follows: **United States** (age limit 21), 1 liter of alcohol; **Canada** (age limit 19), 1.5 liters of wine, 1.14 liters of hard liquor, or up to 8.5 liters of beer; **United Kingdom** (age limit 18), 1 liter of hard liquor, 2 liters of wine or beer; **Australia** (age limit 18), 2.5 liters of any alcohol; **New Zealand** (age limit 17), 4.5 liters of wine or beer, up to three bottles of liquor (max. 1.125 liters per bottle).

The **duty-free limits on tobacco** products by country are as follows: **United States** (age limit 18), 200 cigarettes or 100 cigars; **Canada** (age limit 21), 200 cigarettes, 100 cigars; **United Kingdom** (age limit 17), 200 cigarettes, 100 cigarillos, 50 cigars, 250 grams of tobacco; **Australia** (age limit 18), one open pack of cigarettes and one unopened pack of up to 25; **New Zealand** (age limit 17), 50 cigarettes or 50 grams of tobacco.

Bringing alcohol or tobacco may affect your overall duty-free amount. Check your government's customs website for specifics.

CONSULATES AND EMBASSIES

If you lose your passport or have an emergency, you will need to contact your government's consulate or embassy. The **U.S. Consulate in Oaxaca City** (Alcalá 407, toll-free Mex. tel. 800/681-9374, 10am-3pm Mon.-Thurs.) is across the Andador from Santo Domingo.

Citizens of Canada, the United Kingdom, Australia, and New Zealand will have to contact their **embassies in Mexico City.** Their contact information is as follows: **Canada** (Schiller 529, Colonia Bosque de Chapultepec, Mexico City, tel. 555/724-7900, mxico@international.gc.ca, 9am-12pm and

2:30pm-4pm Mon.-Fri.); **United Kingdom** (Río Lerma 71, tel. 555/242-8500, ukinmexico. info@fco.gov.uk, 8am-4pm Mon.-Thurs., 8am-1:30pm Fri.); **Australia** (Rubén Darío 55, Colonia Polanco, tel. 551/101-2200, embaustmex@yahoo.com.mx, 8:30am-5:15pm Mon.-Fri.); and **New Zealand** (Jaime Balmes 8, Colonia Polanco, tel. 555/283-9460, 9:30am-5pm Mon.-Fri.).

Chances are slight, but those on longer trips that include Central America may need the services of the **Consulate General of Guatemala** (Álamos 1215, Colonia Reforma, Oaxaca City, tel. 951/132-5949, consoaxaca@minex.gob.gt).

CAR PERMIT

If you plan on driving to Oaxaca, you will need to obtain a Mexico Temporary Vehicle Importation Permit (TIP), as well as a Mexican car insurance policy. The only institution that provides this permit is the national bank of the army called **Banjercito.** Banjercito has offices at border crossings, and can process your application when you arrive. You can also try to apply for the TIP online (www. banjercito.com.mx/registroVehiculos/#). The site is in both English and Spanish, but it sometimes doesn't work. Apply online at least 7-10 days in advance to allow time for the permit to arrive in the mail.

To obtain a TIP, you will need a valid passport, your driver's license, tourist visa, the original vehicle title as well as copies, vehicle registration, and proof of a Mexican car insurance policy. The fee for the permit is US$51 (US$45 online), and you will need to make a deposit of US$200-400, depending on how old your car is. Boats or RVs require a separate TIP. You'll find lots of detailed information about obtaining a TIP and buying insurance at **Mexpro.com.**

Your permit will be issued for as long as your tourist visa. This will be your most important document to hold onto in Mexico. Your vehicle can get confiscated without it, a process that could prove more difficult and/or costly than even replacing a passport.

Recreation

ECOTOURISM

Oaxaca is home to some of the best organized ecotourism organizations in Mexico. The megadiverse region of the **Sierra Norte** is the place to go to explore what both nature and the local cultures have to offer. These lofty peaks are home to more ecotourism centers than I have room for in this guidebook. The stars of the bunch are places like **Ixtlán de Juárez,** where the local organization **Ecoturixtlán** has activities both in and out of its ecotourism park just a few minutes out of town. Closer to the valley, the **Pueblos Mancomunados** are the most well organized in the state, probably in the country. I encourage visitors to take advantage of the guides and community workshops, to get to know the people and customs as much as the natural world.

A handful of more recently established tour agencies in **Oaxaca City** have begun to offer fun and culturally enriching tours of the **Valles Centrales,** as well. Instead of taking you through the main gate of an attraction so you can snap the required selfies to prove you've been there, these companies will have you hiking or cycling through the valley to get there. They stop at rickety old highway *comedores* (restaurants), where the food is meant for Oaxacan palates, not simplified or made "safer" for picky tourists, or fused into hip new recipes.

Down on the coast, you'll find lots of **bird-watching, sea turtle conservation, lagoon tours,** and more. Destinations like **Huatulco, Laguna Manialtepec,** and the **Lagunas de Chacahua** are home to large and diverse avian populations that should be

The Sierra Norte's Communal Lands

Private property is forbidden by municipal law in many of the communities in the Sierra Norte. The trails you walk belong to everyone in the town; therefore, it is necessary to **check in with the local ecotourism office** (yes, in every new community you visit) and **pay a small entrance fee.** This fee is included in the price of *cabañas* and other accommodations (for which you'll have to pass by the office to check in anyway), but if you're just going to be in town for the day, stop in and pay the fee.

of interest to everyone from casual birders to professional ornithologists. Many agencies in **Puerto Escondido** offer tours to Laguna Manialtepec to see the bioluminescent phytoplankton that light up the water at night. Mazunte is the place to go to learn more about sea turtles and the local efforts to conserve their habitat. And **La Ventanilla,** just to the west of Mazunte, offers lagoon tours through crocodile-infested waters.

MOUNTAIN BIKING

Mountain biking in Oaxaca is very popular, and only growing more so each day. Agencies in **Oaxaca City** offer cycling tours throughout the Valles Centrales, often combining them with cultural activities, such as stops at *palenques* (mezcal plantations) to learn about the process and taste the wares. Many of the ecotourism centers in the **Sierra Norte,** such as the **Pueblos Mancomunados,** offer mountain bike rentals and guides. Trails here range from wide, two-track mountain roads to rocky, expert-level single-track trails. There's something for everybody.

Down on the coast, don't miss the chance to take a bike through the **Parque Nacional Huatulco,** just to the west of the Bahías de Huatulco, the main tourist area. You can work up a sweat pedaling through the jungle, then

cool off on one of the undeveloped beaches in the park.

With lots of trail maps, route testimonials, photos, and more, the Oaxaca-specific mountain biking website **OaxacaMTB.org** is the most extensive online resource for those who bring their own bike. If you don't bring your own equipment, don't worry. I'm that dorky guy who always annoys people about wearing helmets, so I made sure that every rental and tour agency in this guide provides a *casco* (helmet) for riders.

During high season, you most likely won't be able to just walk into a tour agency and plan a mountain biking tour the next day. Make reservations well ahead of time with Oaxaca City operators. Even in lesser-visited areas, like the Sierra Norte, call ahead at least a few days to a week ahead of time to reserve, so that operators have time to get all the gear in safe, working order.

HORSEBACK RIDING

Through the company **Horseback Mexico** (Murguía 403, Oaxaca City, tel. 951/199-7026, www.horsebackmexico.com), you can do half-day, overnight, and weeklong rides in various locations throughout Oaxaca.

Lots of communities in the Sierra Norte also offer horseback riding. Take a ride from one town to another in the **Pueblos Mancomunados,** or through the eerie, fog-filled valley at **Llano de las Flores.** Call the communities' ecotourism offices well in advance to plan rides.

You can also trot through thick jungle and on the shores of rivers, lagoons, and beaches in **Huatulco, Puerto Escondido,** and **Laguna de Manialtepec,** on the coast.

SURFING, KAYAKING, AND BOAT TOURS

Your number one choice for **surfing** in Oaxaca is **Puerto Escondido,** where the beach break at **Playa Zicatela** is so powerful, consistent, and downright fun that Puerto is regularly in the top 10 of best surfing spots worldwide. Zicatela's waves are best left to the highly experienced and professionals, but the budding part of the beach called **La Punta Zicatela** has much milder waves for those learning the ropes. East down the coast, at **Barra de la Cruz,** you'll find a very consistent point break that curls slowly for hundreds of yards.

Farther east, in El Istmo de Tehuantepec, the town of **Salina Cruz** is home to a handful of very knowledgeable and experienced surf camps that take care of everything from accommodations to food to transportation to the almost two dozen varied and consistent waves between here and Huatulco. Salina Cruz is not as developed for tourism as Puerto Escondido, and there's not much else to do here besides surf, so it is better to plan a trip with the surf camps, rather than just show up with your board.

One reason the sport is so popular here is because many places have long surf seasons in which wave conditions are perfect. A good online resource for finding when waves will be best is **Surf-Forecast.com.**

A couple spots on the coast, such as Huatulco and Laguna de Manialtepec, offer sea and lagoon **kayaking.** This is an excellent way to see the mangrove forests of the lagoon and observe the flocks of seabirds that nest and feed there. And just about anybody with a **boat** on the beach will take you out to see dolphins or explore the secluded, undeveloped coves all up and down the coast.

SNORKELING AND SCUBA DIVING

Huatulco is the ideal spot on the coast to go **snorkeling.** The aquamarine waters of **Playa La Entrega** are calm and clear enough to see lots of tropical fish and other reef-dwelling creatures. Just be careful not to touch the corals. When the tide is low, there is only a few feet of water over them, and the effects of so many snorkelers and swimmers is apparent. **Playa Puerto Angelito,** in Puerto Escondido, is also calm and clear enough to observe sea life, but in general, the Pacific coast here is rough and murky.

Oaxaca isn't as ideal a destination for **scuba diving,** but there are a couple options along the coast. Because of the often dangerous conditions of the water, as well as a pretty unsafe personal experience with a not-so-serious dive center in Puerto Escondido (now defunct), I can't emphasize enough the importance of sticking to the dive centers listed in this guidebook (there aren't many others, anyway). That past experience made me research dive centers here thoroughly, and I only included centers that showed me they follow PADI safety certifications, and that they know where the good diving is. You'll find the best conditions in Huatulco.

As with diving anywhere, be insistent that all safety precautions are taken, and if something besides the ocean seems fishy, don't get in the water.

FISHING

When it comes to fishing, you really don't need a guidebook to find it on the coast. Go to a beach, and it'll find you. Fishermen have been pulling the catch of the day out of the Pacific up and down the coast for who knows how many generations. Just about any one of them who offers to take you out on his boat will know exactly what he's doing, but **Puerto Escondido, Puerto Ángel,** and **Huatulco** are the most popular destination for deep sea fishing.

All fishing guides listed in this guidebook expressed a personal responsibility to adhere to responsible fishing practices. One in Puerto Escondido made it a priority to be vigilant on the water for illegal turtle fishing and educating his clients on the biology and conservation of this beautiful endangered species.

CLIMBING

There are a few great spots for climbing in Oaxaca, but the sport isn't practiced much here, and very few tourism agencies have the necessary equipment. If you come without your own, head to **Ixtlán de Juárez,** in the Sierra Norte, where there is climbing and rappelling in **Parque Ecoturixtlán.**

The ecotourism center in **Capulálpam de Méndez** also has equipment and experienced guides for the cliffs outside town. These are not tall cliffs, and in these locations, climbing is more of a tourist activity than a serious sport.

The best spot I've found for serious climbing is **Apoala,** in La Mixteca, where the cliffs tower as high as 600 meters (1,970 ft) over the canyon floor. You will have to bring your own gear and experience with you, as the folks in town aren't climbers themselves, and they do not offer guides or equipment.

YOGA AND MEDITATION

Major tourist destinations in Oaxaca, such as Oaxaca City and Puerto Escondido, have lots of **yoga studios** and hotels that offer hatha, vinyasa, kundalini, and other styles of yoga, as well as meditation classes. But for full-on **yoga retreats,** there's no better place than **Mazunte.** If you really need to disconnect from the stress, worry, and technology of the daily grind, this is where to do it.

Food

For many travelers, the gastronomy of Oaxaca is so delicious, unique, and creative that it is reason enough to visit. Even within Mexico, Oaxacan cuisine is widely regarded as the best in the nation, causing Oaxaqueños and other Mexicans alike to emit yummy sounds when they talk about it. Oaxaca is truly an endless buffet for those in search of bold flavors, interesting recipes and cooking methods, and, of course, *el picante* (spicy food).

ANTOJITOS

Most of what the rest of the world thinks of as "Mexican food" is really just the tip of the iceberg. Tacos, quesadillas, and enchiladas belong to the subcategory of Mexican cuisine referred to as *antojitos,* or basically snack foods (don't get me wrong, they will fill you up) or fast foods, which is why you'll find so much of this on the street.

Many of the *antojitos* in Oaxaca aren't exclusively Oaxacan. There are lots of **tacos, tostadas,** and **quesadillas** to be eaten here. As is Oaxaca's wont, however, they usually come with a regional twist that adds flavors distinct from other parts of Mexico. A simple quesadilla here will have a few leaves of the potent herb **epazote,** which, aside from the interesting flavor it lends to a dish, also helps reduce gasses during digestion (it is also often mixed in with beans). **Tortas,** or

Mexican bread-roll sandwiches, are, in this author's obviously biased opinion, better in Oaxaca than in other parts of the country, as well.

Oaxaca also has a couple unique takes on the *antojito.* The most notable and most available statewide is the **tlayuda.** This overgrown monstrosity of a quesadilla (or tostada, depending on the cook's style) is the epitome of tortilla-based cuisine. The tortilla, also referred to simply as a *tlayuda,* is generally around 40 cm (16 in) in diameter, and usually a bit tougher than a regular crunchy tostada. Ingredients vary between cooks and regions, but they are most commonly filled or topped with meat, cheese, beans, lettuce or cabbage, tomatoes, avocados, and other veggies. I've even seen sliced hardboiled eggs on a *tlayuda.* The key ingredient, what sets the *tlayuda* apart from its sibling *antojitos,* is something called **asiento.** *Asiento* is the thick, savory stuff left over after frying *chicharrones* (pork rinds), so vegans beware. This sneaky ingredient hidden beneath the mountain of deliciousness on top is what gives a *tlayuda* its distinct flavor and sets it apart from your average taco, quesadilla, and tostada on the street. *Tlayuda* styles differ from region to region, but you'll find the best ones in La Mixteca.

Also unique to Oaxaca, but not as

widespread, are the *garnachas* of El Istmo. Unlike their larger Oaxacan cousins, the tortillas for *garnachas* are small and stout. What sets them apart from other *antojitos* is that the tortilla is deep fried before the other ingredients are placed on top. When done right, the tortilla has a crunchy outer layer, but is still somewhat soft and pliable inside, and the light frying gives it a delicious flavor that complements the shredded beef or *picadillo* (ground beef with potatoes) and *queso istmeño* (a *queso fresco*, or "fresh cheese," from El Istmo). They are usually served with a tangy coleslaw that adds a fresh crunch to the greasy little things.

REGIONAL FOODS

Oaxaca's rugged landscape has kept communities more or less secluded for hundreds, even thousands of years. Because of this, people have had to work with what was close by, which in the gastronomical department means there are lots of regional dishes that one can only find in certain locations, despite the installation of highways in the 20th century that made travel between remote locations easier. This often makes eating here a full-on adventure, and not just one for the taste buds.

For example, you'll very rarely find the *chile de agua* outside **Oaxaca City** and the **Valles Centrales,** which means the chile relleno you order in the Mercado 20 de Noviembre, in downtown Oaxaca, will taste very different from one you order in the neighboring state of Puebla, which will most likely be a *chile poblano.* Don't leave Oaxaca City without trying one.

Places like the **coast, El Istmo,** and **El Papaloapan** in the north are renowned both state- and nationwide for their **seafood.** In these regions of Oaxaca, you can bet on the fact that the fish you ordered for lunch was caught that morning. No offense to the other two, but the best I found was in El Istmo, where seafood dishes are served with *totopos,* the region's light, airy, and hole-ridden take on the crispy tortilla. One key element to the deliciousness of the seafood here is the quality

of the *aderezo,* which means dressing, but in this case means chipotle mayo. It's not unique to El Istmo, but it is the best here, for whatever reason. Another great region for fish meals is the **Sierra Norte,** where countless *trucherías* (trout hatcheries) serve **fresh trout** in a number of tasty and interesting ways.

And then there's *mole.* Although the myth is that there are seven different *mole* recipes in Oaxaca, the truth is that there are so many nuanced regional recipes for the dish that the real number can't be counted. Chef Pilar Cabrera of the Oaxaca City restaurant La Olla once told me that each tiny town in Oaxaca boasts at least one distinct *mole* recipe. One unique regional variation is the soupy, spicy *mole de caderas* (goat *mole,* literally, "*mole* of hips"), a recipe and tradition shared with the Tehuacán region of the neighboring state of Puebla. You'll only find this recipe, which uses the hip and spine bones of the goat and is made with the incredibly flavorful leaves of the avocado tree, in **La Mixteca,** primarily in and around **Huajuapan de León,** and only mid-October–mid-November. The restaurant **Tierra del Sol** in **Oaxaca City,** which specializes in the cuisine of La Mixteca, also serves this dish at this time of year. You might also see it called *huaxmole.*

BEVERAGES

Oaxaca's most famous beverage is hot chocolate, known here simply as **chocolate.** Rare will be the time that the *comedor* you're eating in will not have chocolate as a beverage option. When served hot, it is made with either water (*chocolate de agua*) or milk (*chocolate de leche*), and you can also order it as a *malteada* or *chocomil,* what is generally referred to in the United States as chocolate milk. One of the things that makes Oaxaca so magical to me is that you don't have to wait until the holidays to have a hot chocolate. Here, you'll find the sweet, delicious drink year-round.

But simple hot chocolate or chocolate milk aren't the only drinks made with cacao here. Endemic to Oaxaca City and the Valles Centrales is the wholly Oaxacan drink *tejate.*

Made with cacao, nuts, the seed of the mamey fruit, and a flower called *flor* or *rosita de cacao* (which, funnily enough, is not actually the flower of the cacao plant), this foam-topped beverage may look strange at first glance, but don't let that deter you. It is absolutely delicious, and you won't find it anywhere in the world outside Central Oaxaca. One of the ingredients is the climate. Cool, dry conditions are needed for the ground petals of the *flor de cacao* to turn foamy and rise to the top, so you won't get this chance down on the sultry coast.

Other interesting drinks made with cacao include the **espuma** (literally, "foam") of **Zaachila,** and the **chocolate-atole** of **Teotitlán del Valle** and other communities in the Valle de Tlacolula. These are mixed with the corn-based drink called *atole*, a thick, sweet hot beverage sold on just about every street corner in the country.

The state's **coffee**-producing pride and joy is **Pluma Hidalgo,** in the Sierra Sur, and most of the coffee you try in the state will be from here. Pluma coffee is strong, with bold flavors and a heavy acidity, which, when roasted right (which it usually is), has the perfect acidic bite that doesn't overtake the other flavors in the brew. Other regions, however, such as the Sierra Norte and Sierra Mixe, as well as parts of La Mixteca, also have excellent coffee growing conditions that tend to produce much milder coffees that don't come out as dark as the black gold of Pluma. No matter what kind of coffee you prefer, Oaxaca has a roast for you.

In regions like La Mixteca, the Sierra Norte, and El Istmo, you might have trouble finding espresso-based coffee drinks, as this is a relatively new way to prepare coffee here. Traditionally, and statewide, coffee is prepared in a large ceramic pot, a recipe called *café de olla* (pot coffee). This is usually a much weaker brew, but the Mexican form of brown sugar called *piloncillo* is commonly added to give it sweetness and make up for the lighter taste of the brew. It isn't always presweetened, though, so I usually ask if it's already sweet (*¿Ya está dulce?*).

Anywhere you go in Oaxaca, especially in the *mercados*, you're sure to find a *juguería* (juice bar). In these stalls, you can find **fresh juice** made from the wide variety of tropical fruits that grow in this fertile region.

Oaxaca's most famous alcoholic beverage is **mezcal,** a distillate of the maguey (also called agave) plant. Mezcal is not exclusively Oaxacan. Other states, such as Michoacán and Jalisco (known for its tequila, a type of mezcal), produce quality mezcal, as well. The general consensus around the country, and world, however, is that *palenqueros* (mezcal producers) in Oaxaca do it best. Although you'll be able to find a bottle of the potent stuff anywhere in the state, the real mezcal-crazy region is the **Valles Centrales,** where conditions are best for the types of maguey used to make it. Other parts of Oaxaca, El Istmo for example, have high rates of alcohol consumption, but tend to stick to beer, so if you are interested in tasting and learning more about mezcal, **Oaxaca City** and the surrounding communities are the places to do so. Mezcal culture in Oaxaca has more to do with flavors, culture, and production methods than with getting drunk. You don't shoot mezcal, you sip it.

PICNIC SUPPLIES AND GROCERIES

If you have dietary restrictions, are on a budget, or are just planning a picnic or *asada* (cookout), every single town in Oaxaca will have a *mercado* where fresh fruits, meats, cheeses, and other foodstuffs are sold daily. Since the best cooks in town tend to be in the markets as well, I've noted the markets in just about every town listed in this guide.

I've been told that since agricultural regulations aren't as strict or enforced here in Mexico as they are in the United States, Canada, and the United Kingdom, vegetables here need to be washed with more than water to clean them of pesticides or other harmful chemicals. This isn't to say all of them are covered in pesticides. There is also a lot of organic farming here, but how are you going to be able

Oaxacan Chile Peppers

Mexico's National System of Phytogenic Food Resources and Agriculture (SINAREFI) has counted 64 distinct chile pepper species that grow within the country's borders, making Mexico the nation with the most biodiversity of chiles worldwide. Oaxaca tops the list of states with 25 distinct pepper species that thrive in its deserts, valleys, mountainsides, and hot, humid tropical regions. Some can't be found outside Oaxaca, others are in danger of extinction. Some burn, others transform the soil into more dulcet tones. All are delicious. Here are a few you'll probably see a lot of, and a couple you might not.

Chile de Agua

The *chile de agua* (water chile) is unique to the Valles Centrales. It's usually greenish yellow, and gets bright orange as it matures. These are what is used in all the chiles rellenos, and often in *salsa de molcajete*, a salsa made by grinding the ingredients in mortar and pestles made of igneous stone. *Chile de agua* isn't as easy to come by outside the Valles Centrales, so don't neglect to leave without trying one. They usually have a very mild spice.

Chile Pasilla Mixe

Also called *chile pasilla oaxaqueño*, this species of one of Mexico's most complexly flavored chiles grows in the Mixe region of the Sierra Norte. When fresh, the *pasilla* is called *chile chilaca*. Growers smoke the peppers in wood-fired adobe ovens, and the cloudy days in the mountains don't fully dry them, so they are left in the oven longer than usual to finish the job. This puts the distinctive Oaxacan twist on a pepper whose flavor scuds from sweet to earthy to a distant spice behind it all, just like the clouds on the mountains where it grows. Like the *chile de agua*, you're only likely to find this pepper here in Oaxaca, primarily in the Valles Centrales and mountains to the north, so if you see it on a menu, say yes.

Chile Costeño

As you might guess from the name, you'll find lots of salsas on the coast made with the bright-red *chile costeño*, which usually has a mild spice to it. However, terms in Oaxaca, and Mexico in general, can often be fluid and regional, sometimes used to refer to something different elsewhere. So if you see a yellow *chile costeño*, as they're called around the Jamiltepec region to the west, be warned that it can get pretty hot.

Chile de Onza

This little firecracker, also grown in the Sierra Norte, is short and skinny, and usually packs a punch. Usually yellow, but sometimes flirting with reddish tones, this flame-colored pepper can get up to three times hotter than a jalapeño, so be careful.

Chile Tabiche

This short, triangular pepper, mostly found in Miahuatlán and Ejutla, most often comes in a deep wine red. Fresh *tabiches* are used in salsas and *mole verde*. The dried peppers are used to make dark-red *salsa macha*, a very spicy oil-based salsa with a pulp of dried peppers, herbs, and nuts that settles at the bottom.

Chile Escuchito

Also called *chile paradito* (standing chile) because the little dark-green conical pods grow sticking straight up off the plant. With a fire similar to *chile serrano* or *chile de árbol*, *escuchitos* are typically used in table salsas in Oaxaca City. In the tropical regions to the north, they are sometimes burned to create a smoke that repels mosquitoes, or in infusions that repel spiders, scorpions, and snakes.

Chile Chilhuacle

In Nahuatl, *chilhuacle* means "old chile." This moderately spicy pepper only grows around Cuicatlán, in the region known as La Cañada Chica, the low, arid canyon country to the west of the Sierra

dried chiles for sale in the *mercado*

Mazateca. It is very rare and, as a consequence, quite expensive, as far as chiles go. Because of this, many of the dishes that traditionally include the *chilhuacle* will have *chile guajillo* as a substitute. If you are in La Cañada and find a plate that has this chile in it, do not miss your chance. If you're scouting the markets for them, the fresh ones are green, but they turn red as they mature. When dried, they turn a deeper wine red, and don't become wrinkly like *pasillas* or *guajillos*.

Chile Achilito

This very rare chile pepper also only grows in La Cañada, tending to like the same conditions that favor the *chilhuacle*. It is generally used in dried form for salsas, or sometimes tossed whole into a batch of *barbacoa de borrego* (slow-roasted lamb barbecue). If you think you've had a hard time tracking down *chilhuacles*, you'll struggle even more to find *achilitos*. They are extremely hard to find, even in the communities where it is still cultivated, and not used often in restaurants.

Chile Guajillo

Unlike the previous two, this pepper is by no means endemic to Oaxaca. You'll find it in states as far away as Jalisco and Colima, to the west. But you'll also find it a lot in Oaxaca, especially since it is used as a substitute in *moles* that traditionally call for the *chilhuacle*. This dark-red pepper, the dried form of a pepper called *mirasol* when fresh, is dark brownish red with a leathery texture. Although it tends to have a mild afterburn, it is usually sweeter than it is spicy, making it a great choice for those not accustomed to high amounts of capsaicin, the stuff that gives chiles their fire.

Chile Habanero

Like the *guajillo*, you'll find habaneros all over Mexico, and also in abundance in Oaxaca. Unlike the *guajillo*, however, the habanero is very spicy. Lots of salsas in Oaxaca, especially if they are orange, will have habaneros in them, so if you can't stand the heat, ask what's in the salsa before dousing your taco with it. It is also used as a condiment, usually sliced and mixed with sliced onions in vinegar. It comes in green and red, so be wary. The habanero is the base of my favorite **bottled salsa** from Oaxaca, called **La Mayor,** which is made by the company **El Sabor de Oaxaca** (Teotzapotlán 706, Zaachila, tel. 951/528-7096, www.elsabordeoaxaca.com.mx). You'll find it in many stalls and shops in and around the Mercado Benito Juárez in Oaxaca City. If you're working up a tolerance to the pepper, start with their green one with the word "Kids" on the label.

Pre-Hispanic Oaxacan Food

The richness and variety of Oaxacan food today has much to do with the influence of the Spanish. Without them, there would be no savory pork for the *empanadas de amarillo* of San Antonino Castillo Velasco, no beef for the mind-altering *barbacoa en rollo* of Zaachila, no *quesillo* for the tacos, *tlayudas,* and quesadillas. They even brought the rice to go with the beans. However, if it weren't for the tendency of the Zapotecs, Mixtecs, Mixes, Triques, and the numerous other indigenous peoples of Oaxaca to not let their culture and livelihood go down without a fight, the gastronomy here would be much less varied, creative, fun, and, most importantly, delicious.

The Spanish diet was part and parcel of the conquest, but the conquistadors' attempts to impose their European grub onto the native people of Mexico wasn't as successful as the political, linguistic, and religious components. The magnitude of the biodiversity here gave the creative cooks of pre-Hispanic Oaxaca much to work with, and a lot of what they prepared thousands of years ago is being made the same way today.

For example, people here ate **tamales** stuffed with beans or mixed with the flavorful herb called *chipil.* The practice of entomophagy (eating insects) dates back to, one would assume, the first time someone walked around this land and got hungry, the earliest signs of which are around 7,000 years ago. To this day, you can find women in the Mercado Benito Juárez and other markets all over Oaxaca with mounds of **chapulines** (fried grasshoppers) and **gusanos de maguey** (maguey worms) for sale. If your *tlayuda* is served the ideal way (go to La Mixteca), it'll come with a side of *chapulines,* as well as a few piquant and uniquely flavored herbs like *berroz, pipicha,* and *pápalo,* and the seeds of the *guaje* tree, from which Oaxaca takes its name.

Women from San Andrés Huayapam, just north of Oaxaca City, have been passing down the recipe for the foamy, nutty drink **tejate** to their daughters since long before the town had either the Spanish or Nahuatl names it is known by today. **Chocolate** was one of the items in the Mesoamerican diet that the Spanish actually had no desire to wipe out or replace. The English and Spanish word "chocolate" comes from the Nahuatl *xocolatl,* meaning "bitter water," and many chocolate companies today sell the addictively tasty stuff with chiles, honey, and other local ingredients used to flavor it centuries ago. The sweet, viscous breakfast beverage **champurrado,** the corn-based drink *atole* flavored with chocolate, is likewise from before the conquest.

People along the Coast and in El Istmo have likewise consumed local fauna, such as **iguanas, armadillos,** and **sea turtles** and their eggs, for millennia. Although people still eat these as delicacies in the home, they are not served in restaurants, and due to their presence on endangered species lists, I do not recommend coming to Oaxaca with the intention of eating them.

Probably the most interesting of pre-Hispanic dishes in Oaxaca is the **caldo de piedra,** a seafood stew cooked by dropping a fire-heated river stone into the broth and raw ingredients. Since the isolated town of San Felipe Usila, in El Papaloapan, was never conquered by the Spanish, the recipe has survived as it was thousands of years ago.

to tell from a simple pile of tomatoes in the market? Supermarkets and convenience stores here sell products you can mix with water to clean produce, but simple substances like lime juice or vinegar can be used, as well.

MEALS AND MEALTIMES

A staple of Mexican cuisine is what is called *comida corrida* (set meals, literally something like "food on the run"). This breakfast or lunch option will usually include a few courses, such as soup or pasta and a main dish, and an *agua fresca.* Also called *agua de sabor,* or in conversation, most often simply *agua,* these are juice-like drinks made with fresh fruit and immoderate amounts of sugar. If you want plain old water, you'll have to ask for *agua natural.* Most places that serve *comida corrida* close in the late afternoon, after the lunch rush.

Since the workday starts early for many Mexican folks, **breakfast** (*el desayuno*) is usually eaten quite early. For many people in Oaxaca, breakfast is just a cup of hot chocolate and a *pan de yema* (egg yolk bread served with chocolate). Egg plates, like huevos rancheros or *chilaquiles*, are on the whole called *desayunos*, but some folks will call them *almuerzo*, the word your Spanish textbook told you means "lunch." Some will call **lunch** either el almuerzo or simply *la comida*, the word for food. (Language is a very malleable thing in Oaxaca, used to suit hyperlocal needs for representation, and just when you think you're using the wrong term for something because people in one town call it one thing, you go to the next and everyone says the word you thought it was from the beginning.) Like many Latin American countries, lunch and dinner are generally later than those in the United States, Canada, and the United Kingdom. When I worked in Miahuatlán, we didn't get off for lunch until 2pm, but we had a two-hour siesta, or midday mealtime. **Dinner** (*la cena*) is eaten much later as well, often as late as 9pm or 10pm.

Pay attention to the operating hours of restaurants, as in some places there are de facto rules as to when a certain cuisine is eaten. Many seafood places on the coast, for example, open at 8am and close by 8pm (or sooner). Tacos are more commonly available in the late afternoon until the wee hours of the night, though you shouldn't have problems finding them for lunch.

Accommodations

The accommodations prices listed in this guidebook are the maximum **rack rates** that hotels charge during high season. There is a good chance you'll find good deals (*promociones*), but you probably won't be accommodated if you go around just asking for discounts (*descuentos*).

Many hotel operators in Oaxaca were wary of telling me their rates at first. They don't want people expecting a certain rate just because I wrote it down. So take this as a disclaimer. This is a guide to what you can expect to pay, more or less, when you come. Things like exchange rates or changes of ownership or operational style may cause the prices to be different when you arrive. Do not argue for a rate quoted in the guidebook. In my opinion, most everything in Oaxaca is underpriced, anyway, so it shouldn't be a problem.

MAKING RESERVATIONS

Most of the year, you should be able to walk right into a hotel just about anywhere in Oaxaca and get a room. Even the busiest places in the state, like Oaxaca City, Puerto Escondido, and Huatulco, are pretty empty during low seasons, but if you have a specific hotel in mind, reserve anyway.

There are lots of great websites to get deals on hotels, but when booking online, keep the businesses in mind as much as your own vacation. I received many complaints all over the state about a certain quite famous site that offers free cancellation any time before check-in. I urge you not to take advantage of this, if possible. If you cancel your reservation without time for the hotel to fill the room with another guest, it can negatively affect their business.

You really shouldn't need reservations for regular hotels in regions like La Mixteca, the Sierra Norte, and El Istmo (except in May for El Istmo), but always reserve ahead of time for ecotourism options that include stays in *cabañas*. This is more to ensure that the activities you want to do are ready when you arrive, but you never know. And you don't want to be stuck out of doors in these secluded communities.

I personally recommend booking directly with hotels. This will ensure they have your reservation (I've had online bookings never make it to the front desk), plus it's a great way to practice your Spanish. Many hotels in

High Season in Oaxaca

Here's a quick rundown of the **high tourist seasons in Oaxaca.** If you're coming during these periods, book well in advance, i.e., months. Hotels in Oaxaca City book up months in advance for festivals such as Day of the Dead.

- **Late October and early November:** Day of the Dead
- **Late December and early January:** Christmas and New Year's
- **April:** Semana Santa, or Holy Week; very popular domestic tourism dates
- **May:** month with the most *velas*, traditional raging parties in El Istmo
- **July:** Guelaguetza, festivals in Oaxaca City and many other towns that celebrate local culture
- **July and August:** Summertime!

If you want to **avoid the crowds,** September and October are the best months to come. I basically had Huatulco all to myself one September, and fully recommend coming at this time.

Oaxaca City, Puerto Escondido, and Huatulco have English-speaking staff for booking rooms and other services.

It's worth noting that the gig economy's contribution to accommodations is problematic. Yes, you can stay "with a local" and all that, but a lot of that money goes to the global company and not the local economy. It seems like a way for big companies to skirt costs like hotel taxes, maintenance, and service while taking business away from hotels, many of which here are family-owned operations that have worked long and hard to provide good service to visitors. Keep it local. Keep it personal.

HOTELS

Hotels in Oaxaca range from the basic to the unique and artsy upscale establishments owned by mezcal producers to five-star luxury beach resorts. You've got options here to suit whatever budget and traveling style you like.

When I describe a hotel as "basic," this usually means a bed, private bathroom, a fan, and sometimes TV and Wi-Fi, but don't bet on the internet functioning perfectly in out-of-the-way places like La Mixteca and the north. The best thing about hotels like this is the affordability of privacy. You can often get a private room and bath for less than US$20.

HOSTELS

I was really picky when choosing hostels for this guide. Those listed showed me that they are clean, welcoming, and social without being all-out nightly bacchanals. Most include at least a light breakfast, and many on the coast have full schedules of fun activities, like barbecues, social nights, language exchanges, and more.

CABAÑAS

The primary accommodations in the **mountains** are *cabañas* (cabins). In the higher altitudes, you can expect them to have a fireplace and your reservation to include a load of firewood. Many have potable water in the taps, so ask the manager when you check in. The *cabañas* listed in this guide range from rickety corrugated steel structures with little more than a bed, lightbulb, and dingy shared bathroom (around US$3) to luxurious brick cabins with king beds, hot water, and warmth from the fire (generally no more than US$33). You can get a good idea of how nice a *cabaña* will be from the price.

Down on the **coast,** *cabaña* really means bungalow. Again, there is a wide range of cleanliness and amenities, from rustic shacks in the swampy areas to luxury hilltop villas with spectacular ocean views, balconies, internet, and more. The most basic *cabaña* here is usually about US$10-12 a night, and from there the price can go up quite a bit, depending on how fancy you want your bungalow, with tons of options in between.

HOMESTAYS

For those looking to practice or perfect their Spanish, or to just meet amazing and friendly people and experience their unique culture, there is no better option than the homestay. Forcing yourself to use Spanish all day will increase your vocabulary (key to mastering a language) and get you accustomed to thinking and responding in Spanish. They usually include three home-cooked meals a day, as well. Can't beat that.

The best place for homestays is in the ecotourism communities of the **Sierra Norte**, most notably, the **Pueblos Mancomunados**. Book well in advance to make sure the family is ready to receive you. Spanish schools in **Oaxaca City** also offer homestays as part of their learning packages.

SHORT-TERM RENTALS

You'll find the most short-term rentals directed toward tourists in **Oaxaca City** and the popular destinations on the coast. Depending on the size, condition, amenities, and services offered, this could be the most affordable option for those spending at least a month in one location. You can expect to spend anywhere from US$300-1,000 a month, or more, depending on how luxurious you want your place to be.

You'll also find a lot of rooms for rent in non-touristy towns all over the state. If you're a DIY traveler like myself, and want to truly experience the daily life of a tiny Oaxacan city or town, keep an eye out for signs reading "*Se rentan cuartos*" (**Rooms for rent**). Deal directly with the property owner for rentals like this. Since these will be primarily targeting Oaxacan tenants, you can expect low rates. Just be aware that you get what you pay for.

GUEST RANCHES

The guest ranch option is one of the most limited here in Oaxaca. There is one just outside **Oaxaca City** that focuses on **horseback riding**. Down in the Sierra Sur, around **Pluma Hidalgo,** you'll find *fincas de café* (coffee plantations) that cater to tourists, offering tours of their coffee fields and other fun activities.

CAMPING

The fog-shrouded peaks of the **Sierra Norte** are the best places for camping in Oaxaca. Every ecotourism center listed in this guidebook has a camping option, some of which are more idyllic than others. You can expect to pay US$2-5 per night with your own tent. I've never seen a place charge more than 100 pesos (US$5) for a camping spot. Some have tents for rent, for which you can expect to pay another US$5 or so.

Lots of beach hostels in **Puerto Escondido, Mazunte,** and **Zipolite** offer space to pitch a tent, as well. And in Huatulco's **Bahía Tangolunda,** you can camp out in a small, jungly space between two gigantic five-star resorts, surrounded by huge populations of crabs, iguanas, and tropical seabirds.

I've heard of people just finding a secluded place on a beach somewhere on the coast, and setting up a campsite there, but often with unwelcome results. Still, camping is much safer here than in the rest of Mexico, where it is often confined to fenced-in areas. Stick to the businesses listed in this guide, which offer the freedom of staying outdoors, without feeling like a backyard campout.

HAMMOCKS

For the true budgeting beach bum, there is no more economic option than the **hammock** hung between a couple almond trees in the jungle—a practice that unfortunately is dying out. I often utilized accommodations like this when I lived in Miahuatlán and went down to **Mazunte** for the weekends, but I only saw one place in **Zipolite** that still offered this service when researching for this guidebook. The owner and I lamented the fact that people aren't requesting hammocks like this as much as they did even just a few years ago. However, if people start to request it more, it will become more available again.

Obviously, this option is for those who travel very light and don't bring too many valuables. If you do have something of value you want to keep safe, you can always ask the hostel owner to lock it up in the office for you. The usual rate for a hammock is around 30 pesos (US$1.50), and I've never seen anyone charge more than 40 pesos (US$2) for one, making this the cheapest way to beach bum it on the coast.

Conduct and Customs

Oaxacans are very friendly people, and they respond well to friendly visitors. They like to laugh boisterously and have a good time. Be friendly with them in all your interactions, and you'll have a great trip full of memories of all the wonderful people you met here.

COMMUNICATION STYLES

This friendliness is apparent in your communication styles. It is customary in Mexico to wish someone *Buenos días* (Good morning), *Buenas tardes* (Good afternoon/evening), or *Buenas noches* (Good evening/Goodnight) before beginning a conversation, so always begin with one of these greetings, especially if you're going to make a request.

During my training to become a certified bilingual educator, I learned about the differences in communication styles between English and Spanish speakers. One of the main differences is that whereas English speakers tend to speak, and therefore think, in linear sequences (with a narrative-like beginning, middle, and end, even in everyday conversations), Spanish has a more cyclical pattern to it. Spanish speakers will often come back to a topic in a conversation that a linear-thinking English speaker assumes is finished. This is just a linguistic generality, and doesn't speak for how every Spanish-speaking person thinks and communicates, but the tendency is common enough that awareness of it can make it easier to keep up when learning the language.

BODY LANGUAGE

There really aren't any major differences in the meaning of body language in Mexico and countries like the United States, Canada, and the United Kingdom. The main one that I have noticed is the common gesture here for showing gratitude, which is to display the back of the hand with the fingers in rigid extension. It doesn't correlate directly with an offensive gesture from my culture, but it was slightly alarming at first, and did take a little practice for me to get accustomed to using it in social interactions. If it does take you aback, just remember that the person is saying "Thank you," and not threatening to slap you in the mouth.

Although it isn't too common, you might see a young person make a "V" with their fingers. Visitors from the United Kingdom will most likely be aware that this is not meant offensively, as it is back home, but it seemed worth noting here, just in case.

TERMS OF ADDRESS

The same general politeness you would use at home in the United States or the United Kingdom is expected here in Oaxaca. For example, where you would say "Sir" or "Ma'am" back home, you'll say "*Señor*" or "*Señora*" here in Mexico. To address a younger woman you do not know, say a waitress or girl in a vendor stall in the market, the diminutive "*Señorita*" is acceptable.

If you need to speak to a police officer, you can get their attention by saying "*oficial*"

On Mexican Time

One of the main cultural differences between Mexico and other countries, even Latin American ones, has to do with time. For example, the word *ahorita* (the somehow diminutive of "now") can mean anytime in the next two minutes to tomorrow morning. It is often joked that it can really mean "never." Arriving late for a party or dinner isn't always considered rude. So in general, it is best to know that you are on Mexican time and have patience.

(officer). You might hear people in casual conversation refer to the police as "*poli*," but do not say this directly to a police officer. It would be considered offensive.

When meeting a new person, it is customary and polite to say you're glad to meet them, so after introductions, give a genuine "*Mucho gusto*" to your new acquaintance to keep things cordial.

TABLE MANNERS

When it comes to mealtime in Mexico, politeness extends to strangers, and it is customary to wish that others at a restaurant enjoy their meal. When you both enter and leave a restaurant or food stall, wish the nearby diners a friendly "*Buen provecho*" (Enjoy your meal), and when others say this to you, it is polite to respond with "*Gracias, igualmente*" (Thank you, same to you).

Since a server's entire livelihood is not wholly dependent on tips in Mexico, service can often be slower than foreign visitors would like. Just be patient if something takes longer than you'd like it to. One thing that ends up making wait times at tables longer than foreign visitors would prefer is the fact that servers in Mexico do not bring the check when they assume you are ready to go. This is considered rude here, like they are trying to kick you out. So, when you're ready to head out, get your waiter's attention and say "*La cuenta, por favor*" (Check, please), or give them the writing hand gesture that is more or less the international sign for this request.

PHOTO ETIQUETTE

Like most of us, Oaxacans doing everyday things like working or chilling in the park aren't too keen on having their picture taken without their knowledge or consent. No one wants to be considered a novelty when they're just doing what is normal to them. So, in situations like this—say you want to take a picture of the woman selling *chapulines* (fried grasshoppers) in the market—it is polite to simply ask "*¿Puedo sacar su foto?*" (May I take your picture?) before snapping the shot. This doesn't really apply, however, in public events where people are dressed up and out in public to show off their flashy, colorful costumes and other traditions. Revelers at *calendas* (parades) and other festivities are there for the show, and generally have no problems with their photos being taken.

Health and Safety

DON'T DRINK THE WATER

This may seem obvious to most travelers, but just about every pharmacy doctor in touristy areas will roll their eyes and tell you a story of a foreigner who thought his or her stomach was strong enough to take it. As a rule of thumb, stick to bottled water. If you're staying in one place for an extended period of time, the most economical option is to use a *garrafón* (20-liter hard plastic jug). After paying for a deposit (your rental may already have empty ones to use), you can take the empty jug to a convenience store and get a full one for cheap (about US$1). Or keep an ear out for the guy on his tricycle cruising the streets and shouting "*¡Aguaaaaa!*"

In some places in the Sierra Norte and Sierra Sur, potable water comes from clean mountain springs, and you can drink it straight out of the tap or hose. I've noted this where applicable, but always ask, just to be safe.

VACCINATIONS

There are no vaccine requirements for entering Mexico. However, all visitors to Oaxaca should make sure their routine vaccinations are up-to-date. **Hepatitis A** is a problem in Mexico, and travelers to any part of the country should have at least the first round of shots before entering. **Hepatitis B** is also recommended. If you're planning on going to more remote parts of the state, especially in tropical areas like the coast, El Istmo, and El Papaloapan, you should consider getting vaccinated for **typhoid, dengue,** and **rabies.** Also be aware that mosquitoes here can carry other diseases that do not yet have vaccines, such as **zika** and **chikungunya,** so don't forget bug repellent.

COMMON HEALTH PROBLEMS AND DISEASES

The most common stomach problem for visitors to Mexico is **traveler's diarrhea,** or what is jokingly called "Montezuma's Revenge" (even though the name of the Aztec emperor was actually Moctezuma). This is usually not caused by food prepared in unsanitary conditions, but simply because the stomach is coming into contact with a microbial environment it isn't used to. It usually isn't serious, though it can ruin a day or two of your trip. I recommend trying to wait it out for a day, and if it persists, go to a doctor.

If the problem persists longer, say you get sick every couple weeks for a couple months, it's possible you have a **parasite,** for which antibiotics obviously won't work. There are good one-dose, over-the-counter medications available in every pharmacy for this. Just ask for a *desparasitante* (antiparasitic). If you enjoy street food as much as I do, this information might come in handy.

HEALTH MAINTENANCE

To make sure that your gut bacteria are as strong and healthy as possible when you arrive, begin taking **probiotics** a month or two before your trip.

When you're down here, drink fresh **coconut water** as much as possible. It is naturally antiparasitic, and is also packed full of electrolytes to keep you hydrated. The small bottles of **drinkable yogurt** available in just about every *miscelania* (convenience store) are good for regulating your stomach bugs, as well. The most popular and widely available brand is called Yakult. Drinking one a day can help prevent digestive problems.

Medications and Prescriptions

You should be able to find the same basic over-the-counter medications in pharmacies in Oaxaca that you can back home. Unless you prefer a specific brand, you shouldn't have to worry about bringing your own basic medicines with you. Mexican pharmacies will fill **prescriptions** from foreign doctors; just make sure that you have as much valid documentation as possible and that it is up-to-date. (There is a longstanding myth that Mexican pharmacies will just sell you whatever prescription medication you ask for without a doctor's note. This may have been true long ago, but pharmacies are big business now in Mexico, and every time I've had to fill a prescription, the pharmacist has been very clear on needing the paperwork in order to release the medication.) To save money, ask for the generic (*genérico*) version of the medication you are buying.

Birth control, both preventative and emergency, is available without a prescription in Mexico. In the pharmacy, ask for *pastillas anticonceptivas* (contraceptive pills). Condoms (*condones*) can be bought in any pharmacy and most convenience stores. The emergency contraceptive Plan-B is also called Plan-B here, but you'll have to pronounce the B in Spanish (*beh*). For these and other medications you think you will need while here, research online before you come to find out the equivalent Mexican brand, or at least know what the active ingredient's name is in Spanish.

BEACH SAFETY

The number one safety concern on the coast is the powerful Pacific Ocean. Take warnings about conditions seriously. Even skilled swimmers can get caught in an **undertow,** and undertows can exist even when the ocean seems relatively calm. Surfers, make sure your skill level and confidence are adequate for the waves you attempt to ride. And do not go swimming on Playa Zicatela, in Puerto Escondido—despite the world-renowned size and power of the Mexican Pipeline, lifeguards here still regularly have to pull out swimmers who thought they could hack it. If you just can't wait to take a dip, head to the calmer waters of Playas Marinero and Principal, right next to Zicatela.

As with any hot, tropical region, take the usual precautions to stay healthy. Bring sunscreen and stay hydrated, especially if you drink alcohol.

CREEPY CRAWLERS

Your biggest bug worry down here is going to be **mosquitoes,** which in Oaxaca are known to carry diseases like dengue, chikungunya, and zika (use bug repellent). Other insects here might be frightening in size or appearance, but do not pose serious health risks. **Sand flies** on the beaches are a nuisance and often small enough to get through mosquito nets, so use bug spray if you don't want to itch for a few days. The following concerns are extremely rare, but I mention them because I have experienced them myself once or twice during all the time I've spent in Oaxaca.

Spiders, although very prevalent, are not a serious threat in Oaxaca, and shouldn't cause concern. The deserts of the Valles Centrales are a natural habitat for black widows and brown recluses, but you don't need to take any more precautions than checking your shoes before putting them on, or a towel hung outside to dry before using it. And this is really only a concern in rural areas, or when camping. The rest of Oaxaca's spiders may look scary, but they generally won't bother you (unless you bother them), and if they do, their bite is similar to that of a mosquito. Take similar precautions with shoes and towels for **scorpions,** which are found in the warm regions of the deserts and the coast.

As for **snakes,** be aware that a species of coral snake endemic to Oaxaca lives in the tropical deciduous forests of the Pacific side of the Sierra Madre del Sur and the lowlands of the Istmo de Tehuantepec. A species of rattlesnake also lives in Oaxaca, primarily in the deserts of the Valles Centrales and the Valle de Tehuacán-Cuicatlán. However, I can truthfully say that I've seen more snakes on a

30-minute walk in Texas than I have in all my time hiking in Oaxaca, so there is no need to be alarmed. Just be aware.

Very cheap accommodations, mostly in rural areas, might have **bedbugs.** Although they aren't known to spread diseases, their bites are itchy and irritating. Check the mattress and bedframe for small, dark stains. As with spiders, this is not a serious cause for concern, just a possibility if you plan on staying in the cheapest options available to you, so it is better to be aware. I've only ever found them in one hotel in all my time here.

MEDICAL SERVICES

The most widely available healthcare option is the *consultorio medico* (doctor's office) in many of the *farmacias* (pharmacies). These are adequate for stomach bugs, colds, the flu, minor injuries like small cuts or non-serious burns, and other maladies you'd go to a general practitioner for at home. A consult usually costs no more than US$3, and in some chains they're free, since they expect you to purchase the meds in the pharmacy next door. **Private doctors,** whose signs will also read *consultorio medico,* can also take care of these health issues.

For anything more serious you will need to go to a **hospital.** All the hospitals listed in this guidebook have **24-hour emergency rooms.** Most hospitals in downtown Oaxaca, and those that see lots of tourists on the coast, have English-speaking doctors and staff. If you go to a pharmacy doctor, the visit will most likely be conducted in Spanish, so if you're not confident in your ability to communicate in the language, it's best to take a Spanish speaker with you.

INSURANCE

Since medical care is so affordable in Mexico, it isn't really necessary to take out a traveler's insurance plan, especially for short trips. If you have a medical condition that that requires special attention and could affect you during your trip, however, it might be good to take out a policy. Many resources online

state that if you feel you can afford medical expenses on your trip, it is best not to waste the money on insurance.

If your trip is longer than a few months, or if it involves physically risky activities like surfing, mountain biking, or rock climbing, you might consider taking out a policy. A top-tier global provider is **World Nomads** (www. worldnomads.com). On their website, you can choose your home country and select a plan that is right for your needs.

For the ultimate peace of mind, you can take out a policy with air ambulance provider **Medjet** (toll-free U.S. tel. 800/527-7478, www. medjetassist.com). It's not cheap, but their network of hospitals and air ambulances can get you to the hospital of your choosing back home in case of serious medical conditions.

EARTHQUAKES

Oaxaca is a very seismically active part of the world, and it pays to know what to do in case of an earthquake. The most important thing to do in a seismic event is to remain calm. It might be harder than it sounds, but if you hear the alarm, take a deep breath, and think. Gas lines and appliances are very dangerous in these situations, so put out any flames around you, like stoves, candles, etc. Move away from windows that could break and other loose objects that could fall on you. If you can get to your hotel's *Punto de Reunión* (Meeting Point), make your way there in a calm, ordered fashion. However, during the actual shaking, moving through rooms of a house, and being anywhere near an exterior wall, is not recommended. The best thing to do is drop to your hands and knees so that the shaking won't knock you over. If there is a sturdy desk or table, scurry under it and hold on to a leg, prepared to move with the object, if necessary. If there is no such cover, make your way to an interior wall, away from windows and other objects that could fall on you, cover your neck and head with your arms, and wait out the quake.

There are certain myths about surviving a quake that aren't actually safe. The most

Oaxaca 9-1-1

Mexico has begun using the emergency telephone number 9-1-1 at the national level to connect people to police, fire, and other emergency services. At the time of this writing, the system was still working out some kinks, even in the country's most populous center, Mexico City. In a situation where you need to think fast, try 9-1-1, but if it doesn't work, or the response time is too long, contact the local police department directly. In many small towns, this will be the *agencia municipal*, or local government offices in the center of town.

enduring myth is that doorways are the safest parts of a house, but this is not the case. Neither is the "triangle of life" (crouching next to a piece of furniture in hopes that it will stop a collapsing wall) an effective or safe method. Although it is definitely the most terrifying possibility in an earthquake, total building collapse is extremely rare, and you are much more likely to be harmed by falling objects inside the house than the house itself.

DRUGS

Drugs such as marijuana, cocaine, and heroin are illegal in Oaxaca. The consumption of **hallucinogenic mushrooms** is tolerated by the authorities in the towns of San José del Pacífico (in the Sierra Sur) and Huautla de Jiménez (in the Sierra Mazateca), due to their longstanding use in traditional medicine practices. A stipulation is that the mushrooms be collected, sold, and consumed within the communities. Flouting the stipulation could potentially jeopardize the de facto deals these communities have with the higher authorities, which would not be fair to the people who use the mushrooms religiously or medically, and who have gone through many troubles to preserve this aspect of their culture.

CRIME AND PERSONAL SAFETY

Crime against foreign tourists in Oaxaca is very rare, so much so that as long as you take the same general precautions you would

elsewhere, you should not have to worry about it. Of course, flashy jewelry or other expensive-looking effects may make you a target, as they would anywhere, so leave this stuff at home. Things like nice cameras will not make you a target—just make sure to keep them on your person, and do not leave them sitting unattended in a public place. There is very little chance that you will be violently assaulted for your belongings. Just be aware of your surroundings and keep an eye on your stuff, and you shouldn't have anything to worry about.

As a rule of thumb, stay off the highways at night, unless you're in a bus or *suburban*. Do not drive your own car or a rental on the highways at night, as carjacking is a possibility and should not be underestimated.

Those familiar with other popular tourist destinations in Mexico, such as Cancún and Puerto Vallarta, will know about or maybe have experienced police trying to cheat or otherwise extract bribes from them. I can say from personal experience that this is nowhere near as much a problem in Oaxaca as it is in other major tourist areas. Police in Oaxaca are generally friendly to tourists, and will be polite and cordial with you, as long as you treat them with the same respect.

In general, treating people respectfully is one of the best ways to stay safe. You give respect to get respect. So stick to the Golden Rule, and you'll have a safe and fun trip to Oaxaca.

Travel Tips

WHAT TO PACK

Pack **warm clothing** if you expect to spend some time in the mountains. Places like Cuajimoloyas and San José del Pacífico regularly get down into the 40s (5-10°C), so don't assume Mexico is all heat and pack nothing but shorts and T-shirts.

Pharmacies here should have everything you can find in pharmacies at home, and can fill valid **prescriptions.** Bring extras if you take a harder-to-find medication, or prescriptions to refill while you're here.

Sunscreen and **contact solution** are items that are likely to be more expensive in Mexico than back home. Make sure to buy these before coming here. **Bug repellent,** although not outrageously priced here, can be hard to find, and often only major, chemical-based brands are available. So if you prefer repellents made from natural ingredients, such as lemongrass, bring this from home.

MONEY

Currency

Mexico's national currency is the peso. Its symbol ($) is the same as U.S. dollars, so don't freak out when you see that your hotel room costs $550 (about US$29). In bills, the peso comes in denominations of $20 (blue), $50 (pink), $100 (orange), $500 (brown, or newer blue ones), and the rarer $1,000 (purple). In coins, the peso comes in denominations of $20, $10, $5, $2, and $1. The smallest coins are worth $0.50, or 50 *centavos* (cents).

Exchange Rates

The prices listed in this guidebook are in the equivalent of U.S. dollars at the time of research, during which the rate fluctuated between 18 and 21 pesos on the dollar. At the time of writing, the peso had been bouncing up and down within this range since about 2016, but given the capricious nature of the global economy, the rate could be totally different by the time of publication. Check the website www.xe.com for accurate and up-to-date exchange rates when planning your budget.

Changing money and Atms

A common question is whether it is better to change money at a *casa de cambio* (money exchange center) or withdraw from ATMs. It all depends on your personal banking situation. Check with your bank before coming to see what will be best for you. Some banks partner with Mexican banks so that you don't get charged international ATM fees, others reimburse fees, and some have more favorable exchange rates than others. A *casa de cambio* will charge a fee for the exchange, so depending on your bank's fee system, it might be better to stick to ATMs.

Because of bank fees, it makes more sense to take out larger sums of money. Just be careful doing so. Go immediately from the cash machine to your hotel and store what you don't need for the day in a safe place. For those who go the cash exchange route, be aware of the risk of traveling with so much cash on you, and prepare accordingly. Many hotels have personal safes in the rooms for storing money and other valuables.

Credit Cards and tipping

Many hotels and restaurants in cities accept major credit cards. Don't expect it too much in smaller towns. Check your credit card provider's policy on foreign transactions. If it's high, use cash more than your card for purchases, so as not to rack up fees.

Tipping is not as common in Mexico as in the United States, Canada, and the United Kingdom, but it is customary in more formal restaurants with waiters. A tip of around 10 percent is appropriate. Tipping when paying with a credit card is different from the process in the United States and Canada. Rather than swipe your card and return with a slip to sign that has a line for including the tip, the waiter brings a payment terminal to the table, and you will need to tell him or her how much you want to add as a tip. The easiest is to simply say, *"Con el diez por ciento, por favor"* (With 10 percent added, please). If they did an amazing job, switch out the *diez* for *quince* (15) or *veinte* (20) to show how much you appreciated the service.

COMMUNICATIONS
Phones and Cell Phones
MAKING CALLS IN MEXICO

All phone numbers in Mexico have ten digits, the first two or three of which will be the area code, depending on the region. In Oaxaca, the area codes have three digits, as opposed to Mexico City, which has a two-digit area code and eight-digit phone numbers. Some of the numbers listed in this guide are cell phone numbers from Mexico City, but they have been presented in the three-digit area code format for consistency. All numbers listed that begin with 55 are technically Mexico City numbers.

With a Mexican cell phone number, all you have to do is dial the area code and number. Calling from landlines is a little trickier. To call another landline, dial 01 before the ten-digit phone number listed. The codes to call a mobile phone are 044 and 045, depending on the area codes of both numbers. If one doesn't work, try the other.

INTERNATIONAL CALLS

The country code for Mexico is 52. If you're calling from a cell phone, you'll need to dial the plus sign (+) before the country code for the call to go through. This takes the place of the exit code, which you will need if calling from a landline. So, the **international call format** is: + (or exit code), country code, area code, phone number.

If you're calling from the United States or Canada, your exit code is 011. The exit code for the United Kingdom is 00. Callers from Australia will use the exit code 0011, and

those from New Zealand, 00. The exit code for all Central American countries is also 00, as is Mexico's. To call home from Oaxaca, use the same call format from the previous paragraph.

CELL PHONES

Most populous places in Oaxaca have cell phone service, but don't count on it in the mountains or secluded stretches of highway. Check your roaming rates before you come. If you do need to have internet outside of Wi-Fi hot spots, and your roaming charges are high, you can get a SIM card (*chip*) at a **Telcel** outlet. You will need an official ID (preferably your passport) and a phone that allows you to use other cellular services. I've had phones that had an app that allowed me to safely "jailbreak" my phone for other service providers; others I've had to have jailbroken by someone who knows what they're doing. This can damage your phone if done wrong, so do so at your own risk.

Depending on what phone you have, this can cost US$100 or more, so make sure it is worth your while. Many unofficial cell phone repair stores will do it for you. In Oaxaca City, take Las Casas west to the *periférico*, where you'll find **Unlock Service** (Periférico 108, tel. 951/175-4360, 9:30am-9pm Mon.-Fri., 10am-9pm Sat.). After unblocking your phone (*liberar celular*), you can take it to any Telcel distributor and purchase a *Paquete Amigo Sin Límite,* a prepaid plan that comes out to US$10-20 a month, depending on how much you use it. These plans include unlimited data for social media networks for a specified period of time. I recommend downloading the phone and messaging app called **WhatsApp,** which is basically Latin America's exclusive communications tool. Many businesses here only use this app for calls and texts.

If your phone won't take another carrier's SIM card, you could just **buy a cheap cell phone** with a prepaid Mexican service plan. Although the racks at cell phone distributors are primarily filled with smartphones these days, they will still have a few old-timey button models for as low as US$25-30.

Internet Access

Just about every accommodations option in this guidebook is equipped with Wi-Fi internet; the exceptions have been noted. Internet is spotty in out-of-the-way places, such as in the mountains or lesser-touristed regions such as La Mixteca and El Istmo. If an internet connection is essential to your stay, make sure to check that it works before checking in to your hotel.

Since in-home internet service is relatively expensive in Mexico, many people here go to an internet café (*ciber*) to get online. They are not hard to find; there should be one close to a town's main square. They usually charge around US$0.50 per half hour.

Many towns, especially mountain towns, have opted for a central Wi-Fi connection that is usually based out of the main government building of the town. Local businesses will sell *fichas*, little slips of paper with sign-in information that give you a specified amount of Wi-Fi time. They are generally about US$0.50 per half hour. Some public places like parks and *zócalos* will have free Wi-Fi. Look for the network called "infinitum movil" and access the internet via your Facebook or email account.

Shipping and Postal Service

The Mexican postal service, **Correos de México,** is notorious for being a labyrinth of lost packages and envelopes. For anything more important than a postcard, I do not recommend using this service, especially if time is of the essence. I've had Christmas cards arrive in April.

For important packages, I recommend using one of the international couriers, such as FedEx or DHL, the latter of which usually has slightly lower rates. Make sure to get a tracking number for your package. There's still a good chance it won't arrive on the exact day they tell you at the counter, but it will get there.

OPPORTUNITIES FOR STUDY AND EMPLOYMENT

Studying Spanish in Oaxaca is high on my list of recommended activities here. Visiting Oaxaca is an incredible experience no matter how you do it, but being able to communicate with these kind, intelligent, funny, and infinitely surprising people takes the experience to another level.

Spanish schools in Oaxaca City offer everything from individual classes to weekly and monthly courses to packages that include accommodations, one-on-one instruction, travel planning, and loads of fun cultural activities like dance and cooking classes. Research schools thoroughly. Here you'll find something for all learning types. Some schools have a more traditional classroom style, some only offer one-on-one tutoring, while many focus on immersive, hands-on instruction. Your afternoon class could be something like a trip to the market, where you're in charge of communicating with vendors to buy the ingredients you'll need for the cooking class later. **Puerto Escondido** is another great place to consider learning Spanish. Schools here also offer immersive learning packages, which, of course, include classes on your board in the waves.

Alternatively, if you've already got a good base of Spanish, and just need to put it into practice, consider a **homestay** up in the Pueblos Mancomunados, in the Sierra Norte. You'll have the opportunity to practice at mealtimes and when relaxing in the home of a friendly local family, as well as out on tours with the experienced and knowledgeable guides. Deepen your understanding and broaden your vocabulary on a hike that focuses on diverse flora and fauna of the region, or in a workshop on traditional medicine or baking artisanal bread.

The way I've been able to see so much of the world is by finding employment in a place I want to get to know. The most widely available is teaching English. I taught in a university in Miahuatlán de Porfirio Díaz for over a year, and the experience was one I wouldn't trade for anything. If Oaxaca hooks you as it has done me, teaching English is an excellent option. Immerse yourself in a community, force yourself to speak Spanish daily, and get to know this vibrant and varied culture more deeply than a vacation will allow. The university I taught in belongs to a statewide system of higher learning institutions called **SUNEO** (Sistema de Universidades Estatales de Oaxaca; www. suneo.mx). There are SUNEO campuses in Huajuapan de León, Tuxtepec, Huatulco, Puerto Escondido, and many other parts of the state. Most have English departments. You could try looking for a position on **Idealist.org,** but if you don't see any posts there, you can contact the universities directly.

If the classroom isn't your kind of place, you could always try the classic working at a beachside hostel for room and board. This usually depends on luck, whether or not a place needs help, your level of Spanish, etc.

ACCESS FOR TRAVELERS WITH DISABILITIES

Although accessibility in Oaxaca, and Mexico in general, is not as universal as in countries like the United States, Canada, and the United Kingdom, travelers with disabilities shouldn't let that deter them from coming to experience what this place has to offer. Airlines and a good deal of hotels in Oaxaca City and on the coast are very accommodating to travelers' needs. Very few buildings, however, aside from large beach resorts, have elevators. The colonial architecture of Oaxaca City can present a challenge to those in wheelchairs, but the majority of street corners in the Centro have curb cuts, so mobility is possible.

It is against the law in Mexico for airlines to discriminate against people with disabilities, so you can expect the same accessibility

options as in the United States, Canada, the United Kingdom, and elsewhere.

A good online resource for U.S. travelers with disabilities is **Mobility International USA** (132 E. Broadway, Ste. 343, Eugene, OR 97401, tel. 541/343-1284, www.miusa.org). They can provide destination-specific tips, and also organize cultural, educational, and professional development exchange programs.

In the UK, travelers with disabilities can contact the friendly and experienced staff at **DisabledHolidays.com** (163-167 King St., Dukinfield, SK16 4LF, tel. 0161/804-9898). They can arrange flights, hotels, travel, and more, and guarantee accessibility in all the services they arrange.

For more information on accessibility in Oaxaca, contact the folks at **Piña Palmera** (Playa Zipolite, tel. 951/958-3147, www. pinapalmera.org, 9am-2pm Mon.-Fri.). For over three decades, they have worked to increase social awareness and inclusion and offer skills training to people with physical and mental disabilities in the rural communities of the coast and Sierra Sur. They accept donations and offer volunteer opportunities to those who want to support their very important work.

TRAVELING WITH CHILDREN

Oaxaca is a safe and enjoyable place for those traveling with children. There are lots of fun cultural activities for them in **Oaxaca City** and the **Valles Centrales,** such as workshops on painting *alebrijes* (painted carved wooden figures) or making traditional Oaxacan chocolate. You could take them to the **Árbol del Tule** and have them name the shapes they see in the gigantic tree's trunk. The pyramids at **Monte Albán** and other sites should be of interest to children, as well.

I also recommend the ecotourism centers in the **Sierra Norte** for travelers with kids in tow. You might feel like a kid yourself exploring the cloudy peaks and endless trails in places like **Ixtlán de Juárez** and the **Pueblos Mancomunados.** Most ecotourism centers have a zip line, and many have obstacle courses that look like a lot of fun for both children and parents.

It may be a hard sell to a kid who just started summer vacation, but **learning Spanish** is a great option for children. The earlier a child is exposed to a second language, the easier it will be to learn it. So many schools offer fun, hands-on, immersive instruction, so it won't be like going back to school while on vacation.

Every town in Oaxaca should have a good doctor, in case the children get sick. Basic stuff like stomach problems and colds can be taken care of at pharmacies with an attached doctor's office (*consultorio médico*). If you can't seem to find one, you can ask a local store owner or the nice older folks relaxing outside their homes, "*¿Dónde hay un doctor/médico?*"

Kids tend to sleep pretty well in cars, so you might take advantage of the nighttime bus routes to save on hotel expenses. They also tend to have pretty limited palates, so the intense flavors in Oaxacan cooking might be too much for them. Luckily, chicken soup (*caldo de pollo*) is as Mexican as the taco, and you should be able to find it anywhere. A standard cheese-and-tortilla-only quesadilla is always a good option for satisfying a picky youngster. Hamburgers, hotdogs, and pizzas are also popular enough in Mexico to make them easy to find. If they are daring, try the salsa first, before putting it on their food. Sauces can get pretty spicy down here.

WOMEN TRAVELING ALONE

Oaxaca is a safe place for women traveling alone. That said, harassment toward women both Mexican and foreign is common, mostly taking the form of whistles and *piropos* (catcalls) directed at women in the street. This is not to say that every single Mexican man is going to treat female travelers this way, but the chances of it happening are high, especially for women traveling solo. The best response to this kind of unwanted attention is ignoring it. The chances of physical violence against

female travelers is very low. Violent attacks against foreign tourists in general, although not nonexistent, are extremely rare. Practice the same caution you would at home. Be aware of your surroundings, and make that awareness apparent in your comportment.

SENIOR TRAVELERS

Being the popular snowbird's paradise that it is, Oaxaca City is no stranger to senior travelers, and it is very welcoming to tourists of the *tercer edad* (senior citizens; literally, "the third age"). Destinations on the coast like Puerto Escondido and Huatulco are also popular with senior travelers.

Boston-based **Road Scholar** (11 Ave. de Lafayette, Boston, MA 02111, U.S. tel. 800/454-5769, www.roadscholar.org) offers five different, all-inclusive tours to Oaxaca for seniors. Their tours range 4-15 days and highlight Oaxaca's gastronomy, festivals, history, and culture.

Tour agencies in Oaxaca are also extremely accommodating, and will customize tours to fit any ability level. Check with them to see how they can create a trip that best suits your interests and needs.

For lots of great articles and links to other online resources, check out **TransitionsAbroad.com** and their "Guide for Meaningful Senior Travel Abroad." There is a wealth of information specific to Oaxaca on the site, as well.

LGBTQ TRAVELERS

Oaxaca is very open and welcoming to LGBTQ travelers. Many tour agencies and hotels in Oaxaca City, Tuxtepec, Huajuapan de León, and towns along the coast have received official accreditation from the Federal Secretary of Tourism (SECTUR) for excellence in LGBTQ-oriented travel. You'll find a list of the accredited businesses at the official SECTUR website (www.oaxaca.gob.mx/sectur).

Although tourism in general is less developed in El Istmo, the culture of *muxes*, the third gender widely accepted in that region, is of interest to LGBTQ travelers, and some newer hotels are beginning to target their services toward this traveler group.

Luxury LGBTQ travelers in the United Kingdom should check out the Oaxaca tours at **SameSexHolidays.co.uk**. They offer all-inclusive tours to Oaxaca City for Day of the Dead, one of which includes time in Puerto Escondido to catch some rays.

There are lots of great Oaxaca-specific online resources for LGBTQ travelers. The "Gay Oaxaca Guide" at **QueerInTheWorld. com** has extensive information on hotel and nightlife options in Oaxaca City. Another excellent resource for Oaxaca and Mexico at large is **GayMexicoMap.com**. And, although not specifically dedicated to gay and lesbian travelers, the website **Go-Oaxaca. com** also has a good deal of information for LGBTQ tourism in Oaxaca.

Tourist Information

TOURIST OFFICES

Places with the highest amounts of tourist traffic, such as Oaxaca City, Puerto Escondido, and Huatulco, have numerous tourist information booths in popular areas of town. In Spanish, they'll read Modulo de Información Turística, but they will most likely have information in English, as well. During high seasons in Oaxaca City, the Zócalo and Andador Macedonio Alcalá are crawling with English-speaking representatives from both the state and municipal tourism agencies.

Just about everywhere else in the state, head to local government offices to find tourist information. They are always located by the main square, either called a *plaza* (or *jardín*) *central*, and the offices will either be called the *H. Ayuntamiento*, or the *presidencia* (or *agencia*) *municipal*. Small towns without the resources to support a full-fledged tourism office, many of which are communities that have prohibited the private ownership of property, will coordinate tourism activities out of the *oficina de bienes comunales* (office of communal properties). These and other government offices usually close between 2pm and 4pm (-ish) for the siesta, so try to get there in the morning or late afternoon. These are usually quite sleepy communities, so don't be surprised if no one is in even outside the siesta hours. You might have to ask in another office and spend a bit of time tracking down the right person.

Resources

Glossary

abarrotes: groceries, grocery store

Adoquín: paved pedestrian street, in places like Puerto Escondido and Zipolite

agua de sabor: highly sweetened fruit juice-based drink, also called *agua fresca;* often served with set meals called *comida corrida*

aguamiel: the sweet sap of the mature maguey plant

¡Aguas!: Watch out!

albur: double entendre

alcalde: mayor

alegrías: literally, happinesses, these are sweet snacks made from amaranth, peanuts, cranberries, and other fruits and nuts; commonly sold by street vendors

alebrije: brightly painted carved wooden figures of fantastical creatures, made primarily in Arrazola and Tilcajete

alfarería: pottery

amarillo: literally, yellow, but in Oaxaca is a type of sauce used as filling in empanadas; the best are in San Antonino Castillo Velasco

ámbar: amber

andador: pedestrian walkway

antojitos: Mexican snack foods (e.g., tacos, *tortas,* quesadillas)

arte popular: folk art

artesanías: handicrafts

artesano, artesana: folk artist

asiento: the sediment of pork lard collected after frying the meat; used in *tlayudas* and *memelas,* it is the flavor that sets them apart from tacos, quesadillas, *huaraches,* and other *antojitos*

asunción: the assumption of the Virgin Mary to heaven

atole: thick, sweet, corn-based drink served often with breakfast and sweet breads

autopista: expressway

ayuntamiento: town council

balneario: swimming hole usually formed from a mineral spring or other natural water source, developed into a fun aquatic center

barbacoa: pork, lamb, goat, or sometimes beef (in Zaachila) barbecue; slow-roasted in an earthen oven for up to eight hours

barrio: neighborhood, unofficially; officially neighborhoods are called *colonias*

barro: mud or clay; in the context of folk art, the type of clay used in ceramics, e.g., *barro negro* (black clay) and *barro rojo* (red clay)

berros: watercress; often served with tacos and *tlayudas*

bienes raices: real estate

bola: small crowd of people

boleto: ticket, for bus, plane, admission, etc., but not a traffic ticket (*multa*)

bota: boot

bote: can refer to a small boat, and also a trash bin (*bote de basura*)

brujería: witchcraft

brujo, bruja: warlock, witch

caballero: gentleman

cabaña: cabin

cabecera: town that is the seat of a municipality

cabrón: literally, cuckold, but used both derisively and affectionately among friends

cacique: chief of a *señorío* (pre-Hispanic chiefdom), and still used today for head elders in communities

café de olla: coffee made in a big clay pot; a

staple of *comida corrida* meals, and usually seasoned with *piloncillo*

calavera, calaca: words for the skulls used to decorate altars and homes during Day of the Dead

calenda: riotous parade with costumes, dancing, and live music; celebrates everything from university graduations to cultural festivities

caminata: hike

camionera: bus station

camioneta: covered pickup truck used to transport people and cargo *colectivo* style

campesino: farmworker

canasta: type of woven basket with a handle

canasto: bigger basket, like a hamper

cantera: literally, quarry, but used in Oaxaca to refer to the stone itself; many colonial buildings in Oaxaca City are made of *cantera verde*, green limestone

casa de huéspedes: guesthouse

cascada: waterfall

casta: caste

caudillo: local strongman who uses force to gain political power

cecina: a tasty cut of pork; *cecina enchilada* is the cut marinated in red chiles and other seasonings

cempasúchil: Mexican marigold; the primary decorative flower for Day of the Dead

centro de salud: medical clinic

champurrado: corn-based drink similar to *atole*, but flavored with chocolate

chapulines: grasshoppers; cooked with chiles, lime, garlic, and other ingredients, they are a common snack in Oaxaca

charro: horseman, or cowboy; also used to refer to the outfits worn by mariachi musicians

chilena: musical style popular on the coast near the border with Guerrero, takes heavy influence from a musical genre called *cueca*, brought to the Oaxacan coast by Chilean sailors in the 19th century

chingar: literally, the F-bomb, and as versatile as the corresponding English curse word; e.g., *Me chingó* (He effed me over)

chingón: cool, dope, really good

Churrigueresque: highly ornate baroque Spanish architectural style popular in the late 17th and early 18th centuries, used to decorate many of the Dominican churches in Oaxaca

científicos: literally, scientists, but used to describe Porfirio Díaz and his cohort of technocratic advisors during his dictatorship

coa: type of hoe used for planting corn and other crops

Cocijo: Zapotec god of lightning, thunder, and rain; also referred to as *El Rayo*, or Lightning Bolt

colectivo: literally, collective; used to describe various modes of public transport, such as taxis, *camionetas*, and *subúrbanes*; as opposed to *viaje privado* or *especial* (private or special trip)

colegio: preparatory school

colonia: official administrative neighborhood demonination

comal: flat ceramic griddle used to cook tortillas, eggs, and other foods

comedor: small, family-run restaurant serving set meals called *comida corrida*

comida casera: home-cooked food

comida corrida: set meal in a *comedor*, usually includes a few courses, such as soup or pasta and a main dish, and an *agua de sabor*

compadrazgo: network of social relationships based on godparents (*padrinos* and *madrinas*) and godchildren (*ahijados, ahijadas*)

compadre: buddy, mate, pal

comparsa: group of musicians, dancers, and revelers in the parades called *calendas*

comunal: communal; much of village life in Oaxaca is communal, from event planning to administration to landownership

correo: mail, post office; also, informally, email

criollo: person of Spanish blood born in Mexico during the colonial period

crucero: highway intersection

Cuaresma: the Catholic observance of Lent

cuota: toll

curandero, curandera: shaman, medicine man or woman

dama: lady

desviación: another term used for a highway junction in some regions, most notably the junction of Highways 190 and 125 in La Mixteca

día de plaza: weekly market, also called a *tianguis* or simply *mercado*

Domingo de Ramos: Palm Sunday

ejido: communal farming system

empanada: baked hand pies filled with savory or sweet fillings; *empanadas de amarillo* are a unique Oaxacan food

encomienda: colonial labor system in which a conquistador was awarded land and native workers

enramada: word used in El Istmo for wood and palm thatch huts, called *palapas* elsewhere

epazote: a piquant herb used often in Oaxacan cuisine, primarily in beans for its gas-reduction properties

espuma: literally, foam, but in Zaachila, a foamy chocolate-based beverage

expendio: store

farmacia: pharmacy

fiesta patronal: festival to honor a patron saint

finca: farm, ranch, plantation, especially for coffee in Oaxaca

flor de terciopelo: common name for the velvety, fuchsia cockscomb flowers used widely in Day of the Dead decorations

fonda: food stall in a market

fraccionamiento: housing subdivision

fuero: former judicial trial system specifically for members of the clergy

gachupín: derogatory term for Spanish citizens of New Spain

gasolinera: gas station, petrol station

gente de razón: "people of reason"; an offensive term used to refer to white Spanish and other Hispanicized people during the colonial period

grabado: print made from woodcut, linotype, acid etching, and other various carving methods

gringo: slightly offensive term to refer to citizens of the United States of America

grito: shout, or impassioned exclamation, as in the *Grito de Dolores* by Father Miguel Hidalgo, which sparked the War of Independence

guero: light-skinned person, but not offensive, as some *gringos* often take it to be; Mexicans will call other light-skinned Mexicans *guero*

guías: the stems and leaves of various squash and chayote plants; this is a homonym for the word for "guides," but don't worry, your *sopa de guías* is not made of tour guides

hacienda: large ranch

hamaca: hammock

hechicero, hechicera: literally, sorcerer or sorceress; sometimes used to refer to shamans that conduct indigenous rituals

hojalata: tinplating; material used in a popular folk art in Oaxaca

hongos: literally, fungi, but used to refer to the mushrooms themselves; most often, but not always, hallucinogenic mushrooms

huarache: sandal; also, an *antojito* similar to a taco, but bigger, named as such due to the tortilla's resemblance to the floppy footwear

huipil: traditional embroidered blouse or dress, of which Oaxaca boasts many distinct styles

huitlacoche: tasty edible fungus that grows on corn; served on quesadillas and other *antojitos*

indígena: indigenous person

indio: literally, Indian; used during the colonial period, but now generally out of use, except as a derogatory term

jacal: hut, shack, small house

jaripeo: bull riding, Mexican rodeo

jejenes: small sandflies that live in coastal wetlands; they bite and are often small enough to squeeze through mosquito nets

jícara; jicarita: calabash squash, and the bowls made from their dried shells; the smaller ones (*jicaritas*) are often used to sip mezcal

juguería: juice bar that usually sells *tortas* and other *antojitos*, as well

laguna: lagoon

lancha: small motorboat

licenciado: bachelor's degree; also used as a generic term for a professional person

machismo; macho: hyperbolic and toxic

masculinity; a man who has this perception of himself and his manhood

maguey: succulent from which mezcal is made; generally called agave elsewhere in Mexico

mañanitas: "Las mañanitas" is the song sung on a person's birthday in Mexico

mano: hand; also the pestle used to grind corn and other grains on a *metate*

marmotas de calenda: in the street parades called *calendas,* the *marmotas* (literally, marmots) are the large white globes sporting the name of the *comparsa* (group celebrating)

marquesitas: rolled crepe desserts originally from the Yucatán filled with cream cheese, jams, or *cajeta* (caramel spread); a common nighttime street snack in Oaxaca City

mayordomía; mayordomo: social system in which a person or group of people are chosen to fund and organize a local festival; the person chosen to organize the party

me enchilé: literally, "I chilied myself"; said when you've had too much spicy (*picante*) salsa

memela: flat tortilla-based *antojito* topped with pork lard, salsas, cheese, and sometimes meat

mercado: market

mestizo: caste designation referring to a person of mixed Spanish and indigenous descent

metate: slightly concave grindstone made of igneous stone

mezcal: distillate of the baked hearts of the maguey plant

milagro: miracle; also a small religious icon offered at a saint's altar to accompany a prayer request

milpa: cornfield or the crop itself

mirador: lookout point

molcajete: bowl-shaped mortar and pestle made of igneous stone; the popular style in Oaxaca is carved to look like a pig

mole: from the Nahuatl word *mulli,* meaning "sauce" or "stew"; represents any one of an almost infinite number of complex sauces served with chicken, pork, or other meats or vegetables; the most well-known is *mole negro* (black *mole*), which includes such interesting ingredients as chocolate and ground-up, burnt-to-a-crisp corn tortillas

monos de calenda: in the street parades called *calendas,* the *monos* are the large puppets of men and women operated by dancing partygoers inside

mordida: little bite; slang word for a bribe; also shouted at birthday parties to egg on the guest of honor to take a bite directly from the cake, although it is widely known that someone is going to shove their face in it

mototaxi: a small, three-wheeled, covered vehicle with seating for two or three, used for transportation over short distances, such as within a town or to and from a highway to a nearby town

muxe: a person belonging to a third gender of men raised as women, who take on the social, economic, and labor roles of women in the Zapotec communities of El Istmo

Nahuatl: the language of the Aztecs

nanche: small orange fruit popular in Oaxaca with an interesting flavor, indeed

ofrenda: an altar in a home, business, or public space that honors the memory of loved ones who have passed on during the Day of the Dead; common decorations are marigolds, candles, skulls, and the favorite snacks of the deceased

olla: ceramic pot

órale: versatile Mexican Spanish word that can mean a number of things, from "right on" to "whoa" to "okay"

padrino, padrina: godfather, godmother

palapa: wall-less wooden shack covered with a palm thatch roof; popular on the coast as beach restaurants or simple structures for shade

palenque: distillery

palequeta: a candied peanut bar usually sold by vendors who sell *alegrías* and other snacks on the street

pan: bread

panadería: bakery

panteón: cemetery

pápalo, pipicha: common regional names in Oaxaca for a type of pigweed, or amaranth, of which the stems and leaves are served with tacos and *tlayudas*, especially in La Mixteca

Pascua: Easter holiday celebrated the week proceeding Easter Sunday; schools get this week off too, so always make reservations during the two-week Semana Santa/Pascua holiday

peninsulares: ruling elite of New Spain born on the Iberian Peninsula, as opposed to the *criollos*, born in Mexico

peón: agricultural laborer during the colonial period

periférico: highway that bypasses a dense urban area; called a business loop in the United States

petate: woven palm frond mat used for various household tasks

piciete: strain of tobacco (*Nicotiana rustica*) endemic to Mexico that is cultivated in the Sierra Mazateca; sometimes called Aztec tobacco

piloncillo: super-concentrated brown sugar made from boiled sugarcane, used to sweeten *café de olla* and various candies; goes by names like *panela, papelón, pepa dulce,* and many more in other Spanish-speaking countries

piñata: papier-mâché figure, usually human, animal, or pop culture character, filled with candy and whacked with sticks by blindfolded birthday partygoers to get to the sweets

plan: political manifesto, generally written and submitted by leaders of political parties or factions vying for power

Porfiriato: the 34-year dictatorship of Porfirio Díaz, which began in 1876 and ended with the Mexican Revolution in 1910

posada: the nine-day celebration leading up to Christmas; from December 16 to Christmas Eve, parades, parties, religious processions, and lots and lots of eating commemorate Mary and Joseph's trip to Bethlehem, where Jesus would be born

pozahuanco: an indigenous female garment used like a skirt or dress, primarily in La Mixteca; generally striped with deep cochineal red, indigo blue, and purple

pozole: a hearty stew made with hominy and usually pork, but sometimes beef or chicken, served with shredded lettuce, radishes, oregano, and chili powder

presidencia municipal: the main government or town elder council offices of a town, almost always located beside the main square; also called the *palacio municipal,* or the *H. Ayuntamiento* (Town Council; the H stands for "Honorable")

pueblo: town, village

puente: bridge; also used to refer to a three-day weekend

pulque: alcoholic beverage made by fermenting the sap (*aguamiel*) of a mature maguey plant

quesillo: Oaxacan string cheese with a pleasing tang; perfect for melting right on the griddle

retablo: altarpiece, retable

retorno: highway turnaround

rurales: federal rural police forces created by Porfirio Díaz to contend with *bandidos* (bandits) and quell political rivalries

sal de gusano: worm salt; made with the worms that grow in the hearts (*piñas*) of maguey plants, and served alongside orange slices with glasses of mezcal

Semana Santa: Holy Week, celebrated the week preceding Easter

son istmeño: literally "Sound of the Isthmus," this distinct musical genre is the accompaniment for the three-day parties of El Istmo, called *velas*

suburban: the main mode of interurban transport in Oaxaca, a 12-15-passenger van

taller: workshop for printmaking, ceramics, *alebrijes,* or other arts

tambora: lively bass brand that provides the tunes for the *calendas* (parades); named for the large bass drum called a *tambor*

tapete: rug; the weavers of Teotitlán del Valle, Santa Ana del Valle, and other communities are known for their colorful *tapetes de lana* (wool)

tasajo: a thin cut of beef for tacos, *tlayudas,* and other meals

tejate: foam-topped pre-Hispanic drink that

originated in San Andrés Huayapam, just north of Oaxaca City; made with a number of interesting ingredients, it has a delightful nutty/chocolatey flavor, but is also sometimes flavored with coconuts

telar: loom

temazcal: traditional indigenous sweat lodge; a primary medicinal treatment for a number of ailments in indigenous communities

tenate: woven palm frond baskets, sometimes brightly colored, used for storing tortillas, fruits, or grains

tepache: an alcoholic beverage made from the fermented juice of pineapple skins and *piloncillo*

tequio: communal labor system used to pay tributes and complete public works, such as bridges, roads, causeways, and other infrastructure projects; appropriated by the Spanish and converted into dissimulated slavery

tianguis: street market; in Oaxaca, where some have run weekly for thousands of years, the market day is usually called *día de mercado* or *día de plaza*

tienda de campaña: camping tent; also called a *casa de campaña*

tlacoyo: an *antojito* made of a thick, usually blue corn tortilla, filled with beans or cheese and topped with nopal (cactus), *queso fresco*, and salsa

tlayuda: the paragon of tortilla-based gastronomy, this large quesadilla or tostada-shaped *antojito* is topped with *asiento* (type of pork lard), meat, veggies, cheese, and other ingredients; the term is also used to refer to the giant tortillas themselves

traje típico: traditional indigenous dress or suit

vela: a three-day party thrown in El Istmo to celebrate a trade (e.g., fishermen, masons, farmers) or social group, such as the *muxes*

zócalo: common name for the Plaza de la Constitución, the main square in Mexico City, which has also come to refer to the main squares of cities elsewhere in Mexico; smaller towns have a *plaza, parque,* or *jardín* (garden) *principal*

Spanish Phrasebook

Spanish commonly uses 30 letters—the familiar English 26, plus four straightforward additions: ch, ll, ñ, and rr, which are explained in "Consonants," below.

PRONUNCIATION

Once you learn them, Spanish pronunciation rules—in contrast to English—don't change. Spanish vowels generally sound softer than in English. (*Note:* The capitalized syllables below receive stronger accents.)

Vowels

a like ah, as in "hah": *agua* AH-gooah (water), *pan* PAHN (bread), and *casa* CAH-sah (house)

e like eh, as in "egg": *mesa* MEH-sah (table), *tela* TEH-lah (cloth), and *de* DEH (of, from)

i like ee, as in "need": *diez* dee-EHS (ten), *comida* ko-MEE-dah (meal), and *fin* FEEN (end)

o like oh, as in "go": *peso* PEH-soh (weight), *ocho* OH-choh (eight), and *poco* POH-koh (a bit)

u like oo, as in "cool": *uno* OO-noh (one), *hule* OO-leh (rubber), and *usted* oos-TEHD (you); when it follows a "q" the u is silent; when it follows a different letter and is followed by another vowel, or has an umlaut, it's pronounced like "w"

Consonants

b, d, f, k, l, m, n, p, q, s, t, v, w, x, y, ch pronounced almost as in English; h occurs, but is silent—not pronounced at all

c like k as in "keep": *cuarto* KWAR-toh (room), Tepic teh-PEEK (capital of Nayarit state); when it precedes "e" or "i," pronounce

c like s, as in "sit": *cerveza* sayr-VEH-sah (beer), *encima* ehn-SEE-mah (atop)

g like g as in "gift" when it precedes "a," "o," "u," or a consonant: *gato* GAH-toh (cat), *hago* AH-goh (I do, make); otherwise, pronounce **g** like h as in "hat": *giro* HEE-roh (money order), *gente* HEHN-tay (people)

j like h, as in "has": *Jueves* HWEH-vehs (Thursday), *mejor* meh-HOR (better)

ll like y, as in "yes": *toalla* toh-AH-yah (towel), *ellos* EH-yohs (they, them)

ñ like ny, as in "canyon": *año* AH-nyo (year), *señor* seh-NYOR (Mr., sir)

r is lightly trilled, with tongue at the roof of your mouth like a very light English d, as in "ready": *pero* PEH-doh (but), *tres* TDAYS (three), *cuatro* KOOAH-tdoh (four)

rr like a Spanish r, but with much more emphasis and trill. Let your tongue flap. Practice with *burro* (donkey), *carretera* (highway), and Carrillo (proper name), then really let go with *ferrocarril* (railroad)

z like s, as in "see," never the buzzing sound of an English z: *zócalo* SOH-cah-loh (main square), *zapato* sah-PAH-toh (shoe)

Note: The single small but common exception to all of the above is the pronunciation of Spanish **y** when it's being used as the Spanish word for "and," as in "Ron y Kathy." In such case, pronounce it like the English ee, as in "keep": Ron "ee" Kathy (Ron and Kathy).

Accent

The rule for accent, the relative stress given to syllables within a given word, is straightforward. If a word ends in a vowel, an n, or an s, accent the next-to-last syllable; if not, accent the last syllable.

Pronounce *sombrero* som-BREH-roh (hat), *orden* OHR-dehn (order), and *carretera* kah-reh-TAY-rah (highway) with stress on the next-to-last syllable.

Emphasize the syllable before the -ia or -ias in words that end in these letters with no accent on the i, such as *gracias* GRAH-seeahs (thank you) and *farmacia* far-MAH-seeah (pharmacy). When the i is accented with a *tilde* (accent sign), put the emphasis on the i: *zapatería*

sah-pah-the-REE-ah (shoe store), and *alegría* ah-leh-GREE-ah (happiness).

Otherwise, accent the last syllable: *venir* veh-NEER (to come), *ferrocarril* feh-roh-cah-REEL (railroad), *edad* eh-DAHD (age), and feliz feh-LEES (happy).

Exceptions to the accent rule are always marked with an accent sign: (á, é, í, ó, or ú), such as *teléfono* teh-LEH-foh-noh (telephone), *jabón* hah-BON (soap), and *rápido* RAH-pee-doh (rapid).

BASIC AND COURTEOUS EXPRESSIONS

Most Spanish-speaking people consider formalities important. Whenever approaching anyone for information or some other reason, do not forget the appropriate salutation—good morning, good evening, etc. Standing alone, the greeting *hola* (hello) can sound brusque.

Hello. *Hola.*

Good morning. *Buenos días.*

Good afternoon. *Buenas tardes.*

Good evening. *Buenas noches.*

How are you? *¿Cómo está usted?*

Very well, thank you. *Muy bien, gracias.*

Okay; good. *Bien.*

Not okay; bad. *Mal* or *feo.*

So-so. *Más o menos.*

And you? *¿Y usted?*

Thank you. *Gracias.*

Thank you very much. *Muchas gracias.*

You're very kind. *Muy amable.*

You're welcome. *De nada.*

Goodbye. *Adios.*

See you later. *Hasta luego.*

please *por favor*

yes *sí*

no *no*

I don't know. *No sé.*

Just a moment, please. *Momentito, por favor.*

Excuse me, please (when you're trying to get attention). *Disculpe* or *Con permiso.*

Excuse me (when you've made a boo-boo). *Lo siento* or *Perdón*

The Magic of Spanish Grammar

You may have heard your Spanish teacher ramble on in grammar lessons about reflexive verbs and their pronouns and blah, blah, blah. This can be a difficult aspect of the language to master, especially when you're thinking in grammatical terms. It's better to just think of the magic within the Spanish language, instead.

Reflexive verbs put the action in the object, rather than the person or subject. For example, the verb *gustar* translates to "to like," but it is not a literal one. In Spanish, you do not like pizza, pizza pleases you: *Me gusta la pizza* ("The pizza pleases me"). You don't like other people, other people "fall well" on you: *Me cae bien* ("I like him," but literally, "He falls well on me"). When *gustar* is used with people, it means a romantic or more-than-friendly interest: *Me gustas* ("I like you," in the "like-like" sense). Reflexive verbs can also be a neat linguistic way to avoid blame. For example, in Spanish, you don't drop objects, they fall from your hands: *Se me cayó el celular* ("I dropped my phone," but literally, "The phone fell from me").

Once you start to think about the outside world acting on you in Spanish much more than you act on it in English, things start to click and your learning will speed up significantly. With all this grammatical magic in the language, it's no wonder the literary movement called Magical Realism, popularized by writers such as Colombian Gabriel García Márquez (1927-2014) and Chilean Isabel Allende (b. 1942), originated in Spanish-language literature.

Pleased to meet you. *Mucho gusto.*
How do you say ... in Spanish? *¿Cómo se dice ... en español?*
What is your name? *¿Cómo se llama usted?*
Do you speak English? *¿Habla usted inglés?*
Is English spoken here? (Does anyone here speak English?) *¿Se habla inglés?*
I don't speak Spanish well. *No hablo bien el español.*
I don't understand. *No entiendo.*
My name is ... *Me llamo ...*
Would you like ... *¿Quisiera usted ...*
Let's go to ... *Vamos a ...*

TERMS OF ADDRESS

When in doubt, use the formal *usted* (you) as a form of address.

I *yo*
you (formal) *usted*
you (familiar) *tú*
he/him *él*
she/her *ella*
we/us *nosotros*
you (plural) *ustedes*
they/them *ellos* (all males or mixed gender); *ellas* (all females)
Mr., sir *señor*

Mrs., madam *señora*
miss, young lady *señorita*
wife *esposa*
husband *esposo*
friend *amigo* (male); *amiga* (female)
sweetheart *novio* (male); *novia* (female)
son; daughter *hijo; hija*
brother; sister *hermano; hermana*
father; mother *padre; madre*
grandfather; grandmother *abuelo; abuela*

TRANSPORTATION

Where is ... ? *¿Dónde está ... ?*
How far is it to ... ? *¿A cuánto está ... ?*
from ... to ... *de ... a ...*
How many blocks? *¿Cuántas cuadras?*
Where (Which) is the way to ... ? *¿Dónde está el camino a ... ?* or *¿Cómo llega uno a ... ?* (How does one arrive at ...?)
the bus station *la terminal de autobuses*
the bus stop *la parada de autobuses*
Where is this bus going? *¿Adónde va este autobús?*
the taxi stand *la parada de taxis*
the train station *la estación de ferrocarril*
the boat *el barco*
the launch *lancha; tiburonera*

Getting the Server's Attention

The noun for waiter or waitress is *mesero* or *mesera*, but you won't actually use it when speaking to them, and the forms of address for waitstaff in Mexico might take you some getting used to. If your server is male, you will say *jóven* to get his attention. This literally means "youngster," but it is the word to use no matter the waiter's age.

If your server is female, you will call her *señorita*, again, despite her age. It might seem a little awkward calling a person older than you a young man or young lady, but it won't be for them. It is the proper way to address them in Mexico. Oh, and don't forget to wish a hearty *¡Buen provecho!* (Enjoy your meal!) to the diners around you when you enter and/or leave a restaurant.

the dock *el muelle*
the airport *el aeropuerto*
I'd like a ticket to ... *Quisiera un boleto a ...*
first (second) class *primera (segunda) clase*
round-trip *ida y vuelta*
reservation *reservación*
baggage *equipaje*
Stop here, please. *Pare aquí, por favor.* Or,
  more commonly in Oaxaca, *Baja aquí, por
  favor.*
the entrance *la entrada*
the exit *la salida*
the ticket office *taquilla*
(very) near; far *(muy) cerca; lejos*
to; toward *a* or *hacia*
by; through *por*
from *de*
the right *la derecha*
the left *la izquierda*
straight ahead *derecho; directo*
in front *en frente*
beside *al lado*
behind *atrás*
the corner *la esquina*
the stoplight *la semáforo*
a turn *una vuelta*
right here *aquí* or *acá*
somewhere around here *por acá*
right there *allí* or *allá*
somewhere around there *por allá*
road *el camino*
street; boulevard *calle; bulevar*
block *la cuadra*
highway *carretera*
kilometer *kilómetro*
bridge; toll *puente; cuota*

address *dirección*
north; south *norte; sur*
east; west *oriente (este); poniente (oeste)*

ACCOMMODATIONS

hotel *hotel*
room *cuarto* or *habitación*
Is there a room? *¿Hay cuarto?*
May I (may we) see it? *¿Puedo (podemos)
  verlo?*
What is the rate? *¿Cuál es el precio?*
Is that your best rate? *¿Es su mejor precio?*
Is there something cheaper? *¿Hay algo
  más económico?*
a single room *un cuarto sencillo*
a double room *un cuarto doble*
double bed *cama matrimonial*
twin bed *cama individual*
with private bath *con baño privado*
hot water *agua caliente*
shower *ducha*
towels *toallas*
soap *jabón*
toilet paper *papel higiénico*
blanket *cobija; manta*
sheets *sábanas*
air-conditioned *aire acondicionado*
fan *abanico; ventilador*
key *llave*
manager *gerente*

FOOD

I'm hungry *Tengo hambre.*
I'm thirsty. *Tengo sed.*
menu *carta; menú*
order *orden*

Don't Be a Puedotener!

In English, especially U.S. English, we commonly request goods or services by opening with "Can I have…?" As a Spanish language learner, your initial instinct might be to translate this literally: *¿Puedo tener un taco de camarón?* This is incorrect, and will get you some funny looks. It is not said like this in Spanish, and will only cause confusion. A good go-to for requesting things is *Me da* (Give me), but not in a commanding or pushy way. Say it with a slight intonation of a question and it is a nice, sensible way to get what you want. *Me da un taco de camarón, ¿por favor?* translates literally to "Give me a shrimp taco, please," but has the connotation of a phrase like "Can I have…" or "I'll take…"

glass *vaso*
fork *tenedor*
knife *cuchillo*
spoon *cuchara*
napkin *servilleta*
soft drink *refresco*
coffee *café*
tea *té*
drinking water *agua pura; agua potable*
bottled carbonated water *agua mineral*
bottled uncarbonated water *agua natural*
beer *cerveza*
wine *vino*
milk *leche*
juice *jugo*
cream *crema*
sugar *azúcar*
cheese *queso*
snack *antojito; botana*
breakfast *desayuno*
lunch *almuerzo* or *comida*
daily lunch special *comida corrida* (or *el menú del día* depending on region)
dinner *comida* (often eaten in late afternoon); *cena* (a late-night snack)
the check *la cuenta*
eggs *huevos*

bread *pan*
salad *ensalada*
fruit *fruta*
mango *mango*
watermelon *sandía*
papaya *papaya*
banana *plátano*
apple *manzana*
orange *naranja*
lime *limón*
fish *pescado*
shellfish *mariscos*
shrimp *camarones*
meat (without) *(sin) carne*
chicken *pollo*
pork *carne de puerco* or *carne de cerdo*
beef; steak *res; bistec*
bacon; ham *tocino; jamón*
fried *frito*
roasted *asada*
barbecue; barbecued *barbacoa; al carbon*

SHOPPING

money *dinero*
money-exchange bureau *casa de cambio*
I would like to exchange traveler's checks. *Quisiera cambiar cheques de viajero.*
What is the exchange rate? *¿Cuál es el tipo de cambio?*
How much is the commission? *¿Cuánto cuesta la comisión?*
Do you accept credit cards? *¿Aceptan tarjetas de crédito?*
money order *remesa* or *giro*
How much does it cost? *¿Cuánto cuesta?*
What is your final price? *¿Cuál es su último precio?*
expensive *caro*
cheap *barato; económico*
more *más*
less *menos*
a little *un poco*
too much *demasiado*

HEALTH

Help me please. *Ayúdeme por favor.*
I am ill. *Estoy enfermo.*

Call a doctor. *Llame un doctor.*
Take me to … *Lléveme a …*
hospital *hospital*
drugstore *farmacia*
pain *dolor*
fever *fiebre*
headache *dolor de cabeza*
stomach ache *dolor de estómago*
burn *quemadura*
cramp *calambre*
nausea *náusea*
vomiting *vomitar*
medicine *medicina* or *medicamento*
antibiotic *antibiótico*
pill; tablet *pastilla*
aspirin *aspirina*
ointment; cream *pomada; crema*
bandage *venda*
cotton *algodón*
tampons *tampones*
sanitary napkins use brand name, e.g.,
   Kotex
birth control pills *pastillas anticonceptivas*
contraceptive foam *espuma
   anticonceptiva*
condoms *preservativos; condones*
toothbrush *cepilla de dientesl*
dental floss *hilo dental*
toothpaste *crema* or *pasta dental*
dentist *dentista*
toothache *dolor de muelas*

POST OFFICE AND COMMUNICATIONS

long-distance phone call *llamada de
   larga distancia*
I would like to call … *Quisiera llamar a …*
collect *por cobrar*
station to station *a quien contesta*
person to person *persona a persona*
credit card *tarjeta de crédito*
post office *correo*
general delivery *lista de correo*
letter *carta*
stamp *estampilla, timbre*
postcard *tarjeta*
aerogram *aerograma*
air mail *correo aereo*

registered *registrado*
money order *remesa* or *giro*
package; box *paquete; caja*
string; tape *cuerda; cinta*

AT THE BORDER

border *frontera*
customs *aduana*
immigration *migración*
tourist card *tarjeta de turista*
inspection *inspección; revisión*
passport *pasaporte*
profession *profesión*
marital status *estado civil*
single *soltero*
married; divorced *casado; divorciado*
widowed *viudado*
insurance *seguros*
title *título*
driver's license *licencia de manejar*

AT THE GAS STATION

gas station *gasolinera*
gasoline *gasolina*
unleaded *sin plomo*
full, please *lleno, por favor*
tire *llanta*
tire repair shop *vulcanizadora*
air *aire*
water *agua*
oil (change) *aceite (cambio de)*
grease *grasa*
My … doesn't work. *Mi … no sirve.*
battery *batería*
radiator *radiador*
alternator *alternador*
generator *generador* or *dínamo*
tow truck *grúa*
repair shop *taller mecánico*
tune-up *afinación*
auto parts store *refaccionería*

VERBS

Verbs are the key to getting along in Spanish.
The "you" forms included here are conjugated
for the pronoun *usted*. The regular conjugation
for the informal *tú* have an s on the end, e.g., *tú
compras* (you buy). They employ mostly pre-

dictable forms and come in three classes, which end in *ar, er,* and *ir,* respectively:

to buy *comprar*
I buy, you (he, she, it) buys *compro, compra*
we buy, you (they) buy *compramos, compran*

to eat *comer*
I eat, you (he, she, it) eats *como, come*
we eat, you (they) eat *comemos, comen*

to climb *subir*
I climb, you (he, she, it) climbs *subo, sube*
we climb, you (they) climb *subimos, suben*

Here are more (with irregularities indicated):

to do or make *hacer* (regular except for *hago,* I do or make)
to go *ir* (very irregular: *voy, vas, va, vamos, van*)
to go (walk) *andar*
to love *amar*
to work *trabajar*
to want *desear, querer*
to need *necesitar*
to read *leer*
to write *escribir*
to repair *reparar*
to stop *parar*
to get off (the bus) *bajar*
to arrive *llegar*
to stay (remain) *quedarse*
to stay (lodge) *hospedarse*
to leave *salir* (regular except for *salgo,* I leave)
to look at *mirar*
to look for *buscar* (the "for" is in the verb already, so you don't have to say *por.* Don't say *Estoy buscando por,* just *Estoy buscando...*)
to give *dar* (regular except for *doy,* I give)
to carry *llevar*
to have *tener* (irregular but important: *tengo, tienes, tiene, tenemos, tienen*)

to come *venir* (similarly irregular: *vengo, vienes, viene, venimos, vienen*)

Spanish has two forms of "to be":

to be *estar* (regular except for *estoy,* I am)
to be *ser* (very irregular: *soy, es, somos, son*)

Use *estar* when speaking of location or a temporary state of being: "I am at home." *"Estoy en casa."* "I'm sick." *"Estoy enfermo."* Use *ser* for a permanent state of being: "I am a doctor." *"Soy doctora."*

NUMBERS

zero *cero*
one *uno*
two *dos*
three *tres*
four *cuatro*
five *cinco*
six *seis*
seven *siete*
eight *ocho*
nine *nueve*
10 *diez*
11 *once*
12 *doce*
13 *trece*
14 *catorce*
15 *quince*
16 *dieciseis*
17 *diecisiete*
18 *dieciocho*
19 *diecinueve*
20 *veinte*
21 *veinte y uno* or *veintiuno*
30 *treinta*
40 *cuarenta*
50 *cincuenta*
60 *sesenta*
70 *setenta*
80 *ochenta*
90 *noventa*
100 *ciento*
101 *ciento y uno* or *cientiuno*
200 *doscientos*
500 *quinientos*

1,000 *mil*
10,000 *diez mil*
100,000 *cien mil*
1,000,000 *millón*
billion *mil millones*
one half *medio* or *mitad*
one third *un tercio*
one fourth *un cuarto*

TIME

What time is it? *¿Qué hora es?*
It's one o'clock. *Es la una.*
It's three in the afternoon. *Son las tres
de la tarde.*
It's 4am. *Son las cuatro de la mañana.*
six-thirty *seis y media*
a quarter till eleven *un cuarto para las
once*
a quarter past five *las cinco y cuarto*
a minute *un minuto*
an hour *una hora*

DAYS AND MONTHS

Monday *lunes*
Tuesday *martes*

Wednesday *miércoles*
Thursday *jueves*
Friday *viernes*
Saturday *sábado*
Sunday *domingo*
today *hoy*
tomorrow *mañana*
yesterday *ayer*
January *enero*
February *febrero*
March *marzo*
April *abril*
May *mayo*
June *junio*
July *julio*
August *agosto*
September *septiembre*
October *octubre*
November *noviembre*
December *diciembre*
a week *una semana*
a month *un mes*
after *después*
before *antes*

Suggested Reading

HISTORY

Blanton, Richard, Gary Feinman, Stephen Kowalewski, and Linda Nicholas. *Ancient Oaxaca: The Monte Albán State.* Cambridge, UK: Cambridge University Press, 1999. Although agriculture in the Americas most likely began in the Oaxaca Valley, and the Zapotecs created one of the first writing systems in Mesoamerica, many overall histories of the pre-Hispanic American cultures overlook these important details. The authors of *Ancient Oaxaca* aim to correct this oversight.

Pearce, Kenneth. *A Traveler's History of Mexico*, 2nd edition. New York, NY: Interlink Publishing, 2004. Pierce's condensed account of the convoluted history of Mexico is both precise and detailed where it counts. As the title conveys, the book is the perfect size for lugging around in a backpack while on the road.

Weeks, Charles A. *The Juárez Myth in Mexico.* Tuscaloosa, AL: University of Alabama Press, 1987. Benito Juárez was influential to the development of modern Mexico even after his death in 1872. In his examination of Juárez's life and legacy, Weeks studiously sheds light on how the national memory of Juárez has been altered to serve various political agendas in the century and a half since his presidency.

FICTION

Ford, Richard. *The Ultimate Good Luck*. New York, NY: Vintage Books, 1981. Pulitzer prize-winning American author Richard Ford's second novel is set in Oaxaca during the cocaine smuggling climate of the 1970s. In Oaxaca to bail his girlfriend's brother out of jail, Harry Quinn gets caught up in a menacing and erotic tale of violence and deception.

Sada, Daniel, and Katherine Silver, translator. *Almost Never*. Minneapolis, MN: Graywolf Press, 2012. Originally published in Spanish under the title *Casi Nunca* (2008), Katherine Silver's excellent translation brings the work of this highly respected Mexican author to an English-reading audience. Chilean novelist in Mexico Roberto Bolaño called Sada's work "the most daring" of the writers of his generation, and this novel of a torrid love triangle set on a ranch outside Oaxaca City is no exception to that description.

Wright, Lili. *Dancing with the Tiger*. New York, NY: G. P. Putnam's Sons, 2016. After a grave robber high on methamphetamines discovers what is possibly the death mask of Aztec emperor Moctezuma, Wright's heroine Anna Ramsey flies to Oaxaca to vindicate her father, a disgraced art collector, and discover the truth behind the mask. While chasing the looter, Anna gets mixed up in the criminal underbelly of Mexico's art scene, discovering that we all wear masks, whether they be literal or figurative.

POETRY

Moore, Roger. *Sun and Moon: Poems from Oaxaca, Mexico*. Halifax, Canada: Mount Saint Vincent University Press, 2000. These verses by Canadian poet Roger Moore explore the lives and histories of the indigenous peoples of Oaxaca, weaving ancient stories into the modern society in which Oaxacans find themselves today. Pre-Hispanic ceremonies are juxtaposed next to interactions between Oaxacans and the tourists that come to experience these cultures that have been overlooked politically, economically, and historically.

ARCHAEOLOGY

Ramos, Juan Arturo López, and Owen Ferguson, translator. *Oaxaca: Cradle and Destiny of American Civilization*. Oaxaca: Fernández Pichardo Cultural Foundation, 2017. This recent translation of the Oaxacan historian and author's 2010 Spanish-language book of the same name draws on the best and latest archaeological evidence to reveal the roots of many modern conventions of civic life to Oaxacan origins. Agriculture, writing systems, and urban planning in the Americas have all been traced back to the rugged mountains and valleys of Oaxaca.

Winter, Marcus. *Oaxaca: The Archaeological Record*. Mexico City: Minutiae Mexicana, 1992. Winter's concise account of the peoples of Monte Albán, Mitla, Yagul, and other pre-Hispanic sites in Oaxaca is a good traveling companion for anyone looking to broaden their knowledge of the place's history. Begin your research here, and use the book from the previous entry to place these civilizations in the greater context of Mesoamerican history.

COOKBOOKS AND GASTRONOMY

Kennedy, Diana. *Oaxaca Al Gusto: An Infinite Gastronomy*. Austin, TX: University of Texas Press, 2010. With nine authoritative books on Mexican cuisine in her oeuvre, Diana Kennedy has come to be known as the "Julia Child of Mexican cooking." Kennedy traveled to the remote nooks and crannies of Oaxaca for years, gathering recipes, ingredients, and stories for this, her masterpiece on the ancient and endlessly surprising Oaxacan kitchen.

Martínez, Zarela. *The Food and Life of Oaxaca: Traditional Recipes from Mexico's Heart*. New York, NY: Macmillan

Publishing, 1997. In the same school as Kennedy and other authorities on Mexican food, Zarela Martínez got both her cooking and cookbook writing from her mother. More than just recipes, the book ties every dish to the people and history behind it.

PEOPLE AND CULTURE

Iturbide, Graciela. *Juchitán de las mujeres:1979-1989*. Mexico City: Editorial RM, 2010. This collection of images of the women of Juchitán by prolific Mexican photographer Graciela Iturbide includes bilingual essays about the pictures that have gone on to iconic representations of the city. A statue six blocks north of the main square in Juchitán honors her most striking photo of the series, *Nuestra Señora de las Iguanas* (Our Lady of the Iguanas), of a *juchiteca* with over a half dozen iguanas perched on her head.

Lawrence, D. H. *Mornings in Mexico*. London: Martin Secker, 1927. Although Lawrence's collection of travel essays from Mexico, four of which treat Oaxaca, occasionally dips into the colonially arrogant, even rude, his descriptions of the markets and street life of Oaxaca City are as rich and lively as the scenes they describe. He wrote some of the passages while staying in the hotel now called Casona Oaxaca.

ARTS, CRAFTS, AND ARCHITECTURE

Chibnik, Michael. *Crafting Tradition: The Making and Marketing of Oaxacan Wood Carvings*. Austin, TX: University of Texas Press, 2003. Get the full scoop on the nascent tradition of *alebrijes* in Oaxaca with this, the most exhaustive examination of the very recent history and marketing techniques of this folk art. Chibnik's well-researched text is accompanied by gorgeous photos of these kaleidoscopic wooden creatures.

Mindling, Eric Sebastian. *Oaxaca Stories in Cloth*. Loveland, CO: Thrums Books, 2016. A quick look through the table of contents of Mindling's comprehensive study of the regional embroidery styles in Oaxaca reveals just how extensive his research was. The book introduces the English-speaking world to embroidery styles from all over the state, including many of the hardest-to-reach places.

Wasserspring, Lois. *Oaxacan Ceramics: Traditional Folk Art by Oaxacan Women*. Vancouver, BC: Raincoast Books, 2000. Rather than an exhaustive investigation of the Oaxacan ceramics world at large, Wasserspring decided to focus on six female potters in Santa María Atzompa and Ocotlán de Morelos, connecting their art to their religions, legends, daily lives, and rich imaginations.

GOVERNMENT, POLITICS, AND ECONOMY

Denham, Diana, ed. *Teaching Rebellion: Stories from the Grassroots Mobilization in Oaxaca*. Oakland, CA: PM Press, 2008. Diana Denham is the coordinator of the C.A.S.A. Collective, a Oaxaca-based international solidarity organization. This anthology collects firsthand accounts of stories from the 2006 political movements that erupted into violence and led to the formation of the Popular Assembly of the Peoples of Oaxaca (APPO).

Murphy, Arthur D., and Alex Stepick. *Social Inequality in Oaxaca: A History of Resistance and Change*. Philadelphia, PA: Temple University Press, 1991. Murphy and Stepick's socioeconomic study of Oaxaca in the 1970s and 1980s takes a neighborhood-based approach to follow the lives of residents of Oaxaca City and learn from the challenges they face to get by.

ENVIRONMENT

Grosselet, Manuel, and Georgita Ruiz. *Field Guide to the Birds of Mexico: Volume 2, Birds of Monte Albán and Yagul.* Mexico City: National Institute of Anthropology and History, 2010. The fact that the 173 different bird species included in this extensively detailed bilingual field guide are found on two hills in the Valles Centrales tells you just how rich the avian biodiversity here is. This is an essential guide for ornithologists amateur to professional.

Sacks, Oliver. *Oaxaca Journal.* Washington, DC: National Geographic Society, 2002. Take a drive up to Tuxtepec, and you'll understand neurologist and author Oliver Sacks's fascination with ferns. Visit anywhere in Oaxaca and you'll understand how the travelogue of his trip with a band of fellow fern fanatics ended up including his musings on the origins of mezcal, chocolate, and ceremonial use of hallucinogenic mushrooms, as well as vibrant descriptions of markets and other scenes of Oaxacan life.

Internet Resources

GENERAL INFORMATION

Oaxaca Mio
www.oaxaca-mio.com
Originally in Spanish, this tourism website uses Google's translation program to convert its pages into English. With lots of general information on festivals, activities, hotels, food, and more, it is a great place to browse and find something to fill a day or two on your itinerary.

Visit Mexico
www.visitmexico.com/en/ main-destinations/Oaxaca
This site run by the Mexico Tourism Board also has lots of broad information on visiting Oaxaca. A wealth of high-quality photos accompany the entries, making this another great resource for trip planning on a basic level. You'll need a more detailed source (ahem) to work out the finer details, but if you're just struggling with deciding where to go and what to do, Visit Mexico is a great place to start.

Go-Oaxaca
www.go-oaxaca.com
Since 2003, Go-Oaxaca has provided accurate, up-to-date information on hotels, restaurants, tour operators, culture, and more for those who plan to go to Oaxaca. Hotel listings, although not extensive, are broken up by star rating and style (hostel, B&B, etc.), and the listings of museums and archaeological sites stick to the big hitters (Monte Albán, Santo Domingo, etc.). The best part of the site is its information on festivals like Day of the Dead and the Guelaguetza.

Oaxaca's Tourist Guide
www.oaxaca.com
Although not as pretty as the previously mentioned site, Oaxaca's Tourist Guide goes into much more detail, with sections on indigenous communities, cultural attractions, and lots of ecotourism destinations. There is also a section of travelogues, with personal stories from folks who have experienced the magic of Oaxaca for themselves.

Oaxaca Bed & Breakfast Association
www.oaxacabedandbreakfast.org
This site is run by a group of family-owned B&Bs, most of which are located in Oaxaca City, but a few are elsewhere in the state. This is a great resource for travelers who want to ensure that their money goes to supporting local residents and businesses.

ARTS AND CULTURE

Friends of Oaxacan Folk Art
www.fofa.us

Friends of Oaxacan Folk Art (FOFA) is a non-profit organization dedicated to the preservation and promotion of Oaxaca's rich and varied folk art traditions. Their website is the most extensive online English-language resource on Oaxacan folk art, with sections on ceramics, textiles, jewelry, and 10 other disciplines, as well as the various regional styles within them and profiles of the artists.

Un huipil al día
www.unhuipil.wordpress.com

This Spanish-language blog showcases the various regional embroidery styles of the blouses called *huipiles*. Each entry includes a high-resolution close-up photo of the embroidery, the town in which it was made, and a brief description of the piece. Even if your Spanish isn't on the level to fully understand the descriptions, the site is an excellent resource for learning to recognize these regional artistic styles.

NEWS AND EVENTS

Qué Pasa Oaxaca
www.quepasaoaxaca.com

The digital component of the free bilingual print magazine is the place to find art exhibitions, movie screenings, concerts, festivals, and other events in Oaxaca City. In addition to events listings, the site has articles from the magazine and sections on hotels and Spanish schools. Keep an eye out at businesses in Oaxaca City for a copy of the print edition.

Oaxaca Times
www.oaxacatimes.com

The *Oaxaca Times* has been connecting foreign tourists to contemporary Oaxacan culture since 1988, but the recent tourism boom in the state, driven by factors such as the rise in international popularity of artisanal mezcal and the movie *Coco*, they completely revamped their website. Aside from cultural articles, the site has a classifieds

section for real estate, medical care, and other services.

Oaxaca Events
www.oaxacaevents.com

Hikes, walking tours, card games, poetry readings, mahjong, and much, much more make up the list of events on the calendar on this handy website. If you're doing an extended stay in Oaxaca City or the Valles Centrales, check Oaxaca Events often to get into the groove of social life here.

Cinema Cuervo
www.cinemacuervo.tumblr.com

This mobile cinema club hosts screenings of movies both recent and classic in homes, restaurants, universities, and other locations in Oaxaca City. The site is in Spanish, as are some of the movies, but they also show many popular English-language movies with subtitles. It is a great way to practice your Spanish, both in the viewing and socializing before and after.

OAXACAN COAST

Puerto Escondido Real Estate
& Vacation Rentals
www.puertorealestate.com

Plan your move to or extended stay in paradise with the help of Puerto Escondido Real Estate & Vacation Rentals. Their English-language site has extensive listings of houses, apartments, bungalows, and vacation rentals all over town. You'll also find tons of maps and information on activities, restaurants, transportation, and more.

Tomzap: The Pacific Coast of Mexico
www.tomzap.com/oaxaca.html

This English-language site is dedicated to the Pacific coast of Mexico, specifically the coasts in the states of Jalisco, Colima, and Oaxaca. The listings include information on many communities on the coast, as well as popular destinations in the Valles Centrales and other towns in Oaxaca. There is also lots of information about the wildlife of the region, as well as stories of the recent history of the Oaxacan coast.

The Eye
www.theeyehuatulco.com
This is the online component to the Huatulco-based print magazine that focuses on beach life, urban living, food, lifestyle, history, culture, and more on the coast. The magazine is free, and the website has links to the digital editions of the full magazine.

PARKS AND RECREATION

Ecoturismo Oaxaca
www.ecoturismoenoaxaca.com
Oaxaca is experiencing an ecotourism boom, and communities all over the state are organizing to showcase the best of what their geographies have to offer. This Spanish-language site has information on ecotourism centers big and small, broken up regionally into the coast, La Mixteca, the Valles Centrales, and the Sierras Norte and Sur.

Expediciones Sierra Norte
www.sierranorte.org.mx
This bilingual site is the promotional website for the organization Expediciones Sierra Norte, which coordinates ecotourism in the Pueblos Mancomunados, in the Sierra Norte. You can use it to book trips, but also just to get information about the pueblos, local traditions, and activities they have to offer.

Oaxaca MTB
www.oaxacamtb.org
Cycling is one of the fastest-growing activities

in Oaxaca in recent years. Oaxaca MTB is a wealth of information on trails, rides, organizing, and more. The dozens of trails in its detailed and well-mapped directory are mostly in the hills around San Felipe del Agua, just a few miles north of Oaxaca City. Entries include information on the terrain, altitude, difficulty, and more of each ride.

Surfing in Oaxaca
www.srfer.com/surfing-in-oaxaca
The Oaxaca section of srfer.com is a comprehensive collection of everything surfing along the coast. You'll find wave-specific information on surf spots up and down the coast, as well as seasonal weather details, wind and wave statistics, and profiles of hotels and surf camps.

Surf Forecast
www.surf-forecast.com
Surf Forecast is another global online surf network that has diligently updated information on surf conditions. Unlike Srfer, it doesn't include camp, hotel, or other information related to the sport, but the pull-down navigation menus let you browse specific conditions for 25 breaks along the Oaxacan coast.

Lagunas de Chacahua National Park
www.lagunasdechacahua.com
The official English-language website for the Lagunas de Chacahua National Park has moderately detailed information on the wildlife, especially seabirds and crocodiles, that live in the lagoons, as well as activities like boat tours, surfing, snorkeling, and more. There are also accommodations listings for the town of Chacahua, right on the beach.

Index

List of Maps

Photo Credits

All interior photos © Cody Copeland except page 3 © Carlos Gordillo; page 6 (bottom) © Jesse Kraft | Dreamstime.com; page 7 (top) © Ana Ortiz Acevedo; page 9 (top) © BavFilm.com; (bottom right) © Byelikova | Dreamstime.com; page 12 © OAXACA, MEXICO; page 17 © Liliana Pérez-Brennan; page 18 © OAXACA, MEXICO; page 19 © Liliana Pérez-Brennan; page 25 (top) © Ana Ortiz Acevedo; page 26 (top) © Liliana Pérez-Brennan; page 27 (bottom) © José Luis Marcos; page 35 © Liliana Pérez-Brennan; page 36 © Bernardo Ramonfaur | Dreamstime.com; page 37 (bottom right) © Ana Ortiz Acevedo; page 38 © Carlos Gordillo; page 40 © Liliana Pérez-Brennan; page 41 (top right) © Liliana Pérez-Brennan; page 67 (top left) © Ana Ortiz Acevedo; (top right) © Liliana Pérez-Brennan; page 98 (top left) © Liliana Pérez-Brennan; page 123 (bottom) © Liliana Pérez-Brennan; page 127 (top left) © Liliana Pérez-Brennan; (top right) © Liliana Pérez-Brennan; (bottom) © Ana Ortiz Acevedo; page 131 (bottom) © Zapotrek Hike and Bike; page 145 (top) © José Luis Marcos; (bottom) © José Luis Marcos; page 152 (bottom) © José Luis Marcos; page 154 © Expediciones Sierra Norte; page 156 © Expediciones Sierra Norte; page 165 © José Luis Marcos; page 181 © Liliana Pérez-Brennan; page 194 © BavFilm.com; page 224 (top right) © Hagia Sofia; page 242 © Liliana Pérez-Brennan; page 265 (bottom) © Hagia Sofia; page 276 © Edwin Morales; page 311 © Nelson Morales; page 313 (bottom) © Carlos Gordillo; page 323 © Ana Ortiz Acevedo; page 331 (bottom) © Liliana Pérez-Brennan; page 369 (top right) © Ana Ortiz Acevedo

BAJA

JENNIFER KRAMER

CANCÚN & COZUMEL

LIZA PRADO & GARY CHANDLER

MEXICO CITY

JULIE MEADE

OAXACA

ANDY COPELAND

PUERTO VALLARTA

MADELINE MILNE

SAN MIGUEL DE ALLENDE

JULIE MEADE

TIJUANA, ENSENADA & VALLE DE GUADALUPE WINE COUNTRY

JENNIFER KRAMER

YUCATÁN PENINSULA

GARY CHANDLER

More Mexico & Latin America from Moon

BELIZE

LEBAWIT LILY GIRMA

CARTAGENA & COLOMBIA'S CARIBBEAN COAST

CHILE

STEPH DYSON

COSTA RICA

NIKKI SOLANO

ECUADOR & THE GALÁPAGOS ISLANDS

BETHANY PITTS

GALÁPAGOS ISLANDS

MACHU PICCHU

PATAGONIA

WAYNE BERNHARDSON

FIND YOUR ADVENTURE

MOON

USA
NATIONAL
PARKS

THE COMPLETE GUIDE TO ALL
59 PARKS

BECKY LOMAX

Join our travel community!
Share your adventures using #travelwithmoon

MOON.COM
@MOONGUIDES

ACADIA
NATIONAL PARK

ARCHES &
CANYONLANDS
NATIONAL PARKS

MOON

BANFF
NATIONAL
PARK

HIKE · CAMP · KAYAK

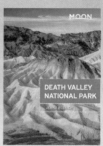

DEATH VALLEY
NATIONAL PARK

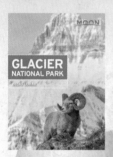

GLACIER
NATIONAL PARK

GRAND
CANYON

MOON

GREAT SMOKY
MOUNTAINS
NATIONAL PARK

HIKE · BIKE · CAMP

MOUNT RUSHMORE
& THE BLACK HILLS

ROCKY MOUNTAIN
NATIONAL PARK

MOON

YELLOWSTONE
& GRAND TETON

HIKE · CAMP
SEE WILDLIFE

YOSEMITE
SEQUOIA &
KINGS CANYON

ZION &
BRYCE

In these books:

- Full coverage of gateway cities and towns
- Itineraries from one day to multiple weeks
- Advice on where to stay (or camp) in and around the parks

GO BIG AND GO BEYOND!

These savvy city guides include strategies to help you see the top sights and find adventure beyond the tourist crowds.

OR TAKE THINGS ONE STEP AT A TIME

#TravelWithMoon

MAP SYMBOLS

▤▤▤ Expressway	○ City/Town	✈ Airport	⚐ Golf Course	
▬▬▬ Primary Road	◉ State Capital	✈ Airfield	🅿 Parking Area	
▭▭▭ Secondary Road	⊛ National Capital	▲ Mountain	🏛 Archaeological Site	
┈┈┈ Unpaved Road	✪ Highlight	✚ Unique Natural Feature	⛪ Church	
┄┄┄ Trail	★ Point of Interest			
┉┉┉ Ferry	• Accommodation	🌊 Waterfall	⛽ Gas Station	
▬▬▬ Railroad	▼ Restaurant/Bar	♠ Park	〰 Glacier	
▤▤▤ Pedestrian Walkway	■ Other Location	🚩 Trailhead	🗺 Mangrove	
▥▥▥ Stairs	▲ Campground	⛷ Skiing Area	▨ Reef	
			〰 Swamp	

CONVERSION TABLES

°C = (°F - 32) / 1.8
°F = (°C x 1.8) + 32
1 inch = 2.54 centimeters (cm)
1 foot = 0.304 meters (m)
1 yard = 0.914 meters
1 mile = 1.6093 kilometers (km)
1 km = 0.6214 miles
1 fathom = 1.8288 m
1 chain = 20.1168 m
1 furlong = 201.168 m
1 acre = 0.4047 hectares
1 sq km = 100 hectares
1 sq mile = 2.59 square km
1 ounce = 28.35 grams
1 pound = 0.4536 kilograms
1 short ton = 0.90718 metric ton
1 short ton = 2,000 pounds
1 long ton = 1.016 metric tons
1 long ton = 2,240 pounds
1 metric ton = 1,000 kilograms
1 quart = 0.94635 liters
1 US gallon = 3.7854 liters
1 Imperial gallon = 4.5459 liters
1 nautical mile = 1.852 km

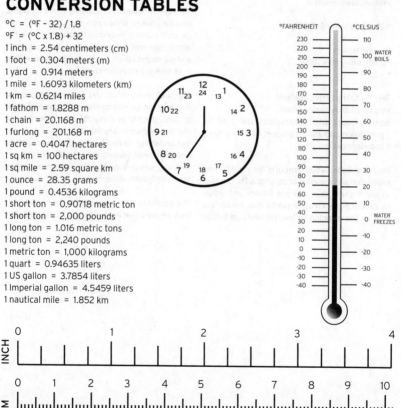

MOON OAXACA

Avalon Travel
Hachette Book Group
1700 Fourth Street
Berkeley, CA 94710, USA
www.moon.com

Editor and Series Manager: Kathryn Ettinger
Acquiring Editor: Nikki Ioakimedes
Copy Editors: Ann Seifert, Linda Cabasin
Graphics and Production Designer:
  Suzanne Albertson
Cover Design: Faceout Studios, Charles Brock
Interior Design: Domini Dragoone
Moon Logo: Tim McGrath
Map Editor: Albert Angulo
Cartographers: Andrew Dolan, Albert Angulo,
  John Culp
Indexer: Greg Jewett

ISBN-13: 978-1-64049-089-5

Printing History
1st Edition — May 2020
5 4 3 2 1

Text © 2020 by Cody Copeland.
Maps © 2020 by Avalon Travel.
Some photos and illustrations are used by
  permission and are the property of the original
  copyright owners.

Hachette Book Group supports the right to free
expression and the value of copyright. The purpose
of copyright is to encourage writers and artists
to produce the creative works that enrich our
culture. The scanning, uploading, and distribution
of this book without permission is a theft of
the author's intellectual property. If you would
like permission to use material from the book
(other than for review purposes), please contact
permissions@hbgusa.com. Thank you for your
support of the author's rights.

Front cover photo: Iglesia Sangre de Cristo in
  Oaxaca City © holgs / Getty Images
Back cover photo: Day of the Dead celebration
  © Kobby Dagan | Dreamstime.com

Printed in China by RR Donnelly

Avalon Travel is a division of Hachette Book Group,
Inc. Moon and the Moon logo are trademarks of
Hachette Book Group, Inc. All other marks and logos
depicted are the property of the original owners.

All recommendations, including those for sights,
activities, hotels, restaurants, and shops, are based
on each author's individual judgment. We do not
accept payment for inclusion in our travel guides,
and our authors don't accept free goods or services
in exchange for positive coverage.

Although every effort was made to ensure that
the information was correct at the time of going
to press, the author and publisher do not assume
and hereby disclaim any liability to any party for any
loss or damage caused by errors, omissions, or any
potential travel disruption due to labor or financial
difficulty, whether such errors or omissions result
from negligence, accident, or any other cause.

The publisher is not responsible for websites (or
their content) that are not owned by the publisher.